BOUNDLESS WINDS OF EMPIRE

Premodern East Asia

PREMODERN EAST ASIA: NEW HORIZONS

This series is dedicated to books that focus on humanistic studies of East Asia before the mid-nineteenth century in fields including literature and cultural and social history, as well as studies of science and technology, the environment, visual cultures, performance, material culture, and gender. The series particularly welcomes works with field-changing and paradigm-shifting potential that adopt interdisciplinary and innovative approaches. Contributors to the series share the premise that creativity in method and rigor in research are preconditions for producing new knowledge that transcends modern disciplinary confines and the framework of the nation-state. In highlighting the complexity and dynamism of premodern societies, these books illuminate the relevance of East Asia to the contemporary world.

Boundless Winds of Empire

*Rhetoric and Ritual in
Early Chosŏn Diplomacy with Ming China*

Sixiang Wang

Columbia University Press   New York

This work was supported by the Core University Program for Korean Studies through the Ministry of Education of the Republic of Korea and the Korean Studies Promotion Service of the Academy of Korean Studies (AKS-2016-OLU-2250006).

Columbia University Press
Publishers Since 1893
New York   Chichester, West Sussex
cup.columbia.edu

Library of Congress Cataloging-in-Publication Data
Names: Wang, Sixiang, author.
Title: Boundless winds of empire : rhetoric and ritual in early Chosŏn diplomacy
    with Ming China / Sixiang Wang.
Description: New York : Columbia University Press, [2023] | Includes bibliographical
    references and index.
Identifiers: LCCN 2022047851 (print) | LCCN 2022047852 (ebook) |
    ISBN 9780231205467 (hardback) | ISBN 9780231205474 (trade paperback) |
    ISBN 9780231556019 (ebook)
Subjects: LCSH: Korea—Foreign relations—China. | China—Foreign relations—Korea. |
    Korea—History—Chosŏn dynasty, 1392–1910. | China—History—Ming dynasty,
    1368–1644. | Diplomatic and consular service—Korea—History.
Classification: LCC DS910.2.C5 W363 2023 (print) | LCC DS910.2.C5 (ebook) |
    DDC 327.519051—dc23/eng/20221012
LC record available at https://lccn.loc.gov/2022047851
LC ebook record available at https://lccn.loc.gov/2022047852

Printed in the United States of America

Cover image: "Seal of the king of Chosŏn" (*Chosŏn kukwang chi in* 朝鮮國王之印). Detail of Dong Qichang (Chinese, 1555–1636), *River and Mountains on a Clear Autumn Day* 江山秋霽圖, c. 1624–27, handscroll, ink on Korean paper; painting only: 38.4 × 136.8 cm (15 1/8 × 53 7/8 in.). The Cleveland Museum of Art, purchase from the J. H. Wade Fund 1959.46, https://www.clevelandart.org/art/1959.46. The striking square stamp on the cover is from a royal seal, granted to Chosŏn's king in 1402 by the Ming emperor. This seal was used to authenticate diplomatic documents that were subsequently sent to the Ming court. Hence, this emblem represents the ritual and rhetorical practices behind this diplomatic relationship. This particular memorial was sent to Ming in 1573. Later, the Ming painter and high official Dong Qichang 董其昌, who coveted Korean memorial paper for use as painting surfaces, appropriated a number of these Korean memorials for this purpose. This imprint comes from one of Dong's most famous landscape paintings. Faint brushwork from the original Korean memorial remains visible on the paper's surface.

Contents

Preface

Boundless Winds of Empire: Rhetoric and Ritual in Early Chosŏn Diplomacy with Ming China is not a definitive recounting of Chosŏn Korea's diplomatic relations with Ming China. Indeed, no book of such modest length can be. There are too many more stories worth telling, too many important historical figures worth revisiting. As such, the book's choice of scenarios and cast of characters will necessarily be somewhat idiosyncratic. Still, the snapshots it takes were chosen with purpose. Each one is framed to capture dynamics of ritual and rhetoric usually overlooked in conventional diplomatic histories.

To draw out these dynamics, the book uses a range of primary materials, in particular court chronicles, diplomatic records, and envoy poetry. It situates Chosŏn diplomacy in decades of English-language historiography on Korea and East Asia, as well as methodological considerations on the place of language and ritual in the history of empire, diplomacy, and sovereignty. While it also introduces readers to the contours of relevant historiography in Korean, Chinese, and Japanese languages, the book's main interlocutors are scholars who have written in English. As such, the book only scratches the surface of what scholarship in Asian languages have to offer. One part a consideration of expedience and two parts a reflection of the author's limitations, the book's discussion should be taken as only one more entry into a long-standing global scholarly conversation and not as its representative summary or definitive synthesis.

To accommodate anglophone readers, the book adopts the following conventions for representing Asian languages. The McCune-Reischauer system, used by the Library of Congress, rather than Revised Romanization, is used to romanize Korean. Pinyin is used for romanization of Chinese. Hepburn is used for Japanese. Many authors use their own, personalized romanizations of names over official schemes, but the bibliography will still defer to the above standards except in instances where the relevant publications are in English. I also follow Western word order for authors with Korean, Chinese, or Japanese names if they publish mainly in English or are based in Western academic institutions: Sixiang Wang, not Wang Sixiang.

The modern Korean and Chinese languages are mutually unintelligible, but they share cognates based on the same Chinese characters, or sinographs. In the past, Chosŏn and Ming elites also spoke different languages, but they wrote in a mutually intelligible written language: classical Chinese, also called literary Sinitic. How best to translate text from this language into English with adequate precision and fidelity is a perennial challenge, so where precise rhetoric is important, sinographs will follow a translated text in brackets to benefit the expert reader (e.g. "literature washes away at once the disgraces of Sui and Tang" [文章一洗隋唐陋]). When terms can be directly identified or defined by a single sinographic compound, such as proper names, they will be given without brackets (e.g., Koguryŏ 高句麗 or "barbarian" 夷). More general readers derive little benefit from long strings of romanization, so sinographic terms are generally not romanized unless there is reason to use the original term in the main text. Unless otherwise indicated, romanization will default to the modern Korean reading in McCune-Reischauer.

The identification of political entities, whether present or historical, often evokes anachronistic or otherwise problematic connotations. For concision and readability, the book adopts the following conventions. Modern nation-state terms such as China, Japan, Korea, and Vietnam either stand in for geographical zones or describe a sense of political continuity tied to lines of monarchical transmission. Imperial Chinese regimes are rendered without the definite article "the": "Ming" as opposed to "the Ming." Like Korean regime names such as Chosŏn, these were properly names of states (*kukho* 國號), comparable to France, Austria, Turkey, rather than dynasties or ruling families (i.e., the Bourbons, the Habsburgs, the Ottomans). Therefore, throughout the text, Chosŏn and Ming, as well as the term "dynasty," refer to either these states or the courts that ruled them. Meanwhile, proper names of persons and places are provided with in-line sinographs without additional punctuation upon first mention. Temple names (*myoho* 廟號) are used for reigning Chosŏn monarchs, except for Yi Sŏnggye. Reign names (C. *nianhao* 年號) are used for Ming monarchs, except Yingzong, who has two reign eras.

Traditional Korean and Chinese sources are generally cited according to fascicle (K. *kwŏn*, C. *juan* 卷) number, followed by folio (with recto-verso information) or page number, depending on the edition used. There are several exceptions. Literary anthologies from the *Han'guk munjip ch'onggan* 한국문집총간, as provided in the *Han'guk kojŏn chonghap* 한국고전종합 DB database (http://db.itkc.or.kr) are cited according to volume and page in the database. Entries from the Chosŏn *Veritable Records* (*Chosŏn wangjo sillok* 朝鮮王朝實錄), including references to the *Yŏnsan'gun ilgi* 燕山君日記 and the *Kwanghaegun ilgi* 光海君日記, drawn from the National Institute of History (*Kuksa p'yŏch'an wiwŏnhoe* 國史編纂委員會) database (http://sillok. history.go.kr/), are cited according to royal title, fascicle, folio, recto and verso, followed by corresponding Julian-Gregorian year, lunar month and date, and entry number, for example, *T'aejo sillok* 1:1a [1392/7/17, 1]. Leap months are noted with an "a" after the numerical month it follows. Note that the last lunar months in the East Asian luni-solar calendar technically fall on the following Gregorian year, but this discrepancy is disregarded in the interest of easier timekeeping for modern readers accustomed to Common Era years. Entries from the Ming *Veritable Records*, abbreviated as MSL, will be cited using the same convention. The book uses CE for "common era" and BCE for "before common era."

The book draws extensively from the Korean compilation of Ming envoy poetry called the *Brilliant Flowers Anthologies* (*Hwanghwajip* 皇華集). It exists in various versions across several editions and reprints. Copies and versions are scattered across archives in Korea, China, Japan, and the United States. The Kyujanggak Archives in Seoul, the Chinese National Library in Beijing, and the Asami collection at the Berkeley campus of the University of California house a large portion of the imprints. To simplify the references, I cite from a modern, punctuated edition collated in China by Zhao Ji in the *Complete Brilliant Flowers Anthologies* (*Zuben Huanghua ji*), published by Zhonghua shuju, which also provides a thorough bibliographic introduction.

ACKNOWLEDGMENTS

The book is a dénouement of a long intellectual journey. The first book of Korean history I ever read was *A New History of Korea*, the 1984 English translation of Yi Ki-baek's *Han'guksa sillon*. It was on the syllabus of a high school East Asian history elective taught by Larry Weiss, who was then head of the upper school at the Horace Mann School in New York, which I attended at the time. It was also there, from the late Tom LaFarge, that I learned not to be afraid of putting words onto paper and murdering one's darlings.

The core idea of this book emerged out of a senior thesis project on Kwŏn Kŭn's envoy poetry supported by Hwisang Cho and Wendy Swartz. They also encouraged me to pursue doctoral studies, which I began with JaHyun Kim Haboush at Columbia. She was and remains a wellspring of inspiration. After her untimely passing, Dorothy Ko, Jungwon Kim, Charles Armstrong, Robert Hymes, and Pamela Smith guided my dissertation to completion, while Theodore Hughes and Jenny Wang Medina provided timely advice at critical junctures that made the future possible.

After setting out into the world, I have been supported by many teachers, colleagues, friends, and institutions. I am grateful to Lee Ik Joo and Kim Ho for encouraging me to publish an early articulation of how I saw the potential contributions of my research in *Yŏksa wa hyŏnsil*. When I was at the University of Pennsylvania, Eugene Park and the James Joo-Kim Program of Korean Studies provided their support for a conference called "Korea with Empire" that opened my thinking to connections beyond my habitual temporal and disciplinary scopes. That year, Frank Chance, Linda Chance, Hsiao-wen Cheng, Fredrick Dickinson, Melissa DiFrancesco, Siyen Fei, Antonio Feros, Jooyeon Hahm,

Robert Hegwood, Debbie Huang, Xiaobai Hu, Ayako Kano, Seok Lee, Alexander Martin, Brendan O'Kane, Nancy Steinhardt, Holly Stephens, Joylon Thomas, and Brian Vivier lent me their ears, shared their company, and provided their guidance.

Thanks to the Mellon Fellowship in the Humanities, I was able to spend three fulfilling years in Palo Alto. Lanier Anderson, J. P. Daughton, and Adrian Daub, who directed the fellowship program at Stanford's Humanities Center, modeled an intellectual generosity that deserves widespread emulation. My fellow Mellons, especially Aileen Robinson, Alanna Hickey, Anne Austin, Colleen Anderson, Elizabeth Marcus, Heather Brink-Roby, Luca Scholz, Mélanie Lamotte, Nicole Hughes, Rebekah Baglini, Shawon Kinew, Willie Costello, as well as David Colmenares, Jessie Howell, and Daniel Ohayon, deserve my gratitude for their companionship, thoughtfulness, and tolerance for my endless digressions. During those years, Dafna Zur took me under her wing and brought me along on her many adventures, while Ronald Egan; Yoshiko Matsumoto; Connie Chin, who is no longer with us; Ai Tran; David Hazard; Linda Galvane; Yanshuo Zhang; Ekaterina Mozhaeva; Josh Groschwitz; Briana Burrows; and Kristin Boyd made me forget the Knight Building once belonged to a business school. I shared my work at Ali Yaycıoğlu's Eurasian Empires Workshop and a number of other occasions where Kären Wigen, Matthew Sommer, Yumi Moon, Tom Mullaney, Alexander Statman, Joseph Seeley, and Russell Burge provided encouraging feedback.

Now at the University of California, Los Angeles, I work with one of the most diverse student bodies in the world. Their curiosity reminds me daily of the value and impact of the humanities in higher education. I am therefore grateful to Chris Hanscom, Namhee Lee, Jennifer Jung-Kim, John Duncan, and Robert Buswell for welcoming me to the Department of Asian Languages and Cultures. Together with Michael Berry, William Bodiford, Torquil Duthie, Nina Duthie, George Dutton, Michael Emmerich, Shoichi Iwasaki, Stephanie Jamison, Min Li, Thu-Huong Nguyen-Vo, Sung-Deuk Oak, Oona Paredes, Shu-Mei Shih, Satoko Shimazaki, Sung-Ock Sohn, Hongyin Tao, they have cultivated an atmosphere of collegiality, fairness, and equity, so that I could happily share Royce Hall with Stephanie Balkwill, Diego Loukota, Huijun Mai, Hyun Suk Park, Yinghui Wu, and Junko Yamazaki. We all owe our thanks to the timely support of

Kevin Hsu, Takamasa Imai, Jimmy Tang, Phuong Truong, Timothy Yu, Fatin Zubi and the tireless Shan Shan Chi-Au, as well as our department chair Seiji Lippit and our dean David Schaberg, who steered the ship through the trying times of the COVID-19 pandemic.

Over the past six or so years, during conferences and talks held at a number of institutions in North America, Europe, and Asia, *Boundless Winds of Empire*, in its many pieces and permutations benefited immensely from the many conversations with Adam Yuet Chau, Alden Young, Andrea Goldman, Andrew Jackson, Anna Shields, Anthony Pagden, Arthur Weststejin, Barbara Wall, Benjamin Elman, Bradley Davis, Brian Steininger, Christina Han, Christine von Oertzen, Christopher Lovins, Dagmar Schäfer, Daham Chung, Daniel Barish, David Kang, David Lurie, Don Baker, Fabian Drixler, Gloria Koo, Gregg Brazinsky, Ihor Pidhainy, Isabelle Sancho, Jack Davey, Jamie Yoo, Jaymin Kim, Ji-young Lee, Jinsoo Ahn, Joanna-Elfving Hwang, Jon Kief, Joshua Fogel, Joshua Van Lieu, Jung Donghun, Juhn Ahn, Kenneth Swope, Kim Geun-tae, Kim Ji-young, Koo Bom-jin, Kyoungjin Bae, Luke Roberts, Macabe Keliher, Mark Frank, Märten Saarela, Melissa Brown, Marion Eggert, Mark Ravina, Martina Deuchler, Matthew Fraleigh, Maura Dykstra, Maya Stiller, Mun Chunyang, Nam-lin Hur, Niansheng Song, Nuri Kim, Oh Soo Chang, Paize Keulemans, Pär Cassel, Park Hyun Soon, Pierre-Emmanuel Roux, Richard Y. Kim, Richard Von Glahn, R. Bin Wong, Ross King, Saeyoung Park, Sam Han, Sarah Schneewind, Sean Han, Sebastian Felten, Sem Vermeersch, Seung-Kyung Kim, Seo-Hyun Park, Se-Woong Koo, Si Nae Park, Sora Kim, Stephanie Kim, Sunkyu Lee, Timothy Brook, Tom Mazanec, Vladimír Glomb, Yijun Wang, Yiming Ha, Young Kyun Oh, Young-key Kim-Renaud, Yuanchong Wang, Weiwei Luo, William Flemming, and the Korea-Vietnam Working Group with Kate Baldanza (who introduced me to the skilled cartographer Ben Pease) and John Phan oriented me to premodern Vietnam. The Chosŏn history field in North America also owes tremendously to Sun Joo Kim and Jisoo Kim for their custodianship and leadership.

No scholar in the humanities can do without the accumulated generosity and labor of the librarians and archivists who have collected and curated the resources we use every day. In particular, the staff and curators of the Kyujanggak Archives, Jangseogak Archives, the Institute for the Translation of Korean Classics, the National Museum of Korea, and the National Institute of Korean History have made the historical heritage of Korea freely accessible to the global public in digital form. The Charles Young Library at the University of California, Los Angeles (UCLA); Stanford's East Asia Library; Penn's Van Pelt Library; Harvard's Yenching Library; Princeton's East Asian Library; Berkeley's C. V. Starr Library; the Asian studies library of the Collège de France; the Columbia University libraries; and the entire ILL system sheltered me for many late hours and dispatched numerous overdue notices. I also extend my begrudging gratitude to Facebook for allowing me to expose my most unhinged ideas to innocent social media users.

Before I was quite ready, Emily Mokros, along with Tristan Brown, organized a manuscript workshop at Berkeley for us in 2018. There, Nicholas Tackett's timely advice regarding how to approach the mechanics of manuscript preparation help relieve a major writer's block. Javier Cha, John S. Lee, Brian Landor, Travis Seifman, Chelsea Wang, Devin Fitzgerald, and Eric Schlussel helped pare away overgrown tendrils from early drafts. Throughout, Ksenia Chizhova's aquarian insights have always left me with much to reflect upon. In 2021, when the book neared its current shape, Zrinka Stahuljak and UCLA's CMRS Center for Early Global Studies hosted a workshop for the manuscript. With the help of Erin Romo, I was able to invite Nhung Tuyet Tran and Christopher Atwood to give their incisive critiques. David Robinson, Eugene Park, and Adam Bohnet also sent perceptive page-by-page comments, which, along with those from four anonymous reviewers, helped sharpen the argument and polish away inconsistencies. Throughout this process, Christine Dunbar of Columbia University Press waited patiently for long-delayed drafts and still guided the book to completion. I thank the support of Columbia University's Center for Korean Research; the Academy of Korean Studies; Christian Winting, Chang Jae Lee, and Kathryn Jorge at Columbia University Press; Ben Kolstad at KGL; and the excellent copy editor Marianne L'Abbate who rescued me from numerous infelicities. Those that still remain are my oversights alone.

Throughout my life, my parents, Denong Wang and Fang Wu, appreciated the need to choose one's directions in life. My partner, Elsa Duval, had to endure the consequences of those choices. So many bad sentences have grated on her nerves, and so many lamebrained whims have exasperated her better judgment. Throughout all this, my children,

Timur and Zoé, have tried in good faith to understand why I would clack for hours on a keyboard to the neglect of other matters.

This was the book I wanted to read many years ago as a Chinese-American teenager in New York. It did not exist at the time, so with everyone's help, I wrote it.

Chronology

Time Line of Events Referenced, 1250s to 1640s

1231–1270	Mongol invasions of Korea
1259	Koryŏ court capitulates to Mongols, future king Wŏnjong sent as hostage
1260	Qubilai becomes great khan of the Mongols, establishes Yuan dynasty
1274	Qubilai's daughter, Qutlugh Kelmish, marries Koryŏ heir apparent, future king Ch'ungnyŏl, inaugurating the Yuan-Koryŏ marriage alliance
1307	Koryŏ ritual reforms to avoid "infringement"
1368	Zhu Yuanzhang conquers Beijing, establishes Ming dynasty in Nanjing, rules as Hongwu
1369	Ming sends envoys to invest King Kongmin
1374	King Kongmin is assassinated
1387	Ming conquers Liaodong
1388	King U of Koryŏ launches invasion of Liaodong; Yi Sŏnggye "returns from Wihwa island" and seizes power
1392	Yi Sŏnggye becomes king, thereby establishing Chosŏn dynasty in Korea
1396	Kwŏn Kŭn's envoy mission

1588	Amended version of Ming *Collected Statutes* printed, concluding Chosŏn's "disputing slander" campaign
1592–1598	Japanese invasion of Korea, Imjin War
1616	Nurhaci of Jianzhou establishes Jin dynasty
1619	Jin defeat Ming-Chosŏn at the battle of Sarhu
1620	Jin conquest of Ming Liaodong
1627	Jin invasion of Korea (First Manchu invasion)
1626	Jiang Yueguang's mission to Chosŏn
1633	Last Ming mission to Chosŏn; final *Brilliant Flowers* printed
1636	Hong Taiji changes Jin dynasty to Qing dynasty, assumes imperial title
1636–1637	Qing invasion of Chosŏn (Second Manchu invasion); Chosŏn capitulates; crown prince sent to Mukden as hostage
1644	Beijing falls to rebels; Chongzhen emperor commits suicide; Manchus enter Beijing

Rulers and Regimes I: Antiquity and the Classical Past

Age of the Sage Kings		?
Yao	堯	?
Shun	舜	?
Xia dynasty	夏	ca. 2000–1600 BCE
Yu	禹	ca. 2000 BCE
Shang dynasty	商	ca. 1600s–1046 BCE
Zhòu	紂	ca. 1050 BCE
Wugeng	武庚	ca. 1050 BCE
Kija (Jizi)	箕子	ca. 1050 BCE
Zhou dynasty	周	1046–256 BCE
King Wen	文王	ca. 1050 BCE
King Wu	武王	1046–1043 BCE
Spring and Autumn period	春秋	771–476 BCE
Warring States period	戰國	476–221 BCE
Qin dynasty	秦	221–206 BCE
Shihuangdi	始皇帝	221–210 BCE
Han dynasty	漢	202 BCE–9 CE; 25–220 CE
Han Wudi	漢武帝	140–87 BCE
Three Kingdoms period	三國	220–280 CE
Jin dynasty	晉	266–420 CE

Rulers and Regimes II: The Korean Dynastic Succession*

Tan'gun Chosŏn	檀君朝鮮	Traditionally 2333 BCE–?
Kija Chosŏn	箕子朝鮮	Traditionally 1050–195 BCE
Wiman Chosŏn	衛滿朝鮮	195–108 BCE
Koguryŏ	高句麗	Traditionally 37 BCE–668 CE
King Tongmyŏng	東明王	Traditionally 37 BCE–19 BCE
Paekche	百濟	Traditionally 18 BCE–660 CE
Silla	新羅	Traditionally 57 BCE–935 CE
Koryŏ	高麗	918–1392
Wang Kŏn (T'aejo)	王建 (太祖)	918–943
King Sukchong	肅宗	1095–1105
King Yejong	睿宗	1105–1122
King Wŏnjong	元宗	1259–1274
King Ch'ungnyŏl	忠烈王	1274–1308
King Kongmin	恭愍王	1351–1374
Sin U†	辛禑	1374–1388
King Kongyang	恭讓王	1389–1392
Chosŏn	朝鮮	1392–1910

* See also "Kings of Chosŏn and Their Reigns" time line.
* According to early Chosŏn historical orthodoxy.
† Treated as pretender in official Chosŏn historiography.

Rulers and Regimes III: Regimes in Northeast Asia (Beijing and Liaodong Region), 400–1800

Koguryŏ	高句麗	37 BCE–668
Sixteen Kingdoms Period	十六國	304–406
Northern Wei	北魏	386–535
Sui dynasty	隋	581–619
Sui Yangdi	隋煬帝	605–617
Tang dynasty	唐	618–907
Tang Taizong	唐太宗	627–649
Parhae (Bohai)	渤海	698–926
Khitan Empire (Liao)	遼	916–1218
Jurchen Empire (Jin)	金	1115–1234
Mongol Empire (Yuan)	元	1206–1388
Chinggis Khan (Yuan Taizu)	元太祖	1206–1227
Qubilai Khan (Yuan Shizu)	元世祖	1260–1294
Ming dynasty*	明	1368–1644
Jianzhou-Later Jin	建州–後金	
Cungšan		?–1467
Li Manju		?–1467
Nurhaci (Qing Taizu)	清太祖	1616–1626
Manchu Empire (Qing)	清	1636–1912
Hong Taiji (Qing Taizong)	清太宗	1636–1643
Jiaqing emperor	嘉慶	1796–1820

* See also "Reigns and Temple Names of the Ming Emperors" time line.

Other Regimes of Note (900–1800)

Southeast Asia

Nanzhao (in Yunnan-Burma)	南詔	738–902
Dali (in Yunnan-Burma)	大理	937–1253
Đại Cồ Việt (in Vietnam)	大瞿越	968–1054
Trần dynasty (in Vietnam)	陳朝 (大越)	1225–1400
Hồ dynasty (in Vietnam)	胡朝 (大越)	1400–1407
Lê dynasty (in Vietnam)	黎朝 (大越)	1427–1789
Champa (Southern Vietnam)	占城	192–1832
Hsenwi (in Burma)	木邦	Seventh century–1888

Mainland East Asia

Southern Tang (in Jiangnan)	南唐	937–976
Wuyue (in Jiangnan)	吳越	907–978
Qian Hongchu (King Zhongyi)	錢弘俶 (忠懿王)	947–978
Song dynasty (in China)	宋	960–1279
Song Taizu	宋太祖	960–976
Song Taizong	宋太宗	976–997
Song Huizong	宋徽宗	1100–1126
Western Xia (in Ningxia/Ordos)	西夏	1038–1227

Maritime East Asia

Ryukyu Kingdom	琉球國	1187–1879
Ashikaga Shogunate (in Japan)	足利幕府	1336–1573
Tokugawa Shogunate (in Japan)	德川幕府	1603–1868

Kings of Chosŏn and Their Reigns

T'aejo	太祖	1392–1398
Chŏngjong	定宗	1398–1400
T'aejong	太宗	1400–1418
Sejong	世宗	1418–1450
Munjong	文宗	1450–1452
Tanjong	端宗	1452–1455
Sejo	世祖	1455–1468
Yejong	睿宗	1468–1469
Sŏngjong	成宗	1469–1494
Yŏnsan'gun	燕山君	1494–1506
Chungjong	中宗	1506–1544
Injong	仁宗	1544–1545
Myŏngjong	明宗	1545–1567
Sŏnjo	宣祖	1567–1608
Kwanghaegun	光海君	1608–1623
Injo	仁祖	1623–1649
Hyojong	孝宗	1649–1659
Hyŏnjong	顯宗	1649–1659
Sukchong	肅宗	1659–1720
Kyŏngjong	景宗	1720–1724
Yŏngjo	英祖	1724–1776
Chŏngjo	正祖	1776–1800
Sunjo	純祖	1800–1834
Hŏnjong	憲宗	1834–1849
Ch'ŏljong	哲宗	1849–1863
Kojong	高宗	1864–1907
Sunjong	純宗	1907–1910

Reigns and Temple Names of the Ming Emperors

Hongwu	洪武	Taizu	太祖	1369–1398
Jianwen	建文	Huizong	惠宗	1398–1402
Yongle	永樂	Chengzu	成祖	1402–1424
Hongxi	洪熙	Renzong	仁宗	1424–1425
Xuande	宣德	Xuanzong	宣宗	1425–1435
Zhengtong	正統	Yingzong	英宗	1435–1449
Jingtai	景泰	Daizong	代宗	1449–1457
Tianshun	天順	Yingzong	英宗	1457–1464
Chenghua	成化	Xianzong	憲宗	1464–1487
Hongzhi	弘治	Xiaozong	孝宗	1487–1505
Zhengde	正德	Wuzong	武宗	1505–1521
Jiajing	嘉靖	Shizong	世宗	1521–1567
Longqing	隆慶	Muzong	穆宗	1567–1572
Wanli	萬曆	Shenzong	神宗	1572–1620
Taichang	泰昌	Guangzong	光宗	1620
Tianqi	天啟	Xizong	熹宗	1620–1627
Chongzhen	崇禎	Sizong	思宗	1627–1644

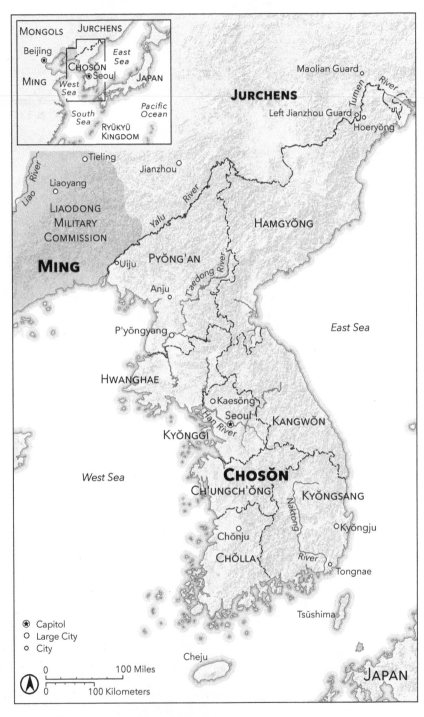

MAP 1 Chosŏn Korea and its neighbors. Map by Ben Pease

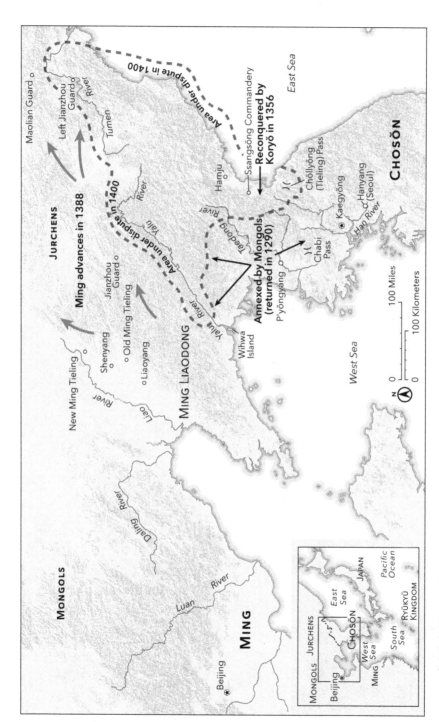

MAP 2 Koryŏ and Ming territorial disputes, ca. 1388. Map by Ben Pease

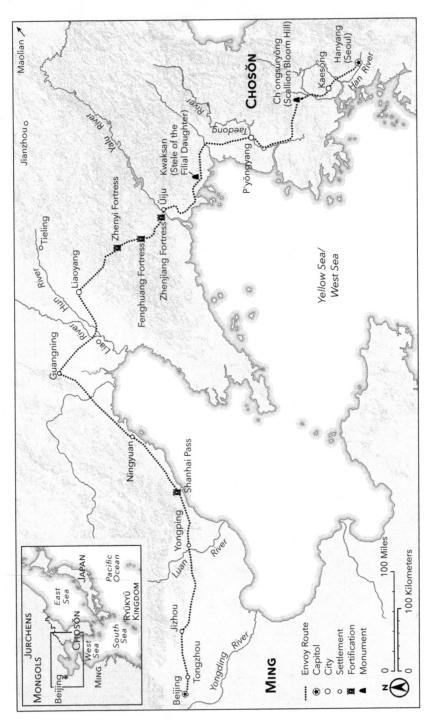

MAP 3 Overland envoy route between Beijing and Seoul, ca. 1580. Map by Ben Pease

BOUNDLESS WINDS OF EMPIRE

Introduction

Korea and the Imperial Tradition

Imperial winds are not bound by limits of the civilized and the barbarian—
Why should the land's lay distinguish one's territory from another's?

皇風不限華夷界 地理何分彼此疆

Imperial rule swept like the wind across the landscape. It paid no heed
to cultural difference, physical terrain, or political boundaries. All-
encompassing and boundless was how the Korean envoy Kwŏn Kŭn
權近 (1352–1409) described Ming (1368–1644) imperial rule in 1396.
Presented to none other than the Ming emperor himself, these lines of
poetry articulated a formula of imperial sovereignty that would have
resonated widely across Eurasia at the time.[1]

Commonplace though it was, the universalizing impulse Kwŏn
Kŭn's couplet expressed was also puzzling. After all, no empire, now or
then, could truly be boundless. However grand the horizons of imperial
aspiration, given enough time and space, they all reach their inevitable ends. So how seriously should anyone, least of all a historian, take
such claims of universal rule? Perhaps court composers like Kwŏn Kŭn
indulged in such panegyrics only to quench the yearnings of fragile
sovereigns or to impress docile subjects with highfalutin propaganda.
But the tension between infinite imagination and finite capacities should
not be written off so easily. At the far, western end of Eurasia, it once
inspired jurists from several nations to debate Spanish Habsburg claims
to world rulership, with long-lasting ramifications for the evolution of

international law.[2] Meanwhile, in northeast Asia, Ming claims of universal rule informed how Korea's rulers and envoys conducted diplomatic relations with their imperial neighbors well after Ming's demise in 1644 and into the twentieth century. In both cases, the salience of these imperial claims extended far beyond the immediate reach of the empires that first staked them. Rhetoric, then, was not merely rhetorical.

THE SHAPE OF EMPIRE

When Kwŏn Kŭn arrived at the Ming court in 1396, he represented the newly established kingdom of Chosŏn (1392–1910). A regime of modest means, Chosŏn ruled a territory and population comparable to Europe's leading monarchies at the time. Confined to the Korean Peninsula and its neighboring littoral, it was dwarfed by its neighbor, the Ming Empire, on every measurable scale. This problem of having an overpowerful neighbor was not uniquely a Korean one. Across the early modern world, most states were not empires with pretensions to universal rule but instead were ephemeral entities that lingered on their margins or teetered in their midst. Among them, few could boast of centuries of political continuity and autonomy. The 200 years of continuous peace that Chosŏn enjoyed with Ming was therefore no small feat, although it is too easily treated as the natural consequence of Korean acquiescence to Ming political and cultural influence. This book tells a different story, one of how Chosŏn's investment in the Ming Empire in fact sheathed a subtle diplomatic and cultural strategy, one apparent only when restored to the thick context of its deployment.

What follows in this book could also be framed as a discussion of how the poetic related to the political in Chosŏn-Ming diplomacy. Critical to the discussion is a recognition that the Ming Empire was not one *thing*. It was instead a contested idea, even as it acquired broad cachet among Ming imperial officials and Chosŏn elites alike. For instance, Kwŏn's couplet projected a vision of empire starkly different from the emperor's own. How the two treated the river that lay between Chosŏn and Ming lands is a case in point. Kwŏn described the Yalu River[3] as "a belt" dividing Korea from Liaoyang in southern Manchuria [長江一帶隔遼陽] only to show how its powers of delimitation had been melted away by imperial influence.[4] In contrast, the emperor, known best by his reign era Hongwu 洪武 (r. 1368–1398, n. Zhu Yuanzhang 朱元璋), saw the river as an eternal frontier, "demarcated since antiquity" [鴨綠江 清界古封]. With its banks "dotted with ruins of ancient fortresses, the traces of wars between long-gone kingdoms" [漢伐可稽明載冊 遼征須 考照遺蹤], the river recalled past hostilities and threatened new ones.[5]

The tone of the emperor's poem was not surprising given decades of strained relations between the emperor and Korea's rulers. Kwŏn Kŭn's 1396 mission in fact came at the heels of yet one more diplomatic crisis. The emperor accused Korean diplomatic missives of being "seemingly in accordance with propriety" but in fact "interspersed with carelessness, frivolity, offense, and insult." He retaliated by detaining Korean envoys and holding them hostage, demanding the Korean king extradited the drafters responsible. Alongside these reactions to the rhetorical slights, whether perceived or actual, the Hongwu emperor also sought to rearrange Korea's position in the imperial landscape. He had once issued an edict that explained why he refused to grant investiture to Kwŏn Kŭn's king, Korea's new ruler. In it, Hongwu explained that "since antiquity," emperors always distinguished carefully between what was considered within their realm and what was beyond.[6] Investiture, described in classical idiom as "dividing earth in wrapped reeds" [分茅胙土], apportioned territorial dominion only to subordinate rulers within the "civilizing influence of China 華夏." Those beyond its bounds were excluded from the rite. Chosŏn's king was ineligible because his country, Korea, was

> . . . separated by mountains and beyond the sea, heaven-made and forged in earth as a country of the eastern barbarians, with conditions distinct and customs different [限山隔海 天造地設 東夷 之邦也 風殊俗異]. If I [as emperor] were to grant to it seals and patents, making it my subject in the witness of ghosts and spirits, would I not be too greedy [朕若賜與印信誥命 令彼臣妾 鬼神監見 無乃貪之甚歟]? On this matter I will be more restrained than the Ancient Sage Kings, and have decided [granting investiture] will not be possible [較之上古聖人 約束一節 決不可爲]. I have commanded in the past that [Korea's] rites should follow its original customs, its laws obeying its former statutes." Allow it to assume its own sovereign rule [儀從本俗 法守舊章 令聽其自爲聲教]. If it so desires, it may intercourse with us; if it is indignant, then we will

cut off all contact—let things be as how things will be [喜則來[往]
怒則絕行 亦聽其自然].[7]

In this, and two earlier imperial missives to Korea, the emperor cast
"China" as the fountainhead of civilization, a place "where moral norms
rested"; Korea, in contrast, was a "barbarian" or *yi* (K. *i* 夷) land plagued
by usurpation and political intrigue, was ultimately "not to be governed
by the Central State 中國."[8] For the Ming emperor, who slipped between
various registers of identification for the political order he represented—"
Central State" 中國, "China" 華夏, "high antiquity" 上古, "within the
civilized fold" 化內—conceived political dominion, civilization, and
perhaps even ethnic identity as coterminous and bounded clearly by
geography. What was "Chinese" was, therefore, "civilized," and therefore
governable and within imperial dominion. In this formulation, the
emperor's role was to enforce these preternatural boundaries.[9]

These imperial proclamations spoke to the emperor's lingering
mistrust of his Korean neighbors. It also raised questions about the
legitimate extent of imperial rule. By articulating why, in principle,
Chosŏn's king should not receive investiture, Hongwu affirmed Korea's
existence as a separate political entity but also relegated it to a cultural
other. He used the term *hua* (K. *hwa* 華) to assert a putative equivalence
between "China" and "civilization" in contradistinction to *yi* in all its
pejorative senses: alien, barbaric, and marginal. In the Ming emperor's
formulation of *hua* and *yi* ("civilized" and "barbarian" might suffice only
as provisional translations) Korean political autonomy was premised
on Chosŏn lying beyond the pale. But when Kwŏn Kŭn insisted that
"imperial winds" should make no distinctions between the "civilized"
hua and the *yi*, did it still make sense to maintain the notion of *yi*
as "barbarian" when the very point was that imperial rule would render
such distinctions meaningless?

The precise valences of the terms *hua* and *yi* depended on the
context of how they are deployed.[10] Chosŏn Koreans might invoke a
universal vision of empire transcending the *hua* and *yi*, only to insist in
the same breath on a stark, even racialized, divide separating themselves
from their Japanese, Jurchen, and Mongol neighbors as barbarian *yi*.[11]
Meanwhile, *hua* could be glossed as cultural "efflorescence," the spatial home of "civilization," or simply a stand-in for a political "China."

When Chosŏn-Ming users employed the term in compounds such as *mohwa* 慕華 "admiring efflorescence," or *chunghwa* 中華 "central efflorescence," they could also superimpose all the above meanings.

A wide semantic range, however, did not mean all uses were equivalent or all meanings conflated. Chosŏn period users, as Pae Usŏng and others argue, availed themselves of this variability to make diverse claims on how Korea related to *hua*. So when Chosŏn elites called their country *So Chunghwa* 小中華, the point was not that Korea was "China" in the miniature, but another, albeit smaller center of cultural efflorescence.[12] What was consistent, however, was how *hua* always marked a target of veneration or emulation, a discursive tool to identify what was culturally and politically legitimate. A quality, rather than ontology, *hua* was manifested by the Ming court, but that did not stop Chosŏn elites from laying claim to it on their own terms.

This variation (which explains in part why they yield no consistent equivalents in English) also testifies to the salience of the ecumenical question the terms represented: how cultural boundaries were to be mapped and managed. "Ecumene," from the Koine Greek *oikoumene* (οἰκουμένη), refers to the known world or the habitable human realm. When Byzantine emperors (and their early modern Muscovite successors) used it to claim dominion over Christendom's confessional community, it evoked contradictory horizons: world rulership that is at once universal and expansive yet limited by cultural or religious membership—coherent only if the two are made coterminous, if "true religion" was established in the whole "known world" with church and empire as one.[13] An analogous tension suffuses the Chinese term *tianxia* (K. *chŏnha* 天下). Suggesting at once universal totality and the political dominion of the emperor, the tension is reflected in the range of English translations attempted for it: "the world," "all-under-heaven," "the realm," or even "the empire," depending on context and the translator's interpretation.[14]

Tianxia had no single shape. As Kwŏn Kŭn's exchange with the emperor suggests, the relationship between imperial power, territorial rule, and cultural difference was a matter of circumstance. When the Mongols "unified all-under-heaven" 混一天下, conquering much of Eurasia in the thirteenth century, they espoused a cosmopolitan vision. They appropriated different religious, cultural, and political traditions as they saw fit, all the while fostering translation and movement among them. The Mongol-Yuan (1206–1388) patronage of Confucian literati culture was a case in point. By the early fourteenth century, the Confucian scholars of the empire counted among their ranks men of Mongol, Chinese, Jurchen, Khitan, Uyghur, Tangut, Parhae, and Korean descent. Kwŏn Kŭn's teacher Yi Saek 李穡 (1328–1396), for instance, had traveled from Korea to the Yuan and passed the civil service exams there, even serving briefly in its bureaucracy.[15] Although the Mongols, after having subjugated the Korean Koryŏ (918–1392) kingdom, limited the ritual prerogatives of its kings, annexed Korean territory, curtailed its institutional autonomy, and "interfered" with Koryŏ's administration, Korea's ecumenical membership was not under question.[16]

The ecumenical configuration advanced in Kwŏn's couplet, therefore, hearkened back to an idealized Yuan-Koryŏ imperial universalism.[17] Kwŏn wished to have his cake and eat it too—that is, to have Chosŏn be both autonomous and belong.[18] Therefore, when Kwŏn Kŭn divested the Yalu River of significance as a boundary separating the "civilized" from the "barbarian," and charged that imperial influence extended beyond natural barriers, Korea's inclusion became a demonstration of Ming's universal reach. But elevating Ming authority to the register of the universal made its territorial claims inconsequential. This transcendence of territorial distinction, far from erasing Korea as a bounded space, preserves its integrity, ironically, by subsuming it under a different scheme of abstraction. Empire was above territory and territory was beneath the dignity of empire.

RITUAL AND RHETORIC IN THE HISTORY OF SINO-KOREAN RELATIONS

Kwŏn Kŭn met only limited success during his diplomatic mission. Although he impressed the Ming emperor with his poetry, he neither obtained the patents of investiture for his king nor secured the release of his detained colleagues. After all, what could a few dozen poems, let alone a single couplet, accomplish?

One purpose of this study is to rethink how efficacy in diplomatic engagement should be appreciated. Addressing specific issues, whether concerning the goods, people, territory, or protocol, was certainly part of any Chosŏn envoy mission. But diplomacy also depended on the cultivation and maintenance of shared frames of reference. Efficacy, in the latter sense, is measured less in whether imperial policies changed at the moment and more in how these frames of reference could be shaped in the long run. Kwŏn's rhetoric might not have coaxed the emperor into changing tack, but as the discussions in this book will show, it was Kwŏn's vision of Ming universal rule (rather than the emperor's) that would dominate Chosŏn-Ming diplomatic rhetoric. In the meantime, the act of investiture, which the emperor had refused to grant even until his death, eventually became a ritual cornerstone of Chosŏn's diplomatic relations with Ming and its Qing (1636–1911) successor. In the long view, no rhetorical or ritual gesture occurred in isolation as discrete statements. They were instead part of an ongoing conversation about the meaning and purpose of empire, one in which Korea's place in the imperial imagination played an important role.

The rhetorical and ritual practices of Korean diplomacy have traditionally been understood in terms of Korean participation in the Chinese "tributary system." As described by American sinologist John K. Fairbank (1907–1991), in this system China's rulers managed relations with their neighbors by enforcing recognition of their superiority as a precondition for commercial and political access. This "Chinese (or East Asian) World Order" provided what political scientist David Kang calls the "rules" and "tools" for resolving conflict.[19] Although the paradigm has invited its share of discontent among historians over the decades, it has recently enjoyed a rebirth in international relations studies.[20] The difference in enthusiasm can be partly explained by the divergent methodological priorities of different disciplines. While historians tend to chafe at overgeneralization, it is precisely how the "tributary system" is able to generalize compelling, if essentialist, "Asian" and "premodern" counterpoint to the fraying Eurocentric and Westphalian nation-state-based model that makes it useful for scholars of international relations.[21]

The "tributary system" presents thorny challenges for understanding Korea's past that go beyond disciplinary differences. If the "tributary system" is "tenacious," its grasp on Korea is particularly strong, especially considering that historians of other regions of East Asia have largely moved on.[22] One reason is the integral role Korea played in establishing the paradigm in the first place. At the outset, Chosŏn relations with imperial China, especially Ming and Qing empires, provided the

Weberian ideal type for the paradigm, with Fairbank once calling it the "primary example, almost the ideal model, of tributary relations," and by extension of East Asian diplomacy before the nineteenth century.[23] Granted, there is some historical basis for thinking about Chosŏn as a "model tributary." Korea's relations with imperial China, unlike those of other polities, have exhibited remarkable institutional continuity. As historian Yuanchong Wang notes, the "Chosŏn model" provided a template that the Manchu Qing Empire deployed in relations with its other vassals.[24] In the meantime, Chosŏn Korean elites who bristled at Manchu domination turned to idealize the previous Chosŏn-Ming relationship as a way to subvert Manchu domination.[25] In short, Chosŏn-Ming relations provide at once an idealized representation of the "tributary system" for multiple parties, the historical antecedent for the "tributary system" as a historiographical paradigm, and its case study par excellence. Now the ouroboros consumes its own tail, creating a tautology: the Chosŏn-Ming relationship has become a model for itself.

This tautology renders the bulk of Chosŏn-Ming history uninteresting. If the scholarly consensus is "the tribute system," once established, "functioned relatively smoothly until the last decade of the sixteenth century," what is there really to see?[26] Indeed, prevailing narratives of the Chosŏn-Ming relationship are interested either in its early years or its tumultuous last decades. The Imjin War of 1592–1598, when Ming helped Chosŏn fend off an invasion from Japan, is used as a stand-in for Chosŏn-Ming relations as a whole. However, the war disrupted Chosŏn and Ming relations and the larger diplomatic order in East Asia in fundamental ways, and it makes little sense to treat the periods before and after in the same breath. Meanwhile, the Manchu invasions of 1627 and 1636 serve to illustrate the dissolution of Chosŏn's ties with Ming and the transition to the Chosŏn-Qing relationship.[27] The volume of scholarship on these episodes could fill a small library; in contrast, the two centuries of peace between the inception of Chosŏn-Ming ties and the Imjin War (the focus of this book) has been comparatively overlooked.

This oversight can be blamed on how cultural practices, such as poetry and ritual, fit into the "tributary system" paradigm. Whereas other participants of the "tributary system," whether Mongol nobles or Japanese merchants, might have paid only lip service, the supposed sincerity of Korean poetic declarations and ritual performances have made it difficult to dismiss the "Chinese World Order" outright—if a Chinese fantasy, it was at least one shared by one of its neighbors.[28] Meanwhile, Chosŏn elites' identification with the cultural ideals and moral values of this order,[29] whether attributed to common Confucian culture or Sinocentric ideology (*Chunghwa chuŭi* 中華主義 in modern Korean or *muhua sixiang* 慕華思想 in modern Chinese), results in a totalizing explanation that turns all things Chinese and Confucian into a singularity. A host of diverse phenomena—everything from Confucian family rites to diplomatic policy—so long as it was an object of Chosŏn appropriation comes to be touted as evidence of Chosŏn's "admiration" 慕.[30]

The "tributary system" has become a black box: a preexisting, unchangeable entity that Koreans could react to, identify with, acknowledge as legitimate, or occasionally circumvent, but not alter. It naturalizes Korean diplomatic practices as the expected consequence of an imposed "system." Under this framework, Chosŏn's ritual and rhetorical activities are at best epiphenomenal reflections of political ideology. They become inert as manifestations of existing hierarchies rather than active processes with "ontological effects" that can "affect material conditions and institutional outcomes." Because the Chosŏn court expended the bulk of its diplomatic efforts on rhetoric and ritual, however, ignoring their role is to dismiss, a priori, the possibility of Korean agency in this relationship. The result is Sinocentrism and cultural essentialism by default: Chosŏn leaned toward Ming China because it was their ideology to gravitate toward China.[31] This explanation is as unsatisfying as an Aristotelian teleology, that objects fall because it is their natural tendency to fall. To understand Chosŏn diplomacy, the black box needs to be opened.

NOT IMPERIAL STATE BUT IMPERIAL TRADITION

If ritual and rhetoric are conceived as able only to express (but not shape) ideology, then Chosŏn-Ming relations as they unfolded could only be the natural consequence of a shared Confucian culture. Within these parameters, only the stereotype that Korean elites aped Chinese high culture can prevail. But suppose imperial ideology and diplomatic norms are treated as open-ended and dynamic. In that case, Chosŏn diplomacy's ceremonial and inscriptional practices should be understood not as reflections of reality but as efforts to shape it.

At this point, a discussion of what this book means by the word "empire" is needed. In common parlance, "empire" usually identifies a large, expansionist state bent on conquest and exploitation.[32] This way of thinking about empire is a poor fit, however, for the book's purpose. Instead of empire as an imperial state, then ensuing discussion will explain why empire is better understood in terms of an imperial tradition.

Ming was undoubtedly a massive state with expansionist ambitions, especially in its early decades. Even after the cant of conquest sputtered in the fifteenth century, it still ruled diverse peoples and commanded enormous material resources. But neither conquest nor profit adequately explains its interactions with Chosŏn. Ming's armies never invaded Korea. No agent of Ming authority—not a single soldier, bureaucrat, or administrator—resided in Chosŏn on a permanent basis. In contrast, their predecessors, the Mongols annexed portions of Koryŏ territory, appointed *darugaci* overseers to supervise Koryŏ's administration, and integrated the Koryŏ elite through marriage and service.[33]

Ming's contrast with the Mongol empire in Korea challenges classical typologies of empire as "formal" and "informal." With domination visible through official, institutional channels, the Mongol-Koryŏ case qualifies as an example of "formal" empire in Michael Doyle's classical typology, but there was nothing about the Ming-Chosŏn arrangement that was "informal." Far from concealing Ming domination, the Chosŏn court explicitly formalized it in ritual and discourse. For instance, the formula "Great King . . . of the State of Chosŏn of Ming" [有明朝鮮國 . . . 大王] was inscribed on the tombstones of Korean monarchs.[34] Indeed, "empire" was never just about armies, taxes, and revenues. As Chris Bayly once put it, the "attitudes, legends, theories, and institutions" created and perpetuated empire in the discursive and mental worlds of those beholden to it.[35] So while the Ming Empire did coerce (in its first century of dealings with Korea, it detained envoys, threatened invasion, and extracted heavy tribute), matters of persuasion, defined by Torquil Duthie as the "administrative and ideological structure for [imperial] subjects to belong to and make sense of their position within the larger world," took on more significance as time went on.[36]

As presaged by Kwŏn's couplet, Chosŏn mattered less to Ming for the material resources it could extract than the role it played in constructing its imperial imaginary. Given the violence intrinsic to any imperial formation, focusing on the coercive aspect of empire-making is usually a historiographical and ethical imperative, but for understanding the Ming Empire in Korea, it creates a methodological barrier by turning a scholar's gaze away from where Korean agency was most possible.

The book therefore needs to anchor its thinking about empire to something other than the idea of an expansive, exploitative state. The very word "empire" appears to foreclose this possibility. After its origins in the Latin *imperium*, the "authority to command," carries militaristic overtones and, as Anthony Pagden explains, implies a related sense of absolute, but territorially defined sovereignty, usually under one ruler.[37] This sense is captured well by its most conventional equivalent in modern East Asian languages, *cheguk* 帝國 (C. *diguo*; J. *teikoku*). Literally, "emperor-state," this term, as well as its many connotations, however, is of exogenous origin. It originated as a calque of the early modern Dutch *Keijzerryk* (or *Kaiserreich* in German) adopted by Japanese Dutch studies in the early nineteenth century.[38]

Absent in East Asian political idiom before then, no one in the period covered by this book would have used this term, let alone conceive of Ming as a *cheguk* or "emperor-state." The compound only became part of the official names of East Asian monarchies in the late nineteenth century: Great Qing Empire (*Da Qing diguo* 大清帝國), Great Nippon Empire (*Dai Nihon teikoku* 大日本帝國) or Korea's Great Han Empire (*Taehan cheguk* 大韓帝國) are all neologisms coined as part of broader adoption of Western symbols of sovereignty.[39] As part of this assemblage of new knowledge, represented, for instance, by translations of Henry Wheaton's (1785–1848) *Elements of International Law* (K. *Man'guk kongpŏp*, C. *Wanguo gongfa* 萬國公法), *cheguk* or "empire" was just one of many neologisms translated as calques from Western languages. These new terms carried with them connotations of a new international order whose discursive conventions have since fundamentally transformed East Asian political vocabulary.[40]

The problem of etymology, then, raises important historiographical and methodological considerations. Indeed, it is still nearly impossible to talk about the East Asian past without using these neologisms and their embedded references to the modern, Western international system, a disease hardly confined to the ivory tower.[41] All the governments of regions that use or once used Chinese characters—China, Taiwan, the Koreas, Japan, Singapore, and Vietnam—assert "sovereignty" (C. *zhuquan*, K. *chukwŏn*, J. *shuken*, V. *Chủ quyền* 主權), another late-nineteenth-century calque translation of a concept of international law, which when projected onto distant pasts (or uninhabited islets) inevitably invests them with anachronistic valences and invented histories.[42] A case in point is how Japan justified its annexation and occupation of Korea by claiming it had always lacked "sovereignty" because of its historical relationship with imperial China. Supposedly evinced by the Chosŏn king's subordination to China's emperors, this anachronism served an obvious political interest in the early twentieth century. After Korean liberation in 1945, much of the intellectual energy expended on Chosŏn's historical relations with China still revolved around recovering some element of Korean sovereignty for the modern nation, usually by blaming the Chosŏn court for disregarding it. With that, the quest for "sovereignty" usually ends abandoned, with the history of Chosŏn diplomacy left in a wasteland of regret and missed opportunity.[43]

The problem with modern ideas of "empire" and "sovereignty" is that they embed another anachronism: that empire should be understood primarily in terms of a large territorial state. To formulate Ming imperial authority in this limited way would have been nonsensical. Chosŏn period usage did speak of Ming as a "superior state" (*sangguk* 上國), but it was also an "imperial court" (or more literally, "august" or "brilliant" court, *hwangjo* 皇朝)[44] whose "winds" (as Kwŏn described it in his poem on the Yalu) translated its authority across territorial divides and natural barriers. What made Ming "imperial" was not its territorial mass but how its authority could transcend these divisions. To delimit imperial authority with territory was an oxymoron.

This incompatibility between Korean conceptions of Ming imperial authority and modern ideas of territorial sovereignty did not mean territorial claims were irrelevant to Chosŏn-Ming diplomacy. In fact, the distinction between Ming as a universal empire with cosmic claims and Chosŏn as a territorial state ruled by a local king was central. This distinction should be pedestrian to any reader familiar with premodern East Asian idioms of sovereignty; nonetheless, it has historically been a stumbling block in attempts to understand Korea's relationship with imperial China by modern scholars and diplomats alike. As nineteenth-century European and American dignitaries complained, Chosŏn's special arrangement with Qing China smacked of the "romance and hyperbole" of "Oriental claims to sovereignty." But how imperial authority is figured Chosŏn diplomatic idiom is only illegible when statehood, sovereignty, and territory are assumed to be coterminous and mutually constitutive (as they are in modern international law).[45]

The casual orientalism notwithstanding, the reality was territorial sovereignty as a legal regime had only recently come into being, even in Europe.[46] In the two centuries between Hugo Grotius (1583–1645) and Wheaton, "empire" was conceived differently. In earlier eras, what was *the* empire for Latinate Europe, the Holy Roman Empire (derided by Voltaire as neither holy, Roman, nor imperial), had little in common, structurally, with these later imperial forms (or with the Ming state in China, for that matter). It did, however, possess a "defining character-istic of empire" that would have made sense to Kwŏn Kŭn. It was, in the words of the historian Peter Wilson, the "absolute refusal to define limits to either its physical extent or its power pretensions." By the time the term "empire" entered East Asia in the nineteenth century, the word in Europe had largely shed this older meaning of a "world order" and became simply a synonym for a large state.[47]

That the rhetoric of empire in Chosŏn-Ming relations can seem so detached from the substance of empire, then, has more to do with mod-ern assumptions about the relationships between territory, authority, and sovereignty than how things, in fact, worked in the past. The leg-acies of these Victorian prejudices aside, there is no fundamental dis-junction between East and West, only the consequences of privileging modern imperial practices as touchstones for historical comparison.[48] So instead of searching for a one-size-fits-all definition of "sovereignty" or "empire" that can apply to all times and all spaces, the historian is bet-ter served by investigating how such claims of authority were sustained and asserted in their context.[49]

The book therefore proposes the following revision to how empire should be understood, at least for the Chosŏn-Ming context. Many scholars of East Asia shy away from the term "empire" not only because of its exogeneity, but because it evokes the world's traumatic encounter with nineteenth-century Western imperialism 帝國主義, which they distinguish (whether appropriately or not) from Qing, Ming, or even Mongol practices of rulership and expansion.[50] But there is no intrinsic reason to privilege expansionist, colonial empires as the default point of comparison, other than that East Asia's confrontation with this imperial form was what introduced "empire" as a term. So instead of the neologism *cheguk*, this book relies on a different anchor for the English word "empire": *t'ong* (C. *tong* 統).

T'ong encapsulates at once the coercive and persuasive dimensions of empire making. It also embeds the dialectical relationship between the exercise of control and expanding horizons of political desire. *T'ong*, as used in various compounds, could point to legal-juridical, military, and administrative mechanisms of enforcement. In modern usage, this control can be spatial; a political regime can "control and administer" (K. *t'ongch'i*, C. *tongzhi* 統治) a region or people. It can also be temporal, as hinted by the deep etymology of *t'ong* as "thread": links of transmission from the present to an origin. This is the sense adapted in the modern word for "tradition" (K. *chŏnt'ong*, C. *chuantong* 傳統), which is usually parsed as "transmitted authority" because of how it connects to another term that intertwines spatial and temporal notions of authority: *chŏngt'ong* (C. *zhengtong* 正統). Often translated as "legitimacy," *chŏngt'ong* delineates a single, orthodox transmission of authority through time, whether of political, scholastic, or genealogical nature.[51] The transmission of the Mandate of Heaven in dynastic succession was thus described as *hwangt'ong* (literally, "august thread," C. *huangtong* 皇統) or *chet'ong* (C. *dit'ong* 帝統), a scheme where connections to the past was what legitimized present imperial control over territories, institutions, and peoples. *T'ong*, by including a diachronic sense of a continuous imperial tradition, exceeds the semantic range suggested by both the classical Latin etymology of "empire" as the power to control and the modern notion of an expansionist state, but it converges with the sense of the medieval Latin *translatio imperii*: the sequential transfer of Rome's imperium to those who claimed to be its successors, whether Charlemagne, the Ottonians, Habsburgs, Byzantines, Ottomans, Romanovs, or Napoleon.[52]

Ming emperors saw themselves as heirs to a continuous imperial tradition passed down since the age of the sage kings. It was also this imperial tradition that animated many of the diplomatic contestations between Ming and Chosŏn. While Chosŏn never challenged Ming's imperial claims, it remained an open question what elements of the imperial tradition were open to the Korean monarchy's appropriation.[53] Narrowly speaking, the "imperial tradition" was simply a line of succession, but to claim it required deploying a repertoire of political technologies for its construction and for lending a sense of timeless majesty to political power.[54] Integrated with techniques of governance, diplomacy, and war making, this repertoire included pageantry, calendars, music, sartorial conventions, and codified rituals.[55] Dynastic histories, classical texts (and their commentaries), literary paeans, and works of statecraft, which document the splendor and exercise of imperial ritual, also constitute a body of knowledge that sustained the transmission of legitimacy. Imperial tradition, writ large, points to this body of knowledge that showed how empire was to function and how it was to be passed down.[56]

Access to this body of knowledge depended on the circulation and literacy of foundational texts in a shared classical language of literary Chinese, or as some prefer, Literary Sinitic. Articulations of political authority in this tradition (ritual practices had broader regional cachet) were legible only within that scriptal zone: the Sinographic cosmopolis of which Korea was a member.[57] It therefore makes sense to speak of East Asian empires in terms of a Sinitic imperial tradition, both to acknowledge the importance of the literary language it depends on and the classical world it references. In this regard, this imperial tradition differs from other repertoires of rule—for instance, Islamicate, Sanskrit, or Persianate traditions—less in terms of practices of rule or even the semiotics of sovereignty, for many parallels, convergences, and moments of cross-fertilization can be observed, especially in the aftermath of one century of Mongol rule.[58] Instead, the critical distinction is in their hermeneutic technologies and normative universes—that is, which bodies of texts and which traditions could be cited to appraise, interpret, and guide political practice.

The advantage of thinking in terms of a Sinitic or East Asian imperial tradition, rather than "Chinese empire," is to accept the existence of a widely shared framework without attributing "Chinese" ethnic essences or national valences to its institutions, practices, or ideas that, by their nature, are transmutable and adaptable. It also avoids the insinuation that whenever someone uses this repertoire, it somehow implies they are or should be subject to some form of Chinese territorial sovereignty.[59] Certainly, the Chinese heartland was the fountainhead of this imperial tradition, but as it was for the Mughals and their Central Asian and Persianate heritage, associations with a region or script did not prevent the translation of political idioms beyond their places of origin.[60] In East Asia, the Sinitic imperial tradition was ultimately claimed by a variety of polities on the Chinese cultural frontier, such as Nanzhao 南詔 (738–902), Dali 大理 (937–1253), Tangut Xia 西夏 (1038–1227), Khitan Liao 遼 (916–1125) and Kara Khitai 黑契丹 (1124–1218) empires. While others, the Jurchen Jin 金 (1115–1234), the Mongol Yuan, and ultimately the Manchu Qing dynasties claimed it in toto when they occupied the Chinese heartland. While these polities have been folded under a national history of China, as Evelyn Rawski points out, the appropriation of this repertoire elsewhere, notably in Korea, Vietnam, and Japan, has since engendered separate national stories.[61]

Any move of analytical terminology from one context to another risks discursive violence. This problem is not unique to "empire," but it is inherent in any attempt to write about the wider world in English, or the past in any modern language, for that matter.[62] It makes no sense to deny, a priori, the appropriateness of transplanted terms for understanding non-Western societies or interpreting "Eastern" ideas any more than it does to insist that any "Western" term must cleave faithfully to their moments of conception.[63] Both extremes privilege the Western historical experience. Instead, there needs to be what JaHyun Kim Haboush calls a "mutual accommodation between the new user and old usage: the new user searches and employs words of best approximation from the Western regime; conversely, the new usage should be assimilated into the old word, and the new usage becomes another possible meaning of this word."[64] In this respect, the historian's quandary is not very different from that of the envoys and interpreters who traveled between the Chosŏn and Ming courts, or any other denizen of a "trading zone" charged with communicating across different linguistic and discursive spaces.[65] Translation is an act of betrayal, but it also produces the necessary, if provisional, shared epistemic space that makes discussion and a more inclusive reckoning of the past possible.

REPERTOIRES OF DIPLOMACY: APPROACHES AND SOURCES

Chosŏn confronted Ming not only as one state to another but also as rival claimants to the classical past with the weight of the imperial tradition behind them. Korea occupied a particular place within the imperial tradition, as a potential object of irredentist ambition. It had once been ruled by the Han dynasty 漢 (202 BCE–221 CE), invaded by the Sui and Tang emperors, and nearly annexed by the Mongols. When the view is stretched to this long arc of historical time, this threat always loomed barely beyond the horizons. Ming never materialized as such a threat, but Korean diplomats and memorial writers, especially in the fifteenth century, did not ignore that possibility. Effective diplomacy meant warding off latent irredentist ambitions over Korea, massaging away the imperial court's jealous monopoly over the symbols of universal and cosmic authority, sidestepping conflicts over a shared frontier, and resolving problems of economic and political access. The Chosŏn court searched for a strategy of engagement that could preserve Korean royal authority and limit Ming claims, all without provoking conflict. The irony was that this strategy hinged on interpolating into Ming processes of empire making.

This book seeks to make sense of this strategy. One way to think about Chosŏn diplomacy is that it was a practical exercise in political theology. That is; it concerned what empire *should* do by determining how imperial action related to values, ideals, and the interpretive traditions that informed its raison d'être. In the most prosaic sense, this strategy was only possible because the Chosŏn court knew the Confucian classics, imperial histories, and the imperial language (literary and spoken Chinese, and during the Yuan period, Mongolian). Shared knowledge facilitated communication, but deploying the discourse of imperial authority implicitly legitimized and strengthened imperial authority. Given the vast differentials of power, where Chosŏn stared down a neighbor twenty times its size, participation in the construction of empire was also used as a weapon of the weak: rather than deny imperial claims outright, it sought to redirect them.

To emphasize Korean agency also rebukes two major tropes in the historiography of Korea's relationship with imperial China. The first is the dichotomies of subservience and resistance typical of both colonialist and nationalist treatments of this history. The second is a Whig history of empire that touts the Sino-Korean peace as an exemplary achievement of China's "virtuous" empire.[66] Both analytical tropes share a Great Powers–centered view of international relations where more modest actors, whether peripheral peoples, marginal states, or middling powers—in this case, Chosŏn Korea—have little meaningful role to play.

An alternative is to shift the gaze from the highest political centers and toward zones of mediation. In these zones, go-betweens (in Chosŏn's case, royal emissaries and their interpreters rather than merchants or clergy) brokered across a range of liminal zones, whether cultural and linguistic frontiers or ungoverned borderlands.[67] Conceived this way, empire ceases to be a typology of political form; instead, it becomes a category of analysis "about political authority relations" as it is negotiated "between a central power and many diverse and differentiated entities," as historical sociologist Karen Barkey puts it. Much as a good economic history is concerned not only with questions of exchange, wealth, value, productivity, and material accretion but also with the institutions, ideas, and discourses surrounding these issues, a history of empire should not "[fixate] on empires as clearly bounded geopolities," but also consider how interactions with "peripheries, local elites, and frontier groups" produce political imaginaries and claims of authority.[68]

In order to emphasize this scale of interaction, this book focuses less on the decisions of kings and emperors than on the envoys and rhetoricians who communicated between them. The chief protagonists in the following pages are Korean envoys like Kwŏn Kŭn. Although the day-to-day operation of diplomacy was carried out by the court's professional interpreters who proverbially "spent their mornings in Seoul and their evenings in Beijing until they die from old age on their journey" [朝漢都 而暮燕京 卒老于行], the envoys who led the embassies were usually well-connected high officials and scions of prestigious aristocratic lineages. They were also the ones who discussed diplomatic policy, performed the rituals, composed diplomatic correspondence, and entertained Ming visitors.[69]

They deployed two main rhetorical modes. The first is autoethnography. In Mary Louise Pratt's original usage, autoethnography "[refers] to instances in which colonized subjects undertake to represent themselves in ways that engage with the colonizer's terms." For colonial elites in Latin America, autoethnographic texts were self-representations constructed "in response to or in dialogue with [the] metropolitan representations" of the Iberian metropole. The Ming-Chosŏn case was by no means colonial, but Korean envoys likewise "collaborat[ed]" with imperial objectives, while "appropriating" imperial idioms and identified them as their own. The essentialism of these autoethnographic moves, as this book will show, were hardly devoid of instrumental calculus and were critical for advancing the agendas of the Chosŏn court and its elites.[70]

The second mode is what this book refers to as the imperializing mode. This rhetorical mode brought the normative elements of the imperial tradition to the negotiation table. It exhorted imperial agents to behave according to their professed values. Both autoethnography and the imperializing mode required the selective and judicious deployment of the imperial tradition to cajole, entice, and ultimately persuade an emperor or his official to a course of action beneficial to the supplicant. The latter, hardly a technique exclusive to Korean envoys, was a tried-and-true tactic for anyone who found themselves in the difficult position to "instruct" monarchs. What was peculiar to the Korean context was how the target of persuasion shifted away from the imperial person. Imperial officials, military officers, eunuch chamberlains, literati ministers, and occasionally even petty functionaries all became possible targets as Korean diplomats foisted the demands of imperial magnanimity onto them.[71]

These rhetorical modes sustained a vivid imperial presence in the Korean diplomatic record. Materialized from Chosŏn diplomatic practice, this record constituted a vast body of knowledge: collections of diplomatic missives, poetry anthologies, travelogues, handbooks, and envoy reports. Kept with an awareness that they would be consulted in the future, a discrete gesture or a momentary act, once documented, became a precedent that could inform the future. Through this cumulative effect, these records of diplomatic activity also became part of the very imperial tradition they sought to intercede in. It is these sources, complemented by official and institutional chronicles from both Chosŏn and Ming, that this book draws upon to craft its argument. Together they reveal how Chosŏn court participated in constructing the Ming Empire, not as passive observers but as integral stakeholders.

The book, therefore, does not provide give a play-by-play account of Chosŏn-Ming diplomacy. Instead, it lays out a new historiographical paradigm where the Chosŏn court's diplomatic strategies take center stage. It foregrounds how, through its use of ritual and rhetoric, the Chosŏn court harnessed the imperial tradition for its own ends and in the process institutionalized certain rhetorical tropes and ritual practices. These choices also mean privileging the collective effort of Chosŏn diplomacy over the diversity of Korean perspectives, opinions, and positions. Although the range of Chosŏn voices represented in this book should suffice as reminders that there was no singular, permanent consensus regarding how diplomacy should be carried out, it remains that, in practice, Korean envoys, interpreters, and court composers acted as agents of the kingdom (whether in practice or in name) and were treated as such by their Ming counterparts. Their position as institutional actors did not mean that other motives, whether personal, ideological, or economic, were irrelevant. Even collective concerns, such as Korea's literary reputation, the success or failure of a diplomatic mission, or the legitimacy of a particular ruler, had enormous implications for the individuals involved. The classic problem of sociology—of how to relate individual action to wider patterns—might be more pronounced given the stakes of diplomacy, but as it is for any context where individual agents operate self-consciously to shape an institutional environment, action informed by prior precedent can also guide future action. Akin to dispositions in a shared habitus, the conventions, tropes, and precedents that the agents of the Chosŏn court constructed and retraced lent a sense of consistency and created what looks like, in retrospect, a systematic diplomatic order.[72]

The emphasis on lines of continuity rather than on points of rupture or difference also means that the book will not insist on any general periodization of how Chosŏn and Ming relations unfolded (for an outline, see chronology on page xv). That does not imply change over time is irrelevant. Indeed, each of the chapters follows an issue or theme with its own historical trajectory. For instance, some chapters engage with the question of ecumenical belonging, which threads through the entire two centuries in question. Other chapters focus on the poetic sociability anchored by court-sponsored literary anthologies, which only emerged after the 1450s.

These issues and themes do not always converge to form neat temporal chunks. Therefore, the book's ten chapters proceed according to a loose chronological order. They are divided into four parts, each focusing on a set of related themes moored to a common moment of inflection. Part I, which covers the prehistory and early decades of Chosŏn-Ming relations, addresses the equivocal legacies of a shared past, which, far from offering a blueprint for peace, required selective reinterpretation and negotiation for stable relations to proceed. Part II looks to the mid-fifteenth century, a period of dynastic instability in both Chosŏn and Ming. It discusses practical aspects of diplomatic activity to show how the very notion of Ming imperial authority could be invoked and used by savvy agents for an ulterior purpose. Part III takes the conversation through the mid-sixteenth century. It shows what rhetorical and ritual strategies Korean envoys and officials adopted as they drew and redrew the ecumenical shape of empire to negotiate and challenge imperial policies. Part IV addresses the enduring discursive legacies of diplomatic rhetoric. Its discussion of literary practice, in particular envoy poetry, reveals how diplomatic discourse and the rituals they narrated invested their relations with the Ming with a moral mythology and a constitutional character, imputing what empire should be and what that meant for Korea's place within it. The book concludes with a brief assessment of this diplomatic universe's afterlife: how the mythology of moral empire that emerged in the fifteenth and sixteenth centuries persisted well after, even up to the contemporary period.

PART I

The Shared Past

In 1368, the Hongwu emperor's armies reached the Mongol imperial capital of Daidu (modern Beijing). The Mongol court abandoned the city with his entourage and retreated north, leaving control of the Chinese heartland to the newly declared Ming dynasty. Meanwhile, the Mongol Empire still held sway in northeast Asia, presenting a diplomatic conundrum for the Korean kingdom of Koryŏ. Its kings, once *küregen*, or sons-in-law, of the Mongol Great Khan, Koryŏ dithered between supporting their Mongol kin in the north and the newly ascendant Ming in China. King Kongmin 恭愍王 (r. 1351–1374) sought good ties with Hongwu, but after his assassination, relations deteriorated, and they were further embittered by the murder of Ming envoys, onerous tribute terms, and Koryŏ's continued relationship with the Mongols.[1]

Over the next decades, Ming asserted control over northeast Asia, defeating forces still loyal to the Mongol Empire. Along with the Liaodong region, Shenyang, once an appanage of Koryŏ princes and settled by people from Koryŏ, fell under Ming control.[2] In 1387, Ming forces defeated Nahacu 納哈出 (?–1388), a Mongol warlord based in the Liao-dong region. To secure Ming's position, Hongwu also established military garrisons along the new frontier, a move that brought Ming and Koryŏ into direct confrontation. Of particular concern was the Tieling Guard 鐵嶺衛, which shared a name with the Ch'ŏllyŏng range 鐵嶺, an area under Koryŏ administration. Once under the Yuan dynasty's Shuangcheng Route Command (K. *Ssangsŏng ch'onggwanbu* 雙城總管府), the region had passed to Koryŏ control when its commander, Yi Chach'un 李子春 (1315–1361), defected to Koryŏ in 1356 (see map 2).[3]

Fearing Ming would use Tieling as a pretext to retake the area, Koryŏ decided to attack Ming-controlled Liaodong. Its army reached the Yalu River in the fifth month of 1388 but found it swelling from heavy rains, impossible to ford. The army stalled on the island of Wihwa. Provisions dwindled. Soldiers deserted. Yi Chach'un's son, Yi Sŏnggye 李成桂 (1335–1408, r. King T'aejo 太祖 of Chosŏn 1392–1398), who was third in command, tried to call off the expedition, but his superiors refused to listen. Rather than carry on, Yi mutinied, turned the army back, seized the capital, purged his political opponents, and deposed the Koryŏ king. In 1392, only four years after his fateful "return from Wihwa island" 威化島回軍, he seized the throne for himself.

From Yi's refusal to ford the Yalu, historians have gleaned his commitment to an ideology where conflict with the Ming Son of Heaven was verboten. Before becoming king, Yi Sŏnggye once declared that for "the small to go against the great is the first mistake."[4] During his fateful return from Wihwa Island, he explained to his troops that "if we violate the territory of the superior country [i.e., the Ming], we will be blamed by the Son of Heaven, and great would be the calamity to befall our dynastic shrines, state altars, and common people."[5] In this view, Chosŏn's tributary relations with Ming were the logical consequence of Yi Sŏnggye's "pro-Ming" tendencies and Chosŏn's "dogmatic devotion to Confucian practice."[6]

Confucian ideology has also been used to explain Koryŏ's demise. Modern historians have described Yi Sŏnggye's supporters in terms of an emerging "middle-sized" landholding elite that adopted Neo-Confucianism as their guiding ideology, although changes in the shape of the ruling elite across the Koryŏ-Chosŏn transition were likely less dramatic and less coherent than usually portrayed.[7] For instance, the core of the aristocracy, of which Kwŏn Kŭn's family is a good example, persisted across the transition.[8] His descent group, the Kwŏn family of Andong 安東權氏 rose to prominence in national politics during the period of Mongol domination.[9] As for Neo-Confucianism,[10] Kwŏn was one of its early proponents in Korea, but many self-identified Neo-Confucians, including Kwŏn's teacher Yi Saek, and his colleagues Chŏng Mongju 鄭夢周 (1337–1392) and Yi Sungin 李崇仁 (1347–1392), opposed Yi Sŏnggye's regime, suffering exile or murder in the process.[11] Neo-Confucian models did inspire reformist policies, but their implementation took place gradually over generations, not months or years.[12] Neo-Confucianism also coexisted with other literati traditions in the learned life of Chosŏn's earliest statesmen. Kwŏn Kŭn provides again a case in point; his capacities ranged across eclectic domains, including mastery of belles lettres that served him well as the new dynasty's chief court composer.[13]

If a "top-down" ideological revolution oversimplifies the dynastic transition in 1392, how useful is it as an explanation for Yi Sŏnggye's diplomacy?[14] The notion of Neo-Confucian "revolution" contains glimmers of truth, but it also rides on an analytical short circuit. It reduces a practice or phenomenon (including diplomacy) to the logical consequence of classical inspiration and Confucian culture. The purpose of part I in this book is to rewire this short circuit by showing how a shared imperial tradition was as much a source of guidance as it was cause for contrition. Its tangle of ambivalent precedents, many of which had proximate origins in Mongol rather than in Sinitic practices of empire making, required a deft handling and a selective paring before they could be applied. In this respect, Confucian classics and a common literary legacy provided not so much serviceable policy models as a repertoire of rhetorical and symbolic tools. Just as speaking a common tongue does not imply uttering the same message, Chosŏn and Ming used common cultural idioms but employed them for divergent purposes. Inasmuch as their rhetoric spoke of a shared ideal of diplomacy, it was a product of Korea's longstanding engagement with the imperial tradition in the first place.

CHAPTER ONE

Serving the Great

By the late fourteenth century, the nearly 500-year-old Koryŏ dynasty had been a long-embattled institution. Already in the twelfth century, its royal house had lost control of the state to a military junta. Between 1260 and 1270, infighting among the junta's leadership led to their overthrow. When royal authority was reestablished, it came at the price of Mongol military intervention.[1] Its rulers then relied on its marital ties with the Mongol imperial family, while Koryŏ's traditional elite bristled under these new arrangements.[2]

After King Kongmin took the throne in 1356, there was an ephemeral resurgence of royal and dynastic authority. He successfully asserted his prerogatives over both the Koryŏ elite and his Mongol cousins, only to face a host of other security challenges, ranging from Chinese Red Turban rebels to marauding Japanese pirates. To handle them, Kongmin relied on military strongmen such as Yi Sŏnggye, but the armies they fielded were bound by personal fealty rather than loyalty to the dynasty.[3] Kongmin was assassinated in 1374. He did not have issue with his primary consort, the Mongol princess Botasiri 寶塔失里 (Princess of Lu 魯國大長公主 ?–1365), which weakened the claims of his heir, King U 禑王 (r. 1375–1388). His opponents stoked rumors over their bloodline, claiming that they were fathered by a Buddhist monk.[4] Most likely fabrications by Yi Sŏnggye's faction who ousted and murdered them, these rumors nevertheless provided the cover for Yi's coalition to seize power in 1388.

The problems that plagued the Koryŏ rulers did not suddenly disappear because a new man was in charge. Yi Sŏnggye still confronted the same fiscal and political challenges as the rulers he overthrew. To refill state coffers, he expropriated Buddhist monasteries and confiscated land held by his political enemies and Koryŏ loyalists.[5] In these endeavors, he was supported by key members of the Koryŏ elite, including Cho Chun 趙浚 (1346–1405), a senior member of the P'yŏngyang Cho 平壤趙氏 descent group who had risen to prominence in the centuries of Mongol rule. Nevertheless, Yi had no real claim to kingship, which explains why Yi first resorted to installing a puppet ruler from the Koryŏ royal house rather than take the throne.[6]

Yi Sŏnggye was also diplomatically isolated. When Yi dispatched envoys to inform Ming that Koryŏ now had a new ruler, Koryŏ loyalists sent a secret missive to the Hongwu emperor in 1391 requesting Ming military intervention to oust Yi Sŏnggye from his position.[7] The Ming court informed Yi Sŏnggye's envoy Cho Pan 趙胖 (1341–1401) of the conspiracy, news that prompted Yi to purge suspected Koryŏ loyalists and take the throne for himself in the seventh month of 1392. To improve relations with Ming, Yi dispatched the news of his accession to the Ming capital with his envoy (again, Cho Pan was selected for the task), relating how the Koryŏ rulers he ousted were illegitimate pretenders who harbored hostile intent toward the imperial court.[8]

After receiving news of Yi's accession, the emperor demanded Yi's regime report post haste the new state's name. Yi Sŏnggye offered the emperor the honors of selecting it. His envoys presented the emperor with the choice between a name connected with Yi's place of birth or an ancient northeast Asian kingdom. The Ming emperor chose the latter: "Chosŏn" 朝鮮, "most beautiful" among the names of "eastern barbarians." Although a promising start, several issues—frontier friction, lack of political recognition, exorbitant tribute terms—proved intractable. A flurry of embassies traveled between the two courts to resolve them. In 1393, Chosŏn returned the golden seal Ming once granted to the Koryŏ King Kongmin. In 1395, Yi Sŏnggye also requested a new seal and patents of investiture (K. komyŏng, C. gaoming 誥命) that would have recognized Yi Sŏnggye as Chosŏn's king and the emperor's vassal. But these efforts earned only a blunt rejection, with the emperor chastising Yi Sŏnggye for failing to properly "serve the great."⁹

Confronted with these diplomatic challenges, Yi Sŏnggye thus expressed his misgivings about the Hongwu emperor to his officials:

> The emperor acquired his realm only because of his vast armies and severe policies. He killed excessively [殺戮過當] so that even his meritorious ministers and chief advisers could not save themselves. He also scrutinizes our small country over and over, making endless and outrageous demands. Now he also accuses me of contrived crimes and threatens me with his troops [而乃屢責我小邦 誅求無厭 今又責我以非罪 而脅我以動兵]—how is this any different from trying to scare a child by screaming [是何異恐喝小兒哉]?

When pressed by his officials about how they would deal with the Ming emperor, Yi Sŏnggye told them he could only "serve him carefully with humble words" [且卑辭謹事之耳].¹⁰ The next years nevertheless put the king's "service to the great" on trial. The Ming emperor remained standoffish, and by 1398, talk of war returned to the Korean court.¹¹ Frustrated Chosŏn officials lamented that, despite the king's "sincere efforts in serving the great," the emperor was still "blowing away hair to look for blemishes," finding any excuse to exert pressure on the fledgling regime.¹² Given these fractious beginnings, it might be surprising that the phrase "serving the great," or *sadae* (C. *shida* 事大), would ever become a shorthand for Chosŏn's diplomacy with the Ming.

Ubiquitous in both imperial and Korean missives, the phrase "serving the great" pointed to both Ming expectations for Korean behavior as well as the self-avowed diplomatic goals of Yi Sŏnggye's descendants. But what in fact did "serving the great" entail? Answering this question is more difficult than might first appear. Tributary hierarchy, ritual correctness, and Korean professions of admiration come to mind. Together they suggest the existence of a ready-made template for diplomatic action, but this chapter contends instead that "serving the great" is better understood as a working shorthand for an array of practices with ambiguous histories.

The following amble through preceding periods offers more a genealogy of the Chosŏn-Ming relationship than its prehistory. By paying attention to literary idioms, political concepts, and diplomatic practices associated with "serving the great," the itinerary it follows reveals several observations: its ambivalent meaning in classical and early imperial sources; an implicit *translatio imperii* whose line plumbs through the northern non-Chinese courts of the Liao, Jin, and Yuan (rather than the Chinese-ruled Song); and the proximate origin of Chosŏn-Ming tributary practices in the Mongol-Koryŏ period. Throughout, Korean diplomatic rhetoric repeatedly anticipated and exceeded imperial expectations, but not always in ways amenable to imperial objectives.

SERVING THE GREAT AND INVESTING THE FAR

In the twentieth century, *sadae* became a bad word. It represented centuries of Korean subordination to China's emperors, an ideology (*sadae chuŭi* 事大主義) that relinquished national sovereignty and self-determination. It explained Korea's national weakness in the face of Japanese imperialist encroachment and colonial occupation (1910–1945). During and after the Cold War (1947–1989), *sadae* in both North and South Korean political discourse was "flunkeyism." It discredited anyone perceived as advocating cultural or political submission to the great powers: the Soviet Union, the United States, and the People's Republic of China.[13] The valences that informed colonial and postcolonial disavowals of *sadae* have little relevance to actual diplomatic relations in the fifteenth and sixteenth century, but this obvious anachronism overshadows a more subtle but arguably more misleading abuse of temporality: the attempt to understand *sadae* in Chosŏn through the term's *locus classicus* in seminal Confucian texts.[14]

These attempts typically begin with the *Mencius*, where it is stated: "it requires a wise prince to be able, with a small country, to serve a large one." From this statement, it is then concluded Mencius offers a viable path for stable relations between a "great state" and a "small state"— so long as the "small" acknowledged this hierarchy, the "great" would reciprocate by "succoring the small" 字小. This hoary origin also infuses the notion of "serving the great" with timeless normativity, a point marshaled as further evidence of Korean internalization of the supposedly "Confucian hierarchical scheme of foreign relations between a superior China and a subordinate Korea."[15]

But a classical reference cannot stand for a concept's meaning. Politics, no monopoly of Confucian moralists, drew lessons as much from past bloodshed as its words of wisdom—a point evident to all those in service to Chosŏn's founders who flouted Confucian ideals of dynastic loyalty and agnatic primogeniture in their quest for power. Even in the Mencian context, service to the great was of dubious moral and strategic value. When the ruler of the small state of Teng asked Mencius for advice on how to deal with his warlike neighbors after he had already "exhausted himself in serving greater states," the sage gave a decidedly unsatisfying answer: rather than abandon his people and seek life, the king should be "prepared to die for them."[16] Indeed, as Fuma Susumu and Peter Yun point out, the moral framework for *sadae* might have classical origins, but its adoption by the Koryŏ and Chosŏn courts was a logical strategic shift in response to challenges of Mongol and later Ming hegemony in the region.[17]

The idea of *sadae* then describes a general template for state-to-state interactions rather than moral clarity about them per se. Elsewhere in the classical corpus, the term is also clouded by a sense of expediency. The traditions of the *Spring and Autumn Annals* upheld reciprocity between the "great" and the "small," but deference to a great power proved a dubious guarantee of a small state's survival.[18] Shared in these texts was a pessimism about the multistate political situation in the Eastern Zhou period. By the time these texts were written, the classical *fengjian* 封建, or "feudal" model of investing hereditary local rulers beholden to a universal king, was already obsolete.[19]

Sadae rarely met its promise of providing safety to small states in a stable interstate system. Nevertheless, it represented a classical paradigm of sovereign authority sitting atop a hierarchical, feudal, multistate order, one that stood in stark contrast with what came after. When the Qin 秦 state destroyed its rivals, it implemented a new paradigm of imperial governance through a centrally appointed bureaucracy. This *junxian* 郡縣, or "commanderies and counties" system, was also accompanied by a new discourse of imperial (rather than kingly) sovereignty that formed the basis of future imperial claims.[20] When the Han empire conquered the proto-Korean state of Wiman Chosŏn 衛滿朝鮮 (194 BCE–109 BCE) and established a series of commanderies 郡 (C. *jun*) over its territories, it also integrated the northern half of the Korean peninsula into this system.[21] Nonetheless, vestiges of a hereditary, feudal appointment system survived in the Han's "loose rein" (C. *jimi* 羈縻) approach to political communities beyond its direct administration, granting both virtual offices in the imperial bureaucracy as well as titles of nobility to their leaders.[22] So even after the kingdom of Koguryŏ 高句麗 (traditionally 37 BCE–668 CE) removed the last vestige of imperial *junxian* administration on the peninsula by conquering the remaining commanderies in the fourth century, signs of imperial authority persisted through this "loose rein" diplomatic framework. Aspiring imperial states on the mainland still invested peninsular rulers with "loose rein" titles combining hereditary and bureaucratic modes of ranking, for instance, this title granted to the ruler of the southwestern Korean kingdom Paekche 百濟 (traditionally 18 BCE–660): "Bearer of the tally, supreme commander of the military affairs of Paekche, the general who tranquilizes the east, the King (*wang*) of Paekche" 持節督百濟諸軍事綏東將軍百濟王.[23]

Imperial investiture of Korean rulers, whether as "king of Koryŏ" 高麗國王, or later, "king of Chosŏn" 朝鮮國王, continued these earlier "loose rein" conventions. Investiture, which reciprocated "service to the great," anchored early modern Korean-imperial relations,[24] but they seldom anticipated long-lasting bilateral ties in earlier periods. Instead, investiture of a foreign ruler implicitly marked a limit to an empire's administrative and military capabilities. When faced with military setbacks, the Sui and Tang emperors invested Koguryŏ kings as a delaying tactic, but in times of imperial strength, the memory of Han dominion provided a pretext for irredentist campaigns such as the one that eventually destroyed Koguryŏ kings in 668. Neither could generations of investiture from imperial rulers save Paekche from destruction in the same war. In the meantime, the rulers of the southeastern Korean kingdom of Silla 新羅 (traditionally 57 BCE–935) only received regular investiture after Tang armies were expelled from the region.[25]

Elsewhere along the Tang frontier, documents of investiture proved just as expedient. The occasional exhortations to "serve the great" in extant Tang investiture missives to the Turgesh (C. 突騎施 699–766), Uyghur (C. 迴鶻, 742–848), and Kyrgyz (C. 黠戛斯 ca. 700–900) khanates, all major military rivals, revealed the precarity rather than the security of imperial pretenses to universal rule.[26] Inasmuch as "service to the great" demanded submission to empire, it more often underscored its failure to occur, such as when the Tang court articulated the casus belli against the Nanzhao kingdom who had sacked Chengdu in Sichuan.[27] Praising someone for "serving the great," a tell-tale sign of eroding imperial authority, also became a way for late Tang officials, such as Li Shangyin 李商隱 (813–858, more famous for his love of poetry), to cajole the empire's military governors, de facto rulers of their own realms, to remain loyal.[28]

Later, these same military governors dismembered the Tang, becoming rival warlords in the subsequent interregnum. During this so-called Five Dynasties and Ten Kingdoms period (907–960), rulers with imperial ambition found valuable investiture for boosting the standing of their shaky regimes. Through investiture, they could transform other rulers, both near and far, into putative vassals. Northern claimants invested Wang Kŏn 王建 (877–943, r. T'aejo 高麗太祖 918–943), the founder of the Koryŏ dynasty as "king" (wang), praising his "diligent service to the great."[29] They did the same with their southern rivals. When the short-lived Later Han 後漢 (947–951) invested Qian Hongchu 錢宏俶 (r. 948–978), the ruler of the Wuyue 吳越 kingdom based in Hangzhou, they called on him to "serve the great with reverence" and be an "eternal vassal."[30] According to the late Chosŏn polymath Yi Ik 李瀷 (1681–1763), Wuyue's experience provided the best historical parallel for Korea's diplomatic relationship with China's imperial rulers. Like Chosŏn rulers, Wuyue's king remained content with the royal title of wang, never assumed the imperial title of huangdi (K. hwangje 皇帝), and recognized the suzerainty of whoever happened to be most powerful in the north China plain.[31] This modesty avoided triggering the anxieties of imperial claimants who might launch punitive expeditions or wars of conquest when others appropriated their precious symbols. The Later Han's successor, the Later Zhou 後周 (951–960), was enforcing its monopoly on this title when it attacked the Southern Tang 南唐 (937–975) regime in Jinling (modern Nanjing). It demanded that the Southern Tang follow the example of the Wuyue kingdom by observing the ancient "rites of the vassal state." Because the Southern Tang ruler had "flouted the [duty] of serving the great" by assuming the title of huangdi, the Later Zhou believed itself justified in seeking Tang's destruction.[32]

The Zhou missive to Southern Tang spoke through a telos of reunification, in which imperial symbols were the exclusive property of the future reunifier. In the meantime, "serving the great" was upheld as a viable path of self-preservation for lesser regimes. Zhou's successor, the Song dynasty, conquered Later Shu 後蜀 (934–965) because of its "dereliction in the propriety of the small serving the great," while the Song emperor Taizong 宋太宗 (r. 967–997) later assured Southern Tang before his advancing armies that "if another [ruler] would serve me according to [these] rites, why would I bother attacking him?"[33] To sue for peace, the Southern Tang ruler relinquished his imperial pretensions, agreed to tribute obligations, and even helped convince other southern rulers to accept Song suzerainty. But the Song emperor's assurances proved transient. Song armies again marched on Southern Tang in 975. Tang envoys sought an explanation: "as the small, my lord has served the great as a child would serve his father" only to have the Song emperor retort, "can a father and son be of two different families?"[34] In the Song quest to reconstitute unified imperial rule, it brooked no rival claimants. It allowed rival states to exist until it was finally powerful enough to destroy them. Here, Yi Ik's comparison of Chosŏn with Wuyue reached its limits. What difference did "serving the great" make for Qian Hongchu, when in the end, his kingdom, like Southern Tang and all the other minor regimes in southern China, was annexed by Song?

Of course, in time, Song accepted the reality of other imperial claimants. It was defeated in the far south by Đại Cồ Việt 大瞿越 (965–1054) in 981 and the seminomadic Khitan Liao Empire in the north in 1005. But military setbacks did not end irredentist desire. The Liao-controlled "sixteen prefectures" in the Beijing and northern Shanxi region remained its object.[35] This irredentist logic supplied no intrinsic reason why large swathes of Vietnam or Korea, both regions once under imperial *junxian* administration, should stay permanently beyond the imperial pale. Whether Song would have sought to reconquer Korea as it did Vietnam had it been able to defeat the Khitans and extend its frontier to the Yalu River is anyone's guess. Still, Koryŏ's elimination did at least occasionally enter the fantasies of Song literati.[36] In a diplomatic paradigm driven by imperial restoration, promises of enduring, reciprocal relations earned by service to the great were temporary expedients at best.

From its classical origins to China's medieval history, "serving the great" carried an ambivalent legacy. It described situations of hierarchy between regimes but offered no script for how their relations ought to be carried out. It was normative inasmuch as it assumed diplomacy would be hierarchical (virtually a universal assumption before the modern era) but offered little in the way of ideological consistency or a path to regime survival for a weaker power. For Chosŏn's earlier rulers to insist on "serving the great" therefore did not mean they conceived of a predefined road map delineated by classical models. Its ubiquity in Chosŏn-Ming diplomatic discourse was instead a result of rhetorical reification: deliberate efforts by Chosŏn's diplomats (and their Ming interlocutors) to create norms and precedents around the term. In other words, *sadae* is better thought of as shorthand for the diplomacy Chosŏn believed to be effective, not the dogma of the past.

THE DIPLOMATIC MEMORIAL

As far as the past was usable, Korea's previous relations with imperial neighbors offered the best guide for action. Chosŏn's immediate predecessor, Koryŏ, had ties with the Song dynasty and its northern rivals, the Khitan Liao and Jurchen Jin. During this period of "China among equals," each of these courts claimed the imperial title, reinventing their Tang predecessors' ritual and political repertoires in the process.[37] Just as no one emperor monopolized the imperial tradition, no dynasty enjoyed Koryŏ's declarations of allegiance exclusively.

For Koryŏ to navigate this "post-universalistic world" required a diplomatic skillfulness. This skill, however, was best found not in a "keen awareness of the *distinction* [emphasis added] between rhetoric and reality," as one historian has put it, but instead their interplay.[38] According to the Chosŏn official Sŏ Kŏjŏng 徐居正 (1420–1488), Koryŏ's diplomatic successes relied on the power of "writings and letters" to shape reality, steering Koryŏ away from "national calamity" and allowing its "envoys to meet as peers the talented men of the Central Plain."[39] Not surprisingly, Sŏ Kŏjŏng included a large number of diplomatic missives in his monumental anthology, the *Literary Selections of the East* (*Tongmunsŏn* 東文選). Of the 130 volumes in the collection, he devoted fourteen to diplomatic missives, in particular, a formal genre written in four-six parallel rhyme-prose 四六騈文 called *p'yo* (C. *biao* 表).

These missives were a staple of foreign correspondence during the Koryŏ and Chosŏn periods. However, the term *p'yo* did not originally refer to diplomatic epistles. According to the sixth-century *Literary Selections* (*Wenxuan* 文選, the Chinese anthology that inspired Sŏ Kŏjŏng's), the form was an "expression" 表, a way to "clarify affairs and matters to enlighten one's lord in fulfillment of the obligations of loyalty"[40] By the thirteenth century, this form had become a standard element in imperial liturgy. Imperial officials presented these "expressions" to the emperor on important occasions, such as the imperial birthday, the new year, or the commemoration of an auspicious omen. Ming protocols also provided their presentation from "vassal kings," particularly Korea, Vietnam, and Ryūkyū.[41] Therefore, when faraway rulers presented "expressions," they were also understood to be signaling political submission, an understanding captured by the refrain "presenting memorials to declare [oneself] a vassal" (C. *fengbiao chengchen* 奉表稱臣), ubiquitous in imperial chronicles.[42]

By and large, congratulatory missives were rhetorically formulaic, with the wording largely fixed for routine annual presentations.[43] Diplomatic *p'yo* from Korea, however, carried a much more comprehensive range of functions. They also related diplomatic concerns (*chinjŏng p'yo* 陳情表), made requests of the imperial court (*chuch'ŏng p'yo* 奏請表), or rendered gratitude for imperial favors (*saŭn p'yo* 謝恩表). Before delving into the crux of their immediate diplomatic objective (the portion usually preserved in surviving anthologies), Korean memorials always restated the nature of Korea's relationship with the imperial court. When these memorials recycled old language, their transcriptions in later records might omit this framing language with a well-placed ellipses 云云; even so, there was more to this boilerplate language than mere formula.

Two diplomatic memorials, one a mock memorial and another a real one, will serve as an illustration. The first mock memorial was written by Sun Di 孫覿 (1081–1169), a Song imperial official. With this memorial, its author achieved the highest score among all the candidates of the 1114 Erudite 博學宏詞 exams, which were held in celebration of an anticipated Koryŏ embassy.[44] For the examination, the writer had to imagine himself as the king of Koryŏ thanking the emperor Huizong 徽宗 (1100–1126) for the gift of his newly forged *Dashengyue* 大晟樂, a set of musical instruments that promised to revive the tunes of the classical past.[45] It survives as an example text in a Southern Song–period literary composition guide, where it is lauded for elegant use of allusions and chains of parallel constructions of the *biao*'s ornate, but demanding, rhyme prose:

> If in the opening phrases, one only mentioned such phrases as "favor extending to distant countries" [寵逮遠邦] like a second-rate writer would, it would be weak and powerless. Therefore, [Sun Di] took the meaning of these words and transformed them. [The phrases] "[You] granted the letters [of investiture] and for a myriad leagues culture all is unified" [十行賜札 萬里同文] are what [I mean]. One has only to read these two phrases to see the big picture.

The structure of the piece was equally important:

> He first speaks of how the distant barbarians are not worthy enough to know elegant music [遠夷不足以知雅樂] and then narrates the splendor of the musical performance and the favor of bestowal. One can use this as a model for any memorial [expressing thanks] for receiving gifts as one of the four barbarians [凡四夷受賜表 皆可倣此].

Like an actual Koryŏ memorial, the text adopted the voice of the Koryŏ king. The Song court composer imagined that the "barbarian" ruler, once ignorant of civilized ways, would now benefit from the empire's civilizing power. With this conclusion, the memorial's wording perfectly captured the moment with its extensive use of "classical allusions" and "aphoristic phrasing."[46] This mock memorial reduced empire to its most basic clichés: humble and ignorant barbarians are basking in the light of civilization emanating from the imperial court.

As a figment of imperial imagination, the mock memorial captured what was desired from a diplomatic letter. The second memorial, which Koryŏ presented to Huizong after the gift in 1116, is a genuine example of Koryŏ's autoethnographic strategy.[47] Although the actual memorial featured identical turns of phrase drawn from predictable classical references, their use shifted the meaning profoundly, amounting to an outright inversion of the imperial cliché. From its opening lines alone, it is clear the Koryŏ king Yejong (睿宗 r. 1105–1122) was no ignorant barbarian to be overawed:

> Your Servant has heard that when Xuanyuan [the Yellow Thearch, Huangdi] created the *Xianchi* and [the Sage King] Yu completed the *Daxia* [軒造咸池 禹成大夏], they used their bodies for their measures and forged tripods to test their sounds.[48] Before the Zhou period, all followed their rules. After the Han dynasty, all failed in their transmission. The [corrupt sounds] of the Zheng and Wei burgeoned, and the *Airs and Elegantiae* [i.e., the proper music of *The Book of Songs*] were long broken [自漢而下 即失其傳 鄭衛以興 風雅久絶].[49] The many scholars could not approximate them; ensuing generations could not develop them. But the Way was never enacted in vain, and its principles only awaited [an able ruler].

> Now, Your Majesty the Emperor, wise and sagely, having achieved brilliance through sincerity, took up the remonstrance of recluses, absolved the confusion of measurements, and followed the legacy of the ancient kings. And so, [You] achieved the balance of the Yellow Bell [黃鍾之均],[50] adorning it with the five modes, disseminating it with the eight instruments. Promulgating them in the altars and shrines, the various spirits submit. Proclaiming them in the imperial court, the commoners and officials are harmonious. [With this, you] illuminated the achievements of an age and revived the fallen paragons of antiquity [薦之郊廟而衆神格 奏於朝廷而庶尹諧 以明一代之成功 以起千古之墜典].[51]

No less an encomium to imperial virtue, the memorial also inserted Koryŏ into Huizong's cultural revival project. Koryŏ's king could hear the resonances of its tunes. He could also appreciate their significance because he and the emperor shared links to the classical past. With a shared stake in Huizong's project, Koryŏ's king was committed to amplifying its effect, a point elaborated in the ensuing verses. Through "the enduring echoes of the bells and chimes" [制鏞磬之遺響], Koryŏ, too, would "use the ocarina and flute to set straight the sounds" [用塤篪之正音], replicating the newly revived classical standards. The *Dashengyue*'s spread would bring "great peace that flows in unison with heaven and earth" for "transmissions [lasting] a hundred generations," a cause of celebration for both "ruler and subject" alike [乃至和平 與天地以同流 傳之百世 爲君臣之相悅]. Grateful though the Koryŏ king was, he appreciated Huizong less for being generously included in his endeavor than the wider benefit the emperor's project would have for the whole civilized world.

In both memorials, correct music regulated the realm, able to mollify barbarian peoples and supernatural beings alike. Sun Di likened the *Dashengyue* to "the dance of feathers and shields." A motif for the power of "civil virtue" 文德 (K. *mundŏk*, C. *wende*), it was an allusion to a passage in the *Counsels of Yu* (*Dayu mo* 大禹謨) concerning the Sage ruler Shun 舜 and his war against the *miao*-aboriginals 苗.[52] Instead of using violence, Shun heeded the advice of his counselor Yu to demonstrate "entire sincerity" [至誠感神 矧茲有苗] to move the spirits. Taking heed, Shun led back his army and "broadly diffused civil virtue and danced with shields and feathers on the two staircases [in his palace courtyard] and in seventy days the Miao came to submit" [帝乃誕敷文德 舞干羽于兩階 七旬有苗格].[53] When the Koryŏ memorial alluded to the same passage, the emphasis was on Huizong's efforts to model himself after Shun rather than the spontaneity of Koryŏ's submission. Huizong's music could harmonize emotional and moral resonances, but the Koryŏ letter arrived only because the Koryŏ king Yejong had deliberately sought out Huizong's *Dashengyue* to burnish the cultural splendor of his court. As his memorial suggested, Koryŏ was a participant in Huizong's project, not a passive beneficiary.[54]

The two memorials employed identical classical tropes but in palpably different ways. Although not always evident beneath the ornate flourishes of the four-six parallel prose, these differences expose a tension between imperial expectation and Korean performance. The mock memorial captured imperial expectations, but it did not represent the *shared* norms produced by actual diplomatic exchange. Meanwhile, the writers of Korean memorials played to imperial desire, but not before claiming a piece of the imperial tradition for themselves.

RECOGNIZING THE IMPERIAL TRANSMISSION

The life of the *p'yo* memorial as a genre followed the trajectory of Korea's relationship to the imperial tradition. In Huizong's reign, the Song dynasty had briefly reasserted itself in the northeast Asian diplomatic scene. But for decades, it was the Khitan Liao court that received the obeisance of Koryŏ's kings. It was through correspondences with the Liao court, therefore, that their composers had been honing their rhetorical craft, where they likened Koryŏ's "service to the great" to the myriad constellations "revolving around the North Star."[55]

Song's efforts to bring Koryŏ to its fold achieved only limited success: Koryŏ refused to side with Song in Huizong's disastrous irredentist war against Liao, which only created an opportunity for the Jurchens (K. *Yŏjin*, C. *Nüzhen* 女真) to destroy Liao in 1125 and sack Song's capital in 1127. When the Jurchens, who once "served" Liao and Koryŏ, assumed the imperial mantle and established the Jin dynasty, Koryŏ reluctantly dispatched tribute missions and *p'yo* memorials to their emperor, continuing a diplomatic arrangement based on "old Liao institutions."[56] This arrangement effectively cut off Song from Koryŏ. Official ties between them were never rekindled, even after Song had reestablished itself in southern China.[57]

It was, in fact, Koryŏ's relations with Liao, Jin, and later the Mongol-Yuan (and not Song) that provided the precedents for Chosŏn's dealings with Ming. Whether due to archival loss or because the branches of the past had been pruned for a more singular view of the past, the documents collected in the *Selections of the East* did not always mark the texts clearly as intended for an imperial Jin audience, even though, until Chosŏn's ties with Ming, it was with Jin that Korea maintained the most stable diplomatic relations.[58] By contrast, the *Selections of the East* accentuated the short periods of interaction with Song, understandable given how Song culture provided intellectual and literary inspiration for Chosŏn's elites. At the same time, the "barbarian" courts of Liao and Jin were targets of repudiation if they were mentioned at all. Nonetheless, surviving *p'yo* still traced a strand of dynastic transmission, a Han-Tang *translatio imperii*, claimed by both the Northern Song and Khitan Liao, that threaded through the Jurchen Jin (but circumventing the Southern Song) and later to be tied together by the Mongol Empire.[59]

The Korean *p'yo* was an instrument for recognizing when the imperial mandate had transferred. A Koryŏ memorial pledging eternal allegiance to a moribund Jin in 1233 was followed the very next year by one swearing allegiance to the very agent of its demise, the Mongol Great Khan. The two were laced with identical tropes of immortal imperial destiny, even as the latter celebrated the very forces that had been decried as "insolent brutes" in the former document.[60] The persistence of this genre and its thematic recycling, seemingly without regard for the identity of the imperial audience, appears to disconnect the text from the world beyond its pages. But it is precisely this rhetorical consistency across dynastic rupture that urges against its summary dismissal. In the Jin and Mongol letters, the will to timelessness—the apparently ahistorical vision of empire—was what imbued them with their rhetorical power. Koryŏ articulated Mongol rulership within the ethos and modality of imperial rule that it had once granted the Liao and Jin emperors. By engaging with the Mongols under these terms, Koryŏ attempted to revive an imperial tradition extinguished with Jin's recent destruction. Even before the Mongols began to appropriate this tradition in earnest, Koryŏ memorials already exhorted their Great Khan to inhabit the role of benevolent universal emperor and true heir to the Han and Tang emperors of yore.[61]

Early Mongol rulers, of course, had their ideas about what imperial rule should look like and how Koryŏ should acknowledge their suzerainty.[62] The old Liao and Jin precedents that Koryŏ sought to follow did not fulfill Mongol expectations. Koryŏ was supposed to comply with a set of non-negotiable demands from the Mongols, the so-called Six Obligations 六事, which together involved accepting a *darugaci* overseer, establishing post stations, providing troops, supplying provisions, submitting census registries, and sending hostages (including the heir apparent). In Koryŏ's case, demands also included personal attendance at the imperial court from the Koryŏ king and abandoning the island stronghold of Kanghwa Island. When hard-pressed by Mongol armies, the Koryŏ court agreed to these terms but tarried on their fulfillment or relied on outright deception: sending an impostor heir apparent.[63]

Alongside these delaying tactics, the Koryŏ court employed the imperializing mode. In a strategy of preemption, they situated the Mongols within a preexisting imperial tradition, but one the Mongols had yet to embrace. Koryŏ diplomatic memorials from this period did not so much legitimize Mongol imperium than seek to fashion the terms on which imperial authority would be predicated.[64] In 1259, the Koryŏ court finally sent the actual heir apparent, the future king Wŏnjong 元宗 (1260–1274), as a hostage. His arrival coincided with a war of succession between two contenders for the position of Great Khan. The eventual victor was Qubilai (1215–1294, r. Yuan Shizu 元世祖 1260–1294), who when taking power in 1260 issued the Mongol Empire's first reign era in the Sinitic imperial mode: *zhongtong* 中統, or "Central Rule."[65] This gesture, along with the selective adoption of other trappings in the Sinitic imperial tradition, was celebrated by the Koryŏ *p'yo* delivered to congratulate Qubilai's accession. Its author, the Koryŏ official Kim Ku 金坵 (1211–1278), infused the text with the rhetorical urge to lead one's conqueror captive:

> After a thousand ages, a new beginning arrives like the rising sun. [All those who] call the four seas home are recipients of Heaven's protection; upon the commencement of this new rule, they celebrate in unison. Having succeeded generations of Accomplished Sages, with wisdom divine in decisiveness, He cultivates the civil and sets aside the whip of war, while dances of shields and feathers fill the two stairs. He administers government and disburses benevolence, gathering the tribute ships of myriad countries [神謀果斷 修文偃革 舞干羽于兩階 發政施仁 湊梯航於萬國]. The Exalted Mandate is restored, and His august fortune augmented. Upon thinking that I, Your servant, on account of my return to inherit this fiefdom [祇襲藩封], am unable to be among those prostrating like crabs before Your Court and can only gaze towards its throne room, I [now] doubly show my sincere joy with an exuberance that moves mountains like a sea turtle's clap.[66]

Qubilai's accession augured a new beginning. Having restored the "exalted Mandate [of Heaven]," his boundless sovereignty was now celebrated by "myriad countries," of which Koryŏ was one. The memorial then praised the Mongol ruler through several humdrum classical allusions that abandoned his achievements in the realm of abstract grandiosity. But when these statements are weighed against the tumult that plagued Koryŏ-Mongol relations in preceding decades, it becomes clear they did more than exalt empire or profess loyalty. Belying their conventionality, this string of tropes encoded a specific version of imperial authority. It praised the emperor for bringing peace, an oblique reminder of the Mongol invasions that devastated Koryŏ. It celebrated his cultivation of civil virtue only to repudiate military aggression. It compared him to King Shun, who secured the submission of his Miao enemies through the "dances of shields and feathers," but in a departure from the *locus classicus*, shifted agency away from the conqueror to the submitter. Koryŏ came to submit not in awe of military prowess but to recognize a ruler who set aside the "whip" of war. Koryŏ's submission confirmed Qubilai's imperial claims, but only because he allowed peace to reign.

Through this clever arrangement of unexceptional tropes, Kim Ku's memorial transformed submission into a sanction of a new imperial order. A classicizing rhetoric coded its message, but by doubling as an appeal to a shared political tradition, it anticipated its true audience: not the Great Khan himself but the Confucian-minded officials at his court. Alongside these formal memorials, Kim Ku also composed letters to Wang E 王鶚 (1190–1273), a former Jin official who saw service in Qubilai's court as an opportunity to revive long-defunct imperial rituals.[67] In these letters, Kim described Wang E and others like him as cultural saviors, designating their erstwhile Mongol overlords as both marginal interlopers and targets of their common civilizing project. Supposedly, Wang E "would sigh and lament at being unable to meet the writer in person" whenever he read Kim Ku's memorials.[68] Their mutual identification as men of letters carved a channel for political negotiation and cooperation, one that involved establishing Koryŏ as a symbol of the imperial tradition Wang E and his colleagues tried to revive.[69]

The Korean *p'yo* did not so much *describe* relations as perform them through a rhetorical enactment of a relationship that bound both parties.[70] Illustrating his process is a *p'yo* thanking the Mongol emperor for repatriating the Koryŏ heir apparent so that he could take the Koryŏ throne after his father's death:

> You comforted me in many ways, many times more than usual. As such, I returned without injury, and gratitude overwhelms my heart. As soon as I arrived in my humble fief, you bestowed upon me enlightened instructions to honor me.[71]

The letter then enumerated these instructions, which had been promulgated to assert the Koryŏ king's prerogatives:

> [Your] edict said, "Your old territory will be restored, and you will eternally be [our] eastern vassal" [完復舊疆 永爲東藩]. Receiving the extended beneficence from this Sagely Dawn, I will now continue to guard the lands of my forebears.

The selective quotation of Qubilai's edict recast the khan's assurances to Wŏnjong as guarantees of Koryŏ's perpetual existence. This reminder implored the emperor and his servants to stay true to their word, an agreement sealed by both Qubilai's original edict and the emotional response of Koryŏ's subjects:

> 'If you set straight your territory and boundaries and settle the hearts of your people, then my armies will not come ever again [亟正疆界 以定民心 我師不復蹂垠矣]. Now that I have made such a declaration, I will certainly not eat my words.' A grand declaration thus made; the utmost benevolence can be seen. With the arrival of one letter wrapped in silk, a whole nation's tears fall at once [綸綍之俄傳 滿國涕洟之俱墮].

Qubilai's support of the Koryŏ throne and his promise not to attack Koryŏ became an act of benevolence that moved even "trees and stones." The Koryŏ ruler and his descendants would "die to repay" it with an oath sworn "upon the mountains and seas" that would "be observed for eternity." When paeans of empire spoke of benevolent rule, literary and civil virtue, universal sovereignty, and reciprocity, they were not fanciful descriptions but exhortations in an imperializing mode. They demanded empire to fulfill its political commitments.

Evoking classical injunctions also extrapolated Qubilai's policies into more general principles. However trite at first glance, the rhetorical tropes used in the Koryŏ memorial transmuted a momentary political agreement into a covenant with normative constants. In doing so, the Koryŏ ruler extracted an eternal mandate for himself and his descendants, at least within the rhetorical universe of diplomatic correspondence. After Qubilai's death, Koryŏ diplomatic correspondence condensed the thrust of Qubilai's edicts into "the old precedents of emperor Shizu" (K. *Sejo kuje* 世祖舊制), ones which Koryŏ officials repeatedly deployed to defend the kingdom's territorial integrity, the well-being of its monarchs, and the sanctity of its indigenous customs.[72]

In the course of Koryŏ's century-long existence as a Mongol client state, not all these entreaties necessarily worked nor were they the only recourse of Koryŏ's rulers. The Koryŏ royal house also participated in Mongol political institutions and acculturated to its cultural idioms, perhaps symbolized best by the royal family's adoption of Mongol hairstyle and dress (a sartorial transformation Chosŏn period chroniclers depicted as a moment of national tragedy).[73] They also continued to comply with tribute demands and contributions to Mongol military campaigns, including the costly and disastrous invasions of Japan in 1274 and 1281. But even these concessions to Mongol domination existed in a diplomatic context where Koryŏ's preservation acquired normative weight. Not a temporary reprieve from inevitable destruction nor a precarious survival scrounged from the emperor's pleasure, Koryŏ's integrity became a matter of imperial duty and ancestral law, a matter of obligation for later khans and imperial officials alike. Koryŏ, once a territory to be conquered, had integrated its preservation into the logic of imperial rule.[74]

THE MING MEMORIAL AFFAIR

Once compiled together in Sŏ Kŏjŏng's *Literary Selections of the East*, *p'yo* memorials became a device of knowledge. Later court composers now had a centuries-long record of templates for speaking and negotiating with empire even in moments of extreme duress. This accumulation also endowed a generic coherence to the literary form, as well as the rhetorical techniques they modeled, techniques whose effectiveness was validated by the reaction of those who received them. Indeed, Wang E was not the only reader who noted the deft rhetoric of these memorials. Even the Hongwu emperor, for all his wariness of his eastern neighbors, once praised the Koryŏ loyalist and martyr Yi Sungin for writing a memorial with "crafted and poignant diction" [表辭精切].[75]

Well into the sixteenth century, Chosŏn memorials continued to earn praise from Ming officials who read them. When the Jiajing 嘉靖 (r. 1521–1567) emperor narrowly avoided assassination by his harem in 1542, the Chosŏn court submitted a memorial of congratulations celebrating the emperor's "successful destruction of the rebels." The Ming Grand Secretary Yan Song 嚴嵩 (1480–1567) lauded the missive for its tactful handling of such a sensitive matter, unlike the "inappropriately worded memorials" from other foreign states.[76]

It is unclear which foreign states Yan Song had in mind. In general, letters from beyond the Sinitic ecumene often required manipulation to avert the possibility of offense,[77] a task that fell on the Ming court's Translator's Institute (Siyi guan 四夷館). When providing a Chinese translation of letters written in foreign scripts, these translations could ensure that the resulting text would conform to the conventions of imperial rhetoric.[78] Korean letters, on the other hand, never had to undergo translation, always arriving ready-made for imperial consumption, so there was never a suspicion that their language was contrived by wily translators.[79] Envoys from places such as Japan and Vietnam, other societies with a rich Sinitic literary tradition, also presented memorials, but their ties with the Ming court were tenuous, disrupted at times with outright hostility. Only the Ryūkyūan kingdom matched Chosŏn in the regularity of participation, but Chosŏn's embassies (about three a year) were still more frequent than the Ryūkyūan missions (about one every year or two).[80]

Unlike memorials presented by their own officials, the imperial court could not directly mandate the contents or timing, let alone the arrival of these documents from foreign rulers. But lack of control only burnished their symbolic significance because their spontaneous arrival affirmed the far reach of imperial authority and the force of its moral attraction, the very clichés repeated in the text of the missives themselves. With regularity, frequency, and verve, Korean memorials performed a sincere genuine loyalty. And given that this paper trail extends back for over a millennium, these *p'yo* might appear only to confirm the long-standing stereotype of Korea as the empire's most loyal vassal.[81] But with so much of this image hinging on Korean literary mastery, one might also ask, if Korean writers were good enough to burnish empire through their rhetoric, what prevented them from using their talents for something more?

Korean mastery meant any flaw could only mean irreverence. And these "documents of expression" were so bound up with the construction of imperial authority that when they offended, they struck at the heart of its ideological edifice. In 1394, the Hongwu emperor who once praised the skill of Korean composers now suspected them of subterfuge. He charged that a Chosŏn *p'yo* was "laced with insulting and offensive phrases" and asked, "is this really the sincerity of the small serving the great?" [雜以侵侮之辭 以小事大之誠 果如是乎].[82] The emperor could not decide whether these composers acted on royal orders or if they had connived on their own. Still, he did identify Yi Sŏnggye's chief minister Chŏng Tojŏn 鄭道傳 (1342–1398) as the main culprit, demanding his extradition. Chosŏn diverted blame to "ignorant" and "unskilled" court composers, some of whom it sent to Ming to face interrogation in Chŏng's place. As the so-called memorial affair 表箋事件 unfolded, the imperial dragnet plumbed down the hierarchy of Korean officialdom, implicating its interpreters, functionaries, and scribes.[83] Meanwhile, the Hongwu emperor detained, exiled, and even executed Korean envoys sent to defuse the situation. Kwŏn Kŭn, whose poetry was discussed in the introduction, had been sent for this precise purpose in 1396 and was one of the few to return unscathed.[84]

The emperor's scrutiny was probably misplaced. After all, the fledgling Chosŏn, hoping for Ming support, had no reason to sabotage ties through provocations (although perhaps officials sympathetic to the old dynasty did). Even so, how Chosŏn's memorials exactly "violated the propriety of serving the great" remains something of a mystery. One widely repeated but contested theory is that these memorials ran afoul of a paranoid emperor by inadvertently bringing attention to his humble origins through untoward puns. Korean sinologist Pak Wŏnho links the affair to a broader early Ming literary inquisition, although other scholars, such as Chan Hok-lam, contend that the very idea of an early Ming literary inquisition had been embellished from untrustworthy sixteenth- and seventeenth-century accounts of the emperor's reign. Although Korean records, including the private writings of Sŏ Kŏjŏng (who was also Kwŏn Kŭn's grandson), supports the idea of lèse-majesté through insulting puns, it remains that nothing to that effect could be gleaned from the memorial that caused the brouhaha in the first place.[85]

Whatever the broader circumstances of the Ming emperor's reaction, it is clear that something was wrong with the wording. Later Ming correspondences made one cause of offense explicit. They homed in on what they called an "irresponsible allusion to the affairs of Zhòu 紂 (traditional r. 1075–1046 BCE)," the last tyrannical ruler of the Shang dynasty (ca. 1600–1046 BCE). If this allusion was indeed the cause of offense, then it was ironically the very name the emperor had chosen himself for Yi Sŏnggye's new dynasty that led to the problem: Chosŏn. The offending p'yo waxed poetic about how the name had been used even in "the ancient time of Kija" [昔在箕子之世 已有朝鮮之稱].[86] In the classical tradition, Kija 箕子 (or Jizi in Chinese, fl. eleventh century BCE) was a prince who tried to convince the tyrannical king Zhòu to change his ways, but the tyrant did not listen and imprisoned Kija. When Zhòu was defeated by King Wu 周武王 (r. 1046 BCE–1043 BCE), Kija was freed. He then transmitted to King Wu the *Great Plan* (*Hongfan* 洪範), an outline of the ways of wise rulership. In recompense, King Wu enfeoffed Kija in a land far to the east called Chaoxian 朝鮮—that is Chosŏn.[87]

Although most likely mythological rather than historical (an issue to be further discussed in chapter 10), the story of Kija's journey east linked the new Chosŏn state to the classical past in the Korean memorial. But the Ming court must have latched on to a different set of analogs: the tyrant Zhòu and King Wu who had overthrown him. If Yi Sŏnggye's Chosŏn was the latter-day realm of Kija, who then was the Ming emperor? Was he the benighted tyrant or the new ruler who received Kija's instructions? Neither option would have sat well with the aging Hongwu emperor, ever concerned about shoring up monarchical authority over the learned elite.[88]

What ultimately triggered the emperor will always remain a matter of speculation. Nonetheless, the Kija allusion is a reminder of the inherent volatility of a shared past, a fact Korean memorial writers were keenly aware of. As the compiler of Korea's *Literary Selections*, Sŏ Kŏjŏng noted, Hongwu was not the first emperor to take offense at a historical allusion in a Korean memorial nor would he be the last. But at least with the *Literary Selections* as a guide, later composers would know how best to approach the imperial ear.[89]

Perhaps, in light of the *p'yo*'s longer history, the Hongwu emperor had good reason to be suspicious of Korean memorials. Where the emperor had erred was to seek irreverence in petty insults and hidden references. If subversion were truly afoot, it manifested at once more grandly and more subtly than he had appreciated. On the surface, these memorials all performed loyalty to one imperial dynasty or another. Their timely presentation at ritual occasions signaled "observation of the proper lunation" 尊正朔, so-called because the second new moon after the solstice marked the first day of the New Year: that is, following the current imperial calendar and employing the imperial reign eras 年號 that marked the passing years. With the control of time an expression of cosmic authority, Korean use of the imperial calendar was to accept the imperial court's temporal domination in exchange for spatial integrity.[90]

Dynastic time framed these diplomatic memorials, but their form, practice, and rhetoric gestured toward eternity. Their classical allusions reached backward in time to the age of sage kings, and their profession of everlasting loyalty looked forward to an infinite future. Tropes of eternity in Korean diplomatic rhetoric might appear to reinforce the idea of Chosŏn as a "model" vassal, but this "model" was not cast in full form out of a preexisting mold. As this chapter shows, it coalesced gradually from a long-standing engagement with the imperial tradition, borne out by the itinerary of the Korean diplomatic memorial in its history.

What does it mean, then, for a Korean diplomatic memorial to belong within dynastic time but for the genre to transcend it? To think of empire as timeless is to conceive it as transcending momentary exigencies and persisting beyond the temporal limits of mortal reckoning. To measure an imperial order with a cosmic scale naturalized its claims to authority and fastened them to universal constants that lay outside dynastic temporality.[91] But if timelessness eternalized empire, then refrains that called Koryŏ and later Chosŏn to "always be the eastern vassal" [永爲東藩] did the same to Korea's place in the imagination of immortal imperium. If Korea was not only a vassal of Ming but of eternal empire (whoever might its momentary ruler be), it could only mean it too was coeval with the sage kings and the classical tradition. For the early Chosŏn court and its founding statesmen, their Eastern Kingdom (K. *Tongguk* 東國) ruled the Samhan 三韓, the land of Verdant Hills (K. *Ch'ŏnggu* 靑丘). It possessed its own, distinct *translatio imperii*, one which hearkened back to the days of Kija, passing through the Three Kingdoms and Koryŏ.[92] So when a Chosŏn *p'yo* declared that the king would as the emperor's "subject reverently hold fast the Verdant Hills to ever more fulfill [his] duty as the vassal of the Han court [臣謹當恪守靑丘 益殫漢藩之職]," it evoked an imperial order that transcended dynastic time. But Korea also existed outside that time. It too was supposed to be eternal.[93]

CHAPTER TWO

Terms of Authority

Ming officials once warned Yi Sŏnggye that past emperors—whether of Han, Sui, and Tang or Liao, Jin, and Yuan—had all sent their armies against Korea at the slightest offenses. For Yi Sŏnggye, whom the Ming emperor saw as a usurper (and therefore guilty of the greatest possible moral offense), these were not idle threats.[1] But for all the saber rattling, a Ming war with Korea never materialized. In the leap fifth month of 1398, during the height of tensions, the Hongwu emperor died. In the eighth month, the Chosŏn prince Yi Pangwŏn 李芳遠 (1367–1422) instigated a coup d'état that led to his father's abdication and the brutal murder of two younger brothers. Yi Pangwŏn installed a reluctant older brother on the throne, only to replace him shortly after, becoming Chosŏn's third king, T'aejong (太宗 r. 1400–1418). Meanwhile, Hongwu's grandson and chosen successor, the Jianwen 建文 emperor Zhu Yunwen 朱允炆 (1377–?, r. 1398–1402), in an attempt to consolidate power, provoked a rebellion from his ambitious uncle, the prince of Yan, Zhu Di 朱棣 (1360–1424).

In one year, the political landscape had changed dramatically. With uncle challenging nephew for the throne, Ming plunged into civil war. Jianwen called on T'aejong's support, who presented thousands of warhorses as tribute. In recompense for this "utmost sincere service to the great," Jianwen's envoys presented the patents of investiture that Hongwu withheld from T'aejong's father.[2] But in 1402, Zhu Di defeated Jianwen and assumed the throne as the Yongle 永樂 emperor (r. 1402–1424). Yongle issued T'aejong another patent of investiture to replace those granted by the nephew he ousted. His envoys also presented T'aejong with regalia of "nine emblems" 九章, an honor reserved only for Ming's first-ranked imperial princes (C. *qinwang* 親王). The imperial edict explained that Chosŏn's king, as a ruler of a "faraway domain" among the "four barbarians," would have been entitled to only five or seven emblems. In light of T'aejong's "loyalty and devotion," the emperor was willing to overlook the fact that the Korean king was "not [the emperor's] own flesh and blood" and grant him this exceptional honor.[3] With one usurper investing another, the early Chosŏn crisis of legitimacy was effectively over.

It is easy to attribute the long peace of the ensuing centuries as the logical consequence of this initial rapprochement. This view persists because of two presumptions about the nature of Chosŏn-Ming diplomacy. The first is that Ming's disposition toward Chosŏn was inherently peaceful. After all, the Hongwu emperor listed Korea among the countries "never to be invaded" [不征之國] in his *Ancestral Injunctions* (*Huang Ming zuxun* 皇明祖訓) to warn his successors against the pitfalls of military adventurism.[4] But his son Yongle, having already disregarded his father's wishes by usurping the throne, also undermined the "foreign policy framework" his father had laid down.[5] Flouting his father's injunctions, he conquered Vietnam in 1407, a country that too was on the list of places "never to be invaded."[6]

The second is the notion that, as long as Chosŏn accepted tributary relations with Ming, it had no fear of Ming aggression. But as Chosŏn's early struggles with the Ming court show, it was Ming who kept Chosŏn at arm's length. The iconic three embassies a year that had become fairly routine by the mid-fifteenth century—to express felicitations and present gifts for the new year (*hajŏngsa* 賀正使), the imperial birthday (*sŏngjŏlsa* 聖節使), and the birthday of the heir apparent (*ch'ŏnch'usa* 千秋使)—is often described as being "required" by Ming, but their regularity depended on precedent rather than a legalistic obligation: no imperial order or statute *mandated* these missions. The first Ming emperor originally ordered Koryŏ (and later Chosŏn) to send no more than *one* embassy *every three* years.[7]

When relations with Chosŏn soured, Hongwu even barred Chosŏn missions from entering Ming territory altogether. Hongwu took issue with a Korean ambassador for having "prostrated incorrectly" in front of him. As punishment, the emperor subjected him to a round of heavy flogging. The pitiable ambassador, who had nearly died from the beating, was then denied the services of Ming waystations and had to travel on foot back to Korea from the imperial capital Nanjing.[8] After this incident, the emperor ordered his frontier officials to refuse entry to embassies sent by the Chosŏn court. Even though its embassies were repeatedly turned away at the frontier between 1393 and 1397, the Chosŏn court still insisted that three annual missions (which had been the practice for Koryŏ and Mongol relations) were "proper" and continued to send them anyway. The Ming emperor justified his poor treatment of Korean envoys because they did not behave properly; what tributary propriety entailed was still a matter of negotiation. If Chosŏn and Ming avoided armed conflict because they finally agreed on what was tributary propriety, they did not begin their relationship with a shared vision of what that might be.[9]

In sum, neither Chosŏn nor Ming possessed the luxury of hindsight afforded to modern observers. In retrospect, it might even appear Chosŏn could have done more to arrogate symbols of Korean sovereignty, however they were defined. Indeed, lamentations to this effect have become something of a trope in modern Korean popular culture and academic historiography alike.[10] But this sentiment too presumes foreknowledge, both of Ming's inherent pacifism (or weakness) and the historical inevitability of Korean ethnonationalism. So instead of judging the Chosŏn court's considerations and objectives from hindsight, it is important to situate the scholar's inquiry under the cover of a hazy future. Unlike moderns looking back today, Chosŏn's rulers, officials, and diplomats did not know how their relationship with the Ming would unfold, nor did they take Ming's peaceful disposition for granted. Only when this sense of uncertainty is restored can Chosŏn's accommodation of Ming imperial authority be properly understood.

That does not mean, however, that the modern preoccupation with Korean sovereignty is misplaced. The dilemma of how Korean political authority should interface with Ming imperial claims was indeed a perennial concern of Chosŏn statecraft, although the way it was resolved rarely followed an ethnocentric or nationalist program. Throughout the late fourteenth and early fifteenth centuries, this issue manifested most poignantly in anxieties surrounding the latent threat of imperial irredentism and the problem of ritual infringement. As this chapter will show, these two sources of anxiety animated controversies across a wide range of areas, including language, astronomy, and music, and not just diplomacy per se, in part because they were all critical to how Korea was to be conceived as an integral, albeit distinct, entity in a universal imperial order.

THE IRREDENTIST SPECTER

King T'aejong witnessed Ming at the height of its military power. Throughout the early fifteenth century, Ming fought numerous wars along its frontiers. When news of one, Yongle's invasion of Vietnam in 1407, reached Chosŏn, it elicited some consternation. As one official remarked, a "small country" like Vietnam "could [not] have stood a chance" against "all the troops under heaven." Court officials proposed to construct forts and stockpile provisions in case Ming attacked Korea too, but T'aejong urged calm. The Yongle emperor, who "loved vainglory and relished triumph," would indeed exploit any small failure in recognizing his superiority to "launch an invasion," but T'aejong believed that, as long as the emperor's pride was satisfied, Chosŏn could avoid the calamity suffered by the Vietnamese.[11] Rather than make war preparations, T'aejong organized a special round of civil service examinations requiring candidates to write mock memorials to congratulate the emperor's victories. When Ming envoys arrived several weeks later to announce Yongle's victory over Vietnam, Chosŏn was ready to dispatch an embassy bearing a memorial of congratulations (*hap'yo* 賀表) for the triumphant emperor.[12]

After receiving this embassy, Yongle tasked a returning Chosŏn envoy to reassure the king. According to the emperor, T'aejong being "a bookish man," would "misunderstand" his war as an act of aggression. The envoy was therefore supposed to "explain the matter clearly to [his] king" that conquest was never the emperor's intent. Instead, Yongle claimed he intervened only on behalf of the Trần 陳 dynasty (1225–1400), who had been usurped by Lê Quý Ly 黎季犛 (aka Hồ Quý

Ly 胡季犛 1336–1407).[13] Lê, however, killed all of the Trần scions. "The enormity of Lê Quý Ly's villainy" left the emperor no legitimate heirs to invest as king and "no choice" but to annex Vietnam as a Ming province.[14] Vietnam had once been ruled by the Han and Tang dynasties so in the emperor's eyes, the annexation was justified as a restoration of imperial rule.[15] These were weak assurances because T'aejong too was a usurper, having helped his father overthrow Koryŏ and seized the throne by eliminating his brothers, not to mention that the Korean peninsula too had at times come under imperial rule.[16]

The irredentist specter reared its head again during Yongle's 1413 campaign against the Mongols. Yun Pong 尹鳳 (fl. 1400–1450), a Korean-born eunuch working in the Ming palace, informed Chosŏn that once the Mongolian campaign concluded, the emperor would order the construction of three thousand warships for a seaborne invasion of Japan.[17] The tip (of uncertain credibility) alarmed T'aejong's court. Some officials believed this meant the Ming emperor also had designs on Chosŏn. They proposed that military officers be dispatched to the Yalu River and Korea's southeastern coast to make war preparations. T'aejong, unconvinced of a Ming threat, answered that the emperor "had not lately treated [Chosŏn] any differently from before."[18]

The debate continued for several days. The minister Ha Yun 河崙 (1347–1416) reminded the king that emperors in the past dangled false promises to rivals before picking them off one by one. Ha mentioned only Qin Shihuangdi 秦始皇帝 (r. 221–210 BCE) by name, the first emperor who unified China (although a passing amble through imperial history yields many more examples of this divide-and-conquer strategy). Ha Yun begged the king to fortify the capital city; another official even suggested forging a defensive alliance with Japan.

T'aejong, in contrast, believed these measures would be pointless. In his reckoning, the emperor had "disobeyed his father's commands and seized the throne himself . . . attacked Vietnam to the south and the wastelands of the north," overextending himself politically and military. The king asked: "with what leisure was he to turn his attention east?" And given the vast gulf of power between Chosŏn and Ming, "if the situation deteriorated to the point that all left to be done was to hold fast to our capital city," there would be no Chosŏn to speak of. In the event of an invasion, the king could only accept that "all things are due their rise and fall." At that juncture, he would simply "raise troops to meet the emperor in the field." What good, the king asked, would come from "waiting behind our walls?"[19]

Rather than gamble on the battlefield, it was far better to prevent such threats from materializing in the first place. To preserve his patrimony, T'aejong, like his father, placed his faith in diplomacy, that is, to "serve the great sincerely." By contrast, "stockpiling grain and training troops" were last resorts. The long period of peace that followed bore the fruit of diplomacy, but it was not a forgone conclusion. Hindsight might praise T'aejong for his foresight and scoff at Ha Yun for failing to recognize the Ming's peaceable disposition; regardless of how they might be judged after the fact, it remains that at the time there was no ready consensus or obvious course of action. To opt for diplomacy, T'aejong had to overrule his dissenting officials. Decrying the invasion of Vietnam as a "moral error," he trusted neither Ming's moral restraint nor good intentions. He did, however, assess the motivations behind the Ming wars, identifying border security as the reason for the Mongolian campaign. "Serving the great" was a considered choice and not the preferred option of those who counseled him.[20]

When the Yongle emperor died in 1424 during his final campaign in Mongolia, his grandiose ambitions perished with him. Over the next decades, Ming military power waned. The prospect of outright imperial aggression receded, but the irredentist specter never quite dissipated. In 1481, Chosŏn learned from its emissaries that Ming planned to construct a new fortress in Liaodong in order to protect Chosŏn embassies from marauding Jurchens. A retired official named Yang Sŏngji 梁誠之 (1415–1482) called for dispatching a mission to Beijing to convince Ming to rescind these orders. He argued that past Korean dynasties had maintained their political independence either because their imperial neighbors were distracted by rival powers or because Korea held its own on the battlefield. Now, with the new courier stations and fortifications being constructed in Liaodong, Ming extended its military reach and narrowed the geographical buffer with Chosŏn. With only "one day's distance" between the new Ming fortress and the Yalu River, Yang worried one day it could present a threat to Korea. "For now," he writes, relations with Ming were good, but "how are we to know that five hundred years hence there will not be [a ruler] who abuses arms and indulges in violence? Or one who loves vainglory and relishes triumph?" Yang Sŏngji urged the court to shift the shortsighted temporal scale of its political calculus to a risk horizon measured in centuries. This future threat took the form of an emperor in Yongle's mold. Chosŏn was safe for now, but there was no telling when another ambitious emperor might set his sights on Korea.

Without foreknowledge of how things would unfold, Yang could only speculate into the far distance with the mirror of history. On this matter, even his colleagues found this horizon of risk too slim for initiating diplomatic action. They shared Yang's long-term concerns but were reluctant to rock the boat when relations with Ming were largely positive. They believed Yang was overreacting.[21]

According to political scientist Brantly Womack, bilateral ties characterized by extreme asymmetries of power present different risks and stakes for each party. The weaker party (Chosŏn) posed no existential threat to its counterpart (Ming), but the latter could inflict great harm on, if not entirely destroy, the former. With any misstep potentially disastrous, Chosŏn had an incentive to scrutinize the Ming's every move before deciding on a course of action. On the other hand, because Chosŏn was one of many entities along Ming's vast frontier, Korean matters seldom received Ming's dedicated attention. Therefore, Ming policies toward Chosŏn were more likely to be "uncoordinated," as different arms of the Ming state enacted their own, even contradictory policies. Left unchecked, this combination of "overattention" and "inattention" could be deadly. When Ming sent ambiguous, conflicting signals that were interpreted in Chosŏn through the lens of heightened attention, a minor point of tension could have snowballed into a wider confrontation.[22]

So was Yang showing judicious foresight, or did he fall into the trap of "overattention"? It is impossible to tell without resorting to the counterfactuals of an alternate timeline. Had Chosŏn-Ming relations developed along a different trajectory, the Ming presence in the Liaodong region might very well have served as a bridgehead for an invasion of the Korean peninsula. As it turned out (and beyond the strategic horizon of anyone in the early fifteenth century), when Ming troops did cross the Yalu from Liaodong in 1592, it was to rescue Korea from an invasion from Japan, a place Chosŏn officials once countenanced as a source of allies against Ming aggression.

The Ming annexation of Vietnam was justified in part by an irredentist claim. In theory, the same casus belli could also have been invoked for Chosŏn: Han rule, Tang annexation, and Mongol dominion marked the Korean peninsula as a target for reconquest. Ming never directly invoked these legacies to seek Korea's subjugation, but their shadow still loomed over the words and actions of the Hongwu and Yongle emperors. The fear was they might be reawakened with the right kind of provocation. One such provocation was ritual infringement (K. *chamwŏl*, C. *jianyue* 僭越).

Ritual infringement occurred when a lesser entity assumed prerogatives belonging to a higher power. A commoner who donned imperial dragon robes offers an obvious, egregious example, but in practice, the problem usually involved scenarios where status and authority were less clearly defined or where boundaries needed to be maintained to prevent usurpation: an ambitious courtier playing sovereign or a vassal king aspiring to greater heights. During the Ming occupation of Vietnam, imperial forces confiscated or destroyed countless records and books because of Vietnamese claims of "political equality" with the Ming. Although Ming sought to preserve works such as maps and gazetteers that aided its governance of the area, anything that "promoted Vietnamese rites and customs" and all stelae erected by Vietnamese authorities were marked for destruction: "not a single character was to be preserved."[23] When Ming withdrew from Vietnam, its officials still complained about how its Lê 黎 (1427–1789) and Mạc 莫 (1527–1592) rulers, despite having rekindled diplomatic ties with Ming, continued to "infringe" 僭號 on Ming prerogatives by using imperial titles.[24]

It was impossible, however, for Chosŏn to steer completely clear of imperial prerogatives. Chosŏn, like Vietnam, drew upon a wellspring of statecraft and rulership shared with Ming. The *p'yo* discussed in chapter 1 is a case in point. When the king dispatched diplomatic memorials to Ming according to its ritual calendar, he also received similarly worded congratulations from his own officials for the same occasions. But instead of *p'yo*, these documents were called *chŏn* 箋 (C. *jian*). In terms of form, the *p'yo* and *chŏn* were identical—their only difference was in nomenclature, where the Confucian notion of "righting names" (*chŏngmyŏng* 正名) enforced a distinction between high and low. Only emperors were entitled to receive *p'yo*, while lesser royalty, from his consorts to his heirs as well as the king of Korea, could receive only *chŏn*.[25]

Memorials presented to the Korean king still walked a tightrope when invoking a shared imperial tradition. They affirmed the distinction between king and emperor by praising the Chosŏn king for his "careful devotion to the emperor" [小心於事帝]. But they also envisioned the Chosŏn king as heir to the same imperial tradition. The king is said to "revere the models of the Tang court" [慕唐朝之典], and his "ceremony" is described as "identical to that of the palaces of Han" [同漢殿之儀].[26] In language that could have suited a Ming emperor, they lauded the king for "succeeding heaven's [mandate], ascending to a supreme [position]," and "inaugurating [his own] inheritance of a new illustrious throne" [繼天立極 誕膺景祚之新].[27] Like the emperor, Chosŏn's king fulfilled "the lessons of the *Great Plan*" [講洪範之訓辭], a reference to the foundational classical text outlining monarchical rule attributed to Kija.[28] Because the same classicizing idiom described rulership in both Chosŏn and the Ming, the lexical overlap itself is unsurprising, but it also meant that a memorial congratulating an emperor could serve as a model for one addressed to a Korean king, or vice versa.

Here was arguably the central dilemma of Chosŏn kingship. Because the ritual and rhetorical idiom of Korean kingship drew from the same classical wellspring as the Ming Empire, how could Korean cultural and political legitimacy be maintained without appearing to challenge imperial authority?[29] How could Korea's rulers assert their claims to the lessons of the sage kings while also steering clear of the Ming's monopoly of their legacies? What determines what is accessible or off-limits to a lesser ruler? The Chosŏn court trod carefully around these dilemmas, often leaving them unresolved. To avoid potential conflict with Ming, it sometimes enforced ritual distinctions internally to clarify the status distinction between "king" and "emperor." But its diplomats were just as likely to conceal and obfuscate where perceived violations might occur.

Infringement had always been an issue of diplomatic import, but it was less urgent for Korea before the Mongol conquests. In the era of "China among equals" spanning the tenth to thirteenth centuries, diplomacy was multilateral rather than unipolar. Many regimes employed the paraphernalia and symbols of imperium. No one state monopolized imperial privileges. The Song rivalry with the Khitan Liao and the Jurchen Jin empires is the most well known, but the rulers of Dali to its southwest, Dai Viet to its southeast, and the Tangut Xia to its northwest also assumed the imperial trifecta of reign eras (to mark the calendar), temple names, and the imperial title of *di* (K. *che* 帝).[30] Koryŏ was coy about the title of *di*. Still, it did occasionally adopt reign eras. It also made full use of "temple names" (C. *miaohao*; K. *myoho* 廟號), that is, posthumous titles ending in the suffix *-zu* 祖 ("progenitor," K. *-jo*) or *-zong* 宗 ("ancestor," K. *-jong*) as in Taizu (K. T'aejo) or Shizong (K. Sejong) (a practice continued in Chosŏn). As the "Son of Heaven, East of the Sea" 海東天子, they also duplicated the imperial ritual program, donning themselves in imperial-style regalia and receiving *p'yo* from their subjects.

When Chosŏn compiled the official history of Koryŏ, its officials considered the Koryŏ conventions to be "infringing" upon imperial prerogatives; however, this perspective was anachronistic. Koryŏ rulers would not have seen such practices as seizing what was not rightly in their possession. Arguably, Koryŏ's rulers remained lower in the status hierarchy than their Liao, Jin, and Song counterparts, but an important difference between Koryŏ in the twelfth-century context and Chosŏn in the fifteenth-century context was the degree to which boundaries between emperor and king had been clarified. Koryŏ can only be said to muddle this distinction if the line between the two had been clearly drawn in the first place (which it was not).[31]

The situation changed after the Mongol conquests. The decades that followed saw a gradual erosion of Koryŏ royal prerogatives. Koryŏ had surrendered to the Mongols in 1259, but its courtly rituals only became a subject of controversy in 1299. That year, a conflict between the Koryŏ king and his son led to an investigation carried out by Körgis 闊里吉思, an imperial official dispatched by the Mongol-Yuan imperial court. Upon his arrival, he saw much that offended him.[32] Koryŏ staffed thousands of officials in an extensive state apparatus that rivaled Yuan's in extent. Koryŏ court ceremonies also involved "grand meetings, canopied carriages, dragon screens, and retinues" reminiscent of imperial pageantry. Among these acts of "excessive infringement," most egregious was how Koryŏ officials assembled before the king to perform the *shanhu* 山呼, clamoring in unison wishes of long-life to the sovereign as they kowtowed at his feet "exactly" as would be done for the emperor.[33]

Körgis's criticisms elicited calls by Yuan officials to annex Koryŏ formally into imperial administration and abolish the Koryŏ kingship altogether. Resounding protests by Koryŏ officials, as well as appeals to Qubilai Khan's promise to "preserve" Koryŏ's institutions, staved off these moves but with the price of symbolic effacement.[34] The Mongol-Yuan court ordered Koryŏ to reform its institutional nomenclature to avoid infringement. Following Tang period conventions, the Koryŏ administration had long adopted the Six Ministries system, or *yukpu* (C. *liubu* 六部), paralleling the institutional structure of the Yuan court. Now any government agency that duplicated the name of an imperial agency had to be renamed. The Ministry of Rites, once called the *yebu* (C. *libu* 禮部) and its minister the *yebu sangsŏ* (C. *libu shangshu* 禮部尚書), were now dubbed the *yejo* 禮曹 and the *yejo p'ansŏ* 禮曹判書, respectively.[35] Koryŏ also abandoned temple names for deceased kings, content only to request a *siho* 諡號 (C. *shihao*), posthumous honorifics from the imperial court. Granted by rulers to exceptional subjects after their deaths, a *siho* was usually a sign of honor (rarely, it could also be used to humiliate vanquished enemies), but in this case, it was also a sign of subordination to imperial rule. Previous Korean rulers were granted *siho* only by their successors, but after these early thirteenth-century reforms, they were granted by the imperial court. These changes reinforced the identity of Koryŏ's monarchs as princes of the empire, a convention that persisted into the Chosŏn-Ming period.[36]

In the following years, additional reforms to court ritual further reinforced the Koryŏ king's inferior status vis-à-vis the Mongol emperor. In 1307, the royal birthday was renamed from *sŏngjŏl* 聖節 ("Sagely Festival") to *tanil* 誕日 ("Day of Inception"), reserving the former term for the *imperial* birthday. A new "palace gazing rite" 望闕禮 (*manggwŏllye*) was implemented: on the first day of every New Year, Koryŏ rulers led their officials into the palace courtyard and prostrated toward the direction of the imperial capital, which was indicated with a sign marked "palace" 闕 (*kwŏl*). This ritual innovation, which established the

Mongol capital, Daidu, as their axis mundi, was continued by Chosŏn in its relations with Ming.[37]

The early fourteenth-century reforms trod a fine line. Koryŏ retained political autonomy but ceded its symbols to a jealous imperial monopoly. But even after these changes, it remained clear, even to imperial officials, that Koryŏ was a *state*. One Chinese official at the Mongol court remarked that Koryŏ was unique in "all-under-heaven" for maintaining its Ancestral Temples and Altar of Land and Grain, ritual spaces ensuring dynastic and political integrity. None of these, not even the fact that Koryŏ collected its own taxes within its territory, was a cause for concern to this imperial official.[38]

What mattered to empire was not Koryŏ's statehood but something else altogether. The Mongols have earned a reputation for their pragmatic approach to conquest and rule. According to this view, once they had submitted to Mongol authority and were compliant with the delivery of tribute, local notables could remain in power and manage their affairs as they wished. The Koryŏ state's continued survival is a case in point.[39] But this supposed pragmatism was also deeply enveloped with ideological considerations. Mongol-Yuan rule might not have enforced uniformity among its constituents, tolerating uneven patchworks of administrative practices and cultural norms. Koryŏ's administrative autonomy and cultural difference posed no problems, but ritual prerogatives were another matter. The Mongol-Yuan court enforced the symbols of imperial supremacy, transforming the idioms of Korean kingship in the process.

The attention paid to symbolic and discursive affronts to imperial authority, as opposed to fiscal or administrative control, is in some sense typical for premodern political configurations. In Benedict Anderson's discussion of "imagined communities," what distinguishes "premodern" societies from modern nation-states is how "kingship organizes everything around a high center"—in this case, Daidu and later Beijing, as defined by the palace-gazing rite. But while the boundaries of "sovereignty" conceived in this manner were often "imperceptible" on the ground, they were instead made conspicuous elsewhere. As Mongol-Yuan concern with infringement suggests, ritual, not territorial administration, was what embossed the lines of authority.[40]

SHENGJIAO AS SOVEREIGNTY

At its heart, ritual infringement was a problem of sovereignty. Of course, "sovereignty" is a troubled concept, burdened with historiographical baggage and layers of ambiguity.[41] Just as no pre-nineteenth-century East Asian emperor spoke of his domain as an "emperor-state" (*cheguk* or *diguo*, modern translations of the word "empire"), no East Asian polity of this period spoke of "sovereignty" (at least not rendered as *zhuquan* or *chukwŏn*). This disjunction, however, has more to do with lacking a shared linguistic genealogy with the European word than the absence of what historian Chen Li has called "sovereign thinking and practice." Instead, as Li notes, any "social, cultural, or legal construct that claims higher authority for a state or imperial formation over another state or political community" has the potential to be an instrument of sovereignty. The search for sovereignty, once freed from the term's European genealogy, becomes a heuristic query for cognate practices and ways of thinking, as opposed to a philological wild-goose chase for a nonexistent Chosŏn-Ming precursor to a modern legal concept.[42] The productive question to ask then is, How was higher authority identified and claimed in that historical context? And because a claim of *higher* authority always implies rival sources of authority to be subsumed, the search must begin where authority was contested.

Quibbles over protocol and exacting debates over esoteric rituals, turns of phrase in poetry, and divergent interpretations of ancient history—these were how such contestation occurred. These "aesthetic" symbols of authority appear deceptively trivial compared to the matters of territory, resources, and military power, but these were how the "scaffolding of sovereignty" was constructed.[43] These symbols, whether expressed in ritual or rhetoric, elicited such anxiety in the context of imperial infringement because they not only represented and manifested authority; authority was having the prerogative to use these very symbols.[44]

When it came to their use, Koryŏ-Mongol precedents still held sway over Chosŏn-Ming arrangements. What changed was how the Chosŏn court proactively observed these precedents, even without imperial intervention. King T'aejong, for instance, went further than his Koryŏ predecessors to avoid "infringing the Central State." Before receiving patents of investiture from the Jianwen emperor, he abolished the noble titles of duke (K. *kong* 公) and marquis (K. *hu* 侯) to avoid duplicating Ming usage.[45] In 1411, T'aejong dispatched envoys who relayed a message to the Ming Ministry of Rites. It explained that Chosŏn's state rituals still followed Koryŏ practices. Uncertain about what Ming had mandated for its vassal states, T'aejong hoped the Ming Ministry of Rites would promulgate these regulations to Chosŏn.[46]

By deferring to Ming ritual authority, it would seem T'aejong had relinquished his own. At the same time, the ritual sites he enumerated were the ancestral temples, the Altars of Land and Grain, shrines to the mountains and rivers, and the Confucian temple, which represented, respectively, the Yi ruling house's dynastic legitimacy, Chosŏn's independent existence, Korea's territorial integrity, and finally membership in a Confucian cultural world. Of these, T'aejong did not ask for imperial approval but recognition. If Ming were to promulgate protocols for these rituals, it would have lent imperial guarantee over the claims of authority implied by these ritual programs.

Thus were the contours of Chosŏn's strategy: it sought to deploy Ming authority as a way to shore up its own. But imperial authority was not always easily borrowed. T'aejong's embassy returned in 1412 with only a message from the emperor that Chosŏn should only "follow its own customs" [從他本俗], suggesting Ming relinquished its stake in these matters.[47] The wording hearkened back to Qubilai's guarantee that Koryŏ could "preserve its original customs," a phrase the Koryŏ court redeployed to argue for its dynastic and territorial integrity when both were under threat. The 1412 Ming missive, on the other hand, echoed a more proximate precedent: the Ming Hongwu emperor's declaration that Chosŏn's "rites should follow its original customs; its laws obeying its former statutes," the very one issued to deny Yi Sŏnggye's investiture on the basis of Korean cultural difference. The Hongwu emperor, in a second missive from 1396, acknowledged Chosŏn "should be invested with a king" but only if the "character of its ruler improved." As long as Chosŏn, in his eyes, remained "stubborn, querulous, cunning and deceiving," he would leave Chosŏn "to exercise its own *shengjiao* (K. *sŏnggyo* 聲教)."[48] Because relinquishing imperial authority over Chosŏn was also a rejection of its ecumenical belonging and political legitimacy, it was no wonder then that King T'aejong sought to reaffirm both through imperial approval.

The term Hongwu used, *shengjiao*, warrants explanation. Like many classical terms, *shengjiao* eludes straightforward translation. It is best understood as a node in a constellation of concepts linking cultural power to sovereign authority.[49] Its locus classicus was a passage in the *Tribute of Yu*, from the *Book of Documents* where it is stated: "On the east, flowing to the sea, on the west, extending to the moving sands, to the far northern and southern limits; thus his *shengjiao* spread through the four seas [東漸于海 西被于流沙 朔南暨 聲教訖于四海].[50] In the discussion of this passage in the influential *Supplement to the Extended Meaning of the Greater Learning* (*Daxue yanyi bu* 大學衍義補), the influential mid-Ming statesman and classical scholar Qiu Jun 丘濬 (1420–1495) equated *shengjiao* with the "rule of an enlightened stage" whose "moral transformation" 化 extended to the farthest reaches of the habitable world bound by sands and seas. In this scheme, *sheng* and *jiao* were complementary mechanisms. The former is "heard by those afar," while the latter are models of action "emulated from afar." Moral transformation occurred, not through direct intercession but when words (*sheng*) and action (*jiao*) inspired others to admiration and emulation.[51] According to Qiu Jun, it was Ming's successful *shengjiao* that caused Chosŏn to "reverently submit to the imperial court and to pay tribute every season, without neglecting their ritual duties," a living example of the classical ideals he expounded.[52]

In Qiu's formulation, geography established natural limits to the extension of *shengjiao*. For a statecraft thinker who believed "reining in the barbarians" [馭夷狄] was the most urgent matter confronting the Ming Empire, there were also implicit limits to imperial power and its cultural authority. There were distant, barren reaches, the so-called *huangfu* (K: *hwangbok* 荒服), that civilizing influence could not reach. Even so, Qiu Jun still held Chosŏn as evidence of Ming's expansive *shengjiao*, a contrast to the Ming founder Hongwu who excluded Chosŏn from his *shengjiao*. Even if the two might have agreed on the necessity of maintaining "the distinction between the civilized and the barbarian" [華夷之辯], they did not agree whether Chosŏn lay within or without the limits of imperial influence.[53] By the late fifteenth century, the Chosŏn court managed to be both inside and outside at the same time, melding both ecumenical schemes. Its rulers received Ming investiture but still "exercised its own *shengjiao*." If denial of investiture meant withholding Ming's civilizing influence, acceptance of investiture should have reinscribed Chosŏn under it, but this phraseology was now used to assert Korea's political and cultural autonomy.[54]

In this respect, the term *shengjiao* might be the best Sino-Korean stand-in for the sovereign concept, encapsulating both manifestations of the monarch's authority through ritual display and his moral charge as civilizer. While broadly understandable as "cultural authority," it also combined two distinct concepts in East Asian political thinking. They are what historian Shao-Yun Yang describes as the difference between "folkways and custom" (C. *fengsu*, K. *p'ungsok* 風俗) and "ritual propriety and moral duty" (C. *liyi*, K. *yeŭi* 禮儀). The former captured aspects of culture that varied across time and space. In contrast, the latter was normative, continuous with the classical tradition. By virtue of being universal and immutable, its possession was what distinguished the civilized from the "barbarians."[55]

By commanding *shengjiao*, Korean sovereignty was indeed its own, even if it was keyed to a universal mode. The Ming court, like its predecessors, did send copies of major imperial commissions of philosophy and history to Korea, often at Chosŏn's request.[56] Imperial rescripts accompanying these gifts even implored Korean elites to "read the books diligently."[57] But Chosŏn's king and officials never needed imperial exhortation to "read books." The Chosŏn court positioned itself as a civilizing agent. Its activist officials implemented a range of interventions to shore up ritual propriety and transform local customs, while local elites celebrated Confucian paragons, attacked heterodox religious practices, reformed local marriage patterns, adopted Zhu Xi's family rituals, and established local centers of learning.[58] As the court official Cho Wi 曹偉 (1454–1503) once stated, the Chosŏn court's method of "civilization, transformation, enlightenment and guidance" [教化開導] had reached the sagely standards set by the Zhou and surpassed the heights attained by former imperial dynasties, like Han and Tang.[59]

Nevertheless, diplomatic rhetoric still insisted that the emperor's *shengjiao* did extend to Korea. Even if a diplomatic conceit, the superimposition of Ming authority over the Chosŏn court still raised some thorny questions. To what degree did Chosŏn royal agency conflict with imperial prerogatives? Should Chosŏn institutions conform to Ming standards or classical ideals? What leeway did the Chosŏn king have in determining his ritual practices? Should existing Korean practices be reformed according to Ming practices? These questions of constitutional import animated court discussion from the dynasty's founding, but it was really in the reign of King T'aejong's son Sejong 世宗 (r. 1418–1450) that they were hashed out in earnest. During these decades, the Chosŏn court triangulated classical prescriptions, contemporary Ming practice, and native customs to revamp state ceremonies, royal marriage practices, and diplomatic protocols. At the same time, belief in the legitimacy of Korea's institutions and local traditions allowed Chosŏn officials to defend them, even against the occasional criticism of Ming officials. A full accounting of these programs, and the controversies they incited, is impossible here (each deserves their dedicated study), but a brief discussion of three issues—sky rituals, the invention of the Korean alphabet, and female musicians at court—will suffice to illustrate the tension between royal agency and imperial authority.

King Sejong's Heavens

In 1370, the Hongwu emperor dispatched envoys to Koryŏ to perform sacrifices to its mountains and rivers. The logic was, now that Koryŏ had become a Ming vassal, the spirits of its mountains and rivers needed to be honored alongside "those of the Central State."[60] In a 1393 missive sent to Yi Sŏnggye, Hongwu invoked those same mountain and river spirits as witnesses to the new king's "misdeeds," crimes that Hongwu also planned to "report" to the Supreme Emperor 上帝 to receive sanction for a punitive expedition. Notable in these appeals to divine authority is how accountability was apportioned: Yi Sŏnggye would be judged by the local gods of the "mountains and rivers," but Hongwu's mandate for war derived from the ultimate celestial deity.[61]

This distinction between kingly and imperial authority also animated debates in Chosŏn over the propriety of the celestial sacrifice rite (chech'ŏn 祭天). Inherited from Koryŏ, it involved a round altar (wŏn'gu 圜丘) that, like the Heavenly Altar (C. Tiantan 天壇) used in imperial rites, represented the celestial abode's circular shape. Officials opposed to its performance insisted that only the Ming emperor, as universal ruler, communed directly with "heaven." In contrast, the Korean king was a "vassal lord" (C. *zhuhou*, K. *chehu* 諸侯) who, according to the *Book of Rites* (*Liji* 禮記), could only venerate the mountains and rivers in the direction of his apportioned terrestrial domain.[62]

The distinction between a terrestrial ruler and the Ming emperor as cosmic sovereign was not as straightforward as the formula above would imply. Claiming the sky risked infringing imperial authority, but early Chosŏn rulers were not keen to abandon the heavens altogether.[63] Yi Sŏnggye's new regime had been justified through a celestial mandate, unsurprising given the close association between sky ritual and sovereign power in classical political discourse.[64] The famous 1395 star chart, the *Positions of the Heavenly Bodies in Their Natural Order and Allocated Celestial Fields* (*Chŏnsang yŏlch'a punya chi to* 天象列次分野之圖), carved in a stone stele shortly after Chosŏn's establishment, lauded the new king's efforts to "correct the central star" as following in the footsteps of the ancient sage kings Yao and Shun.[65]

With cosmology at the very heart of kingship, the question was how to accommodate these competing sovereign claims. Some officials, such as Pyŏn Kyeryang 卞季良 (1369–1430), argued that Chosŏn need not observe the imperial monopoly at all. In his view, Korea's rulers received a *translatio imperii* distinct from China's emperors. And since the first of their kind, the legendary Tan'gun was himself offspring of a sky deity, Chosŏn's political existence was due to this cosmopolitical link to the heavens, not because its land had been "apportioned for enfeoffment by the Son of Heaven" [蓋自天而降焉 非天子分封之也].[66] Others proposed a compromise that respected the distinction between king and emperor while preserving sky rituals for Korea's king. Just as Chosŏn apportioned the earth, it could also partition the heavens by performing rites only for the Blue God 青帝 of the eastern sky.[67]

Both these options were ultimately rejected.[68] Although King Sejong's son King Sejo 世祖 (r. 1455–1468) briefly revived the round-altar sky rituals, he left no record of why he abruptly abandoned them in 1464.[69] Even decades after, Chosŏn officials remained peevish about potential charges of infringement. In 1483, a deputy of a Ming envoy, bedridden with illness, asked the interpreter Kim Chŏ 金渚 to relay a message to the Chosŏn court. The envoy wished for a sacrifice to heaven to be conducted on his behalf. Kim Chŏ explained this was impossible because "sacrifices to heaven are the affair of the Son of Heaven." Therefore, in Korea the king "sacrifices solely to the mountains and rivers, while his subjects pray to their ancestors." Kim Chŏ's political correctness only elicited a dismissive retort from the Ming envoy's deputy. With only a Daoist astral ritual, not an imperial one, in mind, he scoffed "even common men erect altars to pray to heaven; what use is there to sacrifice to one's ancestors?"[70]

Evidently, the Ming court tolerated a wide range of sky cults. The sky's role in timekeeping remained, in theory, however, an imperial prerogative, as did astronomy—the quantitative and observational study of celestial objects that was critical for its creation.[71] Time was also of practical diplomatic consequence. Ming promulgated the Great Concordance Calendar (*Datongli* 大統曆) to Korea, which, by accepting it, "observed the proper lunation,"[72] an act that signified a vassal ruler's subordination.[73] In contrast, when Ming launched its invasion of Vietnam in 1407, it accused its rulers of only "pretending to accept the proper lunation" and "burning the imperial calendars" promulgated to their country. These offenses, when combined with Vietnamese rulers issuing their own reign eras to mark the years, were seen as an attempt to "challenge the Central State as equals" [抗衡於中國]—the ultimate justification for imperial reprisal.[74]

Both the jealous monopoly and the universalizing thrust of imperial astronomy created practical difficulties for the Chosŏn court. After all, the calendar informed everyday timekeeping, the agricultural cycle, as well as the selection of auspicious days for marriage, burial, and sacrifice. The imperial calendar was promulgated annually in the ninth month, with copies conveyed to Chosŏn with a returning embassy. Their timing, however, meant that not every calendar would arrive in time for the New Year in Korea, creating a practical problem that could be resolved only if the Chosŏn court calculated its own calendar.[75] Moreover, the promulgated versions of the Ming Great Concordance Calendar (which was based on the Yuan Season Granting calendar 授時曆) did not detail how the calendar was derived, so Chosŏn could not simply follow its computus to reproduce it for future years. When its astronomers relied on tables from an earlier calendrical system to make calculations, discrepancies between the Korean and the Ming calendars were unavoidable, desynchronizing Ming and Chosŏn time.[76] In 1432, a predicted solar eclipse occurred two days late,[77] which spurred King Sejong to initiate a massive astronomical project involving the construction of a complete set of astronomical instruments—everything from sundials, clepsydras, gnomons, and armillary spheres—for the Royal Observatory to take their measurements.[78]

The sky's sovereign implications prevented Sejong from seeking Ming advice for his project. Korean astronomers, for instance, were unfamiliar with the use of arc-sagitta ratios in relevant calculations, so Sejong considered dispatching an official to consult the Ming astronomical office. The problem, as one official raised, was the potential impropriety of broaching the subject in China (although the king suggested the inquiry could be posed narrowly as a theoretical, mathematical question).[79] King Sejong also ordered his officials to conceal knowledge of his astronomical project from Ming emissaries, again wary of breaching the imperial monopoly.[80]

Regardless, the project continued. Sejong's astronomers did consult a wide range of astronomical texts from Ming, including the *Muslim Calendrical System* (*Huihui lifa* 回回曆法) employed by Muslim astronomers in China.[81] More precise measurements of the sunrise and sunset in Seoul determined the altitude of the North Pole from the capital to be 38 ⅙ (三十八度少弱) degrees (also a measure of geographical latitude). This figure was crucial for calculating whether a predicted eclipse would be visible. These, among other astronomical and geographical differences, explained the discrepancy between the timing of celestial phenomena. This systematic recalibration of the Chosŏn calendrical system from the ground up, including modifications for the movements of the sun and moon and also the five visible planets, was later compiled together as the *Calculation of the Motions of the Seven Celestial Determinants* in 1442 (*Ch'ilchŏngsan* 七政算).[82]

Sky rituals and celestial measurement, with their connection to political authority, have elicited much scholarly discussion on whether Chosŏn initiative in these areas should be understood as asserting political independence from Ming.[83] Sejong conceived of accurate measurement and management of time to be integral to his royal duty, but he also wished for the Korean calculations to result in a calendar that conformed to the imperial one. But it is unclear whether his desire to synchronize Korean with imperial time was motivated by fealty to Ming, a desire to match it in astronomical achievement, or practical considerations of calendrical synchronization. If it was about demonstrating political subordination, it is striking that no extant Korean calendars from before the Imjin War bears the mark of the Ming imperial reign era; they resort only to the sexagenary dating system.[84]

The Chosŏn calendar's relationship to Ming authority was therefore ambiguous, and likely purposely so. However Korean celestial initiatives are to be interpreted, they nonetheless revealed the long shadow cast by the notion of a superior, imperial authority overhead. Royal imperatives conflicted with imperial prerogative precisely because Chosŏn and Ming drew on a common idiom of political authority that now needed to be differentiated. In the face of Ming universal authority, the problem was what was still open to appropriation and how Korean kingship could assert its civilizing prerogatives.

King Sejong's Alphabet

Ming authority was not the only constraint on Korean kingship. In Chosŏn period discourse, Ming models were worthy of emulation because they were "institutions of a temporal ruler" (K. *siwang chi che* 時王之制). His rules were effective for the ecumenical world only for the time being. Classical 古 norms, on the other hand, were, in theory, permanent and unchanging.[85] In Ming, monarchical authority and classical precedent could overlap and clash, but in Chosŏn, the temporal authority of the Ming court created an additional axis of discretion; the Chosŏn ruler had to account for classical, Korean, as well as Ming models.[86] As hinted by the proposal to apportion heaven by venerating only the "Blue God of the East," the idiom of authority for early Chosŏn rulers moored Korean kingship to spatial rather than temporal constructs. Combined with attention to local variation in customs and mores (K. *t'osŏk* 土俗 or K. *t'op'ung* 土風), this discourse of localness sanctioned deviance from imperial and classical authority without declaring total cleavage from it.[87]

One project legitimized by "local custom" was the Korean script invented by King Sejong in 1443. Later promulgated in 1446, the script was a better fit than Chinese characters for the morphological features of the Korean language. Classical Chinese (or Literary Sinitic) is isolating, analytic, and lexically monosyllabic, and it observes a subject-verb-object word order. In contrast, Middle Korean is (as is modern Korean) synthetic, agglutinative, and lexically polysyllabic, and it observes a subject-object-verb word order.[88] According to the bilingual promulgation edict of the alphabet, which Sejong called *The Correct Sounds to Teach the People* (*Hunmin chŏng'ŭm* 訓民正音):

> The sounds of our country are different from that of the Central State [China]. They do not correspond to the literary script [i.e., Sinitic] [國之語音 異乎中國 與文字不相流通; 나랏·말·ᄊᆞ미·中듕國귁·에·달아· 文문字ᄍᆞ·와·로·서르ᄉᆞᄆᆞᆺ디·아니·ᄒᆞᆯᄊᆡ·]. And so, the unlearned people have things to say, but there are many who are in the end unable to express themselves. Looking upon this with pity, I have newly created twenty-eight letters in hopes that they will be easy for people to practice and convenient for their everyday use.[89]

In the usual understanding of the alphabet's history, this passage is treated as evidence of Sejong's nationalist agenda and a populist effort to "democratize" literacy. While it *was* an embrace of Korean distinctiveness and an effort to spread literacy, the idea that it also sought a cultural break from "China" is not as straightforward as this narrative assumes.[90]

The alphabet was still rooted in Sinitic concepts, visible in the cosmological and phonological framework that justified its creation. In promulgating the script, King Sejong and his advisers were keen to identify cosmological correspondences in its phonological system. He matched the three basic vowels ᅵ , ᅳ, ᆞ to heaven, earth, and man while associating the five-part consonant system with each of the five phases 五行. It also shoehorned Middle Chinese phonological distinctions between "turbid" and "clear" consonants into Korean, and also preserved the square-shaped syllable as a graphical unit, an aesthetic choice with no precedent in existing alphabetic scripts.[91]

That King Sejong rooted his alphabet in in existing phonological science does not detract from its ingenuity, but it does reframe the alphabet's purpose. It was as much about rendering "local" language as it was for establishing a standardized convention for the pronunciation of Chinese characters in his kingdom. To achieve this, Sejong's alphabet departed radically from the initial-final method of the *fanqie* 反切 system used in Sinitic phonology since the sixth century. In Sejong's alphabetic system (in contrast to an abugida or syllabary), each grapheme represented one phonetic element. When glossing Chinese characters, it relied on fixed phonological values, an advantage over the *fanqie* system, which had to reference the pronunciation of other characters. As Gari Ledyard proposes, this innovation was aided by familiarity with other alphabetic writing systems such as 'Phags-pa or Old Uyghur.[92]

The alphabet was the culmination of the king's long-standing interest in phonology. Like royal investment in astronomy, it was incited by awareness of discrepancies among contemporary Chinese conventions, classical models, and Korean practices. When the Koryŏ court was deeply enmeshed in Mongol imperial politics in the early fourteenth century, there was no shortage of multilingual elites who could use Chinese and Mongolian, but by the fifteenth century, that generation had largely died out. The Chosŏn court, anxious about the linguistic training of diplomatic personnel, requested several times to send students to Ming China for study, only to be rebuffed on the grounds that Chosŏn was to enact *shengjiao* on its own terms.[93] What the Ming did provide the Chosŏn court was the *Correct Rhymes of Hongwu Reign* (*Hongwu zhengyun* 洪武正韻). Promulgated by the Ming court in 1375, it represented a comprehensive catalog of Chinese phonology, meant to "restore . . . the elegant sounds" supposedly corrupted by a century of Mongol rule. In practice, it meant elevating the learned speech patterns of the Jianghuai 江淮 region (the Hongwu emperor's place of origin and the site of the original Ming capital) to a universal standard. King Sejong's courtiers who worked with the king on the alphabet, notably Sin Sukchu 申叔舟 (1417–1475) and 成三問 (1418–1456), also created a version of the *Hongwu Rhymes* that included glosses in the Korean alphabet to distinguish between "standard" and "vulgar" varieties of contemporary spoken Chinese.[94]

King Sejong was not content to conform to Ming convention—phonology for Sejong was as much about rendering actual speech as providing a tool for recording the *proper* pronunciation of Chinese graphs. So when King Sejong's court published their own glossary, the *Correct Rhymes of the Eastern Kingdom* (*Tongguk chŏng'un* 東國正韻),

it departed from the *Hongwu* glosses. Its express purpose was to correct common errors that had accumulated with time: the conflation of similar-looking characters, the confusion of similar-sounding phonemes, the replacement of one homophone with another, and the haphazard use of vernacular readings. These efforts at correction nonetheless entailed an embrace of local difference. Korea, "the East, is encompassed by rivers and mountains and is a realm of its own, with wind and air different from the Central State." Because what was "breathed" here was different, so too would the sounds of their language differ. These local differences notwithstanding, "the [distinction] between clear and turbid [consonants] and the four tones" still followed classical models.[95]

The goal of the *Eastern Kingdom*, therefore, was not to align Korean readings to contemporary Ming standards. It was to establish a Korean phonological system continuous with earlier precedents. In other words, the *Eastern Kingdom* provided Korea with its own version of a classicizing phonology. As a technical achievement, it was hypercorrect: it preserved phonemic distinctions that had long fallen out of use in China; although it was based on a Korean sound system, it prescribed phonological ideals that were impossible to put into practice.[96] Even if its standards were artificial, it nevertheless made the point that Chosŏn should forge links with the classical past on its own rather than on Ming terms.

Sejong's alphabet had its detractors. One group of officials led by Ch'oe Malli 崔萬理 (?–1445) believed the new vernacular script would displace the Chinese writing system and have Korea join the "barbarians." For them, sharing a script 同文 with China was an emblem of civilized status. In his words, one should "use Chinese ways to transform barbarians" (*yong ha pyŏn i* 用夏變夷), never to use "barbarian ways to transform the Chinese." King Sejong did not take to Ch'oe protests well, punishing him and dismissing him from office.[97] This opposition has led King Sejong to be lionized as a progressive nationalist dedicated to Korea's native culture, while Ch'oe Malli has been vilified as a conservative, Sinophilic ideologue bent on keeping literacy away from non-elites.[98] These caricatures, however, both assume in error that "Chinese" (as used in the term *yong ha pyŏn i*) was posed in contradistinction to "Korean." In fact, Chosŏn elite identification with "China" was not as a foreign other. Rather than ethnic transformation, it was to align Korean practices with universal standards of "ritual and propriety" represented by the classical past.[99]

In the early fifteenth century, the urgency of this transformation would have been compounded by a desire to escape the taint of a century of Mongol (and thus "barbarian") influence. These changes also involved cutting away at the cultural and ethnic diversity generated in the Mongol era in favor of a classicizing ideal of "ritual and propriety." For instance, this included reforming sartorial practices by removing elements of so-called barbarian dress. Tibetan Buddhism, once patronized by Koryŏ kings, disappeared from Korea.[100] Leaders of Korea's Muslim 回回 minority participated in court ceremonies wearing their distinctive dress until 1427, when they were ordered to abandon their traditional sartorial and religious practices as well as assimilate by intermarrying with locals.[101] From this perspective, one can understand why King Sejong's innovative Korean alphabet, which drew on linguistic innovations with origins beyond the Sinitic ecumene, provoked such consternation upon its invention, even when one of its explicit purposes was to transmit Confucian moral values. Counterintuitively, it "used barbarian ways" to civilize Korea.[102]

Despite Ch'oe and Sejong's disagreements, the two had more in common than might first appear. Their difference was not that one valued Sinitic culture whereas the other did not. Instead, it was whether an intermediary technology, in this case, a new script, would become a bridge or a barrier. For Ch'oe, if the king had truly wanted to maintain continuity with the classical past, he should have modeled after Chinese institutions, not create his own.[103] Indeed, Ch'oe's chief worry that the new alphabet would interfere with the direct reading of the classics was borne out in the next two centuries with the emergence of vernacular aids for interpreting and vocalizing the classics (ŏnhae 諺解).[104]

Another underlying subtext (which may explain King Sejong's harsh treatment of Ch'oe) was that Ch'oe directly challenged the king's royal prerogative on this matter. In East Asia, inventing national scripts was historically an act of sovereignty. It had been undertaken by the Khitan, Tangut, Jurchen, and Mongol emperors to whom Ch'oe compared Sejong in his protest.[105] Once the Korean alphabet came into existence, its immediate application was indeed to buttress dynastic authority.

The first attempt to use the alphabet was to render a Korean-language court eulogy celebrating Chosŏn's dynastic founders: the *Songs of Flying Dragons* (*Yong pi ŏ chŏn'ga* 龍飛御天歌) in 1447.[106] Later, in 1481, the court used the alphabet to produce bilingual editions of the *Illustrated Guide to the Three Bonds* (*Samgang haengsildo* 三綱行實圖), a Confucian morality primer embodying the court's role in the civilizing process.[107] Linguistic difference might have inspired the alphabet's invention, but what mattered was how best to reconcile Korean difference with classical models and the scope of the royal prerogative to do so.

King Sejong's Musicians

Female musicians and performers were an integral part of Chosŏn court ceremonial.[108] Their employment, however, had invited controversy from the day the dynasty was established. On the day of Yi Sŏnggye's accession, reform-minded officials called for their elimination as a "pernicious legacy of the previous dynasty" and argued female performers "injured the solemnity of the royal retinue."[109] Music performed by women was, along with hunting, amusing diversions, and palatial construction, among "the paths leading to all sorts of neglectfulness and licentiousness."[110] In this male-centered Confucian discourse, music was meant to regulate unstable emotions; music performed by women would only stir them.[111]

These moral campaigns curtailed, but never eliminated, the use of female musicians. The institution continued through the end of the Chosŏn dynasty, with controversies over their propriety remaining unresolved. It also persisted because it was both a sign of Chosŏn's "local customs" and a symbol of royal prerogative, especially during diplomatic encounters.[112] For instance, King Sejong agreed to end their use in many state ceremonies, including the New Year rituals and the reception of Jurchen and Japanese envoys.[113] In 1435, Chosŏn officials argued that, because the Ming court did not employ women as court musicians, abolition would be in "observance of Chinese institutions."[114] King Sejong resisted this move, however, remarking on how difficult it would be to replace female musicians. The court initiated training programs for young men and eunuchs, but the results were unsatisfactory. The new musicians were deemed unfit to receive Ming dignitaries.[115]

The Chosŏn court went back and forth on this issue. When a Ming emissary was received by female musicians in 1450, he upbraided his hosts for following a "barbarian custom" 夷風 unfit for a "country of propriety and righteousness" 禮儀之邦.[116] Chosŏn officials, smarting from this "grave insult," renewed their efforts to abolish the practice, but as long as practical alternatives were unavailable, the court refused to abandon the use of female musicians altogether.[117] King Sejong's son King Sejo rolled back his father's officials' attempts to replace female musicians, arguing that public rituals should revert to "ancestral precedent."[118] For him, disapprobation from Ming envoys was also no reason to alter Chosŏn's customs. In his words, the "role of the celestial emissary is only to proclaim edicts—how could he change our old customs as well?"[119] Sejo likely viewed the institution as representing royal prerogative. He brought them even to the main throne room, the Hall of Diligent Governance 勤政殿, despite the predictable protests of his officials.[120]

Controversies over female musicians revolved around the issue of boundaries. Chosŏn officials who protested the use of female musicians conceived their presence in terms of a public-private dichotomy. Korean rulers could employ them as long as they were excluded from public (kong 公) life, that is, the zone of official, impartial activity. Female musicians were therefore tolerable as long as they were limited to the king's personal (sa) 私 life or banquets within the inner palace; although in practice, royal action regularly blurred this distinction.[121] Given this dichotomy, it becomes all the more surprising that diplomacy with Ming, a sine qua non site of public and national import, would be the domain where the institution of female musicians was consistently preserved. What did it mean if something regarded as the king's personal domain now infiltrated the ritual space of diplomacy?

Here the issue of female musicians raises the question of whether diplomacy belonged in the realm of the "public" or the "personal." For modern nation-states, diplomacy is a "public" activity, but the language of Chosŏn-Ming diplomatic documents always inscribed relations in terms of personal ties between rulers.[122] Moreover, in the early fifteenth century, Chosŏn rulers also interacted with the emperor's personal representatives, the eunuchs of imperial inner palace.[123] Controversies over female musicians in diplomatic ceremonies, then, might hint at a broader, if largely unspoken, tension around the nature of diplomacy. Protests by the officialdom treated diplomacy as the realm of "public" interest and official governance rather than the personal prerogative of the ruler. In the meantime, as will be discussed in chapters 5 and 6, Chosŏn's ties with the Ming court gradually became less about direct personal connections and more about bureaucratic processes and their rhetorical constructs, even if the interpersonal touch remained integral to their function.

Female musicians exposed the instability of boundaries. Besides transgressing gender norms, they also marked Korean cultural difference from Ming norms and called into question royal prerogatives. Ironically, for Chosŏn's rulers who resisted the reformist impulses of their officials, it was precisely the potential of female musicians to mark difference that was worth emphasizing. When they appealed to local tradition over the censure of both visiting Ming envoys and their own Confucian-minded reformers, they also asserted a royal prerogative to define limits to programs of cultural reform, even ones enacted on the auspices of conformity to universal, civilized standards. It may have been for this reason that rulers seeking to strengthen royal authority, such as Sejo, expanded rather than curtailed the use of female musicians.[124] As was the case for Sejong's astronomical and linguistic projects, both Ming and classical authority played an ambivalent role in the controversy.

Shortly after Chosŏn's founding, the fledgling dynasty sought assurances from a hostile and threatening Ming. Whether these efforts were what earned Chosŏn its long peace with Ming is a matter of speculation, but they are reminders that Chosŏn did not take stable relations for granted. The diplomatic template they adopted drew from Koryŏ-Yuan period arrangements, where the subordination of kingship to imperial authority was not itself an ideological problem, but what it entailed in specific institutional terms remained unclear. Ming authorities were of little help in resolving these issues: Chosŏn was mainly on its own when it came to designing what a "vassal" state should look like.

In Chosŏn, the boundaries of infringement were largely self-policed. That the Chosŏn state rituals accommodated Ming imperial authority has been taken as evidence for the emergence of *sadae*, not as a strategy but as an ideology. That many of these reforms, in particular the abandonment of celestial rites and the prerogative of punitive military expeditions, occurred during the reign of the great King Sejong has even sparked nationalistic condemnation of this generally sacrosanct figure.[125] At the same time, however, other political symbols that could have been diplomatically controversial—the use of temple names for rulers and the extent of Chosŏn's ancestral temples that far exceeded classical prescriptions—were preserved.[126]

This selective accommodation suggests something altogether different at work than loyalty to Ming or obedience to classical authority. It points to how even pragmatic calculations toward accommodating Ming power could become over the decades a source of thorny constitutional dilemmas for Chosŏn's rulers. They had to thread the needle between asserting royal prerogative and avoiding imperial infringement, even as they tied kingship to the cultural inheritance of the classical past. They had to comb through Korea's intertwined history with the imperial tradition by untangling its ambiguities, braiding together its multivalent threads, and cutting away its unwanted loose ends.

The tensions emerging from this process could spill out into court debates and are on full view in Korean historical records. In the arena of diplomacy, however, Chosŏn envoys had to communicate ritual deference, ecumenical belonging, and political autonomy in the same voice. On the receiving end, the Ming court treated these communications as fulfilling classical ideals of barbarians spontaneously submitting to imperial virtue. Scholars since the twentieth century, on the other hand, have attributed Korean self-policing to the ascendancy of Zhu Xi Neo-Confucianism in early Chosŏn intellectual and political culture.[127] While Ming imperial self-importance is easy to grasp, the Neo-Confucian explanation is confusing because there is nothing immediately obvious in the Neo-Confucian intellectual tradition, with its emphasis on gentry independence in scholarly and moral authority, that directly and specifically informed Chosŏn's diplomatic policy. Nevertheless, the Neo-Confucian explanation is on point in one crucial sense: Chosŏn diplomacy regularly appealed to a universal and rational political order, one consistent with the abstract and moral principles that underpinned a scholastic's vision of human affairs.[128] As will be discussed in later chapters, this moral order overlapped, but was not coterminous with Ming imperial authority. Rather than a way of appeasing Ming by equating imperial authority with moral order, Korean investment in this sense of order secured Chosŏn's position as a member of the civilized world and carved out room for Chosŏn's political survival and cultural agency. As will be discussed in the next few chapters, this order was not an empty abstraction: it had palpable consequences for the praxis of diplomacy.

PART II

The Practice of Diplomacy

In 1395, Chosŏn envoys presented gifts of horses to the Ming Prince of Yan (the future Yongle emperor). When his father, the Hongwu emperor, learned of this, he had the Chosŏn envoys apprehended and exiled to Yunnan. He charged, "[H]ow could the King of Chosŏn [be allowed to] have private relations?"[1] This statement recalled an adage in the *Record of Rites* (*Liji* 禮記) that asserted "subjects of others do not have outside relations" [人臣無外交] lest he acquires for himself "two lords."[2] This notion of sovereign monopoly over foreign contact manifested in two similar but distinct idioms: the avoidance of "private relations" (K. *sagyo*, C. *sijiao* 私交) and the injunction against "outside relations" (K. *oegyo*, C. *waijiao* 外交). Their coexistence also points to a latent tension in Chosŏn-Ming diplomacy. Investiture formalized the Chosŏn king as the Ming emperor's subject, a point reinforced in the diction of diplomatic memorials and imperial decrees alike.[3] So if his status as a Ming subject is to be taken literally, it would seem to disqualify Chosŏn's king from conducting foreign relations altogether. But if the Chosŏn king were really a Ming subject, why should contact between him and another Ming subject be forbidden under this scheme?[4]

This seeming incongruence has more to do with how these words are used in modern East Asia than how diplomacy worked in the fifteenth and sixteenth centuries. Its resolution requires revisiting what was meant by "outside relations." As *oegyo*, it is the cognate term in East Asia for "diplomacy" in the modern sense of the word. Chosŏn's emissaries were certainly conducting "diplomacy" with Ming, in the technical sense that they were carrying credentials (*diploma*) from one court to another, but there were important differences. Neither the Chosŏn nor the Ming courts maintained a dedicated organ for foreign affairs, as is typical in the modern nation-state system. For instance, the Ming Messenger's Office 行人司 dispatched messengers to rulers of distant kingdoms, imperial princes in the provinces, and local officials. Visiting dignitaries were handled by various agencies under the Ministry of Rites (C. *libu* 禮部), the same ministry that managed all matters of ceremony. Meanwhile, the Chosŏn court's own Ministry of Rites (K. *yejo* 禮曹) administered relations with Jurchens, Ryukyuans, and Japanese under the framework of "neighborly relations" (*kyorin* 交鄰).[5] On both institutional and discursive levels, the operant distinction was not one between the "domestic" and the "foreign." Instead, it was a relative framing of "inner" and "outer" that intersected with a hierarchical distinction between the Ming emperor as universal sovereign and the Chosŏn's king as his vassal. Through synecdoche, this subordination meant the Chosŏn state was the "small country" (*sobang* 小邦) to Ming, the "superior state" (*sangguk* 上國). So even if the Hongwu emperor treated relations with Chosŏn as "outside relations," it did not preclude him from arrogating the authority to detain and punish its envoys.

Behind the imperial claim to universal authority was anxiety over blurred boundaries and murky loyalties. Notwithstanding Hongwu's injunction against personal "outside relations" (and true to the emperor's fears), imperial personnel did prove pliable to cooptation. One reason was simply how frequently Chosŏn embassies traveled to Beijing. Chosŏn envoys traveled to Ming 1,118 times over 200 years of active diplomacy between the two courts. Between the three regular annual missions, embassies also traveled across the Yalu to handle royal and imperial succession; render gratitude; petition the imperial throne; resolve border conflicts; escort captives, shipwrecks, extradited criminals; and present gifts, including live tribute, both animal and human.[6] In contrast, imperial envoys visited about once a year in the first half of the fifteenth century and only once or twice every decade by the sixteenth century.[7] Because "coming to court" 來朝 established the Ming capital as an axis mundi, the proportional increase in Chosŏn's burden has been interpreted as a decline in reciprocity and therefore an increasing hierarchical distance between the Ming emperor as universal ruler and the Chosŏn king as his vassal.[8]

These envoy missions indeed enabled Korean access to trade goods and political legitimacy, but a valuable third resource—information—should not be neglected. Commercial goods, smuggled for private gain, rarely benefited official coffers, while the royal need for imperial legitimation was most keenly felt only when withheld. Information, on the other hand, was what allowed diplomacy to function. Like their counterparts in early modern Europe, Korean envoys conducted "honored espionage," but rather than doing so via resident legations,[9] the precursor to permanent plenipotentiary representation in modern diplomacy, they did so through ad hoc embassies.[10] Traveling overland over 3,000 Korean *ri* (roughly 1,200 km) in forty or so days from Seoul to Beijing, a single embassy's total time in Ming territory could easily approach 100 days (see map 3). With a baseline of three missions a year, a Chosŏn embassy was in Ming territory for about half the calendar year. From the perspective of intelligence gathering, the slow pace of foot travel only offered more opportunities.[11]

The information flow was also augmented by the envoy mission's organization. Official statutes required the embassy's secretary (*sŏjanggwan* 書狀官) to keep records and submit reports of what they have seen and heard in their sojourn.[12] In general, the chief envoy and his vice envoy stayed with the mission for its entire duration, but their staff, especially the official interpreters (*t'ongsa* 通事) accompanying them, enjoyed more flexibility.[13] One could be detached from the embassy to travel back to Seoul in advance to relay these reports, allowing the court to react quickly to urgent news.[14] Once the "advance interpreter" (*sŏllae t'ongsa* 先來通事) reached Chosŏn territory, he could cover the distance between Ŭiju and Seoul on horseback in as little as three days.[15]

Frequent and regular embassies to Ming also afforded advantages to the Chosŏn court. They could cultivate ties with imperial agents: precisely the kind of "private" and "outside" relations the Hongwu emperor deplored. To illustrate how these arrangements worked in practice, the chapters in part II turn to the rise and rule of Yi Yu 李瑈 (1417–1468), Great Prince Suyang 首陽大君.[16] Better known to history as Chosŏn's King Sejo, Suyang's dramatic rise and bloody reign still incite controversy today, but less commonly appreciated is his agile use of diplomacy, first to take the throne (chapter 3) and later to prosecute his vendetta against his northern neighbors (chapter 4). His cooptation of Ming institutions, imperial personnel, and diplomatic discourse was fairly typical of Chosŏn's rulers, but where Suyang stood out was how nakedly instrumental his appropriation of empire had been.

CHAPTER THREE

Beneath the Veneer

Dynastic crises have a way of heightening diplomatic communication. Each time a throne changed hands, an embassy traveled between Ming and Chosŏn. In 1449, there was one such crisis at the Ming court. The Oirat leader Esen Taishi (1407–1454) destroyed the Ming army at Tumu 土木 and captured Emperor Yingzong 英宗 (r. 1436–1449, 1457–1464). Esen tried to blackmail the Ming court with his captive emperor. Rather than give in, Ming officials installed Yingzong's younger brother on the throne as the Jingtai emperor 景泰 (r. 1450–1457).[1] Another such crisis was Prince Suyang's usurpation of his nephew Yi Hongwi 李弘暐 (1441–1457), known to history as Tanjong 端宗 (r. 1452–1455). The two crises set off a flurry of embassies, whether to announce accession, bestow investiture, render gratitude, or send tribute, making the 1450s one of the most active periods of Chosŏn-Ming diplomatic contact, and an opportunity to illustrate how much the balance of agency was in the Chosŏn court's favor.

Before Ming had decided how to announce the Jingtai accession, Chosŏn learned about these events from its returning envoy (see table 3.1 for a timeline). King Sejong's court worried that the conflict would spill over to Ming's northeast frontier and put Chosŏn in danger, although news that Esen's armies traveled westward instead allayed those fears. Defense preparations were suspended as a result.[2] The court also mulled the proper diplomatic response. At first, it resolved to mourn the emperor's abduction, but historical and statutory texts offered no guidance for such an exceptional turn of events. It settled on dispatching two separate, parallel embassies. This way they could maintain a separation between auspicious and inauspicious occasions: one embassy to congratulate the Jingtai accession and one embassy to present condolences for the Ming's recent misfortune. But then, unconfirmed reports arrived stating that Yingzong had returned to Beijing and would soon be restored to the throne. If true, both embassies would have to be recalled. A courier traveled post haste to catch up with the already departed congratulations embassy, instructing it to remain at the frontier town of Ŭiju until further notice. Meanwhile, an official interpreter traveled to Ming Liaodong to verify the news. Only when it was determined to be false did the embassy proceed.[3]

A steady flow of new information allowed the Chosŏn court to adjust its diplomatic posturing. When the Ming capital was in Nanjing, the journey could take up to three months each way. The capital's move to Beijing in 1421 shortened the travel time between the capital to Seoul to about one month each way. This compression of time meant that a traveling embassy could relay a message about major events at the Ming court well before their disclosure through official channels. In the fifth month of 1452, the Jingtai emperor deposed his nephew as heir apparent in favor of his son. In this case, the Ming did not dispatch an envoy to inform Chosŏn until early in the seventh month, but Chosŏn already dispatched an embassy to congratulate the newly crowned prince by the middle of the sixth month, over one month before the Ming emissary even crossed the Yalu into Chosŏn.[4] The Chosŏn court learned of these developments two weeks before the Ming embassy even left Beijing, only twenty-two days after its occurrence. This information, relayed by an embassy still on the way back from Beijing, allowed Chosŏn to quickly inform another embassy, already en route to the Ming, to alter the wording of its documents to change the recipient of the gifts to the new crown prince.[5] Meanwhile, Chosŏn prepared another embassy to congratulate the Ming on the prince's investiture.[6] The result was virtual prescience; Chosŏn could almost bend space and time to give their diplomats room to maneuver.

Chosŏn could not match the Ming's size or power, but it did retain an advantage in the flow of information.[7] This was the advantage Suyang

TABLE 3.1

Events Related to the Investiture of Jingtai's Heir in 1452

Event	Year
Jingtai replaces the crown prince.	Second day of the fifth month
Chosŏn learns of development.	Twenty-fourth of the fifth month
Chosŏn dispatches envoy to congratulate Jingtai.	Fifteenth day of the sixth month
Ming envoy departs for Seoul with announcement.	Fourth day of the seventh month
Arrival of Ming envoy on Korean frontier.	Seventh day of the eighth month
Arrival of Ming emissary in Seoul.	Twenty-first of the eighth month

exploited in his dealings with Ming. In 1452, Suyang traveled to Beijing to "render gratitude" (saŭn 謝恩) to the Ming court for investing his teenage nephew, Tanjong as Chosŏn's new king, known to history as Tanjong 端宗 (r. 1452–1455). Upon his return, he seized power and eventually the throne for himself, a path to kingship littered with the corpses of high officials, his princely kin, and eventually the nephew he deposed.[8] But Suyang did not merely take the throne. He also did so with Ming's blessings. As this chapter argues, Suyang's path to the throne cannot be understood without an appreciation of how pliable the instruments of empire were in the hands of a savvy agent.

SUYANG'S MISSION

After the Tumu debacle, Ming needed to proclaim the accession of the new emperor and his new reign era, Jingtai, across its realm and to its vassals. Chosŏn learned from its traveling envoys that bearing this proclamation to Korea would be Ni Qian 倪謙 (1415–1479), expositor-in-waiting of the Hanlin Academy 翰林侍講, accompanied by vice envoy Sima Xun 司馬恂 (?–1466).[9] When Ni arrived in Chosŏn shortly before the New Year, he was dismayed to discover that neither the

Chosŏn king, Sejong, nor his crown prince (the future King Munjong 文宗 r. 1450–1452) would receive him. Both, according to his Korean minders, were bedridden with illness, a claim that only invited his suspicion. He feared that because of the "recent incidents," Chosŏn might now "harbor a second heart" [輒懷二心], one that entertained grander political or ideological designs than Ming could tolerate.[10]

Indeed, failing to meet the king would have placed the envoy in dire straits. The imperial emissary had to proclaim the edict to the correct recipient, even on pain of death, as one Ming envoy to Champa later discovered.[11] Ni Qian avoided this sorry fate. Prince Suyang, as the next most senior member of the royal family, offered to conduct the reception ritual in his father's stead. To safeguard against possible accusations of dereliction, Ni detailed in the travelogue his efforts to demand Chosŏn's compliance while speaking glowingly of Suyang's performance and the Chosŏn court's "sincerity" in serving Ming.[12] Thanks in part to Prince Suyang, Ni accomplished his mission. He wrote a travelogue documenting the affair and returned with poems written in his honor by Chosŏn court's most eminent literati, Sin Sukchu, Chŏng Inji 鄭麟趾 (1396–1478), and Sŏng Sammun.[13]

Shortly after Ni Qian's departure, in the spring of 1450, Suyang's father, King Sejong, passed away. His successor, the sickly Munjong, ruled barely two years before leaving the throne to his son Tanjong. When Tanjong received Ming envoys bringing his patents of investiture 1452, his uncle Suyang again discharged state functions by entertaining the visiting envoys.[14] Through his interactions with Ming emissaries, Suyang built a reputation among Ming officials, but it was his personal embassy in 1452 on to seek imperial investiture of the nephew he eventually deposed that burnished his image as a loyal vassal in imperial eyes.

The quality of surviving sources muddles the circumstances of the 1452 embassy.[15] After the death of each king, a committee of venerable officials compiled the *Veritable Records* 實錄 of his reign, a text meant only for the eyes of posterity.[16] But Suyang's embassy occurred during the reign of his nephew. The *Veritable Records* for Tanjong's reign, properly called the *Chronicles of Prince Nosan* 魯山君日記 (referring to Tanjong by his princely rather than royal title) were left to be compiled not by the court of his chosen successor but the very individuals who conspired in his demise.[17] The exact dates of compilation are unknown, but it was most likely completed alongside King Sejo's *Veritable Records* during the reign of Suyang's grandson, Sŏngjong 成宗 (r. 1469–1494). Their compilers would have had every reason to cast Suyang in a positive light; the project's supervisors were Sin Sukchu and Han Myŏnghoe 韓明澮 (1415–1487), among Suyang's chief supporters and the architects of his fateful coup.[18]

According to the *Chronicles of Prince Nosan*, Suyang volunteered himself when the court debated whom to dispatch for the 1452 mission. His enemies, his younger brother Great Prince Anp'yŏng 安平大君 (Yi Yong 李瑢, 1418–1453) and two of the state councilors, Hwangbo In 皇甫仁 (?–1453) and Kim Chongsŏ 金宗瑞 (1383–1453), disapproved. Suyang's advisers also believed his absence from court would leave an opening for his enemies to act. Suyang prevailed over these objections. He even convinced Hwangbo In and Kim Chongsŏ to send their sons along with him.[19] Hwangbo and Kim might have thought it helpful to have eyes and ears on Suyang's mission, but Suyang intended to use them as hostages—as long as their safety was in his hands, Hwangbo and Kim would not act while Suyang was abroad.[20]

After a number of send-off banquets thrown by the court, royal kinsmen, and high-officials Suyang departed from Seoul on the twelfth day of the tenth month.[21] Over the next thirty or so days, they proceeded gradually through the waystations and settlements dotting Korea's western coast. At P'yŏngyang and the frontier town of Ŭiju, they rested and met local officials who entertained them with banquets.[22] His correspondences and interactions with Chosŏn's elite previewed what opportunities this trip provided for the ambitious prince—not so much the logistics of conspiracy but symbolic ascendancy: Suyang's arrogation of royal destiny.[23]

THE ROAD THROUGH LIAODONG

Accompanying Suyang on his mission as his scribe was Sin Sukchu. Sin had traveled on many occasions to Ming on behalf of King Sejong. Not only was he a seasoned diplomat, he also possessed what was becoming a rare skill among Chosŏn civil officials—competence in spoken Chinese.[24] Sin was already known in Ming court circles as one of the Chosŏn literati who exchanged poems with the Ming emissary Ni Qian in 1450.[25]

The diary Sin kept did not survive, but it was likely the basis of the *Veritable Records* account of Suyang's mission. A dubious piece hagiography, many of its details strain belief, but some historical value can still be extracted, if it is read simultaneously as a post facto retelling in service of Suyang's legitimation and naively as a factual record of his journey. Likewise, no surviving fifteenth-century envoy travelogue features a day-to-day accounting of an embassy's journey, but reading the *Veritable Records'* account of Suyang's journey alongside more detailed early sixteenth-century accounts allows a composite impression of the quotidian matters of what the embassy was like.[26] What "really happened" will remain elusive, but what symbolic, cultural, and social resources Suyang appropriated during his journey will become abundantly clear, as will his method for transforming diplomatic encounters into political resources.[27]

Before crossing the Yalu River with his entourage, Suyang rested in Ŭiju for at least a few days. When he crossed, likely after lunchtime, an interpreter was dispatched ahead of the main body to deliver what was euphemistically called *injŏng* 人情, gifts for cultivating "personal feelings" with Ming officials. In return, the Korean entourage received lodging, transportation, and provisions, including even poultry and livestock for meat.[28] In the following days, Suyang kept order within his ranks, impressing onlookers as they followed the chain of waystations in Liaodong. The embassy traveled between thirty-five and eighty *ri* a day, but not every stopover was at a waystation. At times, the entourage camped out or holed up at private residences, including the estates of Ming local officials, which after repeated visits by Korean embassies became their regular stopovers (see map 3).[29]

After eight days, the entourage arrived in Liaoyang, the seat of the Liaodong Regional Commission 遼東都指揮使司, the highest-ranking Ming office in the region. There, the "Chinese gathered like a wall, all to take a glimpse at [Suyang]," while the Jurchens looking from afar called him a "Buddha," impressed by his bearing. Ming officers tried to intervene to no avail: even when "a hundred batons came down" to clear the road, the crowd would not disperse. At a banquet held in his honor, his decorum and composure also earned the admiration of Regional Commissioner 都指揮使 Wang Xiang 王祥 (?–1457), who chided his subordinates for failing to measure up to Suyang in grace and bearing. Through the rest of the journey from Liaodong to Beijing, Suyang received poems, gifts, and words of praise from all those he encountered.

As frequent travelers in these waystations, Korean embassies relied on Ming locals, particularly the military, for their speedy conduit. The passing years only thickened these ties. When Wang Xiang died in 1457, Chosŏn sent envoys to offer condolences and present gifts to defray the funeral expenses. Even decades later, in 1533, Chosŏn ambassadors stopped by Wang Xiang's tomb to pay their respects.[30] When a Chosŏn embassy was waylaid by "bandits" in 1478, likely a Jurchen raiding party or a company of Ming deserters, the Liaodong commissioner dispatched a punitive expedition to hunt them down. When the embassy returned from Beijing, the Liaodong commander showed the chief Korean envoy the severed heads of the culprits.[31] No wonder then that Ming officers occasionally sought Chosŏn's help in their official careers. Later that year, Regional Commander Han Bin 韓贇 (?), soon to be sacked from this post, implored a passing Chosŏn envoy to have the Korean king submit a favorable report to the emperor of his "ability to defend against Jurchen incursions" as a last-ditch attempt to keep his job.[32]

In Liaodong, ties bound by *injŏng* or "personal feeling" crossed into realms of official concern. As one Chosŏn high official put it, Liaodong was the source of "all information related to the Central Court."[33] Here, even sensitive matters concerning Ming court politics and border disturbances passed from Ming military officers to a Korean embassy.[34] News, although valued, was not always reliable. One Chosŏn envoy Chŏng Hwan 丁焕 (1497–1540) accused a Ming officer of passing along false information in hopes that his embassy would share with him some of their oil paper. Chŏng was undoubtedly frustrated because, by then, his entourage had already exhausted their own supply from these incessant requests.[35]

After Liaoyang, the next major stop on Suyang's embassy was Shanhai Pass, the gateway into the Ming interior. There, in the words of one Chosŏn traveler, they could "gaze northward to the Great Wall, which cutting across the foothills, rose and fell with the landscape, its shape like a white dragon curled in wait, overlooking the great sea in all its boundless expanse."[36] At this vital threshold, the official in charge, a secretary appointed by the Ministry of War 山海關兵部主事, could expect a share of Korean largess. At times refined objects, rather than commodities, sustained this relationship. When Kang Hŭiyŏn 姜希顏 (1417–1464), a Korean official known for his calligraphy and painting, passed by the area, he made a gift of his work to the secretary Yang Ju 楊琚. When Kang Hŭiyŏn's younger brother Kang Hŭimaeng 姜希孟 (1424–1483) traveled to the same road years later, he brought with him a poem of his brother's to give to Yang, who treated him exceptionally well during his stay.[37]

State-to-state relations overlapped with personal ties, and so too did the line between friendly exchange and outright corruption become blurred. In 1461, a Chosŏn emissary returned with requests of stationery by the same Yang Ju and of composite bows by Dong Xing 董興, the regional commander of Guangning 廣寧總兵. Chosŏn's high officials rebuffed Yang's requests because of his "low rank" but complied with Dong's because Dong "directly managed matters [pertaining] to our country [i.e., Korea]."[38] Although these gifts violated Ming prohibitions against trading weapons, they were still rather commonplace. Chosŏn even granted an informal request for deerskins, composite bows, and over 100 arrows for the Liaodong commissioner.[39] That said, several months later, the court rebuffed a similar request made by a son of a Liaodong military judge.[40]

As "personal feelings" proliferated over time, they created the obligation of more gifts commensurate with the thickening ties, opening the door to graft and extortion. Each passing embassy, each favor from the Liaodong military became an economic opportunity.[41] "Personal feelings" also provided cover for a burgeoning clandestine trade lucrative for all who traveled to Ming under official auspices, including Chosŏn's envoys and interpreters.[42] In the reign of Suyang's grandson, Sŏngjong 成宗 (1469–1494), Korea's censors lambasted these practices as a source of moral corruption and a burden on the Korean waystation system, which relied on surplus labor in the form of corvée to function.[43] But in the face of these protests, Sin Sukchu, who had been Suyang's scribe in the 1452 mission, retorted: "When traveling these many thousands of leagues, how can we dispense with personal feelings" [萬里之行 豈無人情]?[44]

To the seasoned diplomat, the routinized quid pro quo had not debased some preexisting system—it *was* the system. Later diplomatic handbooks such as the seventeenth-century *Compendium of the Interpreter's Bureau* (*T'ongmun'gwan chi* 通文館志) included comprehensive, standardized lists of items, the so-called personal feelings earmarked for imperial officials along the tribute path.[45] Actual exchanges unlikely conformed to the letter of the rule, for any number of gift exchanges easily exceeded the prescribed quantities.[46] Nonetheless, formalizing these practices through clear precedents reflected a desire to draw, distinguish, and enforce a boundary between acceptable practice and a breach of custom, even if the line was more often than not fluid and indeterminate.

AT THE EMPEROR'S COURT

Once in the Ming capital, the Korean embassy usually stayed at Yuhe Hostel 玉河館, one of two residences in Beijing housing envoys from abroad.[47] There, its envoys might exchange poems with sojourners from Ryūkyū and Vietnam if the timing of their embassies coincided.[48] Suyang encountered only a company of *yain* 野人 (literally, "men of the wilds"), likely Jurchens living along the Chosŏn frontier. Throughout the fifteenth century, their leaders received ranks and titles from the Chosŏn court if they came to present their tribute; in this case, the leaders of the *yain* promised to pay their respects to Suyang again once he returned to Korea. An older fellow even exclaimed in delight that he had the good fortune to see a living "Buddha" in person before his death.[49]

These, and other encounters, underscored Suyang's effect on all those who met him. The *Veritable Records* mentions several banquets held in Suyang's honor, including an official welcoming reception 下馬宴 and a send-off party 上馬宴, usually hosted by a minister of the Ministry of Rites.[50] In the fifteenth century, the envoy was also received at the residence of imperial eunuchs, usually natives of Korea who were sent as tribute to Ming as children.[51] The envoy Yi Inson 李仁孫 (1395–1463), who went several months after Suyang to Beijing, was feted at the residence of Yun Pong 尹鳳 (fl. The 1430s–1460s), then the highest-ranking Korean eunuch at the Ming court.[52] The account of Suyang's embassy makes no mention of such a meeting, a conspicuous omission whose significance will be noted later.

The banquets became another opportunity to showcase the effusive admiration Suyang earned from his hosts. He declined offers of musical entertainment because the mourning period for his brother, Munjong, had yet to end. He also refused gifts, explaining "a virtuous man 君子 loves men for their virtue, not their wealth." Impressed, one of Suyang's hosts explained that he had adorned the banquet table with plum, bamboo, and pine because they, as symbols of virtue, "befit a virtuous man" like Suyang. The mission culminated with the imperial audience in the Forbidden City, but even there, Prince Suyang's steady virtue inspired the spontaneous admiration of all around, much as the wind bends the grass before it. When Suyang entered the palace grounds, the "eight elephants moved back several steps in unison."[53] Meanwhile, Suyang's regal aura fostered convenient misunderstandings over his exact identity. Ming officials began to address him as "king" (*wang* 王) or "your majesty" (C. *dianxia* 殿下), titles appropriate for Ming princes, but in Korea they were properly reserved for the ruling monarch, not a mere prince envoy. With even canny beasts susceptible to his charisma, these likely innocent mistakes were treated as spontaneous reactions to his virtue, casting a beam of royal destiny on Suyang's person.[54]

Despite this regal aura, Suyang still took care not to outshine the spotlight on his loyalty to Ming. When imperial gifts arrived, the Ming official in charge asked Suyang to remain seated out of deference to his royal status. He also suggested that Suyang need not perform the "rites of obeisance" personally, and it would suffice if one of his underlings did the kneeling and prostration in his stead. Suyang refused. He declared "gifts from the emperor ought to be received in person" and performed these gestures himself. The Ming officials who witnessed this performance exclaimed, "The son of the Chosŏn king is a scion of noble essence." His "wisdom and virtue far surpass the average person," and he was in all ways superior to another foreign prince from the Burmese kingdom of Hsenwi, whom they dismissed as "nothing extraordinary."[55]

The *Veritable Records* underscores the extraordinariness of Suyang's comportment. It was fairly typical, however, for how a Chosŏn envoy was expected to behave. Official histories and unofficial miscellanies (*chapki* 雜記) alike relate anecdotes about how the mien of many an envoy could impress a Ming observer with their "understanding of ritual." Once, Han Myŏnghoe received a gift of wine from the Korean king in the presence of Ming officials. When the messenger bearing the libation first arrived, Han bowed four times before taking his seat. When the messenger raised the cup to bequeath it to Han, he again prostrated before receiving it. As in Suyang's case, Han Myŏnghoe's actions confused Ming Chinese observers, for whom the rite was unfamiliar. But once the Korean interpreter spelled it out as a way to "pay obeisance to a ruler's gift," his actions became legible as an embodiment of ethical character and moral intent. A Ming Confucian scholar who witnessed Han's act "sighed in praise" and remarked that Chosŏn was "indeed, as others have said, a country of propriety and righteousness."[56]

Han Myŏnghoe did not necessarily perform for imperial eyes, but it was precisely the vocal acclaim of Ming observers that made Han's behavior worthy of note in the *Veritable Records*. What it documented was the spontaneous response to virtuous behavior, the same trope that was repeated throughout the account of Suyang's trip to Beijing. What set Suyang apart from Han was how these responses augured his eventual accession. Because his virtue was recognizable to barbarians, beasts, and bureaucrats alike, and the naturalness of royal destiny was thus secured, the exact circumstances of his path to the throne became a moot point.

DOUBLE TRUTHS

Suyang held an archery contest with his men outside the capital gates upon their return to Seoul. Suyang bested his followers. None could hit his mark, while the prince landed seven arrows in a straw man erected 130 paces away. After receiving exhortations to "loyalty and righteousness" from his deputies (a coded reference to his impending conspiracy), he answered them with a long poem celebrating their journey to Ming. In the last lines, Suyang hinted at loftier political designs: "On [my] return, the court and country will be renewed, / and the royal house will be at peace." He then implored his companions to "aid [him] in [fulfilling his] ambitions" with reassurances that he would not "forget the virtuous men" who supported him. The *Veritable Records* portrays Suyang's coup as a last-resort countermeasure, not planned until the ninth month of 1453, several weeks before he made his move.[57] But this account of Suyang's embassy and its return speaks with foreknowledge of Suyang's eventual ascent, revealing his coup to be a premeditated act.

On the tenth day of the tenth month, Suyang instigated his coup. Assistant State Councilor Kim Chongsŏ and his son were ambushed and killed outside their home. The conspirators also moved swiftly against their allies, killing the Chief State Councilor Hwangbo In. The pretext was that Kim and Hwangbo were plotting to place Prince Anp'yŏng, Suyang's younger brother, on the throne. With the reins of state in hand, Suyang then ordered Anp'yŏng's execution.[58]

Ming records make no mention of Suyang's violent coup or the bloody reprisals that followed. By contrast, Ming palace intrigue and political plots were narrated in the Chosŏn court's official records with salacious detail—poisoners in the seraglio, murderous imperial rampages, and a palace woman who in her dying breath cursed the emperor's shriveled penis—reported by returning envoys (and in one case, a repatriated Korean palace woman) who mixed hearsay with their firsthand observations.[59] Consider also the Korean treatment of roughly concurrent political developments at the Ming court after the Tumu debacle. In 1452, Esen Taishi returned Emperor Yingzong to Ming, but with the throne now in his brother Jingtai's hands, Yingzong was placed under house arrest. But in 1457, on the eve of Jingtai's death, disgruntled officials "stormed the gates" (C. *duomen zhi bian* 奪門之變) of the palace and reinstated Yingzong in a coup; however, Yingzong remained under the thumb of the cabal that placed him in power. In 1461, he faced a coup of his own when the palace eunuch Cao Jixiang 曹吉祥 (?–1461) instigated a military mutiny in Beijing. As historian David Robinson notes, its suppression left several thousand dead on the streets, with eight hundred or so dismembered corpses left strewn and exposed—all details reported by Chosŏn envoys who visited Beijing in the aftermath. For the next three days, it rained, and "the water, mixed with blood, flooded the forbidden palace."[60] The Korean envoy report made no additional comment, only appending Yingzong's declaration of victory over the "rebels." In response, Chosŏn sent another envoy to congratulate the emperor on his recent triumph, singing the same praises of august majesty and eternal peace as any other memorial would.[61]

The gap between Korean awareness of Ming affairs and Ming knowledge of Korean politics is again reminiscent of the politics of "overattention" and "inattention" characteristic of asymmetrical relations: Chosŏn paid close attention to Ming affairs because Ming was its most important diplomatic partner, while Chosŏn could rarely sustain the Ming court's concerted and focused attention. Even if knowledge of Suyang's coup circulated among Ming officials, it might not have been important enough to enter the empire's most authoritative chronicle. But as will be soon discussed (and elaborated upon further in chapter 6), asymmetries of attention explains only so much. There were other factors at work when it comes to differences in how Chosŏn-Ming diplomatic history is represented in Korean and Chinese sources.

There is, for one, the distinct style of the early Chosŏn *Veritable Records*. Verbose, and keen to relate feuds of opinion, Chosŏn records, especially from the fifteenth century, tend to delve into greater detail than the laconic Ming *Veritable Records* from the same period.[62] While the Chosŏn *Veritable Records* took care to present a narrative legitimizing Suyang's rise, it also recounted meticulously the planning, execution, and rationalization of the coup, details that celebrate Suyang's acumen and decisiveness but also undermine the official story of his rise.

Another, arguably more critical factor is the attention Chosŏn actors devoted to performing for the diplomatic stage. In Suyang's case, the difference in Chosŏn's domestic records and the diplomatic record shared with Ming could be traced to a version of events Suyang's supporters crafted for Ming consumption. In the coup's aftermath, Suyang portrayed himself as his nephew's protector, even arranging a marriage for the young king. He dispatched embassies to Ming as usual, including one requesting investiture for Tanjong's new queen in the tenth month of 1454.[63] In the fourth month of 1455 arrived a Ming embassy bearing the patents of investiture for her, the first mission since Suyang's coup. The leaders of the embassy were the vice director 少監 Ko Pu 高黼 (fl. 1455–1457) and the palace attendant 內史 Chŏng Tong 鄭同 (fl. 1455–1480), both Korean eunuchs who had been sent as children to the Ming as tribute.[64] No extant records speak to prior contact between Suyang and the palace eunuchs (the narrative of Suyang's mission makes no mention of interface with Korean-born eunuchs), but they had entertained no illusions about who was the power behind the throne. To Sin Sukchu, they praised Suyang's "wisdom and brilliance," exclaimed that "all-under-heaven has heard of Prince Suyang" and hoped to visit him before meeting the boy king. Suyang declined the overture and insisted they observe proprieties and see the king first.[65]

In the *Veritable Records*, Suyang's refusal illustrated the prince's continued deference to the rightful king. But when Suyang met the eunuchs, the *Veritable Records* returned to burnishing Suyang's aura of royal destiny, much in the same way as it had done in its account of Suyang's embassy. During their audience with Suyang, Sin Sukchu arrived with liquor to entertain the emissaries. He also brought a letter supposedly written by King Tanjong that claimed Suyang had already been "entrusted with the affairs of state after having accomplished great deeds." The emissaries answered that they had come to Chosŏn to "witness the loyalty and sincerity of Suyang." They then turned to Suyang and said: "His Majesty [Emperor Jingtai] has said that Suyang has accomplished great deeds. All-under-heaven knows the merit of Suyang. The Emperor knows all of this. How did we hear of this? It was talked about all over at the imperial court, and thus we know of it in detail. All-under-heaven compares Prince Suyang to Li Jing 李靖 (571–649) of the Tang."[66]

With the comparison to the Tang official Li Jing, the emissaries' words presented Suyang as a loyal official, competent in both civil and military affairs.[67] Suyang declined the compliment, crediting the "immense virtue of the Emperor" and the "grand fortune of His Highness [Tanjong]" for protecting the "altars of state." He explained that "the rebellious ministers had earned their own deaths" and he deserved no "merit" in the matter. In the ensuing conversation, however, the eunuchs insisted that nothing could have been accomplished "without Prince Suyang," and the details of what was exchanged during the banquet, along with "what the king has said of [Suyang's] merits" should be reported to the emperor. Suyang also agreed that "this banquet should be made known to the emperor."

The words exchanged, as they are recorded, were oblique and suggestive. When Suyang insisted that the banquet be reported to the emperor, he implied the emperor needed to be assured of Suyang's virtues and merit. He was referring to the contents of Tanjong's royal letter, which Sin Sukchu brought to show Suyang acted out of loyalty and with the king's approval. After all, according to his imperial guests, the emperor already knew what had transpired. But it is here that the account's coherence breaks down. What assurance did the emperor need, if there was already universal recognition of his deeds? During their conversations, the Ming emissaries claimed they had discovered Suyang's coup d'état only after the fact. But they also claimed that when Suyang left Beijing, tribute-bearing *yain* also dispersed. Ming officials, having found it strange, inquired after the reason for their sudden departure. They were told the *yain* hurried back because they caught word of a rebellion by Prince Anp'yŏng and were worried the conflict would spill over into their "backyard." In the conversation, Suyang concurred with this version of events. While it implied the crisis was imminent, Suyang only moved against his enemies months after his return. If the emissaries' retelling were truthful, it would mean the *yain* possessed a foreknowledge of the impending contest that even Suyang lacked.[68]

To reconcile these contradictions, one could accept the *Records* as is: that Anp'yŏng's intent to rebel was so transparent that it was obvious even to the Jurchens and Ming officials—a convenient justification for Suyang fratricidal reprisal. But how would this information have been transmitted in the first place? One possibility would have been Suyang's own embassy. Suyang's entourage could have spread rumors to this effect to Ming officials and Jurchen tribute-bearers alike, but given that the sons of Hwangbo In and Kim Chongsŏ had accompanied Suyang on this mission, it would have had to be done discreetly, lest they report Suyang's plan back to their fathers. The emissaries either learned the details of the coup d'état only after having arrived in Chosŏn, or they were informed by the embassy that Suyang dispatched to request investiture for Tanjong's queen. Regardless of how the Korean eunuch emissaries became privy to the situation, they parroted Suyang's narrative justifying his rise.

The evidence for their collusion is indirect but strong. The *Veritable Records* do not state what, if any, political deal was being hammered out. Eager to curry favor with the new powerholders in Chosŏn, the emissaries brought their most valuable gifts of silk and ivory to Suyang, not the young king.[69] In return, Suyang provisioned gyrfalcons and other exquisite tribute, items the eunuchs could use to garner imperial favor. He also granted their relatives in Korea emoluments and court ranks.[70] Chosŏn's kings (see figure 3.1 for Chosŏn royal succession) routinely dispensed these privileges, but this time they did not issue from a regal hand.

From the eunuch emissaries, Suyang likely sought support for his accession. Suyang held his nephew's abdication rite for the eleventh day in the leap sixth month of 1455, one day after they disbursed titles and honors to the Ming envoys' relatives.[71] For the twenty-seventh day of the same month, the *Records* relates a curious episode. A Ming officer was to return to Beijing ahead of the main body of the embassy. Tanjong, who had in theory already abdicated, invited him for an audience to relate his *intent* to do so. The boy-king stated: "My uncle Suyang has achieved great things for the state—his virtue and renown make him suitable for taking up such an important duty. I have already asked him to take care of the affairs of state. I now intend to send someone to report this matter [to the emperor]."[72] This entry is undoubtedly compromised by layers of filtering—at this point, Suyang fully controlled the organs of state: the young former king could have been coerced, his words willfully misrepresented, and the entire conversation could even have been fabricated.[73] At any rate, two days later, a Chosŏn embassy departed to request "permission" from the Ming for the fait accompli.[74] The rapidity of these developments (a diplomatic mission could take weeks if not months to prepare) could only mean that Suyang's court had long been ready for this moment.

It is unclear from the sequence of events represented in the *Records* whether the eunuchs Ko Pu and Chŏng Tong were aware of Suyang's orchestration behind the scenes. Regardless, Suyang had secured them as witnesses for his nephew's desire to abdicate so that the Ming court would view the transition as legitimate. If the Chosŏn *Veritable Records* are to be believed, the Ming envoys were yet unaware a royal transition had already taken place. If they were in the know, they would have had to feign ignorance to preserve the integrity of the narrative spun by Suyang and his supporters. Whether they were textual fabrications or political performances, these episodes in the *Records* still testify to the importance of controlling the narrative for an imperial audience.

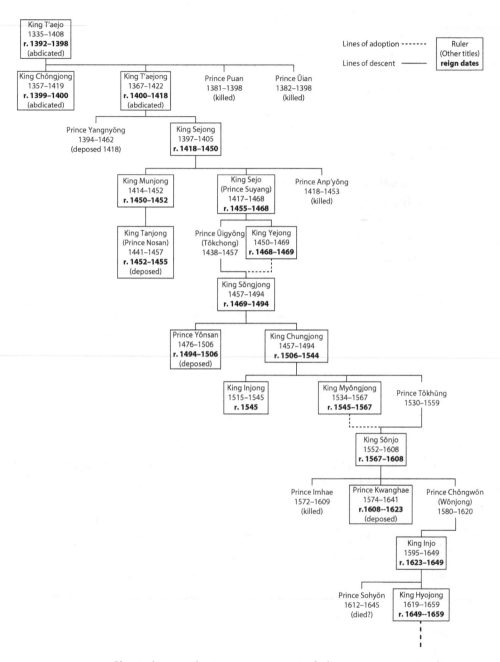

FIGURE 3.1 Chosŏn kings and princes, 1392–1650, including major succession disputes. Illustration by author.

Suyang maintained a deferent, avuncular presence until the envoys' departure. His nephew retained ritual precedence, for instance, in dealings with the Ming envoys.[75] Without formal Ming recognition for his accession, Suyang refrained from infringing on his nephew's prerogatives, at least not in the presence of imperial envoys.[76] But once they departed and his own embassy requesting investiture was en route to Beijing, Suyang quickly dropped the pretense. Only two days after the eunuchs' departure, Suyang donned the royal robes and proceeded to invest his nephew as "Grand Supreme King" (*T'aesangwang* 太上王), the honorary title for retired monarchs, and granted the corresponding title to his nephew's consort, who had only several months ago received Ming recognition as Chosŏn's queen consort.[77]

In the tenth month of 1455, an imperial edict arrived, announcing tentative support of the abdication. The suspicious circumstance evidently raised some red flags in Beijing, for it cautioned the now deposed boy-king to guard against "deception by evil words" and "perfidious designs." But Tanjong was no longer in a position to "investigate the behavior and character" of Suyang, as the edict implored him to do. Its closing words, "Oh King, be vigilant! Oh King, be vigilant!" had come too late.[78]

SECURING INVESTITURE

It is possible that the Ming court was aware of Suyang's plotting. Ming eunuch envoys might have reported the circumstances of Suyang's rise, but no firm evidence of that knowledge survives in extant Ming records. Despite the suspicions voiced by the Ming court in the 1455 edict, the Ming chronicles mention only a request for abdication and the imperial court's subsequent approval. The drafters of these edicts and the compilers of these histories were civil officials employed in the imperial bureaucracy, either at the Ministry of Rites or the Hanlin Academy, not palace eunuchs who had the emperor's ear. Winning over palace eunuchs did not guarantee support from the Ministry of Rites, and vice versa. But the Ming bureaucracy had no independent channel of information from Chosŏn. Its members would have had no grounds to deny Tanjong's apparently legitimate requests or to overrule the testimony of the emperor's agents. In the official Ming record, Tanjong abdicated voluntarily.[79]

The Ming edict "permitting" the abdication referred to Suyang as a "temporary overseer of the affairs of state 權署國事." Suyang still needed recognition as king of Chosŏn through a rite of investiture. Suyang charged Sin Sukchu, the secretary of his 1452 mission, with leading an embassy to request the patents of investiture, royal robes, and seal. Sin Sukchu did not disappoint. On the third day of the second month of 1456, an interpreter from Sin's entourage arrived in Seoul to report the imminent arrival of the Ming envoys, Yun Pong and Kim Hŭng 金興 (both Korean-born eunuchs), who carried the patents of investiture for Chosŏn's new king and queen. When Suyang received Sin's envoy report, he replied with the following: "I have received your report, and I can see that your ardent dedication and deft responses have helped me accomplish this great matter. This has brought me immense joy." The report's contents do not survive, but whatever Sin had done, it was enough.[80]

Once the imperial emissaries arrived and delivered the patents and the imperial proclamation, Suyang had become king in Ming's eyes. And like Korean eunuchs who came before, the new ruler, better known to history as King Sejo, granted them numerous requests, including gifts of slaves. He even bestowed an aristocratic choronym, or *pon'gwan*, for Yun's relatives. He also helped Yun procure young eunuchs for service in the Ming imperial palace. Nine, along with a gyrfalcon, were selected as tribute. Although chattel, these eunuchs ensured that the Chosŏn court's relationship with the Ming inner palace would continue.[81]

Sejo also owed much to his support from the officialdom and influential royal clansmen.[82] For the embassy offering gratitude for investiture, Sejo appointed Han Hwak 韓確 (1400–1456) as chief emissary.[83] He had supported Sejo's coup as a junior minister of the State Council, for which he was rewarded with merit subject (*kongsin* 功臣) status and given the third-highest ranking post in the State Council 議政府.[84] Han's support of Suyang was also unsurprising, given their affinal ties—Han's daughter had married Suyang's son, later the heir apparent. Han was also chosen to lead the gratitude embassy because he was *imperial* kin.[85]

Ties with Ming eunuchs already granted Suyang a channel of communication with the Ming inner palace. Through Han Hwak, the connection went even deeper (see figure 3.2). Two of Han's sisters had entered the Ming imperial harem. The elder married the Yongle emperor but

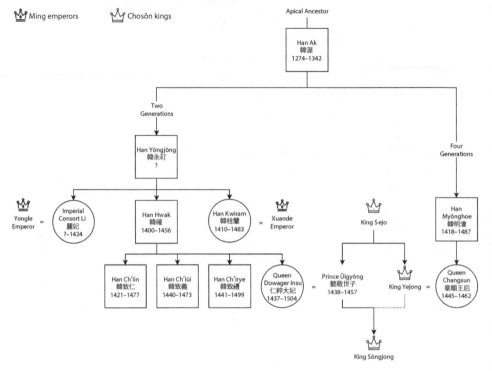

FIGURE 3.2 The Han family of Ch'ŏngju and their royal relations. Illustration by author.

was forced to commit suicide upon his death, following the emperor and his favorite concubines to their early graves.[86] A second sister, Han Kwiram (C: Han Guilan 韓桂蘭 c.1413–1483), was selected to be a consort of Zhu Zhanji 朱瞻基 (1399–1435), the Xuande 宣德 emperor (r. 1425–1435). Before her departure in 1427, the fourteen-year-old cursed her older brother, accusing him of "having sold one sister after another in search of rank and privilege." She then sliced her sleeping mat in half, to show her resolution in cutting off ties to the family that "sold" her.[87]

But unlike her older sister, Han Kwiram lived out her natural life. Her husband never graced her chamber, and she continued to serve in the palace, becoming the confidante of Empress Xiaosu 孝肅皇后 (1430–1504), the mother of the Chenghua emperor 成化 (r. 1465–1487). Later, having evidently set aside whatever resentment she harbored toward her natal family, she wielded the influence she possessed as a senior palace woman to support her brother and his descendants, which in time included Sejo's heirs.[88] Because of these imperial connections, Han Hwak enjoyed rare prestige as both a Chosŏn high official and an honorary member of the Ming officialdom. He had been granted a courtesy appointment as vice minister of the Court of Imperial Entertainment 光祿寺少卿 after his first sister became a member of the Yongle emperor's harem.[89]

After Han Hwak's mission, the Ming court was ready to invest Sejo as Chosŏn's king. With the arrival of the investiture embassy nigh, what remained of Sejo's political opposition made a desperate gamble. They planned to disrupt the investiture. A cabal, which counted among its members the scholar-official Sŏng Sammun (the same Sŏng Sammun who had exchanged verses with Ni Qian in 1450 and conducted linguistic research with King Sejong), plotted to oust Sejo when the Ming embassy was still in Chosŏn. If Sŏng and his accomplices had been successful, they could then have approached the imperial envoys and enumerated Sejo's crimes and exposed his duplicity. They could have restored Tanjong while using the Ming envoys to bear witness to why the king the emperor was hoping to invest had to be deposed.[90]

They failed. The plot was discovered. Sejo had Sŏng and his coconspirators arrested and executed. Their final act earned them the collective moniker of the Six Loyal Officials (*yuksin* 六臣). Sŏng Sammun, in particular, thanks to an apocryphal attribution to the authorship of a vernacular *sijo* poem, is equated with loyalty in popular historical memory. But their failure to restore the boy-king might have instead ensured his demise. Once the Ming envoys departed, Sejo moved against his nephew. Officials loyal to Sejo petitioned to punish his nephew Tanjong:

> Disaster and chaos have ensued once again, while the state and dynasty still could not be brought to peace. But heaven impelled the will of the former king [Tanjong] and had the throne pass to Your Majesty [Sejo], which guarded against disaster and chaos. The Emperor too bequeathed the patents of investiture to the eastern palace [of the heir apparent]. How could this have been achieved by the efforts of men? It was the command of heaven and the silent protection of the ancestors.

Sejo's rule was proclaimed as a dynastic necessity. Ming approval was exalted as divine sanction. Denied, however, were the human efforts and political contingencies that brought him to the throne. The petition then turned the language of imperial sanction against Sejo's enemies. It accused the "former king," Tanjong, of collaborating with the "cabalists" of the already dead Prince Anp'yŏng. Having "long heard of their wicked plots," the boy-king stood idle, refusing to "expose them for their crimes and villainy." Tanjong, by turning against his uncle, had "disobeyed heaven's command and opposed the wills of men." Whether "royal kith and kin, the high ministers, the hundred officials, or the commoners," all condemned him. Whether "the former kings in heaven" or the "divinities of the mountains and rivers," all have abandoned him. Even Ming would chastise him for his misdeeds. In the name of the Yi dynastic house, the common weal, and imperial authority, Sejo sent his nephew into exile.[91] Isolated and vulnerable, the young former king was forced to commit suicide within a year. He was seventeen.[92]

Ming had effectively become an accomplice to regicide. For this, it had King Sejo to thank. At each stage of his rise to power, Sejo manipulated diplomacy to his advantage. He made the most of Korean connections to the Ming court to secure his political position. In these human networks, the bonds of interest could cut against court-centered loyalties, but personal ties alone could not have brought his plans to fruition. He also hijacked the mechanisms of empire: the symbols of imperial authority, Chosŏn's diplomatic machinery, and the eyes and mouths of Ming ambassadors. To employ them, of course, required the orchestration of entire institutional apparatuses. They were not exactly free-floating resources available for anyone to use at will. In theory the power to call upon imperial resources through diplomacy belonged solely to the Korean king, but as Sejo's rise reveals, it could nonetheless slip away from a monarch's hands. Likewise, Chosŏn envoys and interpreters, Ming ambassadors, and frontier military officials also could profit handsomely from diplomatic interchange. In this respect, Sejo just found a way to profit a little more than the others. Even Sejo's opponents tried to use empire against him. Though they failed, they too recognized the importance of crafting a narrative that would be palpable to the imperial court to achieve their ends.

What the situation looked like from Ming's perspective remains a matter of speculation. Sparse imperial records relate nothing about the precise circumstances of Sejo's rise beyond what the Chosŏn court had presented. But one need not presume Ming was hoodwinked by Sejo's diplomacy to appreciate its effect. Matters of Korean succession were in theory subject to imperial approval, a fiction Sejo worked carefully to maintain. What Sejo successfully demonstrated through his diplomacy was not the legitimacy of his accession but his loyalty to the Ming court. More the better that he also supplied a narrative of his rise that could sit comfortably in the shared diplomatic record.

But what did it really mean to be loyal? In Sejo's case, loyalty to Ming did not translate into compliance. Indeed, Sejo could be as irreverent toward Ming authority as his politics were beholden to it. The next chapter continues the discussion of Sejo's appropriation of imperial authority. As king, Sejo's actions continued to generate parallel but contradictory narratives in the historical record, a dissonance that is best appreciated not by forcing harmonization to a single chord but an appreciation of its disparate parts.

CHAPTER FOUR

In Empire's Name

Official records in Chosŏn and Ming diverged on how and why Sejo took power. They amounted to two sets of "public transcripts" of these events. The first transcript was the Chosŏn court's own official records of the events. The Chosŏn *Veritable Records*'s narrative legitimized Sejo's rise, even as it recounted the meticulous planning, execution, and rationalization of his coup, including how Sejo manipulated his Ming contacts. The other was the shared Chosŏn-Ming diplomatic record reflected in the official correspondence between them. There, Sejo received his nephew's abdication only at the behest of country-men, with no mention of the political circumstances of the affair. No deception occurred; no imperial authority flouted. As "public tran-scripts," both recount the "open interaction between subordinates and those who dominate," but occlude the power dynamics that might have threatened the relationship. Inasmuch as they did diverge, they were also preoccupied with different kinds of threats: the question of Sejo's royal legitimacy in the former and the sanctity of Ming authority in the latter.[1]

The coexistence of parallel but contradicting "public transcripts" is not unique to Chosŏn-Ming relations. It is akin to the *uchi* 內 (or J. *naishō* 內証) and *omote* 表 information regime of Tokugawa Japan (1603–1867) described by historian Luke Roberts. In this regime, local lords' records of key political events (the *uchi* version) diverged from the *omote* narratives maintained by central, shogunal authorities. The shared "façade truth" in the *omote* narrative kept the peace between local lords and their erstwhile superior, the shogun, because it allowed potentially subversive local realities to persist without challenging his authority. In the Chosŏn-Ming case, the separate existence of a shared and mutually agreed upon, although ultimately partially fabricated, history of their relations provided the ritual and discursive interface through which diplomatic ties could be conducted.[2]

Here again the notion of asymmetrical relations, applicable both to the Tokugawa and Chosŏn-Ming case, is instructive. Drastic power differentials between two sides make for volatile bilateral relations. To achieve stability, both sides recognize the lopsided nature of the power balance and commit to maintaining what political scientist Brantly Womack calls "sleeves of normalcy": channels of negotiation, crosscutting social ties, respect for past precedents, and in the Chosŏn case, shared rhetorical tropes and ritual practices.[3] Even a patently "false" narrative of the relationship, as long as it was mutually acceptable, could still anchor the relationship by keeping divergent realities at bay. Rather than merely ideological conceit, façade truths were necessary for sustaining a *diplomatic* reality through which Chosŏn and Ming could negotiate; act; and, as will be discussed in this chapter, make war.[4]

In the fifteenth century, Chosŏn came into repeated conflicts with its northern neighbors, resulting in a number of Ming-led coalition wars against them.[5] Appearing in Chosŏn court records as *yain* (literally, "wild men") these northerners, most likely speakers of a Tungusic language, were ethnopolitical heirs of the Jurchens who established the Jin Empire in the thirteenth century and the predecessors of the Manchus who established the Qing Empire in the seventeenth century, although their ethnic, linguistic, and cultural composition in the fifteenth and sixteenth centuries is likely more diverse and complex than these connections might imply.[6]

The two main groups in conflict with Chosŏn in the 1450s and 1460s, when they were distinguished at all in Chosŏn sources, possessed distinct ethnonyms. They were the Uriyangqad (K: *Oryanghap* 兀良哈) of the Maolian Guard 毛憐衛, based in the upper Tumen Valley, and the Jurchens of the three Jianzhou Guards 建州衛, located further west along the Longgong mountain range.[7] Chosŏn and Ming sources call their units of political organization "guards," identifying them as sub-units in the Ming military bureaucracy. In practice, they were autono-mous polities organized along the "loose-rein," or *jimi* system, each ruled by an aristocratic house whose ancestors had served as hereditary local rulers under the Mongol Empire, if not earlier. The region was already under only nominal Ming authority by the 1449 debacle at Tumu, which further weakened the Ming military presence in the region and encour-aged sporadic raids for slaves and plunder in Liaodong and along the Korean frontier.[8]

Under King Sejong and King Sejo, Chosŏn also adopted aggressive policies toward Jianzhou and the Uriyangqad of Maolian. When hostil-ities escalated in the 1460s, Ming tried repeatedly to mediate between Chosŏn and its northern neighbors. Although Sejo always performed the role of Ming's loyal vassal, he had no qualms flouting imperial author-ity when he found advantage to be gained. Perhaps emboldened by the successful diplomacy surrounding his accession, Sejo continued trying to co-opt Ming envoys to pursue his objectives, a tactic that demanded rhetorical finesse. As with Sejo's coup, Chosŏn and Ming accounts again diverge regarding the Chosŏn-Uriyangqad-Jurchen conflicts. These dif-ferences reflected the perspectives of these two courts as well as how Chosŏn's leaders deliberately constructed a diplomatic reality conducive to their ends.

To illustrate this process, this chapter will follow the Chosŏn court's role in a series of diplomatic crises leading up to the joint Ming-Chosŏn attack on Jianzhou in 1467. Sejo and his officials tried to nudge the Ming court's position from a neutral arbiter among its vassals into a guardian of a universal political order, an imperium of perpetual peace willing to wage war to preserve it. Invoking this sense of universal imperium justified the war making that allowed Chosŏn to pursue vendettas against the Uriyangqad and Jurchens while at the same time excluding them as legitimate political actors in the diplo-matic concert. These rhetorical strategies suggest the need to think about the Ming-Chosŏn coalition war not simply in terms of shared military interest but also through the world building it engaged in and the kinds of violence it enabled.

COMPETING WITH THE IMPERIAL COURT:
CHEN JIAYOU'S MISSION OF 1459

In the late fourteenth and early fifteenth centuries, Chosŏn and Ming competed for influence in their shared Manchurian frontier.[9] After all, the founder of the Chosŏn, Yi Sŏnggye, hailed from the region. Now, Yi Sŏnggye's descendants ruled Korea, but three generations of his ancestors served as hereditary local officials of the Mongol Empire, not unlike the forebears of the Jianzhou and Maolian leaders who controlled the region.[10] Toward them, the Chosŏn court employed "loose rein" polices, enticing their leaders to pay homage in Seoul while granting them gifts, titles, and trade privileges, much as the Ming court was also doing in the region.[11]

The "loose rein" approach made the most of the disjointed political alignments among these frontier polities. While one leader might lead a war band to raid Chosŏn border towns, another group might offer intelligence and even personnel for Chosŏn's frontier military.[12] Sejo's usurpation, however, disrupted the balance of power in Chosŏn's northern frontier. Kim Chongsŏ, whom his father Sejong had relied on for carrying out his northern frontier policy, was killed in Sejo's coup. Kim's successor in the north, the general Yi Chingok 李澄玉 (or 澂玉 ?–1453) rebelled with the support of Jurchen leaders in an attempt to oust Sejo in 1453. According to court accounts, Yi Chingok even styled himself Emperor of the Great Jin 大金皇帝, evoking the long-gone Jurchen Empire to secure Jurchen support, which proved as ephemeral as Yi Chingok's insurrection. It collapsed after Yi Chingok's assassination, but Chosŏn's northeastern frontier was now in disarray.[13]

Sejo's efforts to reassert control over the region caught Ming's attention. It discovered that Sejo had granted Chosŏn titles to the Jianzhou Left Guard's commissioner-in-chief Cungšan (童山, also 董山 and 充善; ?–1467) and others.[14] Because Cungšan was ostensibly a Ming vassal like the Chosŏn king, Sejo's "private grants" were perceived as an affront to Ming authority. In 1459, the Ming dispatched an emissary, Chen Jiayou 陳嘉猷 (1421–1467), to upbraid the Korean king for maintaining relations with Jurchen leaders.

To prepare, Sejo's officials quickly ascertained both the timing of the impending embassy and the contents of the Ming missive. Sejo and his officials had long decided that enticing "the submission of the *yain*" was "the best strategy" for managing the frontier.[15] They were not inclined to acquiesce to Ming demands.[16] Chen Jiayou, a Ming civil official without personal ties to Chosŏn, was impervious to the titles and honors dangled before Korean-born eunuchs, but Sejo's court surmised he might yet be swayed by well-chosen gifts.[17] Meanwhile, Sejo received regular updates from Pak Wŏnhyŏng 朴元亨 (1411–1469), Chen's Chosŏn escort. Pak described Chen as "haughty and arrogant, apt to make mistakes," faults in character the Chosŏn court could exploit.[18] Pak also forestalled Chen's progress through the country. The envoy insisted on reaching Seoul within ten days; he arrived only after fourteen days on the road in Chosŏn, affording Sejo the extra time to conceal his dealings with the Jurchens. When Chen's embassy reached Korea, several *yain* notables were still lingering in Seoul. Sejo dispersed them so their presence would not rouse the envoy's suspicions.[19]

Whether Chen Jiayou detected these manipulations is unclear. As with Sejo's usurpation, Ming accounts reverted to a sanitized narrative of the affair. They depicted Sejo as a docile vassal who readily "admitted his faults in trepidation," an impression traceable to how Sejo presented himself.[20] When confronted by Chen Jiayou, Sejo described his court as a helpless victim who "for a long time" had "no choice" in the matter. He explained that "this ilk," referring to the *yain*, have "the faces of men but the hearts of beasts" [人面獸心], so "if we do allow them [to come to us], they will certainly instigate border conflicts." Chen then demanded Sejo report the names of the *yain* leaders who received Korean titles. When Sejo offered them, he received assurances from Chen that Ming will "order" these leaders to refrain from contacting Chosŏn in the future."[21]

Sejo's memorial also adopted a docile posture. Writing that he was "overcome with trepidation," he declared his border policies were not "private dealings with outsiders" nor did he intend to "deceive the [imperial] court." It was only to avoid further "border conflicts." Apologizing for these actions, Sejo declared that "from now on, if they beg for permission to come [to my court], Your Servant will show them the imperial edict, and refuse them."[22] A returning Chosŏn embassy later returned with Ming's response. The rescript contained a stern warning: "for Chosŏn to give titles to those who have received imperial offices is to compete with the imperial court" [與朝廷抗衡]. Ming officials, if aware of Sejo's duplicity, refrained from being more explicit in the missive, exhorting the Chosŏn king to make good on his declarations of loyalty by "cutting off private dealings."[23]

Chen's mission might have nudged Chosŏn frontier policy in the long run. It showed a gradual but noticeable retrenchment after these interventions. By the early sixteenth century, Jurchen leaders no longer assembled en masse at the Chosŏn capital as tribute bearers, although official contact persisted.[24] In the short term, however, Chosŏn was far from compliant. Despite the pledge to desist, Sejo remained proactive toward his *yain* neighbors, in particular the Uriyangqad of Maolian.

THE DEATH OF LANG BORGHAN: ZHANG NING'S MISSION OF 1460

Less than a year after Chen Jiayou left Chosŏn, Sejo captured an Uriyangqad leader, Lang Borghan (浪孛兒罕 ?–1459).[25] Lang behaved irreverently during a previous visit to Korea, and Chosŏn officials decided the offense could not go unpunished.[26] They lured him back to Chosŏn with the promise of titles and gifts, providing frontier officials a chance to ambush him. Borghan's subordinates begged for leniency, reminding Chosŏn that Borghan "received high rank from China," having received from Ming the title of Assistant Commissioner of the Maolian Guard 毛憐衛都督僉事. Chosŏn authorities had him executed anyway.[27] King Sejo, flouting Ming warnings against contact with erstwhile imperial vassals, then rewarded the Uriyangqad and Jurchens who helped him apprehend Lang Borghan. He also ordered the execution of Lang Borghan's male descendants.[28]

The situation escalated over the next few months. The assistant commissioner of Jianzhou, Li Manju 李滿柱 (?–1467), informed Chosŏn that a leader of the Hūlun 火剌溫 planned to raise an army to invade Chosŏn to avenge Lang Borghan. His last surviving son, Abca 阿比車, had eluded Chosŏn capture and took refuge with the Hūlun. In response, Chosŏn promised the Hūlun leader titles and rewards if he were to betray Abca and hand him over, but to no avail.[29] In the spring of the following year (1460), Chosŏn envoys returned from Ming with news that two regional commissioners of the Jianzhou and Maolian guards had protested the Chosŏn killing of Lang Borghan to Ming. They also told Ming they wished to assemble a coalition numbering some 6,000 soldiers to "seek vengeance" for Lang Borghan.[30]

These tidings of war spurred both Ming and Chosŏn into action. A Chosŏn embassy arrived in Ming to explain why Chosŏn had killed Lang Borghan. According to the embassy, Borghan was a resident of Chosŏn's Hoeryŏng region and was executed "according to the law" because he had "secretively plotted rebellion, conspired with outsiders, and enticed his own kind" into conspiracy.[31] Meanwhile, the Jianzhou commander Cungšan visited the Chosŏn envoys in Beijing and divulged more frontier news, notwithstanding Ming "prohibitions" against their intercourse.[32]

The Ming court responded by dispatching another embassy to Chosŏn, this time led by Zhang Ning 張寧 (1426–1496) and assisted by Wu Zhong 武忠 (?–1470), an ethnically Jurchen military officer of the Embroidered Guard 錦衣衛.[33] Usually, when embassies departed, Ming officials informed Chosŏn through notices called p'aemun 牌文 (C. paiwen), but one was not issued in this case. Zhang Ning's mission was supposed to be "secret," but this time, as on other occasions, a Chosŏn embassy still en route in Ming territory identified the staffing, purpose, and planned timetable of Zhang's embassy, giving Chosŏn time to prepare. Chosŏn then adopted the same strategy it had used with the 1459 embassy led by Chen Jiayou.[34]

When Zhang Ning first arrived in Korea, he did what he could to burnish Ming authority. He put on airs, quibbled about protocols, and refused to socialize with his Korean counterparts. After Zhang met the king in person, his attitude softened. Sejo's eloquence, his lavish gifts, and the erudite company of Chosŏn's court scholars coaxed the Ming envoy to relax his rigid stance.[35] Zhang proclaimed the imperial edict, which was sympathetic to Sejo's position. Rather than chastise the king, it merely asked whether the Maolian's accusations were true and implored Sejo to "not cover up anything."

In the reception that followed, Zhang tried to probe further. Zhang asked the king to dismiss the Korean interpreter. He either found his skills inadequate or feared he was dissembling for the king. He asked the king to communicate to him directly in writing. The king's attendants prepared the stationery so the two could continue their conversation on paper. Sejo tried to redirect the conversation, reiterating Chosŏn's long-standing hopes of Korean students to study in China and declared his unwavering loyalty to the emperor.[36] The envoy, on the other hand, went to the crux of the matter and demanded that Sejo explain himself for "wantonly killing" a high-ranking imperial officer. During their discussion, Sejo never acknowledged this point. He instead insisted Lang Borghan was in fact "a person of [this] country." Killing him was no different from executing a common criminal.

Zhang Ning did not press the matter. Reminding the king that the emperor only wished for peace, he said, "Chosŏn has always been a country of propriety and righteousness 禮義之邦 (K. yeŭi chi pang, C. liyi zhi bang), and ever since the reign of Emperor Taizu [Hongwu], the ceremony and esteem accorded to Chosŏn could not be compared to other states." He then told the king that if he could explain the matter in detail to the emperor, Ming could "prevent them [i.e., Jianzhou and Maolian] from seeking vengeance."[37]

Zhang and Sejo agreed to draft separate memorials to the emperor, but in mutual consultation. The Korean memorial, which underwent several drafts for Zhang's review and approval, proceeded from the king's stance that he acted within his jurisdiction. It also made no mention of Lang Borghan's Ming affiliations or Chosŏn's prior knowledge of this fact.[38] Zhang's own memorial repeated Sejo's version of events but added that the king "truly did not know that [Lang] had received an office [from Ming]" and believed he was only "enacting the laws of his own country" to punish a rebel. Vouching for the king's honesty and sincerity, Zhang described Sejo as "consistent from beginning to end, concealing and embellishing nothing."[39] The declaration that nothing was obscured really pointed to a contrary, dissimulated reality. Zhang, by convincing Sejo to express regret over the killing, might have done all he needed to do. After Zhang's mission, the Ming responded with another edict that urged Chosŏn to discuss peace terms with the Uriyangqad and avoid escalation.[40]

These two memorials worked together to sidestep the affront to imperial authority. To pursue the issue of whether Chosŏn had knowingly flouted Ming authority would have benefited no one, save the aggrieved Uriyangqad. As historian Matthew Mosca has argued, it was rarely in the interest of imperial officials in charge of frontier affairs to bring matters of controversy to light. Exposition to the imperial court seldom led to rewards for honesty. It only invited accusations of incompetence. As long as the official could keep the matter under wraps or resolve it quickly, packaging the resolution in a narrative palatable to the imperial center was a far better expedient.[41]

The same observation applies to imperial envoys. Zhang Ning returned to Ming with a triumphal narrative. According to his supporters at the Ming court, the mission "guided [Koreans] through a show of force and display of virtue, laying out his warnings of calamity and his tidings of fortune." Zhang brought the foreign ruler to heel so that he and his subjects looked upon each other with "startled expression" and "admired Zhang Ning as Mount Tai or the Great Dipper." As a result, the Koreans were "ever more respectful of the imperial court." To Zhang's adulators, his mission was equal to "no less than a hundred thousand troops sweeping across the Yalu River" [不減重兵 十萬 橫行鴨綠].[42]

An effect of Zhang Ning and Sejo's cooperation was a change in how the dispute was framed. No longer was it about conflicting Ming and Chosŏn jurisdiction but about Chosŏn's cultural allegiance and ecumenical inclusion. Once Zhang and Sejo had reached a mutual understanding, the rest of the trip was spent sightseeing and exchanging poetry with Chosŏn officials. One day was a boat outing on the Han River, the next an excursion to the Confucian Academy. A visit to the royal palace concluded with the Chosŏn king reminding Zhang of the numerous imperial favors Korea had received, Chosŏn's steadfast loyalty to the Ming, and prior imperial edicts sanctioning the "annihilation" of any *yain* who dared violate Korean territory.[43] Chosŏn diplomacy depended on cultivating cultural affinity, in part by excluding their northern neighbors from shared ecumenical horizons. Even if these horizons did not predetermine the outcome of this multilateral conflict, appeals to them did shift Ming policy in Chosŏn's favor, at enormous expense to those excluded.

Sejo again proved an able operator of the diplomatic system. As he had done to secure his throne, King Sejo at once disregarded Ming authority and appropriated its symbols. He also abused Ming trust. As Zhang Ning told Sejo, "Of countries beyond the sea, there are more than just one. But who among them serves the great state with utmost sincerity as you? For this reason the imperial court has called [Korea] a country of propriety and righteousness; the emperor treats it like his own family."[44]

Were Ming envoys, whether literati like Zhang Ning and Chen Jiayou or Korean-born eunuchs like Yun Pong and Kim Hŭng, necessarily so naive about King Sejo's motivations as their pronouncements appeared to suggest? If not, and they were aware of Sejo's machinations, were they then knowingly complicit in maintaining diplomacy's façade truths? Just as Ming records made no mention of Sejo's usurpation, Ming records preserved the sanctity of imperial authority. Cowed by a virtuous imperial envoy, the Chosŏn king quickly acknowledged his transgressions and returned to being a compliant subject.

MING AS MEDIATOR: MA JIAN'S MISSION OF 1461

If Zhang Ning's mission was meant to end the hostilities between Chosŏn and the Maolian Uriyangqad, it failed. A back-and-forth ensued over the next few months. Ming tried to coax Chosŏn into reconciling with the Maolian. A Ming edict reprimanded Chosŏn for not first reporting Lang Borghan's alleged crimes to the imperial court before meting out its own justice. It then tried to convince Sejo to correct his "mistake" by returning captive members of Lang Borghan's family to Abca. After all, Chosŏn, being a "country of propriety and righteousness," would certainly behave graciously and never "ignore the command of the emperor."[45]

In the face of such cajoling, Chosŏn maintained an outward deference, but it did not comply. Chosŏn told Ming it had already released some captives, but making peace with Abca was pointless because Chosŏn's military had already killed him when he attacked the Korean frontier town of Kyŏngsŏng 鏡城. In the meantime, it informed Ming that Uriyangqad raids continued unabated, leaving Korean civilians dead and their livestock plundered.[46] Ming could express displeasure and demand Chosŏn's compliance, but a pretext, an excuse, or some other deft rhetorical ploy could always be plied to Chosŏn's advantage. As Sin Sukchu advised his king, "when the emperor sends edicts," all that needed to be done was to say Chosŏn "will reverently obey," but if Ming authority required flouting, there was "no need to fret for a lack of words" [何患無辭].[47]

What exactly were these capacious "words"? To answer this question, the rest of this chapter will focus on the rhetoric used by Chosŏn and Ming amid a sharp escalation of border tensions, one that culminated in a joint Ming-Chosŏn attack on Jianzhou in 1467. This rhetoric, which emphasized Korea and Ming's shared place in the civilized world, revolved around Chosŏn's identification as a *yeŭi chi pang*, a "country of propriety and righteousness," a refrain that invested diplomacy with wider civilizational stakes. This civilizational discourse also raised the idea of the Ming's role in enacting cosmic justice, of war as a corrective to disorder.

As part of an attempt to mediate between its vassals, Ming dispatched an envoy to Maolian in the seventh month of 1460. From their governor in Hamgil, Chosŏn learned that the envoy Ma Jian 馬鑑 had proclaimed an edict ordering the Jurchen and Uriyangqad to return the captives and booty they had seized during their frontier raids. Ma Jian promised them Chosŏn would do the same. Their leaders, however, answered they would comply only if Chosŏn released its captives and hostages first. This demand enraged the Ming envoy. He declared, "Chosŏn is a country of propriety and righteousness; if you return what you captured, how could Chosŏn not return what they captured?" In the wake of his mission, he also dispatched a message to the Chosŏn frontier interpreter's office in Hoeryŏng, explaining that he originally wanted a Chosŏn official to witness the proclamation but feared that the "*yain*, with their wild hearts of wolves," would instigate a conflict and risk the life of the Korean representative.[48]

Ma Jian held deep-seated reservations about the trustworthiness of the Maolian Uriyangqad. In contrast, Chosŏn's status as a "civilized" country was why, at least rhetorically, he believed it would behave in good faith. But this trust was misplaced because Chosŏn proved just as, if not more, perfidious. At the very moment Ma Jian was trying to broker peace, Sejo had already ordered Sin Sukchu, recently appointed governor of the northeast frontier region, to attack Maolian. The Ming envoy's unexpected presence now placed the campaign in jeopardy. Sejo's officials wavered, unsure whether it would be wise to follow through. They also learned that several hundred Jianzhou Jurchens accompanied Ma Jian and were now dispersed among the Maolian Uriyangqad, meaning an attack would risk spreading the conflict to them as well.

Against their reservations, Sejo decided to send a delegation to invite the Ming envoy into Chosŏn. He hoped that Ma Jian would travel through Korean territory under Korean escort on his return trip, thereby clearing the way for an attack. If the Ming envoy refused, the delegation could scare him into thinking the Jurchens and Uriyangqad were plotting his murder. If the envoy could not be enticed, the attack would proceed anyway. The Jianzhou Jurchens could also be persuaded to stand down out of "respect for the Ming envoy," but if they insisted on fighting alongside the Maolian, they could be killed as well. His own officials were skeptical of the conspiracy's feasibility, but Sejo believed that, because the Ming envoy's presence ensured all the Maolian leaders were in one place, it was an "opportunity that could not be missed." Writing to Sin Sukchu that "indecision is the great enemy of military plans," Sejo planned to use the Ming envoy as bait.[49]

While Ming was still hoping to mediate the conflict, Chosŏn's king saw only an opportunity to pursue a vendetta. Meanwhile, his frontier commander Sin replied quickly with reassurances meant to allay the court's indecision. Sin explained that he had "weighed the risks and advantages" of the surprise attack. He concluded it was necessary to attack as soon as possible. Sin's reasoning was as follows. Any further delay would harm the morale of his troops. The Uriyangqad of Maolian had raided Chosŏn repeatedly so a show of force as necessary. It was important to demonstrate Korean military strength to the Ming envoy lest the imperial court come to believe that the Maolian *yain* had no respect for Chosŏn. And as long as the Ming envoy was present, they would also be caught off guard. As for the impropriety of launching an attack in the envoy's presence, Sin believed that if the envoy could be convinced to take Chosŏn's side, all the blame could be pinned on the Maolian. If the envoy proved recalcitrant, Chosŏn could always supply the Ming envoy with misinformation to confound his judgment. "With the fault theirs and rightness with us," Sin argued, the attack could always be justified by "necessity." Meanwhile, his forces stood ready.[50]

Despite the Machiavellian contrivance and to Sejo's chagrin, the expedition did not go as planned. Chosŏn could not convince Ma Jian to travel through Chosŏn or delay his return long enough for Sin Sukchu's army to come into position. By the time they arrived in Maolian, the envoy had departed and the Jurchens and Uriyangqad had dispersed.[51]

The setback disappointed but did not dissuade King Sejo. Only days later, he dispatched envoys to Ming to seek imperial sanction for a war against the Uriyangqad. He listed the repeated Maolian raids over the past year and even fished up decades-old Ming edicts dating from 1373 and 1410 that had permitted Chosŏn and its predecessor, Koryŏ, to attack the Uriyangqad. The edicts, according to Sejo, implicitly recognized Chosŏn territorial claims over the lands the Maolian Guard occupied. The same embassy also requested Ming to allow Korean students to study at the National Academy 國子監 (C. *Guozijian*) in Beijing. Hardly a coincidence, it was another reminder to Ming of their shared cultural commitments and what made Koreans different from the Jurchens and the Uriyangqad.[52]

The Ming court rejected both requests. It still hoped to deescalate the crisis.[53] An imperial rescript sent later in the winter of 1460 claimed the Maolian leaders had agreed to repatriate their Chosŏn captives and "never dare make trouble with Chosŏn or seek revenge." In the edict, the emperor took the voice of a universal sovereign, one that made no distinction between his subjects. He proclaimed to Chosŏn: "I succor the four seas and treat all with the same benevolence (C. *yi shi tongren* 一視同仁); I have ordered you to make peace truly because I wish that the people of both places can pursue each their livelihoods in safety."[54]

This lofty imperial gesture failed to convince either the Maolian nobles or the Chosŏn court to put aside their differences. It did, however, extract Korean professions of compliance in front of Ming authorities. Maolian nobles were now sure of Chosŏn retaliation, decided to abandon the Hoeryŏng region altogether, and moved west to join the Jianzhou. Chosŏn now worried about an emerging Jianzhou-Maolian alliance. In the second month of 1461, Chosŏn envoys to Ming encountered a tribute embassy from Li Manju, commander of the Jianzhou Guard Jurchens. Another Jianzhou noble Cungšan, commander of the Jianzhou Left Guard, who was leading the mission, assured Chosŏn it would not join forces with the Maolian against Chosŏn despite having been tempted to do so.[55]

From Cungšan, they learned the "various *yain* of the Maolian" had plans to ambush Chosŏn envoys en route to Ming. The Korean embassy then decided to report the matter to Ming authorities in Liaodong. The original draft of the statement prepared for Ming described the

Maolian exiles in Jianzhou as being motivated by "vengeance" 報復, but the embassy objected to this characterization. To speak of "vengeance," which alluded to Sejo's killing of Lang Borghan, implied that the Maolian had grounds for grievance against Chosŏn. At the same time, mentioning the Jianzhou Jurchens alongside the Maolian risked dragging Jianzhou into their feud. The wording was then revised by the embassy to omit any mention of Jianzhou, isolating the Maolian exiles diplomatically. More important, it described their motivation as "desiring loot." By thus reducing them to the stereotype of frontier marauders, Chosŏn's diplomats denied their capacity for political agency—no legitimate cause could rally them, only their thirst for plunder.[56]

The Chosŏn court bided its time. As before, Chosŏn officials advised the king to continue to observe the kingdom's long-standing policy of "serving the greater state with utmost sincerity," but only by professing compliance with Ming mediation efforts. In the same breath, they also advised the king to "watch the situation." If the Maolian continued to "attack our borders, it would still not be too late to launch a full invasion."[57] Chosŏn therefore needed the Maolian to break the truce so it could move forward with the invasion without appearing to violate Ming injunctions. Chosŏn tried to provoke the Uriyangqad into a raid. When a band of Udege 兀狄哈 (one of the Yeren Jurchen groups based in the far north, around the upper Amur River) reached the Chosŏn frontier in 1461, the court decided to welcome them in spite of Ming prohibitions, allowing a select contingent to proceed to Seoul. Anxious that refusing them altogether might push the Udege to join the Uriyangqad, Chosŏn would rather risk diplomatic confrontation with Ming than lose leverage over its northern neighbors. Once they arrived in Seoul, the Chosŏn court also informed them that it intended to "punish the Uriyangqad for their betrayal of the country" and encouraged the Udege to attack the Uriyangqad, making no secret of Chosŏn hostility toward them.[58]

The provocation Chosŏn was waiting for occurred in the ninth month of 1461. Chosŏn received a warning from Jianzhou's Li Manju that three Maolian Uriyangqad leaders had assembled a raiding party. Under the guise of a hunting expedition, they prepared to waylay the Korean embassy en route to Beijing. Li Manju, likely wishing to steer clear of the fray, explained that these Uriyangqad, who were Lang

Borghan's kin, had relocated to Jianzhou only several years ago and were therefore not his affiliates. Thus alerted to the threat, Chosŏn began to take precautions. It provided stronger armed escorts to its embassies. It also augmented the garrison and increased the gunpowder stockpiles of Ŭiju, the furthest stronghold on the Korean side of the Yalu. Chosŏn also hoped Li Manju could convince the Maolian in Jianzhou to stand down, although Li Manju likely had little control over these new arrivals.[59] Only two days after the Chosŏn court received this message (and before its policies could be implemented), the court received news from the governor of P'yŏngan province that a small band of mounted raiders, about fifteen strong, attacked a village in Ŭiju, burning the grain stocks and taking peasants as captives.[60] True to the intelligence Li Manju provided, more attacks followed in the weeks to come.[61]

Chosŏn reported the matter to Ming. It dispatched an embassy led by a high-ranking official who carried gifts to the emperor, the empress dowager, the empress, and the heir apparent. In the report, Chosŏn claimed that "*yain* from Jianzhou killed forty men and women working in the harvest; captured one hundred and thirty individuals, men, women, and children; captured thirty-seven horses, and one hundred and twenty-five heads of cattle."[62] In the next month, the Chosŏn learned from Li Duri 李豆里, the son of Li Manju, that the Jianzhou would repatriate the captured people and livestock but warned that another Jurchen noble wished to raid Chosŏn later in the winter.[63] This larger raid involved at least seven hundred horsemen. Besides capturing booty and slaves, they even laid siege to a walled border town.[64]

What began with Chosŏn's execution of one Maolian chief now escalated into a much broader conflict involving multiple belligerents. In the spring of the following year (1462), Chosŏn reported these developments to the Ming court. At first, Chosŏn hoped a Ming intercession could convince the Jianzhou leaders to return captive Koreans but realized, if repatriation were coordinated, a Chosŏn punitive expedition against the Maolian would prove difficult to justify.[65] More worrying was other *yain* leaders would see the Maolian's successful raiding as evidence of Chosŏn weakness, an invitation for them to join the fray. A returning embassy from Beijing reported overhearing Haixi Tatars discussing the Maolian's successes and planning their own raids "once the snow melted and the grass sprouted."[66] Meanwhile, the Maolian raids also spilled into Ming territory. The Maolian leader Zhao Samboo 趙三波, who had led the raids on Chosŏn in 1461 to "avenge" Lang Borghan, now plundered the Ming frontier as well. Ming efforts to reconcile Maolian with Chosŏn had come to naught; now Ming officials warned Zhao that Ming forces in Liaodong would join the Koreans to destroy him if he did not desist.[67]

Chosŏn's killing of Lang Borghan lit the fuse, but it cannot alone explain the wider escalation. During this period, Ming frontier policies and malfeasance by Ming frontier officers, known for extorting Jurchen tribute missions, antagonized the Jianzhou elite.[68] These frontier dynamics deserve a dedicated study and, given the surviving materials, it may be impossible to reconstruct the political calculus of Jianzhou's leadership with any reliability. Perhaps Li Manju and Cungšan had failed to rein in their followers. They might have conceived of raiding as a bargaining chip for negotiating with Ming and Chosŏn. They might have used the raids to protest unfair dealings by the Liaodong military elites. After all, trade with Ming and Chosŏn was important to the local economy, and Jurchen nobles relied on it to consolidate power over their rivals. Or Li Manju and Cungšan might have feared retaliation, given that Chosŏn and Ming had sent military expeditions to the area in the past. Regardless, it is clear Jianzhou's leaders wished to avoid full-scale military confrontation with Chosŏn or Ming.[69]

From Li Manju's missives to Chosŏn, it seemed he, as the highest-ranking leader of the Jianzhou Central Guard, wished to remain in Chosŏn's and Ming's good graces. Li informed Chosŏn that he had imprisoned the Maolian leaders responsible for the raids on Chosŏn and promised to return everything that was captured. In return, he asked that Chosŏn refrain from attacking them if Ming were to send a punitive expedition. In another letter, Li tried to explain the many difficulties his people have had with Ming in recent years. He also reminded the Chosŏn court of his many gestures of friendship, including how he tried to prevent Zhao Samboo from attacking Chosŏn by reporting his designs to the Ming court. He also thanked the Chosŏn king for granting emoluments to his relative Cungšan (incidentally, the very act that led to Ming intervention in Chosŏn's Jurchen policy). Chosŏn's answer was much less gracious: "whether or not we campaign against you is up to us; whether you live or die is up to you."[70]

To Chosŏn, Li Manju had already demonstrated that he was either unwilling or unable to keep his subordinates in check. Sporadic raiding continued along the Ming-Chosŏn-Jianzhou frontier over the next few years. Chosŏn discussed retaliatory measures but remained on the defensive, unwilling to move forward without Ming blessings. Maolian raiders even threatened Ming ambassadors who were sent to Korea to proclaim the accession of the Chenghua emperor 成化 (r. 1464–1487) in 1464.[71]

With a new emperor on the throne, Ming wished to avert a wider conflict. In the spring of 1465, Jianzhou Jurchens informed Ming that Chosŏn was preparing for an invasion. In response, Ming again urged Sejo to refrain from military action. The emperor, "as the master of all-under-heaven, who sees all with the same benevolence, without regard to distance . . . truly does not wish that the people of the two regions suffer the calamity of war." Ming again reminded Sejo that the root cause was the Korean killing of Lang Borghan. They counseled the king to "defend his borders so that they no longer dare attack," instead of "venting a moment's anger by launching troops across the border." Still trying to mediate the conflict, Ming announced it had also ordered the Jianzhou to cease "mobilization of men and horses without cause." Chosŏn had no interest in backing down. It decided again that it would "use troops when the moment is right," and come up with the words to justify their actions to Ming when necessary.[72]

THE JUSTICE OF WAR: ATTACK ON JIANZHOU

In time, the Ming court came to see things Sejo's way. Incursions into Ming became more frequent and deadly by 1467.[73] Even so, the Jianzhou, Maolian, and Haixi leaders still professed loyalty to Ming. Confronted with this apparent duplicity, frontier officials suggested they could be appeased to avoid trouble for the moment.[74] Prominent leaders, such as Cungšan, were offered higher imperial titles and trade permits. But once in Ming territory, Cungšan's bad behavior at a banquet was used as a pretext for his apprehension in the fourth month of 1467.[75]

With Cungšan in custody, Ming coordinated with Chosŏn an attack on Jianzhou, authorizing the expedition in the fifth month of 1467.[76] In a missive dispatched by the Ming Liaodong commander, Chosŏn was called on to join an expedition to "punish and eliminate the barbarian bandits" [夷寇]. The same missive stated that Chosŏn "harbored grievance toward the Jianzhou for generations" and "no more delay should come when it comes to the righteous cause of its vengeance." Only a few years ago, Chosŏn was blamed for instigating the conflict; now the fault rested entirely with their common enemies.[77]

Chosŏn had been waiting for this moment. Its frontier armies had long been ready for such an attack.[78] Ming forces destroyed the feeble Jianzhou resistance, while a Chosŏn army numbering some ten thousand soldiers attacked Li Manju's home base, capturing him and killing his son Günaqa 古納哈, along with many kinsmen. They also beheaded 286 others, butchered livestock, and torched hundreds of dwellings. Li Manju was decapitated. His head was dispatched to Beijing, along with the left ears severed from their enemies and a number of live captives, including women and children.[79]

While this campaign unfolded, Ming considered keeping Cungšan as a hostage. It later decided to put him to death as an example instead. When the edict arrived announcing that he should be punished for his "crimes," Cungšan and his entourage attacked the Ming officials present but were subdued and massacred in the ensuing scuffle. With these acts, Ming and Chosŏn decimated the Jianzhou aristocracy. Survivors were exiled to Ming's southwest frontier. Although Ming soon invested Cungšan and Li Manju's relatives to take over, Jianzhou's power had effectively been broken (although Cungšan's direct descendants would later found the Qing dynasty that destroyed Ming and subjugated Chosŏn).[80]

To recount the war here is not to settle accounts for any party, whether Chosŏn, Jianzhou, Maolian, or Ming. Nevertheless, the way Chosŏn and Ming framed this military action squarely placed the blame at the feet of their northern neighbors. Together, they justified their 1467 attack on Jianzhou as an act of *zhengfa* (K. *chŏngpŏl* 征伐), a punitive expedition to restore universal order. As was the case elsewhere in East Asia, the discourse of *zhengfa* legitimized retributive violence by the state, but in classical terms, the punitive war was properly the emperor's sole prerogative.[81] If he wished for others to conduct war on his behalf, he would bestow the ceremonial battle-ax (C. *fuyue* 斧鉞) to a deputy.[82] In the first decades of the Chosŏn period, Korean kings arrogated this authority through the rituals and rhetoric of *zhengfa*. King Sejong acted in the name of universal justice when his armies invaded Tsūshima in 1419 and when they attacked the Jurchens in 1433. Although these moves established the king of Chosŏn as a moral center, at least vis-à-vis its immediate neighbors,[83] these rituals did not position the king as a *supreme* authority. Unlike Ming war ritual, which involved sacrificing to heaven, in 1433, the Chosŏn court sacrificed only to rivers and mountains in advance of troop deployment.[84]

In Chosŏn's case, the reluctance to link war to cosmic authority suggested at least abstract limitations to its scope. By the 1467 war, the Chosŏn court had abandoned the rituals associated with *zhengfa* altogether. No such ritual was included in the *Five Rites and Ceremonies of State* (*Kukcho oryeŭi* 國朝五禮儀) compiled during King Sejong's reign and completed in 1474. Rather than assert an independent prerogative for war, the rituals surrounding the 1467 campaign reinforced the idea that Chosŏn carried out retributive violence only under Ming auspices. Indeed, the 1467 Chosŏn campaign concluded with the presentation of captives and severed enemy body parts to Ming. As the Chosŏn envoy Ŏ Segyŏm 魚世謙 (1430–1500) and his staff explained to a Ming frontier official in 1480 after another frontier war, "to present severed heads to the sovereign's court, this is the ancient way" [獻馘王庭 古也], which again subsumed the Korean court's war making under Ming authority.[85]

Given the Chosŏn court's deference to Ming authority, it is easy to lose sight of how the 1467 war also fulfilled King Sejo's own objectives. Sejo had for years endeavored to bring Ming into the fray. From the perspective of Chosŏn diplomacy, Sejo had succeeded in summoning imperial forces to prosecute a war he had long desired.[86] To achieve this end, his invocation of imperial authority was expedient, but the rhetoric he and his Ming counterparts used had wider diplomatic implications. The *zhengfa* paradigm of war went hand in hand with Ming universal authority. The Ming emperor in theory treated all his subjects, whether within or without his administrative realm with the same "moral excellence," but the emperor could still pursue warfare to punish those who erred.[87]

Warfare conducted under the above paradigm is conceptually distinct from the ideal of just war in the Westphalian international system. According to just war theorist Michael Walzer, the latter was a "a rule-governed activity" where both sides, usually sovereign states, possessed the same legal and moral "permissiveness to kill." Warfare under Ming imperial auspices more resembles the situation after Second World War. War has become "crime and punishment" or "military law enforcement," where the targets of violence are not other sovereign entities but violators of an international order—separatist regimes, terrorist organizations, pirate enclaves, rogue states—that are not afforded such recognition as legitimate political actors.[88]

The 1467 war is therefore more akin to the "police actions" in the contemporary postmodern condition, where war is carried out to "castigate" violators of the "utopia of perpetual peace."[89] Jianzhou was undoubtedly a political community, but under the Ming mandate of war, it was bereft of political agency, becoming merely "usurping caitiffs" 逆虜 who "conspired with the various barbarians to violate the way of Heaven." Chosŏn then was called on to join the "great army to thrust into their nests and caverns, and wipe out their seeds and kind, so that the rage of heaven and the gods can be satiated and the resentment of living beings relieved" [搗其巢穴 絶其種類 以謝天神之怒 以雪生靈之憤].[90]

The bellicose rhetoric, with all its dehumanizing genocidal exuberance, was not just puffery. These former subjects of Ming empire, once to be "treated with the same benevolence" under the emperor, now had their eligibility for imperial protection revoked. The inclusive idiom of universal empire gave way to an exclusive political idiom that could authorize murderous reprisal. This shift created, as historian Chung Daham argues, a "state of exception," one that identified the Jurchens as having exited the ecumenical fold, becoming bestial and monstrous. In the rhetoric of war, they were not even human let alone a legitimate political community.[91]

In contrast, Ming's exhortations to war always portrayed Chosŏn as an obliging partner in the effort to correct the world. "As a country of propriety and righteousness, who, from the time of its ancestors, reverently obeyed the imperial court, loved good and hated evil, sharing with us the same heart,"[92] it could only be "moved to wrath at the sight of such rebellion"[93] When Chosŏn's forces marched north to join the Ming attack, the Ming envoy Bai Yong 白顒, who was in Seoul at the time, praised the Chosŏn as follows: "Although there are many vassal states under heaven, the court has always seen your country as a state of propriety and righteousness; and though there are many vassal kings, the court has always seen you as the [most] wise." And now, with the

"Jianzhou extinguished, the hearts of the Maolian and Haixi will be filled with terror upon witnessing this," achieving the expedition's purpose.[94]

Although the war's executors acted on behalf of two different states, Ming and Chosŏn, the sense of imperial order they restored transcended both. That order was, in theory, coterminous with the Ming imperial authority but extended beyond the reach of its state apparatus. Empire was therefore a shared institution. To be able to access it, Chosŏn kings and diplomats needed to speak through its discursive conventions. Casting its conflicts with the Maolian Uriyangqad and the Jianzhou Jurchens as between civilization and barbarism was a case in point. Rhetoric that framed conflict in ecumenical terms would find analogues in many imperial contexts: Roman, Byzantine, Ottoman, and Anglo-American, to offer a few examples,[95] but what is notable here is who activated this discourse. It was not an imperial state but a vassal to seek its own ends. So even if the imperial order was Ming-centered, the Ming court was not the only entity invested in its enactment. Chosŏn also invested in it, and even the Jianzhou and Maolian appealed to it, though with much less success.

In this regard, Chosŏn's identification as a "country of propriety and righteousness" was not as an idle sobriquet. It, like many of the conventions of rhetoric discussed in this book, in fact sustained the salient, if contrived, diplomatic reality Chosŏn relied on. Given the stakes, it is no wonder Chosŏn never took this identification for granted. It went to great lengths to maintain this image and to convince (with varying degrees of success) Ming rulers, officials, and even literati to see their Korean counterparts as peers, not in political power or authority but in civilization. The desire for this status, of course, had much to do with the cultural and intellectual orientations of the Chosŏn elite, but this autoethnographic performance was also of immense practical, if not existential, consequence. To be included in the empire's ecumenical fold meant staying in Ming's good graces. Sejo and his advisers also knew that to fall outside that fold was to risk becoming like Li Manju, Cungšan, and the people they led: targets of imperial wrath. If managing Chosŏn's image in imperial eyes was critical to the task, so too must be the management of imperial discourse about Chosŏn; only then could imperial power be made accountable—the subject of the next part of the book and its three chapters.

PART III

Ecumenical Boundaries

When the envoy Hŏ Pong 許篈 (1551–1588) left Beijing in 1576, his entourage was exempted from the usual inspections. Previous inspectors searched their luggage for smuggled goods. This time, the two Ming officials in charge, a vice director of the Bureau of Receptions 主客司員外 and a secretary of the Bureau of Equipment of Communications 車駕司主事, asked only that the Koreans report the contents of their belongings. They declared that, unlike other states, Chosŏn "had always observed propriety and righteousness," and so their envoys would "certainly not be willing to purchase prohibited items." The statement was as specious in logic as it was false in description. Koreans often did smuggle. And according to the Chosŏn interpreter Ŏ Sukkwŏn 魚叔權 (fl. 1533–1554), catching or accusing a Korean embassy of doing so became a way for Ming officials to make a handsome profit. To avoid search and seizure, a Korean embassy might surrender goods worth up to "seven or eight thousand ounces of silver." Why would these officials then both overlook potential transgressions *and* forgo a chance to enrich themselves?[1]

It is impossible to know whether these officials were honest, lazy, or naïve. Nevertheless, their actions do illustrate how ecumenical boundaries informed applications of policy. By pointing to Chosŏn's cultural difference from other states, they employed the classical distinction between the "civilized" and the "barbarian" (K. *hwa i chi pyŏn*, C. *hua yi zhi bian* 華夷之辨) to justify their decision. At times, this distinction mapped alongside the spatial dichotomy of "in" (K. *nae*, C. *nei* 內) and "out" (K. *oe*, C. *wai* 外). The "civilized" corresponded with "in," those integral, included, and intimately attached to the political-moral center of empire. Meanwhile, the "barbarian," along with the "out," encompassed all things excluded as foreign, extraneous, marginal, and distant.

These correspondences did not always coalesce, however, into clear ecumenical schemes. Korea's wavering position in it is a case in point. When the early Ming statesman Song Lian 宋濂 (1310–1381) wrote that Korea *"ought* to be treated like the central domains of China, not to be spoken of as one of the outer states" [正當以中夏視之 未可以外國例言之也], he implied a disjunction between actual status and appropriate practice.[2] Likewise, the official *Ming History*, written well after the Ming's fall, offered this retrospective: "although Chosŏn was called a subordinate state during the Ming, it was no different from a realm within its borders" [朝鮮在明雖稱屬國 而無異域內]. Chosŏn was "viewed just like the internal realm" [視同內服], a turn of phrase that at once signified inclusion but also implied that this inclusion was provisional.[3] Expressed in both these statements, made near the date of Ming's foundation and a generation after its demise, was Chosŏn's exceptional status, but one that was premised on its exclusion as the default. Since exception was premised on ecumenical exclusion as the default, Chosŏn could still revert to "outsider" status and be lumped with the "barbarians."

Korea's unstable position in Ming ecumenical imagination was not so much ambiguous as it was contingent and relative. As the Korean official Yun Ŭnp'o 尹殷輔 (fl. 1494–1539) noted, "the Central Court treats us as an outer vassal state beyond the sea, and does *not* see us like its internal realm" [中朝以我國爲海外藩邦 不視同內服], the exact inverse of the *Ming History*'s formulation.[4] That Korean perception and (later) imperial orthodoxy could so diverge on the issue is in part because the spatialized alignment of *hua-yi* relied on analogies and heuristics rather than fixed definitions with certain ontologies. The resulting categories were fluid because they depended on context and how they relate different entities to one another.[5] So even though *hua-yi* ecumenical schemes sometimes posited that cultural and spatial distinctions were coterminous, they did not produce coherent overlaps between cultural, geographic, or political identification. Instead, at least in the context of imperial policy, the rhetoric of inclusion and exclusion differentiated the tool kits appropriate for dealing with a particular group.

The flexibility of this discourse, however, did not mean its categories were infinitely malleable. When Chosŏn diplomats demanded inclusion, they always implied the exclusion of others who were further away from the imperial fold or less civilized in cultural attainment. In most cases, they had in mind their immediate neighbors: the Jurchens and Mongols to the north and the Japanese across the sea. As the discussion of Ming attempts to mediate the Chosŏn-Jianzhou-Maolian conflicts in chapter 4 shows, whether a group was excluded as "outer barbarians" or "inner subjects" in imperial discourse depended on the political purpose of the declaration. What this discourse preserved was a consistent world view for motivating or justifying imperial action, even when it obfuscated the specific power politics behind each situation.[6]

Korea's ecumenical status could vary while the hierarchical logic it was based on remained in place. In practical terms, this meant it was not always clear, even to imperial officials, how Chosŏn should be treated. An imperial agent knew to follow the axioms of "using barbarians to fight barbarians" [以夷制夷], the moral necessity of "revering the sovereign and expelling barbarians" [尊王攘夷]. But they were also compelled to "cherish men from afar" [懷柔遠人]. After all, according to the *Analects*, "when men from afar do not submit, one should cultivate civil virtue to bring them" [故遠人不服 則修文德以來之].[7] But were Koreans *hua* or *yi*? Were Koreans "men from afar" deserving of imperial munificence or wily barbarians to be kept at arm's length? With no fixed answer to these questions, it meant that Ming officials, both petty and grand, could switch to the appropriate discourse to justify their preferred policies, motivated by anything from high-minded principles to naked profit seeking.

Chapters 5 to 7 discuss how a rhetoric of ecumenical belonging (best captured by this refrain of Korea as a "country of propriety and righteousness") had material consequences for the practice of diplomacy. In each of the cases, status had tangible and visible effects on the design, interpretation, and execution of imperial policies. These effects help explain why a discourse of ritual propriety became a cornerstone of Chosŏn's autoethnographic strategies. As the relationship unfolded over the centuries, safeguarding Chosŏn's ecumenical status also became a diplomatic goal in its own right—a development with broader consequences for how Korean royal prerogatives came to be reconciled with Ming imperial authority.

CHAPTER FIVE

Cajoling Empire

Chosŏn's envoys experienced the Ming Empire not as a monolith but as a makeshift contraption assembled through joints of uneven strength. They encountered frontier military officers, waystation managers, and petty functionaries who had different interests in a Korean embassy's conduct. In Beijing, they met high ministers, palace eunuchs, and occasionally, even the emperor himself, each of whom operated in a distinct institutional context. Within their domains of authority, any of these actors could exercise broad discretion in how they treated sojourners from afar. For Chosŏn visitors, Ming policy could seemingly turn on a dime, depending on who was in charge at the moment. To make matters worse, they had few ways to pressure them (bribes and gifts helped, but they could be costly and risky) into changing tack.

One device in an envoy's toolbox that proved reliable was rhetoric. Ready at a moment's notice, it was useful because it could access the idioms that informed imperial precedents. Although empire had a helter-skelter quality to it, the narratives about what it was supposed to be and how it was supposed to act revolved around a set of axioms with origins in the shared classical tradition. Together, these axioms, such as "cherishing men from afar" [懷柔遠人] and "impartial compassion" [一視同仁], lent an air of coherence to imperial rule. When a Chosŏn envoy invoked them, he opened a discursive space to negotiate with Ming officials and emperors alike. Because good imperial policy reflected the wisdom of these axioms, Ming, as a virtuous empire, would observe their guidance as a matter of course. In this imperializing mode of persuasion, the Chosŏn envoy restated what an emperor and his empire *should* do in order to protest particular imperial policies without challenging the premise of imperial authority as such.

This chapter discusses how Chosŏn diplomats employed the imperializing mode to negotiate with different imperial agents. To convince emperors to overrule their own officials, leverage well-placed brokers to intercede on their behalf, and coax Ming bureaucrats to alter long-standing regulations meant taking different approaches and navigating distinct institutional environments. Nevertheless, the rhetorical tools brought to bear remained markedly consistent. Alongside language cajoling imperial actors to confirm imperial ideals, certain refrains, including assertions of Korea's status as a "country of propriety and righteousness," became commonplace, even boilerplate.[1]

Rhetoric was so repetitive not because the terms of Chosŏn-Ming diplomacy were inherently stable, but because imperial agents entertained wide-ranging ideas of how Koreans should be treated. Before the imperializing mode could be summoned to compel favorable terms or challenge specific policies, a Chosŏn envoy first had to confront this variability. As this chapter argues, rhetorical reification in diplomatic discourse, especially in the restating of Korea's ecumenical belonging, did not so much reflect a singular Chosŏn-Ming diplomatic ideology but instead Chosŏn efforts to manage the vagaries of diplomacy in practice.

THE EMPEROR'S PRIDE

In the first decades of the Ming dynasty, emperors took a personal interest in diplomacy. For instance, they spoke directly to Chosŏn emissaries in the audiences they held. The emissaries in turn carried home orally transmitted messages from the emperor to Chosŏn's king.[2] In return, the rhetoric of written appeals played to an attentive imperial ear. As Kwŏn Kŭn did so in the poems written for the Hongwu emperor discussed in this book's introduction,[3] he also had done so years earlier in 1388. In the diplomatic missive he drafted addressing the territorial dispute over Ch'ŏllyŏng (Tieling in Chinese, see map 2), he appealed to the emperor's personal magnanimity.[4] According to Kwŏn, his statement that "[Korea] has long dutifully observed duties of a feudal lord; our land has already entered the imperial domain" was what convinced the emperor to relent.[5]

Kwŏn might have overestimated the impact of his words, but Ming court chronicles still confirm how they had captured the emperor's attention. Hongwu sneered at what he called the Korean propensity to "instigate controversy," but did not wish to "squabble" with "little barbarians." Although moved by condescension rather than magnanimity, the emperor agreed with Kwŏn Kŭn that wrangling with Koreans over territory was beneath imperial dignity.[6] After the appeal, Hongwu reaffirmed the Yalu River as their border and reorganized the military outposts in the region. The Ming military also moved the Tieling Guard further northwest to modern Tieling, the city in modern Liaoning whose name shares the same characters as Korea's Ch'ŏllyŏng. Two places with the same name preserved two convenient fictions: Ming succeeded in bringing Tieling back under imperial administration while Korea fended off Ming encroachment by keeping Ch'ŏllyŏng for itself.[7]

The frontier remained a source of friction, however. In 1404, a dispute flared up, this time over Hamju 咸州, the region once under the Ssangsŏng commandery and the original power base of Chosŏn's dynastic ancestors. Ming officials claimed it had once been under Liao and Jin rule and now proposed establishing military outposts there to assert imperial territorial claims. In protest, Chosŏn envoys countered with historical evidence of Korean jurisdiction over the area. They also reused Kwŏn's rhetorical formula. Appealing to imperial magnanimity, they implored the Yongle emperor "not to discriminate what is beyond his civilizing influence" and "treat all with equal benevolence" [不分化外 一視同仁]. If those outside the emperor's direct rule were still imperial subjects, then Chosŏn, already the emperor's loyal vassal, only governed lands already under imperial sovereignty. The emperor reportedly exclaimed, "The land of Chosŏn is already in my control; what point is there for me to contest this?" He canceled plans to place Hamju under Ming jurisdiction, despite grumbling from his officials.[8] Korean acts of "open obeisance and secret defiance," as one historian describes it, exploited Ming's "vain self-importance" as a self-styled "celestial court."

On the other hand, imperial readiness to concede territorial claims in favor of a rhetorical victory also meant more than flattery was at work: Chosŏn envoys, by participating in the rhetorical construction of imperial authority, also bent it to their own ends.[9]

To live by the word also meant dying by the word. A mercurial emperor could countermand his officials at will, but Chosŏn was vulnerable to the same caprice. In 1421, Chosŏn presented a memorial requesting that the gold and silver tribute be commuted.[10] It called on the emperor to intercede as would a loving father who had heard the pleas of his suffering child. It explained that, because the purpose of tribute was "only to show obeisance and show sincerity," so even "local produce and cloth bolts" should suffice because what mattered were not material riches but the "utmost sentiment" between parent and child.[11] This request, for all its impassioned rhetoric, failed because it never reached the emperor. At the time, the emperor was upset by the wording of another, unrelated Korean memorial so the envoys did not dare present this appeal.[12]

Chosŏn tried again in 1429. It appealed to Yongle's grandson, the Xuande emperor. Now standing in their way was the Ming minister of finance, Jian Yi 蹇義 (1363–1435), who argued the gold and silver tribute was the "iron law" of the Ming's founder Hongwu so it could not be changed.[13] The Chosŏn memorial drafters anticipated this obstacle because their appeal now recalled one occasion when the Hongwu emperor turned away gold and silver, using it as evidence of the emperor's "original intent." A cherry-picked precedent misrepresented the Hongwu emperor's policies, but it sufficed to neutralize Jian Yi's point.[14] The Xuande emperor accepted the Korean appeal, noting Chosŏn's "utmost sincerity in serving the great" and the necessity of considering the "situation of faraway people."[15]

Besides preempting possible objections, the Chosŏn court anticipated the imperial gaze. In advance of the campaign to commute the tribute of specie, Chosŏn proscribed gold and silver ornamentation in official court garb and ritual implements. Moralists at home already decried the use of gold and silver through calls to virtuous austerity, but diplomatic appeals focused exclusively on their scarcity in Korea. To be believable, Chosŏn could not provide evidence to the contrary, lest Ming visitors return with reports exulting Korea's metallic wealth.[16]

Still, all the strategizing was moot if no emperor could devote attention to Korean affairs.

Early Ming rulers like Hongwu, Jianwen, Yongle, and Xuande turned to foreign relations to augment their authority. This attention also meant Korean envoys enjoyed privileged access to their ears. Generous treatment of Koreans demonstrated the emperor's magnanimity, an opportunity Koreans readily provided by inviting them to "embrace the righteousness of grand unification and cherish those afar to bring them to submission" [懷大同之義 柔遠能邇].[17] In return, Chosŏn promised to acknowledge their "receipt of imperial influence with joyful celebrations in percussion and dance" [懽欣皷舞於聖化之中].[18]

By the late fifteenth century, the imperial person faded into the backdrop of the diplomatic stage. Initiative fell into the laps of his underlings, and diplomacy became a contested object between palace eunuchs and the literati-controlled bureaucracy. In such an environment, Chosŏn envoys could no longer count on their memorials to reach the emperor's desk. These appeals, once directed to a single, interested central figure, now had to contend with a host of many, sometimes indifferent actors.

THE BROKER'S DUES

Imperial caprice was not the only source of volatility. Imperial agents exercised wide discretion over the interpretation of an imperial directive (see figure 5.1). In the first month of 1477, the Chosŏn court received a report from its envoys in Beijing that Ming officials had apprehended a Chosŏn interpreter for smuggling water buffalo (*Bubalus bubalis*) horns. Along with fish, glue, and wood, these horns were used by bowyers to fabricate war bows.[19]

Ming prohibited the export of horns, but the interpreter circumvented the ban by buying from the black market. To do so, he enlisted the brokers who provisioned the Yuhe Hostel 玉河館 where the Chosŏn entourage lodged. Ming military officials caught wind of the affair and launched a surprise inspection. They confiscated the contraband and embezzled the cash seized from the bust. The Ming court declared that, because there was no crime in selling these items to Korea, a "country of propriety and righteousness," the arrested interpreter was to be released. It nevertheless ordered the trade ban enforced lest the items fall into the hands of "Wildmen 野人 and Tartars 㺚子."[20] The horn dealers and Ming functionaries abetting the smuggling were less fortunate. The Ming court flogged each 100 times and dispatched them to frontier military duty.[21]

The affair alarmed the Chosŏn court. Water buffalo did not live in Korea, while the horns of native Korean oxen (*Bos taurus coreanae*) were too small for making bows. Because Ming provided Korea with its only reliable supply of this strategic resource, the Chosŏn court had tacitly encouraged the smuggling.[22] Now that the clandestine trade was exposed, it could no longer count on the black market nor could its envoys claim plausible deniability.[23] When the embassy returned to Seoul, the court had the interpreter flogged, not for smuggling but for doing so with "carelessness and indiscretion."[24]

The crackdown also revealed the ambiguity of Korea's ecumenical status. If the Korean interpreter was granted clemency only because he represented a "country of propriety and righteousness," what did it mean if rules targeting "Wildmen and Tartars" were now applied to Chosŏn Koreans? Implied here was a warning: if Korea were indeed a civilized country, it would not disobey Ming regulations by engaging in prohibited activities. Korea's "outside" status might have indicated its political autonomy, but now it caused Korea to be lumped with the "barbarians" Chosŏn detested.

In debates over how best to protest the prohibitions, court officials differed on tactics but agreed it was vital to distinguish Koreans from other foreigners. One official reasoned that, because Ming had always prohibited envoys of "outer states" 外國 from carrying weapons into Ming territory but still allowed Koreans to bear arms, they could argue Koreans were also implicitly exempted from the weapons embargo.[25] Another minister, Hyŏn Sŏkkyu 玄碩圭 (1403–1480), recalled that the Hongwu emperor once bequeathed cannons to Chosŏn. From that precedent, it could be argued that the Ming founder "had treated our country as a [part of his own] family" and was therefore not subject to prohibitions for "outsiders." Nevertheless, Hyŏn believed it would be a tall order to convince Ming officials with such arguments. Hyŏn reminded his colleagues that the famous Song dynasty scholar-official Su Shi 蘇軾 (1037–1101) had once "treated our country like 'outer barbarians' 外夷,

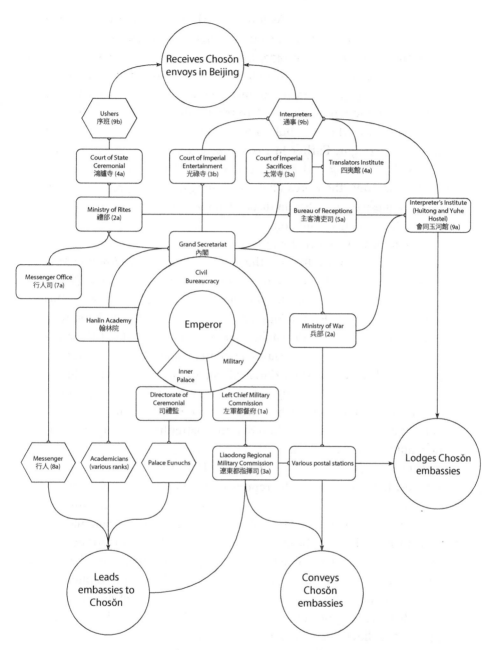

FIGURE 5.1 Ming imperial institutions involved with Chosŏn diplomacy, ca. 1500. Illustration by author.

begrudging us even books." As long as such notions prevailed among Ming literati officials, a lasting solution would remain elusive.[26]

In the eighth month of 1477, the embassy appealing these restrictions departed for Ming.[27] In Beijing, they discovered that both the Ming minister of war and the minister of works opposed exempting Chosŏn from the arms embargo.[28] To resolve this issue, Chosŏn needed more than clever rhetoric, but an unexpected turn of events provided the relief it sought. Earlier in the same year, the Korean-born Ming eunuch Chŏng Tong had led an embassy to Korea. At the behest of Han Kwiram, now the Korean lady-in-waiting of the Empress Dowager, Chŏng requested that Chosŏn dispatch a member of her family to lead the next Korean envoy mission.[29]

Her family, which had supported King Sejo's coup in 1453, had only grown more powerful over the years (see figure 3.1). Another Han daughter, a niece of Han Kwiram, was Queen Dowager Sohye 昭惠王后 (1437–1504), the mother of Chosŏn's current monarch, Sŏngjong.[30] This meant Kwiram was also the king's grandaunt. Sŏngjong, obliging with his grandaunt's request, dispatched his maternal uncle (and Kwiram's nephew) Han Ch'irye 韓致禮 (1441–1499) to Beijing. His mission arrived only a week before[31] so when Han's colleagues ran into problems lifting the embargo, Chŏng Tong suggested that Han Ch'irye write a personal letter to his aunt, asking for her intervention. Han Kwiram soon wrote back to her nephew, assuring him that the matter had the emperor's ear and would soon be resolved.[32]

King Sŏngjong initially celebrated Han Ch'irye's success. His methods, however, earned the reproach of Chosŏn's officials. Han had brought excessive quantities of goods (including 200 folding fans and 300 brimmed hats) intended as gifts for his aunt Han Kwiram and the eunuch Chŏng Tong, or bribes for Ming officials. According to the censorate, an agency responsible for checking official malfeasance, he also overstepped his proscribed duties and interfered with the diplomatic portfolio of his colleagues. He also circumvented official bureaucratic channels by relying on ties with the inner palace, a move his political opponents believed had "embarrassed the state."[33]

The question of Chosŏn's esteem in Ming eyes again came to the fore. The court wished to sway Ming policy by demonstrating Chosŏn's dutifulness. If the policy now changed only because of bribery or personal ties, the damage to the country's reputation "far exceeded the benefit of acquiring horns." To the Chosŏn censorate, it was precisely these perceptions of unreliability that had elicited the ban in the first place. Han had undercut a reputation carefully cultivated over generations to achieve a momentary goal. In this logic, observation of propriety to shift Ming perceptions, not covert tactics of expedience, was the only proper method and the only viable long-term solution.[34]

As the wording of the Ming edict suggested, Ming policymakers still lumped Korea with other "outsiders." It granted an exemption to Chosŏn on the order of fifty units a year. A compromise between Chosŏn demands and the Ming bureaucracy's reservations, the edict reiterated that buffalo horns were prohibited in principle to foreign peoples, but Korea would not be treated in the same category as the "nomads of the north."[35] Chosŏn had "observed the proper lunations, was dutiful in tribute and steadfast in a vassal's duties, and was] different from the various barbarians" [朝鮮奉正朔 謹朝貢 恪守臣節 與諸 夷不同]. Lest Koreans lose their "heart of submission," Ming allowed this limited quota.[36]

Korean distinction from the other "barbarians" was a matter of degree, not of kind. It was still contingent on Chosŏn's good behavior, a point that the censorate officials made sure to belabor. At any rate, fifty horns a year was still a meager quantity—only one or two bows can be made from one horn. Again, King Sŏngjong found his connection to the Ming inner palace too valuable to ignore. In 1481, the Chosŏn court, despite the protests of some of its high officials, sent Second State Councilor Han Myŏnghoe, a senior statesman, a veteran of the Sejo court, and a (very) distant cousin of Han Kwiram, to appeal the matter again.[37] In a personal letter, where he addressed Han Kwiram as aunt 姑孃 and called himself her nephew 姪男, he still couched his appeal in imperial precedent. Given Chosŏn's continuous "reverence in serving the [Ming] court and reception of deep imperial favor," Han only hoped that the emperor would follow in the footsteps of his ancestors who had "granted armaments to Chosŏn without suspicion."[38]

Tropes of kinship in diplomatic correspondence were themselves unremarkable; what *was* remarkable was how they were used. To couch the relationship between emperor and vassal in terms of virtual kinship evoked paternalistic sympathy, but now the discourse of imperial magnanimity seeped into a supposedly personal letter between actual kin. In it, Han Myŏnghoe no longer exhorted the emperor but called upon a relative to embody the empire's highest ideals. The imperializing mode had expanded its targets so that its magnanimity was no longer only an emperor's trait. As the ensuing examples will show, imperial magnanimity had also become an institutional mission.

THE BUREAUCRAT'S IDEAS

After Han Myŏnghoe's mission in 1481, Ming raised the horn quota to two hundred a year. The next few years also saw Ming and Chosŏn coordination in military operations against the Jianzhou Jurchens, which helped alleviate Ming anxieties about exporting buffalo horns to Chosŏn.[39] In 1482, the Ming Minister of Rites even officially exempted Korean embassies from baggage inspections because Chosŏn, "as a country of propriety and righteousness," should not be subject to these restrictions.[40]

The reprieve, however, would not last. Profiteering by Ming military officers motivated in part the initial crackdown of 1477. Allotting trade through quotas only created more opportunities for arbitrage and extortion. In 1495, a Ming frontier official again confiscated horns from a Chosŏn embassy. The ambassador protested, claiming the quantity fell within the legal limit of two hundred. The official returned the items, but the Chosŏn party counted only 106; nearly half were missing.[41] The justifications for these prohibitions turned on where Korea belonged in an unstable ecumenical schema. However, sudden reversals had as much to do with fickle imperial policy as they did with the entrenched interests of those charged with their execution.

Ming security concerns mixed with the lure of a profitable racket to produce another set of troublesome regulations in 1522. A director of the Ming Ministry of Rites, Sun Cun 孫存 (1491–1547), discovered a Korean interpreter had bought books published by the imperial printers. They included the *Gazetteer of the Ming's Great Unification* (*Da Ming yitong zhi* 大明一統志), an imperially commissioned atlas of the entire Ming realm.[42]

Alarmed, Sun, who was also in charge of the Ming Bureau of Receptions 主客司, implemented the so-called gate restriction policy (C. *menjin*;

K. *mun'gŭm* 門禁). This curfew policy barred foreign envoys from traveling and trading freely in Beijing. Henceforth, members of the Chosŏn embassy required written permission from his office before setting foot outside the Yuhe Hostel.[43] Like his Song predecessor Su Shi, who believed that Koryŏ envoys, by acquiring books, maps, and documents, would access information "inappropriate for foreign barbarians" (C. *fanyi* 蕃夷), Sun restricted Korean access to protect his country from the prying eyes of untrustworthy outlanders.[44] As Hyŏn Sŏkkyu had presaged decades earlier, the Ming now begrudged even books to Koreans because they perceived them as foreign.

Much like the horn restrictions, the rules did not emerge as part of a carefully coordinated imperial policy but an ad hoc decision. The travel ban also embroiled Chosŏn embassies with another layer of Ming institutional politics: interpersonal and interagency squabbles. When first confronted with the ban, the Chosŏn court decided against using the highest diplomatic channels, even though the king was personally affected by the rule (rare medical ingredients he required, such as live scorpions, were now impossible to procure). Rather than submit an official *p'yo* memorial on the king's behalf, it ordered the envoys to petition the Ming Ministry of Rites in their delegated capacity.[45] Initial overtures seemed successful. The Ming minister Xi Shu 席書 (1461–1527) agreed to lift the restrictions. Chosŏn emissaries, however, found the superintendent of the Yuhe Hostel 提督會同館主事 Chen Bangcheng 陳邦佩 (fl. 1520) was less cooperative.[46]

Chen still obstructed the movement of Korean ambassadors and even reduced the Korean allotment of buffalo horns to fifty sets a year. In 1525, when Korean officials protested, noting that Minister Xi, in theory, his superior, had already granted them special permission, Chen responded vulgarly (Chosŏn records took care to preserve the tone and register of his speech):

> Don't you tell me that 'cause you reported this to Minister Xi that I'm gonna let you head-severed-bitch-boned-curs go out. Even if you memorialized the imperial court, I still wouldn't let you bitch-boned-curs go out! [休說爾稟席尚書 我便放爾這些砍頭的狗骨頭出[去] 爾便奏與朝廷 我與不放爾這些狗骨頭出去].[47]

Chen's vituperation of the Korean official was overheard by one of his colleagues, a Ming interpreter of Persian language 回回通事 named Hu Shishen 胡士紳.[48]

Interpreter Hu reported the incident to the imperial court. In his report, he impeached Chen for exposing his "ignorance of affairs and propriety" when he verbally abused the Korean embassy. Hu argued that the duty of the "high and low officials of the Central State" was to "cherish those from afar" and ensure that "foreign barbarians, even if stupid as dogs or sheep, will turn and submit to the imperial court." Chen's "rashness and incompetence" would instead cause "the barbarians of the four directions to develop grievances deep as rivers and seas." Chen's behavior "earned their mockery" and would induce them to "betray" the imperial court.[49] Hu's memorial, which called Koreans "barbarians" and compared them to livestock, trafficked in the same dehumanizing language as Chen, but it articulated a vastly different philosophy on how the imperial court should manage foreign relations. For Hu, granting outsiders access to imperial goods, especially knowledge, could demonstrate Ming magnanimity and instill a sense of gratitude. For those who proscribed Korean activity, access was precisely the problem.[50]

The impeachment was successful. Chen Bangcheng and his supervisor, Bureau of Receptions director Chen Jiuchuan 陳九川 (fl. 1514–1522), were arrested and replaced. The affair's unfolding likely had little to do with Ming responsiveness to Korean grievance and more with a wider political rift at the Ming court: the Great Rites Controversy (C. *Da li yi* 大禮議). Later historical accounts accused Hu Shishen of manufacturing the exchange to pursue a personal vendetta against Chen Bangcheng. The resulting scandal gave the Ming minister Xi Shu a pretext to move against Chen Bangcheng's supervisor Chen Jiuchuan. A mid-Ming chronicle of its diplomatic relations, the *Comprehensive Record of Diverse Realms* (*Shuyu zhouzi lu* 殊域周咨錄), did not deny Chen Bangcheng's abusive behavior but excused it because the Korean embassy "was conniving with Ming interpreters [i.e., Hu] and in cahoots with powerful Ming officials [i.e., Xi]."[51] For his part, Hu Shishen might not have been as corrupt as these accounts suggest. On another occasion, the court had commended him for honesty because he had refused bribes from Ottoman (Rūmi 魯迷) envoys. As an official whose work involved dealing with foreign dignitaries, interpreter Hu might have genuinely found Chen Bangcheng's actions deplorable.[52]

In this case, Ming infighting benefited the Korean embassy. But interagency conflict might have been the root of the embassy's troubles in the first place. Whereas Chen Bangcheng oversaw the Bureau of Receptions, Hu was a low-ranking functionary attached to the Court of State Ceremonial 鴻臚寺. Both agencies answered to the Ministry of Rites with theoretically distinct jurisdictions, but their responsibilities overlapped when it came to the entertainment of foreign envoys. In this period, the Bureau of Receptions managed the envoy hostels, while the Court of State Ceremonial arranged for imperial banquets and related entertainments.[53] In the meantime, the Ministry of Rites also fought with the Ministry of War over control of the Yuhe Hostel, with interpreters like Hu Shishen bristling at the war ministry's interference. For Chosŏn, however, this was more than just a problem with administrative procedure.

After Chen's impeachment, a new bureau director permitted the Koreans to trade, but as the 1534 Chosŏn envoy So Seyang 蘇世讓 (1486–1562) would discover, the travel restrictions were still enforced. So and his entourage arrived at the Yuhe Hostel on the twenty-sixth day of the second month. He immediately appealed the policy by speaking to the Bureau of Reception director and the hostel superintendent. They instructed him to raise the issue with the Ministry of Rites. On the fourth day of the leap second month, So requested the Hostel Superintendent Zhang Ao 張鰲 (fl. 1521–1534) to forward his petition to the ministry. Soon, So Seyang heard rumors that local merchants offered kickbacks amounting to half their profits to the superintendent for permission to do business with foreign emissaries. Without the gate restrictions, the merchants would lose their monopoly and the superintendent his racket. Further observation confirmed Superintendent Zhang's duplicity, and So Seyang now believed his petition had been suppressed.[54]

Like other Korean emissaries, So had to navigate an imperial bureaucracy whose opacity left desperate supplicants with few options. Rather than wait in silence, So took matters into his own hands. On the thirteenth of the month, nine days after he first approached Zhang Ao, a welcoming banquet was held for the Chosŏn embassy. Presiding over it was Ming Minister of Rites Xia Yan 夏言 (1482–1548). So Seyang approached the minister, prostrated, and professed his gratitude, first for considering his petition and second for the imperial edict that would lift the prohibition.

The gesture was curious. In his diary, So related how he was convinced the petition was never delivered to Xia. Thus, he had even less reason to think an imperial Ming edict was forthcoming. For him to mention the edict to Xia could only mean he was testing whether Xia had actually received his petition. To So's relief (and despite his pessimism), Xia assured him that the matter had already been discussed. A few days later, on the seventeenth day of the same month, an imperial edict was proclaimed, permitting Korean emissaries' freedom of travel once every five days. The hostel superintendent also allowed So and his entourage to travel out, although still only under close supervision.[55]

So Seyang's appeal asserted what might be termed Korean exceptionalism.[56] From past affairs, So distilled (and constructed) a tradition of Ming granting exemptions to Korean embassies:

> Since our country roughly understands ritual and ceremony and serves the great with utmost sincerity, the [imperial] court has treated it as its internal realm [有同內服]. Whenever our country's envoys come to the capital, they move about freely and never see restrictions or limitations. This [practice] has continued until now. We have acted respectfully, reverently, and obediently for over one hundred years, never once transgressing. Only in recent years did the prohibitions extend to us, confining us to our hostels behind locked doors. Even with official orders or for public business, only one or two interpreters are permitted to come and go at set times under the watch of the hostel guards with special papers. [These policies] contravene the former precedents [有礙舊式].

In his retelling, limits to the movement of envoys in the capital had been enforced when a Jurchen emissary had murdered "other barbarians," but at the time the Ming Ministry of Rites exempted Chosŏn from these restrictions, noting that it "always observed propriety and righteousness, serving the court dutifully." Confining Korean embassies like "prisoners" therefore "not only violated the rules of old practices," but also undermined "the intent of past emperors to treat [Korea] favorably." Accordingly, Ming should lift the "meaningless restriction" against Korean embassies.[57]

It was now up to Ming to rectify the situation by demonstrating its magnanimity. Koreans as "distant men who come awed by righteousness" have now been "completely disappointed." [遠人慕義之望 殊用缺然] because officious administrators "stubbornly refused to observe" established precedents.[58] What a pity then if a "momentary policy" would both violate "the old precedents of the former emperors" and disappoint Korea's long-standing "admiration for righteousness!" So Seyang "badgered on about these minor matters," not because resolving them would "profit" him or Chosŏn. Instead, he explained, they had everything to do with Ming's own priorities:

> Whether you sequester us brings no benefit or loss to us except in one matter. We only believe that if we are treated with the same compassion and without distinctions between what is inside or outside [一視之仁 罔有內外], and if we are allowed to visit and travel without restriction, we will be able to witness rituals and ceremonies, investigate the substance of civilization, and be infused with transformative culture [薰炙遷化]. Thus, to benefit us with this enlightenment will truly actualize the utmost virtue of cherishing [men from afar] [實敦懷柔之至德]. It will spread the total sincerity of our service [事大之盡誠] to the great across our distant marches so that we will always carry the grace [of the imperial] spirit for ten thousand generations in mutual harmony.[59]

So Seyang made no mention of why the gate restriction policy was implemented in the first place, eliding both Ming security concerns and the underlying profiteering. But by doing so, he had changed the subject. Ming security concerns revealed anxiety over Korea's liminal, not-yet-civilized but not-quite-barbarian status in their ecumenical schema. So's arguments, on the other hand, propounded a vision of universal magnanimity that imputed the proper exercise of imperial authority. What was a problem of Chosŏn's ecumenical ambiguity became a matter of Ming imperial obligations: whether it had truly succeeded in cherishing distant men and civilizing the world.

In the proposal to the imperial court, Minister Xia repeated So's rhetorical framing, one squarely within the imperializing mode of Korean diplomatic appeals. He noted that Korean knowledge of "ritual and ceremony" distinguished their emissaries from "barbarian envoys of other places" [他處夷使]. But even as he commended So's desire to be "infused with the transformative culture" of the imperial capital and used it as evidence for his "sincere veneration of the superior state" [仰慕上國之誠], Xia Yan maintained that "the language and dress of distant men are different" and will thus "easily transgress the state's prohibitions" [遠人言服既殊 易罹國禁]. Balancing security concerns with So's arguments, he settled on one unrestricted day out of five, a compromise that "would neither disappoint the sentiments of distant men nor render futile the laws of the Central State" [庶幾不拂遠人之情 不廢中國之法].[60]

For Chosŏn envoys, the new policy was only a marginal improvement. Ming bureaucrats knew full well they used diplomatic missions as cover for illicit trade. For this reason, one modern interpretation understands relaxed restrictions as merely a tip of the hat to So Seyang's eloquence. Contradictory responses by Ming agencies, in this view, were not evidence of bureaucratic dysfunction but instead a case of administrative doublespeak. Ming officials conceded matters of symbolic import to maintain "correct" political ideology in their statements without needing to compromise on issues of concrete import.[61]

In contrast, Yan Congjian 嚴從簡 (fl. 1559–1574), a Ming official who served the Messenger's Office 行人司 (and the author of the *Comprehensive Record of Diverse Realms*) was far less generous. He charged Ming policymakers with undermining state security through this compromise. He believed Xia Yan and others only cooperated to avoid the fate of Chen Bangcheng, whom Hu Shishen had impeached on behalf of the Koreans. Lumping Hu Shishen with corrupt hostel attendants, he believed, meant that they were "teaching" So Seyang how to write his appeal because of its rhetorical similarities to Shishen's 1524 impeachment of Chen Bangcheng.[62]

The above latter-day interpretations diverged in their judgments of Ming bureaucratic competence. They shared the same disregard, however, for Korean agency. The first dismissed So and his petition as ineffectual; the second saw him as a pawn of a wily Ming bureaucrat.

But did So Seyang really need to be tutored on how to use the imperializing mode? After all, this rhetorical technique had been central to Korean diplomatic memorials, the very same communiqués that So Seyang himself had composed on other occasions. That So Seyang's agency is so disregarded by both Ming elites and later historians is perhaps unsurprising. Their preoccupation with Ming court politics makes it easy to overlook dynamics at the scale of the nitty-gritty—the very place where a Korean envoy and his entourage had the most room to maneuver. Meanwhile, overlooking the realm of quotidian diplomacy also misses a broader implication of So Seyang's exchange with Xia Yan from the Korean perspective.

Xia Yan's exemption still reproduced So's reasoning and, in principle, Korea's entitlement to exceptional treatment. His responsiveness, even if only lip service, reinforced the normativity of So's argument. Certainly, the effect on the gate restrictions itself was limited. Chosŏn envoys continued to suffer sporadic attempts to tighten them. The 1537 envoy Chŏng Hwan 丁煥 (1497–1540) virtually reenacted So Seyang's mission. Finding even the purchase of "vegetables and everyday items" difficult, Chŏng lamented the severity of the restrictions he faced, which, like So Seyang, he protested to limited effect.[63] The relief So and other envoys obtained, however nominal, nevertheless added to the growing body of imperial precedents that granted this exception, ensuring its validity for future diplomatic encounters. The appeal's success was therefore palpable less in the alteration of Ming policy than how it reoriented its frame of reference.

Korean diplomatic rhetoric was repetitive because it sought to reify a particular notion of Chosŏn's place in the imperial order. The *Topical Speeches of the Interpreter's Hall* (*Sangwŏn cheŏ* 象院題語), a Chinese-language interpreter's training textbook of mid-sixteenth-century provenance, collected stock statements in colloquial Chinese on various subjects of diplomatic import. Arranged by category, it included basic Ming and Chosŏn history, the bureaucratic structures of both states, outlines of diplomatic protocols, as well as canned responses to inquiries from Ming officials. One such stock statement was a generic oral appeal to an unnamed Ming official for easing the gate restrictions. It addressed the unnamed Ming official with the colloquial honorific, *laoye* 老爺. Like So Seyang's petition to Xia Yan, it spoke of Korea's "constant observation of ritual and law" and how, despite being a country from "beyond the sea," Chosŏn had always been treated exceptionally by Ming, "just like a princely court of the internal domain" [優禮厚待比海內王府一般]. Therefore, when Koreans came to the Ming, they always felt that it was "just like coming home to one's father and mother" [所以我們人到這裏 父母家一般]. But:

> From the old days until now, we've always followed the rules. We never, ever did a single thing that violated the rules [一些兒也沒有違法的事]. During the years of the Zhengde 正德 (1505–1521) reign, there was a Director Sun of the Bureau of Receptions. Who knows what it was about, but he got very angry. And without reporting to the ministries or writing a memorial, he just decided all on his own to not let us come and go.

The complaint conflated the actions of Sun Cun, Chen Bangcheng, and Zhang Ao. Then it collapsed the time line of the appeals made to Xi Shu and Xia Yan into one generic narrative. Each element was grounded in an actual event, but it played fast and loose with chronology and omitted key details (for instance, Xia Yan never granted Koreans complete freedom of movement, not to mention a false sense of Ming policy consistency) to conclude that "in recent years things have gotten so strict, even more, stringent than before" [這幾年又門禁 好生嚴緊 比在前越發緊了]. In this fuzzy rehashing, this arbitrary imposition treated Koreans "the same as Tartars," and "hurt the rules of the former emperors," so the unnamed Ming official, the *laoye*, ought to "investigate past precedents and open the doors in according to them, so as to cherish men from afar" [望老爺查看舊例 依舊開門 柔遠人自行出入了].[64]

A stock argument against a recurring problem, the prepared speech promoted a specific vision of imperial duty while inventing a tradition of reified precedents for guiding action. This repetitive rhetoric established constancy and continuity in an asymmetrical political context where Chosŏn envoys had few, if any, alternatives for holding Ming officials accountable. But inasmuch as rhetoric could effectively dampen the volatility of the diplomatic environment, it was worth repeating, if only to remind imperial agents of the norms Chosŏn envoys wished they would observe.

Chosŏn envoys exalted the majesty and infallibility of Ming rule in order to constrain its arbitrariness within a guiding framework. Notably, this imperializing mode, once commonplace in the *p'yo* memorials addressed to emperors, persisted even when Chosŏn relied on informal communication channels with the emperor's subordinates. Snippets and phrases from the classical corpus had spilled out of the formal memorial, while flourishes from paeans to an emperor's virtue now harangued his humblest servants. They had become, to borrow the wording of anthropologist Karin Barber, "available for repetition or recreation in other contexts," infusing authority to statements made across a range of diplomatic registers and contexts. Rather than a simple repetition of "inert given[s]" of unchanging tradition, this transfer of enduring motifs required "constant activity and creativity" an act of "investment" in a particular rhetorical strategy.[65] The result was an illusion of ideological coherence.

Therefore, ecumenical language in diplomatic rhetoric is paradoxically both relativist and dogmatic. It is relativist in the sense that Korea's status shifted depending on context. Rather than an ontological determination, they were heuristics to guide pragmatic considerations. It was also dogmatic in that virtually no imperial policy and no discussion of such policy was free from this language. This combination of relativism and dogmatism meant that changes in Ming policies also entailed reframing Chosŏn's ecumenical status. Casting Korea as "barbarian" meant it was subject to the empire's cultural and political exclusions. For Chosŏn's envoys, the way to manage this problem was an autoethnographic strategy: to represent Korea's image in imperial eyes in a consistent and even reductive manner so that it aligns with the desired position on this ecumenical scheme, a point to be discussed further in the next chapter.

CHAPTER SIX

Representing Korea

There was no single "Ming" perspective on Chosŏn's ecumenical position. It also meant, for Chosŏn envoys, how best to describe their relationship with Ming depended on the situation. Much as Ming officials relied on different formulations to deal with Chosŏn depending on circumstance, so too might Chosŏn envoys pivot their rhetoric to accomplish their goals. Indeed, at times, Chosŏn envoys found that occupying an outsider position was conducive to their ends. When So Seyang protested hostel regulations, he cast Koreans as "men from afar" to invoke the imperial mission of transforming "barbarians" with civilizing influence.

Implying Korean cultural difference and inferiority, however expedient, also stoked other anxieties. In 1539, a Ming official processing paperwork to repatriate Korean shipwrecks referred to them as "barbarian persons" [夷人], a choice of words his Chosŏn counterpart Kwŏn Pŏl 權橃 (1478–1548) protested. He informed the Ming official that Korea had "for a long time used Chinese ways to change the barbarian" [用夏變夷有自來矣] so the use of this moniker in the official document made him "uneasy." The Ming official "laughed" and agreed to alter the wording from "barbarian persons" to "outside country" [外國]. The Ming official might not have intended to offend, but his offhand response to Kwŏn also suggested that, for him, the distinction between "barbarian" and "outside" was inconsetial: both were markers of foreignness. If the Korean envoy would be satisfied by one over another, it made no difference to him which to use. For Chosŏn envoys such as Kwŏn Pŏl, however, the matter was critical. Rather than hypsitivity to unintended slights, they understood that consistent terminology ensconced policy precedents, especially in official correspondence. With imperial agents themselves so casual about the matter, it was doubly important for Chosŏn officials to maintain a consistent position, especially for a Ming audience.[1]

The Chosŏn court's attention to consistency also produced a reductive, if not altogether stereotyped, image of Korea for imperial consumption. Typical of autoethnographic techniques, their envoys employed an essentialist rhetoric, one which fixed particular attributes—civilized, morally proper, and loyal to the empire—to Chosŏn identity. As this chapter will discuss, reminding Ming officials that Chosŏn was a "country of propriety and righteousness" was as strategic as it was useful. Beyond asserting Korea's cultural membership as a point of pride, it also anchored a discourse of reciprocity that made negotiations with Ming officials possible.[2] To appreciate how this worked requires remembering that empire did not begin and end with the Ming state. At least, in theory, an imperial tradition existed whose authority, by dint of putative antiquity and universal force, could bind Ming to common ideals, standards, and practices. At least rhetorically, through this discourse of reciprocity, the Chosŏn court could hold Ming accountable to a certain, if often imprecise, standard.

The cases to be discussed in this chapter concern the use of reciprocal discourse. First is the experience of a shipwrecked Korean official, Ch'oe Pu 崔溥 (1454–1504). Although not a royal envoy, he regularly interacted with Ming officials to ensure his safe repatriation to Korea. Ch'oe Pu's experiences and observations in China have been examined exhaustively by other scholars, but what is worth revisiting is how he also employed the rhetorical and ritual techniques of diplomacy in a distinctively different context.[3] Second is the so-called disputing slander (pyŏnmu 辯誣) campaign, a centuries-long diplomatic effort by the Chosŏn court to have Ming expunge mentions of regicide in narratives of Chosŏn's founding. Finally, the chapter turns to the attempts by the envoy Pak Sŭngim 朴承任 (1517–1586) to redress what he perceived to be an insult to Chosŏn's dignity as a result of a sudden change in ritual protocol. In each case, these Chosŏn officials insisted fastidiously on ritual propriety, an obsession easily explained away as Confucian ideological zealotry, when in fact they were also part and parcel of a broader strategy of diplomatic negotiation.

DRIFTING ACROSS THE SEA

Early in the spring of 1488, the Chosŏn official Ch'oe Pu learned that his father had died. Having been posted to Cheju 濟州 island only a few months before, he now had to rush home to Naju 羅州 in mourning. He boarded a ship that set sail for the mainland, but a sudden storm blew it off course, ripping its sails. After days of floating adrift, Ch'oe and his crew landed in Linhai 臨海, a county along the coast in Ming Zhejiang. In early modern East Asia, the appearance of castaways initiated a flurry of diplomatic activity, usually concluding in the safe repatriation of the stranded individuals. But before Ch'oe Pu could be repatriated, he and his entourage had to be conducted through Ming's official waystation system.[4]

The imperial agents Ch'oe encountered in the Ming interior, unlike those posted in Liaodong or Beijing, did not have experience handling Korean visitors. There were no cross-border ties, no Korean-speaking interpreters, and no "personal feeling." Ch'oe could, however, draw one arrow from an envoy's quiver: rhetoric. Like Chosŏn's official envoys, he too availed himself of autoethnographic and imperializing rhetoric. When he encountered difficulties with Ming officials, he used his words.

According to Ch'oe's diary, *Record of Drifting Across the Sea* (*P'yohaerok* 漂海錄),[5] when one of his Ming escorts, an official by the name of Yang Wang 楊旺, ordered the flogging of a member of his entourage, Ch'oe protested:

[Your] job is to escort us on our journey. Now, you inflict the penalty of flogging. Is there a legal statute pertaining to those from another country 異國人? The members of my entourage are as blinds and mutes; though they may commit infractions, you ought to explain the matter to them and treat them well.

Yet, you hurt them with beatings. This is no way for the superior state to conduct passage for men from distant places [非上國護送遠人之道也].[6]

According to Ch'oe, the browbeating left Yang embarrassed and speechless. In chastising Ming officials for failing to "cherish men from afar," he also articulated a particular vision of Ming sovereignty:

> My Chosŏn is a land far away, beyond the seas, but its clothing, caps, and matters of civilization, are identical to that of the Central State. And so we should not be treated as from an outside country in the first place [蓋我朝鮮 地雖海外 衣冠文物 悉同中國 則不可以外國視也]. This is not to mention that the Great Ming has unified all under its rule. Even the nomads of the north and tribesmen of the south are part of the family; all under this single heaven are my brothers, so how can distance in space be the basis of inclusion and exclusion [況今大明一統 胡越爲家 則一天之下 皆吾兄弟 豈以地之遠近 分內外哉]?

Ming's expansive sovereignty was bundled with obligations to all those who came under its rule. Rather than draw distinctions among peoples because of distance and culture, the onus was on Ming to nurture them through impartial compassion. But as Ch'oe insisted, Chosŏn was doubly deserving of imperial favor precisely because its civilization was "identical" to Ming's and because of its long-standing service as a loyal subject. Surely, if even "nomads and tribesmen" were owed this benefit, how could Koreans be excluded?

Driving the point home, Ch'oe reminded the Ming official that his duty as a "servant of the Son of Heaven" was to "nurture the small state [of Chosŏn] with benevolence" because that was the original intent of his sovereign and the raison d'être of his rule.[7] For an imperial agent to be reminded of his obligations by a foreign visitor exuded a delicate irony: the erstwhile outsider had become more invested in the proper operation of empire than the imperial official. Under other circumstances, Chosŏn officials might have sought special treatment due to Korea's distance and difference. Now, Ch'oe appealed to a universal magnanimity that could erase the distinction between "outside" and "inside."

The appeal rested on this reciprocal logic: imperial duty is compelled because Chosŏn's fulfilled its obligations.

This logic is also crucial for understanding Ch'oe's punctilious observation of decorum, even when it offended Ming officials and risked scuttling his chances to return home. Ch'oe, observing the mourning period for his father, maintained his mourning attire for the duration of his time abroad. When his underlings panicked, thinking that they would be mistaken for Japanese pirates and killed, he even refused their entreaties for him to put on his court robes, which would have expeditiously identified him as a Chosŏn official.[8] When offered another chance to clear up his identity by confirming the personal name of Chosŏn's king, Ch'oe again refused on the grounds that it was lèse-majesté for subjects to speak or write their sovereign's sacred name. His interrogator, a Ming local official, assured him that this taboo need not be observed in Ming territory, but Ch'oe answered that as a "servant of Chosŏn," he could not "change his ways" or "betray his country" simply because it had left its territory.[9] In Beijing, Ch'oe again refused to change out of his mourning garments into "auspicious garb" in advance of an audience with the emperor. Considering the precedents, the move carried considerable risk (in 1397, a Chosŏn envoy had been executed by the Hongwu emperor for wearing mourning garb for a Korean queen). To the dismay of his handlers, he spurned the imperial invitation, letting his underlings enter the palace to meet the emperor instead. He agreed to change out of his mourning clothes for only one, final imperial audience, right before Ch'oe's group was bound for repatriation.[10]

Ch'oe's observance of these taboos reflected his commitment to Confucian principles, as many scholars have noted. Indeed, Ch'oe belonged to a coterie of activist officials in the Chosŏn court who strove to implement Zhu Xi's family rituals in Korea.[11] As a Chosŏn subject, aware of Korea's marginal place in Ming eyes, Ch'oe was "zealous to prove [his] worth," feeling a "compulsion to prove by word and deed [his] utter Confucianism." But the fact that he would assert filial devotion and loyalty to his king, even if it meant defying imperial authority, requires an explanation beyond "sectarian fervor."[12]

Ch'oe's obstinacy performed also for an imperial gaze. Upon making landfall in China, he reminded his underlings that despite their abject condition as shipwrecks, they must always be ready to demonstrate that

"Our Country is one of propriety and righteousness." His underlings were to pay careful attention to hierarchical distinctions, always prostrating to one another according to rank. In front of curious onlookers, they should always do so with their hands clasped in their sleeves.[13] These gestures, along with holding observance of mourning, reminded their Ming handlers that they were civilized people deserving to be treated accordingly. At the same time, as denizens of "another country" 異國, their observance of propriety implied the universality of the values they embodied, one that, by extension, should have guided the actions of Ming officials.

Ch'oe, like the Chosŏn royal envoy, implored Ming officials to make good on their duty to "cherish men from afar." This imperializing mode appealed to imperial duty, while its effectiveness depended on autoethnographic collaboration and appropriation of imperial idioms. Likewise, the Chosŏn court presented Korea as a "country of propriety and righteousness" to activate the reciprocal appeal to an imperial idiom. No wonder then that the Chosŏn interpreter Ŏ Sukkwŏn showed such dismay when he saw in 1547 how a group of Korean embassy retainers "carried bamboo sticks" to intimidate and beat the Ming wardens in charge of the waystations. After the Ming wardens fled from their posts in fear, one Chinese official remarked, "I never thought that people from a country of propriety and righteousness could be as uncivilized as this."[14] One could also imagine Ch'oe Pu's mortification had he lived to hear of this affair.

As will soon be discussed, Korea's image in imperial eyes was a delicate mirage, one that required far more than incidental gestures or rhetorical platitudes to sustain. It required regular touching up and consistent investment on an *institutional* level, efforts that both determined and depended on the effectiveness of Chosŏn diplomacy as a whole.

THE DISPUTING SLANDER CAMPAIGN

In 1506, a coup d'état overthrew the unpopular king, Yi Yung 李㦕 (1476–1506), better known to history as Prince Yŏnsan 燕山君 (r. 1494–1506). The conspirators placed on the throne his teenage brother Yi Yŏk 李懌 (1488–1544), who reigned as King Chungjong 中宗 (r. 1506–1544). In a series of events reminiscent of Sejo's coup from half a century earlier, the Chosŏn court also went to great lengths to secure a document of investiture from Ming. This time, however, it was not an adult usurper consolidating his power, but a cabal of senior statesmen looking back on Sejo's methods for guidance on how to secure their new regime.[15]

The envoys they dispatched were given precise instructions regarding how to dissimulate. Some matters were to be relayed truthfully, but they had to deliver a fabricated account of the circumstances of Yŏnsan's abdication. They informed Ming court officials and palace eunuchs alike that the king had long suffered from debilitating seizures, which had only worsened after his heir's recent death (in fact, his four sons, all young children, were executed at the behest of the high officials with the reluctant approval of their uncle, the new king).[16] Historian David Robinson, who discusses how the Chosŏn court "lobbied" Ming eunuchs to ensure Chungjong's recognition, has noted the discrepancy between Chinese and Korean records regarding these events. As was the case for King Sejo's accession, Ming accounts suggest investiture was granted for "the purest of reasons." With the reasons for succession clear, "there was no need to investigate, for the Koreans were honest; there was no mention of bribery or lobbying for the Chinese were magnanimous and scrupulous."[17]

An envoy report in the Chosŏn *Veritable Records* tells a different story. Ming officials suspected "conspiracy" 謀作, to which the envoys provided their scripted retort, asking incredulously, "how could there be such a thing in Our Country, a country of propriety and righteousness?" [我國禮義之邦 豈有如此等事]. A lively discussion ensued at the Ming court. One low-ranking official proposed sending an imperial doctor to treat the king's illness in recompense for the king's "dutiful reverence towards the imperial court," although it was unclear whether he was motivated by friendly regard for a neighboring monarch or sought to use it as a ploy to ascertain the truth. Others proposed withholding investiture from Chungjong as long as Yŏnsan was still alive. The chief ministers ruled against all these options. They reasoned that, although Chosŏn was a "country of propriety and righteousness, it was still a foreign state" [朝鮮禮義之邦 然亦是外國], its affairs beyond Ming's capacity to interfere and "must not be dealt with in this manner" [外國事不可如此]. Rhetorically, Korea's civilized status precluded the possibility of usurpation, but it opened the door to Ming intervention.

On the other hand, foreignness placed Korea beyond the pale and outside Ming concern, allowing the court to set aside its reservations and abandon further investigation.[18]

As was the case for Sejo's usurpation, the true circumstances surrounding Yŏnsan's abdication were not so much concealed as they were overwritten. Korean records reveal that Ming suspicion could not be avoided altogether, but even so, no trace of Chosŏn malfeasance remains in surviving Ming accounts, again leaving two parallel but contradictory public transcripts of the affair. In Chosŏn and in its official history, Yŏnsan was an evil tyrant who deserved to be overthrown. In the shared Chosŏn-Ming diplomatic narrative, Yŏnsan was a dutiful king and loyal vassal who became too sick to rule.[19]

Maintaining these contradictory but simultaneous realities required careful orchestration. When Ming emissaries did arrive to invest Chungjong in 1508, they brought imperial gifts to the "retired king." By then, Yŏnsan had already been dead for nearly two years.[20] When the envoys asked to pay the "sick king" a visit, Chosŏn officials refused, informing them (as they were instructed) that the king was utterly "dependent on the help of others for everyday life"—he could neither drink, eat, urinate, nor defecate on his own. Quartered in the inner palace and attended to by the dowager queen, the king was in no shape to receive an imperial envoy.[21] For all intents and purposes, Yŏnsan's retirement (and continued existence) had become a diplomatic fact, a conceit shared between Chosŏn and Ming. Even decades later, Ming embassies continued bringing gifts to the "retired king," while Chosŏn maintained he was alive.[22]

Even after Chungjong died in 1544, Yŏnsan lived on in the diplomatic record. But why did Chosŏn insist that Yŏnsan persist in suspended animation?[23] For one, reporting Yŏnsan's death to the Ming would have invited an imperial embassy to invest the deposed ruler with a *siho* 諡號, the posthumous honorific title due to a former ruler. Not requesting one upon a report of death or rejecting them outright would have exposed the duplicity. On the other hand, to receive them would have provoked a ritual crisis at the Chosŏn court. After all, in Ming eyes, Yŏnsan ruled as a legitimate king, even if he had been expunged from the line of legitimate monarchs in Chosŏn.

To be sure, not every Chosŏn official approved of the charade. After Chungjong's reign, an anonymous compiler of his *Veritable Records* asserted that Chosŏn should have reported Yŏnsan's crimes to Ming from the very beginning and avoided this entire mess. Now, every act of deception only required further concealment of its deception" [因循掩覆].[24] By 1544, a Chosŏn censorate official named Chŏng Hwang 丁熿 (1512–1560) argued that Ming still considered Chosŏn as one among the "outer barbarians" [外夷], and could care less about the details of Korean succession. On the contrary, it was the "retired" king's astounding "longevity" that now stretched credibility.[25] Chŏng Hwang's was only half right: by 1562, it became clear to the Chosŏn court that Yŏnsan, dead for five decades, had been entirely forgotten by Ming because its envoys had not inquired after the "retired king" for years.[26]

Chŏng Hwang's argument relied on a logic of alterity. Ming perception of Korea as other and beyond should have afforded it leeway in matters of succession, enabling the charade to continue. But the very idea that Chosŏn should be treated as an "outer barbarian" was anathema to Chosŏn's other diplomatic priorities. During Chungjong's reign, another diplomatic affair explains why Yŏnsan had to be kept "alive" in the sixteenth-century version of suspended animation: the "disputing slander" campaign.

The "slander" in question was how Ming documented the Chosŏn dynasty's foundation. According to the Hongwu emperor's *Ancestral Injunctions*, its founders did so through regicide and usurpation, an allegation that made its way into other Ming official documents.[27] Chosŏn protested this charge as early as 1402, and it received assurances that changes would be made, and with the Yongle emperor's express approval, the matter was assumed resolved. The 1461 *Gazetteer of the Ming's Great Unification* reflected Chosŏn's demands, but in 1518, returning envoys from Beijing discovered that they reappeared in the *Collected Statutes of the Great Ming* (*Da Ming Huidian* 大明會典), spurring King Chungjong to initiate another round of diplomatic protests.[28]

The "corrections" that Chosŏn requested would have whitewashed the dynasty's bloody rise. Still, the Ming version did mix up several crucial details. For one, it erroneously identified Yi Sŏnggye as the offspring of an overpowerful minister Yi Inim 李仁任 (?–1388) (Yi Sŏnggye was, in fact, the son of a military strongman, Yi Chach'un). It was also not entirely true that Yi Sŏnggye had "assassinated the four kings"—King Kongmin's death in 1374 had nothing to do with Yi Sŏnggye—but the fates of the other three, U 禑 (r. 1374–1388), Ch'ang 昌 (r. 1388–1389), and Kongyang 恭讓 (r. 1389–1392) were another matter. The official Chosŏn position treated U and Ch'ang as sons of a Buddhist monk rather than legitimate scions of the Wang royal house (and being usurpers, their murder was technically not regicide).[29] Chosŏn also blamed them for instigating conflict with Ming, which was why Yi Sŏnggye ousted them in favor of a legitimate scion of the Wang 王 royal house, King Kong-yang, who later abdicated in Yi's favor.[30]

When the Chosŏn court sought to "correct" the Ming understanding of these events in 1402, it claimed King Kongyang "lived out his natural years." In reality, Kongyang was strangled to death on Yi Sŏnggye's orders. Most remaining male members of the Koryŏ royal family were drowned in the sea, having been thrown overboard while en route to their promised site of exile and refuge—all details recorded in the Chosŏn dynasty's own chronicles.[31] Distant members of the Wang royal clan still at large were hunted down and killed. Those who had received the royal surname as honors were ordered to revert to their original surnames. Those who happened to have the Wang surname but who were unconnected to the royal family were compelled to adopt the names of their maternal lineages.[32] Through outright killings and discursive effacement, Chosŏn eliminated its Koryŏ predecessors.[33]

Neither the Ming understanding nor the Chosŏn corrections conformed to reality. Ming allegations contained more truth in them than Chosŏn could allow. Its description of Yi Sŏnggye as a regicidal usurper undercut the politically correct narrative of Chosŏn's virtuous beginnings, but the sense of indignation on the part of the Chosŏn court was likely genuine. Although the sordid details of conspiracy and murder were recorded in the *Veritable Records*, given the limited access granted to the text, not even the king and high officials were necessarily privy to its secrets.[34] Indeed, when King Chungjong first learned of the Ming account of Chosŏn's founding, he expressed an incredulity that could only be explained by kingly naïveté: "how could my ancestors have done *this sort of thing?*"[35]

Charging the royal ancestors with usurpation was doubly troubling because of Chungjong's path to the throne. However confident (or anxious) Chungjong was of the legitimacy of his accession, the circumstances had never been disclosed to Ming. When Chungjong's court discussed their strategy for "disputing slander," they were concerned whether Ming would revisit the abdications of Prince Yŏnsan and even Sejo's nephew Tanjong from a century ago. The royal secretary Kim Chŏngguk 金正國 (1485–1541) mainly was unconcerned. He believed the envoys need not "embellish or fabricate" because if the true circumstances were discovered, they could always refer to the examples of Yi Yin 伊尹 (fl. seventeenth century BCE) and the Duke of Zhou 周公 (fl. eleventh century BCE). These ancient paragons replaced incompetent or tyrannical rulers with virtuous ones. As long as the moral basis of the irregular succession was clarified, the controversies surrounding Chosŏn's founding could also be resolved.

The state councilor Sin Yonggae 申用溉 (1463–1519) disagreed. He argued that Korea's diplomatic posturing thus far had relied on consistent dissimulation. As the grandson of Sin Sukchu (one of Sejo's coconspirators) and a scion of a family at the center of court power for generations, Sin Yonggae likely knew too well how Chosŏn's moral reputation was suspended tenuously by a web of lies. Revealing the truth of Yŏnsan's demise now would discredit the shared diplomatic narrative Chosŏn's officials and envoy had worked so hard to maintain. Unraveling the truth of the 1506 coup would also upend the accepted narrative of Tanjong's abdication in 1455, not to mention the story of the dynasty's founding the court now hoped to advance.[36]

The "disputing slander" mission in 1518 confronted several obstacles in Beijing. It was first stalled by the Zhengde emperor's extended absence. The petition also hinged on the Yongle period approval of the first emendation. Ming officials, however, could not confirm it from their own records. Only a ledger found in the personal possession of a low-ranking clerk contained a record of the Korean appeal from 100 years before. A more delicate problem inherent to acts of censorship was that spelling out what exact words were the cause of offense would also preserve them for posterity.[37] The problem even extended to whether the 1518 appeal itself should be kept in Ming records, which would also call attention to the offending details. Therefore, the Chosŏn envoy Nam Kon 南袞 (1471–1523) also requested Ming officials expunge the original allegations entirely from any record of this embassy. The envoys returned to Chosŏn with an imperial rescript acknowledging the errors in the Ming documents and promising emendation, but without any mention of what these mistakes actually were.[38]

To succeed in this mission, Nam Kon pled his case through informal channels as well. The official memorials addressed to the emperor obfuscated the circumstances of Chosŏn's rise, adhering to the orthodox narrative. Nam did the same in the letter he presented to Mao Cheng 毛澄 (1460–1523), the chief minister of the Ming Ministry of Rites. Rather than "prove" the Ming narrative incorrect with evidence, he relied on a different approach:

> We, the state of Chosŏn, are by the edge of the sea. Though we are faraway and humble, we have communicated with the Central State for generations and are well-versed in the teachings of poetry, writing, propriety, and righteousness. We respect rectified names and value moral relations. It has been a long time since we have "used Chinese ways to transform barbarian ways." Now, the time of the sagely dynasty [i.e., the Ming], its eastward transmission of civilization has reached us first . . . But as for assassination and rebellion—these are the greatest evils in all the world. No man can tolerate them; no law can forgive them. . . . As for how my country's founding ancestors treated the Wang house—all its details are clear in my petitions—they did not even menace them with even a hairbreadth's force, but yet they have now suffered [this] evil reputation. . . . It turns Korea into a lair of rebels.[39]

Korea's state of civilization and loyal service to the Ming meant that it was inconceivable for the dynasty to be founded in sin. Chosŏn was, by definition, incapable of guilt. Nam's a priori logic relied on an essentialist determination of Chosŏn's fundamental character. It smacked of sophistry, but was nonetheless rhetorically effective.

For one, the appeal adopted the positionality of an aggrieved supplicant in a legal plaint. Because assassination and rebellion were slanderous impossibilities in his circular reasoning, the damage it caused Chosŏn's moral reputation resulted in an emotional grievance (K. wŏn 冤, K. ŏguram 억울함) that compelled the just sovereign to alleviate. Ming, as Chosŏn's overlord, was thus obligated to intercede on Chosŏn's behalf.[40] Such grievance, if unchecked, would also hurt Ming's own reputation:

> What would then become of all that [Chosŏn] has learned from the Central State? The poetry, writing, propriety, righteousness? The moral relations and the rectified names [詩書禮義之教安在 綱常安在 名分安在]? [Those in the future who read these lines] would certainly all say: "Chosŏn is a country of assassins and rebels!" They would also say: "could it be that a country of assassins and rebels were among countries that paid tribute [to Ming]" [弒逆之邦 亦在朝貢之列乎]?

Nam transformed a controversy over Korea's reputation into one about the present prestige and future historical legacy of Ming. With this line of rhetorical questioning, Nam hit the crux of the matter. As a diplomatic issue, Korea's portrayal was not one of moral accountability or historical truth, but one of representation, reputation, and political correctness. If the situation were not "corrected," neither Chosŏn nor Ming could escape the searing judgment of later generations. Should "this small country suffer [the injustice of] an ill-deserved reputation" [小邦曖昧之名], then Ming, by "nurturing this small country," would have supported its immoral regime. A loyal Chosŏn was as the "feathers and regalia" of the Ming court [朝廷羽儀], and in this metonymic logic, tarnishing this imperial ornament was to spoil the empire. As long as the two courts were bound through a communion of tributary ritual, an immoral vassal could only mean an immoral empire. If the indignation of slander suffered by one led to the infamy of the other, then only by insisting that Chosŏn was pristine could the Ming remain immaculate.[41]

Ming, for its part, agreed to expunge the record, but following through with the promised revision was another matter. The *Collected Statutes* had only recently been printed at great expense; the court had no intention of reprinting it only for these revisions. Chosŏn was told to await the next edition for the approved revisions. Lest Ming forget its commitments, Chosŏn envoys continued the "disputing slander" campaign, expanding its scope from Ming official records to even private Chinese publications. When a new edition of the *Collected Statutes* was reprinted with the desired corrections in 1588, it seemed the matter could finally be laid to rest, only to reemerge a century later once the Qing dynasty published the official *Ming History*, which included both the offending narrative and a record of Chosŏn's centuries-long campaign to dispute them.[42]

The "disputing slander" campaign was ineffectual if efficacy is measured in terms of immediate results. It was also unsuccessful in the long run, given how the bowdlerized narrative failed to take hold. As one modern scholar observes, this failure reveals the concrete constraints confronted by Chosŏn envoys, who lacked any coercive leverage over Ming officials. As for why Chosŏn continued to protest, the usual explanation was that these "disputing slander" campaigns were tied to an overriding anxiety over the Chungjong court's political legitimacy, one which repairing Chosŏn's reputation at the Ming court could offset. In this view, the court's efforts to "huddle under the Ming umbrella," as historian Seung B. Kye put it, was to burnish royal authority through an imperial proxy, a response to Chungjong's anxieties over his authority at home.[43]

However, legitimacy conceived in this manner is too abstract and too mechanistic. It assumes the legitimacy of Chosŏn rulers at home depended on Ming approval, which could therefore compensate proportionally for Chungjong's deficit of legitimacy.[44] Several observations point to a more complex interplay of a Chosŏn king's domestic authority, diplomatic standing, and Chosŏn's general reputation. First, Chosŏn rulers desired Ming recognition in the form of investiture, but the rite confirmed royal authority rather than enabled it. Chosŏn kings always held their accession ceremonies before requesting and receiving the Ming patents of investiture that supposedly granted imperial permission for a new king to take power. Second, Ming knowledge of Chosŏn's violent origins did not stop Ming's recognition of Chosŏn for the last century. Chungjong, unlike his ancestor Yi Sŏnggye, received Ming investiture and reigned with Ming's full blessings. Finally, accounts of usurpation and dynastic ignominy, if they circulated as popular tracts, could, in theory, embolden would-be rebels, but in this case, it was formalized in an authoritative imperial text, generally inaccessible except to officials at the very center of power.[45] Together, these caveats suggest the "disputing slander" campaign coalesced not from perceived threats to Chungjong's regime but from something more.

One immediate threat posed by this account was that it would upend the delicate image of Chosŏn manicured over generations in the shared diplomatic record. Seen in this respect, the diplomatic urgency behind the "disputing slander" campaign was the need to protect past investments. A comparison might be made to contemporary disputes over strategically and economically insignificant maritime rock formations. In the modern legal regime of territorial sovereignty, incursions against claimed space must be defended at every juncture lest the disputed space default to another's control.[46] Likewise, assaults on Chosŏn's claims to "propriety and righteousness" must also be protested lest Korea's position default to that of an "outside barbarian," no different from other foreign peoples.

TO BE OUTSIDE THE HALBERD GATES

Pak Sŭngim, a disciple of the influential sixteenth-century philosopher Yi Hwang 李滉 (1501–1570), embroiled himself in a diplomatic dispute during an embassy to Beijing in 1569. Ming officials of the Court of Ceremonial had altered the protocols for the winter solstice ceremonies. In the past, Chosŏn officials, arrayed right behind Ming court officials, took part in the rites within the main palace compound. Now, Chosŏn envoys were "barred from entering the Gate of August Supremacy 皇極門" and forced to participate in the first courtyard after the Meridian Gate 午門.[47]

Worse, the Chosŏn emissaries were now placed behind scholars without official rank and untitled commoners. Because proximity to the emperor expressed prestige and distance corresponded with descending rank, Chosŏn envoys had now been ritually demoted. Whereas past protocols esteemed their status as royal officials, placing them only one step below imperial officials, the new rules underscored their status as outsiders. In the new scheme, Ming subjects, however humble, took precedence over Koreans as visitors from afar.

Pak protested the new protocol to the Ming ministry secretary in charge 主事 from the Board of Rites. In his petition, he first established what he took to be a proper understanding of Chosŏn's relationship with the Ming court before explaining why the new rules were such an affront. He explained that Chosŏn was "in name an outer vassal but in substance the same as [the Ming's] internal realm" [名爲外藩 實同內服]. This special status was due to Chosŏn's "loyalty and deference" and "admiration of righteousness," which Ming recognized [鑑其忠順 嘉其慕義] by "affording it ritual distinction from other countries" [遇以殊禮 別於他邦]. Overturning long-established precedents so suddenly now upset the distinctions between "the esteemed and the base," leaving "men from afar trembling in confusion over the reason" [遠人惶惑 罔知厥由]. Although they could "for the moment follow these new orders" [姑循新令], acquiescence would require "hiding and enduring [their distress], with shame on their face, sweat on their backs, and so ashamed that they could bear themselves" [隱忍遷就 靦面汗背 無地容措]. They could only "wonder with trepidation" what "crime" Chosŏn committed to deserve this treatment.[48]

Belying this rhetoric of helplessness was Pak's efforts to appeal to different bodies of the Ming government. He already demanded an explanation from the ministry's bureau director 郎中, who was "surprised by the recklessness of the change" [亦訝其變易之輕率] and ordered Koreans to be restored to their original position. These appeals, however, only made matters worse because Pak's entourage fell victim to bureaucratic malfeasance. The functionaries at the Court of Ceremonial (see figure 5.1) retaliated against these complaints by placing the Korean delegation even further away. Now, the Koreans were made to stand "beyond the halberd thresholds" [止之戟門之外] to find themselves among other tribute-bearers (most likely Mongols and Jurchens) Pak scorned as "left-lapeled, bestial-odored brutes" [左衽羶醜]. No longer a question of declining grades of prestige, the incident now concerned Chosŏn's identity as a civilized country.

His rhetoric took on a more forceful tenor once he finished recounting these events. Rather than adopt the rhetoric of a supplicant, Pak now spoke as a furious sermoner, fully convinced of the moral and ideological correctness of his position:

Howsoever the superior state receives its vassals and subjects necessarily involves compromises and alterations. Even so, since the time of the *Spring and Autumn Annals*, it was unheard of for vassals who came to their king's court to be degraded and humiliated by being placed behind the dregs of the base.

Those in charge of court rituals should always observe the old precedents with resolve, like the hardness of metal or stone. If it had
been a matter that fomented corruption or interfered with government or harmed the interests [of the state], then they should have
memorialized the matter. It would then have to be delegated to the
relevant ministries, who could debate and decide on a policy to
be proposed for imperial approval. Then it could be promulgated,
informing all, so there would have been no confusion or surprise.
If things had been decided this way, then it would be in accordance
with propriety, and [we] men of afar would have nothing more to
say of it [如是則處事得體 遠人無辭矣].

Having laid down to the Ming official what proper government procedure should look like, he then described what he saw to be a mockery
of due process. Rather than underlings obeying higher authority, Ming
officials acted in caprice:

But today, the imperial court knows nothing of the matter. The
relevant ministry does not debate the matter. There is neither
half a line of documentation nor a single explanation offered. We
were forced by the ceremonial officials with tongues flailing and
arms waving. They destroyed the old rules long decided by previous reigns and changed a harmless, existing law in a spur of the
moment.[49]

Again, Pak feigned incredulity. He "reflected on the matter over and
over, and could not arrive at an understanding." The only conclusion he
could draw was that Ming officials "saw us as lowly messengers from
distant marches, ignorant and without learning, so they [believed] they
could order us around with impunity" [必以爲偏荒賤价 蔑無知識 呼
來斥去 誰敢違逆 所以隨意指使而然也]. If their ill treatment could
be explained only by their discrimination toward Koreans, Pak then
showed, by insisting on proper procedure, that Koreans were fully aware
of the standards of proper governance.

He also made a bolder claim: Ming agencies should be held accountable to Chosŏn expectations. Whenever the imperial court received
embassies, "every announcement and every instruction should be a matter

of decorum and propriety. Every move forward and backward is tied to a question of rank and authority" [然竊謂朝廷接待外國 其一號一令 實體統所關 一進一退 乃等威所係]. As for arbitrary alterations to established protocol, Pak asked, "[D]o they not harm decorum and propriety? Do they not disappoint our feelings of admiration" [豈不妨於體統 而缺於慕望之心乎]?

Ming bureaucratic procedure should also be accountable to Chosŏn because its ruler had fulfilled all his obligations. In a logic that fits what, for instance, has been described as "role ethics," where hierarchy worked only as much as each entity performs appropriately to his position,[50] Pak reminded the Ming official that the "government of a [sage] King only promotes when there is good . . . and punishes only when there is fault" [王者之政 有善然後升陟 . . . 有罪然後降黜]." Meanwhile, the Chosŏn king has "served the great with utmost sincerity for many generations" and was guilty of "no transgressions," as demonstrated by the extant edicts of generations of Ming emperors who have "treated us with munificence and exception, praising and rewarding us." Korea had been faultless and consistent; any change on the Ming's part was a failure to behave correctly. It was the court's *duty* to treat Korea with decorum and propriety because it was what an imperial court *ought* to do in the first place.

Pak then drove home his appeal by describing the disaster that would follow Ming's failure to observe its obligations. The result was a cascading moral collapse that would leave nothing untouched:

> My country's prince had always feared the authority of heaven . . . [If he were to hear of this matter], he would certainly be alarmed and distraught . . . Along with all the officials and people of our country, he would agitate over this, unable to sleep or eat in peace.

> My ruler guards his small country and must attend to affairs from dawn to dusk. Since he cannot come [to the emperor] in person, he orders one or two of his retainers to present tribute offerings. Though we retainers are lowly, we are, in fact, the representatives of our ruler and are only well-treated because of him. Now we have lost our positions in the ranks and are left to pay our obeisance outside the gates. Though it appears [only we] retainers have lost

our places, it is in fact the disgrace of our ruler. Though it appears that only the Court of Ceremonial who humiliates us retainers, it is in fact the imperial court who, for no reason, humiliates our small country . . . The humble mission of one whose status is lowly like mine is not worth considering, but [what is at stake] is the munificent intent of the Imperial Court and my ruler's purely sincere admiration from afar, which has all come to naught.[51]

Ming records make no note of this affair, but according to the Chosŏn *Veritable Records*, the Ministry of Rites "restored the rank order to their proper place, and made it standard for perpetuity."[52] This appeal was as close to a constitutional treatise of Chosŏn-Ming relations as could be, an essay on how an imperial court *should* treat its loyal vassals. It was the Korean envoy who described what empire should be and why.

A gulf between professed ideals and diplomatic circumstance is never in itself surprising. What is worthy of note, however, is the intensity Chosŏn envoys invested in these ideals compared to their Ming counterparts. At times, the keenest purveyors of these imperial ideals were Korean sojourners who sought to hold reluctant Ming emperors and officials accountable, and not the empire's officials. When the Chosŏn diplomat Hŏ Pong complained of Ming policies, he said it was "regrettable" that they "fell short of the idea of impartial benevolence and treating the 'inner' and 'outer' without discrimination" [有缺於一視同仁 罔間內外之意]. Poor treatment of Korea was a betrayal of the impartiality and commitment to ecumenical inclusion implied by Ming's claim to empire.[53]

As Chosŏn and Ming diplomacy unfolded, two general patterns can be observed over these two centuries of peace. The first was how the tropes of moral empire had also come to reify an idea of what Chosŏn and Ming's relationship was and what obligations it entailed. Chosŏn's consistent performance of its civilized status and repeated demand for imperial accountability provided a shared nomos, or normative universe, to which both Chosŏn and Ming were beholden and through which representatives of both states could stake claims. With the rules of empire transcending both, the details of status, ceremony, and diction came to mean more than what was proper or effective diplomacy: they became matters of constitutional import, critical to the sense of what their shared political order meant.[54]

These patterns also reveal something critical about Chosŏn diplomatic strategy. It relied on the reproduction of certain tropes concerning Korea's relationship with empire: Korea's identity as a "country of propriety and righteousness" and a "loyal vassal," and the Ming's responsibility as a magnanimous overlord. These tropes were then reiterated by the rescripts and reactions of Ming officials themselves, lending credence to their effectiveness as diplomatic tools. As shown in this book so far, these tropes were deployed in negotiations over virtually every conceivable issue—bullion tribute, the arms trade, freedom of movement, ritual status, treatment of shipwrecks, investiture, usurpation, and historiographical portrayal. Whether rhetoric made the critical difference in any specific case is, of course, open to interpretation (and what theory of political causality one subscribes to), but at the very least Chosŏn's diplomats firmly believed in their importance of well-chosen words.

In their diplomatic rhetoric, certain tropes stand out for their ubiquity, a basso continuo that underlies every movement. Given these repeated statements of Chosŏn loyalty, Ming magnanimity, and common civilization, it might be tempting to see each as a defining characteristic of the Ming-Chosŏn tributary system. But again, it is worth remembering that diplomatic rhetoric was not descriptive; it was performative. Consistent rhetoric did not indicate a coherent system imposed on an otherwise messy diplomatic reality. On the contrary, the causal chain ran in the opposite direction: Chosŏn and Ming actors co-constructed and co-invested in a set of tropes that could withstand the vicissitudes of imperial politics. In turn, their reified diplomatic discourse addressed practical concerns obliquely by shaping a normative regime of Korea's relationship to empire. Chosŏn diplomacy worked not because it followed the tributary system's norms but because it helped create them in the first place.

CHAPTER SEVEN

Contests of Ritual

Pak Sŭngim could not have lodged his complaint (see chapter 6) in a vacuum. He needed a shared normative universe. By the same token, maintaining this universe had become, in practice, one of the main imperatives of repeated Korean embassies to the imperial court over the centuries. At the very least, its maintenance was necessary to the envoys who staked claims within it. These claims could be articulated through writing and speech, as the examples in the previous chapters have shown, but they could also be performed through the symbolic and gestural language of the diplomatic ceremony.[1]

Ceremony falls under the rubric of *ye* 禮 (C. *li*). A term usually translated as "ritual" or "propriety," it encompassed actual, performed ceremonies (K. *ŭirye*, C. *yili* 儀禮); the formal system (K. *yeche*, C. *lizhi* 禮制) behind these rites; as well as informal social conventions that disciplined body, speech, and composure (*chŏl* 節).[2] *Ye*, in this respect, is also normative.[3] When it came to Chosŏn-Ming diplomacy, rituals were proper when they affirmed Chosŏn loyalty and recognized Ming supremacy, in accordance with what both Chosŏn statesmen and Ming officials called *sadae chi rye* 事大之禮, or the "Rites for Serving the Greater [State]."

It was one thing to agree on what a ceremony should affirm or recognize. It was another, however, to coordinate how it would do so in practice. From regalia, banners, musical programs, seating positions, and the handling and wording of documents down to the number of kowtows, the sheer number of factors and variables meant it was easier to imagine coherence than to actualize it.[4] As discussed in chapter 2, significant discrepancies remained as late as the mid-fifteenth century. The codification of Chosŏn court ceremony in the *Five Rites* could resolve them only up to a point. Diplomatic rites, after all, were always coproductions; both Ming and Chosŏn participants needed to perform together, but what the Chosŏn court determined to be proper did not always concur with a Ming visitor's convictions.

A Ming envoy's proclamation of an imperial decree in Korea is a case in point. At this delicate moment, rhetoric and gesture came together to assemble competing cosmological, cultural, and political claims in one ceremonial space. Not surprisingly, the ritual invited controversy. For instance, its prelude, the suburban reception rite (*kyoyŏng* 郊迎), which involved the Korean king welcoming the imperial entourage outside the gates of the royal city, had been a contested object from its inception during the Mongol invasions in the thirteenth century until its very last iteration conducted to welcome Qing diplomats in 1890.[5]

Ritual contestations often concerned details that appear downright trifling to those with no stake in their outcome. But if, following sinologist Michael Puett, ritual "acknowledges authority relations and their consequences," then quibbles to an outsider in fact touched on fundamental constitutional questions. For those invested in its performance, a ritual operated in the "subjunctive," organizing the actions of its participants "as if" the social world created by self-conscious ritual action were the real one.[6]

These contests concerning how Chosŏn *should* relate to the Ming Empire indeed brought to bear a wide range of authoritative sources, including classical injunctions, imperial statutes, the imperial envoy's discretion, the Chosŏn king's obligations, and shared diplomatic precedent. The varied sources also implied multiple, competing notions of Chosŏn's kingly authority. For instance, was it derived primarily from cosmological sources, earned from a monopoly of cultural authority in the territory it governed, or simply granted by the Ming, as an acknowledgment of their status as imperial vassals? What if the imperial envoy in question was of Korean origin—to what degree did he owe obeisance to the Chosŏn king?[7]

As this chapter shows, these questions were never fully resolved, and the attendant issues remained in flux, explaining in part why generations of Ming envoys revisited and contested envoy reception protocols.[8] And despite the repeated wrangling, there were no serious attempts by Ming or Chosŏn actors to disrupt the envoy reception ritual in actual performance, suggesting a shared desire to ensure its seamless execution. Nonetheless, even when a working consensus over its significance had been achieved for the moment, accounts of ritual often diverged in Ming envoy diaries and Chosŏn official records. In these rival textual representations, the very fact that Ming envoys contested Korean diplomatic protocol became an integral component in the performance of Ming authority, one that the Korean court was fully aware of and even abetted.

UNSTEADY SIGNALS

Ceremony in contemporary international relations usually conceals differences of power. Flags of two sovereign states are always flown at the same height; heads of state speak from podiums of equal size, regardless of the size of their nuclear arsenals or gross domestic products.[9] In contrast, the rituals of Chosŏn-Ming diplomacy, when viewed in terms of their relationship to power, translate differences of power into hierarchies of status. Making status explicit managed the volatility inherent to this asymmetrical relationship. If the unilateral alteration of shared precedents could provoke misunderstanding and conflict, stable "signals"—envoys performing the expected rituals, proclaiming the expected edicts, and delivering the expected memorials—maintained the relationship.[10]

In practice, the signals of ritual were less steady than might first appear. In fact, they were often muddled by the very envoys responsible for tuning them. In general, a Ming embassy sent to Chosŏn always proclaimed some kind of imperial decree. The choice of who to lead them depended on the circumstance. Envoys from the literati-staffed bureaucracy arrived when proclamations (K. *cho*, C. *zhao* 詔) concerned imperial succession. To deliver other edicts (K. *ch'ik*, C. *chi* 勅) and patents of investiture for the Korean royal family,[11] the principal envoy was usually a palace eunuch, accompanied by a literati official from the Messenger's Office who served as a vice emissary.[12]

Until the early sixteenth century, the eunuchs sent as imperial envoys to Chosŏn were mostly Korean-born. In the first century rule, the Ming court generally sent eunuch-envoys to their places of ethnic origin or cultural affinity. In some cases, these eunuchs from far-flung regions entered imperial service as prisoners of war, as was the case for two famous early Ming eunuchs: the admiral Zheng He 鄭和 (1371–1433), who was born into a Muslim aristocratic family in Yunnan, and the Forbidden City's architect Ruan An 阮安 (V. Nguyễn An, 1381–1453) from Vietnam. Both were captured after the Ming conquests of their homeland and castrated (in imperial China, the process entailed the complete removal of male genitalia, not just the testes).[13] Korean eunuchs, on the other hand, were sent as children or teenagers by the Chosŏn court. A continuation of Koryŏ-Yuan period patterns, their arrival at first accompanied the presentation of young women to the imperial harem, though this human tribute of eunuchs persisted well after Chosŏn sent the last Korean woman to serve the Ming palace in 1427.[14] The last group of enslaved boys was sent in 1483, after which the Korean-born imperial eunuch would eventually cease to exist.[15] As one Chosŏn king crudely remarked, "there are no seeds for such things" [此物無種]—a statement that also reflected their subhuman status in the eyes of Chosŏn elites. But as long they were available for service, they remained important mediators between the Ming and Chosŏn courts.[16]

Ties to both courts, which made Korean eunuchs useful for diplomacy, also proved a source of trouble. When Ming envoys proclaimed imperial decrees, they occupied the superior position of north, with a south-facing orientation. Meanwhile, the Chosŏn king and his officials adopted inferior orientations. In proclamation ceremonies, the envoy was a proxy for the emperor's voice so eunuch envoys behaved no differently from their literati colleagues. Once outside this formal ceremonial context, the eunuchs' place of origin became an issue. In 1435, when hosting a banquet for the Korean-born imperial envoys Yi Ch'ung 李忠, Kim Kak 金角, and Kim Pok 金福, Prince Suyang arranged for them to face south, as was "according to precedent." Yi Ch'ung, however, declined and said, "I was originally a slave of this country, and now your excellency the prince comes to comfort me, how dare I face south?" Improvising, Prince Suyang and the Ming envoy sat opposite one another, sitting according to east-west positions of parity instead.[17]

By 1468, what had once been a ritual improvisation now became an established precedent. It eventually grabbed the attention of a Ming investigating censor posted in Liaodong named Hou Ying 侯英 (1430–?). He accused Korean eunuchs of harboring residual loyalty to the Chosŏn court. Explaining that these eunuchs were originally "people of the country of Chosŏn," whose "ancestral graves, parents, brothers, and relatives are all in that land," he believed they would "prostrate to [its] king and ask for favors, greatly undermining the prestige of the Central State."[18]

This whistleblowing prompted an official moratorium on employing Korean eunuchs as envoys, but it was either quickly lifted or never seriously enforced. When the Korean eunuch Chŏng Tong traveled to Chosŏn in 1481, he behaved in the exact manner Hou described in his protests over a decade earlier. When Chŏng was received in the confines of the royal quarters, Chŏng insisted the Chosŏn king occupy the superior "south-facing" position. The king declined, arguing such a "breach of precedent" would make Chosŏn "no different from the Jurchens or Mongols." Chŏng, however, retorted that, because he was a "native" 土民 of Korea, it was only right that he "face north" in observance of the "rites of ruler and subject." Chŏng then led the other Korean eunuchs to kowtow to the Korean king. They remained prone on the floor, refusing to stand until the Chosŏn ruler accepted their obeisance.[19]

As Hou Ying had observed, Korean eunuchs had good reason to perform subordination. For them, an envoy mission was a rare homecoming, a chance to be briefly reunited with family. It was an opportunity to request emoluments for relatives and stipends for aging parents they could no longer care for. Obeisance expressed as affinity to homeland might very well have been rooted in genuine sentiment, even if only because the Korean ruler was the best guarantor for their family's well-being.[20] For this (and their penchant for extorting treasure in the emperor's name), Chosŏn court officials judged Korean eunuchs harshly. Still, they also opened a communication channel to Ming's inner palace and the emperor too valuable and volatile to ignore.[21]

The behavior of Korean eunuchs and the fraught symbiosis they enjoyed with the Chosŏn court raised two issues surrounding diplomatic ritual. First, even if Ming claims to universal sovereignty were respected, there was no a priori consensus over where imperial authority ended and Korean royal prerogatives began. Second, ritual acts are not reducible to an "instrumental information code that conveys descriptive messages." Analogous to what this book has argued regarding rhetoric's constitutive and generative relationship to power, ritual instantiates authority claims rather than only describing them. Because ritual was what generated an "ordered world" that would otherwise revert to a "broken state," ritual accommodations to Korean royal dignity threatened imperial authority by positing other possible normative orders, in this case, one in which the universal reach of imperial authority could be set aside in the face of other imperatives of fealty. But as will be soon discussed, momentary suspension of rival claims and the accommodation of coexisting alternatives were central, even critical, to the practice of diplomatic ritual.[22]

THE SUBURBAN RECEPTION

Ming envoys expected the Chosŏn king to venture outside his capital to welcome him.[23] Departing from earlier Chinese imperial practice, the Ming court had codified this expectation in the ritual protocols for its vassal states. In 1370, only two years after the Ming foundation, they were promulgated to Koryŏ as the *Ceremonial Protocols for Vassal States* (*Fanguo yizhu* 藩國儀注). This early date of codification and promulgation, when coupled with an East Asian discourse of political ritual that emphasizes rectitude and timelessness, gives the false impression that the Ming system of diplomatic ritual was birthed fully-formed at the moment of inception. In fact, the 1370 protocols underwent multiple revisions (the text of the original protocols promulgated to Korea are no longer extant). Neither did they cover all ritual contingencies, so the Chosŏn court maintained its own, often more detailed protocols. The existences of multiple protocol texts meant inconsistencies and differences of interpretation needed to be hashed out on the ground before every diplomatic encounter.[24]

The rituals of Chosŏn and Ming diplomacy, more provisional than what might be assumed, were also more innovative than they appear at first glance. They did have earlier antecedents, but they were not transplanted directly from the Confucian classics or even earlier Chinese imperial practices. The Korean king's performance of the suburban reception, for instance, amalgamated preexisting East Asian conventions with Mongol practices in thirteenth century. The idea first appeared in the historical record in 1219, when Mongol emissaries arrived in the Koryŏ capital Kaesŏng bearing a letter from the Great Khan. Koryŏ officials tried to receive them as they would have a Jurchen Jin ambassador. Decked in full ceremonial garb, they would line the street from Sŏnŭi Gate, the capital's west gate, to the Koryŏ palace in welcome. The Koryŏ king would await their arrival at the entrance of his palace to receive them. Upon their meeting, the king and the emissary would greet one another as peers, both bowing with clasped hands. The imperial emissary would then take up a ritually superior position, standing while the Korean king prostrated to receive the still-sealed document from the emissary. Afterward, the document would be moved to the king's quarters for "viewing" by the king and his officials.[25]

Koryŏ officials tried but failed to enforce these protocols. They wrested only half-hearted compliance from their Mongol guests, who entertained different ideas about how they were to be received. As the Southern Song official Zhao Gong 趙珙 observed in 1221, when heralds of Mongol rulers traveled through conquered lands, the authority figures of the citadel or settlement in question were to "[kneel] down to greet them in the suburbs."[26] In the Koryŏ case, the Mongol emissaries were sent by a Mongol commander whose army had been assisted by Koryŏ forces in exterminating a rump state founded by Khitan refugees. Although they did not represent the Great Khan, they demanded that the Koryŏ king venture out of the city to welcome them.[27] Without some form of suburban reception, the Mongol emissaries refused to enter the city.

They relented only after repeated entreaties from Koryŏ interpreters. When they did enter the city, they refused to dismount from their horses, riding their way to their hostel. The next day, the envoys wore "fur garments and hats, with bows and arrows" at their sides during the court audience. The chief emissary marched up to the raised platform of the king's throne and grabbed the king's hand, into which he placed a letter he had been holding in his bosom. These actions by "hideous caitiffs" alarmed the Koryŏ officials, who now feared for the safety of the royal person. The Mongol emissaries were escorted out. The next day, they were coaxed to change into court garb for a private audience with the Koryŏ king.[28]

Understood in Geertzian terms, where ritual instantiates relations of power, the transgression of the sovereign body in the presence of his courtiers threatened as much the royal person as the hierarchies he anchored.[29] From the vantage of the *Koryŏ History*, where the account of the encounter is preserved, the violated sovereign body prefigured the dismemberment of the Koryŏ state, the scattering of its people as captives and refugees, and the subordination of the kingdom to the Mongol Empire in the decades to follow. Even so, it was unclear whether the chronicler understood the clash of ceremonial convention as a deliberate provocation or the fumbling of an ignorant "barbarian" interloper.[30] Mongol emissaries acted as personal messengers of the khan or other leaders and preferred to deliver their messages orally.[31] Meanwhile, as Chinese observers from this period noted, Mongol "courtesy" upon meeting was to "embrace" instead of bowing with clasped hands.[32] Considering the Mongol preference for oral delivery and bodily immediacy alongside a Koryŏ-Jin diplomatic protocol that involved neither, what did the emissary's final act of offense mean? Could grabbing the king's hand as he handed the document have been intended as a gesture of sincerity rather than a deliberate provocation?[33]

Whether the Mongol emissaries committed a gaffe, a provocation, or some combination of both, the incident underscores the opacity of textual representations of ritual encounters. Terse descriptions, such as those drawn from the *Koryŏ History* above, often comprised the total record of these encounters. Instead of transparent records, these descriptions of ritual reveal more reliably the historiographical agenda of those who left them.[34]

For the *Koryŏ History*'s Chosŏn compilers, their agenda is visible in the details selected for mention. The account of another ritual encounter, one from 1231 during the Mongol siege of the Koryŏ capital, notes how the Koryŏ king, although desperate to sue for peace, only dispatched high officials to welcome Mongol emissaries at the city gates. But upon their arrival, the king descended the palace steps to receive them; to show his deference, he adopted the inferior north-facing position while allowing the emissary to face south (another departure from Liao-Jin period precedents, in which the Koryŏ ruler "faced west").[35] The chief Mongol emissary, however, graciously refused to take a position superior to the Koryŏ king (foreshadowing the preservation of Koryŏ's political autonomy) but offended the Koryŏ court by refusing to change out of "fur clothes and felt caps," opting only to don the courtly "violet damask" over their original attire.[36] The envoys' untoward behavior, as well as the harsh tribute terms they communicated, made diplomatic breakdown and the resumption of war inevitable. The subtext here and elsewhere in the *Koryŏ History* was that the Mongols were yet unready for imperial rule. Koryŏ honored the Mongols, who agreed to preserve Koryŏ's political existence, but their ignorance of civilized protocol rendered them unready suzerains.[37]

Although these accounts of ritual breakdown spoke to Chosŏn period priorities, they were not wholly untethered from Koryŏ-Mongol political realities. When Koryŏ finally secured peace with the Mongol Empire, it was under the auspices of a Korean royal restoration, supported by Mongol military power. In the ensuing decades, the Koryŏ court implemented a number of ritual reforms (as discussed in chapters 1 and 2) to clarify the Koryŏ kingship's subordination to the Mongol court. During this period, however, the marriage of Koryŏ heir apparent, the future King Ch'ungnyŏl 忠烈王 (r. 1274–1308), to Qubilai Khan's daughter, Qutlugh Kelmish 忽都魯揭里迷失 (Princess of Qi 齊國公主, 1259–1297), introduced other complications to the issue of hierarchy. In 1269, because of the proposed marriage, the Mongol emissary Qïtï 黑的 refused to "rival in ceremony" 抗禮 the Koryŏ king and insisted that the Koryŏ king take the superior south-facing position during a banquet. He explained that the Koryŏ ruler was now a member of the Great Khan's family, while he, an emissary, was merely the khan's "servant." They settled on an arrangement of parity, where the two faced one another as peers.[38] The king, no longer to be "rivaled" by a mere envoy, could once again "face south" as sovereign, leading the "people of [Koryŏ] to rejoice."[39] The Koryŏ king's newfound membership in the khan's family meant that the emissary, as the great khan's servant, was now also a "servant" of the Koryŏ king.

Here, as elsewhere, the question of subordination was one of status, not of political loyalties or concrete resources that could be brought to bear. Nevertheless, ritual status mattered constitutionally, that is, in how Koryŏ and its ruler were organized under an overarching imperial structure. In 1274, Ch'ungnyŏl again "faced south" during a banquet thrown for the imperial emissary and the *darugaci*, the Mongol overseer. This time, the two guests disagreed on the degree of the Koryŏ king's elevation. The emissary received the king's offer of wine by prostrating, but the *darugaci* received the libation standing. He argued that the Koryŏ king's elevation depended on his status as *küregen*, or imperial son-in-law, but because the princess was not present, the Koryŏ ruler could not enjoy those privileges.[40] Before his accession, Ch'ungnyŏl "never traveled outside the city gates" to welcome imperial officials. After his accession, however, imperial officials warned that King Ch'ungnyŏl had now become the ruler of an *oeguk*, or "outer state" and was therefore obligated to perform the suburban reception of the imperial emissary like any local official bound to the duties of his position.[41]

Superimposed on the Koryŏ ruler were two different schemes of hierarchy.[42] Marriage elevated Ch'ungnyŏl as an affine of the Mongol Golden Family, which in turn implied Koryŏ was a princely appanage granted to one of its own. On the other hand, Koryŏ's status as an "outer state" required its ruler to perform subordination to the Great Khan's emissaries.[43] That a prince consort enjoyed greater privileges than a ruler of a state might seem counterintuitive, but only because the term "outer state," cognate with modern East Asian terms for "foreign country," implies sovereign statehood and peer status in contemporary international relations, a conception anachronistic to the thirteenth-century Mongol context. From the Mongol perspective, kingdoms ruled by princes married to the Chinggisid line, whether Mongolian, Turkic, or Korean, formed a screen around the Mongolian homeland. Koryŏ's distinct governing institutions qualified it as a separate state, but it did not free it from imperial authority. "Outside" status and the condition of statehood signified only the degree of distance from what was "interior" 內, a measure of political and familial proximity to the Chinggisid ruling house. For Ch'ungnyŏl, his prestige as an affine depended on his inclusion in the Mongol imperial order, one which reinforced Koryŏ's status as an "obedient" or "submitted" (Mong. *il*) state.[44] In short, a ruler of an "outer" state was still an imperial subject, and the performance of the suburban reception demonstrated his subordination, a logic preserved in later Chosŏn-Ming diplomatic ritual.

The Mongols were not unique in claiming universal rule over "outside" and "inside." The early conquest ideology of the Mongols, which understood peoples and polities beyond their control as "defiant" (Mong. *bulġa*) enemies-yet-to-be-conquered, later merged with a Sinitic idiom that elevated the emperor above all others.[45] Although the Ming founders cast their new regime as a break from the Mongol past, Ming still inherited Mongol period ritual innovations in its diplomacy with Korea. These included the expectation that Korean royals perform the suburban reception and that imperial emissaries proclaim orally the decrees they carried to Korea. What also persisted in Ming-Chosŏn diplomacy were the constitutional issues raised by the competing schemes of hierarchy embedded in these rituals.

So even though Chosŏn never secured a marriage alliance with its imperial suzerain, the dual status of the Korean king as both a local official and a (virtual) member of the imperial family remained. If the Ming ritual regalia issued to Korea's rulers, namely, a nine-inch scepter, nine-beaded crown, nine-emblem royal robes, and golden seal with a tortoise handle, were any indication, his ritual status was somewhere between that of a first- and second-rank Ming imperial prince. Indeed, one Ming envoy even stated that "the emperor sees the king as if he were [the emperor's] own child."[46] Meanwhile, Mongol-Koryŏ protocols for writing, addressing, and sending diplomatic documents, which deputized the Korean ruler as an official in the imperial bureaucracy, were inherited in the Chosŏn court, who communicated with Ming agencies such as the Ministry of Rites and the Liaodong Military Commission as peers.[47]

Neither scheme called into question the Chosŏn ruler's subordination to the Ming emperor. Less clear was how Chosŏn should relate to other Ming entities. The suburban reception, for instance, raised several questions that did not invite obvious answers: what was the relative precedence of the Korean king to the imperial messenger? Was the Korean king welcoming the emperor's delegate himself or only the imperial missive he was bearing? Did the envoy's status as an imperial delegate persist after the conclusion of the ritual? Did different kinds of imperial missives require distinct treatment? How should the Chosŏn king's other ritual obligations interact with the reception rite?

In 1401, envoys arrived from the Ming bearing an imperial proclamation of a new calendar. Later in the same year, another set of envoys brought the patents of investiture. In line with earlier precedents, King T'aejong led his officials outside the capital city gates to welcome the envoys.[48] In 1402, another Ming ambassador expected the king to do the same for him. But not only did he demand the king "welcome him upon the road" but also descend from his horse first before receiving him, an act the Chosŏn court interpreted as a sign of deference. King T'aejong remarked that the ambassador did not bring an imperial proclamation (*cho*), only a lateral missive (K. *chamun*, C. *ziwen* 咨文) from the Ming Ministry of War. It would have been a violation of "ritual" for him as a "vassal king" to show him deference by dismounting. Rather than contest the matter, the ever-pragmatic T'aejong sidestepped it by waiting for the envoy in an encampment outside the city. Since the king was no longer mounted to begin with, the envoy had to be the one to alight from his mount in front of him. By manipulating the ritual context, T'aejong satisfied the letter of the envoy's request—that the king dismount first outside the city—but made it appear that the envoy was the one deferring to the king's dignity.[49]

The compromise avoided further wrangling but left the ritual question of precedence unresolved. Meanwhile, unforeseen exigencies required creating new precedents, leading to finer ritual distinctions over time. When Chen Dun 陳鈍 (fl. 1453–1457) arrived in 1452 to proclaim the accession of a new Ming heir apparent, the mission coincided with the mourning period of King Munjong. The rites of bereavement required his successor Tanjong to wear mourning garb. Chen insisted, however, that Tanjong don "auspicious clothes" 吉服 appropriate for a celebratory occasion. He argued, "[I]n ritual, the low cannot abrogate the high." Mourning a dead king was a local, Korean affair, but "the investiture of the imperial heir apparent is to be celebrated by all-under-heaven."[50]

Chen treated the issue as one of hierarchy: the superiority of Ming prerogatives over Korean ones. At odds now were also two universalizing moral forces that demanded compliance: the sanctity of mourning as an expression of filial devotion in Confucian ritualism and the ascendancy of imperial authority that subsumed all lesser claims of authority.[51] To accommodate both ritual needs, the Chosŏn reception committee agreed to wear auspicious garb when receiving the Ming edict and to change into mourning clothes thereafter. The usual celebratory fanfare, including acrobats, musical performances, and festive canopies, were canceled, although the envoy insisted music should still be performed during the ceremony itself.[52]

There was, however, another complication. What should Tanjong wear during the proclamation ceremony? Tanjong's father had only recently died, making him the first Chosŏn king to receive an imperial proclamation appointing an imperial heir apparent *before* having first received Ming investiture for himself. The envoy suggested he wear the "robes of a crown prince" to receive the edict because the king had yet to be formally recognized by Ming as Chosŏn's king.[53] Chosŏn court officials objected. They declared it better for the king to receive the edict in the regal (rather than the princely) attire of scarlet robes 絳紗袍 capped with a winged-crown 翼善冠. Korean officials also proposed that musicians and instruments could only be arrayed during the edict's proclamation, but they should remain silent. To support this position, they leaned on classical precedents. The *Book of Rites* and the *Spring and Autumn Annals* both stated that "a ruler does not play music upon the death of his minister," therefore the emperor's emissary should likewise refrain from music upon the death of the Korean king, who was, by analogy, the emperor's minister.[54]

Meanwhile, the negotiations continued. On the day of the suburban reception and edict proclamation, numerous details remained unresolved. A few ad hoc adjustments were made along the way. The Ming envoy thought the entire Chosŏn welcoming entourage would wear auspicious garb, but he found that the attendants, soldiers, and banner carriers wore black-colored, round-collar hempen tunics—not the color of mourning but still too plain for the envoy's liking. Calling the garb "inauspicious," the envoy requested the retinue change their garments. To this, his Chosŏn minder answered: "[I]n the edict of the Ming founder to our country, we are permitted to follow our original customs in ritual; we have always used hempen collared tunics as auspicious garb." When the envoy learned that the king was not to kowtow five times but only three times to the edict, his Chosŏn minder again invoked the Ming founder by referring to the *Ceremonial Protocols for Vassal States* promulgated to Koryŏ in 1370, which required only three. Chen Dun then asked the king to perform four kowtows instead in a compromise that Chosŏn officials also found acceptable. The Ming envoy then objected to other matters, but again the Chosŏn court deferred to the *Protocols*. Chen, dubious, demanded to see the text of the document.

Once he verified its authenticity, he explained that Ming had since altered its ritual codes. Chosŏn should therefore reform its ritual practice according to current practice. Korean officials then professed no knowledge of the new codes. Absent a formal promulgation from the Ming, they "dared not wantonly alter the protocol" simply because of an envoy's demands. This argument convinced the Ming official to relent on this point. Once the details were agreed upon, the king arrived to welcome the emissary in his mourning robes but changed out of them to a plain, white, round-collared tunic, along with a winged crown, only at the last possible moment. After the ritual's conclusion, the king then changed back into his mourning robes and retired. His uncle, Prince Suyang (the future King Sejo), took the king's place as host, a compromise where the envoy was esteemed by the presence of a senior royal while the king avoided being present at a festive banquet in mourning robes.[55]

Throughout this episode, both the Chosŏn court and the Ming envoys insisted that *they* were the ones adhering to ritual principles. They agreed on the supremacy of Ming ritual authority and Chosŏn's duty to mourn but differed on when and how to give way to another. Chen Dun and his staff accused their Korean hosts of "defiance" and decried the "harm" to imperial ceremony. Like other Ming envoys who did not get their way, they threatened to leave Korea without proclaiming the edict. Chosŏn officials, for their part, retorted that they only insisted on ritual propriety because Korea "singularly followed civilized (*hwa*) institutions and observed civilized (*hwa*) customs" [一遵華制 欽慕華風]. Mourning the dead king was about common civilizational norms that even the Ming envoy ought to respect. Chen Dun and his staff turned this logic on its head:

> It is for this exact reason the Central State does not proclaim its edicts to other states beyond the sea [海外他國] and only proclaims it to Chosŏn. When it comes to music, it is only necessary to cease licentious sounds [rather than all music]. It would have

been fine if you did not ask me about this issue and did it your way. Now that you ask me to agree to something outside of ritual [問余以禮外之事], how dare I arbitrarily permit it [安敢擅許之]?

Chen Dun and his Chosŏn hosts agreed that propriety should be observed. They could not agree, however, on whose conception was correct and which authorities should be followed.[56] Multiple sources of authority—classical texts, Korean royal prerogative, Confucian family rituals—collided in the very moment that was supposed to align them. Even imperial authority drew from competing sources: the Ming envoy's judgment, existing Ming statutes, and orders from the Ming founder. In the end, Chosŏn deferred to the envoy on the matter of music, while Chen Dun gave way on the kowtow. Not stipulated in advance by any authoritative source, the result was less a coherent synthesis than a compromise of the moment.

The 1452 affair was not an isolated incident. Inasmuch as diplomatic ritual was a codified system, it was an open-ended one that was never fully completed—unsurprising given the variability of diplomatic exigency and the possibility that any envoy could always raise new objections. In 1488, the Ming dispatched Dong Yue 董越, (1430–1502) to proclaim the accession of the Hongzhi emperor. Having ascertained Dong's reputation for fastidiousness, Chosŏn officials anticipated a ritual dispute over whether the Chosŏn heir apparent, then a youth of twelve years, should participate in the rites. To avoid potential complications, they preemptively alerted the Ming envoy that the heir was ill.[57] Dong made no fuss about the heir apparent, but to Chosŏn's surprise, he raised another set of issues. Most of the issues were quickly resolved with compromises satisfying both sides.[58]

One matter, however, proved more trying. Dong Yue was displeased that the king would be seated in a palanquin when conducting the suburban reception. He proposed that the king either remain on foot or, failing that, be on horseback instead. He asked his hosts, "[I]f the Chosŏn king were to proclaim his instructions within his realm, would his subject receiving his instructions be carried on a palanquin?" In Dong's reckoning, the Ming emperor was to Chosŏn's king as the king was to his officials; what would be verboten to a Chosŏn official should also be to Chosŏn's king.

Some Chosŏn officials advised King Sŏngjong to accept the envoy's request, but the court mainly was opposed to this modification. The arguments were wide-ranging. One argument from the Chosŏn side was the palanquin was a "ceremonial implement" that "dignified" the rite. Receiving an imperial edict was a "great occasion"—for the king to be in his saddle would only ruin its "solemnity" and "injure Ming's magnificence." Another identified the palanquin as a modern equivalent to the horse-drawn chariot, permitted by classical texts for ceremonial use by the "various vassals of the Son of Heaven." Still others believed the Ming envoy's objections were arbitrary because no other envoy found reason to challenge this long-established precedent. No Ming ritual text, and certainly not the 1370 *Protocols*, explicitly prohibited the use of the palanquin.[59] Because the Ming envoy objected "without basis," Chosŏn could again argue it did not dare "lightly alter ancient precedents."[60]

When faced with Korean recalcitrance, Dong's predecessors Ni Qian and Chen Dun threatened to return to the Ming with the edict undelivered, but Dong Yue employed a subtler tactic. He and his deputy said, "[T]he king can decide whether he rides a palanquin or horse." If he chose the latter, "we would walk on foot," and if the imperial court learned that "we walked on foot" while the king "rode in a palanquin," it would be obvious that the ritual was conducted "incorrectly." They then reminded Chosŏn that even Ming imperial princes did not receive edicts in a palanquin. They then sighed, lamenting that "the institutions of this country beyond the sea" are indeed "different" from that of China.[61]

In the face of this cajoling, Hŏ Chong 許琮 (1434–1494), the Korean official accompanying the envoys, spoke to them privately. He told them that if the Korean king were to stand outside the capital gates on foot in the manner of a Ming imperial prince, his "officials and subjects would harbor resentment" at what they would perceive to be the degradation of Korean royal dignity at the hands of the emperor's envoys.[62] Hŏ's candid statement prompted Dong to agree to the following compromise: because the envoys arrived with two different kinds of imperial decrees—a proclamation (*cho*) and an edict (*ch'ik*), with the former declaring the imperial succession and the latter a command directed at the Korean king, they decided two separate rituals should be performed by the king, one for each decree. The king could welcome the proclamation on his palanquin, but the edict would be received on horseback because it was addressed to the Korean king specifically.[63] The Chosŏn king and Ming envoys performed two rituals for the same occasion, the Hongzhi emperor's accession.

The palanquin controversy of 1488 concluded with a creative manipulation of the ritual facts. The new ceremonial distinction this manipulation generated allowed both king and envoy to maintain their original stances on the ritual, but it did not receive universal acceptance.[64] In 1558, another Ming envoy refused to admit any ritual distinction between the two kinds of decrees. He asserted that "proclamations and edicts are all the same, how can they be viewed differently?" With the Ming envoy's stubborn refusal on a host of other technical matters, King Myŏngjong 明宗 (r. 1545–1567) threw up his hands and said, "[I]f the envoys so insist on their views, and they do not harm ritual propriety in a major way, we should just follow what they want and change accordingly."[65]

This sort of wrangling had become an expected accessory to Ming envoy missions. With that, the attention devoted to these rituals also shifted away from the protocols themselves or even the hierarchies they instantiated, to the process of contestation itself. With the lines of battle arrayed on shifting sands, each new contestation only led to the proliferation of new precedents. And as will soon be discussed, they also became a literary trope, a central element in the narratives left by Ming envoys of their sojourns to Korean.

TO SECURE SUBMISSION WITH THEIR TONGUES ALONE

Why did generations of Ming envoys contest these rituals? These contestations could very well have been a result of Ming uncertainty over what protocols to follow. Besides the discrepancies between the 1370 *Protocols* and later Ming statutes, notably the *Assembled Rituals of the Great Ming* (*Daming jili* 大明集禮), the latter's instructions were also far more schematic than what the Chosŏn court provided in its ritual codes, which likely left Ming envoys in a lurch when their ideas conflicted with Korean expectations.[66]

Moreover, imperial embassies were infrequent affairs. The word "ritual" might evoke a sense of regularity and repetition, but imperial accession and investiture occurred only as frequently as the life spans and reigns of kings and emperors were short. During the long reigns of the Jiajing (r. 1521–1567) and Wanli 萬曆 (r. 1572–1620) emperors, decades separated one mission from another. According to the 1537 Ming envoy Gong Yongqing (龔用卿, 1500–1563), he had tried to locate records of previous Ming embassies before departing for Korea. Finding the documentation of ritual protocols lacking, he kept his own *Record of an Embassy to Chosŏn* (*Shi Chaoxian lu* 使朝鮮錄) to save his successors the trouble.[67]

Herein lies a critical caveat to how these ritual contestations should be understood. They are only known in detail today because the parties involved found the terms of contention worthy of preservation. Therefore, what exists in the historical record is not "ritual" as such but its "textual practice." This distinction, as one scholar of medieval European ritual has argued, requires taking stock of these accounts of ritual not as sources to reconstruct what took place but as indicators of what *stakes* the authors had in representing them.[68] And when the "effects and consequences of such symbolic acts are not under anyone's full control," as another medievalist puts it, their extended afterlife in the textual record only adds another layer of complexity to the interpretive process.[69]

Accounts of these ritual contests survive in three different source bases. The first is the official transcript of these discussions in the Chosŏn *Veritable Records*. Chosŏn officials also occasionally left accounts in their private writings, as did Sŏng Hyŏn 成俔 (1439–1504), who had little good to say of one envoy named Ai Pu 艾璞 (1451–1513) who had more pedantry than character.[70] While official records from Chosŏn take care to document the procedure of each embassy as well as the circumstances of disputes when they arose, not all Ming records mentioned them, let alone delve into the finer details of the ritual contention. Despite his extended ritual dispute with the Chosŏn court, Dong Yue's memoir recounts only that Chosŏn had performed the necessary rites to show its "loyalty and reverence" that befit Ming's "esteem of the Eastern country."[71] If these contestations show a Ming interest in using ritual contests to affirm Ming's "superior identity" and confirm Chosŏn commitment to the "status quo" of the tributary arrangement, then it makes sense for the imperial ritual to appear unchallenged. If the aim is to have Koreans "[display] compliance" in the diplomatic arena, as political scientist Ji-Young Lee has argued, then indeed nothing would be gained from revealing how the Chosŏn court pushed back against Ming demands.[72]

Dutifulness to the empire therefore does not quite explain the eagerness of Ming envoys to incite these ritual controversies. The bulk of any Ming envoy travelogue was poetry and prose documenting their sojourn, as well as epistles exchanged with their Korean hosts, much of which also entered their personal literary anthologies.[73] A literati envoy, usually an official of middling rank, likely saw a mission as a stepping stone in what hopefully was a long, illustrious official career. The rare opportunity to travel abroad and exchange letters with Koreans could also burnish their reputations as men of letters. From this perspective, an explanation of Ming envoy behavior should not be reduced to their official roles alone; their ambitions also need to be considered.

The Chosŏn court knew full well that an envoy's behavior was wrapped up with their literati identity. As King Sejo once said, "[T]hese literati know only of the exploits [of the Han dynasty general and emissary] Ban Chao 班超 (32–102 CE)" and therefore believed they could, like him, "secure the submission of barbarians with their tongues alone" [此儒等徒知 班超之使外國 宣漢德 能以口舌順服夷狄].[74] They wished to live out a scholar-official's fantasy, where, by dint of personal virtue and literary skill, they could overcome the recalcitrance of any foreign prince, a trope that recurred in texts ranging from biographies of real envoys to a fictionalized account of an imperial embassy to Korea in a late seventeenth-century popular novel set in the Ming period.[75] For King Sejo, this desire to reenact Ban Chao's feats explained why a Ming envoy often harped on ceremonial detail, but it also came with a touch of irony because Chosŏn's ready compliance was, in fact, a *problem* for an envoy who saw his mission as an opportunity to develop his reputation. If the model envoy was supposed to teach Koreans proper ritual, what merit could the ambitious envoy achieve if Chosŏn already behaved properly?

This irony explains two things. It explains the moving goalposts of ritual compliance: why a set of protocols agreed upon by one group of envoys would be deemed inadequate by a successor. As one Chosŏn official remarked in 1488, these contests allowed a Ming envoy to "gloat about his achievements" by claiming he had succeeded in "correcting" Chosŏn's "long-time failure to observe ritual."[76] It also explains why records of such disputes did occasionally appear in Ming envoy accounts; they were narrated into the very trope King Sejo had disparaged: that the Ming envoys had cowed the Koreans with only caviling words.

In 1626, during the embassy of Jiang Yueguang 姜曰廣 (1584–1649) to announce the investiture of a Ming heir apparent, this trope took on new significance for the Ming court. Several years before, in 1619, a joint Ming-Chosŏn military expedition against the newly established Jurchen kingdom of Latter Jin 後金 ended in disastrous defeat.[77] In the aftermath, the Jurchen ruler Nurhaci 努爾哈齊 (r. Qing Taizu 清太祖, 1616–1626) wrested control over Ming Liaodong, cutting off Chosŏn's land route to Ming and disrupting the once regular tribute missions from Chosŏn. The delicate military and diplomatic situation only amplified the urgency for Jiang, who saw the mission as a chance to reassert Ming authority over Chosŏn.[78]

When Jiang arrived, he also encountered a ritual situation similar to Chen Dun's 1452 embassy, as well as Xu Guo's 許國 (1527–1596) 1567 mission: at the time King Injo 仁祖 (r. 1623–1649) was mourning the death of his mother.[79] According to Jiang's account of the embassy, the Chosŏn court wished to use the king's bereavement as an excuse to avoid performing the proper rites. Jiang objected to their proposal for the king to "not prostrate and keep his plain clothes of mourning." He argued:

"The celebration of the imperial court is a public matter; the mourning of your state is a private matter. As a subject, how can he abrogate public duty with private obligations" [朝慶公也 國喪私也 為臣子者不得以私廢公]?

The king responded as follows: "Loyalty and filial piety follow one way; private feelings are consistent with obligations to lord and father."

I answered: "Has the king not heard of the principle of transferring filiality to loyalty? Moreover, a three-year mourning period can be continued at any time, but the proclamation of an imperial decree can only occur on this day. Is the king unable to exert one day's worth of sincerity for his ruler?"

The king responded: "This small country is far away beyond the seas; its ritual garments are not complete, please understand."

I answered: "This is only an excuse! Your esteemed country has long been exalted beyond the seas for its civilization and culture [以聲名文物 見美海外久矣]; how can anyone believe that its ruler, the leader of his people, would be lacking in garments? Moreover, what has become of the embroidered robes, silks, and satins that our ancestral emperors have bequeathed upon you? How else are they to be used?"

The king responded: "It is but one month into the period of mourning; my heart is ill at ease. What to do?"

I answered: "If the king is not at ease with propriety, might he then be at ease with impropriety [不安於禮 顧安於非禮耶]? If I had been charged with proclaiming this edict to Japan or Ryūkyū, I would not make such demands. Even if the ceremonies and protocols are flawed, I have heard that the Celestial Court treats barbarians according to their custom, allowing them to their own sovereign teachings; this is to understand them [待夷狄任其俗 自為 聲教 體也]. But Chosŏn has received the teachings of the Central Efflorescence. . . . Do you not realize, I, the envoy, exalt the king with the rites of civilization, so what does it mean if the king still insists on following barbarian customs instead [豈不聞使者以華 禮 厚國王而國王 反以夷俗自處 其謂之何]?"

Finally Jiang told the king: "If the envoy knows [what is wrong] and does not speak, or he speaks but without conviction, then the envoy is at fault; if the envoy has explained what is correct, but could not succeed, then the fault remains with the king. If the king does not change his garments, then the edict will not be proclaimed. O King, reflect upon this with care!" With these words, the king finally relented, stating: "How dare I not follow your orders and change my garments?" Taken at face value, it appeared that King Injo could offer only the meekest of excuses, before being overawed by the Ming envoy's arguments.[80]

As would be expected, the Chosŏn *Veritable Records* presents a different version of events. For the day of the ritual, it only states the "proclamation and edict were received according to the [proper] ceremony." It reports a face-to-face "conversation" between Jiang and the king, but only after the ritual's conclusion, with the envoy graciously assuring the king that he could put on his mourning robes again once the auspicious day of the imperial proclamation was over. Initially, the Chosŏn king did insist on wearing plain black robes to the ritual; although the Ming envoy protested, it was the Chosŏn court's own officials who coaxed the king to comply with the envoy's requests to change into dragon robes, unsurprising given how Chosŏn officials had debated (and disagreed) over the proper way to accommodate diplomacy with mourning long before they received any notice from the Ming envoy. Absent from the Chosŏn records was anything like the castigation of Korean recalcitrance present in Jiang's diary, save one instance where the envoy objected to the court's use of indigo-colored paper in correspondence with him.[81]

Jiang's dramatized version transformed a mutual consultation into a one-sided show of rhetorical force. Whereas Dong Yue's account of the 1488 incident minimized the issues of controversy recorded in the Chosŏn annals, the Ming envoy in 1626 placed the spotlight on the controversy to burnish his image. Inhabiting a persona of heroic condescension, he parried the Chosŏn king's objections with an unbending appeal to what he presents to be the self-evident, morally correct ritual solution. Jiang's reasoning appealed to Ming sovereign claims, but the divergence between his account and Korean records also pointed to motivations far beyond loyalty to imperial interests. Jiang revealed a desire to follow in the footsteps of those who came before; for instance, he called for the local officials in Anju 安州 to perform what he called the "Heavenly Bridge Rite" 天橋禮, only to discover, likely to his embarrassment, that, far from a settled ceremonial precedent, it had been contrived by one Ming eunuch to extort treasure from locals. The reputation-conscious Jiang backed off.[82]

What mattered in these contests was not only whether Chosŏn performed subordination but whether the envoys could measure up to those who came before him. For the envoy, this involved a demonstration of his virtue that engaged Korea's rulers in this dance of recalcitrance, reluctance, and finally compliance. With the dance too becoming something of a ritual of its own, the affirmation of imperial authority too was about performing to the narratives that legitimized its exercise. The trope of a Ming envoy standing steadfast in the face of Korean opposition but in the end prevailing over their errors was precisely one such narrative. But here in 1626, as elsewhere, the performed ritual then was only half the story, a prelude to the trope's textual afterlife as proof of Ming's moral empire.

When Hou Ying protested the employment of Korean eunuchs as envoys, he believed that the blurring of ritual boundaries would cause Koreans to look down on the Ming court. He stated that, in Korea, "there are many who study books and understand ritual." If "the wrong men"—eunuchs—were sent, Koreans would "slight us." The "right" men for the job, in his mind, were other literati officials because only they could be trusted with conducting themselves properly and demand the same from Korea.[83] Indeed, Ming literati like Chen Dun, Dong Yue, and Jiang Yueguang did pay attention to ritual decorum, but that did not mean the ambiguities surrounding diplomatic ritual would disappear. In seeking to resolve areas of ambiguities, they also opened new arenas of contention.

These persistent contests also reveal how Ming claims of supremacy had to be confirmed with Korean participation. Rather than a one-sided Ming imposition, they were produced and reproduced through an iterative process of renegotiation, a "rule-based contestation," one that "selectively . . . reject[s], embrace[s], and internalize[s]" a set of institutions and values. As international relations scholar Seo-Hyun Park argues, it is precisely this process that produces the underlying "constitutional structure" of a hierarchical order.[84] Its production, however, did not preclude manipulation, dissimulation, and makeshift compromises. As this book argues elsewhere (see chapters 1, 5, 8, 9) regarding rhetoric, such disjunctions between political experience and idealized representation pointed not to flaws in the program but to ritual's very function in maintaining a shared framework of interaction.

Through the course of diplomatic interaction, claims of authority, whether by the Korean court or imperial agents, were never fully reconciled. Although proscribed by shared norms and common textual authorities, diplomatic ritual was not a closed, complete system. Like a Mandelbrot fractal, new but familiar patterns are revealed with every shift of perspective and additional degree of scrutiny. As the subject of contention moved to yet another detail of the ritual program, the Chosŏn court offered yet another concession to erratic Ming demands.

Tempting though it is to interpret these concessions as Chosŏn giving ground on sovereign prerogatives, this interpretation makes sense only if there were a stable perch to track which signs were "sovereign" and which were not. When the meaning of these signs were themselves subject to negotiation and transformation, such a vantage proves elusive, especially in the long arc of historical time. In other words, there is no unequivocal way to determine whether this or that change to diplomatic ritual was asserting or denying Korean sovereignty because the symbolic meaning of each element of a ritual program could always be subject to revision. A palanquin, a horse, a robe, the presence or absence of music, the use of this or that color—they could all be inconsequential details, until someone decided they were not.

Particular ritual elements could be contested, but what remained stable was the expectation that the diplomatic ritual affirmed Ming supremacy. This expectation also envisioned the relationship as one that operated in the world of *as if*s. It was one where the Korean court behaved *as if* Ming ruled Korea, *as if* its imperial rule were perfect, *as if* Chosŏn were its most loyal vassal, and *as if* this arrangement were eternal. In parallel with the rhetorical motifs of continuity and eternity discussed elsewhere in this book (especially chapters 1, 8, and 10), ritual instantiated a sense of order that transcended the political discretions of the moment. Contestations always referenced notions that existed outside imperial fiat and sought conformity with supposedly timeless patterns, whether elaborated in the classics or ensconced in shared precedent. At work was a constitutional logic, one in which the central question was not whether Chosŏn belonged to that order but where and how Chosŏn could operate within it—a question that will be discussed in the next chapter and that animated the literary expression of Chosŏn's relations with the Ming court in the envoy poetry of the *Brilliant Flowers*.

PART IV

An Empire of Letters

To arrange the visits of Ming envoys, the Chosŏn court relied on an ad hoc agency called the Reception Commission 迎接都監. Comprised of senior officials, including at times the chief councilors, it administered and negotiated ceremonial protocols, mobilized personnel, assembled the honor guard, and managed victual details down to the dishes and table setting at every banquet.[1] The commission also oversaw the escorts provided to the Ming entourage. Chosŏn appointed a reception envoy 遠接使 who traveled up to Ŭiju on the southern bank of the Yalu to await its arrival. As the leader of the welcoming party, he also accompanied the Ming envoys through the entire length of their stay in Korea. He usually served as their hostel companion 館伴, residing with the Ming envoys at their living quarters at every leg of their journey. While arranging the embassy's daily activities, he reported directly to the kingdom's highest authorities, either the Reception Commission or even the king himself.[2]

Chosŏn might have complained about the strict regulations its envoys faced in Beijing, but it imposed an even more stringent regime on their Ming guests. Under constant surveillance, a Ming envoy could not travel freely in Chosŏn and, like Korean visitors to Beijing, he was sequestered in his hostel, the Hall of Great Peace 太平館, after arriving in Seoul. A significant difference, however, was the dignity accorded to Ming visitors. Unlike Chosŏn visitors to Ming, Ming visitors were not guarded by low-ranking minders and protocol officers but were instead accompanied by high officials who reported directly to Chosŏn's king. In a context where interactions remained closely monitored and highly orchestrated, the Chosŏn court's honored guests could only see and hear what was divulged to them. Chosŏn officials who contacted Ming emissaries without prior approval or who divulged sensitive matters were severely punished, even with death.[3] Of course, seals on the flow of information could never be airtight, but compared to the multilateral diplomatic environment of early modern Europe or late nineteenth-century East Asia, where the circulation of the information supplied fodder for counternarratives that might supplant an official story, the early Chosŏn court still exercised a remarkable degree of control over what was communicated to its visitors.[4]

The number of Ming embassies dwindled significantly in the sixteenth century. In the early fifteenth century, Korean eunuchs some-times traveled several times a year to extract tribute at the behest of their imperial masters, but these missions ended (along with the eunuch tribute), leaving only occasional imperial embassies conducted for matters related to monarchical succession in both Ming and Chosŏn. Sometimes taking place only a couple of times every decade, such an embassy, which lasted a few short weeks, provided the only window of direct imperial knowledge of the country, a scenario conducive to the autoethnographic reproduction of Korea's stereotyped image as a civilized, literate, and halcyon society organized around the dictates of the Confucian classics.

Central to this hackneyed image was how Chosŏn "approximated" 侔擬 Ming civilization. As the Ming envoy Dong Yue had remarked in his 1488 *Description of Chosŏn* (*Chaoxian fu* 朝鮮賦), Korea was a place whose defining characteristics—the efflorescence of Chinese literary culture, the recruitment of officials through an exam system, and the use of "gowns and caps" in ritual ceremonies—were all reminiscent of the best Ming practices. Even when Dong noticed stark differences between Chosŏn and Ming, for example, the existence of the *yangban* aristocracy, the absence of metallic currency, and the ban on widow remarriage, he still attributed them to Korea having "observed the Central State and copying it." For Dong Yue and other Ming envoys who viewed Korea through "imperial eyes," Chosŏn "propriety and righteousness" mattered ultimately as a demonstration of Ming's civilizing power.[5]

The primacy of Ming's civilization power was not only a figment of the Ming envoy's imagination. The idea pervaded the diplomatic record. It was articulated in the presence of the envoy's Korean hosts and augmented by the compositions of Chosŏn's own poet-officials. The Chosŏn court assembled these exchanges in a series of compilations called the *Brilliant Flowers Anthologies* (*Hwanghwajip* 皇華集). Produced after each literati-led envoy mission between 1457 and 1633 (twenty-five times, as well as one retrospective anthology of the 1450 mission), these anthologies together comprise 6,500 individual pieces of prose and verse, ranging from brief quatrains to extended meditations sustained over sixty or seventy couplets.[6]

The *Brilliant Flowers* was a monument to the "literary diplomacy" (C. *shifu waijiao*, K. *sibu oegyo* 詩賦外交), a style of diplomacy long associated with the "ideal" form of tributary relations that Chosŏn-Ming relations represented. Scholars have contrasted this "literary diplomacy" to the early Ming's assertive (and acquisitive) diplomacy until the debacle at Tumu in 1449. In this view, decades of military decline and weaker emperors allowed the reins of diplomacy to pass from the eunuchs of the inner palace, bound by personal loyalty to the emperor, to Ming's literati-controlled bureaucracy. The persistence of Korean eunuch-led embassies through the Zhengde reigns belies this simplistic picture of transition, but if diplomacy in the intervening period between 1449 and 1521 can be seen as a tug-of-war between two imperial modes—the patrimonial style of emperors and eunuchs versus the bureaucratic style of literati Grand Secretaries—then the *Brilliant Flowers* is emblematic of the ideals of civil rule and literary virtue, or *wende* 文德 (K. *mundŏk*) celebrated by the latter.[7]

Although the larger pattern holds over the two centuries of Chosŏn-Ming relations, "literary diplomacy" should not be idealized either in moral or historical terms. Poetry was no more inherent to Chosŏn-Ming diplomacy than the extortions of Ming envoys were an aberration. Poetry and the values did nevertheless bind the educated elites of the two courts together, while largely excluding other actors who played essential roles in diplomacy—Korea's professional interpreters, court painters, the military men of Liaodong, Ming eunuchs, anonymous porters, and female entertainers—but could not participate as social equals in its literary culture. Inasmuch as the era of the *Brilliant Flowers* represented any "ideal," it was one envisioned by Confucian men of letters. that the diplomatic record testifies to this ideal was in part because these elite men of letters were who left the literary testimonies to that ideal in the first place. All this is to say, the exclusivity of the *Brilliant Flowers* was by design—it was a way to perpetuate am mythology of Ming's civilizing agency and moral imperium.

The following chapters concern how this mythology was constructed through the literary sociability of the *Brilliant Flowers*. They also reveal what ends it served and what contradictions it generated. Chapter 8 addresses the multivocality of the *Brilliant Flowers* by showing how it juxtaposed a variety of narratives regarding Chosŏn vis-à-vis imperial authority, allowing them to exist in superimposition rather than as a monolith. Chapter 9 turns to the synecdochal relationship between an envoy's literary performance of personal virtue and the ideal of a moral empire based on *wende*, a performance with an afterlife that far outlasted the Ming dynasty itself. Chapter 10 turns to the spatial and physical embodiment of envoy writing. It discusses how the Chosŏn court used a sociability of space to claim ancient history and enlist Ming envoy-poets to anchor its political identity.

CHAPTER EIGHT

The Brilliant Flowers

The Chosŏn court abolished the poetry section of its civil service exams in 1444 because of its "frivolity" compared to classical scholarship. But the section was restored in 1453, three years after Ni Qian's mission in 1450, which reminded the court how important poetic craft could be for diplomacy.[1] Chosŏn investment in literary diplomacy at first responded to changing winds at the Ming court, even though the later role it played in nurturing its growth should not be overlooked. The result was a mutually reinforcing dynamic: with poetry becoming inseparable from diplomacy, Ming too was encouraged to interact with Chosŏn through this channel. Just as Chosŏn selected talented writers to accompany Ming visitors, Ming too selected men of literary ability to satisfy Korean expectations.[2] Neither an accidental conjunction nor a mere barometer of Ming political shifts, the fact that the *Brilliant Flowers* endured over two centuries was a desired outcome of Chosŏn's approach to diplomacy.

Although a *Brilliant Flowers* anthology exists for Ni Qian's mission in 1450, it was printed retroactively. The first time the Chosŏn court created a *Brilliant Flowers* anthology was 1457, when one was printed after the embassy announcing Emperor Yingzong's restoration to the throne. The emperor had returned to power after a long captivity, first with the Oirats and later under house arrest in Beijing. The sparse records from the period leave no explanation for why the Chosŏn court produced the 1457 anthology, but its material history leaves some clues. Originally printed using the metal Kabin 甲寅 font of 1434, each individual edition of *Brilliant Flowers* could be typeset quickly after the conclusion of an embassy, but compared to carved woodblock printing, the print runs were short (likely in the dozens) and ephemeral. Metal typography's slow rate of printing (around forty sheets a day) and the fact that the metal type would be disassembled after a print run was finished meant that the state likely printed only enough copies for an immediate purpose, enough to serve as mementos for visiting envoys and as gifts to Ming notables and to stock the Chosŏn's court libraries—and not much more.[3] The anthology was never intended for wide distribution and was more likely a personal favor to the envoys Chen Jian 陳鑑 (1415–1471) and Gao Run 高閏 (fl. 1457) than a propaganda effort intended for a wider imperial audience.[4] Nevertheless, the anthology, as a diplomatic gift, could have reaffirmed Chosŏn fealty to an embattled Ming dynastic house. Or King Sejo, anxious about his legitimacy, published this anthology to remind Ming of his obedience.[5]

Whatever motivated its creation, the *Brilliant Flowers* grew over time into something much bigger than the anthologies' physical tomes. Ming embassies to Korea, unlike the ritually timed Korean embassies to Beijing, were ad hoc responses to singular concerns. Nonetheless, they generated their own rhythms, timed not to the clockwork of ritual but to the prosody of a lyrical poem. With every generation, a new cohort of Ming and Chosŏn literati revisited spaces once trod by their predecessors, recycling their old rhymes, tropes, and themes. As their intercourse bound literary and political concerns in this exclusive social space, they also wove a web of personal connections and intertextual links in China and Korea.[6] After repeated compilations and reprinting, the anthologies ceased only with the end of Chosŏn-Ming relations in 1633.[7]

What then did envoy poetry accomplish? When a Ming official could see his Chosŏn counterparts as fellow men of letters, it assured Chosŏn's status as a civilized realm in Ming imperial imagination. Poetry anchored that shared cultural imaginary, a cosmopolis bound by shared cultural transmission and sustained by a common script.[8] Literary exchange also fostered a sense of coevality—a lateral, horizontal sense of belonging instead of the hierarchical, vertical subordination instantiated in formal diplomatic rituals. To be sure, the *Brilliant Flowers* still coded hierarchy in its very material form. In its typesetting, the anthologies elevated references to the Ming emperor two spaces, while mention of Chosŏn's king or the imperial emissary received only one space of elevation, a convention observed in other records of diplomacy from the period. Still, the practices surrounding the *Brilliant Flowers* posited alternative ways to inscribe the imperial envoy's relationship to Korea—that of peers in cultural attainment.[9]

These two scales of integration, one horizontal and the other vertical, touch on a central question of the *Brilliant Flowers*: how does literary production relate to imperial ideology? The polysemy of its title, *hwanghwa* (C. *huanghua* 皇華), is a case in point. Its components, breaking down into *hwang* (august, brilliant, or imperial) and *hwa* (efflorescence, civilization, or China), allow for several interpretations, but in any combination, even as "august efflorescence" (arguably the least politically explicit possibility), links literary and cultural power to imperial authority. Yet the most politically explicit rendering of the term *hwanghwa* as "imperial China" (in the instinct of a modern reader) was a valence never invoked in the *Brilliant Flowers* themselves.[10] Instead, the title drew attention to a piece in the *Book of Songs* (*Shijing* 詩經) whose affective image (C. *xing* 興) of flowers blooming brilliantly across the landscape (C. *huanghuangzhe hua* 皇皇者華) evoked a Zhou royal emissary who traveled tirelessly to the many feudal states to procure virtuous men for his ruler.[11]

These crossings between past and present, empire and poetry, Chosŏn and Ming were also fostered by the literary sociability of these anthologies. In every sense a joint production, Ming envoys and their Chosŏn interlocutors gathered to harmonize their celebrations of Ming rule. By extension, they advanced a distinct narrative of what empire was and should be. This chapter will show how, within the circumscribed social space of diplomatic poetry, Ming envoys and their Chosŏn hosts calibrated their visions of empire. At stake was never the legitimacy of the Ming's claim to empire per se but the configuration of the claim, precisely how questions of territoriality, ecumenical belonging, political authority, and the emperor as sovereign were interconnected.

Poetry had long been a mainstay of East Asian diplomatic practice.[12] Even rare literary anthologies surviving from the twelfth century include a handful of poems written by Jin imperial officials addressing their Koryŏ counterparts.[13] Koryŏ and Chosŏn envoys (as well as Vietnamese envoys) included such poems in their personal travelogues of their sojourns to China.[14] There was also Kwŏn Kŭn's celebrated exchange with the Hongwu emperor. Its original manuscript (now lost) also invited colophons from Ming visitors to Korea,[15] who in turn capped verses with Korea's kings.[16]

Several features set the *Brilliant Flowers* apart from its antecedents. Before the *Brilliant Flowers*, Chosŏn-Ming envoy poems appeared only in individual anthologies 別集 published by returning envoys as part of their collected works. Ming envoys tended to showcase their own writing, including only a selection of Korean poems. This selectivity, exhibited in the envoy Ni Qian's travelogue, became a sore issue in Korea. The Chosŏn statesman Sŏ Kŏjŏng concluded that Ni "sought to make himself look better by highlighting his own poetry over that of great Chosŏn writers."[17] The *Brilliant Flowers*, by contrast, was a result of state investment in literary sociability; it always juxtaposed the works of Chosŏn courtiers with those of the envoys they entertained (see table 8.1).

Reminders of the envoy poem's social character pervaded the prefaces, titles, and postscripts in the *Brilliant Flowers*. Indeed, the typical *Brilliant Flowers* poem was exchanged as *ch'aun* (C. *ciyun* 次韻) or rhyme-matched verses.[18] The 1460 envoy Zhang Ning described the practice as one of recent provenance, dating only as far back as the Song poet Su Shi, but when he ascended the Pavilion of a Myriad Scenes 萬景樓 and saw the hanging inscriptions of the 1457 envoy Chen Jian describing his ascent to the same lookout, he could not "avoid following the custom."[19]

Ming envoys continued to read, comment on, and respond to the verses of their predecessors during the whole length of their journey. When an envoy wrote in the footsteps of his predecessors to secure his position among their ranks, any site treated by one envoy could inspire dozens more in the decades to follow. As they revisited old themes with recycled rhymes, they linked themselves to every Ming embassy that

TABLE 8.1
The Brilliant Flowers and Ming Embassies

Year of Embassy	Chief Envoy	Deputy Envoy	Korean Welcoming Emissary (*wŏnjŏpsa*)	Fascicle in 1773 Edition of *Brilliant Flowers*
1449–1450	Ni Qian 倪謙 (1415–1479)	Sima Xun 司馬恂 (?–1466)	Chŏng Inji 鄭麟趾 (1396–1478)	1
1457	Chen Jian 陳鑑 (1415–1471)	Gao Run 高閏 (fl. 1457)	Pak Wŏnhyŏng 朴元亨 (1411–1469)	2–3
1459	Chen Jiayou 陳嘉猷 (1421–1467)		Pak Wŏnhyŏng	4
1460	Zhang Ning 張寧 (1426–1496)	Wu Zhong 武忠 (?–1470)	Pak Wŏnhyŏng	5
1464	Jin Shi 金湜 (fl. 1441–1467)	Zhang Cheng 張珹 (1425–1470)	Pak Wŏnhyŏng	6–7
1476	Qi Shun 祁順 (1434–1497)	Zhang Jin 張瑾 (1448–1481)	Sŏ Kŏjŏng 徐居正 (1420–1488)	8–9
1488	Dong Yue 董越 (1430–1502)	Wang Chang 王敞 (1453–1515)	Hŏ Chong 許琮 (1434–1494)	10–12
1492	*	Ai Pu 艾璞 (1450–1512)	No Kongp'il 盧公弼 (1445–1516)	13
1506	Xu Mu 徐穆 (1467–1511)		Im Sahong 任士洪 (1445–1506)	13
1521	Tang Gao 唐皋 (1469–1526)	Shi Dao 史道 (1485–1554)	Yi Haeng 李荇 (1478–1534)	14–17
1537	Gong Yongqing 龔用卿 (1500–1563)	Wu Ximeng 吳希孟 (1508–?)	Chŏng Saryong 鄭士龍 (1491–1570)	18–22
1539	Hua Cha 華察 (1497–1574)	Xue Tingchong 薛廷籠 (fl. 1532–1539)	So Seyang 蘇世讓 (1486–1562)	23–27
1545	*	Zhang Chengxian 張承憲 (?)	Sin Kwanghan 申光漢 (1484–1555)	28
1546	*	Wang He 王鶴 (1516–?)	Chŏng Saryong	29

(continued)

TABLE 8.1 (*Continued*)
The Brilliant Flowers and Ming Embassies

Year of Embassy	Chief Envoy	Deputy Envoy	Korean Welcoming Emissary (*wŏnjŏpsa*)	Fascicle in 1773 Edition of *Brilliant Flowers*
1567	Xu Guo 許國 (1527–1596)	Wei Shiliang 魏時亮 (1529–1585)	Pak Ch'ungwŏn 朴忠元 (1507–1581)	30
1568	*	Ou Xiji 歐希稷 (1534–?)	Pak Sun 朴淳 (1523–1589)	31
1568	Cheng Xian 成憲 (?)	Wang Xi 王璽 (?)	Pak Sun	32
1573	Han Shineng 韓世能 (1528–1598)	Chen Sanmo 陳三謨 (?)	Chŏng Yugil 鄭惟吉 (1515–1588)	33–34
1582	Huang Hongxian 黃洪憲 (1541–1600)	Wang Jingmin 王敬民 (?)	Yi I 李珥 (1536–1584)	35–36
1602	Gu Tianjun 顧天埈 (1561–?)	Cui Tingjian 崔廷健 (?)	Yi Homin 李好閔 (1553–1634)	37
1606	Zhu Zhifan 朱之蕃 (1558–1626)	Liang Younian 梁有年 (?–1614)	Yu Kŭn 柳根 (1549–1627)	38–42
1609	Xiong Hua 熊化 (?–1649)		Yu Kŭn	43
1621	Liu Hongxun 劉鴻訓 (1565–1634)	Yang Daoyin 楊道寅 (?)	Yi Ich'ŏm 李爾瞻 (1560–1623)	**
1626	Jiang Yueguang 姜曰廣 (1584–1649)	Wang Mengyin 王夢尹 (1649)	Kim Ryu 金鎏 (1571–1648)	44–47
1633	Cheng Long 程龍 (?–1637)		Sin Kyeyŏng 申啓榮 (1577–1669)	48–50

Table based on Zhao Ii, *Zuben Huanghua ji* 足本皇華集 (Nanjing: Fenghuang chubanshe, 2013), 1779–1958; Du Huiyue, *Mingdai wenchen chushi Chaoxian yu "Huanghuaji"* (Beijing: Renmin chubanshe, 2010), 18–19.
*Chief envoy not literatus
**Lost in Chosŏn

came before. As the 1476 Ming envoy Qi Shun put it when he passed by Shanhai Pass: "an envoy from the central academy comes here once again / and loves to put old subjects in new verses" [中臺使節今重到愛把新詩續舊體].[20] Ming envoys recognized how their work in Korea could secure lasting, even posthumous reputations, and they eagerly adorned Korean edifices and scenic vistas (a practice to be discussed further in chapter 10).

Not every matched verse required consulting a physical, epigraphic inscription. Many envoys did just as well with earlier editions of the *Brilliant Flowers*. In the spring of 1537, as the court awaited the arrival of the Ming envoys Gong Yongqing and Wu Ximeng 吳希孟 (1508–?), their welcoming envoy So Seyang reported: "[T]he celestial emissaries chant poems by day and scribble by night, likely composing poems." Consulting the compositions of their predecessors, they prepared poems for the sites and scenes that awaited them on the journey ahead. Ming envoys usually matched the rhymes of their predecessors, while Chosŏn officials matched the rhymes of their guests. So when the Ming envoys then unleashed their poems "all at once," the Korean welcoming committee could not "withstand" the deluge. Thus, So Seyang urged his superiors in Seoul to distribute copies of the *Brilliant Flowers* beforehand so they could prepare their own matching verses. This ploy could only work because all parties knew which poems would be matched in the first place.[21]

The demands of impromptu virtuosity frustrated even experienced court composers.[22] Chosŏn officials retold the infelicities committed by Ming envoys and venerable Korean officials alike. Kim Suon 金守溫 (1409–1481), whose essays once impressed a Ming envoy in his youth, embarrassed himself twenty years later during the 1476 Ming embassy. When it was his turn to compose a verse using words rhyming with "pile" 堆, he "murmured bitterly and furrowed his brows." Declaring that his "spirit was exhausted," Kim penned an uninspired "fine wine in a thousand bottles and meat in a hundred piles" [崇酒千瓶肉百堆]. When he wrote another poem about rain clouds gathering overhead, the bemused Ming envoy Qi Shun 祁順 (1434–1497) exclaimed the rain had arrived to "wash the meat in a hundred piles."[23] These and other similar anecdotes about ghostwriting, recycling old verses, and mistakes in prosody appeared as firsthand recollections and circulated as hearsay before finding their way in Korean compilations of "remarks on poetry" (K. *sihwa* 詩話).[24]

One oft-repeated anecdote in these "remarks on poetry" is an encounter between Qi Shun and the venerable Sŏ Kŏjŏng, who served as his reception envoy. Sŏ had heard Qi was a skilled poet but was unimpressed by Qi's compositions during their journey, believing they had all been written in advance. Taking Qi to be a "mediocre" poet, Sŏ Kŏjŏng hatched a plan to embarrass his guest during a planned boat outing.[25] Sŏ prepared a regulated verse for the occasion. He asked to reverse the usual custom of allowing the Ming envoy to compose his poem first. Qi Shun agreed. When the wine was about half-finished, "Sŏ began to chant softly, pretending that he was in the middle of thinking up a poem." With brush in hand, he wrote a poem with the couplet, "the wind and moon do not follow the yellow crane away; / the mist and waves often send forth white gulls over" [風月不隨黃鶴去 煙波長送白鷗來], and invited Qi to match it. Sŏ had employed a rhyme scheme yet to be used for the occasion, so he believed the Ming ambassador would be caught off guard.

Rather than "raise his flag of capitulation," Qi picked up a brush without hesitation and wrote a verse of his own. His "powerful and untrammeled" calligraphy was impressive, but it was his couplet: "the terrain of Paekche ends by the river's edge / the fountains of Odae spring from the heavens" [百濟地形臨水盡 五臺泉脈自天來] that astonished his hosts. The lines had incorporated Korea's history and geography in a parallel couplet crafted with formal precision. In such a couplet, the second line had to match the syntax and semantic categories of the first; numbers were paired with numbers, verbs with verbs, natural objects with other natural objects. In the first line, the territory of the ancient Korean state Paekche, whose name means "a hundred fords," was delimited by the Han River. In the second line, Odae Mountain, literally the "five terraces," matched the "hundred fords," while "spring from the heavens" matched "end by the river's edge." A perfect syntactic parallel doubled as accurate geographical description: Odae Mountain was near the Han River's source.[26]

Sŏ's rivalry with Qi elicited reactions ranging from romanticization to jesting ridicule.[27] According to a later sixteenth-century account, weeks of trying to best one another nurtured a mutual appreciation.

When the two left their boats and returned to the riverside, Sŏ composed a long verse in the ancient style, to which Qi Shun matched line by line without rest, finally convincing Sŏ that Qi's talent was genuine. Sŏ also received his share of praises. Qi said that "even in China, Sŏ would be among the four or five best," a reputation Qi helped build upon his return to China. The account even compared Qi Shun and Sŏ Kŏjŏng's rivalry to that between the two military geniuses Zhuge Liang 諸葛亮 (181–234) and Sima Yi 司馬懿 (179–251). As portrayed in the *Romance of the Three Kingdoms*, their "polite airs and deference remained amid the banners and drums of war."[28] These stories undoubtedly contain embellished details (even if their authors were often personal acquaintances); nevertheless, such tales of literary virtuosity (and perfidy) at least speak to the broader cultural import of these exchanges.

The last poems were usually exchanged along the southern banks of the Yalu River, right before the Ming envoys returned to China. By and large in a lyrical form[29] that is expressive of emotion, these verses spoke of "lingering thoughts of separation" [繾綣之意], manifested in images of the once lush riverbank turning barren from their despondent longing for the departing envoy. Their streaming tears showed mutual appreciation as literary peers, if not genuine affection and friendship, but this poetry was an act of social performance.[30] With their attention to both a present and future audience, and not meditations of private sentiment, these poetic expressions of friendship went beyond the personal—the sense of social parity they proffered was what allowed them to share a common literary tradition, one that now bore the burden of diplomacy.

LANDSCAPE AND HISTORY

Poetry reflected the political ideals of Chosŏn-Ming relations because they were crafted to do so. In 1460, when the envoy Zhang Ning ascended the Hall of Great Peace (*T'aep'yŏnggwan* 太平館), the site of the envoy's residence in Seoul, he claimed by "looking off into the far distance," even the "imperial capital" was visible—the imperial center, as the axis mundi, lay barely over the horizon, however removed its physical presence. Therefore, the envoy's visual sweep spanned across Korea's "efflorescent peaks" over all its "three thousand leagues," compressing the kingdom's entire landscape into his gaze. That same gaze overlaid past and present, reaching far back into historical time to recognize Korea as "territory once enfeoffed as the Han's domain" [輿圖盡屬漢提封] and Ming as heir to Zhou's "statutes and models" [厝周典則]. An imagined panorama fused with the physical landscape: "the affairs of men, the scenery and objects, mountains and rivers," some "hidden," some "apparent" were all revealed to the Ming envoy's "mind and eye" [天時人事 景物山川 幽顯雖殊 心目俱至].

Behind the physical scenery (the "apparent" 顯) was the correlative cosmology (the "hidden" 幽) that granted coherence to the imperial worldview.[31] In this cosmology, universal empire *was* natural and perpetual, a point reinforced by its litany of parallel couplets. "When heaven and earth provide, all receive its benefit"—it was a matter of course that "whether civilized or barbarian, none do not pay obeisance to the source" [天地有恩同覆載 華夷無處不朝宗]. As the "Eastern Land where the culture of letters has always been good," Chosŏn served eternally as the Ming's "vassal screen." Still, it was the "wonders bequeathed" by "the Central Court since long ago" that explained its "decorum of virtue" and why its "ceremonies modeled after Sagely Forms" [由來東土文風好 自昔中朝賜予隆 藩屏皇家崇節度 儀形聖範恤疲癃]. Korea's cultural efflorescence depended on the graces of the timeless "Central Court," a point reiterated by connecting the generative force of spring to the cultural power of Ming rule in the landscape's depiction. Again, the union of natural and cultural generation rendered geographical distance and cultural difference irrelevant: "the road reaches the ends of the water and land, and the sounds of the country are different; / [but] spring [still] fills heaven and earth, and the scenery is all the same [路窮水陸鄉音別 春滿乾坤景色同]."[32]

Zhang's musings make it clear how an envoy poem could affirm loyalty to the imperial system, even without necessarily stating it outright. As literary scholar Stephen Owen notes, poetry, especially the Regulated Verse 律詩, required the "assimilation of the correlative cosmology" that justified its existence.[33] Most visible in the analogical juxtaposition of corresponding pairs in the parallel couplet in Zhang's encomium, the correlative cosmology is also reminiscent of the Towers and Pavilions style 台閣體. A reference to the imperial grand secretariat 內閣, the style was so named because of its association with court academicians who served there during the early Ming.[34] A typical Towers and Pavilion poem, often written on an emperor's command, described lavish banquets, magnificent hunts, and scenic vistas visited by the imperial entourage. By extolling imperial achievements, their purpose was to "adorn the Great Peace" 黼黻太平. Written during social gatherings, often at scenic vistas, they inscribed political aspiration in descriptions of landscape.[35]

The fact that poems in the *Brilliant Flowers* share features with Ming academic poetry is to be expected. Both were products of courtly sociability, but the link is even more direct. In fact, the mid- to late fifteenth-century Ming envoys who helped ensconce the *Brilliant Flowers* tradition, especially Ni Qian and Zhang Ning, were well-known practitioners of this style. And because Ming envoy-poets were also court academicians, this link remained strong, even after the Towers and Pavilions style fell out of fashion.[36] The style's life cycle is usually described in terms of the crest and fall of Ming power: it came into vogue when the Ming Empire was ascendant, but after the mid-fifteenth century, with imperial retrenchment and dynastic unrest, its hifalutin rhetoric became "tedious" artifacts of courtly conceit. But as David Robinson has argued, this style of encomium, even in its heyday, was never simply about praising the emperor and certainly not about describing actual conditions. Instead, it articulated a moral vision of political order espoused by its authors. That the imperial person fell short of these ideals was perhaps part of the point.[37]

Therefore, it is not enough to say a poem praised empire; one must ask what *kind* of empire it promoted. To pose the same question to the *Brilliant Flowers* would also mean asking how Korea fits into that vision. In Zhang Ning's musings on the Hall of Great Peace, it was how Korea reaffirmed Ming claims on the imperial and classical past by showing where it surpassed its predecessors. It is articulated by the Ming official Xue Yingqi 薛應旂 (1500–1575) in his preface for the now lost travelogue of his friend Wu Ximeng, the vice envoy of the 1537 mission:

> Chosŏn of today was once the country of Jizi [Kija] in the Zhou. During the Han, it was the prefectures of Lelang and Xuantu. It was always a place where civilizing transformation reached [聲教 所暨之地]. When the [Koguryŏ] dictator [Yŏn'gaesomun 淵蓋蘇文

?–665] brought tumult during the Zhenguan period (627–649), the dispatch of China's troops could not be avoided . . . Only with the rise of Our Ming did they sincerely turn towards transformation and come to submit ahead of the various barbarians [迨我明興輸忱向化 為諸夷先至]—a great triumph of Our Emperor's diffusion of culture [誕敷大慶].[38]

A prevalent motif in the *Brilliant Flowers*, the Ming is superior to its predecessors because it achieved Korea's submission peacefully by dint of literary and cultural prowess. In contrast, empires of the past, such as Han and Tang, had to rely on the force of arms.

To laud Ming superiority over its predecessors implied other imperial possibilities were less desirable. Xue Yingqi addressed only other Ming gentry-scholars, but when the 1476 envoy Qi Shun made the same point to his Korean hosts, it provoked troubling associations. In his twenty-couplet-long historical meditation on P'yŏngyang (C. *Pingrang huaigu* 平壤懷古), the city's history became a microcosm for Korea's relations with past imperial dynasties. He spoke of how the "barbarian Yuan" indulged in "immoral" wars of expansion that "sought to swallow" Korea's lands [胡元不道圖吞併] and whose annexation of the P'yŏngyang area corrupted these "borderlands with animal stench." Ming, in contrast, knew to "succor the small" 字小. "Delighting in heaven" 樂天, it achieved the Mencian ideal of how a great state was to treat a smaller neighbor.[39] He (erroneously) credited Ming with reverting P'yŏngyang to Korean control, a munificent act that distinguished Ming from its barbarous Mongol predecessors. The resulting peace allowed Ming's cultural attainments to diffuse to Korea, raising it to new heights of civilization.[40]

Qi's ruminations concluded with the Ming-Yuan comparison, but they tapped further into the reservoir of the past. As he showed off his (imperfect) erudition, he roused the specter of imperial irredentism. P'yŏngyang had been the site of Lelang, one of the Han Commanderies and later Koguryŏ's capital.[41] Although he decried the Sui dynasty for "raising troops three times to harry in vain," he praised the Tang generals Xue Rengui 薛仁貴 (614–683) and Su Dingfang 蘇定方 (592–667) for their astounding victories at Kŭmsan and P'aesu, which led to Koguryŏ's demise [金山得捷薛仁貴 浿水成功蘇定方].[42] The Sui and

Tang invasions, however, were not remembered in Korea as glorious military achievements, but acts of aggression.

Qi Shun did not mention the Tang-Silla war (670–676), which broke out shortly after Koguryŏ's defeat. Nevertheless, this celebration of Tang military achievements would have evoked its memory. Here again, the treatment of the war in the received imperial and Korean historical traditions diverge drastically. According to the *Historical Records of the Three Kingdoms* (*Samguk sagi* 三國史記) written by Kim Pusik 金富軾 (1075–1151), Silla preserved its independence by defeating Tang forces that occupied the peninsula. Only by first securing its territorial integrity did Silla agree to recognize the Tang as suzerain.[43] Meanwhile, in the Chinese imperial histories (the basis of Qi Shun's knowledge), Tang humbled Silla into submission, allowing it autonomy only after it acknowledged Tang suzerainty. In Qi's understanding of history, Silla never fought off Tang. Indeed, even Korea's revanchist successes against the Yuan Mongols in the mid-fourteenth century became a gift from Ming—imperial favor had become the sole explanation for Korea's survival.[44]

Sŏ Kŏjŏng, as Qi's minder and companion, responded to these verses with a poem of his own. It opened with effusive praise of the Ming's civil virtue. It only returned to the subject of history toward the end of the piece in the fifteenth couplet, where the line "Sui and Tang abused arms—[stuff] of laughing trifles" [隋唐黷武笑區區] delivered a pithy dismissal.[45] Tang succeeded where Sui failed, but Sŏ rejected that success as pointless warmongering. Over the following days, Qi and Sŏ came to converge on this issue. Qi, in his "Miscellaneous Songs on Chosŏn" (*Chaoxian za yong* 朝鮮雜詠) now also repudiated military aggression, denouncing Tang as well. Meanwhile, Sŏ reiterated the ignominy Tang suffered for having attacked Koguryŏ.[46] Sŏ's view, of course, was not a uniquely Korean perspective on imperial aggression. Imperial officials over the centuries have also used the Sui and Tang invasions of Korea as cautionary tales for ambitious emperors. What Sŏ had done here was to remind Qi Shun that he was celebrating the wrong kind of imperial glory.[47]

Hints of similar controversy are difficult to detect elsewhere in the *Brilliant Flowers*, so where they can be whiffed indicates a breach of an unspoken consensus. Here a contested past bubbled up to disturb a placid present; the hidden was made apparent momentarily. Panegyrics praising civil rule, literary culture, and perpetual peace suppressed a different imperial logic of military might and territorial conquest. In this respect, Sŏ Kŏjŏng's retorts targeted less Qi Shun's poem per se but the logics of empire making he esteemed. Martial prowess was no complement to civil virtue; it was its antithesis.

Sui, Tang, and the Mongols were inferior to Ming because they treated Korea the wrong way. And what better testament to Ming's superiority than the *Brilliant Flowers*?[48] It at once acclaimed the glorious present and pacified the turbulent past. As Sŏ Kŏjŏng wrote elsewhere, it was "literature [that] washes away at once the disgraces of Sui and Tang" [文章一洗隋唐陋].[49] Or in the words of another Chosŏn poet-official Yi Haeng 李荇 (1478–1534): "one line of (or: from) the Brilliant Flower(s) is enough / there is no need for ten-thousand troops to pass" [皇華一句足 不必萬兵過]. The "brilliant flowers," through its double entendre as both the imperial envoy's sobriquet and the anthology's title, had made the force of arms obsolete.[50]

EASTWARD FLOW OR EASTERN SPRING?

Praising Ming's civil and literary virtues also elevated the envoy who personified them. At times, the envoy's person even overshadowed the emperor whose will he represented. The 1537 envoy Gong Yongqing thus described his crossing of the Yalu River (see figure 8.1):

> On the road to Puyŏ [i.e., Korea] the spring wind arrives early;
> Along the Yalu's banks bloom poplar and willow.
> All is because civilizing influence belongs to one rule;
> For myriad years, the vassal screen [Korea] shall protect the imperial house.

扶餘道上春風早 鴨綠江頭楊柳花
自是文風歸一統 萬年藩屏衛皇家

Gong's treatment of Yalu as a "natural barrier that limits the Central Effloresence" [遂令天塹限中華] recalled its treatment in Kwŏn Kŭn's 1396 poem on the river. In Kwŏn's earlier poem, the river's ability to

FIGURE 8.1 Detail of "Welcoming the imperial proclamation at Ŭisun Station" (*Ŭisun'gwan yŏngjo to* 義順館迎詔圖), ca. 1573. Chosŏn officials led by the welcoming commissioner Chŏng Yugil 鄭惟吉 (1515–1588) gather on the banks of the Yalu River to welcome the entourage of the Ming envoy Han Shineng. Leaves in album, colored ink; 46 × 38.5 cm. Kyujanggak Archives, 古貫 4250-108. Courtesy of the Kyujanggak Institute for Korean Studies.

divide the civilized and the barbarian in in the face of empire's prevailing winds, in Gong's later poem, the imperial envoy became the spring wind that awakened the flowers on the river's banks.[51] The herald embodied the empire's civilizing influence, replacing the imperial person in this cosmic analogy.

The replacement was figurative but found its analog in diplomatic praxis. Early Ming emperors left personal imprints on diplomacy, whether by demanding tribute, deciding policy, or dedicating poems to Korean visitors. By the age of the *Brilliant Flowers*, emperors had faded into the background, relegated to the literary register of convention and abstraction: sagely, benevolent, perfect, and shorn of specific qualities. The disembodiment is partly explained by the timing of these literati-led embassies, occurring only upon the accession of a new emperor or, in the case of the 1537 mission, the birth of the Ming heir apparent. At these junctures that were critical for dynastic renewal, at stake was not the emperor as a *person* but how he, as an institution, continued the imperial tradition.

Neither was empire in the *Brilliant Flowers* about territorial rule. When Gong, in his Yalu poem, stated that "all" was because of Ming's universal rule, he meant Ming was the ultimate source of civilization, a point he restated during a visit to the shrine of Confucius in P'yŏng-yang. There he wrote, "the East [Korea] holds on to the teachings of civilization" [東方守文教] because "imperial transformation reveres the literati style" that inspires emulation. Korean cultural achievement was meaningful primarily as evidence of civilization's "gradual flow" from Ming [皇化重儒風 漸摩知所效].[52] A particularly contrived expression of this trope was Qi Shun's rumination on the significance of portents in his "Rhapsody on Phoenix Hill (*Fengshan fu* 鳳山賦)." Old legends of alighting phoenixes described only "fleeting marvels," but their appearance in Korea, on the other hand, could somehow demonstrate "the complete triumph" of Ming's "cultural power" that "extended from the Nine Realms within to the distant marches without."[53]

Chosŏn officials, by matching such verses, indulged the envoys' conceits of imagination. With literary sociability encouraging harmonization above contention, imperial encomium ceased to be an exercise in self-adulation. If Ming literati appreciated Korean poetry exchanges as "testimonies to Korea's civilization" and "the success of the Ming dynasty's propagation of civil and Confucian culture to faraway lands," as literary scholar Du Huiyue puts it, where does it leave Chosŏn officials? Were they content only to bask in Ming's shining light? What about the Chosŏn court's own civilizing mission? Was Korea only to "turn towards civilization" (*hwanghwa* 向化) but not produce its own?[54]

When Chosŏn officials fashioned imperial authority, they also staked their own claims on Ming's civilizing process. Kim Suon, in his response to Qi Shun's "Rhapsody on Phoenix Hill," stated, "[T]hough our country is said to be [but] one corner [of the world], it is first to receive the eastward flow of civilization" [國雖曰一隅 然東漸之化 實先被焉], a statement anticipating the Neo-Confucian philosopher-cum-statesman Yi Hwang's even bolder assertion in the 1568 *Brilliant Flowers*: "With the Great Ming on high, the eight frontiers are united; but as for the foremost and preeminent recipient of the eastward flow of the civilization, there is none who is closer than We, the East" [大明當天 八荒同軌 而東漸之化 首被而尤洽者 莫近於我東]. Ming rule was universal, but it was still partial to Korea, who received its pristine, dawn-break glow.[55]

These poems had as much to do with imperial authority as with Korea's civilizational claims. That Chosŏn officials nimbly adapted tropes of imperial encomium to serve their situation is in itself unsurprising. After all, both poetry and empire had been the subject of Korean appropriation and reinvention for centuries. It also bears reminding that the assertions of Ming monopoly were always only *claims* of cultural authority. At play were two narratives of how that authority worked. The first of "eastward transmission" underscores Ming influence. The second of native autonomy centers the civilizing mission of Korean kingship. The tension between the two is crucial for appreciating the cultural work accomplished in the *Brilliant Flowers*.

Here, the case of the filial daughter of Kwaksan in Pyŏng'an province is instructive (see map 3). In 1422, the Chosŏn court erected a stele and memorial gate 旌閭 to honor a local daughter named Kim Sawŏl 金四月. Her mother had suffered from seizures, so when Kim learned human flesh could relieve them, she severed her own finger to feed to her mother, curing her. Kim Sawŏl was most likely inspired by autochthonous religious ideas rather than Confucian teachings, but that did not stop either Ming or Chosŏn from appropriating her as a symbol of their respective civilizing projects.[56]

The stele in her honor stood in Kwaksan 郭山, a small town located on the road between Ŭiju and P'yŏngyang, a path every Ming embassy had to take as they proceeded to Seoul. Upon seeing the stele, many Ming envoys left poems to celebrate Kim Sawŏl's extraordinary filial devotion. The first to do so was Ni Qian.[57] For him, Kim Sawŏl proved that Ming grace, by reaching as far as Korea, "did not distinguish between the civilized and the barbarian [始知帝降衷 不以華夷別]" (see figure 8.2).

Ni's companion, the Chosŏn official Sin Sukchu, saw the matter differently (see figure 8.3). It was his king who "affirmed filial principles," who "praised the beautiful to admonish future men," who "carved [her deeds] in stone to set them apart," and who "raised models so that all will have their place." A filial child like Kim Sawŏl validated the Chosŏn court's efforts to encourage Confucian social mores. Now that the Chosŏn king had erected these monuments to celebrate her virtue, the

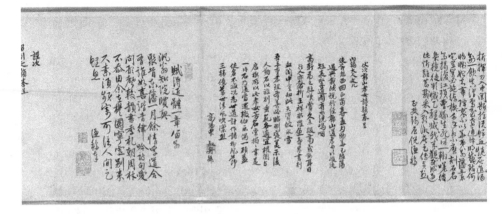

FIGURE 8.2 Poem on the filial daughter of Kwaksan by Ni Qian, in author's calligraphy. Detail of "Scroll of poetry exchanged during an embassy to Chosŏn" (*Pongsa Chosŏn ch'anghwa sigwŏn* 奉使朝鮮倡和詩卷), 1450. Handscroll, ink on paper; 33 × 1600 cm. National Museum of Korea, 신수 14149. Courtesy of the National Museum of Korea.

FIGURE 8.3 "Verses to match [Ni's] Filial Daughter of Kwaksan," by Sin Sukchu, in author's calligraphy. Detail of "Scroll of poetry exchanged during an embassy to Chosŏn," 1450. Courtesy of the National Museum of Korea.

Ming envoy should use his privileged position also to praise the success of Korea's civilizing project with "poems that uplift customs and virtues," so that "in Korea, for a million and myriad generations, / A clear wind will blow among the stalwart and righteous" [作詩樹風節 三韓億萬世 清風吹凜烈]. Sin diverted the outward and downward impetus of the civilizing process in the Ming envoy's poem in favor of Korean royal initiative, granting the Ming envoy only the power to vindicate virtue through its representation.[58]

Ni Qian's poems inspired his successors to follow in his footsteps. Poems written by his successors also tended to subordinate Korean agency, treating it as a proxy to Ming's civilizing project. As Gong Yongqing put it, the filial daughter was proof that "imperial airs extended beyond the Nine Reaches" to reach Korea, "the eastern vassal" [皇風自是式九圍 澤被東藩乃如此].[59] In this logic, the more praises he heaped on Chosŏn, the greater Ming's accomplishments, so when Gong's vice envoy Wu Ximeng declared that the virtue of Korea's "gentlemen" must have been beyond reproach, because "even the women [of Chosŏn] are like this" [東方女流尚如此 因誠君子倫理敦], the words still carried a sense of imperial triumphalism.[60] That is not to say that the Chosŏn court's role was completely effaced. A line in the 1521 Ming envoy Shi Dao's 史道 (1485–1554) poem echoed Sin Sukchu's poem by placing the spotlight on Chosŏn's ruler: "the vassal king affirms moral teachings; / filial principles flow" to the people of the East [藩王重名教 孝理漸東民].[61]

Kim Sawŏl captured the tensions between two different sources of cultural (and therefore political) authority in microcosm. To release this tension, the *Brilliant Flowers* did not so much seek a reconciliation. Instead, as it did with the problem of historical memory, envoy poetry offered a deferral of meaning:

Who knew that this one girl
Would alone be collected among the envoy's poems?
I heard that Confucius had once said,
"Virtue will certainly have its neighbors."
Though [this] small country is a different land,
Its denizens are also subjects of the imperial house.
Its people all devote themselves,
To better understand Kingly transformations.

那知一女子 獨取扵諮詢
我聞孔氏說 惟德必有隣
小邦雖異土 亦是皇家民
斯民各盡性 益知王化諄.[62]

According to these lines written by the Chosŏn official Yi Haeng in the 1521 anthology, Kim Sawŏl's filial actions assured the ecumenical inclusion of the "denizens" of Chosŏn as "subjects of the imperial house" despite geographical distance and cultural differences. However, what Yi Haeng meant by "Kingly transformations" 王化 was ambiguous. Were these the moral teachings of antiquity's Sage Kings? Did they point to the cultural authority of Ming rule? Or did they refer to the civilizing efforts of Chosŏn's own king?

All three interpretations existed in superimposition, but here, as elsewhere, the literary agency of the envoy stole the limelight. Yi Haeng, in a different poem, wrote:

The starry chariot has traveled far—where does it go?
Its path leads to the Verdant Hills [Korea] for collecting poems.
Sagely Transformation has flowed to the east; every family is virtuous
   and righteous.
Now, there is more than what [you have seen] on Kwaksan's stele.

星軺跋涉向何之 路入青丘為探詩
聖化東漸家節義 如今不獨郭山碑.[63]

So successful was the flow of civilization that virtuous individuals like Kim Sawŏl were everywhere, but it was the envoy whose act of "collecting poems" that truly mattered. As another poem put it, the envoy, by "troubling himself with a brush" [更煩椽筆為題詩], had preserved Kim Sawŏl's "fragrant name" for a "thousand ages," replacing the physical monument as the primary testament of her virtue [芳名定自流千古 不必堅頑數尺碑].[64] Envoy poetry elevated Chosŏn and Ming civilizing projects to a literary register. Instead of diverging as rival projects in competition, they now converged into a common project of literary reenactment.

REENACTING THE *BOOK OF SONGS*

Ming envoys celebrated the filial daughter as performance of their duty to "collect poems." A classical trope associated with the tradition of the *Book of Songs*, the duty to collect poems evoked its first section, the

"Airs of the States" (*Guofeng* 國風), which contained verses collected by Zhou royal emissaries to document the moral conditions of the feudal states they visited. Ming envoys, such as the vice emissary of the 1537 mission, Xue Tingchong 薛廷寵 (fl. 1532–1539), also described their paeans to the filial daughter in these terms, as *guofeng*, a modern "air of the state" that documented the country's customs. In this analogy, Ming was the Zhou of yore while Chosŏn was one of Zhou's feudal states. The envoy in turn was like a Zhou emissary who "searched all around" in Korea for "beautiful customs" to render in verse.[65]

The analogy between now and then borrowed classical sanction, but it could go only so far. After all, the poems of the *Brilliant Flowers* were the envoy's own compositions, not local folk songs. Nevertheless, the analogy circumscribed diplomacy with significance beyond the present moment. In So Seyang's matching poem to Xue's piece, the envoy's writing called on the classical past to invest the imperial embassy to Korea with a timeless moral mission:

The envoy in one glance gathers the people's customs,
For a myriad ages, his writing will be as the seas and mountains.
In the East, the principle of filial devotion has been recorded since
    antiquity,
Ever more that the Sagely Ming now tends the jade candle.
The "Cry of Fishhawks" begins: the origin of civilization;
When women behave properly, men follow their model.

皇華一顧採民風 萬古文章同海岳
東方孝理著自古 況今聖明調玉燭
関雎首開風化原 女子有行男私淑

The "cry of fishhawks" 關雎 pointed to the first poem of "Airs," the very beginning of the *Book of Songs*'s moral lessons, and by extension, the origin of civilization itself. Ming guarded the transmission of civilization, while the envoy ensured that Korea's role in sustaining would be documented for posterity.[66]

When the analogy with the classical past transformed Chosŏn's king into the modern equivalent of Zhou's feudal vassal, it signified much more than Korean loyalty or subordination to Ming. Prefaces written by Sŏ Kŏjŏng for two different envoy poetry collections expound on the implications of this analogy. To open the first preface, written for 1476 *Brilliant Flowers* anthology, Sŏ wrote: "when the Kingly Way flourishes, the 'Odes' 雅 and 'Hymns' 頌 of the *Songs* are composed, and so the traces of perfect rule can thus be investigated." As evidence of moral empire, envoy poetry demonstrated that Ming's "reign over the world" had "spread civilization within and beyond the seas" and made the whole world its vassal. Chosŏn "served the Great State with utmost sincerity" precisely because Ming "does not abuse distant men as barbarians," treating Chosŏn as it deserved to be treated. Although it was a "small country," it was blessed with "the marvel of Kija's enduring spirit [古箕子存神之妙]." Having received "civilizing influence for generations," Chosŏn could therefore produce poetry that was "certainly not inferior to the Airs of Gui 檜 and Cao 曹." And because the *Songs* included verses from even these "minor" states, surely Chosŏn would deserve inclusion in the modern iteration of the *Book of Songs*, the *Brilliant Flowers*. Implied here was a claim of direct continuity with the classical past, one that would have made Chosŏn and Ming coeval heirs to a shared antiquity.[67]

Whatever the political hierarchies, classical models still mediated Ming cultural authority. They were the touchstones for evaluating both Chosŏn and Ming success in their emulation, a point implicit in the second preface to the personal anthology (the anthology is no longer extant) of Pak Wŏnhyŏng, Sŏ's' senior colleague who had received several groups of Ming envoys during his career. In it, Sŏ Kŏjŏng celebrated Korea's "flourishing of ritual and music" [禮樂文章之盛]" for "approximating that of the Central Efflorescence" [侔擬中華], a statement, that, at first glance, appears to suggest Korean conformity to Ming models. But by speaking of how Korea's men of talent were on par with "ancient worthies and ministers," he suggested Chosŏn and Ming drew from a shared wellspring of antiquity. Sŏ still accepted the primacy of the "Revered and August Ming," whose universal authority extended "from within the seas to beyond," but its relationship to Korea's efflorescence was not causal. Instead, it was reciprocal and mediated. Ming "regards Chosŏn as a feudal lord of the interior, while the two gaze upon one another with gifts and tribute" [乃眷朝鮮 比之內諸侯 錫貢相望]." The emperor "succors the four seas as one family" [天子仁聖 四海一家],

while Korea's king "has borne heaven's mandate ever since the beginning, serving the Great State with utmost sincerity" [我殿下膺天興運至誠事大]. This complementary relationship, then, required the coordination of men endowed with "literary refinement and ritual decorum" [文辭禮儀]. Through their "chanting of poems and skill in response [誦詩專對], esteem was brought to our king" [尊王人之體] and "glorified in the court of the Son of Heaven" [揚休天子之庭]. Again, it was the Korean literatus-cum-courtier, precisely individuals like Sŏ Kŏjŏng and Pak Wŏnhyŏng, who held the relationship together."[68]

Indeed, the *Brilliant Flowers* often centered heralds and mediators, even at the expense of the imperial authority they represented. Sŏ's preface to the 1476 *Brilliant Flowers* spoke briefly of the envoy mission's overt purpose—the announcement of the Ming heir apparent investiture—only to wax on about the envoy as a collector of poems when they "descended to the broad plains and gazed upon the surrounding scenery" or "observed with their eyes the mountains and rivers, the lay of the land, the people's mores and the customs of the country." Comparisons to the composers of the "Four Steeds" (C. *Si mu* 四牡) and the "Brilliant Flowers," two verses related to traveling envoys in the *Songs*, invested Ming visitors with this task of classical reenactment, but in doing so, they also reserved an integral role for Korea: only by presenting these poems that documented Chosŏn's beautiful customs could the envoys "carry on the upright [legacies] of the 'Odes of Zhou.'" The encomiums to empire in the *Brilliant Flowers*, never only celebrations of Ming rule, also served Chosŏn's autoethnographic strategies—the imperial envoy had been enlisted by his Chosŏn hosts to support Korea's claim to antiquity.[69]

What made Sŏ's articulation of this agenda remarkable was how explicitly Chosŏn's claim to antiquity was asserted. Other preface writers, before and after, were more attenuated, although they exuded no less confidence in Korea's civilizational worth. When Yi Hwang wrote his preface to the 1568 *Brilliant Flowers*, he attributed Ming's imperial favor to Chosŏn's "generations of loyal behavior, apparent in its observance of a vassal's duties" [我東世篤忠藎 明修侯度]. But when it came to the question of civilization's "eastward flow," he stated: "The Eastern Kingdom, with its territory and lands inscribed by heaven [天畫壤地], occupies a place far by the sea's edge. It was, however, the place where Kija was

enfeoffed and the place where Confucius had wished to live [箕子之所
受封 孔聖之所欲居]. Long it has deserved to be called [a place of] propriety, righteousness, and manifest civility."[70] Korea's physical separation
from the imperial center was a matter of preternatural determination.
Still, it was merely geographic. What mattered instead was Chosŏn's own
cultural attainments, admired by none other than Confucius himself.
The moral order that legitimized Chosŏn's vassal status vis-à-vis the
Ming also cast them as peers in civilization.

In the preface to the 1476 *Brilliant Flowers*, Sŏ also wrote that the
anthology's poems "originated from the reality of one's emotions and
sentiments" [本乎性情之眞]. This was an echo of the preface to the Mao
commentaries (*Mao shi* 毛詩) of the *Songs*, where the lyrical poem (K.
si, C. *shi* 詩) was charged with emotional immediacy and therefore represented the author's sentiments and intentions (C. *shi yan zhi* 詩言
志).[71] In this literary paradigm, the envoy poem becomes evidence of the
Chosŏn court's sincerity, its genuine loyalty to Ming. What else could
be a more convincing demonstration of Korean "admiration" 慕 of all
things Ming and Chinese if not the poems that profess it?[72]

   This chapter's discussion confounds this interpretation. The envoy
poets of the *Brilliant Flowers* maintained a pretense of emotional immediacy throughout their compositions. The envoy-poet, however, was
ever aware of the public nature of his verses. Although this awareness
need not preclude authentic sentiment, it always had to manage the dual
expectations of Ming and the Chosŏn court. In reality, the typical envoy
poem was a carefully manicured artifact tailored to social and political
demands rather than a spontaneous expression of sentiment.

   Another issue is that the central figure of the *Brilliant Flowers* was
not the Chosŏn official but his guests, the Ming envoys. In this case, does
it really make sense to see the *Brilliant Flowers* as primarily showcasing
Chosŏn responses to Ming virtue? The usual imperial trope of diplomatic encounters involved barbarian peoples and distant rulers submitting in awe of the emperor's civilizing power, but in the *Brilliant Flowers*,
this trope was just as often reserved. Here instead was an imperial agent
responding to the civilization of an erstwhile "barbarian" foreign state.
In other words, what was being celebrated in the anthology was in fact
how Chosŏn inspired the imperial official to praise its virtue.

The Chosŏn court, by printing the *Brilliant Flowers*, burnished the literary reputations of individual Ming envoys, tailoring their poetry to suit the envoy's person, playing to the envoy's desires. Beyond flattering visiting envoys, producing the *Brilliant Flowers* also enlisted these envoys to partake in the Chosŏn court's own autoethnographic agenda with appreciable effect. The poetry of the *Brilliant Flowers*, for instance, is scattered throughout the section devoted to Korea in the early seventeenth-century treatise on Ming foreign relations, the *Comprehensive Record of Diverse Realms*, contrasting sharply to its accounts of Japan and Vietnam (or farther beyond). Whereas other regions (the Ryūkyūs excepted) were portrayed as sources of endless trouble, the presence of envoy poetry in Chosŏn diverted the usual ethnographic gaze habituated to viewing "diverse realms" 殊域 as inhabited by morally and culturally inferior "others." Instead, it sharpened a common vision, one where Ming and Chosŏn worked toward a shared purpose: the edification and valorization of moral empire.[73]

To serve a range of agendas, the vision of moral empire clarified in the *Brilliant Flowers* did not imagine what empire *was*. Instead, Ming envoys and their Chosŏn interlocutors offered many, sometimes divergent, views on what it *should be*. A veneer of high imperial rhetoric celebrating the beautiful and the virtuous glazed over possible sources of animosity and conflict. This rhetorical construct maintained a social space that supposedly paralleled the tranquil relations between the two courts. They reified Chosŏn's identity as a loyal Ming vassal, yet they also reinscribed Ming imperial claims so that its authority manifested not from the force of arms or the extraction of tribute but from its civilizing process. Modern scholars have rightly treated the *Brilliant Flowers* as a way to "adorn the state" (*munjang hwaguk* 文章華國), but the target of literary adornment was not so much the Korean kingdom as it was the shape of the Ming Empire.[74]

Envoy poetry was therefore not a medium for *describing* Ming's empire but what sustained it in the diplomatic context. Put differently, it was as much a means of envoy exchange as one of its chief purposes: envoys gathered *in order to create* these paeans to empire. Meanwhile, this social space, nurtured by poetry exchange, locked Chosŏn officials and their Ming counterparts into an act of coproduction. Although each participant entertained their preferred narratives, what mattered was their sublimation in the *Brilliant Flowers* to the literary enterprise. Poetry ensured that variety did not dissolve into dissonance. At least within the space of a couplet or quatrain, it was harmonized in deference to the literary act. Inasmuch as a coherent vision did come into being from these poems, it only needed to work for a while. Once the banquets and pleasure outings ended and the envoy-poets returned to their respective places, they were free to think and write as they would, but not without bringing with them a piece of the grand, if ephemeral, production they helped reenact.

CHAPTER NINE

The Envoy's Virtue

The Ming envoy Gong Yongqing behaved badly at the royal banquet. He complained about the food and told the king that the seafood was poorly seasoned. When King Chungjong graciously apologized for his "unskilled" kitchen staff, Gong obtusely offered to present his own, presumably superior recipe. He had already irked his hosts when he requested courtesans to serve him during the banquet, but what he did next was the last straw.

As the evening wound down, Gong Yongqing offered to dedicate a piece of his calligraphy to the king. While the paper was being prepared, Gong asked the Korean interpreter to "find two young courtesans to hold candles" and four more to dance in front of him. When they arrived, Gong complained that one courtesan was taller than the others and had the mismatched woman replaced. When he noticed the flowers adorning the coiffure of one of the women, he asked for them to be removed, lest they "catch fire," a pretext for catching a better glimpse of the courtesan's face. As Gong prepared to write, he

> stared at the courtesan who was holding the candle. His heart was unsteady. He then wet his big brush with ink and flicked it towards the courtesan, spraying the ink on the courtesan's clothing and face [心不自定 以大筆濡墨 向妓而揮之 墨濺于妓之衣及面上].

Then he called the courtesan forth to stand for a long time at the desk in front [of him]. He wielded his brush as if to write something down. [But], he did not land his brush, continuing to tease her while holding his brush. Only after a long time did he stop [弄筆談謔 良久乃已].[1]

His manipulation of a wet brush in front of a woman's body—the innuendo of erotic desire—comes through as strongly in the original as it does in English translation. With the solemnity of the royal banquet thus spoiled by the envoy's "unbridled emotions," the "palace hall became boisterous and unsettled." The court officials were paralyzed in disbelief at the scene they had just witnessed.

Led by the Chief Censor Kwŏn Ye 權輗 (1495–1549), they approached the king. Chosŏn should, of course, "treat the imperial envoy with the utmost respect," but it should, on no account, indulge "great errors in decorum." According to Kwŏn, on this occasion, the envoy behaved "like a crazy person." He had "called forth a courtesan," hoping to "take her for his pleasure," a prelude to "something greatly insulting and vile." Although "emperors and feudal lords are distinct [in rank]," they were both "rulers" and deserved better. The king urged calm. Once Gong Yongqing completed his inscription, the king tried to dismiss the courtesans from the scene. The envoy, likely oblivious to the commotion, insisted that the women stay behind because his deputy also wanted to dedicate a piece. Meanwhile, court officials continued to whisper complaints to the king of the "celestial envoys' many failures of ceremony."[2]

The next day, the king tried to mollify his court. He issued an edict stating his "shock" at the envoys' "wild transgressions." But the king also chastised his officials for insisting that he intervene and confront the envoy. Chungjong explained that as a "vassal king," he could not reproach the emperor's emissaries. Instead, "tolerance and forbearance, and to bid them farewell on good terms" was all he could do. The censorial officials were now to drop the matter, lest the envoy discover their continued protests and be "provoked to anger." There was no telling what a peeved envoy might report to the emperor. The envoys were only in Korea for a few weeks. However offensive Gong's behavior, they were a passing affair. Enduring a few moments of frustration was a small price to pay to maintain cordial relations with Ming.[3]

But was it true that Chosŏn had no recourse when it came to misbehaving envoys? To answer this question requires venturing beyond the realm of formal tributary rituals and official missives. It requires taking stock of diplomacy's informal practices and unspoken conventions. Gong Yongqing violated "propriety" because he did not behave as an envoy was expected. His insistence on female company brought the suggestion of inordinate male desire, when his task was to perform a different kind of masculinity, that of homosocial bonding where men of letters built their relationship around expressions of literary refinement. In the presence of female beauty, he was to be a model of restraint, someone impervious to both erotic and (as will be discussed later in this chapter) material temptation.

Self-restraint in the face of erotic allurement and austerity in the face of material temptation made an envoy virtuous, but only ostentatious performance of this restraint, whether in actual deed or literary flourish, could ensure a reputation would last. The *Brilliant Flowers* afforded envoys a chance to raise themselves as exemplars for their successors. That did not always mean, however, that actions matched words. Ming accounts of exemplary envoy behavior, often based on literary performances in the *Brilliant Flowers*, became a predictable formula, one often contradicted by records left by their Korean hosts. Meanwhile, these discrepancies between words, actions, and memory, which emerged from the tension between moral performance and literary representation, provided the necessary openings to construct, not just an envoy's personal reputation, but also the myth of Ming as a moral empire.

SPURNING THE COURTESANS

Chosŏn records, whether the official histories or private memoirs, offer candid evaluations of an envoy's character. The Chosŏn official Sŏng Hyŏn thus wrote of the 1467 envoys he entertained: "[the vice-envoy] Zhang Cheng 張珹 (1425–1470) was good at writing poems, but whenever he saw a courtesan, he would happily look at her, smiling." His colleague Jin Shi 金湜 (fl. 1441–1467) had the sin of "greed" 貪, but Zhang Cheng's chief failing was "lust" 色.[4] In contrast, the *Veritable Records* speaks glowingly of the 1401 envoys Zhang Jin 章瑾 and Duanmu Li 端木禮. The two were "honest and upright; their outward manifestation of propriety was reverent and circumspect. They moved and stopped without error [and so], the people of [our country] loved and admired them."[5] This praise had much to do with how Zhang Jin and Duanmu Li performed in the face of erotic temptation. They refused to be entertained by female performers. Only at the banquet held in their honor, when the Chosŏn king insisted that the women represented Korea's "local custom" 鄉風, did they agree only to watch a brief performance.[6]

As discussed in chapter 2, the propriety of the court's female performers had been a long-standing controversy. It also proved to be a touchy subject for Ming envoys.[7] Their presence indeed surprised Zhang Jin and Duanmu Li, but mostly due to the perfidy of one of their predecessors, Lu Yong 陸顒. The Jianwen emperor once asked Lu whether it was true that the Chosŏn court used "female musicians to bewitch [imperial] envoys," as Koryŏ had supposedly done to Yuan emissaries. Lu, who had, in fact, taken a Korean courtesan as a lover during his visit, concealed the matter by telling the emperor that in Korea, "the rites and music are no different from that of China" and no female musicians were employed. The emperor, believing Lu, dispatched him on another embassy to Chosŏn. On the way, he ran into Zhang Jin and Duanmu Li, who had just seen a performance by female musicians in Chosŏn. They threatened to report Lu for deceiving the emperor. At this juncture, Lu's assistant Zhu Mengxian 祝孟獻 (1334–1412) defended him. He said to Zhang: "[Y]ou have held on to your pure virtue 清節, but why [must] you scold Lu Yong?" The worthiness of an envoy, Zhu insisted, was a matter for Chosŏn to judge—and judge it would.[8]

The above conversation, likely overheard by Chosŏn's interpreters, only entered Korean official records to explain Lu's subsequent behavior. Once he arrived in Korea, he "became ill of mind and unable to drink or eat," afraid that he would be punished upon his return to Ming. The length of his stay only worsened his condition, leading him to "act without self-control" and speak "mad words." In this frail moment, he turned to his Korean lover for comfort. He "held her hand" and burst into tears. He cried: "I thought I would die before I could see you again." One night, he tried to kill himself by hanging, but because Ming envoys were under constant surveillance by their minders, Lu Yong was rescued and placed under closer guard. Several days later, he attempted an escape, slipping away under cover of darkness, only to be recovered by a patrol unit early the next morning.[9] Desperate, he begged the king to save him. Kneeling on the ground and kowtowing many times "with extreme consternation and sincerity," he asked the king to help fake his death and then report it as fact to the emperor, all to avoid returning home to face the consequences.[10]

No extant records discuss what became of Lu once he eventually returned to Ming, although it seems he managed to continue his official career.[11] Nevertheless, other envoys took precautions not to falter in the same way. Duanmu Li's younger brother Duanmu Zhi 端木智 also enjoyed the company of courtesans, but to ensure that no one would report him to the emperor, he "called forth courtesans to tempt" his fellow envoys. One took the bait, but the other, Zhu Mengxian, Lu's old assistant, proceeded more cautiously. Duanmu invited Zhu to his room when the courtesans were present, but Zhu was content only to drink and listen to the music. He did not, however, "indulge" in sex. For this reason, the Chosŏn *Veritable Records* calls Duanmu Zhi "licentious, lecherous, arrogant and deceitful" but praised Zhu for being "pure, austere, and guarded."[12]

For the Chosŏn chronicler, sexual restraint reflected inner moral integrity. Even so, an envoy could be too austere. One Ming envoy told a Chosŏn official that "all the literati of China who heard of Lu Yong ridicule him," but he went too far to avoid being lumped with Lu Yong's ilk. He even refused to exchange poems with Korean officials because, in his reckoning, any sociability, whether facilitated by poetry, wine, or women, might compromise his integrity.[13] A period when Ming envoys refused both courtesans and poems, the first half of the fifteenth century has left very few pieces of envoy poetry compared to later eras.[14]

When Ni Qian's embassy of 1450 brought envoy poetry back to diplomacy, the problem of female performers also received a literary solution. Ni wrote two "poems to refuse courtesans" 卻妓詩 to explain why he could not accept their company, setting a precedent for subsequent envoys. In six of the next ten literati-led missions, Ming envoys composed poems in this manner until Gong Yongqing broke this tradition with his outrageous behavior during his 1537 mission.[15] These poems, collected in the *Brilliant Flowers*, treated "female music" 女樂 as a vessel of corruption because its provocation of (male) sexual desire conflicted with music's normative ritual function of emotional regulation.[16] As Ni Qian put it, "Cloud-like tresses and rainbow skirts arrayed with pipes and strings" [雲鬢霓裳列管絃] tempted the virtuous envoy who was able to turn them all away as would the "rigid wind" scatter the "rain" or a "brilliant sun" evaporate the "mist" (moisture being a euphemism for sex) [剛風吹散陽臺雨 烈日衝開洛浦煙].[17]

If a woman's music could bewitch the listener and invite corruption, where did that leave his Korean hosts who had offered it to him? Did the gesture of refusal preserve the envoy's virtue at their expense? Chosŏn's moral position proved a delicate matter, an impasse Ni's second poem tried to circumvent by writing "Chosŏn upheld ritual and valued the imperial court" [朝鮮秉禮重朝廷]. If female musicians were still a valid expression of Korean hospitality, then the issue at stake was no longer the impropriety of female music but the envoy's indifference to sensuality.[18] But Ni's logic turned on itself; if the envoy was incorruptible in the first place, what harm would there have been to hear their music?

Not always so easy to sidestep, the tension between authentic inner virtue and performative display emerged again in Qi Shun's exchange with Sŏ Kŏjŏng in 1476. As Qi Shun had done with his poems on Korea's fractious history with the imperial past, he now came the closest to laying bare the underlying moral tension:

> Why must graceful beauties emerge from the fine screen?
> Ritual is a weighty matter, while sensual pleasure is a trifle.
> Bewitching beauty moves men—sure to cause swift calamity;
> Licentious sounds bring chaos to elegance—you are too ruthless!
> Destiny once brought regret over an ode to the "Wind and Light";
> In fallen spirits, I have in vain acquired a faithless name.
> I would rather be like Han Yu, and drink to a game of letters—
> Once drunk, we can sing our verses, and have purity yet remain.

綺羅何用出娉婷 禮重由來色是輕
尤物移人應速禍 淫聲亂雅太無情
因緣舊愧風光曲 落魄空贏薄幸名
爭似昌黎文字飲 醉來歌詠有餘清.[19]

The poem recalled the Song dynasty official Tao Gu 陶穀 (903–970), who compromised himself by falling in with a courtesan during an embassy to the Southern Tang. After a liaison with a local woman at a waystation, he composed for her a love song titled "The Wind and Light are Good" ("Feng guang hao" 風光好). When he arrived at the Tang court, he tried to demonstrate his virtue by refusing court entertainers, but at an official banquet, the woman from the waystation reappeared to serve him wine, singing the same song Tao had written for her. It turned out the woman he met at the waystation was an agent of the Tang minister Han Xizai 韓熙載 (902–970), sent to entrap and embarrass the sanctimonious scholar Tao.[20]

Unlike scholar Tao, Qi insisted that his refusal was no moral pretense and a genuine reflection of his moral character. By allowing female performers to approach him, his hosts would only lead others to compare him to the late Tang poet Du Mu 杜牧 (803–852), who notoriously dallied among courtesans during his exile.[21] He would instead follow the example of Confucian statesman Han Yu 韓愈 (768–824), who chided the "wealthy youth of Chang'an" for only "seeking drunkenness among red skirts" and not learning how to "drink to letters."[22]

A friendship between gentlemen needed only the aid of lettered congeniality that a woman's presence could only spoil. Qi's poem thus delivered a reproach to his host through its allusions, but reducing "female music" to "licentious sounds" that "bring chaos to elegance" touched a raw nerve in his host, Sŏ Kŏjŏng. If Qi sought the "weight" of ritual over sensual frivolity, he also imputed a corresponding deficiency in Chosŏn's ritual regime. In response, Sŏ defended the use of "female music" and turned the Ming envoy's self-declared integrity against him. In one couplet, he wrote: "bowels of iron are not disturbed by graceful beauty; / not all is over whether ritual is weighty or trivial" [鐵腸元不撓娉婷 不是都迷禮重輕]. The genuinely virtuous had nothing to fear from temptation. Since the envoy's heart was "doubly pure," there was no reason to speak of the transgressions of "scholar Tao" [莫說風光陶學士 信君心迹本雙清].[23]

Sŏ's response shifted the burden of moral restraint back to the envoy. A poem of the 1464 Ming envoy Jin Shi mocked his predecessor Chen Jian for assuming female musicians offered pleasures of "clouds and rain," when it was the envoy himself who was "entangled in [such a] dream." Jin, in contrast, claimed he knew how to maintain appropriate boundaries, because "with the wind clear and moon bright, on a normal night / It has always been that, at a public hostel, we sleep alone"

[清風明月尋常夜 公館從來慣獨眠]. Jin, like Sŏ Kŏjŏng, saw the more virtuous envoy as he who remained unmoved in the face of female allure, not the one who used poetry to grandstand on a false moral premise. In this case, however, Jin was giving himself the lassitude to watch their performance.[24]

Ming envoys wished to at least appear irreproachable. In this regard, they performed as much for their Chosŏn hosts as the Ming court. In 1460, the envoy Zhang Ning ran to some trouble with his assistant Wu Zhong, a military officer from the Embroidered Guard who technically outranked him. Zhang wanted nothing to do with female entertainers, but Wu demanded their company. After one banquet, Zhang invited the courtesans to the envoy's lodge to appease him. Meanwhile, he swore to his welcoming emissary Pak Wŏnhyŏng that "even a sliver of intimacy would make [us] no different from dogs or sheep." When night fell, Zhang "chased the courtesans out one by one." He declared to Wu Zhong that the women were there only to serve him drinks. Before retiring, Zhang locked the doors of their quarters from the inside, leaving a frustrated Wu Zhong alone in his room. Zhang then told Pak Wŏnhyŏng that all this was done to ensure no suspicions lingered over the moral integrity of the Ming envoys.[25]

These performances of virtue invited suspicion of hypocrisy and posturing, anxiety over which suffused the performances themselves. When Qi Shun was again offered the company of courtesans, this time after a royal banquet, he wrote to the Korean king: "on my way here, I had written poems turning them away; [now] I worry that I was not believed." To Qi, it might have appeared that the Chosŏn court was deliberately testing his moral fiber by offering him opportunities to transgress. He insisted again in two quatrains that his "heart and bowels" were made of "iron and stone." Thus unstirred by "irrelevant flowers," the only fragrant company he would keep were "cold winter plums," a symbol of unwavering virtue.[26]

POLITICS OF REPUTATION

Whether Chosŏn deliberately used offers of female musicians as a gauge for an envoy's integrity is hard to say. What is clearer was how restraint (C. *jie*, K. *chŏl* 節) in the face of temptation, whether erotic or material, had become part of an idealized persona which, along with literary achievement, was integral to the social identity of Ming gentry-officials. Given the increasing politicization of personal virtue at the Ming court, which, according to historian Ying Zhang, reached its zenith in the seventeenth century, it was also unsurprising that Ming envoys (as well as their colleagues who wrote about them) paid enormous attention to cultivating this image.[27] As will soon be discussed, whether they also cared about their reputation in Korea or only for a domestic audience varied from envoy to envoy. Indeed, Ming envoys ran the gamut between bold-faced hypocrisy to total sincerity, but even with this great variation in behavior, they shared expectations with Chosŏn for how an imperial envoy *should be*, even if real ones, more often than not, fell far short of those ideals.

Alongside sexual restraint, how an envoy responded to gifts prepared by the Chosŏn court, which ranged from mundane, everyday items to opulence rivaling the emperor's tribute, provided the basis of moral judgment by their Korean hosts. The standards depended, however, on the envoy's social background. In general, the Chosŏn court expected literati envoys to behave well and took it as a matter of course that palace eunuchs would behave poorly. Frustrated by the outrageous demands of the Korean-born eunuch Chŏng Tong, King Sŏngjong once complained: "[I]f he were a [literati] court official, how would things have come to this!"[28] An official agreed with this generalization: "court officials comport themselves with restraint, righteousness, honesty, and dignity," but "eunuchs were generally greedy and voracious."[29] That said, female musicians only became an issue of concern for literati emissaries, perhaps because the problem of erotic enticement was assumed moot when the envoy was a eunuch. Before the Ming envoy Dong Yue even set foot in Korea, the court assumed that he, as a "court official," would "certainly refuse female music."[30] Ming envoys too observed this social boundary, so Dong Yue, when he demanded better treatment from his Korean hosts, scoffed that he was not a "eunuch from your country."[31]

Literati identity was scant assurance of model behavior. Literati envoys could prove just as acquisitive. They also demanded gifts and favors from their Korean hosts, a problem only exacerbated by the Ming economy's rapid commercialization after the sixteenth century and the influx of silver specie into Korea during the Imjin War.[32] The most notorious was probably Gu Tianjun 顧天埈 (1561–?). He "publicly demanded over a thousand taels of silver" and even resold his gifts, whether of "food, drink, utensils, or dishware" before returning to Ming. Gu's behavior prompted the anonymous compiler of the *Veritable Records* to lament: "[A]t that time, greed was the custom at the imperial court; bribery and graft were done openly."[33] The court historian appended a poem, attributed to one of Gu's servants, satirizing the envoy's behavior:

> Like a hound he came; like the wind he flew.
> From Chosŏn snatched he until all was through.
> But the green hills there he could not move,
> So into painted pictures, all of them he drew.

來如獵狗去如風 收拾朝鮮一罄空
惟有青山移不動 將來描入畫圖中[34]

Although a standard seven-character quatrain, the ditty possessed a limerick's wit. It compared the envoy's behavior to that of a ravenous hunting dog. The rapacious envoy would have seized even Korea's landscape had it been possible. Only because it was not did he settle for their sketched renditions.

The historian's judgment supplied a poetic justice that could not have been exacted at the moment. Even so, what mattered was less Gu's egregious behavior than what would happen to the norms he violated, which had consequences for future embassies. Even the most acquisitive eunuch ambassadors observed precedent when they made their demands, as one Chosŏn official noted, but if even scholar-officials such as Gu sank to these new lows, what hope remained that their social inferiors would behave? With nothing to restrain their greed, the eunuchs were expected to behave "ten times worse." Chosŏn officials therefore anticipated future expenditures on the order of ten thousand taels of silver and over one thousand catties of ginseng. Already an excessive amount of treasure, it proved to be only a fraction of what the eunuch Liu Yong 劉用, in fact, was able to extort (around sixty thousand taels) in 1609 by calling on Chosŏn to recompense the Ming for having "rescued" Korea during the Imjin War.[35]

There were also Ming envoys who embodied the other extreme. Among men who cultivated an air of restraint and austerity there were even those whose deeds matched the reputations they desired. In the tenth month of 1537, a Korean embassy returning from Beijing passed the night in Tongzhou 通州 at a private inn. The Korean envoys struck up a conversation with the innkeeper, where they shared their opinion of the Ming envoy Gong Yongqing, who had just concluded his mission to Korea. The innkeeper found Gong and his assistant "dissolute and given to drunkenness;" when they had passed by his home, they showed "no self-restraint," and so they certainly would have demanded many things from the Chosŏn king. Likely unwilling to speak ill of imperial officials, the Korean envoy Chŏng Saryong 鄭士龍 (1491–1570) retorted that Gong and his assistant had "come to our country and not taken a single item . . . the two men were austere and virtuous and were viewed admirably by all in our country." The innkeeper, finding the statement disingenuous, remarked: "[W]hen they went [to Korea], they only had four or five porters," but they returned with "thirty or forty." "What," he asked rhetorically, "could they have been carrying?" The host then waxed nostalgic about the 1521 envoy Tang Gao 唐皋 (1469–1526). According to him, when Tang returned from Korea, he brought nothing but a calligraphy brush. Unfortunately, he lamented, this same honesty later cost Tang his official career. He was dismissed from office because he spoke out against corruption in court. When he died soon after, "his family had not a single ounce of silver to their name." He lamented that a man of such integrity "would likely not come to this world again."[36]

Chosŏn records corroborated this assessment of Tang. When Tang's entourage was en route to Korea, the Chosŏn court already noticed they carried only fourteen pieces of luggage, minuscule compared to the four hundred pieces brought in 1483 by the eunuch envoy Chŏng Tong or the veritable caravan of Gu Tianjun, which was so overloaded that its conveyance "exhausted the northwest region of Korea."[37] When Tang arrived, he declared that, because he came to "spread the emperor's munificence," disturbing the "people" would "pervert" his embassy's purpose. He therefore indulged in no excesses, even refusing wine at meals.[38] In Seoul, King Chungjong insisted to Tang that he accept the gifts of stationery, explaining that "brushes, inkstones, paper, and ink are but small trifles for use in the study" and would not "harm one's integrity." Tang still refused. He answered that he was selected for this mission because of his "strict adherence to principles and rules," so even accepting "small things" would still be to "deceive the imperial court."[39]

The envoy's gestures left a deep impression on Chungjong and his ministers. According to Ŏ Sukkwŏn, who served as Tang's interpreter during the 1521 embassy, the envoy, although reserved, was a fine poet who eagerly engaged in verse exchange with his Korean counterparts.[40] When he departed Seoul, he also left a letter to King Chungjong explaining why he declined his gifts. The poem it enclosed contained the following lines:

> [T]hough I refused your entreaties to stay,
> Once parted, I think only of your benevolence;
> I gaze upon Xuantu [i.e., Korea] with longing eyes
> As I fly away from these white peaks.
> Such feelings will never disappear—
> What need is there to carve them in resolute stone?

留時雖阻意 去後但懷仁
遠送玄菟目 常飛白岳身
此情元不朽 何啻在貞珉.[41]

The state councilor Nam Kon considered it remarkable that a "celestial envoy was so moved" as to dedicate a parting poem to the king. He suggested Tang be presented with additional gifts of stationery and medicine. Receiving these orders, the officials escorting Tang Gao to the border informed him that the king "had been dispirited, even unable to sleep" after their "hurried parting." The king hoped the envoy would accept these tokens as an expression of his "lingering feelings."[42] Tang declined again, resolving to "adhere to ritual." At his escort's insistence, Tang "dared accept" the stationery, a calligraphy template, and "nothing more," while his vice emissary Shi Dao accepted one brush and one inkstick. Tang accepted pouches of medical herbs but opened them in front of his deputies so that all could see no treasure was inside.

Tang's final gesture suggested that the Ming court back home was ultimately the intended audience of his actions. Charged as these interactions were with emotive language, these performances of both virtue and sentiment relied on literary craft to dissipate any doubts looming over his honesty. To be effective (and to strike the right tone to avoid offending his hosts), Tang treated material objects as incontrovertible with intangible sentiments. In this moral economy, Tang and the king exchanged only adoration; his luggage was light, but he left Korea heavy with "feelings never to disappear."[43]

Tang's investment in these performances exceeded that of other envoys, but the rhetoric he used was fairly common. Decades earlier, the 1476 envoy Qi Shun articulated a similar incontrovertibility of sentiment and object. In his parting letters to King Sŏngjong, Qi expressed concern that the king "could not completely know" his reason for refusing gifts. Qi explained it was not because he wished to "contravene [the king's] generous intentions":

> But how could the friendship of gentlemen be sustained only through material things? To send someone off with gifts—that is the ceremony of the king. I treasure my heart that covets not. Both host and guest have done their utmost according to their station and should have no shame. This ought to be enough, but I may yet be unable to free myself from the fault of irreverence.[44]

When the Korean royal secretary presented Qi with a coat of marten fur, Qi wrote another letter where he reasoned the king must have "taken his refusal to be a false and empty gesture," having ignored them only to send more riches from afar. He recalled the austerity of Yan Ying 晏嬰 (578 BCE–500 BCE) who for thirty years "wore only one vixen coat." Because "material objects can be exhausted, but feelings are inexhaustible," what bound him to the king, according to Qi Shun, were "feelings, not objects."[45]

In Qi's understanding, it was decorous for the king to offer, while it was the envoy's duty to refuse. But the resolve in the literary refusal often occluded the flexibility of the actual exchange. Qi did, in fact, accept many gifts from the Chosŏn court, although he took care to moderate their quantity. Elsewhere, Qi invoked an altogether different discourse of emotion and materiality, conceiving the two as exchangeable.[46] He claimed he was obliged to "appreciate the generosity and sincerity" of the king. Daring not "wantonly waste the products of nature," he had no choice but to "humbly accept one or two parts" while returning the rest, all to show that he would not "forget [the king's] care."[47]

Literary articulations of refusal balanced the cultivation of a virtuous reputation with maintaining cordial relations with one's hosts. A cynical reading could treat this rhetoric as a way to acquire both wealth and reputation, although outright refusal to engage with the Korean court could itself cause offense. The 1495 envoy Wang Xianchen 王獻臣 (fl. 1490–1513, later more famous for his Humble Administrator's Garden 拙政園 in Suzhou), rankled his Korean hosts for his pedantry in matters of protocol and total rejection of gestures of goodwill from his Chosŏn hosts.[48] Without a literary accompaniment, refusing such gestures rejected the sentiments they were meant to represent.

Virtue and literary craft were therefore two sides of the same coin, at least when it came to an envoy's reputation in Korea. Qi Shun's escort, Sŏ Kŏjŏng, praised Qi for a "distilled and proper" style of writing that reflected his virtue in deeds. Sŏ had plenty of points of comparison because, over the course of his official career, he had interacted with dozens of other Ming envoys for whom he often left pithy assessments in his *Miscellaneous Records of the Brush Garden* (*P'irwŏn chapki* 筆苑 雜記). The 1450 envoy Ni Qian was "understanding and friendly," while his assistant Sima Xun was "frugal and upright." Sima was inferior to Ni in literary reputation but surpassed him in "deeds and virtue." One envoy named Jiang Hao 姜浩 (1443–?) behaved well but "lacked literary elegance." But the possession of the latter could not make up for deficiencies in the former. The 1467 envoy Jin Shi had "a practiced hand in seven-character verses," and his calligraphy and painting were said to be "excellent and sublime," but his "virtue and deeds were deplorable." With his "greedy nature," he even personally stuffed his luggage with "miscellaneous items like dried meat and fruit." Because he demanded many metal implements from the Chosŏn court, they often jokingly referred to him as the "brass dishware literati-merchant" [鍮器長商士]. Brushes and inkstones reflected the literati's station, but such everyday goods profaned the envoy's mission. On the contrary, the 1460 envoy Zhang Ning was "a little forced in his words and deeds," taking his refusals of Korean gifts a little too far. But like Sŏng Hyŏn, who described him as "gallant and majestic, spirited and untrammeled," Sŏ also found him a worthy gentleman.[49]

Against this ledger of moral virtue and literary talent, the voracious Gu Tianjun and the perfectly restrained Tang Gao were truly outliers. Few Ming envoys went to either extreme because acquisitiveness damaged one's image while outstanding literary ability could mitigate a negative impression. Neither quality was enough to condemn or exalt alone. Most telling is to whom Sŏ consigned the most virulent condemnation: the 1457 envoy Gao Run. During Gao's mission, Sŏ Kŏjŏng was a junior court official and had an opportunity to peek at Gao Run's personal travelogue. He found poems with titles such as "Thinking of my parents" 思親詞, "Given gifts of clothing, but did not accept" 送衣不受詩, "Refusing courtesans" 却妓詩, and "Visiting Confucius" 謁宣聖詩. These, Sŏ believed, would be used to "angle for a reputation" upon the envoy's return to China.

Many envoys wrote similar poems, but Gao was infuriating because of his blatant hypocrisy. Gao craved both material goods and a spotless reputation. From topknot wigs to eating utensils, Gao Run "demanded items without cease."[50] But Gao was also careful to limit his requests to items small enough to be hidden from public view, so when the king bequeathed him a horse and saddle, items too large to be squirreled away in a sack, Gao would, as Sŏ predicted, decline them with a poem. Sŏ found this behavior to be "deceitful and perfidious, unbecoming of a proper envoy," and "tactless to the extreme" [人之無狀至此哉]. Even more frustrating to the young Sŏ Kŏjŏng was how Chosŏn officials humored Gao's pretensions. Sŏ lamented: "Could Chosŏn be so insignificant and powerless that not a single person could distinguish between right and wrong, [allowing him] to act as fraudulently as such?" Sŏ was finally vindicated, however, with the printing of the *Brilliant Flowers.* Sŏ noticed that Gao was "initially quite pleased," but when he came across the poem he had written to thank the king for his gifts, the envoy "turned colorless with rage." With such a poem in the anthology, Gao could no longer claim he had taken nothing from Korea.[51]

IMAGINED PAVILIONS

Sŏ Kŏjŏng disdained Gao for making no effort to match in deed the aura of virtue he cultivated in his writing. To Sŏ's chagrin, Gao Run eventually succeeded in this quest for renown. Gao's hometown gazetteer 方志 described him as an honest and frugal man, using his purported behavior in Chosŏn as an illustration. It asserted not only that he returned from Korea with nothing save a poetry anthology but also claimed the Chosŏn court was so impressed that it erected a "Refusing Gold Pavilion" 郤金亭 to honor his memory. Given Gao's awful reputation in Korea, this claim is hard to believe, but it would have been only one of many such pavilions that were peppered across Korea's landscape, if late imperial Chinese biographies of Ming envoys are to be believed.[52]

Reputations of personal virtue continued to be made after these envoys returned across the Yalu River and even after they left the world of the living. Gifts rejected and courtesans spurned once upon a time in Korea continued to shape an envoy's posthumous reputation in China.[53] The funerary epitaph 墓誌銘 of the 1476 envoy Qi Shun juxtaposed sexual restraint and frugal behavior, portraying him as a man who received the emperor's praise for "resolutely refused all the presentations of female entertainers and gifts of gold and silk."[54] A later sixteenth-century gazetteer provided an even more embellished account of Qi Shun's 1476 trip. In it, Qi Shun's "resolute refusal" of "saddles, horses, gold, silks, and entertainment" caused the "ruler and ministers of Korea to look upon each other in such amazement" that they constructed a pavilion in his honor. Although Korean accounts of Qi's trip confirm this positive impression, the idea that Qi traveled to Korea on "a single steed," as well as the pavilion constructed in his name, were outright fabrications.[55]

"Refusing Gold Pavilions" that appeared in such biographical accounts supposedly provided material evidence of exemplary behavior. Even more of these pavilions came into existence in later Qing period records to honor even more Ming envoys. An eighteenth-century provincial gazetteer of Zhejiang claimed that "the people of Chosŏn erected a 'Refusing Gold Pavilion'" for the 1582 envoy Huang Hongxian 黃洪憲 (1541–1600).[56] The legend of a "Refusing Gold Gateway" constructed for the 1568 vice envoy Wang Xi 王璽 who also "refused gifts of treasures and jewels" persisted well into the nineteenth century.[57]

According to these Chinese accounts, there should have been dozens of such Refusing Gold Pavilions in Korea. Chosŏn sources suggest there were exactly zero. In 1488, when the shipwrecked Ch'oe Pu was still stranded in China, he was approached by a relative of the 1460 envoy Zhang Ning who asked about a "Refusing Gold Pavilion Poem" in the *Brilliant Flowers*. Such a poem did not exist in Zhang's *Brilliant*

Flowers anthology, although Ch'oe Pu satisfied the man by reciting another poem from Zhang's collection.[58] Pavilions of this sort were not mentioned again in surviving Korean records until 1626. That year, the envoy Jiang Yueguang asked his Korean welcoming emissary Kim Ryu 金瑬 (1571–1648) to take him to see the Refusing Gold Pavilion and the Refusing Gold Bridge that honored the 1567 envoy Xu Guo. The request perplexed the Chosŏn court. Knowing of no such edifices, it ordered Kim Ryu simply to tell Jiang that "Envoy Xu was lofty and virtuous like a clear wind, foremost in all of China," and Chosŏn would never have dared to bequeath him treasure.[59]

Jiang took offense, however, and found it "extremely strange" that Chosŏn's officials had forgotten Xu Guo's "virtuous deeds." Even in China, he had heard that Xu Guo accepted only two sets of silver-shafted and silver-handled brushes, only to throw the silver trimmings into the water as he crossed the Yalu. Suspecting that his hosts refused to show him the sites because they had let the monuments fall into disrepair, Jiang Yueguang volunteered to commit his personal funds to their restoration. Upon this request, the Chosŏn Welcoming Commission proposed that "we should point at any small pavilion and call it the 'Refusing Gold Pavilion,' and invite the Ming envoy to leave his own inscriptions on the spot." The court thought this plan "fit the contingency of the situation" but took the dissimulation a bit too far. It rejected this course of action.[60]

Kim Ryu could not take Jiang Yueguang to see Xu Guo's pavilion because it never existed. In time, Jiang Yueguang himself received an imaginary Korean pavilion dedicated to his name. When the Chosŏn writer and painter Cho Yŏngsŏk 趙榮祐 (1686–1761) came across a Chinese account describing Jiang's pavilion, he scoffed: "In our country [Korea], we have never heard of these 'Refusing Gold Pavilions . . . this is how incredible such rumors can be!"[61]

These Korean pavilions indeed were figments of Ming imagination, but their textual proliferation reflected a convergence of actual practices. In Chosŏn, there were memorial sites that honored Ming officials, but they were constructed in the wake of the Imjin War to honor Ming soldiers and officers who defended Korea.[62] There were also scenic vistas, stone monuments, and even pavilions associated with Ming envoys. Rather than built to honor the virtue of specific envoys, they were usually existing sites that Ming envoys adorned with their calligraphy or poetry (a practice to be discussed further in the next chapter).[63] In Ming, however, pavilions, gateways, steles, and other monuments honoring respected local officials (or to cajole existing ones into behaving according to those standards) were common sights in the provinces.[64] Among them included presumably actual Refusing Gold Pavilions honoring an official's honesty. Although amid the "image politics" of the period, it should be noted that they provoked contentious questions over authenticity even among Ming contemporaries: did such pavilions actually exist? Did the honored officials in fact behave virtuously? And, if so, did they do so only to chase a reputation?[65]

Refusing Gold Pavilions might never have existed in Korea, but they testified to the discursive potency of Ming envoy reputations. They endured well beyond an envoy's sojourn or even his lifetime through the tropes of material austerity and sexual restraint employed by epitaph and gazetteer writers alike. Indeed, Jiang Yueguang only needed to turn to a predecessor's funerary epitaph to corroborate his belief that they had "not even accepted a single item offered as a gift."[66] These refrains even issued from the hands of the Ming court's most venerable Ming statesmen, such as Grand Secretary Li Dongyang 李東陽 (1447–1516) and the preeminent scholar-official Wang Shizhen 王世貞 (1526–1590).[67] So when Wang Shizhen stated that the 1539 envoy Hua Cha 華察 (1497–1574) "refused all bribes at the Yalu River" and called his act a "great affair, recorded in the unofficial histories of Korea," he not only dramatized a conventional narrative with new tropes but also burnished the credibility of such accounts.[68] With so many luminaries having written about so many pavilions, why should Jiang Yueguang ever have doubted their existence?

The Ming literati community turned the Refusing Gold Pavilions into another literary device of empire. In their narratives, the gift-refusing, courtesan-spurning imperial envoy became a synecdoche for the moral character of imperial rule. These tales of virtue then brought home the transformative influence these envoys had on those they encountered. Throughout these narratives, the envoy is portrayed as "instructing" his barbarian charges, civilizing them through his virtuous displays and moral exhortations. The 1488 vice envoy Wang Chang 王敞 (1453–1515) taught a lesson to the Koreans when he refused performances of female entertainers at a banquet. His words—"the Son of Heaven has only recently entered the afterlife; how could I bear to hear this?"—caused the Korean "ruler and his officials to look upon each other in shame, withdrawing the female musicians."[69] Here, as elsewhere, Korean "ruler and ministers" were either shamed or awestruck by the envoy's behavior. Another Ming period account, the tombstone inscription of an official named Ge Shouli 葛守禮 (1505–1578), followed a similar arc. In this case, it was a visiting Korean envoy who brought him gifts, which he refused. So impressed by Ge's integrity, the Korean envoy supposedly reported to Korea's king, who "erected a memorial gate on the border to honor his virtue."[70]

As icons for the myth of moral empire, these imaginary edifices were built not only by Chosŏn rulers. Gazetteers from the Ming and later Qing periods also spoke of monuments erected by Vietnamese monarchs, Ryūkyūan kings, and aboriginal chieftains. Like the pavilions in Korea, it was unlikely any of these existed, but their propagation across such wide geographical and diverse cultural zones only highlights their tenacity in Ming literati imagination.[71] Ornaments of a stereotyped narrative rather than actual structures of wood and stone, these paper pavilions were a consequence of a central imperial myth that has been discussed throughout this book, one that also appears again and again in the diplomatic record: how with words alone, the barbarians could be brought to submission.

Given how often the man behind the story fell short of the image, it is tempting to disregard these accounts of exemplary Ming envoys as immaterial hooey. Even when there was deed to match the word, the self-conscious fashioning smacked of hypocrisy. But these are not reasons to dismiss them. Both fiction and hypocrisy had a role in shaping diplomatic conventions. Because Ming officials and the envoy's Korean hosts imagined a shared, if stereotyped ideal, deviations in deed required either dissimulation or self-deception by a wayward envoy. Even the most unscrupulous still couched his behavior within a cultural idiom of self-restraint. After all, hypocrisy existed only when there were ideals to undermine in the first place.

Tropes of refused gifts, spurned courtesans, and imagined pavilions also produced an enduring mythology of empire that outlasted the Ming dynasty itself. In 1799, long after Ming's fall, the Qing emperor Jiaqing 嘉慶 (r. 1796–1820) ordered his emissaries to Chosŏn to behave according to earlier Ming paragons, prohibiting them from "taking even a single thing" from Chosŏn. On their return, they proudly reported to the emperor that they had carried out his orders to the letter. They refused every single gift, even though the Chosŏn court's messengers had followed them all the way to the Yalu River, insisting that they accept them. To the envoys' surprise, the emperor was displeased. He scolded them: "if they had gone this far, you should have at least taken something instead of leaving the vassal state offended." The emperor then docked the envoys' salaries for one year as punishment.[72]

In this blend of fact and fable, a single gesture might have had a minuscule effect in the grand scheme of things. But as one scholar says of ritual in imperial China: "no one makes up ritual or symbol any more than anyone makes up language." As "collective products worked out by numberless anonymous men over long periods of time," malleability did not imply "infinite flexibility."[73] With their accumulation, even a single gesture could shape how a future envoy mission played out. Ritualized practices, like language, also shifted with the accretion of minute changes.

But as the Jiaqing emperor's reaction to his envoys' behavior showed, it was one thing to recognize a precedent and another to act upon them well. Appropriate action required not so much adherence to fixed rules but modeling one's behavior on past exemplars. As Yan Congjian put it in his treatise on the Ming envoy office, a good imperial envoy was one who "did not stain his great reputation and whose stalwart virtue 駿傑 sufficed as a formula or model." What best illustrated this ideal were the deeds of actual envoys.[74] Although Yan largely refrained from repeating outlandish acts in his accounts, when it came to establishing precedents for envoy behavior, exemplary acts that never occurred could work just as well as a model if the posthumous biographies discussed in this chapter are any indication.

Finally, the myth of the virtuous envoy also contributed to the long-standing generalization of a Chinese-centered tributary order as one sustained by cultural attraction. The idea of Chosŏn admiration of Ming culture (and, by extension, Korean admiration of Chinese civilization, *mohwa* or *muhua* 慕華) was also reproduced by these accounts.

But if these gestures of virtue are understood in terms of ritual practice, as operating in the "subjunctive," they also highlight the oft-occluded dynamic: the intense Korean investment in the imperative of moral empire. The Chosŏn court presented gifts and courtesans, even expecting them to be declined. They also always represented Ming envoys in a positive light in diplomatic correspondence, regardless of what transpired. This outwardly cynical behavior that enabled an envoy's hypocrisy still proceeded "as if" Ming envoys were moral paragons.[75] By doing so, the Chosŏn court did not "admire" from a distance but negotiated a shared imperial ideal. When it came to constructing the Refusing Gold Pavilions in imperial imagination, Chosŏn might have been an unwitting accomplice; its interpolation into the ideals they represented, however, was deliberate.

CHAPTER TEN

The East Does Not Submit

Not all pavilions were figments of Ming imagination. Imperial envoys did leave their mark on Korea's landscape, just not in the manner described in their epitaphs. All along the envoy route, Chosŏn officials invited Ming envoys to dedicate poems 詩, rhapsodies 辭賦, and travel accounts 記 to commemorate their visits. Most of these pieces entered the pages of the *Brilliant Flowers*, while some also adorned the rafters of pavilions or were carved into stone steles. Virtually every stop along the envoy route received some literary treatment, but it was P'yŏngyang, the largest city in northern Korea, that received the most attention.

The sites envoys visited in P'yŏngyang were often associated with hoary legends. Ming envoys unfamiliar with local lore would have learned of these stories after ascending the Pavilion of Floating Emerald 浮碧樓. On its rafters hung the famous poem of the Koryŏ writer Yi Saek recounting how the demigod founder of Koguryŏ, King Tongmyŏng 東明王 (r. 37 BCE–19 BCE), launched himself into the sky from Heaven Gazing Rock 朝天石, riding the *kirin* he reared in a nearby underground cavern called Unicorn Grotto 麒麟窟.[1] Ming envoys also visited the shrine of Korea's mythical first king, Tan'gun 檀君[2] and the temple and tomb of the sage Kija.[3]

Chosŏn used all three figures, Tan'gun, Kija, and Tongmyŏng, to claim antiquity. Since at least the Koryŏ period, they represented a native trajectory of dynastic and cultural succession. In a rhyming chronology of Chinese and Korean rulers, the Koryŏ statesman Yi Sŭnghyu 李承休 (1214–1259) established a line of succession beginning with Tan'gun to inscribe for Korea a "heaven and earth" distinct from China [遼東別有 一乾坤 斗與中朝區以分]. But rather than cleavage, Yi claimed parity: Korea was the "lesser central efflorescence" (*so Chunghwa* 小中華) due only to its smaller size, not inferior cultural attainment.[4]

To Ming envoys, however, Tan'gun and Tongmyŏng were unfamiliar figures. Only a handful left dedications for them. Only Kija, a prominent figure in the classical tradition, always received their homage. The 1539 envoys Hua Cha and Xue Tingchong bowed only with their hands clasped 揖 when they visited Tan'gun's shrine, but for Kija, they performed four kneeling prostrations 四拜, the same level of obeisance shown to Confucius himself.[5] Kija's relative esteem also matched the sheer volume of writing about him, as opposed to Tan'gun or Tongmyŏng.[6]

Kija's significance for the ideology of Chosŏn diplomacy has long been noted, but less appreciated was his role in diplomacy's social dynamics.[7] As an important classical figure, Kija lived in the world of texts and the imaginations of learned men, but the tomb and shrine in P'yŏngyang gave him a physical presence in Korea. That presence intertwined the numerous pieces of writing dedicated to him by Ming envoys with, to borrow Henri Lefebvre's terminology, "spatial practice." In turn, these envoy inscriptions bound these physical monuments in a wider web of historical imagination through connections to other texts in the poetic and exegetical tradition surrounding Kija.[8] As this chapter will show, the Chosŏn court and its diplomats deployed these connections in their autoethnographic strategies. In this case, these strategies went beyond the rhetorical. They manipulated space and sociability to enlist Ming envoys in their efforts to authenticate Korea's links to Kija, and by extension, Chosŏn's claim to political autonomy.

THE KIJA MYTHOS

Kija probably never existed. Absent support from modern archaeology or philology, the lore surrounding him is better treated by modern scholarship as mythos, one whose significance is as a source of moral lessons and symbolic resonances for Chosŏn elites and their Ming interloctuors.[9] In this respect, Kija has been understood primarily as a "cultural symbol" of "a shared culture" 同文 in Korea's relations with China. As historian Kim Han'gyu elaborates, it was "because Korea received the ablutions of Chinese civilization through Kija" that Ming envoys "recognized it to be a country that shared with China its culture and institutions" [同文同軌].[10]

In Ming imperial imaginary, Kija's actions anticipated Ming's civilizing influence over the country. Take, for example, the Xuande 宣德 (r. 1425–1435) emperor's endearingly literal poem written on the subject of "Chosŏn Sending Envoys to Present Tribute:"[11]

> East of the sea—the vassal kingdom of ancient Koryŏ;
> Its writing, civilization, clothing and caps, far surpass the barbarians
>   of the four [directions].
> Traveling far to join us here, the envoys are often sent;
> Filling the court with crates of tribute, they are also ceremonious.
> I hear that Kija's teachings yet remain,
> And I feel that Puyŏ's old customs have changed.
> To make sure they leave with much and arrive with little I will do,
> So that in P'yŏngyang too, the same spring light will shine.

> 海東蕃國古高麗 文物衣冠邁四夷
> 遠道會同頻遣使 充庭筐篚亦多儀
> 還聞箕子遺風在 已覺夫餘舊俗移
> 厚往薄來吾所務 當今平壤共春熙

This piece of sovereign doggerel described how "Kija's teachings" had transformed the barbarian Puyŏ people into the civilized (and loyal) Chosŏn he knew. In this poem, Kija at once reinforced Chosŏn's vassal status and symbolized Ming's universal, civilizing power.[12] No wonder then that Chosŏn reverence of Kija has also been interpreted as evidence of its elites being "mired in an ideology of 'admiring China' 慕華主義."[13] On the other hand, in line with the Yi Sŭnghyu's chronology of kings, sixteenth-century Chosŏn scholar-officials also asserted, through Kija, Korea's independent transmission of cultural and moral legitimacy from antiquity. According to historian Han Youngwoo, this orthodox "transmission of the Way" (tot'ong 道統) inscribed a political and cultural space for a Korea separate from Chinese imperial authority.[14] How could Kija simultaneously represent both Chosŏn's affinity to China and its distinction from it?

The contradiction appears only if all valences of "China" 中國— cultural, historical, political, geographic, and ethnolinguistic—collapse into a singularity. A necessary condition for Chinese nationalism, this semantic collapse had occurred as early as the eleventh century. But given that Chosŏn Korean elites had their own cultural and political stakes in the idea of "China," there is no reason to assume they shared Chinese nationalist understandings about the meaning of "China's" constituent parts and how they interacted with one another.[15] Here Kija's role as a "cultural symbol" that connected Korea to "China" is instructive because it only makes sense if the latter is disaggregated into its constituent parts. There is "China" as a political imaginary of successive imperial dynasties, "China" as a symbol for the classical world and the civilizational values it inspired, "China" as a referent to the imperial state that claimed a monopoly over all of the above, and "China" as the territory ruled by said state. Only with these distinctions in mind does Kija's role become recognizable as part of an autoethnographic strategy, one which Alexander Woodside describes as a form of "boundary maintenance" used by states on the imperial periphery such as Dai Viet and Chosŏn "against Chinese hegemony."[16]

Demarcating boundaries, whether cultural, territorial, or conceptual, was only half the program. Chosŏn Korean elites also sought recognition from Ming as cultural peers, so whatever bounded space they inscribed could not only militate against Chinese or imperial claims. It also had to make sense in imperial discourse. Kija's place in the classical tradition allowed Chosŏn to do both: assert Korean independence and cultural belonging in a manner comprehensible and acceptable to an imperial audience. As discussed in chapter 8, diplomatic encounters permitted no luxury of solipsism. Even if both Chosŏn and Ming officials were free to ply divergent narratives in their own records, they still had to harmonize in the social moment of the encounter. Accordingly, boundaries demarcated in the envoy poetry of the *Brilliant Flowers* were rarely embossed in stark relief. They are perceptible only if the implications of particular literary and historical allusions (and their precise juxtapositions) are taken to heart.

Any properly educated literatus would have recognized the reca-pitulation of Kija's story in a typical Chosŏn-Ming envoy poem.[17] They invariably drew upon standard classical references. According to the *Book of Documents* (*Shang shu* 尚書, the *Records of the Grand Historian* (*Shiji* 史記), and their commentaries, Kija was a clansman of the tyrannical last ruler of the Shang dynasty, Zhòu 紂 (not to be confused with Zhou 周, the name of the dynasty that overthrew him). Along with Bigan 比干 (fl. c. 1050? BCE), another Shang prince, Kija admonished Zhòu for his decadence, which one envoy poem by Dong Yue evoked by mentioning "ivory chopsticks," pleasure pavilions, and ponds filled with wine [象箸當年託意深 臺池那復救荒淫]. Tyrant Zhòu, weary of Bigan's remonstration, "said angrily, 'I have heard that a sage's heart has seven chambers' and dismembered Bigan to view his heart." Witnessing Bigan's demise, Kija "grew fearful and feigned mad-ness" and suffered only imprisonment. When King Wu overthrew the tyrant, he released Kija from captivity. Kija then transmitted to Wu the teachings of the Sage King Yu through the *Great Plan*, which provided the new ruler a guide for rulership [禹範一篇陳大道].[18] In this ren-dition, Kija showed dynastic loyalty, represented the minister's moral prerogative to remonstrate with wayward rulers, and served as a vector for the transmission of political knowledge.

Kija's portrayal in historical texts did not cohere perfectly with his status as a moral exemplar.[19] Confucius upheld Kija as a moral exemplar for speaking up to the tyrant, even ranking him alongside Bigan as one of the "three benevolent" paragons (C. *sanren*, K. *samin* 三仁).[20] But among them, only Bigan gave his life for the cause. According to the *Grand Historian*, Bigan even found Kija's loyalty inadequate because he told him that "as a subject to a ruler, one has no choice but to remon-strate [against his misdeeds] unto death" [為人臣者 不得不以死爭].[21] According to the scholar of early China Michael Nylan, the Kija story raises a "host of moral quandaries," including, "when is loyalty to family less important than loyalty to community? How may a corrupt reign be restored to goodness?" It also asks, When does "a higher duty to the Right" supersede "conventional obligations?"[22]

These questions gave plenty for Chosŏn and Ming envoys to con-sider in their literary meditations. Dong Yue's poem, for instance, insisted Kija's feigned lunacy too were "sacrifices" of a "stalwart heart"

[誰云披髮佯狂態 不是捐軀獻靖心]. Kija did not die for a moral cause like Bigan, but his actions were equal to Bigan's martyrdom because both offered their "hearts": as part of his body in Bigan's case and as the seat of psycho-moral knowledge in Kija's. These points of moral tension in the Kija mythos found their resolution in Kija's connection with Korea. In many envoy poems, Kija's actions after entrusting the empire to King Wu compensated for where his sacrifice fell short of Bigan's.[23] According to the commentarial tradition, Kija was heartbroken by his dynasty's demise and left his homeland for a place called Chaoxian 朝鮮.[24] There, Kija received investiture from King Wu of Zhou and established a state. And by promulgating his "instructions in eight points" 八條之敎 to the locals, he brought civilization to Chaoxian as well. According to the third century Chinese *Record of the Three Kingdoms (Sanguo zhi* 三國志), Kija's descendants ruled until they were usurped by a Chinese exile named Weiman (K. Wiman 衛滿).[25]

The story of Kija represented the eventual triumph of the kingly way over despotism. That said, the figure of a remonstrating official ignored to the end by his sovereign might have resonated with both Chosŏn and Ming officials in another way. For those confronting monarchs who turned a deaf ear to their counsel, Kija promised eventual vindication, even as he embodied the personal tragedy that often befell the remonstrators. With these motifs, several Ming envoy poems invested a sense of pathos in this historical figure. For the 1476 envoy Zhang Jin 張瑾 (1448–1481), visiting the "desolate tomb" in P'yŏngyang that "faced the setting sun" [平壤荒墳對夕陽] was an opportunity to lament Kija's fate. Kija's "loyalty and righteousness" only earned his ruler's "recalcitrance" [當時忠義忤商王]. Left to "suffer as a slave" in vain, Kija had to witness the destruction of the state he tried to save [隱忍為奴社稷亡]. Although in old age "he received investiture from the sage king Wu," his submission left him "with no face" to see the Shang founder "in the yellow springs" of the underworld [白首有封逢聖武 黃泉無面見成湯]. Although Kija's name has persisted, those who bring him sacrifices could not help but feel pain for his fate [千古三人傳不朽 椒漿奠罷使人傷].[26]

Sŏ Kŏjŏng, his Korean welcoming emissary, objected to this reading. For him, Kija's act of civilizing Korea brought closure to the sage's life by confirming his moral intentions. To speak of losing face in death undermined the moral message of Kija's life. Sŏ reminded Zhang Jin that what ultimately mattered was Kija's contributions to the Confucian way, validated by the "millennia of ritual veneration" he enjoyed thereafter, so there was no reason to be "moved to sadness in vain" [丹荔黃蕉千載 祀 空令過客為悲傷].[27] Other Ming envoys gravitated toward the same resolution when they came to "pay their respects" to Kija. They too "gradually felt their emotions swell," only to be relieved that Kija's "legacy" had "flowed here" [我來拜謁頻增感 遺化漸洏遍海陬].[28] Through these interlocking references, Kija explained Korea; Korea also explained Kija. Korea had become part of the classical past and its interpretation, but only if it could be safely assumed that Korea was really Chosŏn, an assumption, as will be explained, was less safe than might first appear.

THE PRODUCTION OF SPACE

Analogous to the idea that Kija was Korea's civilizer was the notion that Ming envoys enacted the empire's civilizing mission, an analogy reinforced by Chosŏn-Ming spatial practice. In 1574, when the Chosŏn official Hŏ Pong traveled through Korea, he noted how many of the scenic areas of the country had been named by visiting Ming envoys. The 1567 envoy Wei Shiliang 魏時亮 (1529–1585) chose the name Moon Admiring Veranda 弄月軒 for an older pavilion, while Gentleman's Hall 君子堂 became the Pavilion of Gathering Cool 納凉亭 after the 1573 envoy Han Shineng 韓世能 (1528–1598) inscribed a placard with the new name.[29] The most famous was Scallion Bloom Hill 蔥秀山 in Hwanghae Province (see map 3), which had been named by the 1488 envoy Dong Yue when he dedicated a travel account to the spot.[30] Once Scallion Bloom Hill was named through Dong Yue's dedication, the Chosŏn court erected a stele with his inscription, inviting more visits and literary ruminations from Ming envoys.[31] Facing it was Emerald Screen Hill 翠屏山, where another stele bearing an inscription by a Ming envoy stood.[32]

By the end of the sixteenth century, a cluster of Ming epigraphy had gathered around the site. Another Chosŏn official linked the natural splendors of the area to the generative power of Ming writing. In describing the scenery of Scallion Bloom Hill, he asked rhetorically, "Among all the scholars of China / whose brush was like a rafter," powerful enough to give life to this scene [中朝諸學士 誰是筆如椽]?[33] These and other sites adorned by the writing and calligraphy of Ming envoys had become celebrated locations in Chosŏn's literary geography.[34]

These inscriptional practices also enabled Ming pretensions of universal empire. As the 1537 envoy Gong Yongqing wrote, such sites "would have fallen into obscurity in this eastern land" if they had not left traces of their ink [幸有吾人為賦詩 不然泯沒在東土]. Their writing, they believed, was a civilizing act that instilled meaning in an empty landscape.[35] This experience, however, was one curated deliberately for imperial eyes. When Gong Yongqing visited Korea, he requested blank, multicolored hanging boards to be prepared in advance of his arrival at the capital. The Korean interpreter misunderstood his request and furnished him with blank scrolls instead.[36] The carte blanche Chosŏn provided was both figurative and literal because the court also cleared the literary landscape for the envoy. The court prevented "any books" written by Koreans or "ancient texts containing the prefaces or post-faces by Korean writers" from being shown to Ming envoys without advance permission.[37]

Compositions by Korean officials and literati that adorned pavil-ions, waystations, and vistas were subject to the same policy. Although stone steles remained in place, wooden plaques that hung on rafters and entryways could be removed at will.[38] According to Kwŏn Ŭngin 權應仁 (1517–?) and Hŏ Kyun 許筠 (1569–1618), both officials, who participated extensively in diplomacy, only the placard containing the parting poem titled "The Taedong River" 大同江 by the Koryŏ poet, Chŏng Chisang 鄭知常 (?–1135) remained hanging at the Pavilion of Floating Emer-ald 浮碧樓 when a Ming embassy passed through.[39] Removing Korean writing, however, conflicted with the desire to burnish the reputation of Korean writers in Ming eyes. Chŏng Saryŏng once interceded to keep Yi Saek's poem on the Temple of Eternal Brightness 永明寺 in place, but only because the Ming envoy Ni Qian had once praised it as "no inferior" to Chŏng Chisang's poem, which hung in the same spot (see figure 10.1). All in all, whatever Ming envoys saw in Korea had been crafted for their gaze.[40]

With the landscape denuded of native literary flourish, Ming envoys saw instead one redolent with their own. Rhyme-matching ensured each site visited would gradually accumulate inscriptions over time.[41] The 1450 envoy Ni Qian left an inscription that inspired the 1452 envoy Chen

FIGURE 10.1 View of the Taedong River from Moran Peak, overlooking the Pavilion of Floating Emerald (Pupyŏngnu 浮碧樓) and the Temple of Eternal Brightness (Yŏngmyŏngsa 永明寺). "P'yŏngyang Morandae," 1921. Photograph in *Shasinjō*: Chōsen 寫眞帖-朝鮮. Chōsen sōtokufu 朝鮮總督府. Seoul Museum of History 서 27618. Courtesy of the Seoul Museum of History.

Dun to insist that his own compositions be hung at the envoy hostel in Seoul.[42] Chosŏn also encouraged this accumulation. In 1464, the court ordered local officials along the road from the frontier to the capital to hang the placards with Ming envoy writing before the embassy's return to the Ming.[43] Envoys could therefore see their own works adorning the waystations and pavilions that they wrote upon their arrival.[44] Since Ming literati envoys generally never traveled to Chosŏn again, seeing these plaques hanging alongside those of their predecessors was one way they could know for sure that they would continue to be celebrated in Korea. By 1488, the envoy Wang Chang already noticed that the walls of one waystation were now covered with "ink, thick with poems left in leisure" [壁間濃墨閒留題] by his predecessors.[45]

Together, these sites embodied the collective traces left by generations of Ming envoys. If the publication of the *Brilliant Flowers* linked them across time through genre and text, these sites granted their links physical form, leaving the pages of the *Brilliant Flowers* to become part of the landscape. Once their inscriptions began to decorate the pavilions, waystations, and vistas in stone steles and wooden plaques, they accumulated a sense of temporal depth and regularity to once-in-a-generation diplomatic encounters (see figures 10.2 and 10.3). This sense, however, depended on investment from the Chosŏn court whose representatives brought imperial envoys to the same sites as their predecessors, inviting them to perform in their shadow. Once the visitors agreed to follow suit, spatial practice acquired an illocutionary effect. The result was something more concrete and enduring than the social moments that inspired them.[46]

Through these spatial practices, the Chosŏn court cast Ming envoys as latter-day Kijas, agents of civilization's "eastward flow" 東漸 from China to Korea. But these spatial practices also undercut the congruence

FIGURE 10.2 "Hall of Illuminated Virtue" (Myŏngnyundang 明倫堂), 1606. Zhu Zhifan 朱之蕃 (1558–1626). Hanging board with calligraphy. Outside the lecture hall of the Chosŏn royal academy, the Sŏnggyun'gwan 成均館, currently in the grounds of Sunggyunkwan University. Photograph by author.

FIGURE 10.3 Poem by Zhu Zhifan, 1606. Hanging board with calligraphy. Interior rafter of Myŏngnyundang. Photograph by Dorothy Ko.

between the Kija mythos and the Ming imperial narrative. First, the Chosŏn court, never a passive accessory, relinquished the power to inscribe only for the duration of a Ming envoy mission. Ming writing monopolized Korean spaces, but Korean writing returned to their former places once the envoys departed. The fiction of Ming as sole civilizer was maintained only for as long as Ming eyes were looking. Second, Kija's tomb and shrine, unlike renamed hills and vistas, did not occupy a supposedly unadorned landscape but were in the city of P'yŏngyang, a place with a layered past that told a story of cultural and political continuity. These two caveats, one related to Korean intention and the other to spatial context, point to a third issue, that of inscriptional practice. Repeated in situ inscription imbued a site with a transtemporal significance. The meaning of any single piece of verse was not limited in the discrete context of its composition or its immediate audience but was self-consciously one element in a wider social matrix and ongoing tradition.

A FORGED ANTIQUITY

The Chosŏn court invested in the narrative of Ming envoys as contemporary instantiations of the civilizing process. But what, besides goodwill from the Ming court, did Chosŏn gain from this investment? Understanding what was at work requires appreciating how the Kija mythos transformed P'yŏngyang into a site of representation, a place whose significance resonated far beyond its immediate spatial context. As suggested earlier in this chapter, Ming envoys recapitulated Kija's story, but by doing so in P'yŏngyang at Kija's tomb and shrine, they also underscored and authenticated what was originally a marginal detail in that narrative: Korea's link to classical antiquity.

Korea had become part of the classical past and its interpretation, but only if Kija's Chaoxian was really Korea, an assumption that must not be taken for granted. Before the twentieth century, it was common to refer to Korea as the "country of Kija" 箕子之國 and the city of P'yŏngyang as the "city of Kija" 箕城.[47] The connection appears self-evident partly because the name of the Chosŏn dynasty matches the name of Kija's kingdom, Chaoxian. From Ming envoy poems to standard early Chosŏn histories, Kija's Chaoxian, the kingdom of Wiman, and the Korean state of Chosŏn were ontologically continuous. In turn, Chosŏn/Chaoxian has become synonymous with Korea as a cultural, political, and geographic entity, stable across time periods and in all modern East Asian languages. The stability of these associations today, along with the importance of Kija for Chosŏn's political ideology, make it difficult to appreciate how tenuous this connection once was.

The identification of Chosŏn Korea with Kija was not a foregone conclusion. It was an equivalence produced through a deliberate historiographical, ideological, and diplomatic strategy. The dynasty's founders likely desired a connection with Kija when they presented "Chosŏn" as one of two options to the Ming Hongwu emperor as candidates to replace "Koryŏ" as the "title" 國號 of the new state.[48] Before this fourteenth-century adoption, Chosŏn/Chaoxian had not been the formal name for any state for sixteen hundred years, the last one being the state of Wiman, which the Han Empire destroyed. During the Koryŏ period, the name was used in titles of honor such as "Duke of Chosŏn" 朝鮮公, it was not conceived as an alternative name for the Koryŏ state, even as it identified Chosŏn as one of its antecedents.[49]

Earlier states based in the Korean peninsula also claimed Kija but faced obstacles when doing so. Koguryŏ adopted a cult of Kija worship, likely as an ancestral deity, but contemporary Chinese observers considered it a form of "inordinate worship" 淫祀.[50] In the eleventh century, the Koryŏ ruler Sukchong 肅宗 (r. 1095–1105) constructed the Tomb of Kija in P'yŏngyang to establish his kingdom as Koguryŏ's successor, directing his ambitions northward toward its frontier with the Khitan-ruled Liao in Manchuria.[51] In the meantime, Liao identified its eastern capital, Liaoyang, not P'yŏngyang, as the site of Kija Chaoxian's citadel, indirectly claiming Koguryŏ's legacy for itself. Like Chosŏn Korea would do later, the Liao court also credited Kija with bringing "civilization" to this region. Rival Liao and Koryŏ claims over Kija, and the cultural and political legacy of Koguryŏ come as no surprise given their parallel and competing claims over Manchuria.[52]

The Kija tomb built by Sukchong in P'yŏngyang was a cenotaph (see figure 10.4). After all, if, as modern scholars argue, Kija's journey to Chaoxian was no more than an anachronistic reading of earlier sources, no tomb in Korea could have interred this ancient sage.[53] Indeed, there were plenty of skeptics even before the modern era. One commentary of the *Grand Historian* identified Meng County 蒙縣 in China's Shandong region as the location of Kija's burial. The existence of another tomb in an authoritative source must have made the Korean tomb's authenticity suspect for imperial visitors, though only a few openly voiced any doubts. One who did was a Yuan envoy who passed through P'yŏngyang in 1366:[54]

FIGURE 10.4 Kija's Tomb, P'yŏngyang, ca. 1908–1922 [?]. Photograph by Shannon McCune. USC Digital Library. Pacific Rim Archive Collection. Courtesy of the University of Southern California, on behalf of the USC Libraries Special Collection.

On a hill in the lands of Lu, pine and cypress stand;
A loyal soul will be known by ghosts and spirits for eternity.
At night, I sit on my horse on the path to Chaoxian—
I can almost hear the song of the Ripening Wheat.[55]

魯士一丘松栢在 忠魂萬古鬼神知
晚來立馬朝鮮道 髣髴猶聞麥秀詩

Pine and cypresses represented virtue's endurance and were metonyms for tombs and graveyards. That they stood in Lu (i.e., Shandong) and not in Chaoxian meant the envoy could *almost* feel Kija's spiritual presence in Korea, even if his actual remains were elsewhere. One Ming envoy did call it a "perfidious burial" and told his hosts that "no descendants of Kija" lived in Korea, a remark the Chosŏn king dismissed as "ignorant."[56] This unnamed Ming envoy might have committed a diplomatic faux pas, but his doubts were shared by others in Ming China, including one sixteenth-century scholar who called King Wu's investiture of Kija in Chaoxian "utterly ridiculous."[57] The point here is not that the Koryŏ tomb was real or that the Shandong tomb was not, or vice versa (both were cenotaphs). At stake instead was the status of Korea's connection to Kija. If the Kija tomb in Korea were real, the connection would be unassailable. But what if the tomb was counterfeit? What did that mean for Chosŏn's link to Kija?[58]

The tomb's provenance also troubled the Chosŏn court. King Sejong was wary of the vast temporal gulf between his time and Kija's tomb. In 1419, he ordered a new stele to be inscribed by the tomb's side. Its author, Pyŏn Kyeryang, recapped the Kija narrative and wrote proudly that Kija, who "contributed to the Way," and the "teacher of King Wu," was not "enfeoffed anywhere else, but in [Our] Chosŏn," whose populace had once "directly received his daily teachings." Treating Kija's presence as "heaven's generosity towards the East," Pyŏn asserted a seamless continuity between the Chaoxian of yore and the Chosŏn of his day. Kija's teachings had crossed the gulf of time, enduring over millennia.[59]

Not all were convinced by Pyŏn's assertions. Some court officials protested the stele's erection. They argued that the so-called Tomb of Kija was but a "legend passed on by the locals." To insist on the tomb's authenticity without "written records as a basis" and "several thousand years" separating Kija from the present would "not be the way to show proper reverence." Against these reservations, Pyŏn still urged that the stele be placed by the tomb, as initially intended, but the king dithered on the matter, and in 1428 moved it beside the shrine instead.[60] Decades later, King Sŏngjong once asked the local governor to investigate the tomb's provenance, including when it was first asserted to be Kija's tomb and what documentary basis existed for this assertion. No records survive from this investigation, but it was unlikely anything definitive could have been discovered.[61] Ultimately, Chosŏn stepped back from the issue, leaving the tomb's authenticity unresolved.

Meanwhile, the tomb remained to sustain associations with Kija. The 1582 Ming vice emissary Wang Jingmin 王敬民 once related to his Korean host, the Neo-Confucian scholar-official Yi I 李珥 (1536–1584), how excited he was to "lodge so close to Kija's ancient ruins," but he confessed "ignorance of the details" of Kija's activities in Korea. Yi I produced a copy of the *True Annals of Kija* (*Kija silgi* 箕子實紀) that he penned, a text meant to authenticate Chosŏn's link to Kija.[62] According to Yi I's biographers, the envoy was thoroughly impressed by the work, exclaiming that "there was no document like this in China," words of compliment that, if taken out of context, might have suggested incredulity instead.[63]

Did Wang Jingmin's inquiry stem from curiosity or skepticism? Regardless, Chosŏn's connection to Kija was at stake. Yi I and other early Chosŏn statesmen based their confidence on established textual authority. They "broadly investigated books of classics, histories, and philosophers" and "assembled the facts and the discourses of sages and wise men"[64] to find ample support for Korea's connection to Kija from canonical authorities but their research offered little in the way of resolving remaining lacunae in the Kija mythos. For example, these works spoke of Kija's "instructions in eight points" proclaimed in Chaoxian, but no one could ever enumerate them. Even Yi I could list them only "in brief," giving only three.[65] Another work, one which Yi I's *True Annals* relied on, the *Record of Kija* (*Kija chi* 箕子志), included an apocryphal chronology of Kija's forty-one descendants and their royal titles and reign dates for the period they purportedly ruled Korea, information drawn from the genealogy of a local elite family claiming descent from Kija.[66] Its author, the one-time governor of P'yŏngyang and compiler of its earliest extant gazetteer, Yun Tusu 尹斗壽 (1533–1601), once wrote of the city: "The people who remain [here now]—though we do not know from whom they descended—*should* all be the progeny of those who once received his teachings."[67]

Apocryphal sources, later embellishments, and unverifiable details entered these accounts. Chosŏn period scholar-statesmen such as Pyŏn Kyeryang, Yi I, and Yun Tusu, were most likely aware of these evidentiary problems, but they were motivated by a desire to authenticate the link to Kija and availed themselves of the limited resources they had on hand. But in this enterprise, they were also aided by another powerful source of authority: imperial officials. When Ming envoys visited P'yŏngyang, they already saw an array of edifices and inscriptions celebrating Kija, but by paying homage to Kija's shrine and tomb and dedicating their poems and elegies, they only strengthened their effect.[68]

As early as 1457, Ming envoys felt compelled to deliver their elegy after having "read the masterpieces of those who have come before."[69]

Visiting "Korea and paying respects to [Kija's] old shrine" [人到三韓 謁舊祠], Ming envoys like Chen Jiayou equated the "Eastern fief" of their day, Korea, with the "ancient country where [Kija] was enfeoffed, / whose people's customs were just as they were before" [東藩自是分封 國 民俗依然似昔時]. Meanwhile, these compositions declaring Korea to be "truly the place of the master's fiefdom" adorned the shrine hall as evidence of continuity.[70] By 1539, when the envoy Xue Tingchong visited P'yŏngyang, he saw not only Pyŏn's stele protected by a small pavilion but also the "writings of great men from the Central Court in new plaques and old hangings" [新匾舊揭 胥中朝鉅公題詠].[71] Rectangular fields in P'yŏngyang were taken to be remnants of the "well fields" 井田 the sage had implemented, which led one Ming envoys to remark that "until today the people of P'yŏngyang / still know the influence of the Shang" [至今平壤民 猶識商家風].[72]

The old tomb was of dubious origin, but imperial inscriptions affirmed if not P'yŏngyang as the site of Kija's sepulcher then at least Chosŏn's claims to Kija's legacy. Whatever doubt a Ming envoy harbored had to be suspended when he performed his ablutions in front of Kija's tomb or wrote a dedication to the shrine. Otherwise, he would have had to contradict an entire tradition constructed over decades by his predecessors and peers. If the imperial gaze of Ming envoys provoked anxiety over Kija's authenticity, the Chosŏn court, by endowing Ming envoy writing with the physical form, now enlisted that very gaze as a palliative for that same anxiety. Together with the tomb and shrine, the inscriptions of Ming envoys transformed a once tenuous claim into a shared and certain truth.

REWRITING THE CLASSICS

When it came to forging a classical past, Koryŏ and Chosŏn Koreans would have found ample company among societies elsewhere in Eurasia. Geoffrey of Monmouth (ca. 1100–1155) traced Britain's origin to an adventuring son of the Trojan hero Aeneas (and progenitor of the Romans) in order to claim an antiquity for Britain that rivaled Rome, a claim held fast long after the Galfridian myth had been debunked.[73] The value of these antiquarian connections, however, went beyond asserting cultural prestige. They also established a *translation imperii* that provided a historical justification for the existence of a political community. In this regard, the Kija mythos is reminiscent of the the *Privilegium Maius* created at the behest of Rudolf IV (r. 1358–1365), the Habsburg ruler of Austria. Through a set of forged documents, it invented legal precedents dating back to Julius Caesar and Nero, one that guaranteed Austria's territorial integrity and legal autonomy from Rome, and by extension the laws of its latter-day successor, the Holy Roman Empire.[74]

As was the case for the *Privilegium Maius*, the Kija mythos advanced a claim for privileged membership within an imperial order, not separation from it. But instead of invented legal precedents, Kija worked through poetry, diplomatic ritual, and classical exegesis. The ablutions and elegies performed by Ming envoys lent imperial sanction to the idea that Kija's Chaoxian was the precursor to Chosŏn, they also implicitly agreed that Korea was transhistorical, that it existed since the age of the classics. As Pyŏn Kyeryang's stele in P'yŏngyang put it, Kija's was the "only" reason why "the writing, civilization, ritual, and music of the East have approximated that of the Central States for over two thousand years now" [吾東方文物禮樂 侔擬中國 迨今二千餘祀 惟箕子之 敎是賴]. Kija, by expounding the *Great Plan* to King Wu of Zhou had also transmitted to him the imperial tradition now inherited by Ming; now by bringing civilization to Korea, Kija also created a separate "eastern" strand of political transmission distinct from the "Central States" (a claim which also implicitly diminished the potential civilizing role of later imperial dynasties). Korea became a separate but culturally equipollent political entity.[75]

Korea was now coeval with empire, but this also raised further questions. If both Chosŏn and Ming were common heirs of the classical past, what did this imply for Chosŏn's relationship to imperial authority in the present? On this issue, Kija was ambiguous. For one, Kija championed a moral good that trumped obedience to the monarch Kija's relationship with King Wu, who freed him, presented yet another problem. According to the *Shiji*, after Kija transmitted the *Great Plan* to him, King Wu "invested Kija in Chaoxian, but did not make [him his] subject (C. *buchen*, K. *pulsin* 不臣)" [於是武王乃封箕子於朝鮮而不臣也], implying Kija's new state was beyond the pale of King Wu's authority. Syntactical ambiguity also permits reading "Kija," not "King Wu," as the agent. In that case, it would not have been King Wu who "did not make [him his] subject" in a show of magnanimity, but Kija who defied King Wu by "not serving [him]."[76] The latter interpretation found expression in the envoy Dong Yue's second poem on Kija. In lingering loyalty to the Shang, he "the Jade Horse[77] refused to serve in the court of the Western Zhou (Wu's kingdom)," so "with cap and gowns," the trappings of civilized life, he "raised pure standards in the Eastern Kingdom" instead [玉馬西周不共朝 冠裳東國儼青標].[78]

Dong Yue's was only one possible reading. Even the received exegetical tradition diverged on how to understand *buchen* and what it meant for Kija's relationship with King Wu. The term *buchen*, used elsewhere, could mean rebellion and thus carried strong negative connotations incompatible with the sage's impeccable virtue. Early commentaries to the *Great Plan* in the *Great Tradition of the Book of Documents* (*Shangshu dazhuan* 尚書大傳) avoided portraying Kija's departure to Chaoxian in those terms. In contrast to the *Grand Historian*, it claimed that "since Kija had received the investiture of the Zhou, he could not avoid observing the rites of a subject" and therefore came to pay tribute three times every ten years.[79]

In this version, Kija's observance of a subject's rites emerged out of moral obligation toward the Zhou king Wu, the logical result of accepting its investiture. In the seventh and eighth centuries, Kija's investiture had been used by the Sui and Tang empires to justify invasions of Koguryŏ as irredentist wars to reclaim old imperial territories. The Sui statesman Pei Ju 裴矩 (547–627) declared that Koguryŏ was where the Zhou enfeoffed Kija (and these territories were also formerly under Han rule), but it "now refused to serve [*buchen*]" and therefore deserved imperial retribution.[80] For Chosŏn, which desired imperial recognition as cultural equals and assurance of political autonomy, this version of Kija presented a quandary.

Kija linked Korea to antiquity but also raised the specter of irredentism. The two versions of Kija posited two different views on the meaning of investiture. But even where investiture did not entail submission to Zhou authority, as in the *Grand Historian*, Kija's freedom was still premised upon King Wu's generosity. Neither version left much room for Korean political agency.

In the stele erected in P'yŏngyang, Pyŏn Kyeryang managed nevertheless to carve out that room with a bit of syntactical innovation. Pyŏn restated the canonical story, but explained that "when King Wu of Zhou defeated Yin (Shang)," he invested Kija "in our state, in order to allow him to follow his will of not being a subject" [封殷太師于我邦 遂其不臣之志也].[81] Here Pyŏn did not use the compound *buchen* in a causative sense, where a generous Zhou king "did not make [Kija his] subject," but instead used it to describe Kija's moral resolution of refusing to serve, which the Zhou ruler "followed."[82] As the moral will of a virtuous sage, *buchen* was now shorn of negative implications. Investiture too became less a sign of political subservience than a representation of imperial commitment to Kija's political autonomy.[83]

P'yŏn's radical interpretation of *buchen* was reiterated elsewhere. In the *Brilliant Flowers* poems by the Chosŏn official Hŏ Chong, Kija's "receipt of investiture was not to become a servant of the Zhou" [受封非是作周臣], and in "single-minded loyalty, he never paid obeisance west [to the Zhou]" [孤忠終不向西朝].[84] Not surprisingly, some Ming guests disapproved of this interpretation. The 1460 envoy Zhang Ning, who wrote one of the most extensive meditations on Kija, framed his response as a rebuttal to the famous Tang scholar-official Liu Zongyuan's 柳宗元 (773–819) interpretation of Kija's life.[85] Liu Zongyuan posited that if the last tyrannical Shang ruler had died sooner or if the uprising by the Shang prince Wugeng (武庚 fl. eleventh century BCE) had succeeded, Kija would have had a chance to restore his dynasty. A lament of Kija's misfortune, it also implied that Kija's later actions, including his transmission of the *Great Plan* and his exile to Chaoxian, were motivated by lingering loyalty toward his destroyed dynasty.[86]

The problem with Liu's version was that it reduced Kija's loyalty to dynastic fealty. For Zhang, that loyalty ought to be understood as loyalty to a moral and political order that transcended dynastic interests. Kija's great wisdom was expressed in accepting Shang's demise as inevitable. Recognizing the outcome as "heaven's will" explained why he chose to deliver the *Great Plan* to King Wu instead of fixating on the doomed Shang. His "original heart" was also visible through his later actions— even when his clansmen tried to restore Shang, he did not rebel against Zhou authority. Instead, he remained in Chaoxian and "taught the people with regulations and laws, inspired rituals and decorum, and nurtured those in the Eastern land." Zhang then borrowed Pyŏn's unique turn of phrase in his inscription to say how Kija was "from beginning to end able follow his ambition of not submitting [*buchen*] [終始遂其不臣之志]" while dramatically shifting its significance:

> [Kija] brought great benefit to one region. He turned the barbarians to civilization [俾夷為華]. The boons of ethics, mores, ritual, and music have continued until today without decline. For generations, [his country] has received investiture and patents, a state that has lasted for a long time. And the Master [Kija] has enjoyed sacrifices at his temple in perpetuity. All of these things were the gift of the Central State, the Zhou. Ah! How benevolent indeed was the Zhou [皆中國周之賜也 於乎 周亦仁矣哉]!

Zhang Ning, like his Chosŏn hosts, equated Kija's state with Chosŏn. He also affirmed Korea's existence outside dynastic time, but he ascribed its civilization and independence not to Kija's labors, but the Zhou king's benevolence. In this analogical scheme where Zhou was the Central State then, and Ming was the Central State now, Chosŏn's political existence could only be a gift of the Ming Empire.

Although worded as a response to Liu Zongyuan, Zhang's tract ventriloquized a retort of P'yŏn's interpretation of Kija. Yet within the diplomatic channel sustained by the *Brilliant Flowers*, a variety of interpretations could flourish in tandem, so Zhang did not have the last word. As with the other examples discussed in this book, points of tension were rarely made explicit. For instance, the 1521 envoy Tang Gao also disputed the dominant Korean narrative—but indirectly. He wrote that "Kija was a guest" 賓 of King Wu rather than his subject 臣 and thus "was made not to submit." The model here was a relationship based on reciprocity and mutual coexistence: Kija's "state was coeval with the Imperial Ming / with baskets of gifts and tribute of treasures" going between them [國與皇明相終始兮 賜有篚而貢有琛].[87] "Not submitting [*buchen*]" remained King Wu's "gift," but defiance was never Kija's intention. In a rebuke to his Chosŏn hosts and a rejection of Pyŏn's stele, he also claimed Kija had "now acquired a reputation of defiance in vain" [不臣自是周王禮 虛被頑名直至今].[88] Tang's Korean interlocutor, the Chosŏn official Yi Haeng, doubled down on the narrative in Pyŏn's stele. He answered: "The East was once the land of Kija who did not submit, / Where his legacy of loyalty and righteousness remain to this day" [東方原是不臣地 忠義遺風留至今].[89]

Whereas Tang excused Kija for "not serving," Yi Haeng identified refusal to submit itself as an expression of loyalty. In the Kija mythos, the target of loyalty would have been Kija's dynasty, Shang, but how would this analogy work in the present context, where Ming saw itself as the Zhou dynasty's successor?

Reconciling this problem required reframing this analogy. Elsewhere, Yi Haeng wrote that becoming a vassal to the Zhou in Korea was in itself an expression of "not submitting."[90] The only way to make sense of this statement, of how Korea could be a "land that does not submit," could be reconciled with loyalty to empire is to see how Kija delineated, in principle, that imperial authority had limits, even if its precise bounds remained unmarked. What mattered in this formulation was the following: that Chosŏn remained an integral stakeholder of the imperial system and a distinct political entity whose perpetual existence was guaranteed by their shared classical tradition.

Kija accommodated different narratives about Korea's place vis-à-vis empire. These narratives did not coalesce into a precise meaning, even as the Chosŏn court calibrated the Kija mythos to align with its claims of authority. The Chosŏn court's selective adaptation of a specific register within a range of possible interpretations did conflict at times with the expectations of Ming envoys, but during the diplomatic encounter, even contested meanings could coexist in parallel, without any one becoming the definitive, final interpretation. It is here that spatial practice has a role to play: in front of Kija's tomb and shrine, all parties deferred to the rituals of the sage's veneration.

As this chapter has shown, the spatial practices of diplomacy converged with a broader Korean autoethnographic strategy. Allowing the visiting Ming envoy to play the role of civilizer certainly reinforced the Kija mythos, but as one tailored and refined for Chosŏn's ideological and political goals. By encouraging Ming envoys to visit places of Kija worship and leave behind their "representations of space"—poetic and prose portrayals of their homage, the Chosŏn court obliged Ming envoys to authenticate shaky Korean claims and reify particular meanings. The process transformed the sites in P'yŏngyang into a Lefebvrian "representational space" whose meaning resonated well beyond the city's walls.[91] P'yŏngyang stood for Kija, who stood for a Korea coeval with Ming as an essential component of the classical canon. It also stood for a Korea whose existence transcended the vicissitudes of history to become a permanent fixture in the imperial tradition. Through Kija, empire was co-opted rather than subverted; its advances were redirected rather than spurned.

By the turn of the twentieth century, the classical past and the imperial tradition lost their relevance for staking meaningful claims on the diplomatic scene. What changed was not the urgency of maintaining Korea as a distinct political space, but against whom such claims needed to be made. With its rapid imperial decline, Qing China ceased to be a viable political partner or a target of cultural identification. Reform-minded Korean elites demoted China from the home of classical civilization to just another ethnonational entity on the world stage, one which was filled with new existential threats in the form of Western imperialism and a rapidly modernizing Japan.

For a while, Kija maintained its relevance as a political symbol. The embattled King Kojong 高宗 (r. 1864–1907), associations with imperial influence motivated a wholesale rejection of the Kija mythos. As late as 1888, Kojong still sought to draw on Kija to shore up royal authority by upgrading the status of Kija's tomb 墓 to that of a royal mausoleum 陵, strengthening the *translation imperii* through Kija for his embattled monarchy. But for others, Kija became an unwanted vestige of Korea's political and cultural dependency, not an ancient sage representing universal moral aspirations. He was, in the words of the Korean nationalist historian and political activist, Sin Ch'aeho 申采浩 (1880–1936), merely a prince of "China" (K. China, J. Shina 支那).[92] A radical shift from the Chosŏn period, Tan'gun replaced Kija as the premier, historical symbol of an eternal Korea, if not the actual progenitor of the Korean people in both North and South Korea. Kija, on the other hand, has all but disappeared from popular historical imagination.[93]

Ideological repudiation and historiographical rejection have incidentally converged with modern philology and archaeology. Only a minority of serious scholars would accept the story of Kija's eastward migration as history, let alone see Korea as the location of Kija's Chaoxian.[94] Nevertheless, the link between Kija and Chaoxian remains a component of contemporary Chinese claims of *historical* sovereignty over Manchuria, which has clashed with Korean nationalist perceptions of Manchuria as "lost" Korean territory.[95]

Behind these rival nationalisms is a deep irony. Their moves, to expurgate Kija from Korean national history and to assert Kija's historicity in service of either Chinese territorial sovereignty or cultural influence, share an assumption about what the Kija mythos meant. They both treat Kija as a stand-in for China. This is a fundamental misrecognition of the Kija mythos in its Chosŏn context, one possible only because colonial, postcolonial, and ethno-nationalist contexts have stripped away all of Kija's symbolic resonances to leave it as a bare signpost to a moribund "Chinese" imperial system—the very resonances that led the Chosŏn court to manipulate space to strengthen Korea's associations with Kija and to win acknowledgment of these associations from Ming visitors in the first place. Kija, meaning much more than "China," traced for Chosŏn elites a genealogy of descent to a vaunted antiquity that could anchor Korean political claims. In fact, Kija's primary function was precisely what his later detractors criticized it for not doing: establishing a Korean identity that was independent and distinct from China.

Conclusion

The Myth of Moral Empire

The chief strategy of Chosŏn diplomacy was to shape empire and how Korea related to empire. Empire, in this frame of reference, is not reducible to an expansive imperial state but entailed a wider political imagination with stakeholders beyond the outer bounds of imperial control. As was the case for the Chosŏn court, these stakeholders need not be the executors or even the object of an emperor's sovereign claims, but ones who interpolated themselves into the process of empire making. For the Chosŏn court, this interpolation was preemptive and anticipatory rather than reactive. Although Chosŏn did challenge unfavorable imperial policies once they had been enacted, it mostly tried to prevent them from materializing in the first place.

To do so, Chosŏn produced and reified the idea that a proper, moral empire also had to guarantee Korea's political integrity. Along with the trope of Korea's perpetual loyalty, the notion of moral empire framed what was within the realm of imperial possibility. Although these tropes have become emblematic of Chosŏn-Ming relations as a whole, but as this book has shown, they emerged from Chosŏn's engagement with the rhetorical logic and ritual symbolism of empire. If statistical accumulation, economic exploitation, bureaucratic rationalization, military logistics, ritual differentiation, ethnologic categorization, or even panoptic surveillance belonged in the go-to repertoires of an empire's rulers and administrators, then those at the imperial margins, like Chosŏn Korea, counted on a different repertoire. They relied on an imperializing mode of appeal, autoethnographic techniques of representation, and the performance of imperial tropes in ritual and discourse—techniques that did not directly challenge empire, but sought to engage with it, appropriate it, and redirect it

But did this repertoire work? Did Korean engagement with empire and interpolation into the imperial tradition change the course of Korean history? Without the benefit of alternative timelines or parallel realities, the answer must perforce remain speculative. Nonetheless, how the Chosŏn-Ming relationship evolved and later unraveled between the outbreak of the Imjin War in 1592 and the Manchu conquest of China do offer some clues.

IMJIN AND BEYOND

When the Japanese warlord Toyotomi Hideyoshi 豊臣秀吉 (1537–1598) invaded Korea in 1592, he had much grander designs. His primary target was not Chosŏn but Ming. He declared to Chosŏn his will to unify the world under his rule and demanded that it support his venture. Chosŏn rebuffed him, comparing what he proposed "to a son turning against his father;" an unthinkable and gross moral violation.[1] When Hideyoshi's armies landed in Korea, Chosŏn's defenses melted before the onslaught, Ming forces eventually came to Chosŏn's rescue. After six long years, Hideyoshi's armies were turned back, and Chosŏn rule over Korea was restored. If Hideyoshi's invasion was, as is often described, a revisionist effort to dismantle the Ming-centered, Sinocentric world order, Ming's defense of Korea in the Imjin War demonstrated its resilience.[2]

Seen in these terms, Ming intervention appears to be the logical outcome of the tributary system. If Ming wished to reassert its preeminent position in East Asia, it had to support its most "loyal tributary."[3] The Chosŏn king Sŏnjo, for his part, did believe he was entitled to the hegemon's protection because his kingdom had "served the great with utmost sincerity" [事大以至誠] for many generations. As he fled before the advancing Japanese forces, he assured his entourage that if they could but reach Ming Liaodong, imperial armies would undoubtedly come to protect them; however, his courtiers were less confident.

Unsure whether the Ming court would accept an exiled Korean king, let alone lend him support, they dissuaded him from further flight across the Yalu River.[4]

In the meantime, the envoys sent to request aid from Beijing met with difficulties. From how the Ming court discussed the matter, it did not look like aid was forthcoming. One Ming minister insisted that "the Central State should only stand guard at its own gates." Chosŏn might have served Ming loyally, but it was still one among the "barbarians of the four directions" and only the empire's "outer hedge." With an aphoristic touch, he stated: "One has only heard of using the barbarians of the four directions to defend [the realm]" and never "to help the barbarians defend themselves" [聞守在四夷 不聞爲四夷守].[5] Others believed that a war between the Japanese and Korea was an instance of "barbarians fighting one another" [夷狄相攻], making imperial intervention pointless. Some officials even suspected Chosŏn was in cahoots with the Japanese invaders. A Ming envoy was sent to investigate the situation and was convinced otherwise only when the Koreans showed him their wartime correspondence with the Japanese.[6] Whatever the two centuries of tribute missions amounted to, it was not enough.[7]

As the Ming court debated its options, Chosŏn envoys waited anxiously in their hostel in Beijing. They found a sympathetic ear with the Ming minister of war, Shi Xing 石星 (1537–1599). He invited the envoys to his private residence, where they discussed how to convince the Ming court to send aid. In a line of argumentation reminiscent of the diplomatic appeals of Nam Kon and So Seyang decades earlier, he stated that Chosŏn deserved Ming's support because it had "always observed propriety and righteousness," possessed a culture that "approximates the Central Efflorescence," and displayed "flawless reverence for two hundred years."[8] Korean chronicles also credit him for disabusing his colleagues of the idea that Korea was a place beyond the reach and authority of Ming. While he agreed with them that the fate of the "outer states," which were "far beyond the distant marches," was not Ming's proper concern, Chosŏn was exceptional, a place to be treated as part of the Ming's "internal realm" 內服.[9] After Shi had built a coalition of voices to support the Chosŏn cause (which included a Siamese ambassador who pledged his country's military aid), the Ming court decided, with the emperor's personal approval, to intervene.[10]

Shi Xing's case for intervention depended on seeing Korea as integral rather than extraneous to Ming's empire. At one point, the Chosŏn court even offered to integrate the kingdom with the Ming state (literally, "attached to the interior" K. *naebu, C. neifu* 內附) if the invaders could be trounced.[11] Besides counteracting the view that Chosŏn was beyond proper imperial concern, reminders of Chosŏn's perpetual loyalty and invocations of a broader ecumenical imaginary also raised the banner of imperial responsibility: what Ming *owed* its loyal vassals in this time of need. Here, Chosŏn diplomacy worked. Its earlier investment in the Ming Empire paid off. Such appeals were convincing because the narrative they employed had already been reified by centuries of diplomacy before.

To be sure, rhetoric alone was not enough to prevent Chosŏn from being cast away as an extraneous appendage. These appeals, whether by Shi or Chosŏn's envoys, also spoke to security concerns, underscoring Korea's role as a defensive bulwark, a literal "fence and barrier" that protected the Ming heartland, just as lips protect teeth from cold.[12] Amid concern over the risk and cost of military intervention, the Ming court had other reasons to delay aid (Ming forces were tied up elsewhere). The choice to intervene was conceived in strategic and ideological terms, with the decisive factor a matter open to debate. But when the focus is on which calculations were more critical to the Ming decision to rescue Chosŏn, it is easy to forget that the tropes of empire activated at this moment were never intended for this purpose.[13]

The Imjin War was a black swan event. For virtually the entirety of recorded Korean history until then (notwithstanding Meiji Japanese fantasies of Jingū 神功, traditionally, 201–269 CE), existential threats to peninsular regimes always materialized from the north and west. Chosŏn did not invest in the Ming Empire for 200 years so that Ming armies could be summoned to defend Korea. It did so as a talisman *against* imperial intervention. Korea was not ready for a cataclysmic war because two centuries of diplomacy had already staved off the greatest potential threat to its military security: imperial China. What the fifteenth-century architects of Chosŏn diplomacy, the likes of Kwŏn Kŭn, Pyŏn Kyeryang, Sin Sukchu, and Sŏ Kŏjŏng, could have never imagined was that the most crucial invocation of empire in Chosŏn history was not to fend off an imperial army but to invite one to rescue Chosŏn from an unanticipated threat.

Notably, their sixteenth-century successors, the Chosŏn courtiers at the helm during the Imjin War, were uneasy about imperial aid. Even during this existential crisis, Chosŏn officials remained apprehensive about the Ming presence. What if once the Ming army arrived, they never left? As the Imjin War carried on, Ming sidelined the Chosŏn court in peace talks with Hideyoshi. The Chosŏn court opposed these overtures, but Ming officials reminded it that Chosŏn would be defenseless without their armies. Throughout negotiations, Hideyoshi's representatives proposed that the southern half of the Korean peninsula be ceded to Hideyoshi as terms for withdrawal. Although the Ming court never seriously considered this proposal, the fact that this item had even been raised for discussion caused ample consternation at the Chosŏn court.[14]

The war ended with Hideyoshi's death and the Japanese withdrawal in 1598. Its wide-ranging consequences for Chosŏn's relations with Ming are too many to be enumerated here, but for the purposes of this book's discussion, a few are worthy of note. One significant but subtle (and therefore overlooked) effect was the disruption of a delicate if asymmetrical balance between knowledge and power that the Chosŏn court had painstakingly cultivated. For the first time in centuries, hundreds of thousands of imperial subjects—soldiers, officials, traders—set foot in the peninsula.[15] A sizeable body of poetry, maps, history books, literary anthologies, and Korean editions of the classics—all compiled and published in Chosŏn, trickled into Ming China.[16] No longer a faraway land whose vistas entered only the eyes of an occasional imperial emissary, Korea fell under Ming's imperial gaze in a qualitatively different way.

With the imperial gaze thus focused, Chosŏn could no longer count on imperial inattention. For the first time in two centuries, the Ming court intervened directly in matters of Korean succession. It refused to invest Kwanghae 光海君 (r. 1608–1623), Sŏnjo's second son, as Chosŏn's king because Ming officials wished to enforce a rule of primogeniture in dynastic succession. Although the motivation was most likely the terms of an imperial succession dispute in Ming, now Ming officials saw the Chosŏn case as relevant to their own precedents, which ironically touched off a crisis of constitutional proportions in Chosŏn.[17] After the Japanese threat abated, Korea persisted in Ming strategic thinking. The rise of Nurhaci and the resurgence of the Jianzhou Jurchens invited a Ming-Chosŏn punitive expedition of unprecedented scale and unmitigated failure in 1619. The ongoing Jurchen threat even prompted the Ming court to consider dispatching imperial superintendents 監國 to oversee Korean military preparations, an intrusion Chosŏn opposed.[18] Meanwhile, and most pertinent to the issue of rhetoric, was the unfurling of a new slogan in the discursive landscape, one that represented Chosŏn's blood debt for the "recreation" of the kingdom through imperial beneficence [再造之恩]. Used at times by Ming envoys and officials to browbeat the Chosŏn court to comply with Ming demands, it also became a rhetorical cornerstone of Chosŏn domestic politics. As a rallying call for loyalty to Ming, it justified the overthrow of Kwanghae, who was accused of betraying the Ming emperor. And in the eighteenth century, it supplied the rationale for holding state sacrifices to Ming emperors.[19]

In short, the Imjin War reframed how Chosŏn and Ming related to one another. The old fictions of imperial rule evoked by rituals and poetry threatened to become a new reality, setting what Chosŏn considered dangerous new precedents. The Ming collapse in the mid-seventeenth century effectively rendered the issue moot. However shocking Ming's fall was to Chosŏn, it was likely mourned less than what post-Ming narratives of stalwart Korean loyalty to Ming would have posterity believe. After all, Chosŏn monarchs only raised the banner of Ming loyalism with enthusiasm decades after Ming's demise.[20]

The end of the Ming Empire did not mean, however, that Chosŏn ceased to be relevant to imperial legitimation. The Manchu invasions of Korea demonstrate otherwise. In 1636, the Jurchen emperor Hong Taiji (r. Qing Taizong 清太宗 1626–1643) renamed his people the Manchus and assumed the title *huangdi* or emperor, which replaced his former inner Asian style of khan (C. *kehan* 可汗) in Chinese documents issued by his chancellery. In the following winter, he invaded Chosŏn. His forces outmaneuvered Chosŏn's defenses and besieged the Korean king at the mountain fortress of Namhan. The Chosŏn king Injo 仁祖 (r. 1623–1649) capitulated and agreed to a humiliating surrender. For the first time since Koryŏ, a Korean monarch prostrated before a foreign ruler to pay his obeisance. When Hong Taiji withdrew, his armies hauled away royal hostages, captives, and treasure but left the Chosŏn state intact.[21]

Why did Hong Taiji not annex Korea when he had the chance? He certainly had the wherewithal: Hong Taiji continued to batter Ming armies, and his successors went on to conquer China and inner Asia. Perhaps ruling Korea was not worth the trouble if his eyes were set on a grander prize. But before Hong Taiji left, he commissioned a massive stele to be erected at Samjŏn Ford 三田渡, the site where he received King Injo's prostrations.[22] Drafted by Chosŏn officials and approved by Hong Taiji, the Manchu invasion was rewritten as a display of martial and civil virtue. On its face, Korea submitted willingly before imperial majesty. As a result, Hong Taiji magnanimously granted Chosŏn forgiveness for its transgressions, "unwilling to kill or harm [its people]," and thus "preserved [Korea's] ancestral temples" and "protected its living beings."[23] Having so recently assumed the imperial title (and therefore eager to secure recognition for it), Hong Taiji perhaps saw more value in the idea of Korea's submission as a jewel in his crown than as a territory to be ruled as his dominion.[24]

To inherit heaven's mandate properly and claim universal rulership, he had to acquire all the symbols of imperial legitimacy before he could replace Ming. He issued a new imperial calendar, assumed new reign titles, and even come into possession of the lost seals of China's first emperor and the great Chinggis Khan. Even his new dynastic name, Qing (literally, transparent, like water), promised to douse the once brilliant fire of Ming (literally, glowing). In this view, having Ming's former vassals recognize his virtue and destiny was just another way to displace the Ming as the world's true master.[25] But if Hong Taiji needed Korean tribute missions to demonstrate his imperial eligibility, it follows whomever Koreans showed their obeisance would also be the legitimate Son of Heaven. This inversion preserves the logic of imperial legitimation, but it exposes a startling observation about Korea as a component of this process. Could it also be that an empire that could not earn Korea's allegiance was no true empire at all?

This notion of Korea as the empire's first vassal, one that constituted the minimal imperial-tributary dyad, hearkened back to the narratives Koryŏ memorial writers plied to their Mongol overlords—that Koryŏ's survival and autonomy were premised on how it was "first to submit" to Qubilai. Hong Taiji's gesture (at least as narrated by the Chosŏn officials ordered to explain it) had firm antecedents in the imperial tradition. But when viewed against the long history of empire in East Asia, this arrangement was only one of many options. For the Sui and Tang emperors, Korea was an object of reconquest, former imperial territory to be reintegrated. But now, replacing this irredentism was the idea that Korea was the empire's most loyal vassal whose fealty and submission validated the imperial project. For this mechanism of legitimation to work, Korea had to remain autonomous. Hong Taiji, of course, coerced Korea to submit, but with his stele in place, he was content enough that Korea's submission was narrated, in perpetuity, as their willing recognition of his virtue and destiny.[26]

THE PAST HAS NO PROPER NAME

Chosŏn as an eternally loyal vassal, Ming as a paragon moral empire: these two ideas had been reified over the centuries of Chosŏn-Ming diplomacy and repurposed for Chosŏn's relations with the Manchu Qing Empire. Neither formulation is tenable today. Emperors are no more, even if the imperial past remains important to Chinese national identity and cultural pride. In Korea, Chosŏn's ties to empire remain a specter to be exorcised. But whether as an object of nostalgia or a target of disavowal, the imperial past is viewed in these ways because of how historical actors themselves narrated their worlds. After all, it was Chosŏn and Ming diplomats themselves who described their activities in terms of loyalty, propriety, and civilization. They were the ones who reified the idea of Chosŏn "serving the great with utmost sincerity" [至誠事大] and Korea's identity as the empire's "eastern vassal" 東藩.

This book has historicized this process of reification. It shows how these concepts, terms, and slogans endured because they were integral to the discursive and representational strategies of the Chosŏn court. Its diplomats distilled a narrative of Korea's relationship to empire that asserted both Chosŏn's membership in the civilized ecumene and its existence as a separate political entity: an independent state. But this narrative also had to be legible and workable within the diplomatic context. In other words, it also had to be compatible with Ming claims of universal empire. What diplomacy achieved was the reification of a shared set of discursive and ritual symbols that allowed all these claims to the imperial tradition and the classical past to coexist, even if contradictions remained.

But what does it mean to be an independent state and part of empire at the same time? Did performing a particular ritual or using a particular turn of phrase mean Chosŏn was part of Ming? The correct answer to this question has a feeling of quantum uncertainty: yes, no, both, or neither, a superimposition that depends on the motivations and goals of the observer. For the Chosŏn envoy, there were times to claim belonging and there were times to claim distinction; there was not one, definitive version of how Chosŏn related to the Ming Empire, a polysemy made possible by diplomacy as practiced.

As this book has argued, to think of Ming empire requires thinking beyond Ming as an expansive state but in terms of an idealized political imaginary. After all, Chosŏn was interested in Korea's position vis-à-vis, not just a Ming imperium, but an imperial order, one which could have a wide range of local meanings. When Chosŏn and Ming officials encountered one another in a diplomatic "trading zone," they operated through a shared imperial tradition with common conventions and precedents, but sharing each other's vision was not necessary for a diplomatic transaction to proceed. Chosŏn and Ming officials could, for instance, leave with different narratives, as long as the signs they used remained mutually legible and sufficient for "local coordination" when they reconvened; this was the role performed by the rhetorical and ritual practices described in this book. They made diplomacy possible.[27]

The diplomatic encounter required only momentary coherence. Afterwards, it fragments. The diplomatic record, the literary anthologies, the envoy accounts, and the historical memory documented in the texts discussed in this book do not then realign to form a shared transcript. Arguably, this fragmentation was even more pronounced in Chosŏn-Qing relations. The Chosŏn court rejected Qing legitimacy, but on the diplomatic stage, it still behaved as if the Qing emperors were legitimate. The superimposition of two, contradictory parallel transcripts remained stable as long as diplomacy remained mostly bilateral and its narratives securely under official control. Once third-party observers entered the picture, the superimposition was much harder to maintain.

In 1890, while Chosŏn and Qing officials wrangled over the protocols surrounding a number of diplomatic ceremonies, they were both keen to perform and advance their own narratives of what the ceremonies meant for a Western diplomatic audience. As Joshua Van Lieu shows, the eventual collapse of these narratives into a stereotyped Qing view of Chosŏn's timeless submission to Chinese empire had as much to do with Qing propaganda as how it fed into Western orientalist views of an unchanging Asia reproduced in contemporary print media and later academic works alike.[28] Eventually, Qing's defeat in the Sino-Japanese War (1894–1895) was what ultimately extracted Korea from this imperial universe, the semiotic dissolution of the mode of diplomacy described in this book had begun much earlier in the face of new hegemonies, new technologies, and new audiences.

The late nineteenth century also witnessed a shift to a diplomatic regime formalized by international law. Amid the furious diplomatic activity to delineate rights, obligations, and relations between polities in terms of treaties and constitutions, it became a pressing matter for both Chosŏn and Qing officials to "define" the exact nature of their relationship. This definition proved elusive to the very end.[29] Indeed, this problem of definition remains for historians today: what to call this entity, sustained by interlocked institutions, narratives, motifs, and practices, that bound Chosŏn so closely to Ming and then Qing Empire?

Over the last century or so, leading scholars writing in various languages have tried to name and rename it. John K. Fairbank dubbed its institutions the "tributary system" and its ideology the "Chinese world order." Peter Weber-Shäfer called it an "ecumenical empire" (*oikumenischen Reiche*). Hamashita Takeshi described a "regional system" to underscore material and not just political connections sustained by "tributary trade." Fuma Susumu and Chŏn Haejong (and the academic mainstream in South Korea) use some combination of the words "tribute" 朝貢 and "investiture" 冊封. Huang Zhilian referred to it as the "East Asian ritual world" 東亞禮儀世界, while Sinophone scholarship generally uses the term *zongfan* system 宗藩體系. Among theorists in China, Wang Hui folds it under a "supra-systemic society" 跨體系社會. At the same time, Zhang Tingyang calls it the *tianxia* (all-under-heaven) ritual system 天下禮儀體系. Jiang Shigong refers to a "Chinese empire" 中華帝國. In the meantime, Timothy Brook offers a reminder that the term "empire" is exogenous, and argues its best East Asian cognate was the notion of a Great State 大國, which folds in all the institutions and traditions above. The list goes on.[30]

Each formulation will have detractors and supporters. None will survive unscathed from a multilingual scholastic gauntlet of translation, critique, and reinterpretation. Rather than add to this litany of formulations (readers can choose their own), this book has discussed the history of Chosŏn and Ming relations without fixing its name. The reason is simple: to understand how Chosŏn Korea related to the imperial tradition, it was necessary to unravel the reification that was so central to its strategy of diplomacy. Only then could the processes of claims making that Chosŏn invested in be made clear. As Ludwig Wittgenstein's oft-quoted injunction, "Don't think, but look!" suggests, to understand what went on, it is better to examine a preponderance of particular cases, to observe diplomacy's "language-game," rather than derive general definitions from the classical texts or imperial statutes it referenced.[31] Unlike the scholastic legal culture of Grotius, Vittoria, Wheaton, and their successors, seldom do claims in diplomacy proceed deductively from formal, first principles. In early modern East Asia (and elsewhere), practitioners of diplomacy proceed through an experimental and inductive mode.[32] Every time Chosŏn envoys contested a ritual or invoked the imperial tradition (and the textual corpus that sustained it), they were engaged in experiments of what might be termed the political theology of empire: a search for an ulterior, moral ordering of empire that could transcend those who wielded its power.[33]

When Chosŏn rulers, officials, and envoys negotiated Korea's political position vis-à-vis Ming, the issue of empire was not just about Ming imperium but *imperial* order, a question that transcended empire as merely a state-making enterprise.[34] Today, the conversation over the terms of empire continues. Now, in the wake of inflamed geopolitical rivalries, one might ask what lessons this imperial past provides for the present. Is its myth of moral empire a prophecy for a desired future or a portent against foreboding horizons? For those championing Chinese ascendancy, Chosŏn's relationship with Ming is a serviceable past, a proof of concept for a China-led world order's promised benevolence.[35] For China's geopolitical adversaries, the pretense to moral empire is as ludicrous as it is ominous. Such alarms, whether sounded by retired generals or enthused journalists, will always find plenty of cause.[36] Just as no effort is needed to find hypocrisy in Western calls to defend human rights and international law, any cursory reading of the imperial record will yield enough examples of nefariousness and perfidy to undercut the mythology (this book mentions plenty).[37]

Despite the geopolitical rivals and ideological differences at work, there is something held widely in common by all sides of the conversation. They share a penchant for blending imperial myths with the actual past. They disregard the threshold between the past as a site for historical inquiry and the past as a quarry for serviceable truisms. But they were not the first to ignore this threshold. As this book has shown, Chosŏn's diplomats and court composers regularly indulged in the myth of moral empire. For Korea or any other middling power lacking the wherewithal to challenge empire directly, imperial myths provided the best opportunities for effective engagement. Curating imperial myths through a selective reading of the imperial past became a means to bend empire to their ends.

Inclusion in empire was a necessary condition for cajoling empire. Over the centuries, Korean elites, as stakeholders rather than outsiders, helped shape the imperial tradition. The palpable irony of all this is the myth of China's moral empire has persisted even today, partly because generations of Korean diplomats had been repeating it to China's imperial forebears for centuries.[38] The sheer volume of rhetoric uttered and rituals performed to support the myth makes it appear, in hindsight, to be qualitatively true. But to come away with this conclusion is to forget how Korean envoys and memorial drafters used the notion of moral empire in the first place: it was to convince emperors and their agents that behaving according to Korean expectations was the best way to be imperial.

Notes

HHJ   *Hwanghwajip* (足本)皇華集
HMC   (Yŏngin p'yojŏm) *Han'guk munjip chonggan* 影印標點韓國文集叢刊
KS   *Koryŏsa* 高麗史
MSL   *Ming shilu* 明實錄
QSL   Qing shilu 清實錄
QTW   *Quan Tang wen* 全唐文
SSJZS   (Chongkan Song ben) *Shisanjin zhushu* (重刊宋本)十三經注疏
SQKS   *Siku quanshu* 四庫全書
TDYS   *Taedong yasŭng* 大東野乘
TMS   *Tongmunsŏn* 東文選
YHNCJ *Yŏnhaengnok chŏnjip* 燕行錄全集

INTRODUCTION: KOREA AND THE IMPERIAL TRADITION

1. Kwŏn Kŭn, *Yangch'on chip*, 1 in HMC 7:15b; Yuri Pines, Michal Biran, and Jörg Rüpke, eds., *The Limits of Universal Rule: Eurasian Empires Compared* (Cambridge: Cambridge University Press, 2021); For Ottoman case, see A. Nuri Yurdusev, *Ottoman Diplomacy: Conventional or Unconventional?* (New York: Palgrave Macmillan, 2004), 18–20.

2. Anthony Pagden, *Lords of All Worlds: Ideologies of Empire in Spain, Britain and France c. 1500–c. 1800* (New Haven, CT: Yale University Press, 1995), 53–62.

3. For Yalu as frontier, see Jing Liu and Yan Piao, "Expansion, Contestation, and Boundary Making: Chosŏn Korea and Ming China's Border Relations Over the Yalu River Region," *International Journal of Korean History* 25, no. 2 (August 2020): 105–42; Nianshen Song, "A Buffer Against Whom? Rethinking the Qing-Chosŏn Border Region," *Geopolitics* (December 2020), 1–17; Joseph A. Seeley, "Reeds, River Islands, and Inter-Imperial Conflict on the Early Twentieth-Century Sino-Korean Border," *Water History* 12, no. 3 (September 2020): 373–84.

4. Kwŏn Kŭn, *Yangch'on chip*, 1 in HMC 7:15b.

5. Kwŏn Kŭn, *Yangch'on chip*, 1:1a-b in HMC 7:14a. For Kwŏn's mission and alternate interpretation, see Dane Alston, "Emperor and Emissary: The Hongwu Emperor, Kwŏn Kŭn, and the Poetry of Late Fourteenth Century Diplomacy," *Korean Studies* 32 (2008): 119–24, 129–31.

6. Pak Wŏnho[hyo], *Myŏngch'o Chosŏn kwan'gyesa yŏn'gu* (Seoul: Ilchogak, 2002), 5–61; Kim Sunja, *Han'guk chungse Han-Chung kwan'gyesa* (Seoul: Hyean, 2007), 17, 164–70.

7. *T'aejo sillok* 9:4a [1396/3/29,3], http://sillok.history.go.kr/id/waa_10503029_003, accessed February 20, 2021. Although widely cited, the edict is often incorrectly translated, beginning with the modern Korean translation.

8. *T'aejo sillok* 2:14b [1392/11/27, 1].

9. Edward L. Farmer, *Zhu Yuanzhang and Early Ming Legislation: The Reordering of Chinese Society Following the Era of Mongol Rule* (New York: Brill, 1995), 13, 24–31, 81–86.

10. Late Chosŏn discourse about the *yi*-ness of the Qing, the Yongzheng-Qianlong controversies over the meaning of *yi*, the Tokugawa Japanese redefinition of *hua-yi* (J. *ka-i ron*), the legitimacy of Chinese rule in Xinjiang, and the British insistence of *yi* as pejorative are only some important examples. U Kyŏngsŏp, *Chosŏn chunghwa chuŭi ŭi sŏngnip kwa Tong asia* (Seoul: Yuni sŭt'ori, 2013), 15–23; 167–186; Lydia H. Liu, *The Clash of Empires: The Invention of China in Modern World Making* (Cambridge, MA: Harvard University Press, 2004), 31–69; Shao-yun Yang, *The Way of the Barbarians: Redrawing Ethnic Boundaries in Tang and Song China* (Seattle: University of Washington Press, 2019), 8–11. Here one should think about *hua* and *yi* in terms of Ludwig Wittgenstein's idea of "language games" and "family resemblances," rather than fixed definitions with stable, historical referents, see Ludwig Wittgenstein, *Philosophical Investigations*, 4th ed., ed. P. M. S. Hacker and Joachim Schulte (Oxford: Wiley-Blackwell, 2009).

11. As argued in Fuma Susumu, *Chōsen enkōshi to Chōsen tsūshinshi* (Nagoya: Nagoya daigaku shuppankai, 2015), 39–42.

12. Neither were the ethnocentric valences of *hua* that figured so strongly in Chinese usage operant for Koryŏ or Chosŏn Koreans when they identified

with *hua*; see Javier Cha, "The Civilizing Project in Medieval Korea: Neo-Classicism, Nativism, and Figurations of Power" (PhD diss., Harvard University, 2014), 48–57; Pae Usŏng, *Chosŏn kwa Chunghwa : Chosŏn i kkum kkugo sangsang han segye wa munmyŏng* (Kyŏnggi-do P'aju-si: Tolbegae, 2014), 93–109; 546–62; *Sŏngjong sillok* 134:11b [1481/10/17, 1].

13. See the "Eusebian accommodation" by Antontius IV, Patriarch of Constantinople, in his missive to the Vasili I of Moscow, quoted in Francis Oakley, *Kingship* (Oxford: Blackwell, 2005), 81–83; Peter F. Bang and Dariusz Kołodziejczyk, eds., *Universal Empire: A Comparative Approach to Imperial Culture and Representation in Eurasian History* (Cambridge: Cambridge University Press, 2012), 30–33; Peter F. Bang and C. A. Bayly, eds., *Tributary Empires in Global History* (New York: Palgrave Macmillan, 2011), 1–3. For application of "ecumene" to Chinese empire, see Peter Weber-Schäfer, *Oikumene und Imperium: Studien zur Ziviltheologie des chinesischen Kaiserreichs* (Bern: Peter Lang International, 1968).

14. Zhao Tingyang, "Rethinking Empire from the Chinese Concept 'All-under-Heaven' (Tianxia)," in *China Orders the World: Normative Soft Power and Foreign Policy*, ed. William A. Callahan and Elena Barabantseva (Washington, DC: Woodrow Wilson Center Press, 2011); William A. Callahan, "Tianxia, Empire, and the World: Chinese Visions of World Order for the Twenty-First Century," in *China Orders the World*; Ban Wang, *Chinese Visions of World Order: Tianxia, Culture, and World Politics* (Durham, NC: Duke University Press, 2017), 5–7, 231n23.

15. Jesse D. Sloane, "Mapping a Stateless Nation: 'Bohai' Identity in the Twelfth to Fourteenth Centuries," *Journal of Song-Yuan Studies* 44 (2014): 384–400.

16. For an overview, see Kim Tangt'aek, *Wŏn kansŏp ha ŭi Koryŏ chŏngch'isa* (Seoul: Ilchogak, 1998); Kang Hahn Lee, "Shifting Political, Legal, and Institutional Borderlines Between Koryŏ and the Mongol Yuan Empire," *Seoul Journal of Korean Studies* 29, no. 2 (2016): 239–66.

17. Remco E. Breuker, "Within or Without? Ambiguity of Borders and Koryŏ Koreans' Travels During the Liao, Jin, Song, and Yuan," *East Asian History*, no. 38 (2014): 55–61.

18. For an analogous problem in Vietnam, see Kathlene Baldanza, "De-Civilizing Ming China's Southern Border: Vietnam as Lost Province or Barbarian Culture," in *Chinese History in Geographical Perspective*, ed. Jeff Kyong-McClain and Yongtao Du (Lanham, MD: Lexington, 2013), 55–70.

19. John King Fairbank, ed., *The Chinese World Order: Traditional China's Foreign Relations* (Cambridge, MA: Harvard University Press, 1968), 1, 3–4, 9–11; Mark Mancall, "The Ch'ing Tribute System: An Interpretive Essay," in *The Chinese World Order; Traditional China's Foreign Relations*, ed. John King

Fairbank (Cambridge, MA: Harvard University Press, 1968), 63–90; Hae-jong Chun, "Sino-Korean Tributary Relations in the Ch'ing Period," in *The Chinese World Order*, 90–111; David C. Kang, *East Asia Before the West: Five Centuries of Trade and Tribute* (New York: Columbia University Press, 2010), 9–11, 82–93. The "tributary system" is known by a variety of names in East Asian languages under the same paradigm, see Ku Pŏmjin, "Tong Asia kukche chilsŏ ŭi pyŏndong kwa Chosŏn–Ch'ŏng kwan'gye," in *Tong Asia kukche chilsŏ sok ŭi Han-Chung kwan'gyesa: cheŏn kwa mosaek*, ed. Yi Ikchu et. al. (Seoul: Tongbuga yŏksa chaedan, 2010), 293–380.

20. For overemphasizing "tribute" to the detriment of other diplomatic tools, overgeneralizing institutional practices as a "system" across the vastness of dynastic time and imperial space, and being Sinocentric, see critiques in Yuanchong Wang, *Remaking the Chinese Empire: Manchu-Korean Relations, 1616–1911* (Ithaca, NY: Cornell University Press, 2018), 3–9; Morris Rossabi, ed., *China Among Equals: The Middle Kingdom and Its Neighbors, 10th–14th Centuries* (Berkeley: University of California Press, 1983), 4–9; John E. Wills, ed., *China and Maritime Europe, 1500–1800: Trade, Settlement, Diplomacy, and Missions* (Cambridge: Cambridge University Press, 2011), 3–5; Felix Kuhn, "Much More Than Tribute: The Foreign Policy Instruments of the Ming Empire," *Journal of Chinese History* 5, no. 1 (January 2021): 59–82.

21. Kirk W. Larsen, "Comforting Fictions: The Tribute System, the Westphalian Order, and Sino-Korean Relations," *Journal of East Asian Studies* 13, no. 2 (May–August 2013): 236–42, 249–50; Kang, *East Asia Before the West*, 2–8; Ji-Young Lee, *China's Hegemony: Four Hundred Years of East Asian Domination* (New York: Columbia University Press, 2016), 2–11; Feng Zhang, *Chinese Hegemony: Grand Strategy and International Institutions in East Asian History* (Stanford, CA: Stanford University Press, 2015), 1–11, 153–73; Hendrik Spruyt, *The World Imagined: Collective Beliefs and Political Order in the Sinocentric, Islamic and Southeast Asian International Societies* (Cambridge: Cambridge University Press, 2020), 48–54, 74–79.

22. Peter C. Perdue, "The Tenacious Tributary System," *Journal of Contemporary China* 24, no. 96 (November 2015): 1002–14; Saeyoung Park, "Me, Myself, and My Hegemony: The Work of Making the Chinese World Order a Reality," *Harvard Journal of Asiatic Studies* 77, no. 1 (July 2017): 47–72; Joshua Van Lieu, "The Tributary System and the Persistence of Late Victorian Knowledge," *Harvard Journal of Asiatic Studies* 77, no. 1 (July 2017): 76–86.

23. Fairbank, *The Chinese World Order*, 16; Chŏn Haejong, *Han-Chung kwan'gyesa yŏn'gu* (Seoul: Ilchogak, 1970), 50–58; Donald N. Clark, "Sino-Korean Tributary Relations Under the Ming," in *The Ming Dynasty, 1398–1644, Part 2, The Cambridge History of China* (Cambridge: Cambridge University Press,

1998), 272–73; Kirk W. Larsen, *Tradition, Treaties, and Trade: Qing Imperialism and Chosŏn Korea, 1850–1910* (Cambridge, MA: Harvard University Asia Center, 2008), 21–23.

24. Wang, *Remaking the Chinese Empire*, 54–75.

25. Adam Bohnet, "Ruling Ideology and Marginal Subjects: Ming Loyalism and Foreign Lineages in Late Choson Korea," *Journal of Early Modern History* 15, no. 6 (November 2011): 480–83.

26. Clark, "Sino-Korean Tributary Relations," 273, 284. When Chosŏn-Ming relations really "stabilized" depends on who one asks; see Hugh D. Walker, "The Yi-Ming Rapprochement: Sino-Korean Foreign Relations, 1392–1592" (PhD diss., University of California, Los Angeles, 1971), 171–172; Ye Quanhong, *Mingdai qianqi Zhong Han guojiao zhi yanjiu: 1368–1488* (Taipei: Shangwu yinshuguan, 1991), 119, 125–26, 131–34; Philip de Heer, "Three Embassies to Seoul: Sino-Korean Relations in the 15th Century," in *Conflict and Accomodation in Early Modern East Asia: Essays in Honour of Erik Zurcher*, ed. Leonard Blusse and Harriet T. Zurndorfer (Leiden: E.J. Brill, 1993), 243, 255–57; Pak Wŏnho[hyo], *Myŏng ch'o Chosŏn*, 288–90, 294–301; Kim Sunja, *Han'guk chungse*, 14–15. The claim of eventual stabilization is also implied in Kang, *East Asia Before the West*, 93–98; Zhang, *Chinese Hegemony*, 73–84.

27. For authoritative treatments of these episodes, see Han Myŏnggi, *Imjin Waeran kwa Han-Chung kwan'gye* (Seoul: Yŏksa pip'yŏngsa, 1999); Hŏ T'aegu, *Pyŏngja Horan kwa ye, kŭrigo Chunghwa* (Seoul: Somyŏng ch'ulp'an, 2019).

28. For further discussion of this problem, see Hyewon Cha, "Was Joseon a Model or an Exception? Reconsidering the Tributary Relations During Ming China," *Korea Journal* 51, no. 4 (Winter 2011): 33–58.

29. Commonly referred to as "Chosŏn Sinocentrism" 朝鮮中華主義; see Adam Bohnet, *Turning Toward Edification: Foreigners in Chosŏn Korea* (Honolulu: University of Hawai'i Press, 2020), 5–8; Pae Usŏng, *Chosŏn kwa Chunghwa*, 16–22.

30. For the range of meanings, see Sun Weiguo, *Cong "zun Ming" dao "feng Qing": Chaoxian wang chao dui Qing yishi de shanbian (1627–1910)* (Taipei: Taiwan daxue chuban she, 2019), 40–53; Hendrik Spruyt, "Collective Imaginations and International Order: The Contemporary Context of the Chinese Tributary System," *Harvard Journal of Asiatic Studies* 77, no. 1 (July 2017): 21–45. A parallel situation can be observed in the historiography of Vietnam; see Liam C. Kelley, "'Confucianism' in Vietnam: A State of the Field Essay," *Journal of Vietnamese Studies* 1, no. 1–2 (2006): 314–70.

31. For a critique, see Joshua Van Lieu, "Chosŏn-Qing Tributary Discourse: Transgression, Restoration, and Textual Performativity," *Cross-Currents: East Asian History and Culture Review*, no. 27 (June 2018): 81–82; the quote is from Spruyt,

The World Imagined, 62–63; see also Park, "Me, Myself, and My Hegemony," 62–65.

32. As represented in Jane Burbank and Frederick Cooper, *Empires in World History: Power and the Politics of Difference* (Princeton, NJ: Princeton University Press, 2010), 8–11, with the caveat of conquest without "imposing uniformity in culture or administration."

33. William E. Henthorn, *Korea: The Mongol Invasions* (Leiden: Brill, 1963), 194–225; Chŏng Inji, *Koryŏ sa*, ed. Hŏ Sŏngdo (Pukhan sahoe kwahak wŏn, 1998), 90:11a–b.

34. *Sejong sillok* 17:19a–21b [1422/9/6, 3]. In Michael Doyle's typology, suzerainty: empire in "form," but not "substance," belonging to the distant, "feudal" past, but not the present. Dismissal of "formal" elements speaks to a "materialist view of international order" shared by both realist and liberal theories that view "the distribution of power becomes virtually the only relevant feature of the international system." As Hendrik Spruyt explains, little room remains for traditions, beliefs, emotions, and other cultural factors that inform "intersubjective meaning" and "collective imagination," the very arenas formalized ritual and discourse have a critical role to play. The problem is only exacerbated when the international society in question follows the "logics of organization that differed significantly from the Westphalian model" that begins with the sovereign, territorial states as their building blocks. See Michael W Doyle, *Empires* (Ithaca, NY: Cornell University Press, 1996), 30–47, especially 42–43; 135–36; Spruyt, *The World Imagined*, 22–23; 54–61; 74–79; Saeyoung Park, "Long Live the Tributary System!: The Future of Studying East Asian Foreign Relations," *Harvard Journal of Asiatic Studies* 77, no. 1 (July 2017): 14–17; Jean-Marc Coicaud, "The Question of Emotions and Passions in Mainstream International Relations, and Beyond," in *Emotions in International Politics: Beyond Mainstream International Relations*, ed. Yohan Ariffin, Jean-Marc Coicaud, and Vesselin Popovski (Cambridge: Cambridge University Press, 2017), 14–17.

35. C. A. Bayly, *Imperial Meridian: The British Empire and the World, 1780–1830* (London: Longman, 1989), 15.

36. A statement that applies to the rhetorical needs of the medieval Japanese court as it does to any other political formation; see Torquil Duthie, *Man'yōshū and the Imperial Imagination in Early Japan* (Leiden: Brill, 2014), 1–5.

37. Pagden, *Lords of All Worlds*, 12–17.

38. For a comprehensive history of this process, see Lan Hongyue, "'Di guo' gainian zai Hanwenquan de fanyi yu liu chuan: cong Momu Riben dao Qingmo Zhongguo," *Zhongyang yanjiu yuan lishi yuyan yanjiusuo jikan* 93, no. 1 (March 2022): 213–43.

39. Liu, *The Clash of Empires*, 108–39; Lydia H. Liu, *Translingual Practice: Literature, National Culture, and Translated Modernity—China, 1900–1937* (Stanford, CA: Stanford University Press, 1995), 27–42, 259–352, especially. p. 269; Andre Schmid, *Korea Between Empires, 1895–1919* (New York: Columbia University Press, 2002), 75–78; Mark Ravina, *To Stand with the Nations of the World: Japan's Meiji Restoration in World History* (Oxford: Oxford University Press, 2017), 203–6. Yan Fu 嚴復 (1854–1921) preferred the transliteration *yingbai'er* 英拜兒 to the neologism *diguo*. *Da Qing diguo* first appears in the Qing *Veritable Records* in 1909: "We, as the Commander-in-Chief of the Army and Navies of the Great Qing Empire . . ." Note the peculiar idiom of sovereignty in this document that echoes, for instance, the language of the American Constitution describing the function of the president. QSL *Xuantong zhengji* 宣統政紀 14:286a; U.S. Constitution, article II, § 1.1. Europeans did not use "empire" to describe China until the 1650s; see Timothy Brook, "Great States," *Journal of Asian Studies* 75, no. 4 (November 2016): 963.

40. Liu, *The Clash of Empires*, 33–40; Henry Wheaton, *Elements of International Law*, ed. Richard Henry Dana and Theodore Dwight Woolsey (Gale, Making of Modern Law, 1866). The problem of faux indigeneity also plagues recent attempts to indigenize the concept of "tributary system" with East Asian language terminology such as the Chinese term *zongfan* 宗藩, which are also modern neologisms. As it appears in Chosŏn, Ming, and Qing sources, *zongfan* refers to nobles of the royal lines and has little to do with tributary practices; for an explanation, see Wang, *Remaking the Chinese Empire*, 3–6.

41. David C. Kang, "Getting Asia Wrong: The Need for New Analytical Frameworks," *International Security* 27, no. 4 (2003): 57–85; David C. Kang and Xinru Ma, "Power Transitions: Thucydides Didn't Live in East Asia," *Washington Quarterly* 41, no. 1 (January 2018): 137–54.

42. Ravina, *To Stand with the Nations of the World*, 210–12.

43. Alexis Dudden, *Japan's Colonization of Korea: Discourse and Power* (Honolulu: University of Hawai'i Press, 2005), 60–62; Henry Em, *The Great Enterprise: Sovereignty and Historiography in Modern Korea* (Durham, NC: Duke University Press, 2013), 40–52.

44. But never an "emperor state," 皇國, or 皇帝國.

45. Larsen, *Tradition, Treaties, and Trade*, 23.

46. Lauren A. Benton, *A Search for Sovereignty: Law and Geography in European Empires, 1400–1900* (Cambridge: Cambridge University Press, 2010).

47. Peter H. Wilson, *Heart of Europe: A History of the Holy Roman Empire* (Cambridge, MA: Belknap Press, 2016), 4, 162–163; Pagden, *Lords of All Worlds*, 14, 24–27.

48. Van Lieu, "The Tributary System," 87–92.

49. Zvi Ben-Dor Benite, Stefanos Geroulanos, and Nicole Jerr, eds., *The Scaffolding of Sovereignty: Global and Aesthetic Perspectives on the History of a Concept* (New York: Columbia University Press, 2017).

50. A critical point in orthodox national historiography in China; for discussions, see Lan Hongyue, "'Di guo' gainian zai Hanwenquan de fanyi yu liuchuan: Cong Mumo Riben dao Qingmo Zhongguo," 248–259; Wang, *Remaking the Chinese Empire*, 9–18; Brook, "Great States"; Larsen, *Tradition, Treaties, and Trade*, 8–22; Bin Wong, *China Transformed: Historical Change and the Limits of European Experience*, 1st ed. (Ithaca, NY: Cornell University Press, 2000), 127–48. In contrast, some use "imperial" to highlight moments of aggressive military expansion, especially in competition with other territorial empires; see Peter C. Perdue, *China Marches West: The Qing Conquest of Central Eurasia* (Cambridge, MA: Belknap Press, 2005), xiv, 9–14, 497–510.

51. Hok-lam Chan, *Legitimation in Imperial China: Discussions Under the Jurchen-Chin Dynasty (1115–1234)* (Seattle: University of Washington Press, 1984), 19–48.

52. But without the eschatological implications of the term, see Wilson, *Heart of Europe*, 37–42.

53. Remco E. Breuker, "Koryŏ as an Independent Realm: The Emperor's Clothes," *Korean Studies* 27, no. 1 (January 2003): 48–84.

54. For a definition of "imperial repertoires," see Burbank and Cooper, *Empires in World History*, 3–11.

55. JaHyun Kim Haboush, "Contesting Chinese Time, Nationalizing Temporal Space: Temporal Inscription in Late Chosŏn Korea," in *Time, Temporality and Imperial Transition: East Asia Form Ming to Qing*, ed. Lynn A. Struve, Asian Interactions and Comparisons (Honolulu: University of Hawai'i Press, 2005), 115–41; Joseph S. C. Lam, "Huizong's Dashengyue, a Musical Performance of Emperorship and Officialdom," in *Emperor Huizong and Late Northern Song China : The Politics of Culture and the Culture of Politics*, ed. Patricia Buckley Ebrey and Maggie Bickford (Cambridge, MA: Harvard University Asia Center, 2006), 395–452; Howard J Wechsler, *Offerings of Jade and Silk: Ritual and Symbol in the Legitimation of the T'ang Dynasty* (New Haven, CT: Yale University Press, 1985); James Louis Hevia, "Sovereignty and Subject: Constituting Relationships of Power in Qing Guest Ritual," in *Body, Subject & Power in China*, ed. Angela Zito and Tani E. Barlow (Chicago: University of Chicago Press, 1994).

56. Sixiang Wang, "What Tang Taizong Could Not Do: The Korean Surrender of 1259 and the Imperial Tradition," *T'oung Pao* 104, no. 3–4 (October 2018): 338–83.

57. Victor H. Mair, "Buddhism and the Rise of the Written Vernacular in East Asia: The Making of National Languages," *Journal of Asian Studies* 53, no. 3 (1994): 707–51; Ross King, "Ditching 'Diglossia': Describing Ecologies of the Spoken and

Inscribed in Pre-Modern Korea," *Sungkyun Journal of East Asian Studies* 15, no. 1 (2015): 1–19.

58. For the Islamicate, Sanskrit, and Persianate traditions, see Sheldon Pollock, *The Language of the Gods in the World of Men: Sanskrit, Culture, and Power in Premodern India* (Berkeley: University of California Press, 2009), 1–75; Brinkley Morris Messick, *The Calligraphic State: Textual Domination and History in a Muslim Society* (Berkeley: University of California Press, 1993), 15–36, 135–66; Audrey Truschke, *Culture of Encounters: Sanskrit at the Mughal Court* (New York: Columbia University Press, 2016), 6–10. For the aftermath of the Mongol rule, see Thomas T. Allsen, *Culture and Conquest in Mongol Eurasia* (Cambridge: Cambridge University Press, 2001); Ayşe Zarakol, *Before the West: The Rise and Fall of Eastern World Orders* (Cambridge: Cambridge University Press, 2022).

59. A reconciliation of the two camps in the protracted "Sinicization" debate, as suggested by Richard J. Smith, *Mapping China and Managing the World: Culture, Cartography and Cosmology in Late Imperial Times* (London: Routledge, 2013), 10–14. See Ping-Ti Ho, "In Defense of Sinicization: A Rebuttal of Evelyn Rawski's 'Reenvisioning the Qing,'" *Journal of Asian Studies* 57, no. 1 (1998): 123–55; Evelyn S. Rawski, "Reenvisioning the Qing: The Significance of the Qing Period in Chinese History," *Journal of Asian Studies* 55, no. 4 (November 1996): 829–50.

60. Truschke, *Culture of Encounters*, 142–65; Stewart Gordon, ed., *Robes of Honour: Khilat In Pre-Colonial and Colonial India* (New Delhi: Oxford University Press, 2003).

61. Evelyn S. Rawski, *Early Modern China and Northeast Asia: Cross-Border Perspectives* (Cambridge: Cambridge University Press, 2015).

62. Or in the application of social scientific concepts, for instance, the debate surrounding "civil society" and "public sphere" in Chosŏn Korea and Qing China; see JaHyun Kim Haboush, "Academies and Civil Society in Chosŏn Korea," in *La société civile face à l'État: dans les traditions chinoise, japonaise, coréenne et vietnamienne*, ed. Léon Vandermeersch (Paris: École Française d'Extrême-Orient, 1994), 383–92; John B. Duncan, "The Problematic Modernity of Confucianism: The Question of 'Civil Society' in Choson Dynasty Korea," in *Korean Society: Civil Society, Democracy and the State*, ed. Charles K. Armstrong (New York: Routledge, 2002), 38–46.

63. As applied to the "tributary system," see Spruyt, "Collective Imaginations and International Order," 35–38.

64. JaHyun Kim Haboush, *The Great East Asian War of 1592 and the Birth of the Korean Nation*, ed. William Joseph Haboush and Jisoo M. Kim (New York: Columbia University Press, 2016).

65. Sixiang Wang, "Chosŏn's Office of Interpreters: The Apt Response and the Knowledge Culture of Diplomacy," *Journal for the History of Knowledge* 1, no. 1 (December 2020): 10.

66. A staple of Chinese imperial ideology; more recently, both those who laud and lament China's recent geopolitical ascent describe it in terms of traditional imperial models. See discussion in this book's conclusion.

67. E. Natalie Rothman, *Brokering Empire: Trans-Imperial Subjects Between Venice and Istanbul* (Ithaca, NY: Cornell University Press, 2012).

68. Karen Barkey, *Empire of Difference: The Ottomans in Comparative Perspective* (Cambridge: Cambridge University Press, 2008), 9–10; Ann Laura Stoler, Carole McGranahan, and Peter C. Perdue, eds., *Imperial Formations* (Santa Fe, NM: School for Advanced Research Press, 2007), 8–9.

69. Kang Hǔimaeng, *Sasukchae chip*, 8 in HMC 12:118b. I have discussed the Korean interpreter's critical role as a "go-between" elsewhere, see Sixiang Wang, "The Sounds of Our Country: Interpreters, Linguistic Knowledge and the Politics of Language in Early Chosŏn Korea (1392–1592)," in *Rethinking East Asian Languages, Vernaculars, and Literacies, 1000–1919*, ed. Benjamin A. Elman (Leiden: Brill, 2014), 58–95; Wang, "Chosŏn's Office of Interpreters."

70. Mary Louise Pratt, *Imperial Eyes: Travel Writing and Transculturation* (London: Routledge, 1992), 9. Following the "generic norms and tropes" of the metropole was also possible in the "more institutionally rigid contact zone" of China's southwest; see Eloise Wright, "History and Autoethnography: Accounting for the Indigenous Population of Yunnan, 1550–1650," *Journal of Colonialism and Colonial History* 22, no. 1 (2021).

71. "His aim was not to berate, but to cajole"; as described in Garret P. S. Olberding, ed., *Facing the Monarch: Modes of Advice in the Early Chinese Court* (Cambridge, MA: Harvard University Asia Center, 2013), 4–5; 9–10.

72. Pierre Bourdieu, *Language and Symbolic Power*, ed. John Brookshire Thompson, trans. Matthew Adamson and Gino Raymond (Cambridge: Polity Press, 1991), 8–9; 12–14; 196–202. With gratitude to Covell Meyskens for this insight.

PART I. THE SHARED PAST

1. Donald N. Clark, "Sino-Korean Tributary Relations Under the Ming," in *The Ming Dynasty, 1398–1644, Part 2, The Cambridge History of China* (Cambridge: Cambridge University Press, 1998), 273–76. For an overview of Korean diplomacy during the Yuan-Ming transition, see Kim Sunja, *Han'guk chungse*; Fan Yongcong, *Shida yu baoguo: Yuan Ming zhi ji de Zhong Han guanxi* (Hong Kong: Xianggang jiaoyu tushu, 2009); David M. Robinson, "Rethinking the Late

Koryŏ in an International Context," *Korean Studies* 41 (July 2017): 75–98; David M. Robinson, *Korea and the Fall of the Mongol Empire: Alliance, Upheaval, and the Rise of a New East Asian Order* (Cambridge: Cambridge University Press, 2022), 153–245.

2. David M. Robinson, *Empire's Twilight: Northeast Asia Under the Mongols* (Cambridge, MA: Harvard University Asia Center, 2009), 33, 44.

3. Also known by his Mongol name Ulus Buqa, Yi Chach'un hailed from a Koryŏ aristocratic family who had served the Mongols for several generations. Robinson, *Empire's Twilight*, 127–31; Stella Xu, *Reconstructing Ancient Korean History: The Formation of Korean-Ness in the Shadow of History* (London: Lexington Books, 2016), 58–59. *T'aejo sillok* 1:1a–4b [*ch'ongsŏ*, 1–22]. For the Tieling issue, see further discussion in chapter 5 of this book.

4. *T'aejo sillok* 1:21b [*ch'ongsŏ*, 83].

5. *T'aejo sillok* 1:22a [*ch'ongsŏ*, 84].

6. For dogma and Confucianism, see Hugh D. Walker, "The Yi-Ming Rapprochement: Sino-Korean Foreign Relations, 1392–1592" (PhD diss., University of California, Los Angeles, 1971), 203–8.

7. As articulated in T'ae-jin Yi, *The Dynamics of Confucianism and Modernization in Korean History* (Ithaca, NY: East Asia Program, Cornell University, 2007), 3–20.

8. John B. Duncan, *The Origins of the Chosŏn Dynasty* (Seattle: University of Washington Press, 2000), 99–154; John B. Duncan, "The Social Background to the Founding of the Chosŏn Dynasty: Change or Continuity," *Journal of Korean Studies* 6 (1988): 39–79. For emergence of Kwŏn family, see Javier Cha, "To Build a Centralizing Regime: Yangban Aristocracy and Medieval Patrimonialism," *Seoul Journal of Korean Studies* 32, no. 1 (2019): 53–57.

9. Korean descent groups are identified by a patrilineal surname and a choronym (*pon'gwan* 本貫), an ancestral seat (which may be a place of origin or a seat granted by royal decree). Possessing a choronym is a necessary, but not sufficient, condition for elite status. See Eugene Y. Park, *A Family of No Prominence: The Descendants of Pak Tŏkhwa and the Birth of Modern Korea* (Stanford, CA: Stanford University Press, 2014), 9–14.

10. As used in this book, the intellectual tradition identified with Zhu Xi 朱熹 (1130–1200), a narrower definition than usually employed in Chinese historiography. See Peter K. Bol, *Neo-Confucianism in History* (Cambridge, MA: Harvard University Asia Center, 2008), 83–89.

11. *T'aejo sillok* 1:29b [*ch'ongsŏ*, 111], 1:34b [*ch'ongsŏ*, 131], 1:43a [1392/7/28, 3], 1:54a [1392/8/23, 2]; Sixiang Wang, "Loyalty, History, and Empire: Qian Qianyi and His Korean Biographies," in *Representing Lives in East Asia, China and Korea*

1400–1900, ed. Ihor Pidhainy, Grace Fong, and Roger Des Forges (Ithaca, NY: Cornell University East Asia Program, 2018), 302–12.

12. Martina Deuchler, *The Confucian Transformation of Korea: A Study of Society and Ideology* (Cambridge, MA: Council on East Asian Studies, 1992), 92–107; Martina Deuchler, *Under the Ancestors' Eyes: Kinship, Status, and Locality in Premodern Korea* (Cambridge, MA: Harvard University Asia Center, 2015), 67–76; 207.

13. Duncan, *The Origins of the Chosŏn Dynasty*, 246–65. See also the importance of neoclassicism 古文, as opposed to Neo-Confucianism, discussed in Javier Cha, "The Civilizing Project in Medieval Korea: Neo-Classicism, Nativism, and Figurations of Power" (PhD diss., Harvard University, 2014).

14. Odd Arne Westad, *Empire and Righteous Nation: 600 Years of China-Korea Relations.* (Cambridge, MA: Harvard University Press, 2021), 36–37.

1. SERVING THE GREAT

1. Edward J. Shultz, *Generals and Scholars: Military Rule in Medieval Korea* (Honolulu: University of Hawai'i Press, 2000), 28–53; 166–75; Sixiang Wang, "What Tang Taizong Could Not Do: The Korean Surrender of 1259 and the Imperial Tradition," *T'oung Pao* 104, no. 3–4 (October 30, 2018): 344–47.

2. Deuchler, *Under the Ancestors' Eyes*, 43–51; Juhn Y. Ahn, *Buddhas and Ancestors: Religion and Wealth in Fourteenth-Century Korea* (Seattle: University of Washington Press, 2018), 7–10; 81–104.

3. Robinson, *Empire's Twilight*, 124–29; 180–84.

4. Jeong Ho-hun, "Deconstructing the Official History of Koryŏ in Late Chosŏn," *Seoul Journal of Korean Studies* 26, no. 2 (December 2013): 335–60.

5. Duncan, *The Origins of the Chosŏn Dynasty*, 187–91; 206–13. For different view on Buddhist institutions, see Ahn, *Buddhas and Ancestors*, 42–48.

6. Eugene Y. Park, *A Genealogy of Dissent: The Progeny of Fallen Royals in Chosŏn Korea* (Stanford, CA: Stanford University Press, 2018), 11–15; Duncan, *The Origins of the Chosŏn Dynasty*, 100–106; 121–33.

7. Cho Pan, no relation to Cho Chun, was a Koryŏ aristocrat fostered in Beijing, and later served as an official but left for Koryŏ in 1368, the year of the Ming sack of Beijing. His earlier experience as an imperial official and fluency in Chinese and Mongolian was likely why he was chosen as an envoy. *T'aejo sillok* 1:29a [*chŏngsŏ*, 111]; *T'aejong sillok* 2:16b [1401/10/27, 2].

8. *T'aejo sillok* 1:37a [1392/7/17, 1], 1:39a [1392/7/18, 2].

9. *T'aejo sillok* 2:15a [1392/11/29, 1], 3:3b [1393/2/15, 1].

10. *T'aejo sillok* 3:9b [1393/5/25, 2].

11. Pak Wŏnho[hyo], "Myŏngch'o Chosŏn ŭi Yodong kongpŏl kyehoek kwa Chosŏn p'yojŏn munje," *Paeksan hakpo* 19 (1975).

12. *T'aejo sillok* 14:5b [1398/5a/3, 1].

13. For *sadae* in modern Korea, see Michael Robinson, "National Identity and the Thought of Sin Ch'aeho: Sadaejuŭi and Chuch'e in History and Politics," *Journal of Korean Studies* 5 (January 1984): 121–42; Andre Schmid, *Korea Between Empires, 1895–1919* (New York: Columbia University Press, 2002), 129–36; John B. Duncan, "Uses of Confucianism in Modern Korea," in *Rethinking Confucianism: Past and Present in China, Japan, Korea, and Vietnam*, ed. Benjamin A. Elman, John B. Duncan, and Herman Ooms (Los Angeles: UCLA Asian Pacific Monograph Series, 2002), 433–39; 447–48; 460–61; Seo-Hyun Park, "Dueling Nationalisms in North and South Korea," *Palgrave Communications* 5, no. 1 (April 2019): 5.

14. For this reason, earlier generations of South Korean scholars replaced the overly laden *sadae* with the more "neutral" terminology of "tribute" and "investiture" relations (*chogong ch'aekpong*). See Chŏn Haejong, *Han-Chung kwan'gyesa yŏn'gu* (Seoul: Ilchogak, 1970), especially pp. 27, 252–53.

15. *Mencius* 2 in Zhu Xi, *Dianjiao sishu zhangji ju* (Beijing: Zhonghua shuju, 1983), 213. See elaborations in Kirk W. Larsen, *Tradition, Treaties, and Trade: Qing Imperialism and Chosŏn Korea, 1850–1910* (Cambridge, MA: Harvard University Asia Center, 2008), 169; Fuma Susumu, *Chōsen enkōshi to Chōsen tsūshinshi*; Etsuko Hae-jin Kang, *Diplomacy and Ideology in Japanese-Korean Relations: From the Fifteenth to the Eighteenth Century* (New York: Springer, 2016), 168–77; Feng Zhang, *Chinese Hegemony: Grand Strategy and International Institutions in East Asian History* (Stanford, CA: Stanford University Press, 2015), 72–73; 79.

16. Mencius 2 in Zhu Xi, *Dianjiao sishu zhangju ji zhu*, 225.

17. Fuma Susumu, *Chōsen enkōshi to Chōsen tsūshinshi*, 29–32; Peter Yun, "Confucian Ideology and the Tribute System in Chosŏn-Ming Relations," *Sach'ong* 55, no. 9 (2002): 67–88.

18. Yang Bojun, *Chunqiu Zuozhuan zhu* (Beijing: Zhonghua shuju, 1981), 957, 1506, 1642ff; *Guliang zhushu* 穀梁注疏 7:71b in SSJZS; Chen Qiyou, ed., *Han Feizi* (Beijing: Zhonghua shuju, 1958), 2, 152; 19, 1067.

19. *Rites of Zhou*, Xiagong sima 夏宮司馬 in SSJZS 29, 439b. Using "feudal" as translation for *fengjian* is controversial; see Feng Li, *Bureaucracy and the State in Early China: Governing the Western Zhou* (Cambridge: Cambridge University Press, 2013), 288–93.

20. Yuri Pines, *Envisioning Eternal Empire: Chinese Political Thought of the Warring States Period* (Honolulu: University of Hawai'i Press, 2009), 1–4; 15–24; 107–11; Mark E. Lewis, "Warring States: A Political History," in *The Cambridge History of Ancient China*, ed. Michael Loewe and Edward L. Shaughnessy (Cambridge: Cambridge University Press, 1999), 597–604.

21. Charles Holcombe, *The Genesis of East Asia, 221 B.C.–A.D. 907* (Honolulu: Association for Asian Studies and University of Hawai'i Press, 2001), 165–69. For the location of Wiman Chosŏn, see Song Ho Jung, "Old Chosŏn: Its History and Archaeology," in *The Han Commandaries in Early Korean History*, ed. Mark E. Byington, Early Korean Project Occasional Series (Cambridge, MA: Korea Institute, Harvard University, 2013), 52–73; Sima Qian, *Shiji (Xinjiaoben Shiji sanjiazhu bing fubian erzhong)*, Zhongguo xueshu leibian (Taipei: Dingwen shuju, 1981), 115, p. 2985.

22. John King Fairbank, ed., *The Chinese World Order: Traditional China's Foreign Relations* (Cambridge, MA: Harvard University Press, 1968), 8–10; Zhenping Wang, *Tang China in Multi-Polar Asia: A History of Diplomacy and War* (Honolulu: University of Hawai'i Press, 2017), 9–10; 250–54.

23. Yao Cha et al., *Liang shu*, Zhongguo xueshu leibian (Taipei: Dingwen shuju, 1980), 54, p. 804; Zhenping Wang, *Ambassadors from the Islands of Immortals: China-Japan Relations in the Han-Tang Period* (Honolulu: University of Hawai'i Press, 2005), 17–32.

24. Ji-Young Lee, "Diplomatic Ritual as a Power Resource: The Politics of Asymmetry in Early Modern Chinese-Korean Relations," *Journal of East Asian Studies* 13, no. 2 (May–August 2013): 309–36, 377.

25. JaHyun Kim Haboush, "Contesting Chinese Time, Nationalizing Temporal Space: Temporal Inscription in Late Chosŏn Korea," in *Time, Temporality and Imperial Transition: East Asia Form Ming to Qing*, ed. Lynn A. Struve, Asian Interactions and Comparisons (Honolulu: University of Hawai'i Press, 2005), 117–19; Wang, *Tang China in Multi-Polar Asia*, 55–69; 80–86.

26. Dong Gao, *Quan Tang wen*, Scripta Sinica (Beijing: Zhonghua shuju, 1987), 39, 425:1 (hereafter QTW); QTW 75, p. 788:2; QTW 76, p. 801:2; QTW 700, p. 7185:2; QTW 707, p. 7251:2; QTW 665, p. 6759:1; QTW 665, p. 6759:2; QTW 666, p. 6768:2.

27. QTW 85, pp. 892:2–896:2; QTW 103, p. 1054:1–2; QTW 811, p. 8538:2; QTW 827, p. 8714:1: "The small should serve the great; the barbarian should not disturb the civilized" [小當事大 夷不亂華].

28. QTW 774, p. 8068:2; 776, p. 8097:2; See also QTW 837, p. 8812:1. "When the son-of-heaven rules the regions, the feudal lords fulfill their duties, maintaining good relations with its neighbor and serving the great" [天子省方 藩侯述職 睦鄰事大].

29. QTW 108, p. 1104:2–1105:1; QTW 114, p. 1165:1.

30. QTW 121, pp. 1221:1–2.

31. It also served whoever happened to be the "Central State without regard to its conditions" [不問中國之光景如]; see Yi Ik, *Sŏngho sŏnsaeng sasŏl*, ed.

Yi Tonhyŏng, Han'guk kojŏn chonghap DB (Seoul: Han'guk kojŏn pŏnyŏgwŏn, 1978), 24:78a.

32. QTW, 126, p. 1270:1.

33. QTW 876, 891, p. 9308b–9309a; p. 9166b–9167a; 9167a–9196a.

34. Li Tao, *Xu zizhi tongjian changbian* (Beijing: Zhonghua shuju, 2004), 16, 346. According to another source, the emperor declared to the Tang envoy: "All-under-heaven is one family; how can one tolerate the snoring of another by one's sleeping mat?" Ma Guangzu, "Jingding Jiankang zhi" 景定建康志, in *Song Yuan fangzhi congkan*, ed. Zhou Yinghe (Shanghai: Zhonghua shuju, 1990), 13, 1474b.

35. Paul J. Smith, "Irredentism as Political Capital: The New Policies and the Annexation of Tibetan Domains in Hehuang (the Qinghai-Gansu Highlands) under Shenzong and His Sons, 1068–1126," in *Emperor Huizong and Late Northern Song China: The Politics of Culture and the Culture of Politics*, ed. Patricia Buckley Ebrey and Maggie Bickford (Cambridge, MA: Harvard University Asia Center, 2006), 78–130; Nicolas Tackett, *The Origins of the Chinese Nation: Song China and the Forging of an East Asian World Order* (Cambridge: Cambridge University Press, 2017), 143–50, 195–210.

36. Shao-yun Yang, *The Way of the Barbarians: Redrawing Ethnic Boundaries in Tang and Song China* (Seattle: University of Washington Press, 2019), 56.

37. Gungwu Wang, "The Rhetoric of a Lesser Empire: Early Sung Relations with Its Neighbors," in *China Among Equals: The Middle Kingdom and Its Neighbors, 10th–14th Centuries*, ed. Morris Rossabi (Berkeley: University of California Press, 1983), 47–50, 55; Chan, *Legitimation in Imperial China*, 37–38, 81, 103–7; Jae Woo Park, "Early Koryŏ Political Institutions and the International Expansion of Tang and Song Institutions," *Korean Studies* 41 (2017): 12–21.

38. Michael C. Rogers, "National Consciousness in Medieval Korea: The Impact of Liao and Chin on Koryŏ," in *China Among Equals*, ed. Morris Rossabi (Berkeley: University of California Press, 1983), 166.

39. Sŏ Kŏjŏng, ed., *Tongmunsŏn* (Seoul: Kyŏnghŭi ch'ulp'ansa, 1966), (hereafter TMS), sŏ 1b–2a.

40. TMS 31–33; especially 33:1b–2a, 32:22a–b; Xiao Tong and Li Shan, eds., *Wenxuan* (Shanghai: Shanghai guji chubanshe, 2005), 4, 1667.

41. Lin Yaoyu, ed., *Libu zhigao*, SQKS 597–598 (Taipei: Shangwu yinshuguan, 1983), 59:15b–16b, 64:36a; Chŏn Haejong, "Han-Chung chogong kwan'gye kaeron—Han-Chung kwan'gyesa ŭi chogam ŭl wihayŏ—," in *Kodae Han-Chung kwan'gyesa ŭi yŏn'gu* (Seoul: Samjiwŏn, 1987), 53–62. For parallel prose forms as part of Japanese imperial ritual, see Brian Steininger, *Chinese Literary Forms in*

Heian Japan: Poetics and Practice (Cambridge, MA: Harvard University Asia Center, 2017), 15, 61–78.

42. For earliest examples, see Sima Guang, *Zizhi tongjian*, ed. Hu Sansheng, Scripta Sinica (Beijing: Beijing guji chuban she, 1956), 72, pp. 2284, 2290; 176, p. 5483; 281, p. 9188; 283, p. 9242; 284, p. 9294; 285, p. 9310; 287, p. 9364.

43. Kim Chinam, *T'ongmun'gwan chi*, Ko. 古 5120-11-v.1–3 (Kyujanggak Archives, Seoul National University, 1720), 2:12a–15b; note their absence from Kwŏn Kŭn et al., ed., *Koewŏn tŭngnok*, Jangseogak Archives (Changsŏgak) k2-3465, thirteenth to seventeenth centuries.

44. Similar mock memorials were written for exams in 1095 to celebrate a Koryŏ tribute embassy and another in 1100 to celebrate the gift to Koryŏ of the *Taiping yulan* 太平御覽. See Xu Song, and Wang Deyi, eds., *Song huiyao jigao*, Scripta Sinica (Taipei: Zhongyang yanjiuyuan lishi yuyan yanjiusuo, 2008), Xuanju 選舉 12:3, 12:5.

45. Ironically, Huizong's *Dashengyue* was later widely ridiculed as a symbol of imperial excess and a symptom of dynastic decline. See Joseph S. C. Lam, "Huizong's Dashengyue, a Musical Performance of Emperorship and Officialdom," in *Emperor Huizong and Late Northern Song China: The Politics of Culture and the Culture of Politics*, ed. Patricia Buckley Ebrey and Maggie Bickford (Cambridge, MA: Harvard University Asia Center, 2006), 395–452. Huizong also hoped that closer connections with Koryŏ could aid the Song reconquest of Liao-ruled territories. See Michael C. Rogers, "Notes on Koryŏ's Relations with Sung and Liao," *Chindan Hakpo* 12 (1991): 334–35.

46. *Cixue zhinan* in Wang Yinglin, *Yu Hai*, SKQS 943–48 (Taipei: Shangwu yinshuguan, 1983), 203:3a-4b; Chang Tong'ik, *Songdae yŏsa charyo chimnok* (Seoul: Seoul taehakkyo ch'ulp'anbu, 2000), 533.

47. Chŏng Inji, *Koryŏ sa*, 14:14a–15b (hereafter KS).

48. The *Xianchi* 咸池 and *Daxia* 大夏, the perfect music of ancient sage kings.

49. *Analects* 15.10; 17.8.

50. The *huangzhong* 黃鐘 that provided the scale for perfect pitch and harmony.

51. TMS 34:13b–14a.

52. Miao, in classical texts a generic term for the indigenous people of the south, not to be confused as an identifier of any modern ethnic groups. See Norma Diamond, "Defining the Miao: Ming, Qing, and Contemporary Views," in *Cultural Encounters on China's Ethnic Frontiers*, ed. Stevan Harrell (Seattle: University of Washington Press, 1995), 99–100.

53. *Dayu mo* 大禹謨 *Shangshu zhushu* 尚書註疏 4:52b in SSJZS

54. Kim Pyŏngin, "Koryŏ Yejong ŭi t'ongch'i haengwi e nat'anan yuhyŏngjŏk t'ŭkching kwa kŭ chŏngch'ijŏk paegyŏng," *Yŏksa wa kyŏnggye* 79 (June 2011): 35–74.

55. KS 12:13a; 13b.

56. KS 15:11b; 19b. See KS 15:19a–b [1126/9–10]. Remco E. Breuker, *Establishing a Pluralist Society in Medieval Korea, 918–1170: History, Ideology and Identity in the Koryŏ Dynasty* (Leiden: Brill, 2010), 222–31.

57. Koryŏ maintained informal trade ties only with the Southern Song. See Kim Wihyŏn 金渭顯, *Koryŏ sidae taeoe kwan'gyesa yŏn'gu* (Seoul: Kyŏng'in munhwasa, 2004), 245–46, 257–58; Breuker, *Establishing a Pluralist Society*, 248–56.

58. *Sejo sillok* 9:4a [1457/9/10, 2]; Breuker, *Establishing a Pluralist Society*, 263. TMS 33–35, 39:5b–6b, 48:2a–9b; Peter Yun, "Rethinking the Tribute System: Korean States and Northeast Asian Interstate Relations, 600–1600" (PhD diss., University of California, Los Angeles, 1998), 11–16, 146–49.

59. The early Yuan court saw itself primarily as successors to the Liao and Jin, and not the Song. See Chan, Hok-lam, "Wang O (1190–1273)," *Papers on Far Eastern History* 12 (September 1975): 43–70.

60. KS 23:26a–b [1233/3]; Yi Kyubo, *Tongguk Yi Sangguk chip*, 28:23a–23b, 25b–26b, in HMC 1:593a–593c, 594a–b. TMS 39:16b–17b, 39:25b–25a.

61. Wang, "What Tang Taizong Could Not Do," 360–69.

62. Herbert Franke, *From Tribal Chieftain to Universal Emperor and God: The Legitimation of the Yüan Dynasty* (München: Verlag der Baerischen Akademie der Wissenschaften, 1978), 1–25.

63. An ongoing tactic of negotiation; see Yi Ikchu, "Koryŏ-Monggol chŏnjaeng ch'ogi (1231–1232) ŭi Kanghwa hyŏpsang yŏn'gu," *Han'guksa yŏn'gu* 180 (March 2018): 1–31; Chunyuan Li, "Transition Under Ambiguity: Koryŏ-Mongol Relations Around 1260," *International Journal of Korean History* 25, no. 1 (February 2020): 123n3, 129–39.

64. Wang, "What Tang Taizong Could Not Do," 340–53.

65. Franke, *From Tribal Chieftain to Universal Emperor and God*, 26–35.

66. The giant *ao*-sea turtle 鼇 carries continents on its back, thus moving mountains in motion. Kim Ku, *Chip'o chip* 2 in HMC 2:332c. KS 25:13b–14a.

67. TMS 62:5b–7b; Kim Ku, *Chip'o chip*, 3 in HMC 2:362b–363b. Before Kim Ku, the Koryŏ memorial writer Yi Kyubo 李奎報 (1169–1241) wrote to Yelü Chucai 耶律楚材 (1190–1244), a Khitan aristocrat charged with administering northern China on behalf of the Mongols. See Wang, "What Tang Taizong Could Not Do," 362–65.

68. KS 106:14a; Kim Ku, *Chip'o chip*, preface, in HMC 2:323b–c.

69. Xiao Qiqing, *Nei Beiguo er wai Zhongguo: Meng-Yuanshi yanjiu* (Beijing: Zhonghua shuju, 2007), 125–31; Kim Ku, *Chip'o chip*, 3 in HMC 2:361d-362a; 362b. Wang, "What Tang Taizong Could Not Do," 369–76. Li, "Transition Under Ambiguity," 126–29; 139–41.

70. The process, as described by Joshua Van Lieu, employed a combination of "illocutionary force" and performativity. Illocution urges the audience to future action even if such demands are not made explicit in the syntax or semantics of the statement. In the case of *p'yo*, this occurred through performativity, the rhetorical enactment of a relationship that bound both parties. See Joshua Van Lieu, "Chosŏn-Qing Tributary Discourse: Transgression, Restoration, and Textual Performativity," *Cross-Currents: East Asian History and Culture Review*, no. 27 (June 2018): 79–87; John Langshaw Austin, *How to Do Things with Words* (London: Oxford University Press, 1975), 99–120; William P. Alston, *Illocutionary Acts and Sentence Meaning* (Ithaca, NY: Cornell University Press, 2000), 11–30.

71. Kim Ku, *Chip'o chip*, 2 in HMC 2:333a–333d. TMS 32:10a–11b. KS 25:14a–16a. The TMS and *Chip'o chip* reproduce different wordings for Qubilai's edict, suggesting a translation process, possibly from Mongolian.

72. Yi Ikchu, "Koryŏ, Wŏn kwan'gye ŭi kujo e taehan yŏn'gu—sowi 'Sejo kuje' ŭi punsŏk ŭl chungsim ŭro," *Han'guk saron* 36 (1996): 1–51; Li, "Transition Under Ambiguity," 142–49.

73. KS 27:27a.

74. Sixiang Wang, "Emotions in Koryŏ-Mongol Diplomacy: From Covenants of Affect to the Paternal Simile" (December 1, 2021).

75. *T'aejo sillok* 1:54a [1392/8/23, 2]; *T'aejong sillok* 20:33a [1410/10/23, 1].

76. Ŏ Sukkwŏn, *A Korean Storyteller's Miscellany: The Paegwan Chapki of O Sukkwon*, trans. Peter H. Lee (Princeton, NJ: Princeton University Press, 1989), 84; Ŏ Sukkwŏn, *P'aegwan chapki* in TDYS 4, vol. 1:732; Kim An'guk, *Mojae chip*, 9 in HMC 20:162d-163a.

77. Original Burmese, Thai, and Laotian "diplomatic memorials" in Qing period archives exhibit this manufactured conformity to imperial expectation. "Grand Secretariat Archives (Neige daku dang'an)" (Taipei, Fusinian Library, 18th century), 106204, 287678, 117451, 056317, Academia Sinica. After concluding a war with the Qing, the Burmese ruler addressed the Qing emperor as equals in his original letter, but the Chinese translation transforms the Burmese ruler to a Qing vassal. See Yingcong Dai, "A Disguised Defeat: The Myanmar Campaign of the Qing Dynasty," *Modern Asian Studies* 38, no. 1 (February 1, 2004): 173–75. See also the Persian letter incident described in Yan Congjian, *Shuyu zhouzi lu*, ed. Yu Sili (Beijing: Zhonghua shuju, 1993), 394–400.

78. The Ming court's Translator's Institute was often understaffed and/or had poorly trained staff. Thus, reliability remained a perennial challenge. Lü Weiqi, *Siyi guan zengding guanze*, 6 vols. (Beijing University Library: China-America Digital Academic Library (CADAL), 1675) preface 13a–b, 1:6a–b, 2:2a–b, 12:1a–2b, 14b; Carla Nappi, *Translating Early Modern China: Illegible Cities* (London: Oxford University Press, 2021), 16–22.

79. Ye Quanhong, *Mingdai qianqi Zhong Han guojiao zhi yanjiu: 1368–1488* (Taipei: Shangwu yinshuguan, 1991), 84; Sixiang Wang, "What Tang Taizong Could Not Do," 62–63.

80. Gregory Smits, *Maritime Ryukyu, 1050–1650* (Honolulu: University of Hawai'i Press, 2019), 68–69, 135. Although Chosŏn occasionally noted the quality of Vietnamese memorials, see *Sejo sillok* 18:6b [1459/11/1, 1]; *Chungjong sillok* 29:59b [1790/3/27, 2].

81. Clark, "Sino-Korean Tributary Relations," 273; James Louis Hevia, *Cherishing Men from Afar: Qing Guest Ritual and the Macartney Embassy of 1793* (Durham, NC: Duke University Press, 1995), 50; Hae-jong Chun, "Sino-Korean Tributary Relations in the Ch'ing Period," in *The Chinese World Order; Traditional China's Foreign Relations*, ed. John King Fairbank and Ta-tuan Ch'en (Cambridge, MA: Harvard University Press, 1968), 92–93.

82. *T'aejo sillok* 5:6a [1394/2/19, 1]. For other cases, see Chen Long and Shen Zaiquan, "Chaoxian yu Ming Qing biaojian waijiao wenti yanjiu," *Zhongguo bianjiang shidi yanjiu* 20, no. 1 (2010): 61–68.

83. *T'aejo sillok* 9:9a [1396/6/11, 1], 9:9b [1396/6/14, 1], 10:1b [1396/7/19, 1], 14:2b [1398/5/14, 2], 14:5b [1398/5a/03, 1].

84. *T'aejo sillok* 5:6a [1394/2/19, 1]; 9:2a [1396/2/9, 1]; 10:1b [1396/7/19, 1]. For the detainment, exile, and execution of Korean envoys and their attendants, see 9:2a [1396/2/15, 1], 9:4a [1396/3/29, 3], 10:7b [1396/11/6, 1], 11:9b [1397/4/14, 1], 12:8b [1397/11/30, 2], 14:2b, and [1398/5/14]. Most detainees were never repatriated, although one thought dead had in fact been exiled to Yunnan. Of thirteen detained, five returned in 1404. The crews of two Korean merchant ships never returned. See *T'aejong sillok* 4:18a [1402/10/16, 2], 7:11a [1404/3/27, 1].

85. Pak Wŏnho[hyo], "Myŏngch'o ŭi munchaok kwa Chosŏn p'yojŏn munje," in *Myŏngch'o Chosŏn kwan'gyesa yŏn'gu* (Sŏul T'ŭkpyŏlsi: Ilchogak, 2002), 26–29. For banned words, see *Da Yuan shengzheng guochao dianzhang*, Scripta Sinica (Taipei: Guoli gugong bowuyuan, 1976), 28, pp. 1027–29. Kim Sunja, *Han'guk chungse Han-Chung kwan'gyesa* (Seoul: Hyean, 2007), 17; 164–70; Chen Xuelin, *Mingdai renwu yu chuanshuo* (Hong Kong: Zhongwen daxue chubanshe, 1997), 2–5; 5n12; 13–21, also 12n26 for Chan's reading of Korean evidence. See also Hok-lam Chan and Laurie Dennis, "Frenzied Fictions: Popular Beliefs and Political Propaganda in the Written History of Ming Taizu," in *Long Live the Emperor! : Uses of the Ming Founder Across Six Centuries of East Asian History*, ed. Sarah Schneewind (Minneapolis, MN: Society for Ming Studies, 2008), 27–31; Sŏ Kŏjŏng, *P'irwŏn chapki* in TDYS 3, vol. 1:670.

86. *T'aejo sillok* 9:4a [1396/3/29, 3], 3:5a [1393/3/9, 2]. Pak Wŏnho[hyo], *Myŏng ch'o Chosŏn*, 7–9.

87. Sima Qian, *Shiji*, 3, pp. 105–109; 4, pp. 131; 38, pp. 1602–21, especially the Zheng Xuan 鄭玄 (127–200) commentary, p. 1620. See also the commentaries on the *Zhoushu* 周書 in part 12 of the *Shangshu zhushu* 尚書註疏 167a–b in SSJZS. For consistency, the Korean romanization, "Kija," rather than Chinese, "Jizi," is used throughout this book. See further discussion in chapter 10 in this book.

88. Edward L. Farmer, *Zhu Yuanzhang and Early Ming Legislation: The Reordering of Chinese Society Following the Era of Mongol Rule* (New York: E.J. Brill, 1995), 100–103; Edward L. Dreyer, *Early Ming China: A Political History, 1355–1435* (Stanford, CA: Stanford University Press, 1982), 93, 106, 146–48.

89. A Jurchen Jin emperor once took offense when a Koryŏ memorial spoke too directly to the political challenges he faced. See Sŏ Kŏjŏng, *P'irwŏn chapki* 2 in TDYS 3, vol. 1:670. Kim Chongsŏ, *Koryŏsa chŏryo*, ed. Kojŏn kanhaeng hoe (Seoul: Minjok munhwa ch'ujinhoe, 1966 [15th century]), 14 Hŭijong 5 [1209/3]; Chen Long and Shen Zaiquan, "Chaoxian yu Ming Qing biaojian waijiao wenti yanjiu," 66–67.

90. Haboush, "Contesting Chinese Time," 132.

91. David Graeber and Marshall Sahlins, *On Kings* (Chicago: Hau Books, 2017), 2–5.

92. An identity with Koryŏ period origins; see Breuker, *Establishing a Pluralist Society*, 30–40; John B. Duncan, "Proto-Nationalism in Premodern Korea," in *Perspectives on Korea.*, ed. Duk-Soo Park and Sang-Oak Lee (Sydney: Wild Peony, 1998), 214–16; Remco E. Breuker, "The Three in One, the One in Three: The Koryŏ Three Han as a Pre-Modern Nation," *Journal of Inner and East Asian Studies* 2, no. 2 (December 2005): 144–67; Sŏ Inwŏn, "Chosŏn ch'ogi yŏksa insik kwa yŏng'uk insik: 'Tongguk yŏji sŭngnam' ŭl chungsim ŭro," *Yŏksa wa sirhak* 35 (June 2008): 89–116.

93. *Sejo sillok* 43:46b [1467/8/28, 8].

2. TERMS OF AUTHORITY

1. *T'aejo sillok* 5:6a [1394/2/19, 1], 14:2b [1398/7/5, 2]. For discussion of Ming hostility, see Wu Yue, "Waijiao de linian yu waijiao de xianshi: yi Zhu Yuanzhang dui 'buzhengguo' Chaoxian de zhengce wei zhongxin," *Mingshi yanjiu* 11 (2010): 33–43.

2. *T'aejong sillok* 1:16a [1401/2/30, 1]; 1:30b [1401/5/27, 2]; [1401/6/12, 1]. Pak Wŏnho[hyo], *Myŏngch'o Chosŏn kwan'gyesa yŏn'gu* (Seoul: Ilchogak, 2002), 122–30.

3. *T'aejong sillok* 3:11b [1402/2/26, 1]; 5:14b [1403/4/8, 1]. For significance of regalia, see, Chŏng Tonghun, "Myŏngdae ŭi yeje chilsŏ esŏ Chosŏn kugwang ŭi wisang," *Yŏksa wa hyŏnsil* no. 84 (June 2012): 251–92.

4. Zhu Yuanzhang, *Huang Ming zuxun*, Siku quanshu cunmu congshu, shi bu (part 2) 264 (Tainan: Zhuangyan wenhua, 1996), shouzhang 5a–7a. As one historian puts it, "the word 'peaceable' can in no way summarize Zhu Yuanzhang's foreign policy towards Koryŏ and Chosŏn": see Wu Yue, "Waijiao de linian yu waijiao de xianshi: yi Zhu Yuanzhang dui 'buzhengguo' Chaoxian de zhengce wei zhongxin," *Mingshi yanjiu* 11 (2010): 51–54. Neither was there an "a priori Confucian-Mencian strategic cultural preference" for peace in Ming strategic culture; see Alastair Ian Johnston, *Cultural Realism: Strategic Culture and Strategy in Chinese History* (Princeton, NJ: Princeton University Press, 1998), 176, 143–54.

5. Wang Gungwu, "The Cambridge History of China," in *Ming Foreign Relations: Southeast Asia*, ed. Denis C. Twitchett and Frederick W. Mote, vol. 8 (Cambridge: Cambridge University Press, 1998), 311–18.

6. Kathlene Baldanza, "The Ambiguous Border: Early Modern Sino-Viet Relations" (PhD diss., University of Pennsylvania, 2010), 45–49.

7. The third mission was eventually supplanted by the winter solstice mission (*tongjisa* 冬至使). See Chŏn Haejong, "Han-Chung chogong kwan'gye kaeron—Han-Chung kwan'gyesa ŭi chogam ŭl wihayŏ—," in *Kodae Han-Chung kwan'gyesa ŭi yŏn'gu* (Seoul: Samjiwŏn, 1987), 54–60.

8. *T'aejo sillok* 4:6a [1393/8/15, 1].

9. For the Hongwu emperor's expectations, see *T'aejo sillok* 4:7a [1393/9/2/, 1]. For the restoration of three embassies per annum, see *T'aejo sillok* 12:12a [1397/12/28, 1]; Peter Yun, "Rethinking the Tribute System: Korean States and Northeast Asian Interstate Relations, 600–1600" (PhD diss., University of California, Los Angeles, 1998), 146–48, 197–203; Gari Ledyard, "Korean Travelers in China over Four Hundred Years, 1488–1887," *Occasional Papers on Korea*, no. 2 (March 1974): 3–5.

10. Kye Sŭngbŏm, *Chosŏn sidae haeoe p'abyŏng kwa Han-Chung kwan'gye: Chosŏn chibae ch'ŭng ŭi Chungguk insik* (Seoul: P'urŭn yŏksa, 2009), 20–26; 59–64. For historical fantasy in this vein, watch Kim Yujin, *Sin'gijŏn* (CJ Entertainment, 2008); Chu Changmin, *Kwanghae, Wang i toen namja* (CJ Entertainment, 2012).

11. *T'aejong sillok* 13:16b [1407/4/8, 1].

12. *T'aejong sillok* 13:17b [1407/4/18, 1], 13:20b [1407/5/1, 1], 13:23b [1407/5/9, 1].

13. For Lê Quý Ly's name, see John Duong Phan, "Lacquered Words: The Evolution of Vietnamese Under Sinitic Influences from the 1st Century B.C.E. Through the 17th Century C.E." (PhD diss., Cornell University, 2013), 383n289.

14. *T'aejong sillok* 14:19a–20a [1407/8/29, 1].

15. Zhang Tingyu, *Ming shi* (Beijing: Zhonghua shuju, 1974), 321, p. 8315.

16. Yongle was a usurper as well, a moral failing that he may have tried to compensate for by punishing the Lê; see Wang Gungwu, "The Cambridge History of China," 315–16.

17. Shih-shan Henry Tsai, *The Eunuchs in the Ming Dynasty* (Albany, NY: SUNY Press, 1996), 135–39; Sixiang Wang, "Korean Eunuchs as Imperial Envoys: Relations with Chosŏn Through the Zhengde Reign," in *The Ming World*, ed. Kenneth Swope (New York: Routledge, 2020), 135–39.

18. *T'aejong sillok* 26:5a [1413/7/18, 1].

19. *T'aejong sillok* 26:5a [1413/7/19, 1], 26:7b [1413/7/26, 1]. Also of concern was the potential influx of defeated Mongols, who were hemmed in by the Great Wall to the west, to "stream south" toward Chosŏn. The Dongzhen incursions of 1211 and the Red Turban invasions of 1356 began as refugee inflows in the wake of Jin and Mongol imperial collapse; see William E. Henthorn, *Korea: The Mongol Invasions* (Leiden: E.J. Brill, 1963), 14–20; David M. Robinson, *Empire's Twilight: Northeast Asia Under the Mongols* (Cambridge, MA: Harvard University Asia Center, 2009), 147–59.

20. For an example of the "hindsight" view, see Huang Zhilian, *Dong Ya de liyi shijie: Zhongguo fengjianwangchao yu Chaoxian bandao guanxi xingtailun* (Beijing: Zhongguo renmin daxue chuban she, 1994), 291–98. *T'aejong sillok* 27:45b [1414/6/20, 4]

21. *Sŏngjong sillok* 134:11b [1481/10/17, 1]; Jing Liu and Yan Piao, "Expansion, Contestation, and Boundary Making: Chosŏn Korea and Ming China's Border Relations over the Yalu River Region," *International Journal of Korean History* 25, no. 2 (August 30, 2020): 108–15.

22. Brantly Womack, *China and Vietnam: The Politics of Asymmetry* (Cambridge: Cambridge University Press, 2006), 77–81.

23. Alexander Eng and Ann Ong, "Contextualising the Book-Burning Episode During the Ming Invasion and Occupation of Vietnam," in *Southeast Asia in the Fifteenth Century: The China Factor*, ed. Geoff Wade and Laichen Sun (Singapore: NUS Press and Hong Kong University Press, 2010), 155–60.

24. Yan Congjian, *Shuyu zhouzi lu* (Beijing: Gugong bowuyuan tushuguan, 1580), 5:51a–57b.

25. The nomenclature observes no inherent distinction between what is domestic or diplomatic. In Kwŏn Kŭn's collected works, they are listed separately as "*p'yo* and *chŏn* for serving the great" (*sadae p'yojŏn* 事大表箋), and "*p'yo* documents of our [country's] court" (*ponjo chŏnmun* 本朝表文). Note the use of *p'yo* in the latter category, even though not a single *p'yo* is represented in the group, a slippage of terminology that suggests formal interchangeability. See Kwŏn Kŭn, *Yangch'on chip*, 24–25 in HMC 7:237a–250b.

26. Sŏ Kŏjŏng, ed., *Tongmunsŏn* (Seoul: Kyŏnghŭi ch'ulp'ansa, 1966), (hereafter TMS), 32:25b–26a.

27. TMS 32:21a–b.

28. TMS 32:22b–23a; Kwŏn Kŭn, *Yangch'on chip*, 24 in HMC 7:240d.

29. As expressed in Wang Kŏn's *Ten Injunctions* in Chŏng Inji, *Koryŏ sa*, 14:14a–15b (hereafter KS), 2:15b. Charles Holcombe, *The Genesis of East Asia, 221 B.C.–A.D. 907* (Honolulu: Association for Asian Studies and University of Hawai'i Press, 2001), 60–74; 178–82; Nishijima Sadao, *Chūgoku kodai kokka to Higashi Ajia sekai* (Tokyo: Tōkyō Daigaku Shuppankai, 1983). Drawing sovereign models from "outside" is a common practice in human history, see David Graeber and Marshall Sahlins, *On Kings* (Chicago: Hau Books, 2017), 5–7, 144–75, 224–37.

30. Morris Rossabi, ed., *China Among Equals: The Middle Kingdom and Its Neighbors, 10th–14th Centuries* (Berkeley: University of California Press, 1983); Jing-shen Tao, *Two Sons of Heaven: Studies in Sung-Liao Relations* (Tucson: University of Arizona Press, 1988), 17–21, 29–31; Jing-shen Tao, *The Jurchen in Twelfth-Century China: A Study of Sinicization* (Seattle: University of Washington Press, 1977), 41–47.

31. Remco E. Breuker, "Koryŏ as an Independent Realm: The Emperor's Clothes," *Korean Studies* 27, no. 1 (January 2003): 52–58. *Sejong sillok* 11:8a [1421/1/30, 2], 22:6a [1423/12/29, 3]

32. Giwargis is another possible reconstruction of 闊里吉思, see KS 31:28a–b; Lee, "Shifting Borderlines," 250–51.

33. Song Lian, *Yuan shi*, ed. Yang Jialuo (Taipei: Dingwen shuju, 1981), 108, p. 4623.

34. KS 31:28b; Ko Pyŏngik, *Tonga kyosŏpsa ŭi yŏn'gu* (Seoul: Sŏul Taehakkyo ch'ulp'anbu, 1970), 200–216; David M. Robinson, *Korea and the Fall of the Mongol Empire: Alliance, Upheaval, and the Rise of a New East Asian Order*, (Cambridge: Cambridge University Press, 2022), 76–79.

35. KS 32:2a–2b; 32:5a. For related changes in the protocol terminology of diplomatic missives, see Chŏng Tonghun, "Koryŏ-Myŏng oegyo munsŏ sŏsik ŭi sŏngnip kwa paegyŏng," *Han'guk saron* 56 (2010): 139–207.

36. Yi Myŏngmi, "Koryŏ-Mongol kwan'gye wa Koryŏ kugwang wisang ŭi pyŏnhwa" (PhD diss., Seoul National University, 2012), 61–87; 147–52. *T'aejong sillok* 16:7a [1408/8/7, 3]. Yi Sŏnggye's descendants restored the use of temple names, but they continued to use the reformed nomenclature for Chosŏn government institutions and still requested a two-character *siho* from the imperial court after a monarch's death. That said, their successors also appended their own honorifics to the imperially granted *siho*. See An Kihyŏk, "Yŏmal Sŏnch'o tae Chungguk kwan'gye wa Kugwang siho," *Yŏksa wa hyŏnsil* 104 (June 2017): 229–62.

37. Kuwano Eiji, "Kōrai makki no girei to kokusai kankyō tai Min yōhai girei no sōshutsu," *Bulletin of Faculty of Literature, Kurume University, Intercultural Studies* 21 (2004.3): 67–70.

38. Yao Sui, *Muan ji*, SKQS1 1201 (Taipei: Shangwu yinshuguan, 1983), 3:16b–18b; Chang Tong'ik, *Wŏndae Yŏsa charyo chimnok* (Seoul: Sŏul Taehakkyo ch'ulp'anbu, 1997), 127–29.

39. Morris Rossabi, *Khubilai Khan: His Life and Times* (Berkeley: University of California Press, 1988), 71. For Mongol accommodation of Koryŏ, see Lee, "Shifting Borderlines," 244–61; King Kwong Wong, "All Are the Ruler's Domain, but All Are Different: Mongol-Yuan Rule and Koryŏ Sovereignty in the Thirteenth and Fourteenth Centuries," *Seoul Journal of Korean Studies* 34, no. 1 (2021): 1–30.

40. Benedict R. Anderson, *Imagined Communities: Reflections on the Origin and Spread of Nationalism* (London: Verso, 1991), 25–26. For debate, see Wong, "All Are the Ruler's Domain, but All Are Different," 12–22; Kang Hahn Lee, "Discussing David M. Robinson's *Empire's Twilight: Northeast Asia Under the Mongols*," *International Journal of Korean History* 16, no. 1 (2011): 1–24.

41. Hent Kalmo and Quentin Skinner, *Sovereignty in Fragments: The Past, Present and Future of a Contested Concept* (Cambridge: Cambridge University Press, 2010).

42. Li Chen, *Chinese Law in Imperial Eyes: Sovereignty, Justice, and Transcultural Politics* (New York: Columbia University Press, 2016), 12–13.

43. Benite et al., *The Scaffolding of Sovereignty*, 3–29.

44. William Roosen, "Early Modern Diplomatic Ceremonial: A Systems Approach," *Journal of Modern History* 52, no. 3 (1980): 452–76. For an East Asian example of ritual as sovereign formalization, see Macabe Keliher, *The Board of Rites and the Making of Qing China* (Oakland: University of California Press, 2019), 69–81, 162–68.

45. *T'aejong sillok* 1:11a [1401/1/25, 4].

46. *T'aejong sillok* 22:36b [1411/11/7, 1].

47. *T'aejong sillok* 23:30a [1412/5/3, 4].

48. *T'aejo sillok* 9:4a [1396/3/29].

49. Peter K. Bol, *Neo-Confucianism in History* (Cambridge, MA: Harvard University Asia Center, 2008), 144. *Shengjiao* is expanded in glosses as *shengwei jiaohua* 聲威教化. *Jiaohua* 教化, as "civilization," is related to *feng* 風, or "moral influence" as it appears in the "Great Preface" of the *Book of Songs* [風 風也 教也 風以動之 教以化之]. In Chosŏn-Ming diplomatic discourse, *feng* and *hua* 化 describe imperial authority in terms such as *huangfeng* 皇風 and *huanghua* 皇化 by ascribing civilizing agency to the emperor and his rule. A related term is *wen* (Kr. *mun* 文) as literary patterning, the mechanism by which this civilizing process is achieved. See Stephen Owen, *Readings in Chinese Literary Thought* (Cambridge, MA: Council on East Asian Studies, Harvard University Press, 1992), 24–25, for the discussion of 文, 38–39 for the equivalence of 教化 and 風. See also Shao-yun Yang, *The Way of the Barbarians: Redrawing Ethnic Boundaries in Tang and Song China* (Seattle: University of Washington Press,

2019); Sarah Schneewind, *Community Schools and the State in Ming China* (Stanford, CA: Stanford University Press, 2006), 39.

50. *Shangshu zhushu* 尚書注疏 6, 93a–b in SSJZS.

51. Qiu Jun, *Daxue yanyi bu*, SKQS (Taipei: Shangwu yinshu guan, n.d.), 143, p. 1326.

52. Qiu Jun, *Daxue yanyi bu*, 712–13:155, p. 1426; 145, pp. 1346, 1347–48.

53. Aaron Wesley Throness, "To Govern the State and Bring Peace to the Realm: Qiu Jun's (1421–1495) Geographic Statecraft Thought in 15th Century Ming China" (master's thesis, University of British Columbia, 2022), 2–5; 47–59.

54. Ch'oe Chongsŏk, "Chosŏn ch'ogi kukka wisang kwa 'Sŏnggyo chayu,'" *Hanguksa yŏn'gu* 162 (September 2013): 6–12; Mun Chungyang, "15 segi ŭi 'p'ungt'o pudongnon' kwa Chosŏn ŭi koyusŏng," *Hanguksa yŏn'gu* 162 (September 2013): 58–63. The Ming court continued to deny Chosŏn access to Ming using the pretext of cultural difference. The Ming refusal to grant Chosŏn access to its legal regulations, the Ming Code 大明律, was another case in point. *Sejong sillok* 112:30a [1446/6/7, 1].

55. Yang, *The Way of the Barbarians*, 11–24.

56. *Tanjong sillok* 12:13a [1457/9/27, 1].

57. *Sejong sillok* 6:10a [1419/12/7, 3]. For instance, Ming gifted Chosŏn the Neo-Confucian corpus, the *Xingli daquan* 性理大全, see Bol, *Neo-Confucianism in History*, 147–49.

58. As discussed by Martina Deuchler, *The Confucian Transformation of Korea: A Study of Society and Ideology* (Cambridge, MA: Council on East Asian Studies, 1992), 89–128. For example, see *Sejong sillok* 114:16b [1446/10/28, 1]; Young Kyun Oh, *Engraving Virtue: The Printing History of a Premodern Korean Moral Primer* (Leiden: Brill, 2013), 62–84.

59. Cho Wi, *Maegye chip*, 4 in HMC 16:328b.

60. MSL *Taizu* 47:5b [Hongwu 2/12/21]; 48:4b [Hongwu 3/1/10].

61. *T'aejo sillok* 3:9a [1393/5/23, 1].

62. *T'aejo sillok* 2:3a [1392/9/21, 3].

63. Se-Woong Koo, "Making Belief: Religion and the State in Korea, 1392-1960" (PhD diss., Stanford University, 2011), 21–38.

64. *T'aejo sillok* 1:40a [1392/7/20, 3].

65. Joseph Needham, *The Hall of Heavenly Records: Korean Astronomical Instruments and Clocks 1380–1780* (Cambridge: Cambridge University Press, 2004), 154; *Ch'ŏnsang yŏlch'a punya chi to* 天象列次分野之圖, 1395, stele, Ch'angdŏk 12937, National Palace Museum of Korea, Kukbo 228.

66. *T'aejong sillok* 31:44a [1416/6/1, 1].

67. *T'aejong sillok* 22:34a [1411/10/27, 2], 22:44b [1411/12/6, 4], 24:11b [1411/8/28, 1].

68. *Sejong sillok* 125:1b [1449/7/4, 1].

69. *Sejong sillok* 34:6b [1426/11/7, 1], 101:6b [1443/7/10, 3], 105:9b [1444/7/20, 1]. Sejo eventually abolished the heaven worshiping ritual in 1464. See Joon Hur, "The State and Identity Construction in Chosŏn Korea" (PhD diss., University of California, Los Angeles, 2019), 22–25.

70. *Sŏngjong sillok* 157:4a [1483/8/3, 4].

71. While prior imperial dynasties proscribed its knowledge to court-employed specialists, the Ming dynasty expected some familiarity with calendrical techniques from its literati officials. See Nathan Sivin, Kiyosi Yabuuti, and Shigeru Nakayama, *Granting the Seasons: The Chinese Astronomical Reform of 1280, with a Study of Its Many Dimensions and a Translation of Its Records* (New York: Springer, 2009), 35–38; Benjamin A. Elman, *A Cultural History of Civil Examinations in Late Imperial China* (Berkeley: University of California Press, 2000), 463–77; Yonglin Jiang, *The Mandate of Heaven and the Great Ming Code* (Seattle: University of Washington Press, 2013), 75–77.

72. *T'aejong sillok* 5:16a [1403/4/8, 1], 15:5b [1408/2/7, 1]

73. When Koryŏ surrendered to the Mongol Empire, imperial officials wanted to confirm that Koryŏ no longer observed Song lunations. Centuries later, after Ming's destruction, a Ming loyalist was moved to tears when leafing through Korean books that marked time with the Ming calendar. Likewise, the discovery of Korean use of Ming time could miff a Qing emperor, sensitive to insinuations of Manchu illegitimacy. See Wang Yun 王惲, *Qiujian ji*, SQKS 1200–1201 (Taipei: Shangwu yinshuguan, 1983), 82:4b–6b; Qian Qianyi, *Muzhai youxue ji*, ed. Qian Zeng and Qian Zhonglian (Shanghai: Shanghai guji chubanshe, 1996), 46, pp. 1527–28.

74. *T'aejong sillok* 13:20b [1407/5/1, 1]

75. Park Kwon Soo, "Calendar Publishing and Local Science in Chosŏn Korea," in *Science and Confucian Statecraft in East Asia*, ed. Francesca Bray and Jongtae Lim (Leiden: Brill, 2019), 138–41.

76. Eun Hee Lee, "Korean Astronomical Calendar, Chiljeongsan," in *Handbook of Archaeoastronomy and Ethnoastronomy*, ed. Clive L.N. Ruggles (New York: Springer, 2015), 2157–62. *Sejong sillok* 101:4a [1443/7/6, 5]; 156:1a [七政算內外篇].

77. Han Yŏngho, Yi Ŭnhŭi, and Kim Minjŏng, "Sejong ŭi yŏkpŏp chejŏng kwa 'Ch'ilchŏng san,'" *Tongpang hakchi* 168 (2014): 102.

78. Needham, *The Hall of Heavenly Records*, 16–9.

79. *Sejong sillok* 51:22b [1431/3/2, 1]; *Sejong sillok* 56:24a [1432/5/14, 2]; that is, 弧矢割圓法 or 方圓法.

80. Ku Manok, "Chosŏn wangjo ŭi chipkwŏn ch'eje wa kwahak kisul chŏngch'aek: Chosŏn chŏn'gi ch'ŏnmun yŏksanhak ŭi chŏngbi kwajŏng ŭl chungsim ŭro," *Tongpang hakchi* 124 (2004): 235–36.

81. Yunli Shi, "The Korean Adaptation of the Chinese-Islamic Astronomical Tables," *Archive for History of Exact Sciences* 57, no. 1 (2003): 25–60; Li Liang, "Tables of Sunrise and Sunset in Yuan and Ming China (1271–1644) and Their Adoption in Korea," in *Editing and Analysing Numerical Tables: Towards a Digital Information System for the History of Astral Sciences*, ed. Matthieu Husson, Clemency Montelle, and Benno van Dalen (Turnhout, Belgium: Brepols, 2021), 253–85.

82. Note that traditional East Asian calendrical systems used 365.2575 degrees (1 per solar day) instead of 360. The East Asian latitude measurement of 38⅙ degrees for Seoul, when converted to modern units yields approximately 37.61°N, which is less than 0.03° higher than the modern value of 37.58°N for the latitude of the royal palace in Seoul. See Han Yŏngho, Yi Ŭnhŭi, and Kim Minjŏng, "Sejong ŭi yŏkpŏp," 108–109n20; Sivin et al., *Granting the Seasons*, 46–147, 577–79, 488–94.

83. Mun Chungyang, "'Hyangnyŏk' esŏ 'Tongnyŏk' ŭro: Chosŏn hugi chaguk ryŏk ŭr katgocha hanŭn yŏlmang," *Yŏksa hakpo* 218 (June 2013): 239–44; Ku Manok, "Chosŏn wangjo ŭi chipkwŏn che," 231–37; 247–51.

84. Park Kwon Soo, "Calendar Publishing and Local Science in Chosŏn Korea," 130–32.

85. Ch'oe Chongsŏk, "Chosŏn ch'ogi 'siwang chi che' nonŭi kujo ŭi t'ŭkching kwa chunghwa pop'yŏn ŭi ch'ugu," *Chosŏn sidae sa hakpo*, no. 52 (2010): 5–59.

86. For how these differences might unfold, see Yiming Ha, "Public Discourse and Private Sentiment: Ritual Controversies, Ritual Authority, and Political Succession in Ming and Chosŏn," *Ming Studies* (May 2022): 1–26.

87. Soyoung Suh, "Herbs of Our Own Kingdom: Layers of the 'Local' in the Materia Medica of Early Choson Korea," *Asian Medicine* 4, no. 2 (December 2009): 395–422.

88. Iksop Lee and S. Robert Ramsey, *The Korean Language* (Albany: SUNY Press, 2000), 7–13; 31–33.

89. *Sejong sillok* 113:36b [1446/4/29, 4]; Yi To, *Sejong ŏje Hunmin chŏngŭm ŏnhae*, repr., Kyujanggak Archives 가람 古 411.1-H899s (Seoul, 1568), 1a–3a.

90. Ross King, "Nationalism and Language Reform in Korea," in *Nationalism and the Construction of Korean Identity*, ed. Hyung Il Pai and Timothy R. Tangherlini (Berkeley: Institute of East Asian Studies, University of California, 1998), 34–35.

91. Gari Ledyard, *The Korean Language Reform of 1446* (Seoul: Singu Munhwasa, 1998), 277–322.

92. Gari Ledyard, "The International Linguistic Background of the Correct Sounds for the Instruction of the People," in *The Korean Alphabet: Its History and Structure*, ed. Young-Key Kim-Renaud (Honolulu: University of Hawai'i Press, 1997), 31–87.

93. Sixiang Wang, "The Sounds of Our Country: Interpreters, Linguistic Knowledge and the Politics of Language in Early Chosŏn Korea (1392–1592)," in *Rethinking East Asian Languages, Vernaculars, and Literacies, 1000–1919*, ed. Benjamin A. Elman (Leiden: Brill, 2014); Chŏng Taham, "Yŏmal Sŏnch'o ŭi Tongasia chilsŏ wa Chosŏn esŏ ŭi Hanŏ, Hanimun, Hunmin Chŏngŭm," *Han'guksa hakpo* 36 (2009): 269–305.

94. Sin Sukchu, *Pohanjae chip* 15 in HMC 10:126a–126d; Ledyard, *The Korean Language Reform*, 363–64.

95. *Sejong sillok* 117:22a [1447/9/29, 2].

96. Lee and Ramsey, *The Korean Language*, 283–289; Ledyard, *The Korean Language Reform*, 356–58.

97. *Sejong sillok* 103:19b [1444/2/20, 1].

98. Ross King, "North and South Korea," in *Language and National Identity in Asia*, ed. Andrew Simpson (Oxford: Oxford University Press, 2007), 203–4.

99. Mun Chungyang, "15 segi ŭi 'p'ungt'o pudong"; Chŏng Taham, "Yŏmal Sŏnch'o ŭi Tongasia," 286–98.

100. Henrik H. Sorenson, "Lamaism in Korea during the Late Koryŏ Dynasty," *Korea Journal* 33, no. 3 (1993): 67–81.

101. Adam Bohnet, *Turning Toward Edification: Foreigners in Chosŏn Korea* (Honolulu: University of Hawai'i Press, 2020), 47. One Central Asian emigre, Sŏl Changsu 偰長壽 (1340–1399), served as Chosŏn's chief interpreter; see Michael C. Brose, "Uyghur Technologists of Writing and Literacy in Mongol China," *T'oung Pao*, Second Series, 91, no. 4/5 (January 2005): 396–435; Sixiang Wang, "Chosŏn's Office of Interpreters: The Apt Response and the Knowledge Culture of Diplomacy," *Journal for the History of Knowledge* 1, no. 1 (December 17, 2020): 5. Islamic calendrical arts were also incorporated into Korean astronomical practice; see Han Yŏngho, "Chosŏn ŭi Hoehoeryŏkpŏp toip kwa 'Ch'ilchŏngsan oe p'yŏn,'" *Minjok munhwa* 45 (June 2015): 127–60.

102. Pae Usŏng, *Chosŏn kwa Chunghwa: Chosŏn i kkum kkugo sangsang han segye wa munmyŏng* (Kyŏnggi-do P'aju-si: Tolbegae, 2014), 125–27.

103. Sixiang Wang, "Story of the Eastern Chamber: Dilemmas of Vernacular Language and Political Authority in Eighteenth-Century Chosŏn," *Journal of Korean Studies* 24, no. 1 (March 2019): 42.

104. Peter Kornicki, *Languages, Scripts, and Chinese Texts in East Asia* (Oxford: Oxford University Press, 2018), 197–204; Si Nae Park, "The Sound of Learning the Confucian Classics in Chosŏn Korea," *Harvard Journal of Asiatic Studies* 79, no. 1 (2019): 137–40.

105. Xin Wen, "The Road to Literary Culture: Revisiting the Jurchen Language Examination System," *T'oung Pao* 101, no. 1–3 (August 2015): 130–67.

106. Peter H. Lee, *Songs of Flying Dragons: A Critical Reading* (Cambridge, MA: Harvard University Press, 1975), 7–8; 30–33.

107. Oh, *Engraving Virtue*, 55–90; 128–37.

108. An institution that overlapped with the government courtesan system; see Hyun Suk Park, "The Government Courtesan: Status, Gender, and Performance in Late Choson Korea" (PhD diss., University of Chicago, 2015), 1–8; 51–55; 61–63.

109. See *T'aejo sillok*, 1:6b [preface, 35]; *T'aejong sillok* 22:10b [1411/7/15, 1]. For T'aejong's use of *yŏak*, see *T'aejong sillok* 27:15b [1414/2/27, 1], 27:16a [1414/3/6, 1], 27:18b [1414/3/28, 3], 27:21a [1414/4/14, 1]; *T'aejo sillok* 7:9b [1395/4/25, 1], 8:8a [1395/10/5, 1].

110. *T'aejo sillok* 8:9a [1395/10/7, 2].

111. Such attempts to banish female performers from the court were really "camouflage for conflicted male desire for and fear of female sensuality." See Joseph S. C. Lam, "The Presence and Absence of Female Musicians and Music in China," in *Women and Confucian Cultures in Premodern China, Korea, and Japan*, ed. Dorothy Ko, JaHyun Kim Haboush, and Joan R. Piggott (Berkeley: University of California Press, 2003), 97–108.

112. Park, "The Government Courtesan," 64–85.

113. *Sejong sillok* 49:8a [1430/7/28, 2], 56:13a [1432/4/25, 2], 59:1a [1433/1/1, 3].

114. *Sejong sillok* 67:22a [1435/3/7, 4].

115. *Sejong sillok* 54:40a [1431/12/25, 5], 100:6b [1443/4/17, 2], 116:10a [1447/4a/22, 1]. Park, "The Government Courtesan," 64–69.

116. *Munjong sillok* 4:53b [1450/11/22, 7]. See also *Munjong sillok* 13:10a [1452/4/14, 1].

117. The music of the state of Zheng was synonymous with moral decay. See *Munjong sillok* 4:53b [1450/11/22, 7].

118. *Tanjong sillok* 12:14b [1454/10/5, 1].

119. *Sŏngjong sillok* 47:8b [1474/9/21, 2].

120. *Sejo sillok* 13:35b [1458/8/13, 2]. His grandson Sŏngjong also defended the practice, although he again banished female musicians from the Hall of Diligent Governance but retained them for palace banquets. *Sŏngjong sillok* 14:7b [1472/1/15, 5], 36:1a [1473/11/1, 2], 75:21b [1477/1/22, 4], 125:4a [1481/1/5, 2].

121. Not "public" in the Habermasian sense, but one opposed to the zone of private, self-centered action. See JaHyun Kim Haboush, "Academies and Civil Society in Chosŏn Korea," in *La société civile face à l'État: dans les traditions chinoise, japonaise, coréenne et vietnamienne*, ed. Léon Vandermeersch (Paris: École Française d'Extrême-Orient, 1994). For the inner palace as existing outside the jurisdiction of official, public interest, see JaHyun Kim Haboush, "Versions and Subversions: Patriarchy and Polygamy in Korean Narratives," in *Women and Confucian Cultures in Premodern China, Korea, and Japan*, ed. Dorothy Ko,

JaHyun Kim Haboush, and Joan R. Piggott (Berkeley: University of California Press, 2003), 285–88. For ambiguity, the case of extended royal kin (*chongch'in* 宗親) was one example; see *Sŏngjong sillok* 197:7b [1486/11/16, 3], [1486/11/17, 1].

122. Sixiang Wang,. "Emotions in Koryŏ-Mongol Diplomacy: From Covenants of Affect to the Paternal Simile" (December 2021).

123. Chŏng Tonghun, "Myŏngdae ŭi yeje chilsŏ," 255–56; 283–84.

124. Yi Aedŭk, "Chosŏn sidae Yŏnsan'gun ŭi yŏak chedo e kwanhan koch'al," *Muyong hakhoe nonmunjip* 50 (2007): 159–77. For connection to royal power, see Park, "The Government Courtesan," 84–85.

125. Yi Yŏnghun, *Sejong ŭn kwayŏn sŏnggun inga* (P'aju: Paengnyŏn tongan, 2018), 151–56; 160–63.

126. These matters became a diplomatic controversy when brought to the attention of the Ming court during the Imjin War. See Gari Ledyard, "Confucianism and War: The Korean Security Crisis of 1598," *Journal of Korean Studies* 6, no. 1 (1988): 81–119.

127. Peter Yun, "Confucian Ideology and the Tribute System in Chosŏn-Ming Relations," *Sach'ong* 55, no. 9 (2002): 67–88.

128. Bol, *Neo-Confucianism in History*, 115–44; 197–204; Yung Sik Kim, *The Natural Philosophy of Chu Hsi (1130–1200)* (Philadelphia: American Philosophical Society, 2000).

PART II. THE PRACTICE OF DIPLOMACY

1. *T'aejong sillok* 8:12b [1395/11/6, 1].

2. For example, *Sejong sillok* 63:31b [1434/3/21, 4].

3. Donghun Jung, "From a Lord to a Bureaucrat: The Change of Koryŏ King's Status in the Korea-China Relations," *Review of Korean Studies* 19, no. 2 (December 2016): 115–36.

4. Im Hyŏnjin, "Yŏmal Sŏnch'o ŭi tae-Myŏng kwan'gye wa insin mu oegyo kwannyŏm," *Sahak yŏn'gu*, no. 138 (2020): 213–54.

5. As opposed to Chosŏn's ties with Ming, which fell under the scheme of "serving the great," or *sadae*, and which entailed distinct precedents and practices. See Kenneth R. Robinson, "Centering the King of Chosŏn," *Journal of Asian Studies* 59, no. 1 (2000): 110.

6. Regular envoy missions were disrupted after the Manchu conquest of Liaodong in 1620. Tabulations vary. See Chŏn Haejong, "Han-Chung chogong kwan'gye kaeron—Han-Chung kwan'gyesa ŭi chogam ŭl wihayŏ—," in *Kodae Han-Chung kwan'gyesa ŭi yŏn'gu* (Seoul: Samjiwŏn, 1987), 54–60; Gao Yanlin, "Ming chao yu Chaoxian wangchao zhi jian de shichen wanglai," *The Final Research Results Supported by the KFAS International Scholar Exchange Fellowship Program,*

2003–2004, August 13, 2004, 164–92; Figures based on Chŏng Ŭnju, *Chosŏn sidae sahaeng kirokhwa: yet kŭrim ŭro ingnŭn Han-Chung kwan'gye sa* (Seoul: Sahoe p'yŏngnon, 2012).

7. *Sŏngjong sillok* 150:2b [1483/1/3, 5]; T'aejong's reign saw 2.7 Ming missions per year, while Sejong received 1.1 missions per year. Between 1392 and 1492, Chosŏn sent 1.13 missions for every mission received. Chungjong received one embassy every 6.5 years (0.15 per year); his successor Myŏngjong one every 5.5 years (0.18 per year). From 1492 to 1568, Ming envoys arrived once every 4.8 years (0.21 per year). Sŏnjo's reign saw an average of 0.85 embassies per year, but the numbers are inflated by the Imjin War, which saw intense diplomatic contact. Ratios based on Cho Yŏngnok, "Sŏnch'o ŭi Chosŏn ch'ulsin Myŏngsa ko—Sŏngjong cho ŭi tae Myŏng kyosŏp kwa Myŏngsa Chŏng Tong—," *Kuksagwan nonch'ong* 14 (1990): 110, especially n8.

8. Peter Yun, "Rethinking the Tribute System: Korean States and Northeast Asian Interstate Relations, 600–1600" (PhD diss., University of California, Los Angeles, 1998), 115–20; Seung B. Kye, "Huddling Under the Imperial Umbrella: A Korean Approach to Ming China in the Early 1500s," *Journal of Korean Studies* 15, no. 1 (2010): 41–66.

9. Daniela Frigo, ed., *Politics and Diplomacy in Early Modern Italy: The Structure of Diplomatic Practice, 1450–1800*, trans. Adrian Belton, reissue (Cambridge: Cambridge University Press, 2011), 10–11; Ricardo Fubini, "Diplomacy and Government in the Italian City-States of the Fifteenth Century (Florence and Venice)," in *Politics and Diplomacy in Early Modern Italy*, 25–48.

10. Both diplomatic systems emerged contingently from their respective institutional contexts, so there is no reason to think of the absence of one institution as a "limitation" without imposing the anachronistic norms of one set of practices onto another. Kirk W. Larsen, *Tradition, Treaties, and Trade: Qing Imperialism and Chosŏn Korea, 1850–1910* (Cambridge, MA: Harvard University Asia Center, 2008), 13–14, 23–24, 47–52; Kwŏn Inyong, "Myŏng chunggi Chosŏn ŭi ip Myŏng sahaeng—So Seyang ŭi 'Pu Kyŏng ilgi' rŭl t'onghayŏ," *Myŏng-Ch'ongsa yŏn'gu* 19 (2003): 131–32.

11. The distances are 1,186 *ri* from Seoul to Ŭiju and 2,012 *ri* from Seoul to Beijing. Each Korean *ri* corresponds to 393 meters. The distance estimate is computed from the numbers provided in Kim Kyŏngnok, "Chosŏn sidae chogong ch'eje tae Chungguk sahaeng," *Myŏng-Ch'ongsa yŏn'gu* 30 (2008): 107.

12. Synopses of envoys reports from after the seventeenth century survive in Sŭngmunwŏn, ed., *Tongmun hwigo*, Han'guk saryo ch'ongsŏ 24 (Seoul: Kuksa p'yŏnch'an wiwŏnhoe, 1978), vol. 2, pp. 1562–1700. The precedent was established by Cho Malsaeng 趙末生 (1370–1447), the secretary of the 1403 mission; see Kim Chinam, *T'ongmun'gwan chi*, Kyujanggak charyo ch'ongsŏ (Seoul: Sŏul

taehakkyo Kyujanggak Han'gukhak yŏn'guwŏn, 2006), 3:2a–b; Ch'oe Hang and Sŏ Kŏjŏng, eds., *Kyŏngguk taejŏn*, Asami Collection, Korean Rare Book Collection (University of California, Berkeley) Asami 18.10 vol. 1–4 (Seoul, 1603 [15th century]), 3:39b; Yi Sangjŏk, *Yŏnhaeng sarye*, Fonds Maurice Courant, manuscrits coréens n5258 KS 42 (Paris, 1857), 54b.

13. Kim Kyŏngnok, "Chosŏn sidae chogong," 99–106; Yang Yulei, *Yanxing yu Zhong-Chao wenhua guanxi* (Shanghai: Shanghai cishu chubanshe, 2011), 23–25; Sixiang Wang, "Chosŏn's Office of Interpreters: The Apt Response and the Knowledge Culture of Diplomacy," *Journal for the History of Knowledge* 1, no. 1 (December 17, 2020): 8–11.

14. Kim Kyŏngnok, "Chosŏn ch'ogi t'ongsa ŭi hwaldong kwa wisang pyŏnhwa," *Han'guk hakpo* 26, no. 4 (December 2000): 60–61. See *Sejo sillok* 27:15b [1462/2/11, 2]; *Sejo sillok* 29:7a [1462/8/20, 2].

15. Haste taxed both men and horses; in 1468, royal orders limited such rapid travel only to deliver military intelligence. *Sejo sillok* 45:41b [1468/3/26, 1].

16. Chosŏn princely titles reflected their generational and genealogical distance from their closest royal kin. Suyang, as a son borne of King Sejong's primary consort, was therefore a "great prince," *taegun*.

3. BENEATH THE VENEER

1. Philip de Heer, *The Care-Taker Emperor: Aspects of the Imperial Institution in Fifteenth-Century China as Reflected in the Political History of the Reign of Chu Ch'i-Yü* (Leiden: Brill, 1986), 18–42; Phillip H. Woodruff, "Foreign Policy and Frontier Affairs Along the Northeast Frontier of the Ming Dynasty, 1350–1618: Tripartite Relations of the Ming Chinese, Korean Koryo, and Jurchen-Manchu Tribesmen" (PhD diss., University of Chicago, 1995), 157–65.

2. *Sejong sillok* 126:1a [1449/10/1, 1].

3. *Sejong sillok* 125:24a [1449/9/29, 2], 126:3b [1449/10/18, 1].

4. *Tanjong sillok* 2:8a [1452/7/21, 3].

5. *Tanjong sillok* 1:17a [1452/5/24, 1], 1:17b [1452/5/25, 2].

6. *Tanjong sillok* 1:25b [1452/6/15, 2].

7. For elaboration, see Sixiang Wang, "Co-Constructing Empire in Early Chosŏn Korea: Knowledge Production and the Culture of Diplomacy, 1392–1592" (PhD diss., Columbia University, 2015), 179–240.

8. Edward W. Wagner, "The Literati Purges: Case Studies in the Factionalism of the Early Yi Dynasty" (PhD diss., Harvard University, 1959), 42–45; Kim Yŏngdu, "Sillok p'yŏnch'an e nat'anan Sejo chŏngkwŏn ŭi chŏngdangsŏng ch'ugu," *Han'guk sahak sahakpo* 27 (2013): 65–99.

9. *Sejong sillok* 126:10a [1449/12/22, 1].

10. A fear Chosŏn anticipated. See *Sejong sillok* 126:11a [1449/23/24, 1].

11. At the time, the Champa kingdom was in the throes of civil war, and this Ming envoy, unable to find the real ruler, settled for delivering the imperial message to one of his nobles. Upon his return, he was accused of deceiving the imperial court and executed for his negligence. See Zhang Tingyu, *Ming shi* (Beijing: Zhonghua shuju, 1974) (hereafter MS), 324, p. 8389.

12. *Sejong sillok* 127:16b [1450/1a/1, 1]; Ni Qian, *Chaoxian jishi*, Congshu jicheng chubian 3240 (Beijing: Zhonghua shuju, 1985), 6–7, 11; Philip de Heer, "Three Embassies to Seoul: Sino-Korean Relations in the 15th Century," in *Conflict and Accomodation in Early Modern East Asia: Essays in Honour of Erik Zurcher*, ed. Leonard Blusse and Harriet T. Zurndorfer (Leiden: E.J. Brill, 1993), 246, especially n15.

13. Ni Qian, *Liaohai bian* (Beijing: Beijing tushuguan chuban she, 1469), 2:21b–30b; 4:11a–22b.

14. *Tanjong sillok* 2:22a [1452/8/22, 1], 2:29b [1452/8/26, 2].

15. Kim Yŏngdu, "Sillok p'yŏnch'an."

16. For compilation, culling, and censorship of *Veritable Records*, see Hang Nyeong Oh, "The Meaning of Ritual Practices in the Compilation of the Chosŏn Sillok," in *The Institutional Basis of Civil Governance in the Chosŏn Dynasty*, ed. John Duncan (Seoul: Seoul Selection, 2009), 161–79; Graeme R. Reynolds, "Culling Archival Collections in the Koryŏ-Chosŏn Transition," *Journal of Korean Studies* 24, no. 2 (October 2019): 237–44.

17. The *Chronicle* was not renamed to a *Veritable Record* until Tanjong's rehabilitation in 1698, see Yun Chŏng, "Sukchongdae Tanjong ch'upok ŭi chŏngch'isajŏk ŭimi," *Han'guk sasang sahak* 22 (June 2004): 213–17.

18. *Sejo sillok* purok 47a–b; *Sejo sillok* 2:12a [1452/7/28, 2]; Kang Chehun, "Chosŏn ch'ogi hunch'ŏk Han Myŏnghoe ŭi kwanjik saenghwal kwa kŭ t'ŭkching," *Yŏksa wa hyŏnsil* 43 (November 2010): 8–13.

19. *Tanjong sillok* 3:5b [1452/9/10, 2], 3:7b [1452/9/10, 5], 3:11b [1452/9/27, 2].

20. *Tanjong sillok* 3:23b [1452/9a/22, 3], 4:3b [1452/10/5, 3].

21. *Tanjong sillok* 3:25b [1452/9a/27, 4], 4:2a [10/2, 1], 4:5a–b [10/8, 4; 10/10, 2; 10/12, 1].

22. *Tanjong sillok* 4:6a [1452/10/14, 1], 6b [16, 1].

23. Royal kinsmen suggested that Suyang "possessed the mandate of heaven," even as he performed loyalty to the throne. See *Tanjong sillok* 4:5a [1452/10/8, 5], 4:7b [21, 2].

24. Gari Ledyard, "The Korean Language Reform of 1446: The Origin, Background, and Early History of the Korean Alphabet" (PhD diss., University of California, 1966), 81–84.

25. Ni Qian, "Liaohai bian," in *Shi Chaoxian lu*, ed. Yin Mengxia and Yu Hao (Beijing: Beijing tushuguan chubanshe, 2003), 2:22b, p. 565; 2:26a–30a, pp. 572–580.

26. This account draws from So Seyang, "Yanggok pugyŏng ilgi," in *Yŏnhaengnok chŏnjip*, ed. Im Kijung, [1534], vol. 2 (Seoul: Tongguk taehakkyo ch'ulp'anbu, 2001), (hereafter YHNCJ).

27. *Tanjong sillok* 5:18a [1453/2/26, 1].

28. So Seyang, "Yanggok ilgi," in YHNCJ 2, 397.

29. So Seyang, "Yanggok ilgi," in YHNCJ 2, 397–98.

30. *Sejo sillok* 10:11a [1457/11/20, 1; 2]; So Seyang, "Yanggok ilgi," in YHNCJ 2, 398.

31. *Sŏngjong sillok* 88:3b [1478/1/11, 1], 92:23b [1478/5/29, 5].

32. *Sŏngjong sillok* 99:15b [1478/12/21, 3]. During the Imjin War, the Korean court did write on behalf of Ming officers whom they believed acted in Korea's interest. Gari Ledyard, "Confucianism and War: The Korean Security Crisis of 1598," *Journal of Korean Studies* 6, no. 1 (1988), 85–91.

33. *Chungjong sillok* 42:51a [1521/7/21, 1].

34. *Sejo sillok* 45:25b [1468/3/2, 3]; see also *Sejo sillok* 41:8b [1467/2/5, 2].

35. Oiled paper 油芚 protected valuables from moisture and rain. Chŏng Hwan, *Hoesan sŏnsaeng munjip* 2 in HMC (sok), vol. 2:211b–c, 215a, 226b.

36. So Seyang, "Yanggok ilgi," in YHNCJ 2, 400.

37. *Sejo sillok* 34:32a [1464/10/9, 2].

38. *Sejo sillok* 25:14b [1461/8/7, 2].

39. *Sejo sillok* 44:4b [1467/10/6, 2].

40. Because of his connections to the frontier military; see *Sejo sillok* 46:13b [1468/4/30, 1].

41. The Liaodong military often escorted returning envoys. Expecting that Liaodong commanders would also fête their envoys, the Chosŏn court prepared additional gifts for the Liaodong military. See *Sŏngjong sillok* 54:6b [1475/4/14, 1]. See, for example, *Sŏngjong sillok* 9:4b [1471/1/10, 10].

42. Xu Dongri, *Chaoxian chao shichen yanzhong de Zhongguo xingxiang: yi "Yan xing lu" "Chao tian lu" wei zhongxin* (Beijing: Zhonghua shuju, 2010), 101. *Chungjong sillok* 31:3a [1517/12/7, 1]. Chosŏn-Ming period trade volume (as well as the size of embassies) is dwarfed by commerce in the later Chosŏn-Qing period; see Seonmin Kim, *Ginseng and Borderland: Territorial Boundaries and Political Relations Between Qing China and Chosŏn Korea, 1636–1912* (Oakland: University of California Press, 2017), 107–22.

43. *Sŏngjong sillok* 55:1b [1475/5/4, 4], 56:1b [1475/6/2, 3], 55:5b [1475/5/11, 3], 55:12a [1475/5/15, 1].

44. *Sŏngjong sillok* 39:5b [1474/2/7, 1].

45. Kim Chinam, *T'ongmun'gwan chi*, Ko. 古 5120-11-v.1–3 (Kyujanggak Archives, Seoul National University, 1720), 2:7a–9a.
46. Hŏ Pong, "Hagok sŏnsaeng Choch'ŏn'gi," *Hagok chip*, in HMC 58:412a–b.
47. Also known as the Southern Huitong Hostel, it was established in 1441. It was a complex with 387 rooms. See Chen Yiqiu, "Cong Chaoxian shichen de Zhongguo xingji kan Mingday zhonghouqi de Yuhe guan: yi Huitong guan tiduguan wei zhongxin," *Nanjing xiaozhuang xueyuan xuebao* 3 (2014): 57–58.
48. Liam C. Kelley, *Beyond the Bronze Pillars: Envoy Poetry and the Sino-Vietnamese Relationship* (Honolulu: University of Hawai'i Press, 2005). See, for example, Yi Sugwang, *Chipong sŏnsaeng chip* 8, 9 in HMC 66:85a–86d; 93a–94b; So Seyang, "Yanggok ilgi," in YHNCJ 2, 403.
49. The term *yain* is cognate with the Chinese word *Yeren*, an exonym for Tungusic people north of the Songhua River, but Chosŏn period usage tends to treat *yain* as a catchall that includes all Jurchen groups. See Kenneth R. Robinson, "Organizing Japanese and Jurchens in Tribute Systems in Early Chosŏn Korea," *Journal of East Asian Studies* 13, no. 2 (May 2013): 337–60. Even in the mid-sixteenth century, *yain* leaders treated Korean ambassadors with deference; see So Seyang, "Yanggok ilgi," in YNCHJ 2, 404; Pak Chŏngmin, "Yŏnsan'gun—Myŏngjongdae Yŏjinin naejo ŭi chaegŏmt'o," *Yŏksa hakpo* 222 (June 2014): 37–65.
50. Zhang Shizun, "Ming Qing Chaoxian shituan 'xiamayan' he 'shangmayan' kaoshi," *Anshan shifan xueyuan xuebao* 21, no. 05 (2019): 33–34.
51. Sixiang Wang, "Korean Eunuchs as Imperial Envoys: Relations with Chosŏn Through the Zhengde Reign," in *The Ming World*, ed. Kenneth Swope (New York: Routledge, 2020).
52. See *Tanjong sillok* 7:23a [1453/9/21, 1]. The practice continued. The 1481 envoy Yi Sŭngso 李承召 (1422–1484), for instance, dedicated several poems to Korean eunuchs who held banquets for the visiting Korean emissaries at their residences. See Yi Sŭngso, *Samt'an sŏnsaeng chip* 6 in HMC 11:455a–c.
53. 八象; or "all the eight trigrams." The intended meaning is unclear.
54. For example, as sympathetic responses or *ganying* 感應 (K. *kamŭng*). See Yung Sik Kim, *The Natural Philosophy of Chu Hsi (1130–1200)* (Philadelphia: American Philosophical Society, 2000), 122–28.
55. Or Theinni, identified as Mokpang 木方 here, homophonous with Mubang 木邦 in Ming sources. See MS 315, p. 8144. Geoff Wade, "Engaging the South: Ming China and Southeast Asia in the Fifteenth Century," *Journal of the Economic and Social History of the Orient* 51, no. 4 (2008): 595, 600–603.

56. *Sejo sillok* 10:2a–2b [1457/11/10, 1].

57. *Tanjong sillok* 7:25b [1453/9/25/, 1].

58. This incident is usually referred to, euphemistically, as the *"kyeyu* year pacification" (*kyeyu chŏngnan* 癸酉靖難) in Chosŏn sources. *Tanjong sillok* 7:25b [1453/9/25, 1], 8:5b–8:9a [1453/10/10, 1].

59. Wang, "Korean Eunuchs," 464–66. *Sejong sillok* 26:15b [1424/10/17, 2], 68:10b [1435/4/28, 2].

60. *Sejo sillok* 25:20b [1461/8/26, 2]; David M. Robinson, "Politics, Force and Ethnicity in Ming China: Mongols and the Abortive Coup of 1461," *Harvard Journal of Asiatic Studies* 59, no. 1 (June 1999): 113–14.

61. *Sejo sillok* 25:24b [1461/9/6, 1].

62. Unlike the Ming *Records*, which eventually leaked outside the palace, the Chosŏn records remained generally inaccessible through the end of the dynasty. See Sun Weiguo, " 'Ming shilu' yu 'Chaoxian wangchao shilu' zhi bijiao yanjiu," in *Ming Qing shiqi Zhongguo shixue dui Chaoxian de yingxiang: jian lun liangguo xueshu jiaoliu yu haiwai Hanxue* (Shanghai: Shanghai cishu chuban she, 2009). This openness extended to other state archives; see Devin Fitzgerald, "The Ming Open Archive and the Global Reading of Early Modern China" (PhD diss., Harvard University, 2020), 75–106.

63. *Tanjong sillok* 12:15a [1454/10/10, 1].

64. *Tanjong sillok* 13:27b [1455/2/22, 1]. Chŏng's given name is sometimes rendered as T'ong 通.

65. *Tanjong sillok* 14:15b [1455/4/23, 1].

66. *Tanjong sillok* 14:16a [1455/4/27, 2].

67. Liu Ju, *Jiu Tangshu*, ed. Yang Jialuo, Scripta Sinica (Taipei: Dingwen shuju, 1981), 150, pp. 2472–82.

68. *Tanjong sillok* 14:16a [1455/4/27, 2]

69. *Tanjong sillok* 14:15b [1455/4/23, 1], 14:17a [1455/4/28, 1].

70. For examples of gifts, see *Sejo sillok* 1:26b [1455/7/2, 1], 1:33a [1455/7/9, 1]; for falcons, see *Tanjong sillok* 14:18b [1455/5/7, 1], 14:19a [1455/5/8, 2], 14:20a [1455/5/8, 4]; for benefits to relatives, see, for example, *Sejo sillok* 1:24a [1455/6a/24, 2].

71. *Tanjong sillok* 14:29a [1455/6a/10, 3]; *Sejo sillok* 1:9a [1455/6a/11, 1].

72. *Sejo sillok* 1:25a [1455/6a/27, 1].

73. Although this affair is presented as a direct, verbatim representation of the king's desires, nearly all oral interactions in diplomacy were mediated by Chosŏn interpreters. See Sixiang Wang, "The Sounds of Our Country: Interpreters, Linguistic Knowledge and the Politics of Language in Early Chosŏn Korea (1392–1592)," in *Rethinking East Asian Languages, Vernaculars, and Literacies, 1000–1919*, ed. Benjamin A. Elman (Leiden: Brill, 2014), 80–87.

74. *Sejo sillok* 1:25b [1455/6a/29, 2].

75. *Sejo sillok* 1:32b [1455/7/8, 1].

76. *Sejo sillok* 1:33a [1455/7/9, 1].

77. *Sejo sillok* 1.33b [1455/7/11, 1].

78. MSL *Xianzong* 257:5b [1455/8/22]; see also *Sejo sillok* 2:29a [1455/10/13, 3].

79. MSL *Yingzong* 262:2a-b [1455/2/4, 1]; as far as the author can tell, all extant Ming accounts share this lacuna, e.g., Yan Congjian, *Shuyu zhouzi*, 1:10a.

80. *Sejo sillok* 3:8a [1456/2/3, 2]; *Sejo sillok* 3:8a [1456/2/3, 4], 3:13b [1456/2/21, 1].

81. See *Sejo sillok* 3:39a [1456/4/28, 2], 3:38b [1456/4/24, 1], 5:4a [1456/8/16, 3], 3:39b [1456/4/28, 3].

82. Kim T'aeyŏng, "Chosŏn ch'ogi Sejo wangkwŏn ŭi chŏnjesŏng e taehan ilgoch'al," *Hanguksa yŏn'gu* 87 (December 1994): 120–30; 138–44.

83. *Sejo sillok* 3:38a [1456/4/23, 2], 3:38b [1456/4/27, 1].

84. *Tanjong sillok* 9:4b [1453/11/4, 6], 9:8a [1453/11/8, 2].

85. Han Hyojung, ed., *Chŏngju Han ssi chokp'o [sep'o]*, Ko (古) 4650–74 Kyujanggak Archives, Seoul National University, 1617, chart 3, section cham 潛; section to 陶.

86. A tragic fate shared by many Korean palace women. See *Sejong sillok* 26:15b [1424/10/17, 2]. See also *Sejong sillok* 68:10b [1435/4/28, 2]; Wang, "Korean Eunuchs as Imperial Envoys," 464–65.

87. *Sejong sillok* 36:10b [1427/5/1, 3; 4]; Han Hyojung, *Chŏngju Han*, 1a–b, chart 1, section hwang 荒.

88. Cho Yŏngnok, "Sŏnch'o ŭi Chosŏn," 115–22.; *Sŏngjong sillok* 162:2a [1484/1/4, 5]. For the influence of Korean ladies-in-waiting in the early Ming palace, see David M. Robinson, "The Ming Court and the Legacy of the Yuan Mongols," in *Culture, Courtiers, and Competition: The Ming Court (1368–1644)*, ed. David M. Robinson (Cambridge, MA: Harvard University Asia Center, 2008), 382–86, also chap. 7.

89. *Sejong sillok* 27:31a [1425/3/1, 2].

90. The coup d'état was planned for the fourth day of the sixth month. See *Sejo sillok* 4:14a [1456/6/2, 2].

91. *Sejo sillok* 5:32b [1456/12/30].

92. Suyang also ordered the deaths of four other Chosŏn princes who had supported Tanjong. See *Sejo sillok* 9:25a [1457/10/21, 2].

4. IN EMPIRE'S NAME

1. James C. Scott, *Domination and the Arts of Resistance: Hidden Transcripts* (New Haven, CT: Yale University Press, 2008), 3–14.

2. Luke S. Roberts, *Performing the Great Peace: Political Space and Open Secrets in Tokugawa Japan* (Honolulu: Hawai'i University Press, 2015), 6–7, 19–52.

3. Brantly Womack, *China and Vietnam: The Politics of Asymmetry* (Cambridge: Cambridge University Press, 2006), 82–85, 89–92; Ji-Young Lee, "Diplomatic Ritual as a Power Resource: The Politics of Asymmetry in Early Modern Chinese-Korean Relations," *Journal of East Asian Studies* 13, no. 2 (May–August 2013): 377.

4. These multiple "realities" behind Chosŏn-Qing relations confounded Western observers in the nineteenth century, but they are a common feature of diplomatic regimes. Indeed, the truism of "organized hypocrisy" applies just as well to premodern East Asia as it does to twentieth-century sovereignty. Joshua Van Lieu, "The Politics of Condolence: Contested Representations of Tribute in Late Nineteenth-Century Chosŏn-Qing Relations," *Journal of Korean Studies* 14, no. 1 (2009): 83–115; Stephen D. Krasner, *Sovereignty: Organized Hypocrisy* (Princeton, NJ: Princeton University Press, 1999).

5. Kye Sŭngbŏm, *Chosŏn sidae haeoe p'abyŏng kwa Han-Chung kwan'gye: Chosŏn chibae ch'ŭng ŭi Chungguk insik* (Seoul: P'urŭn yŏksa, 2009), 94–113.

6. Adam Bohnet, *Turning Toward Edification: Foreigners in Chosŏn Korea* (Honolulu: University of Hawai'i Press, 2020), 35–41.

7. The nomenclature is often inconsistent, reflecting the Chosŏn court's own struggles in understanding the ethnopolitical landscape of their frontiers. Note that the Uriyangqad identified here are likely distinct from the Uriyangqad Mongols in Liaoxi. See Phillip H. Woodruff, "Status and Lineage Among Jurchens of the Korean Northeast in the Mid-Fifteenth Century," *Central and Inner Asian Studies* 1, no. 1 (1987): 117–32. For use of these ethnonyms in Chosŏn period sources, see Kim Chuwŏn, "Kugyŏk Chosŏn wangjo sillok e nat'anan pŏnyŏgŏ 'orangk'ae' e taehayŏ," *Han'guk ŏnŏ hakhoe haksul taehoeji* (2006): 54–62; Kang Chaejŏl and Yi Poggyu, "Orangk'ae (Oryanghap) ŏwŏn sŏlhwa yŏn'gu," *Pigyo minsok hak* 22 (February 2002): 181–218. For the aristocratic state rather than "tribes," see David Sneath, *The Headless State: Aristocratic Orders, Kinship Society, and Misrepresentations of Nomadic Inner Asia* (New York: Columbia University Press, 2007); Gertraude Roth Li, "State Building Before 1644," in *The Cambridge History of China*, vol. 9, ed. Willard J. Peterson (Cambridge: Cambridge University Press, 2002), 10–12; 16–18.

8. Donald N. Clark, "Sino-Korean Tributary Relations under the Ming," in *The Ming Dynasty, 1398–1644, Part 2, The Cambridge History of China* (Cambridge: Cambridge University Press, 1998), 289; Phillip H. Woodruff, "Foreign Policy and Frontier Affairs Along the Northeast Frontier of the Ming Dynasty, 1350–1618: Tripartite Relations of the Ming Chinese, Korean Koryo, and Jurchen-Manchu Tribesmen" (PhD diss., University of Chicago, 1995), 153–67.

9. "Manchurian" is anachronistic; this shared northeast Eurasian frontier has yet to be properly named. See Nianshen Song, "Northeast Eurasia as Historical

Center: Exploration of a Joint Frontier," *Asia-Pacific Journal: Japan Focus* 13, no. 44.2 (November 2015): 1–18.

10. Diao Shuren, "Jingtai, Tianshun nianjian Jianzhou sanwei Nüzhen yu Ming chao, Chaoxian guanxi," *Sahak ch'onggan*, no. 1 (2010): 101–7; Woodruff, "Foreign Policy and Frontier Affairs," 80–119.

11. Kenneth R. Robinson, "Policies of Practicality: The Choson Court's Regulation of Contact with Japanese and Jurchens, 1392–1580s" (PhD diss., University of Hawai'i, 1997), 25–79; 181–217; Kenneth R. Robinson, "Organizing Japanese and Jurchens in Tribute Systems in Early Chosŏn Korea," *Journal of East Asian Studies* 13, no. 2 (May 2013): 337–60.

12. Cho Yongch'ŏl, "Chosŏn ch'ogi Yŏjin kwan'gye ŭi pyŏnhwa wa tongbungmyŏn chiyŏk chinch'ul kwajŏng: Sejong 14 nyŏn (1432) Yŏngbukchin sŏlchi ijŏn sigi rŭl chungsim ŭro," *Yŏksa hakpo* 233 (2017.3): 39–73; Han Sŏngju, *Chosŏn chŏn'gi sujik Yŏjinin yŏn'gu* (Seoul: *Kyŏngin munhwasa*, 2011), 18–36, 47–51, 156–71; Woodruff, "Foreign Policy and Frontier Affairs," 165–96.

13. Hŏ Pong, *Haedong yaŏn*, 2 in TDYS 7, p. 622; Ch'a Ch'ŏllo, *Osan sŏllim ch'ogo*, in TDYS 5, pp. 512–513; Woodruff, "Foreign Policy and Frontier Affairs," 163–64. *Tanjong sillok* 8:28a [1453/10/25, 3], 10:21b [1454/1/24, 3].

14. Romanizing Jurchen names rendered in sinographic materials is a challenge. Where lexical units or common names are identifiable, they are represented in Manchu, based on Stary, *A Dictionary of Manchu Names*—an imperfect solution, but preferable to *pinyin* or McCune Reischauer romanization. I thank Chris Atwood for help in this area. See Giovanni Stary, *A Dictionary of Manchu Names: A Name-Index to the Manchu Version of the* "Complete Genealogies of the Manchu Clans and Families of the Eight Banners" (Wiesbaden: Harrassowitz, 2000).

15. *Sejo sillok* 15:24b [1459/3/25].

16. *Sejo sillok* 15:22b [1459/3/14, 4].

17. *Sejo sillok* 15:22b [1459/3/15, 3].

18. *Sejo sillok* 15:25a [1459/3/27, 4].

19. *Sejo sillok* 15:23a [1459/3/17, 1].

20. From Chen Jiayou's obituary, see MSL *Xianzong* 47:1a [1467/10/1, 6].

21. *Sejo sillok* 16:1b [1459/4/8, 1].

22. *Sejo sillok* 16:7a [1459/4/16, 1].

23. *Sejo sillok* 17:5b [1459/7/19, 1].

24. Sun Joo Kim, ed., "Residence and Foreign Relations in the Peninsular Northeast During the Fifteenth and Sixteenth Centuries," in *The Northern Region of Korea: History, Identity & Culture* (Seattle: University of Washington Press, 2010), 31–33; Han Sŏngju, *Chosŏn chŏn'gi sujik Yŏjinin yŏn'gu*, 151–52, 175–84, 196–205, 232–39, 246–49; Pak Chŏngmin, "Yŏnsan'gun—Myŏngjongdae Yŏjinin naejo ŭi chaegŏmt'o," *Yŏksa hakpo* 222 (June 2014): 47–60.

25. Borghan 孛兒罕 appears to be "willow," while the character 浪 is used as a surname.

26. *Sejo sillok* 17:18a [1459/8/24, 2].

27. *Sejo sillok* 17:15a [1459/8/23]; Woodruff, "Foreign Policy and Frontier Affairs," 167–68.

28. *Sejo sillok* 17:20l [1459/8/28, 1]. For a summary of Chosŏn-Maolian relations, see Li Bo, "Maolian wei yu Ming, Chaoxian de guanxi yanjiu" (Master's thesis, Changchun, *Dongbei shifan daxue*, 2011).

29. *Sejo sillok* 18:14a [1459/11/24, 1].

30. *Sejo sillok* 19:15a [1460/2/6, 4].

31. *Sejo sillok* 19:17a [1460/2/10, 4].

32. See *Sejo sillok* 19:15a [1460/2/6, 4].

33. MSL *Xianzong* 85:2b [1470/11/12, 1].

34. *Sejo sillok* 15:25a [1459/3/27, 4]; 19:11b [1460/2/4, 1]; *Sŏngjong sillok* 109:17b [1479/10/29, 3], 109:18b [1479/10/30, 4].

35. For gifts, see *Sejo sillok* 19:34a [1460/3/8, 3], 19:35a [1460/3/9, 3]. Again, Sejo encouraged the envoy to tarry; see 19:31b [1460/3/4, 2].

36. Sixiang Wang, "The Sounds of Our Country: Interpreters, Linguistic Knowledge and the Politics of Language in Early Chosŏn Korea (1392–1592)," in *Rethinking East Asian Languages, Vernaculars, and Literacies, 1000–1919*, ed. Benjamin A. Elman (Leiden: Brill, 2014), 67–71; 80–81.

37. *Sejo sillok* 19:26a [1460/3/2, 1]. For analysis of Zhang's version of events, see Philip de Heer, "Three Embassies to Seoul: Sino-Korean Relations in the 15th Century," in *Conflict and Accomodation in Early Modern East Asia: Essays in Honour of Erik Zurcher*, ed. Leonard Blusse and Harriet T. Zurndorfer (Leiden: E.J. Brill, 1993).

38. *Sejo sillok* 19:31b [1460/3/4, 2].

39. Zhang Ning, *Fengshi lu*, Congshu jicheng chubian 2142 (Shanghai: Shangwu yinshuguan, 1936), 3.

40. *Sejo sillok* 20:16a [1460/4/25, 1].

41. Matthew W. Mosca, *From Frontier Policy to Foreign Policy: The Question of India and the Transformation of Geopolitics in Qing China* (Stanford, CA: Stanford University Press, 2013), 12–14, 166–67. Also consider the fate of the Ming official Zhu Wan, whose antipirate operations earned him the ire of Zhejiang's local gentry; see Roland L. Higgins, "Pirates in Gowns and Caps: Gentry Law-Breaking in the Mid-Ming," *Ming Studies* 1980, no. 1 (January 1980): 30–37; Michael Szonyi, *The Art of Being Governed: Everyday Politics in Late Imperial China* (Princeton, NJ: Princeton University Press, 2017), 91–94.

42. Yan Congjian, *Shuyu zhouzi lu*, ed. Yu Sili (Beijing: Zhonghua shuju, 1993), 20–21; Du Huiyue, *Mingdai wenchen chushi Chaoxian yu "Huanghuaji"* (Beijing: Renmin chubanshe, 2010), 306.

43. *Sejo sillok* 19:32a [1460/3/5, 1]; 19:32b [1460/3/6, 3]; 19:33a [1460/3/6, 4], 19:33a [1460/3/7, 1].
44. *Sejo sillok* 19:43a [1460/3/21, 2].
45. *Sejo sillok* 20:22b [1460/5/11, 1], 20:37b [1460/6/9, 1].
46. *Sejo sillok* 20:41a [1460/6/19, 1].
47. *Sejo sillok* 20:17b [1460/4/26, 3]; *Sejo sillok* 35.20b [1465/3/11, 1]; Yi Kyuch'ŏl, "Sejo tae Moryŏnwi chŏngpŏl ŭi ŭimi wa tae Myŏng insik," *Han'guksa yŏn'gu* 158 (September 2012): 143–44.
48. *Sejo sillok* 21:5a [1460/7/25, 4].
49. *Sejo sillok* 21:1b [1460/7/5, 2], 21:3b [1460/7/16, 1], 21:7a [1460/7/27, 3], 21:7b [1460/7/29, 1], 21:8b [1460/7/29, 3].
50. *Sejo sillok* 21:11a [1460/8/5].
51. *Sejo sillok* 21:12a–13a [1460/8/8, 3], 21:31a [1460/8/8, 4], 21:14b [1460/8/12, 6], 21:15a–15b [1460/8/13, 3], 21:15b [1460/8/13, 4].
52. *Sejo sillok* 21:18b [1460/8/19, 2].
53. *Sejo sillok* 21:21a [1460/8/26, 1].
54. *Sejo sillok* 22:27b [1460/11a/16, 2].
55. *Sejo sillok* 23:16a [1461/2/15, 3].
56. *Sejo sillok* 23:17b [1461/2/17, 1].
57. *Sejo sillok* 25:13a [1461/8/3, 1].
58. *Sejo sillok* 25:18b [1461/8/18, 1].
59. *Sejo sillok* 25:28b [1461/9/15, 2].
60. *Sejo sillok* 25:30b [1461/9/2, 2].
61. *Sejo sillok* 25:32b [1461/9/24, 2].
62. *Sejo sillok* 26:5a [1461/10/10, 2].
63. *Sejo sillok* 26:6a [1461/10/13, 2].
64. *Sejo sillok* 26:28a [1461/12/26]; *Sejo sillok* 26:18b [1461/11/23, 1].
65. *Sejo sillok* 26:19a [1461/11/27, 2], 27:8b [1462/1/27, 1].
66. *Sejo sillok* 27:15b [1462/2/11, 2].
67. *Sejo sillok* 29:7a [1462/8/20, 2].
68. Woodruff, "Foreign Policy and Frontier Affairs," 170–75; Morris Rossabi, *The Jurchen in the Yuan and Ming* (Ithaca, NY: Cornell University, China-Japan Program, 1982).
69. Woodruff, "Foreign Policy and Frontier Affairs," 188–93.
70. *Sejo sillok* 29:33b [1462/12/27, 3].
71. *Sejo sillok* 32:27b [1464/3/7, 2].
72. *Sejo sillok* 35:20b [1465/3/11, 1], 35:27b [1465/3/26, 4].
73. MSL *Xianzong* 38, p. 751 [1467/1/3]; 39, p. 780 [1467/2/8]; 40, p. 811 [1467/3/13], 40, p. 827 [1467/3/28]; 40, p. 851 [1476/4/28].
74. MSL *Xianzong* 38, pp. 751–752 [1467/1/3]; 38, p. 752–753 [1467/1/4].

75. MSL *Xianzong* 38, p. 753 [1467/1/6]; 38, p. 756 [1467/1/13]; 42, p. 860 [1467/5/16].

76. MSL *Xianzong* 42, p. 865 [1467/5/25].

77. *Sejo sillok* 43:37b [1467/8/17, 3].

78. *Sejo sillok* 43:19b [1467/7/23, 7].

79. *Sejo sillok* 44:18b [1467/10/24, 3], 44:15b [1467/10/21, 2].

80. Woodruff, "Foreign Policy and Frontier Affairs," 176–78; Clark, "Sino-Korean Tributary Relations," 268–71; Li, "State Building Before 1644," 14–16, 21–27.

81. "When the Way prevails under heaven, then the rites, music, and punitive expeditions come only from the Son of Heaven" [天下有道 則禮樂征伐自天子出] in *Analects* 16.2.

82. Xu Yikui, *Da Ming jili*, Ming Jiajing print (Scripta Sinica, 1530), 34:2a–b.

83. Chŏng Taham, "'Sadae' wa 'kyorin' kwa 'Sochunghwa' ranŭn t'ŭl ŭi ch'osiganjŏgin kŭrigo Ch'ogongganjŏgin maengrak," *Han'guksa hakpo* 42 (2011.2): 287–323; Chŏng Taham, "Chŏngpŏl iranŭn chŏnjaeng / Chŏngpŏl iranŭn chesa," *Han'guksa hakpo* 52 (August 2013): 282–85; Kenneth R. Robinson, "Centering the King of Chosŏn," *Journal of Asian Studies* 59, no. 1 (2000). For *zhengfa* rite, see *Sejong sillok* 60:25b [1433/5/13, 2]; for a discussion of *fuyue*, see 59:32b [1433/2/23, 3].

84. Chŏng Taham, "Chŏngpŏl," 285–88; 293–99.

85. *Sejo sillok* 44:15 b [1467/10/21, 2]. *Wang* 王 as sovereign is in line with classical usage. Here it refers not to Chosŏn, but the Ming emperor. Ŏ Segyŏm suspected Ming frontier officials wished to take war trophies themselves, so he insisted on conveying the trophies directly to Beijing. Note that Chosŏn presented severed ears, not heads per se; the phrasing again invokes classical practice, where severed enemy heads were burned at ancestral temples, Olivia Milburn, "Headhunting in Ancient China: The History of Violence and Denial of Knowledge," *Bulletin of the School of Oriental and African Studies* 81, no. 1 (February 2018): 107–16.

86. Kye Sŭngbŏm, *Chosŏn sidae haeoe*, 102.

87. Feng Zhang, "Confucian Foreign Policy Traditions in Chinese History," *The Chinese Journal of International Politics* 8, no. 2 (June 2015): 203–5. Under this imperial paradigm, common throughout medieval and early modern East Asia, a "just war"—that is, war conducted with legitimate cause—is always coded as a suppression of rebellion; see Karl F. Friday, *Samurai, Warfare and the State in Early Medieval Japan* (London: Routledge, 2004), 19–33; Alastair Ian Johnston, *Cultural Realism: Strategic Culture and Strategy in Chinese History* (Princeton, NJ: Princeton University Press, 1998), 69–73.

88. Michael Walzer, *Just and Unjust Wars: A Moral Argument with Historical Illustrations* (New York: Basic Books, 2015), 41. The analogy between postmodern and early modern East Asian concepts is only worthy of note because of how far they diverge

from the nation-state-centered notions that inform Walzer's thinking. Indeed, war as "police action" would have resonated across many imperial contexts.

89. Michael Hardt and Antonio Negri, *Empire* (Cambridge, MA: Harvard University Press, 2000), 10–17.

90. *Sejo sillok* 43:56b [1467/9/14, 1].

91. For these two facets to Confucian statecraft in foreign affairs, see Zhang, "Confucian Foreign Policy," 205–10. See the discussion in Chŏng Taham, "Chŏngpŏl," 278–82; Giorgio Agamben, *State of Exception* (Chicago: University of Chicago Press, 2005).

92. *Sejo sillok* 43:37b [1467/8/17, 3].

93. *Sejo sillok* 43:56b [1467/9/14, 1].

94. *Sejo sillok* 43:59b [1467/9/15, 2].

95. Kenneth Pomeranz, "Empire and 'Civilizing' Missions, Past and Present," *Daedalus* 134, no. 2 (Spring 2005): 34–45.

PART III. ECUMENICAL BOUNDARIES

1. Hŏ Pong, "Hagok sŏnsaeng Choch'ŏn'gi" 2 in *Hagok chip*, HMC 58:462c; Ŏ Sukkwŏn, *P'aegwan chapki*, 1 in TDYS 4, 732.

2. Song Lian, *Wenxian ji*, SKQS 1223–24 (Taipei: Shangwu yinshuguan, 1983), 9:42b–44a.

3. MS 320, p. 8307. See also expression by Ming elites: Kim Han'gyu, *Sa Chosŏnnok yŏn'gu: Song, Myŏng, Ch'ŏng sidae Chosŏn sahaengnok ŭi saryojŏk kach'i* (Seoul: Sŏgang taehakkyo ch'ulp'anbu, 2011), 160–64; Ni Qian, *Liaohai bian* (Beijing: Beijing tushuguan chubanshe, 2003), 624–28.

4. *Chungjong sillok* 90:14b [1539/4/7, 1].

5. As a number of scholars have demonstrated; see William A. Callahan, *Sensible Politics: Visualizing International Relations* (New York: Oxford University Press, 2020), 48–50; 224–25; Ge Zhaoguang, *Lishi Zhongguo de nei yu wai: youguan Zhongguo yu zhoubian gai nian de zai chengqing* (Hong Kong: Xianggang zhongwen daxue chubanshe, 2017), 27–66; Lydia H. Liu, *The Clash of Empires: The Invention of China in Modern World Making* (Cambridge, MA: Harvard University Press, 2004), 84–88.

6. Geoff Wade et al., eds., "Civilizational Rhetoric and the Obfuscation of Power Politics," in *Sacred Mandates: Asian International Relations Since Chinggis Khan* (Chicago: University of Chicago Press, 2018), 75–78.

7. *Zhongyong* 21; *Analects* 16.1. For use of this term, see James Louis Hevia, *Cherishing Men from Afar: Qing Guest Ritual and the Macartney Embassy of 1793* (Durham, NC: Duke University Press, 1995), ix, 46, 135, 147, 193, 209. For a discussion of varied connotations, see James Millward, "How Mongolia Matters:

War, Law, and Society," in *How Mongolia Matters: War, Law, and Society*, ed. Morris Rossabi (Leiden: Brill, 2017), 19–34. For the relationship between axiom and policy in Ming statecraft, see Devin Fitzgerald, "The Ming Open Archive and the Global Reading of Early Modern China" (PhD diss., Harvard University, 2020), 39–58.

5. CAJOLING EMPIRE

1. Ku Toyŏng, "Chosŏn chŏn'gi oegyo kwan'gye ŭi hamsu, 'yeŭi chi kuk,'" *Taedong munhwa yŏn'gu*, no. 89 (2015): 174–89.

2. See *T'aejo sillok* 11:4b [1397/3/8, 1]; 15:2a [1398/9/15, 3]; *T'aejo sillok* 1:25a [preface, 86].

3. Kwŏn Kŭn, *Yangch'on chip* 1 in HMC 7:15b.

4. Ming's original Tieling garrison was located on far on the Liaodong side of the Yalu River, but the garrison's military activities extended far enough east across the river to alarm Koryŏ. Pak Wŏnho[hyo], *Myŏngch'o Chosŏn kwan'gyesa yŏn'gu* (Seoul: Ilchogak, 2002), 33–113; Kim Sunja, *Han'guk chungse Han-Chung kwan'gyesa* (Seoul: Hyean, 2007), 54–62, 199–221. MSL *Taizu* 187:6a [1387/12/26]; 189:14a [1388/3/27]. For debate, see Chŏng T'aesang, "Myŏng ŭi Ch'ŏllyŏng-wi wa Koryŏmal kukkyŏng ŭi chaegŏmt'o," *Inmun kwahak yŏn'gu* 58 (September 2018): 189–216.

5. Kim Sunja, *Han'guk chungse*, 105–26; Kwŏn Kŭn, *Yangch'on chip* 24 in HMC 7:237a–237c. *T'aejo sillok* 12:11a [1397/12/24, 2].

6. MSL *Taizu* 190:3a [1388/4/18].

7. MSL *Taizu* 227:1b [1393/4/8]; MS 41, p. 956; Diao Shuren and Bu Zhaojin, "Lun Yuanmo Mingchu Zhongguo yu Gaoli, Chaoxian de bianjie zhi zheng," *Beihua daxue xuebao (Shehui kexue ban)* 2, no. 1 (March 2001): 53–54.

8. *T'aejong sillok* 7:20b–21b [1404/5/19, 4], 35:45a–b [1418/5/4, 2].

9. Diao Shuren and Wang Jian, "Ming chu Maolian wei yu Chaoxian de guanxi," *Dongbei shidi* 1 (2006): 257–58; Diao Shuren and Bu Zhaojin, "Lun Yuanmo," 54–55.

10. Yu Sŭngju, "Chosŏn chŏn'gi tae Myŏng muyŏk i kungnae sanŏp e mich'in yŏnghyang: 15 segi tae Myŏng kŭmŭn chogong kwa kungnae kŭmŭn kwangŏp ŭl chungsim ŭro," *Asea yŏn'gu* 32, no. 2 (July 1989): 30–44.

11. Kwŏn Kŭn et al., ed., *Koewŏn tŭngnok*, Jangseogak Archives (Changsŏgak) k2-3465, thirteenth to seventeenth centuries, 1:4a–b; 9a–9b; Pyŏn Kyeryang, *Ch'unjŏng sŏnsaeng munjip* 9 in HMC 8:129c–130b.

12. Two memorials exist, one attributed to Pyŏn Kyeryang sent in 1420, quoted above, and one to Yu Hyot'ong 俞孝通 (fl. 1408–1431) preserved in Kwŏn Kŭn, *Kwewŏn tŭngnok*, 1:9b–10a. Pyŏn's was never presented, while Yu Hyot'ong's version survives only in truncated form. Yu's was originally a mock memorial written for a special civil service examination in 1427, but it is unclear

whether it was later presented to the Xuande emperor. See also *Sejong sillok* 8:9b [1420/5/2, 2], 35:21b [1427/3/14, 1].

13. *Sejong sillok* 46:13a [1429/11/29, 3].

14. For Ming tribute exactions, see Jin-Han Lee, "The Development of Diplomatic Relations and Trade with Ming in the Last Years of the Koryŏ Dynasty," *International Journal of Korean History* 10 (December 2006): 1–24. Chosŏn envoys were not alone to cite scripture to suit their own purpose. For diverse invocations of the Ming founder's authority, see Sarah Schneewind, ed., *Long Live the Emperor!: Uses of the Ming Founder Across Six Centuries of East Asian History* (Minneapolis, MN: Society for Ming Studies, 2008).

15. *Sejong sillok* 46:13a [1429/11/29, 3].

16. *Sejong sillok* 3:1b [1419/1/6, 4], 13:11b [1421/9/7, 5]. In 1521, court officials raised similar concerns over the Korean use of precious metals for purchasing Chinese goods during tribute missions. Fear that newfound sources of wealth would only attract exorbitant tribute demands from the Ming disincentivized Chosŏn from developing metallic currency, interstate trade, and mineral extraction, even when opportunities to do so presented themselves. For court concerns, see *Chungjong sillok* 42:49a–b [1521/7/17, 1]. For Ming envoy perceptions, see Dong Yue, *Chosŏn pu*, trans. Yun Hojin, Sosu sŏwŏn pon (Kkach'i, 1995), 4b–5a; Seonmin Kim, "Borders and Crossings: Trade, Diplomacy and Ginseng Between Qing China and Choson Korea" (PhD diss., Duke University, 2006), 211–13.

17. Kwŏn Kŭn, *Kwewŏn tŭngnok*, 1:9b–10a.

18. Pyŏn Kyeryang, *Ch'unjŏng chip* 9 in HMC 8:130b; Kwŏn Kŭn, *Kwewŏn tŭngnok*, 1:9a–9b.

19. Pak Hŭihyŏn, "Kakkung kwa hwasal ŭi chejak," *Han'guk minsok hak* 10 (December 1977): 177–215.

20. The terms "Wildmen" and "Tartars" is used to capture the derogatory sense of *yeren* 野人 and *dazi* 㺜子 when applied to Jurchens and Mongols. *Sŏngjong sillok* 75:18b–19a [1477/1/17, 3]; 76:2b [1477/2/4, 3]. See also Ku Toyŏng, "Chosŏn chŏn'gi oegyo," 191–97.

21. *Sŏngjong sillok* 77:2a [1477/2a/6, 2]; Li Shanhong, "Mingdai Huitongguan dui Chaoxian shichen menjin wenti yanjiu," *Lishixue yanjiu* 132, no. 3 (2012): 143–46. See also *Yŏnsangun ilgi* 4:5a [1495/3/10, 4].

22. In later periods, Chosŏn acquired horns brought from Southeast Asia to Nagaski through the Tsūshima trade; see Kim Tongch'ŏl, "Chosŏn hugi suugak muyŏk kwa kakkung kye kongin," *Han'guk munhwa yŏn'gu* 4 (December 1991): 55–110. Buffalo horns are occasionally misidentified as "bows and bugles" in translation; see Ŏ Sukkwŏn, *A Korean Storyteller's Miscellany: The Paegwan*

Chapki of O Sukkwon, trans. Peter H. Lee (Princeton, NJ: Princeton University Press, 1989), 76–77.

23. *Sŏngjong sillok* 85:14a [1477/10/22, 3]. There is no mention of this trade in official records until 1475, when Chosŏn officials initially noticed the Ming clampdown. *Sŏngjong sillok* 56:4a–5a [1475/6/4, 4].

24. *Sŏngjong sillok* 75:25b [1477/1/25, 7], 76:1b [1477/2/3, 3].

25. *Sŏngjong sillok* 75:24b [1477/1/25, 4].

26. *Sŏngjong sillok* 75:25b [1477/1/25, 7].

27. *Sŏngjong sillok* 83:20b [1477/8/26, 3].

28. *Sŏngjong sillok* 88:6a [1478/1/15, 2].

29. *Sŏngjong sillok* 80:7a [1477/5/25, 2], 81:1b [1477/6/2, 3].

30. Han Hyojung, ed., *Ch'ŏngju Han ssi chokp'o [sep'o]*, Ko (古) 4650–74 Kyujang-gak Archives, Seoul National University, 1617, 1a–b, chart 1, section hwang 荒. *Sŏngjong sillok* 80:7a [1477/5/25, 2].

31. The petitioners left Seoul on the twenty-sixth day of the eighth month while Han's mission departed less than a week earlier, on the seventeenth day of the same month. *Sŏngjong sillok* 83:20b [1477/8/26, 3], 83:9a [1477/8/17, 2].

32. *Sŏngjong sillok* 88:3a [1478/1/10, 2], 88:4b [1478/1/12, 1], 88:7a 1478/1/15, 2]. Although Lady Han was Han Ch'irye's aunt, it did not seem they were able to meet in person.

33. *Sŏngjong sillok* 88:5b [1478/1/14, 1], 88:6a [1478/1/15, 2]. For protests, see 88:4b [1478/1/12, 1], 88:5a [1478/1/13, 1].

34. *Sŏngjong sillok* 88:5a [1478/1/13, 1].

35. 胡人 (K. *hoin*) another derogatory term for the non-sedentary peoples of the northern frontier.

36. MSL *Xianzong* 172:3a–b.

37. Or his fourth cousin, once removed; their last common ancestor, Han Ak 韓渥 (1274–1342) was born two centuries ago. See Han Hyojung, *Ch'ŏngju Han*, 1:1a–1b, chart 1 section hwang 荒; chart 2, 1.

38. *Sŏngjong sillok* 128:8b [1481/4/19, 6].

39. MSL *Xianzong* 212:5a [1481/2/23, 3].

40. *Sŏngjong sillok* 145:11a [1482/8a/13, 3].

41. *Yŏnsangun ilgi* 4:5a [1495/3/10, 4].

42. *Chungjong sillok* 44:22a [1522/2/3, 3]. Sun Cun is better known for having authored the *Methods of Reading the Great Ming Code* (*Da Ming lü dufa* 大明律讀法). MS 99, p. 2398; Ŏ Sukkwŏn, *P'aegwan* 1 in TDYS 4, pp. 729–30. For Korean interest in the Ming *Gazetteer*, see Alexander Van Zandt Akin, "Printed Maps in Late Ming Publishing Culture: A Trans-Regional Perspective" (PhD diss., Harvard University, 2009), 59–62; 269–76.

43. *Chungjong sillok* 53:29b [1525/3/7, 3].

44. Su Shi, *Dongpo quanji*, SKQS 1107–8 (Taipei: Shangwu yinshuguan, 1983), 63:8b–20a; Su Che, *Luancheng ji*, SKQS 1112 (Taipei: Shangwu yinshuguan, 1983), 46:1a–2a; Zhang Fangping, *Lequan ji*, SKQS 252–255 (Taipei: Shangwu yinshuguan, 1970), 27:7b–8a; Chang Tong'ik, *Songdae Yŏsa charyo chimnok* (Seoul: Sŏul taehakkyo ch'ulp'anbu, 2000), 308–12, 314–18, 319.

45. *Chungjong sillok* 53:33b [1525/3/12, 4]. *Chungjong sillok* 54:17a [1525/5/2, 5], 55:51a [1525/11/11, 2].

46. Chen Yiqiu, "Cong Chaoxian shichen de Zhongguo xingji kan Mingdai zhonghouqi de Yuhe guan: yi Huitong guan tiduguan wei zhongxin," *Nanjing xiaozhuang xueyuan xuebao* 3 (2014).

47. *Chungjong sillok* 56:59b [1526/3/19, 5].

48. Hu appears marginal but was embroiled in several diplomatic controversies, including one involving jewel tribute from Muslim merchants; see Yan Congjian, *Shuyu zhouzi lu*, ed. Yu Sili (Beijing: Zhonghua shuju, 1993), 395–409.

49. Hu's memorial was relayed to the Chosŏn king with the return of an embassy in 1526. See *Chungjong sillok* 56:59a–60a [1526/3/19, 5].

50. Restrictions on book buying remained a contentious issue well through the Qing period. In theory, Korean envoys were barred from buying historical and geographical works, but such restrictions were inconsistently enforced. A large number of such books, including a nearly complete copy of the *Ming Veritable Records* entered Korean collections. Sun Weiguo, *Ming Qing shiqi Zhongguo shixue dui Chaoxian de yingxiang: jian lun liangguo xueshu jiaoliu yu haiwai Han xue* (Shanghai: Shanghai cishu chubanshe, 2009), 22–32; Jamie Jungmin Yoo, "Networks of Disquiet: Censorship and the Production of Literature in Eighteenth-Century Korea," *Acta Koreana* 20, no. 1 (2017): 259–67.

51. Traditional historiography portrays Xi Shu and others who took the Jiajing emperor's side in the Great Ritual Controversy unfavorably. See MS 189, p. 5023; Jun Fang, *China's Second Capital: Nanjing Under the Ming, 1368–1644* (New York: Routledge, 2014), 67–68; Yan Congjian, *Shuyu zhouzi*, 1993 1, 29.

52. See MSL *Shizong* 62:5a–b [1526/3/17, 1], 72:8a–b [1527/1/29, 1].

53. Charles O. Hucker, *A Dictionary of Official Titles in Imperial China* (Stanford, CA: Stanford University Press, 1985), 181, 264.

54. Li Shanhong, "Mingdai Huitongguan," 145–46; Wang Jianfeng, "Mingchao tidu Huitongguan zhushi shezhi tanwei," *Liaoning daxue xuebao: zhexue shehui kexue ban* 34, no. 6 (November 2006): 81–82.

55. *Chungjong sillok* 77:24a–26b [1534/4/24, 1]. So Seyang, "Yanggok pugyŏng ilgi," in YHNCJ, pp. 401–3.

56. An exceptionalism that applied to other areas of diplomatic protocol as well, such as Chosŏn envoys' exemption from the Ming tally system. See Chŏng Tonghun, "Myŏngdae chŏn'gi oegyo sajŏl ŭi sinpun chŭngmyŏng pangsik kwa

kukkagan ch'egye," *Myŏng-Ch'ŏng sa yŏn'gu* 10 (October 2013): 21–26. Or as described in Ku Toyŏng, "Chosŏn chŏn'gi oegyo," 174–97, especially 188–90.

57. So's petition does not survive in Korean sources. For So's letter and Xia's petition, see Xia Yan, *Guizhou xiansheng zouyi*, Siku quanshu cunmu congshu, Shi bu (part 2) 60 (Tainan: Zhuangyan wenhua, 1996), 20:20b–22b; Yan Congjian, *Shuyu zhouzi*, 1993, 1, 29–31.

58. The view of the Chosŏn court; see *Chungjong sillok* 77:24a [1534/4/24, 1].

59. Xia Yan, *Guizhou xiansheng zouyi*, 20:21b–22a.

60. Xia Yan, *Guizhou xiansheng zouyi*, 20:22b.

61. Li Shanhong, "Mingdai Huitongguan," 143–46.

62. Yan Congjian, *Shuyu zhouzi*, 1993, 1, pp. 30–31.

63. See the Beijing diary of Chŏng Hwan in Chŏng Hwan, *Hoesan sŏnsaeng munjip*, 2 in HMC b2:217b–222d. The diplomatic chronicle in *Kosa ch'waryo* shows that the 1547 envoys made a similar appeal, see Ŏ Sukkwŏn, *Kosa ch'waryo*, Asami Collection, Korean Rare Book Collection (University of California, Berkeley) 35.7 (Seoul, 17th century [1554]), 1:37a–38b.

64. Sayŏkwŏn, *Sangwŏn cheŏ*, Asami Collection (University of California, Berkeley) 18.61 (Korea, 16th century), 10b–11b.

65. That is, a process of "entextualization," as described in Karin Barber, *The Anthropology of Texts, Persons and Publics: Oral and Written Culture in Africa and Beyond* (Cambridge: Cambridge University Press, 2007), 22; Michael Silverstein and Greg Urban, *Natural Histories of Discourse* (Chicago: University of Chicago Press, 1996), 21.

6. REPRESENTING KOREA

1. Kwŏn Pŏl, *Ch'ungjae sŏnsaeng munjip*, 7 in HMC 19:449b.

2. Here, "strategic essentialism" is not a tactic of social emancipation but it still spoke on behalf of a community beholden to a more powerful entity. That both imperial officials and Korean envoys trafficked in the same stereotypes only reinforced their cachet. For a twentieth-century example, see Jim Glassman, *Drums of War, Drums of Development: The Formation of a Pacific Ruling Class and Industrial Transformation in East and Southeast Asia, 1945–1980* (Leiden: Brill, 2018), 513n13, 535–47.

3. Timothy Brook, *The Confusions of Pleasure: Commerce and Culture in Ming China* (Berkeley: University of California Press, 1998), 44–50; Pak Wŏnho[hyo], *Ch'oe Pu P'yohaerok yŏn'gu* (Seoul: Koryŏ taehakkyo ch'ulp'anbu, 2006).

4. See Ch'oe Pu, *Kŭmnam chip* 1 in HMC 16:422a–433d. For Chosŏn and Ming maritime governance in the Yellow Sea, see Jing Liu, "Beyond the Land:

Maritime Interactions, Border Control, and Regional Powers Between China and Korea, 1500–1637" (PhD diss., Syracuse University, 2019), 27–93.

5. For a full translation, see Ch'oe Pu, *Ch'oe Pu's Diary: A Record of Drifting Across the Sea*, trans. John Thomas Meskill (Tucson: University of Arizona Press, 1965). For an annotated Chinese edition, see Ge Zhenjia, ed., *Cui Pu "Piaohai lu" pingzhu* (Beijing: Xianzhuang shuju, 2002). For a critical discussion, see Pak Wǒnho[hyo], *Ch'oe Pu P'yohaerok yǒn'gu*.

6. Ch'oe Pu, "P'yohae rok," in *Kǔmnanjip* 2 in HMC 16:463a–b.

7. Ch'oe Pu, "P'yohae rok," 1 in HMC 16:443d–444a.

8. Ch'oe Pu, "P'yohae rok," 1 in HMC 16:432b–c, 16:433d–433a, 436a–436d, 437a–b, 437c. See also a similar quandary with the shipwrecked Yi Sǒm 李暹, whom Ming officials suspected of being a pirate in *Sǒngjong sillok* 157:25a–26b [1483/8/22, 6].

9. Ch'oe Pu, "P'yohae rok," 2 in HMC 16:441d–442a.

10. Ch'oe Pu, "P'yohae rok," 3 in HMC 16:482c–484c; *T'aejo sillok* 12:8b [1397/11/30, 2].

11. Ch'oe secured his reputation in 1504 when he was executed for outspokenness against the king. Earlier, his political opponents accused him of "currying renown" in his shipwreck accounts. Milan Hejtmanek, "The Familiar Dead: The Creation of an Intimate Afterlife in Early Chosǒn Korea," in *Death, Mourning, and the Afterlife in Korea: From Ancient to Contemporary Times*, ed. Charlotte Horlyck and Michael J. Pettid (Honolulu: University of Hawai'i Press, 2014), 164–65.

12. As Ch'oe and Chosǒn Neo-Confucians have sometimes been portrayed; see John Thomas Meskill, "A Record of Drifting Across the Sea: P'yohaerok" (PhD diss., Columbia University, 1959), 17–19.

13. Ch'oe Pu, "P'yohae rok," 2 in HMC 16:438c-d, 434b–434d.

14. Ǒ Sukkwǒn, *P'aegwan chapki*, 2 in TDYS, vol. 1:751–752; Ǒ Sukkwǒn 魚叔權, *A Korean Storyteller's Miscellany: The Paegwan Chapki of O Sukkwon*, trans. Peter H. Lee (Princeton, NJ: Princeton University Press, 1989), 43.

15. Edward W Wagner, *The Literati Purges: Political Conflict in Early Yi Korea* (Cambridge, MA: East Asian Research Center, Harvard University Press, 1974), 67–76.

16. For envoy instructions, see *Chungjong sillok* 1:19b [1506/9/21, 6]; see also 1:23a [1506/9/27, 2] for the diplomatic message; for execution, see 1:20b [1506/9/24, 3].

17. David M. Robinson, "Korean Lobbying at the Ming Court: King Chungjong's Usurpation of 1506: A Research Note," *Ming Studies* 41, no. 1 (Spring 1999): 42.

18. See *Chungjong sillok* 2:34a–35b [1507/2/15, 2]. Ming proved more interventionist after the Imjin War, refusing Chosǒn requests for the investiture of Kwanghaegun, first as heir apparent and then as king in order to enforce primogeniture in the early sixteenth century. See Seung B. Kye, "In the Shadow of

the Father: Court Opposition and the Reign of King Kwanghae in Early Seventeenth-Century Choson Korea" (PhD diss., University of Washington, 2006), 42–54, 153–71.

19. This was not unique to Chosŏn. Koryŏ maintained three different narratives of monarchical succession for Liao, Song, and domestic audiences, see Xu Jing, *A Chinese Traveler in Medieval Korea: Xu Jing's Illustrated Account of the Xuanhe Embassy to Koryo*, trans. Sem Vermeersch (Honolulu: University of Hawai'i Press, 2016), 16–17.

20. *Chungjong sillok* 2:35b [1507/2/16, 1]. Seung B. Kye, "Huddling Under the Imperial Umbrella: A Korean Approach to Ming China in the Early 1500s," *Journal of Korean Studies* 15, no. 1 (2010): 54–56. Given the paucity of Ming documentation, there is no way to determine whether the emissaries acted in ignorance or feigned it out of expedience.

21. *Chungjong sillok* 5:29b [1508/2/18, 6], 6:19b [1508/6/8, 1].

22. *Chungjong sillok* 41:27b [1521/1/23, 2], 41:47a [1521/4/10, 4]. The 1521 envoys to Chosŏn, Kim Ŭi 金義 (fl. 1506–1521) and Chin Ho 陳浩 (fl. 1506–1521) were the very same eunuchs that the Chosŏn court "lobbied" to secure Chungjong's investiture. It is difficult to know whether Chosŏn concealed the matter from them, or were they in on the plot.

23. See *Injong sillok* 1:55a [1545/2/27, 3].

24. *Chungjong sillok* 1:65a [1506/12/11, 5], 5:53a [1508/4/15].

25. *Chungjong sillok* 105:44a [1544/12/5, 2].

26. *Myŏngjong sillok* 28:26a [1562/6/27, 1].

27. Zhu Yuanzhang, *Huang Ming zuxun*, Siku quanshu cunmu congshu, shi bu (part 2) 264 (Tainan: Zhuangyan wenhua, 1996), shouzhang 5a–7a.

28. An oversight blamed on a palace fire that destroyed the archives pertaining to this case; see Kuwano Eiji, "Chōsen Chūshūdai niokeru shūkei benfu mondai no sainen," *Bulletin of Faculty of Literature, Kurume University, Intercultural Studies* 25 (2008): 57–58, 63.

29. A claim later challenged even by Chosŏn subjects. See Jeong Ho-hun, "Deconstructing the Official History of Koryŏ in Late Chosŏn," *Seoul Journal of Korean Studies* 26, no. 2 (December 2013).

30. For the Chosŏn petition, see the 1518 petition to the Ming in *Chungjong sillok* 33:51a–52a [1518/6/16, 1].

31. *T'aejo sillok* 5:19a [1394/4/17, 3], [1394/4/15, 1], [1394/4/20, 1], [1394/4/20, 2]. For persecution, see Eugene Y. Park, *A Genealogy of Dissent: The Progeny of Fallen Royals in Chosŏn Korea* (Stanford, CA: Stanford University Press, 2018), 20–27.

32. *T'aejo sillok* 5:19b [1394/4/26, 1].

33. The virtually extinct Koryŏ royal line was later restored by T'aejong; see Park, *A Genealogy of Dissent*, 48–79.

34. Graeme R. Reynolds, "Culling Archival Collections in the Koryŏ-Chosŏn Transition," *Journal of Korean Studies* 24, no. 2 (October 1, 2019): 237–44; Hang Nyeong Oh, "The Meaning of Ritual Practices in the Compilation of the Chosŏn Sillok," in *The Institutional Basis of Civil Governance in the Chosŏn Dynasty*, ed. John Duncan (Seoul: Seoul Selection, 2009).

35. *Chungjong sillok* 32:64b–65b [1518/4/26, 1], 33:5a–33:6a [1518/5/7, 4].

36. *Chungjong sillok* 34:10a–11b [1518/7/14].

37. A case of the Barbra Streisand effect; see Lynn Avery Hunt, ed., *The Invention of Pornography: Obscenity and the Origins of Modernity, 1500–1800* (New York: Zone Books, 1993), 14–18.

38. *Chungjong sillok* 33:51a–52a [1518/6/16, 1], 35:59b [1519/4/7, 1], 35:48b [1519/3/15, 6]. Kuwano Eiji, "Chōsen Chūshūdai," 60–64.

39. *Chungjong sillok* 35:58b [1519/4/7, 1].

40. For the significance of "grievance" in judicial discourse, see Jisoo M. Kim, *The Emotions of Justice: Gender, Status, and Legal Performance in Chosŏn Korea* (Seattle: University of Washington Press, 2015), 3–7, 26–39.

41. *Chungjong sillok* 35:58b [1519/4/7, 1].

42. *Chungjong sillok* 92:58a–60b [1540/1/5, 3]; *Kwanghaegun ilgi* (*chungch'opon*) 33:52a–61a [1615/8a/8, 2]. Sun Weiguo, *Ming Qing shiqi Zhongguo shixue dui Chaoxian de yingxiang: jian lun liangguo xueshu jiaoliu yu haiwai Han xue* (Shanghai: Shanghai cishu chubanshe, 2009), 1–21.

43. Kye, "Huddling Under the Imperial Umbrella."

44. Kwŏn Inyong, "Myŏng chung'gi Chosŏn ŭi chonggye pyŏnmu wa tae Myŏng oegyo," *Myŏng-Ch'ŏng sa yŏn'gu* 24 (October 2005): 96–100; Xu Qixiong, "Shida zhicheng—Cong 16 shijimo 'Zhaoxue guoyi' he 'Renchen qingyuan' kan Chaoxian Li Chao zhengzhi hexin dui Zhongguo de xiangxiang he qixu," in *Cong zhoubian kan Zhongguo*, ed. Ge Zhaoguang and Wenshi yanjiu yuan (Beijing: Zhonghua shuju, 2009), 337–45.

45. John Jorgensen, *The Foresight of Dark Knowing: Chŏng Kam Nok and Insurrectionary Prognostication in Pre-Modern Korea*, Korean Classics Library: Philosophy and Religion (Honolulu: University of Hawai'i Press, 2018).

46. Jon M. Van Dyke, "Legal Issues Related to Sovereignty over Dokdo and Its Maritime Boundary," *Ocean Development & International Law* 38, no. 1–2 (July 2007): 157–224.

47. Once the Gate of Esteeming Heaven 奉天門, now the Gate of Supreme Harmony 太和門, renamed in 1645.

48. Pak Sŭngim, *Sogo sŏnsaeng munjip*, 3 in HMC 36:293d–295a.

49. Pak Sŭngim, *Sogo chip*, 3 in HMC 36:294a–294c.

50. Roger T. Ames, *Confucian Role Ethics: A Vocabulary* (Beijing: Chinese University Press, 2011); Feng Zhang, *Chinese Hegemony: Grand Strategy and*

International Institutions in East Asian History (Stanford, CA: Stanford University Press, 2015), 28–32.

51. Pak Sŭngim, *Sogo chip*, 3 in HMC 36:294c–295a.

52. *Sŏnjo sillok* 3:42–43b [1569/11/29, 2].

53. Hŏ Pong, "Hagok sŏnsaeng Choch'ŏn'gi," in *Hagok chip* 2 in HMC 58:460c–d.

54. Norms as defined in Gary Goertz and Paul F. Diehl, "Toward a Theory of International Norms: Some Conceptual and Measurement Issues," *Journal of Conflict Resolution* 36, no. 4 (1992): 636–39; Robert M Cover, "The Supreme Court, 1982 Term—Foreword: Nomos and Narrative," *Harvard Law Review* 97 (1983): 4–63. I am grateful to Maura Dykstra for this point.

7. CONTESTS OF RITUAL

1. For ritual as claims making elsewhere, see Barbara Stollberg-Rilinger, *The Emperor's Old Clothes: Constitutional History and the Symbolic Language of the Holy Roman Empire*, trans. Thomas Dunlap (New York: Berghahn, 2015), 3–12; Peter L Berger and Thomas Luckmann, *The Social Construction of Reality: A Treatise in the Sociology of Knowledge* (New York: Penguin, 1967), 110–48.

2. Christian Meyer, "Negotiating Rites in Imperial China: The Case of Northern Song Court Ritual Debates from 1034 to 1093," in *Negotiating Rites*, ed. Ute Hüsken and Frank Neubert (New York: Oxford University Press, 2012), 99–115; Angela Zito, *Of Body and Brush: Grand Sacrifice as Text/Performance in Eighteenth-Century China* (Chicago: University of Chicago Press, 1998), 16, 51–57.

3. Often as "correct performance or enactment of the textual script." See Catherine Bell, *Ritual: Perspectives and Dimensions*. Rev. ed. (New York: Oxford University Press, 2009), 38–41, 129–30, 203–4.

4. For changes in the number of kowtows, see Yu Pada, "Chosŏn ch'ogi ŭngchoch'ik kwallyŏn ŭiju ŭi sŏngnip kwa Cho-Myŏng kwan'gye," *Yŏksa minsok hak*, no. 40 (November 2012): 123–60.

5. Joshua Van Lieu, "The Politics of Condolence: Contested Representations of Tribute in Late Nineteenth-Century Chosŏn-Qing Relations," *Journal of Korean Studies* 14, no. 1 (2009).

6. Adam B Seligman et al., *Ritual and Its Consequences: An Essay on the Limits of Sincerity* (New York: Oxford University Press, 2008), 7–16, 20, 24, 30.

7. Han Hyŏngju, "Tae Myŏng ŭirye rŭl t'onghae pon 15 segi Cho–Myŏng kwan'gye," *Yŏksa minsok hak*, no. 28 (November 2008): 39–75.

8. Contestations and disruption help identify the stakes (and stakeholders) behind these ceremonies, especially when different ritual systems collide. See Kathryn McClymond, *Ritual Gone Wrong: What We Learn from Ritual Disruption* (New York: Oxford University Press, 2016), 176–81.

9. The Flag and Seal, Seat of Government, and the States, 4 U.S.C. § 7 (1947).

10. Ji-Young Lee, "Diplomatic Ritual as a Power Resource: The Politics of Asymmetry in Early Modern Chinese-Korean Relations," *Journal of East Asian Studies* 13, no. 2 (May–August 2013): 310–12; Joshua Van Lieu, "Divergent Visions of Serving the Great: The Emergence of Chosŏn-Qing Tributary Relations as a Politics of Representation" (PhD diss., University of Washington, 2010), 17–21, 33–79; Brantly Womack, *China and Vietnam: The Politics of Asymmetry*, (Cambridge: Cambridge University Press, 2006), 82–85.

11. For types of documents, see Sixiang Wang, "Compiling Diplomacy: Record-Keeping and Archival Practices in Chosŏn Korea," *Journal of Korean Studies* 24, no. 2 (September 2019): 258–61.

12. Sun Weiguo, "Shi shuo Ming dai Xingren," *Shixue jikan*, no. 1 (1994): 11–16; Yan Congjian, *Shuyu zhouzi lu*, Reprint, Beijing: Gugong bowuyuan tushuguan, 1580 1:9b.

13. Eunuchs of Muslim heritage were sent to Central Asia, Mongols to Mongolia, Jurchens to Liaodong. See Henry Tsai, *The Eunuchs in the Ming Dynasty* (Albany, NY: SUNY Press, 1996), 119–42; Chŏng Tonghun, "Myŏngdae chŏn'gi oegyo sajŏl ŭi sinpun chŏngmyŏng pangsik kwa kukkagan ch'egye," *Myŏng-Ch'ŏng say ŏn'gu* 10 (October 2013): 1–34; Sun Weiguo, "Lun Mingchu de huanguan waijiao," *Nankai xuebao*, no. 2 (1994): 34–42. For practice and trauma inflicted on castrated persons, see Howard Chang, *After Eunuchs: Science, Medicine, and the Transformation of Sex in Modern China* (New York: Columbia University Press, 2018), 16–69.

14. David M. Robinson, *Empire's Twilight: Northeast Asia Under the Mongols* (Cambridge, MA: Harvard University Asia Center, 2009), 382–86; David M. Robinson, "The Ming Court and the Legacy of the Yuan Mongols," in *Culture, Courtiers, and Competition: The Ming Court (1368–1644)*, ed. David M. Robinson (Cambridge, MA: Harvard University Asia Center, 2008).

15. *Sejong sillok* 36:10b [1427/5/1, 3, 4]; Sixiang Wang, "Korean Eunuchs as Imperial Envoys: Relations with Chosŏn Through the Zhengde Reign," in *The Ming World*, ed. Kenneth Swope (New York: Routledge, 2020), 472–74. Dong Yue suggests that eunuchs in Korea were not deliberately castrated but owed their condition to accident or disease; see Dong Yue, *Chosŏn pu*, trans. Yun Hojin, (Kkach'i, 1995), 2a–b.

16. *T'aejong sillok* 14:14b [1407/8/6].

17. *Sejong sillok* 68:9a–b [1435/4/26, 2–3], 68:10a [1435/4/27, 2].

18. MSL *Xianzong* 6:11a [Chenghua 4, 12/26].

19. *Sŏngjong sillok* 117:3b [1480/5/5, 1]; 129:13b [1481/5/22, 1]. See also *Sejo sillok* 46:6a [1468/4/13].

20. See Wang, "Korean Eunuchs as Imperial Envoys," 466–72.

21. Cho Yŏngnok, "Sŏnch'o ŭi Chosŏn ch'ulsin Myŏngsa ko—Sŏngjong cho ŭi tae Myŏng kyosŏp kwa Myŏngsa Chŏng Tong—," 國史館論叢 14 (1990).

22. Seligman et al., *Ritual and Its Consequences*, 15–16, 30.

23. As discussed in chapter 3, the envoy Ni Qian chastised the Chosŏn court because the king could not receive him in person. Ni Qian, *Chaoxian jishi*, Congshu jicheng chubian 3240 (Beijing: Zhonghua shuju, 1985) 65, 6–7, 11.

24. Silla and Koryŏ reception of imperial envoys, for instance, were not formalized in Tang or Song imperial statutes. See Guo Jiahui, "Tianxia tongli: Mingdai binli de liuchuan yu yuwai shijian de fenzheng," *Taiwan shida lishi xuebao* 59 (June 2018): 5–16, 24–26; Ch'oe Chongsŏk, "Koryŏ malgi, Chosŏn ch'ogi yŏngjo ŭirye e kwanhan saeroun ihae mosaek 'Pŏn'guk ŭiju ŭi sogae wa pogwŏn,'" *Minjok munhwa yŏn'gu* 69 (2015): 274–76, 279–80; Ch'oe Chongsŏk, "Chosŏn ch'ogi yŏngjorye unyŏng kwa Pŏn'guk ŭiju," *Yŏksa wa tamnon* 86 (April 2018): 139–77; Xu Yikui, *Ming jili*, SKQS 649–50 (Taipei: Shangwu yinshuguan, n.d.), 32:11a, 32:14b–15a.

25. KS 65:1a-6a. For the Liao-Jin protocols, see Pak Yunmi, "Koryŏ chŏn'gi oegyo ŭirye esŏ kugwang sŏmyŏn ŭi ŭimi," *Yŏksa wa hyŏnsil*, no. 98 (December 2015): 69–102.

26. Christopher P. Atwood, *The Rise of the Mongols: Five Chinese Sources* (Indianapolis, IN: Hackett, 2021), 86; 89.

27. William E. Henthorn, *Korea: The Mongol Invasions* (Leiden: Brill, 1963), 14–21.

28. Han Chaeyŏn, *Koryŏ kodoching*, repr. [1850] (Asea munhwasa, 1972), 1, 31; KS 22:16b [1219/1].

29. Bell, *Ritual: Perspectives and Dimensions*, 128–29.

30. The latter is a subtext in other Koryŏ records of the Mongol conquests. See Gari Ledyard, "Two Mongol Documents from the Koryŏ Sa," *Journal of the American Oriental Society* 83, no. 2 (1963): 225–39.

31. A conspicuous and lasting legacy of this practice was the insertion into late imperial Chinese practice and Chosŏn-Ming diplomatic protocol an oral proclamation (C. *xuandu*) of the delivered imperial decree; see Miao Dong, "Yuandai shichen yanjiu," (PhD diss., Nankai University, 2010), 3–4, 12, 71–74. Atwood, *The Rise of the Mongols*, 75, 81–82.

32. Atwood, *The Rise of the Mongols*, 104–5; For the "personal" character of the Mongol emissaries, see Miao Dong, "Yuandai shichen," 3–4, 12, 50–59, 74–79.

33. As would a handshake in contemporary Western etiquette; incidentally, a convention that one late nineteenth-century Chinese diplomat visiting the United States found repulsive. The curious Western dinner party, the appalled traveler wrote, required a man not only to "shake a strange woman's hand" as a greeting but also "offer her his arm." Bell, *Ritual: Perspectives and Dimensions*, 260–61. R. David Arkush and Leo Ou-fan Lee, *Land Without Ghosts: Chinese*

Impressions of America from the Mid-Nineteenth Century to the Present (Berkeley: University of California Press, 1989), 16, 55–56.

34. Ritualized acts possess "two loci" of significance: "the short-term experience of the embodied performance, and the long-term struggle over interpretation in speech and writing." See Christina Pössel, "The Magic of Early Medieval Ritual," *Early Medieval Europe* 17, no. 2 (May 2009): 114–16; Philippe Buc, *The Dangers of Ritual Between Early Medieval Texts and Social Scientific Theory* (Princeton, NJ: Princeton University Press, 2009), 3–8.

35. KS 65:1b.

36. KS 23:3b–4a [1231/12].

37. Henthorn, *Korea: The Mongol Invasions*; *Yuan Gaoli jishi* (Taipei: Guangwen shuju, 1972), 5; Song Lian, *Yuan shi*, ed. Yang Jialuo (Taipei: Dingwen shuju, 1981) 208, pp. 4608–4609. For Mongol retaliations after diplomatic breakdown, see Morris Rossabi, *Khubilai Khan: His Life and Times* (Berkeley: University of California Press, 1988), 81, 101; Thomas T. Allsen, "The Rise of the Mongolian Empire and Mongolian Rule in North China," in *The Cambridge History of China Volume 6: Alien Regimes and Border States, 907–1368*, ed. Herbert Franke and Denis C. Twitchett (Cambridge: Cambridge University Press, 1994), 409–10; Charles J Halperin, *Russia and the Mongols: Slavs and the Steppe in Medieval and Early Modern Russia* (Bucureşti: Ed. Academiae Romane, 2007), 185–86.

38. KS 65:10a-10b, 26:27a [1269/11], 27:24a [1271/10].

39. KS 65:11b. A position the king utilized to shore up his own authority vis-à-vis Koryŏ's traditional elite; see Yi Ikchu, "Koryŏ Ch'ungnyŏl wangdae ŭi chŏngch'i sanghwang kwa chŏngch'i seryŏk ŭi sŏngkyŏk," *Han'guk saron* 18 (1988): 168–73.

40. KS 28.2a–b [1274/8].

41. KS 65:11b–12a; Miao Dong, "Yuandai shichen," 89; *Da Yuan shengzheng guochao dianzhang*, Scripta Sinica (Taipei: Guoli gugong bowuyuan, 1976), 28, p. 1035; KS 65:11b–12a.

42. His "dichotomous" existence (*ichŭng chonjae*). See Yi Myŏngmi, "Koryŏ-Mongol kwan'gye wa Koryŏ kugwang wisang ŭi pyŏnhwa" (PhD diss., Seoul National University, 2012), 60–124; Kang Hahn Lee, "Shifting Political, Legal, and Institutional Borderlines Between Koryŏ and the Mongol Yuan Empire," *Seoul Journal of Korean Studies* 29, no. 2 (2016): 246–50.

43. Kim Hodong, *Monggol cheguk kwa Koryŏ: K'ubillai chŏngkwŏn ŭi t'ansaeng kwa Koryŏ ŭi chŏngch'ijŏk wisang* (Seoul: Sŏul taehakkyo ch'ulp'anbu, 2007).

44. A simplification of the dynamics between different idioms of authority in this period; see Timothy Brook, M. C. van Walt van Praag, and Miek Boltjes, eds., *Sacred Mandates: Asian International Relations Since Chinggis Khan* (Chicago: University of Chicago Press, 2018), 49–56; Christopher P. Atwood,

"Legal Norms and Apocalyptic Dreams: Inter-Polity Relations in the Long Mongol Century" (unpublished manuscript, last modified September 6, 2019), 14–15.

45. Herbert Franke, *From Tribal Chieftain to Universal Emperor and God: The Legitimation of the Yüan Dynasty* (München: Verlag der Baerischen Akademie der Wissenschaften, 1978); Atwood, "Legal Norms," 2–3.

46. Chŏng Tonghun, "Myŏngdae ŭi yeje chilsŏ," 263–74; *Sejong sillok* 26:1a [1424/10/3, 2].

47. Chŏng Tonghun, "Koryŏ-Myŏng oegyo munsŏ sŏsik ŭi sŏngnip kwa paegyŏng," *Han'guk saron* 56 (2010).

48. *T'aejong sillok* 1:12b [1401/2/6, 1], 1:32a [1401/6/12, 1].

49. *T'aejong sillok* 1:34b [1402/1/24, 2].

50. *Tanjong sillok* 2:8a [1452/7/21, 3], 2:11a [1452/7/25, 6], 2:16a [1452/8/10, 2, 3], 2:19b [1452/8/18, 2].

51. A conflict that spurred on many ritual disputes in both Chosŏn and Ming; see Yiming Ha, "Public Discourse and Private Sentiment: Ritual Controversies, Ritual Authority, and Political Succession in Ming and Chosŏn," *Ming Studies* (May 2022).

52. *Tanjong sillok* 2:11a [1452/7/26, 1], 2:11b [1452/7/26, 3].

53. *Tanjong sillok* 2:19b [1452/8/18, 2].

54. *Tanjong sillok* 2:19b [1452/8/19, 2].

55. *Tanjong sillok* 2:22a–25b [1452/8/22, 1].

56. *Tanjong sillok* 2:22a [1452/8/21, 4]. Chen here suggests a minor point could be overlooked as long as discrepancies were not pointed out; indeed, the magic of ritual was spoiled by being too literal!

57. *Sŏngjong sillok* 213:11a [1488/2/21, 5], 213:14a [1488/2/29, 2], 214:4b [1488/3/7, 2]. For a thorough discussion of the 1488 disputes, see Yi Kyuch'ŏl, "Chosŏn Sŏngjŏngdae oegyo ŭirye pyŏn'gyŏng e taehan nonŭi wa tae Myŏng ŭisik," *Yŏksa wa hyŏnsil*, no. 98 (December 2015): 169–97.

58. *Sŏngjong sillok* 214:6a [1488/3/10, 1].

59. *Sŏngjong sillok* 214:7a–8b [1488/3/10, 4–5].

60. *Sŏngjong sillok* 214:9b [1488/3/11, 1].

61. *Sŏngjong sillok* 214:11a [1488/3/12, 5].

62. *Sŏngjong sillok* 214:11b [1488/3/12, 6].

63. *Sŏngjong sillok* 214:2a [1488/3/12, 7].

64. *Sŏngjong sillok* 214:14b–15b [1488/3/13, 10; 11].

65. Kim Kwiyŏng, *Tongwŏn chip, munjip* 3 in HMC 37:457b; *Myŏngjong sillok* 24:14a [1558/2/22, 1].

66. Ch'oe Chongsŏk, "Chosŏn ch'ogi," 145–160. Compare Xu Yikui, *Da Ming jili*, 32:11b, 17b–19b, with protocol in *Orye* 五禮, in *Sejong sillok* 132:28a.

67. Gong Yongqing, *Shi Chaoxian lu* (Nanjing: Taofenglou, 1937), xu 1a–b.
68. Buc, *The Dangers of Ritual*, 3–5.
69. Pössel, "The Magic of Early Medieval Ritual," 114–16.
70. Sŏng Hyŏn, *Yongjae ch'onghwa* 1 in TDYS 1, 570.
71. Dong Yue, "Chaoxian zazhi," in *Shi Chaoxian lu*, ed. Yin Mengxia and Yu Hao (Beijing: Beijing tushuguan chubanshe, 2003), 804–6; Philip de Heer, "Three Embassies to Seoul: Sino-Korean Relations in the 15th Century," in *Conflict and Accomodation in Early Modern East Asia: Essays in Honour of Erik Zurcher*, ed. Leonard Blusse and Harriet T. Zurndorfer (Leiden: Brill, 1993), 253n53.
72. Lee, "Diplomatic Ritual as a Power Resource," 311–13; Ji-Young Lee, *China's Hegemony: Four Hundred Years of East Asian Ddomination* (New York: Columbia University Press, 2016), 40–43.
73. For several extant examples, see those collected in Yin Mengxia and Yu Hao, *Shi Chaoxian lu* (Beijing: Beijing tushuguan chubanshe, 2003).
74. *Sejo sillok* 7:40b [1457/5/27, 4]. The original wolf warrior, Ban's aggressive diplomacy briefly reasserted Han hegemony in the Tarim Basin.
75. Jiao Hong, *Guochao xianzheng lu*, Scripta Sinica, Mingdai zhuanji congkan 109–114 (Taipei: Mingwen shuju, 1991), 38, p. 736; 73, p. 626; Tianhua caizi and Siqiao jushi, *Kuaixian bian*, ed. Guoli zhengzhi daxue gudian xiaoshuo yanjiu zhongxin (Taipei: Tianyi chubanshe, 1985), parts 3, 9:3b–4a.
76. *Sŏngjong sillok* 214:8b [1488/3/10, 5].
77. Sun Joo Kim, "Culture of Remembrance in Late Chosŏn Korea: Bringing an Unknown War Hero Back into History," *Journal of Social History* 44, no. 2 (2010): 566–73.
78. Kim Han'gyu, *Sa Chosŏnnok yŏn'gu: Song, Myŏng, Ch'ŏng sidae Chosŏn sahaengnok ŭi saryojŏk kach'i* (Seoul: Sŏgang taehakkyo ch'ulp'anbu, 2011), 356–65.
79. *Injo sillok* 12:18b [1626/3/25, 3].
80. Jiang Yueguang, *Youxuan jishi*, 37–40.
81. *Injo sillok* 13:5a [1626/6/13, 1]. Jiang's travelogue also reproduced a similar conversation; see Jiang Yueguang, *Youxuan jishi*, 41–42. For Chosŏn court debates, see *Injo sillok* 12:45a [1626/5/22, 2], 12:46a [1626/5/26, 2], 13:2a [1626/6/5, 1].
82. *Injo sillok* 13:1a [1626/6/2, 1]. His zeal for moral performativity notwithstanding (perhaps a common trait of Donglin affiliates), Jiang generally behaved honestly in Korea. Later serving as Grand Secretary, he died as a Ming loyalist, committing suicide in 1649 when efforts to restore the Ming dynasty had failed. See Frederic E. Wakeman, *The Great Enterprise: The Manchu Reconstruction of Imperial Order in Seventeenth-Century China* (Berkeley: University of California Press, 1985), 368n158; Ying Zhang, *Confucian Image Politics: Masculine Morality in Seventeenth-Century China* (Seattle: University of Washington Press, 2017), 148–49.

83. MSL *Xianzong* 6:11a [Chenghua 4, 12/26].

84. Seo-Hyun Park, *Sovereignty and Status in East Asian International Relations* (Cambridge: Cambridge University Press, 2017), 25–101, especially 29–30; James Louis Hevia, *Cherishing Men from Afar: Qing Guest Ritual and the Macartney Embassy of 1793* (Durham, NC: Duke University Press, 1995), 130–33; Clifford Geertz, *Negara: The Theatre State in Nineteenth-Century Bali* (Princeton, NJ: Princeton University Press, 1981), 98–136; Bell, *Ritual: Perspectives and Dimensions*, 66–68; Edward Muir, *Ritual in Early Modern Europe* (Cambridge: Cambridge University Press, 2005), 253–55.

PART IV. AN EMPIRE OF LETTERS

1. See, for example, *Sejong sillok* 27:11a [1425/1/20, 4]. More detailed records survive only from the period following the Imjin War. See Yŏngjŏp togam, *Yŏngjŏp togam tochʻŏng ŭigwe*, Kyujanggak Archives (Seoul National University) Kyu 14559 (Seoul, 1634); Kyujanggak Archives (Seoul National University) Kyu 14545, 14546 (Seoul, 1608).

2. See, for example, *Sejo sillok* 15:25a [1459/3/27, 4]; *Yŏnsan'gun ilgi* 50:9a–10b [1503/7/3, 4].

3. *Tanjong sillok* 3:17b [1452/9a/12, 13].

4. Such as in early modern Europe; see Jan Hennings, *Russia and Courtly Europe: Ritual and the Culture of Diplomacy, 1648–1725* (Cambridge: Cambridge University Press, 2016), 22–25, 131–54. Or after the advent of instantaneous communication technology, as both Qing and Chosŏn would learn in the age of the telegraph and international journalism; see Joshua Van Lieu, "The Politics of Condolence: Contested Representations of Tribute in Late Nineteenth-Century Chosŏn-Qing Relations," *Journal of Korean Studies* 14, no. 1 (2009): 97–109.

5. Dong Yue, *Chosŏn pu*, trans. Yun Hojin, Sosu sŏwon pon (Kkachʻi, 1995), 4a–5b; Emma Teng, "Other as Self? The 'Civilized Barbarian' in Dong Yue's *Fu on Korea*," in *Travels in and out of Pre-Modern Korea*, ed. Marion Eggert and Bochumer Jahrbuch Zur Ostasienforschung (Bochum, Germany: Fakultät für Ostasienwissenschaften, Ruhr-Universität Bochum, 2012), 78–81.

6. For publication history, see Kim Kihwa, "'Hwanghwajip' ŭi pʻyŏnchʻan kwa kanhaeng e kwanhan yŏn'gu," *Sŏjihak yŏn'gu* 39 (June 2008): 201–53. Tabulations for the totals are inexact, depending on whether different pieces in one poetic suite or lengthy paratexts are counted individually, and whether the recently rediscovered 1620 *Brilliant Flowers* are included. Sin Tʻaeyŏng, *Myŏng nara sasin ŭn Chosŏn ŭl ŏttŏke poannŭn'ga: "Hwanghwajip" yŏn'gu* (Seoul: Taumsaem, 2005), 1–5; Zhao Ji, *Zuben Huanghua ji* (Nanjing: Fenghuang chubanshe, 2013), 3–4.

7. Wang Keping, "Shifu waijiao zai Ming chao yu Chaoxian guanxi shi shang de zuoyong," *Yanbian daxue xuebao* 44, no. 1 (February 2011): 88–92; Ye Quanhong, *Mingdai qianqi Zhong Han guojiao zhi yanjiu: 1368–1488* (Taipei: Shangwu yinshuguan, 1991), 122, 125–26, 131–34, 146; Philip de Heer, "Three Embassies to Seoul: Sino-Korean Relations in the 15th Century," in *Conflict and Accomodation in Early Modern East Asia: Essays in Honour of Erik Zurcher*, ed. Leonard Blusse and Harriet T. Zurndorfer (Leiden: Brill, 1993), 250–56; Du Huiyue, *Mingdai wenchen chushi Chaoxian yu "Huanghuaji"* (Beijing: Renmin chubanshe, 2010), 66–69, 80–89.

8. THE BRILLIANT FLOWERS

1. Peter H. Lee, *A History of Korean Literature* (New York: Cambridge University Press, 2003), 316–22; Benjamin A. Elman, *A Cultural History of Civil Examinations in Late Imperial China* (Berkeley: University of California Press, 2000), 23; *Chungjong sillok* 40:46b; Yi Ch'angsin 李昌臣 (1449–1506), cautioned his king against neglecting *belles-lettres*, despite "irrelevance to governing the country," precisely for this reason. *Sŏngjong sillok* 122:9a [1480/10/26, 3].

2. Du Huiyue, *Mingdai wenchen*, 98–99. *Chungjong sillok* 83:14a [1536/12/16, 11]; Hong Manjong and Chŏ Sŏngjik, *Shihua conglin jianzhu*, ed. Zhao Ji (Tianjin: Nankai daxue chubanshe, 2006), 225.

3. Young Kyun Oh, *Engraving Virtue: The Printing History of a Premodern Korean Moral Primer* (Leiden: Brill, 2013), 107–8; Kim Kihwa, "Hwanghwajip ŭi p'yŏnch'an," 220–50.

4. An Changni, "Chosŏn chŏn'gi 'Hwanghwajip' mit Myŏng sasin ŭi Chosŏn kwallyŏn sŏjok ch'ulp'an e taehan yŏn'gu," *Kugŏ kyoyuk* 107 (2002): 360–61; Ryu Kisu, "Hwanghwajip ŭi kanhaeng kwa surokdoen Myŏngsa e kwanhan koch'al," *Chungguk hak yŏn'gu* 47 (2009): 93–106.

5. Sin T'aeyŏng, " 'Hwanghwajip' ŭi p'yŏnch'an ŭisik yŏn'gu - sŏmun ŭl chungsim ŭro," *Hanmun hakpo* 5 (2001): 115–44; Du Huiyue, *Mingdai wenchen*, 70–88.

6. For examples of Korean accounts, see Sŏ Kŏjŏng, *P'irwŏn chapki*. In TDYS; Sŏng Hyŏn, *Yongjae ch'onghwa* in TDYS 1.

7. Du Huiyue, *Mingdai wenchen*, 279–80; Zhao Ji, *Zuben* HHJ, 3. References to the *Brilliant Flowers* will be cited by year, followed by location in the *Zuben Huanghua ji*, (hereafter HHJ). They eventually acquired the form of a unified corpus only after the anthologies were reprinted as a complete set in 1773. Note that the 1621 anthology is missing from the 1773 reprinting.

8. Zev Joseph Handel, *Sinography: The Borrowing and Adaptation of the Chinese Script* (Leiden: Brill, 2019), 10–12; Chong-sok Ko and Ross King, *Infected Korean Language, Purity Versus Hybridity: From the Sinographic Cosmopolis to*

Japanese Colonialism to Global English (Amherst, NY: Cambria Press, 2014), 2–3. Or, alternatively, "Sinosphere." See Nanxiu Qian, Richard J. Smith, and Bowei Zhang, eds., *Rethinking the Sinosphere: Poetics, Aesthetics, and Identity Formation* (Amherst, NY: Cambria Press, 2020), xxiii–xxix.

9. Jongmook Lee, "Establishing Friendships Between Competing Civilizations: Exchange of Chinese Poetry in East Asia in the Fifteenth and Sixteenth Centuries," in *Rethinking the Sinosphere Poetics, Aesthetics, and Identity Formation*, ed. Nanxiu Qian, Richard J. Smith, and Bowei Zhang (Amherst, NY: Cambria Press, 2020), 15–20, 26–27.

10. *Hwanghwa* is translated as "imperial flowers" in Lee, "Establishing Friendships."

11. *Shijing*, Mao 163. Similar titles were also used in Vietnamese envoy poetry collections, see Liam C. Kelley, *Beyond the Bronze Pillars: Envoy Poetry and the Sino-Vietnamese Relationship.* (Honolulu: University of Hawai'i Press, 2005), 68, 233.

12. Zhenping Wang, *Ambassadors from the Islands of Immortals: China-Japan Relations in the Han-Tang Period* (Honolulu: University of Hawai'i Press, 2005). For general history, see Piao Zhongjin, *Zhongguo shifu waijiao de qiyuan yu fazhan* (Beijing: Zhishi chanquan chubanshe, 2014).

13. Jin Yufu, ed., *Liaohai congshu* (Shenyang: Liaoshen shushe, 1985), 2540; Chang Tong'ik, *Wŏndae Yŏsa charyo chimnok* (Seoul: Sŏul Taehakkyo ch'ulp'anbu, 1997), 347–60, especially p. 348.

14. Kelley, *Beyond the Bronze Pillars*, 182–192.

15. Kwŏn Kŭn, *Yangch'on chip* in HMC 7:14–21b. *Sejo sillok* 19:33a [1460/3/7, 1]; Zhang Ning, *Fengshi lu*, Congshu jicheng chubian 2142. Shanghai: Shangwu yinshuguan, 1936, 16–17; Kwŏn Kŭn, *Tonggukki*, Kyujanggak Archives (Seoul National University) 가람古貴 951-G995d, 1460, 61b–67b.

16. For example, *T'aejong sillok* 1:33a [1401/6/14, 1]; 4:18b [1402/10/26, 2].

17. Sŏ Kŏjŏng, *P'irwŏn chapki* 2 in TDYS 1:686.

18. Kim Allo, *Hŭiraktang ko* 8 in HMC 21:450c; Kim Wŏnjun, "Chosa wa ŭi ch'aunsi e nat'anan Chipong ŭi ŭisik: Chipong ŭi 'Hwanghwajip ch'aun ŭl t'onghae," *Hanminjok ŏmunhak* 6, no. 44 (2004): 237. At times, officials wrote additional verses to supplement what was already included in the anthology; see *Chungjong sillok* 43:59a [1522/1/20, 4].

19. Zhang Ning, *Fengshi lu*, 2:18.

20. 1476 HHJ, 155–56.

21. *Chungjong sillok* 84:1a [1537/3/2, 1]; Ŏ Sukkwŏn, *A Korean Storyteller's Miscellany: The Paegwan Chapki of O Sukkwon*, trans. Peter H. Lee (Princeton, NJ: Princeton University Press, 1989), 196–97; Du Huiyue, *Mingdai wenchen*, 105–6.

22. There were other such literary "games." A number of *Brilliant Flowers* anthologies include palindromic verses 回文體 that read the same forward and backward. There was also the *Tongp'a ch'e* (*Dongpo ti* 東坡題), another innovation credited to Su Shi. Readers were alerted to the poem's form with specific modifying qualities to yield lines of poetry. For example, a "tall mountain" would be indicated with the glyph for "mountain" written above the usual height, a "red leaf" might be rendered with the glyph for "leaf" in red. See Lee, "Establishing Friendships," 20–26; Colin S. C. Hawes, *The Social Circulation of Poetry in the Mid-Northern Song: Emotional Energy and Literati Self-Cultivation* (Albany, NY: SUNY Press, 2005), 5, 31–44.

23. My gratitude to Javier Cha for first bringing my attention to this anecdote. See Kim Allo, *Hŭiraktang ko* 8 in HMC 21:450c; Hong Manjong and Chŏ Sŏngjik, *Shihua conglin*, 126.

24. Hong Manjong and Chŏ Sŏngjik, *Shihua conglin*, 147, 172, 177. For discussion, see also the preface in Cai Meihua and Zhao Ji, eds., *Hanguo shihua quanbian jiaozhu* (Beijing:Remin wenxue chubanshe, 2012). For the origin of the anecdote collections as a genre, see Jack W. Chen and David Schaberg, eds., *Idle Talk: Gossip and Anecdote in Traditional China* (Berkeley: University of California Press, 2014). For the origins of "remarks on poetry" in the literati tradition, see Ronald Egan, *The Problem of Beauty: Aesthetic Thought and Pursuits in Northern Song Dynasty China* (Cambridge, MA: Harvard University Asia Center, 2006), 60–108.

25. Sŏng Hyŏn, *Yongjae ch'onghwa*, 1 in TDYS 1:569. Kim Allo, *Hŭiraktang ko* 8 in HMC 21:451b.

26. See also Hong Manjong and Chŏ Sŏngjik, *Shihua conglin*, 59. Sŏ's poem was a pastiche of verses by well-known Korean poets. Sŏ probably counted on the Ming envoy's ignorance of the Korean repertoire to impress him with its best lines. See Sin T'aeyŏng, *Myŏng nara sasin*, 92–108; Lee, "Establishing Friendships," 18–20.

27. Sŏ Kŏjŏng, *P'irwŏn chapki* 2 in TDYS 1:685–686; Sŏng Hyŏn, *Yongjae ch'onghwa* 1 in TDYS 1, 567–70; Hong Manjong and Chŏ Sŏngjik, *Shihua conglin*, 59.

28. Kim Allo, *Hŭiraktang ko* 8 in HMC 21:451c-d. The shipwrecked Ch'oe Pu reported that some southern literati had heard of Sŏ Kŏjŏng's name; see Ch'oe Pu, *Kŭmnam chip*, 4 in HMC 16:456d-a; See also Lee, "Establishing Friendships."

29. For genres and forms in the *Brilliant Flowers*, see Du Huiyue, *Mingdai wenchen*, 133–80.

30. 1521 HHJ p. 539; *Chungjong sillok* 43:49b [1521/12/23, 1]; Hong Manjong and Chŏ Sŏngjik, *Shihua conglin*, 154; 1573 HHJ, 206–7; Lee, "Establishing Friendships," 20, 26–27.

31. Correlative cosmology is associated with Zhu Xi Neo-Confucianism, but it is not specific to it and certainly predates it in the poetic tradition. See Yung Sik Kim, *The Natural Philosophy of Chu Hsi (1130–1200)* (Philadelphia: American Philosophical Society, 2000), 42–63.

32. Zhang Ning, *Fengshi lu*, 13–15; 1460 HHJ, pp. 118–119.

33. Stephen Owen, *Traditional Chinese Poetry and Poetics: Omen of the World* (Madison: University of Wisconsin Press, 1985), 27–29.

34. Notably the Three Yangs: Yang Shiqi 楊士奇 (1364–1444), Yang Rong 楊榮 (1371–1440), and Yang Fu 楊溥 (1372–1446). John W. Dardess, *A Ming Society: T'ai-Ho County, Kiangsi, in the Fourteenth to Seventeenth Centuries* (Berkeley: University of California Press, 1996), 199–205; Du Huiyue, *Mingdai wenchen*, 183–202.

35. Li Shenghua, *Chu Ming shige yanjiu* (Beijing: Zhonghua shuju, 2012), 364–66.

36. As were Chen Jian of 1457 and Zhang Ning of 1460; see Du Huiyue, *Mingdai wenchen*, 280–83. The Grand Secretary Li Dongyang 李東陽 (1447–1516), who spearheaded a transformation of academic poetry with his Chaling School poetry (茶陵派), was a junior associate of Ni Qian and the 1488 envoy Dong Yue. See Li Shenghua, *Chu Ming shige*, 357; Li Dongyang, *Li Dongyang ji* (Changsha: Yuelu shushe, 1984), 22, in vol. 2, 322–23; 24 in vol. 3, 354–57, 25 in vol. 3, 361–62.

37. Yoshikawa Kōjirō, *Five Hundred Years of Chinese Poetry, 1150–1650: The Chin, Yuan, and Ming Dynasties* (Princeton, NJ: Princeton University Press, 1989), 122–33; Li Shenghua, *Chu Ming shige*, 357–64; David M. Robinson, *Martial Spectacles of the Ming Court* (Cambridge, MA: Harvard University Asia Center, 2013), 74–79.

38. Xue Yingqi, *Fangshan xiansheng wenlu*, Dongwu shulin jiaokan ben, Siku quanshu cunmu congshu, jibu 102 (Jinan: Qilu shushe, 1997), 9:28b-29b.

39. 1476 HHJ 1, 235–36. Other works of note include his "Short Songs of Kaesŏng" 開城小詠; see 1476 HHJ, 261–66.

40. P'yŏngyang was returned to Koryŏ rule in 1290, with the remaining annexed territories reconquered by Koryŏ in the wake of the Yuan collapse; see Chŏng Inji, *Koryŏ sa*, 30:21a–b (hereafter KS) [1290/3 chŏngmyo].

41. The identification has elicited controversy in some populist circles, but it is well attested to archaeologically. It was also the consensus in the Chosŏn period; see Mark E. Byington, ed., *The Han Commanderies in Early Korean History*, illustrated ed. (Cambridge, MA: Korea Institute, 2014); Andrew Logie, "Diagnosing and Debunking Korean Pseudohistory," *European Journal of Korean Studies* 18, no. 2 (2019): 41, 50–53. *Sejong sillok* 154:2b chiriji.

42. For Xue Rengui, Korea, see W. L. Idema, "Fighting in Korea: Two Early Narrative Treaments of the Story of Xue Rengui," in *Korea in the Middle: Korean*

Studies and Area Studies: Essays in Honour of Boudewjin Walraven, ed. Remco E. Breuker (Leiden: CNWS, 2007), 341–58.

43. Ki-baik Lee, *A New History of Korea* (Seoul: Ilchogak, 1997), 71; JaHyun Kim Haboush, "Contesting Chinese Time, Nationalizing Temporal Space: Temporal Inscription in Late Chosŏn Korea," in *Time, Temporality and Imperial Transition: East Asia Form Ming to Qing*, ed. Lynn A. Struve, Asian Interactions and Comparisons (Honolulu: University of Hawai'i Press, 2005), 118; Kim Pusik, *Samguk sagi* (Han'guksa saryo yŏn'gu so, 2004), 7:16a–17b; Tineke D'Haeseleer, "Tang Taizong in Korea: The Siege of Ansi," *East Asian History*, no. 40 (August 2016): 1–17.

44. See, for instance, the disputed facts of the Tang-Silla wars in Sima Guang, *Zizhi tongjian*, ed. Hu Sansheng and Scripta Sinica (Beijing: Beijing guji chubanshe, 1956), 18, p. 6375; Ouyang Xiu and Song Qi, *Xin Tang shu*, ed. Yang Jialuo (Taipei: Dingwen shuju, 1981), 220, p. 6197; Sun Weiran, "Qiantan Tang-Luo zhanzheng zhong de 'Maixiaocheng zhi zhan,'" *Dongbei shidi* 2 (2010): 43–44.

45. 1476 HHJ, 235–6.

46. 1476 HHJ, 261–4; Sŏ Kŏjŏng, *Saga chip*, Saga sijip p'oyu 四佳詩集補遺 2 in HMC 11:165a–b. For a close reading, see Sin T'aeyŏng, *Myŏng nara sasin*, 108–24. For Chosŏn period interpretations of Sui-Tang invasions of Koguryŏ, see Hyung-Wook Kim, "An Ancient and Glorious Past: Koguryo in the Collective Memories of the Korean People" (PhD diss., University of California, Los Angeles, 2012), 66–78.

47. For martial ideals of Ming empire, see Robinson, *Martial Spectacles*.

48. "Don't copy the Sui and Tang and forget the fundamentals!" [莫學隋唐昧根本] in 1476 HHJ, 268; see also 261, 264; 1539 HHJ, 800–1, 808–9, 835.

49. 1476 HHJ, 269.

50. 1521 HHJ, 474.

51. 1537 HHJ, 576.

52. 1537 HHJ, 597.

53. 1476 HHJ, 218–20.

54. Du Huiyue, *Mingdai wenchen*, 68–69. A loaded term; see Adam Bohnet, *Turning Toward Edification: Foreigners in Chosŏn Korea* (Honolulu: University of Hawai'i Press, 2020), 40–41.

55. 1476 HHJ, 220–2. Kim Suon, *Sigu chip* 4 in HMC 9:111a–111b. Note that the HHJ ascribes this piece to Sŏng Im 成任. See also Yi Hwang, *T'oegye chip*, munjip 42 in HMC 30:435a, 1537 HHJ, 570–1; Kim Allo, *Hŭiraktang ko*, munjip 5, in HMC 21:397a–398b. Examples such as these in the prefaces and text of the HHJ are too numerous to list; see Sin T'aeyŏng, "'Hwanghwajip' ŭi p'yŏnch'an ŭisik"; Yi Sŏkhyŏng, *Chŏhŏn chip* 2 in HMC 9:428d–429b.

56. *Sejong sillok* 16.18a [1422/6/27, 2]. For an extended discussion of this case, see Sixiang Wang, "The Filial Daughter of Kwaksan: Finger Severing, Confucian

Virtues, and Envoy Poetry in Early Chosŏn," *Seoul Journal of Korean Studies* 25, no. 2 (December 2012): 175–212.

57. Ni Qian, *Liaohai bian* (Beijing: Beijing tushuguan chuban she, 1469), 2:25a–25b; pp. 570–571. 1450 HHJ, 38; 1488 HHJ, 344.

58. Sin Sukchu, *Pohanjae*, 12 in HMC 10:98a.

59. 1537 HHJ, 582.

60. 1537 HHJ, 726.

61. 1521 HHJ, 449–550.

62. 1521 HHJ, 449–550.

63. 1521 HHJ, 465.

64. 1521 HHJ, 466.

65. 1539 HHJ 782: 國風歌謠采閨門 皇華使臣徧諏述 我欲獻之列樂官 示爾世世承芳躅; Stephen Owen, *Readings in Chinese Literary Thought* (Cambridge, MA: Harvard University Press, 1992), 37–49; Michael Nylan, *The Five "Confucian" Classics* (New Haven, CT: Yale University Press, 2001), 78–84.

66. 1539 HHJ, 782; Owen, *Readings in Chinese Literary Thought*, 1–2.

67. Sŏ Kŏjŏng, *Saga chip*, munjip 4 in HMC 11:247b–247d. 1476 HHJ, 209–10.

68. Sŏ Kŏjŏng, *Saga chip*, munjip 4 in HMC 11:235a–236b. For an interpretation, see Du Huiyue, *Mingdai wenchen*, 68–70.

69. 1476 HHJ, 209–10.

70. 1568 HHJ, 1065; Yi Hwang, *T'oegye chip*, *munjip* 42 in in HMC 30:435a–b,

71. Owen, *Readings in Chinese Literary Thought*, 37–44.

72. As captured in the term *muhwa zhuyi* 慕華主義 in contemporary Chinese scholarship; see Du Huiyue, *Mingdai wenchen*, 256–63; Sin T'aeyŏng, " 'Hwang-hwajip' ŭi p'yŏnch'an ŭisik," 118.

73. Yan Congjian, *Shuyu zhouzi lu*, (Beijing: Gugong bowuyuan tushuguan, 1580), 1:15a–30b.

74. Sin T'aeyŏng, *Myŏng nara sasin*, 158–59.

9. THE ENVOY'S VIRTUE

1. *Chungjong sillok* 84:24a–29b [1537/3/14, 6–8].

2. *Chungjong sillok* 84:24a–29b [1537/3/14, 6–8].

3. *Chungjong sillok* 32:64b–65b [1518/4/26, 1]; 33:5a–33:6a [1518/5/7, 4].

4. Sŏng Hyŏn, *Yongjae ch'onghwa*, in TDYS 1:567–70.

5. *T'aejong sillok* 1:33b [1401/6/16].

6. *T'aejong sillok* 1:32a–33a [1401/6/12, 1], 1:33a [1401/6/13, 1].

7. In theory, Ming scholar-officials were prohibited by law from marrying courtesans. For courtesans in Ming elite culture, see Harriet T. Zurndorfer, "Prostitutes and

Courtesans in the Confucian Moral Universe of Late Ming China (1550–1644)," *International Review of Social History* 56, no. S19 (December 2011): 197–216.

8. *T'aejong sillok* [1401/8/23, 1].

9. *T'aejong sillok* 2:10a [1401/9/2, 1], 9:12a [1401/9/12, 1]

10. *T'aejong sillok* 2:13a [1401/10/3, 1].

11. MSL *Taizong* 21:7a [1403/6/20].

12. *T'aejong sillok* 3:12a [1402/3/1, 1].

13. *T'aejong sillok* 4:18b [1402/10/26, 2].

14. A few exceptions include T'aejong's poems to Zhang Jin and Duanmu Li in 1402. See *T'aejong sillok* 1:33a [1401/6/14, 1].

15. 1457 HHJ, 57, 59–60; 1464 HHJ, 159, 169–70, 178; 1476 HHJ, 227–28, 230–31, 266–67; 1488 HHJ, 373–74. See also Kim Han'gyu, *Sa Chosŏnnok yŏn'gu: Song, Myŏng, Ch'ŏng sidae Chosŏn sahaengnok ŭi saryojŏk kach'i* (Seoul: Sŏgang tae-hakkyo ch'ulp'anbu, 2011), 150–54; Sin T'aeyŏng, *Myŏng nara sasin ŭn Chosŏn ŭl ŏttŏke poannŭn'ga: "Hwanghwajip" yŏn'gu* (Seoul: Taunsaem, 2005), 227, 228–30. The 1521 envoy Tang Gao also wrote such a poem, but it does not appear in his *Brilliant Flowers*; see Ŏ Sukkwŏn, *P'aegwan chapki*, in TDYS, 775–76.

16. Joseph S. C. Lam, "The Presence and Absence of Female Musicians and Music in China," in *Women and Confucian Cultures in Premodern China, Korea, and Japan*, ed. Dorothy Ko, JaHyun Kim Haboush, and Joan R. Piggott, 97–120 (Berkeley: University of California Press, 2003), 97–108.

17. 1450 HHJ, 31.

18. 1450 HHJ, 34.

19. 1476 HHJ, 227–28.

20. Zheng Wenbao, "Nan Tang jinshi, in *Wudai shishu huibian*, ed. Fu Xuancong (Hangzhou: Hangzhou chubanshe, 2004), 2, pp. 5062–63.

21. Peng Dingqiu, ed., *Quan Tangshi* (Beijing: Zhonghua shuju, 1960), 524, p. 5998 : 十年一覺揚州夢 贏得青樓薄幸名.

22. Peng Dingqiu, *Quan Tangshi*, 337, p. 3774: 長安眾富兒 盤饌羅膻葷 不解文字飲 惟能醉紅裙 . . .

23. 1476 HHJ, 228.

24. 1464 HHJ, 178.

25. In Zhang's words, "it must be believed that Zeng Shen did not commit murder." Observers were amused that Zhang, who was of lower court rank, could domineer Wu in such a way. *Sejo sillok* 19:34a [1460/3/8, 1]; Sŏng Hyŏn, *Yongjae ch'onghwa*, 1 in TDYS 1, 568.

26. HHJ 1476, 266.

27. Zhang, *Confucian Image Politics*, 3–27; 53–57.

28. *Sŏngjong sillok* 116:6a [1480/4/21, 3].

29. *Sŏngjong sillok* 130:19a [1481/6/21, 1].

30. *Sŏngjong sillok* 214:3a [1488/3/3, 3].

31. Ŏ Sukkwŏn, *P'aegwan chapki* in TDYS 4, 772; Ŏ Sukkwŏn, *A Korean Storyteller's Miscellany: The Paegwan Chapki of O Sukkwon*, trans. Peter H. Lee (Princeton, NJ: Princeton University Press, 1989), 216.

32. Han Myŏnggi, *Imjin Waeran kwa Han-Chung kwan'gye* (Seoul: Yŏksa pip'yŏngsa, 1999), 89–98; 198–223.

33. *Sŏnjo sillok* 151:6a [1602/6/14, 2].

34. *Sŏnjo sillok* 148:12a [1602/3/19, 2].

35. *Sŏnjo sillok* 149:7b [1602/4/14, 2]; Han Myŏnggi, *Imjin waeran*, 214–16.

36. Chŏng Hwan, *Hoesan chip*, 2 in HMC part 2, 2:225b–d.

37. *Chungjong sillok* 43:4a–b [1521/11/22, 3]; *Sŏngjong sillok* 155:7b [1483/6/16]; *Sŏnjo sillok* 149:7b [1602/4/14, 2].

38. *Chungjong sillok* 43:11b [1521/11/24, 3].

39. *Chungjong sillok* 43:43a [1521/12/8, 3], [1521/12/9, 3].

40. Ŏ Sukkwŏn, *P'aegwan chapki* 3 in TDYS 4, 763; Ŏ Sukkwŏn, *A Korean Storyteller's Miscellany*, 184–85.

41. *Chungjong sillok* 43:43b [1521/12/10, 2].

42. *Chungjong sillok* 43:44a–b [1521/12/11, 2–3].

43. *Chungjong sillok* 43:46a [1521/12/14, 3].

44. 1476 HHJ, 319.

45. 1476 HHJ, 320.

46. *Sŏngjong sillok* 64:22a [1476/2/27, 3]. Qi Shun's younger brother, who accompanied him, was reluctant to leave Korea so spare and requested, "on behalf of his brother," several bolts of cloth. See *Sŏngjong sillok* 64:24b [1476/2/28, 3].

47. *Sŏngjong sillok* 64:19a [1476/2/22, 3], 64:21b [1476/2/25, 2].

48. *Yŏnsan'gun ilgi* 5:20b-6:7b; Sŏng Hyŏn, *Yongjae ch'onghwa*, 1 in TDYS 1, 570.

49. Sŏ Kŏjŏng, *P'irwŏn chapki*, 2 in TDYS 3, 685.; *Sejo sillok* 19:26a [1460/3/2, 1], 19:31b [1460/3/4, 1]; Sŏng Hyŏn, *Yongjae ch'onghwa*, 1 in TDYS 1, 567–68. *Sejo sillok* 19:33a–34a [1460/3/7, 1, 3].

50. *Sejo sillok* 8:7a [1457/6/13, 1].

51. Sŏ Kŏjŏng, *P'irwŏn chapki*, 2 in TDYS 3, 685–86.

52. Xu Yuanmei, *Shanyin xianzhi*, ed. Zhu Wenhan, Jiaqing 嘉慶本, Zhongguo fangzhi ku (Beijing: Airusheng, 2009), 14, p. 404; Gao Dengxian, ed., *Shanyin xianzhi*, Chinese Rare Book Collection (Library of Congress), 1662, 29:2a–3a.

53. The funerary epitaph of Chen Jian described him as "delighting only in the collection of old books, paintings, and trinkets," elegant pursuits becoming of a man of letters. In "sensuality," he had no interest, for "when [Chen] was sent as an envoy, courtesans were presented to his service, but he wrote a poem to refuse them." The account embellished the affair further: "the barbarians

夷人 were in awe and carved his poem in a plaque [to honor him]," see Jiao
Hong, *Guochao xianzheng lu*, Scripta Sinica, Mingdai zhuanji congkan, 109–14
(Taipei: Mingwen shuju, 1991), 73:13a–15b.

54. Jiao Hong, *Guochao xianzheng*, 86:9a–10a.
55. Guo Fei, *Yue da ji*, Wanli 萬曆本 [16th century], Zhongguo fangzhi ku (Beijing:
    Airusheng, 2009), 18, pp. 1317–18. For earlier example, see Zhao Zan, *Hong-
    zhi guizhou tujing xinzhi*, Hongzhi 弘治本, [15th century], Zhongguo fangzhi
    ku (Beijing: Airusheng, 2009), 6, pp. 264–65.
56. Xue Yingqi and Hu Zongxian, eds., *Zhejiang tongzhi*, Jiajing 嘉靖本 [16th
    century], Zhongguo fangzhi ku (Beijing: Airusheng, 2009), 179, p. 4335.
57. Lu Qiguang and Shao Ziyi, eds., *Jianchang fuzhi*, Tongzhi 同治本, Zhongguo
    fangzhi ku (Beijing: Airusheng, 2009 [19th century]), renwu 8, p. 1762.
58. Ch'oe Pu, *Kŭmnam chip*, 4 in HMC 16:451c.
59. *Injo sillok* 13:3a [1626/6/7, 1].
60. *Injo sillok* 13:4b [1626/6/10, 3].
61. The account in question comes from a book given to Yi Chŏnggwi 李廷龜
    (1564–1635) from a Chinese envoy. See Cho Yŏngsŏk, *Kwanajae ko* 3 in HMC
    part 2, 67:285d.
62. Gari Ledyard, "Confucianism and War: The Korean Security Crisis of 1598,"
    Journal of Korean Studies 6, no. 1 (1988): 113n67; Joshua Van Lieu, "A Farce That
    Wounds Both High and Low: The Guan Yu Cult in Chosŏn-Ming Relations,"
    Journal of Korean Religions 5, no. 2 (December 2014): 56–65.
63. For one Ming envoy's work, see Kim Hongdae, "Chu Chibŏn [Zhu Zhifan]
    ŭi pyŏngo sahaeng (1606) kwa kŭ ŭi sŏhwa yŏn'gu," *Onji nonch'ong* 11 (2004):
    289–95.
64. Sarah Schneewind, "Beyond Flattery: Legitimating Political Participation in a
    Ming Living Shrine," *The Journal of Asian Studies* 72, no. 2 (May 2013): 345–66.
65. Sarah Schneewind, "Pavilions to Celebrate Honest Officials: An Authenticity
    Dilemma in Fifteenth-Century China," *Journal of the Economic and Social His-
    tory of the Orient* 65, no. 1–2 (2022): 164–213; Zhang, *Confucian Image Politics*,
    3–23.
66. Jiao Hong, *Guochao xianzheng*, 17:169a–175b. Even when no pavilions appeared
    in a posthumous biography of the 1521 vice-envoy Shi Dao, it still claimed that
    his refusal of a copy of the *Brilliant Flowers* led the Korean king to "memo-
    rialize his lofty behavior" to the emperor as similar fictions. See Jiao Hong,
    Guochao xianzheng, 39:87a–96b.
67. Jiao Hong, *Guochao xianzheng*, 52:15a–16b.
68. Jiao Hong, *Guochao xianzheng*, 23:9a–14b.
69. Jiao Hong, *Guochao xianzheng*, 38:97a–99b.
70. Jiao Hong, *Guochao xianzheng*, 54:119b–120a.

71. See Deng Yunlong and Li Yourong, *Sanshui xianzhi*, Jiaqing 嘉慶本 [1819], Zhongguo fangzhi ku (Beijing: Airusheng, 2009), 11, 703–5, for a Vietnamese example. See Yang Junqing and Cheng Kai, *Pinghu xianzhi*, Tianqi 天啟本, Zhongguo fangzhi ku (Beijing: Airusheng, 2009), 15, pp. 835–36; Wang Jianxin, Liu Wenqi, and Zhang Anbao, eds., *Chongxiu Yizheng xianzhi*, Daoguang 道光本 [1890], (Beijing: Airusheng, 2009), 36, pp. 2138–39 for Ryūkyūan cases. See Zhu Changtai and Li Ruizhong, eds., *Changshan xianzhi*, Guangxu 光緒 本 [1908]. Zhongguo fangzhi ku (Beijing: Airusheng, 2009), 47, p. 1079; Feng Keyong and Yang Taiheng, *Cixi xianzhi*, Guangxu 光緒本 [1899], Zhongguo fangzhi ku (Beijing: Airusheng, 2009), 28, pp. 2350–51, for local chieftaincies.

72. Song Huijuan, *Qingdai Zhong-Chao zongfan guanxi shanbian yanjiu* (Changchun: Jilin daxue chubanshe, 2007), 86–88; *Qing Renzong shilu*, See *Qing shilu*, Scripta Sinica (Beijing: Zhonghua shuju, 1936), 42 [1799/4/wuxu], 28, p. 515.

73. Howard J. Wechsler, *Offerings of Jade and Silk: Ritual and Symbol in the Legitimation of the T'ang Dynasty* (New Haven, CT: Yale University Press, 1985), 35.

74. Yan Congjian, *Shizhi wenxian tongbian*, National Central Library (Taiwan), 1565, 8:1b–2a.

75. See the discussion in chapter 7 of this book.

10. THE EAST DOES NOT SUBMIT

1. Yi Saek, *Mogŭn'go*, sigo 2 in HMC 3:529d.

2. 1521 HHJ, 519–31. For Tan'gun and Korean origin myths in Koryŏ and Chosŏn, see Stella Xu, *Reconstructing Ancient Korean History: The Formation of Korean-Ness in the Shadow of History* (London: Lexington, 2016), 54–67.

3. One Ming envoy found it strange that a magical steed was reared in an underwater cavern instead of a stable. Tongmyŏng's connection to P'yŏngyang is specious; Koguryŏ's' capital was not located in P'yŏngyang during his reign, as even Chosŏn visitors pointed out. 1537 HHJ, 595; 1539 HHJ, 895; Hŏ Pong, "Hagok sŏnsaeng Choch'ŏn'gi," *Hagok chip* in HMC 58:407a.

4. Yu Sŭnghyu, "Chewang un'gi," in *Koryŏ myŏnghyŏn chip*, repr, [1287] [1939] (Seoul: Sŏnggyun'gwan taehakkyo Taedong munhwa yŏn'guwŏn, 1973), vol. 1, 636–37; Young-woo Han, "Kija Worship in the Koryŏ and Early Yi Dynasties: A Cultural Symbol in the Relationship Between Korea and China," in *The Rise of Neo-Confucianism in Korea*, ed. William Theodore de Bary and JaHyun Kim Haboush (New York: Columbia University Press, 1985), 358.

5. Sin T'aeyŏng, *Myŏng nara sasin ŭn Chosŏn ŭl ŏttŏke poannŭn'ga: "Hwanghwajip" yŏn'gu* (Seoul: Taunsaem, 2005), 196–206.; *Chungjong sillok* 90:10b [1539/4/5, 2]. On the envoy's decorum see 90:16a [1539/4/7, 4]. On the hierarchy

of different nonverbal ritual gestures, see Endymion Porter Wilkinson, *Chinese History: A Manual* (Cambridge, MA: Harvard Asia Center, 2000), 105–6.

6. Pak Ch'unsŏp, *Chosŏn kwa Myŏng nara munsadŭl ŭi Kija tamnon ŭi chŏn'gae: "Hwanghwajip" yŏn'gu* (Seoul: Pangmunsa, 2018), 26–27, 53–60.

7. Du Huiyue, *Mingdai wenchen chushi Chaoxian yu "Huanghuaji"* (Beijing: Renmin chubanshe, 2010), 59–60; Sin T'aeyŏng, *Myŏng nara sasin*, 180–206; Kim Han'gyu, *Sa Chosŏnnok yŏn'gu: Song, Myŏng, Ch'ŏng sidae Chosŏn sahaengnok ŭi saryojŏk kach'i* (Seoul: Sŏgang taehakkyo ch'ulp'anbu, 2011), 156–61.

8. As in Lefebvre's tripartite model of spatial production as "spatial practice," "spatial representation" and "representational space." See Henri Lefebvre, *The Production of Space* (Malden, MA: Wiley, 1992).

9. Niels Christian Nielsen, *Fundamentalism, Mythos, and World Religions* (Albany: SUNY Press, 1993), 32–44; Jae-Hoon Shim, "A New Understanding of Kija Chosŏn as a Historical Anachronism," *Harvard Journal of Asiatic Studies* 62, no. 2 (December 2002): 273–75, 299–305.

10. Kim Han'gyu, *Sa Chosŏnnok*, 157.

11. Zhu Zhanji, *Da Ming Xuanzong huangdi yuzhi ji*, Siku quanshu cunmu congshu, Ji bu (part 4) 24 (Tainan: Zhuangyan wenhua, 1997), 35:7b.

12. Once the Yongle emperor said to his officials, "I often drink, but not to inebriation. Chosŏn is the country where Kija was enfeoffed, a country of propriety and righteousness, and it serves the Great State with sincerity. Today, I am feting the envoys of Chosŏn. I will drink until I am drunk." *Sejong sillok* 26:18a [1424/10/21, 2].

13. Sŏ Inwŏn, "Chosŏn ch'ogi yŏksa insik kwa yŏng'uk insik: 'Tongguk yŏji sŭngnam' ŭl chungsim ŭro," *Yŏksa wa sirhak* 35 (June 2008): 96.

14. Han, "Kija Worship." As Andre Schmid notes, by the seventeenth century, the Kija lore was less about tributary relations, but Chosŏn's independent claim to moral legitimacy. This discourse, however, was already active in earlier periods. See Andre Schmid, *Korea Between Empires, 1895–1919* (New York: Columbia University Press, 2002), 177–80.

15. Ge Zhaoguang, *Zhaizi Zhongguo: chongjian youguan Zhongguo de lishi lunshu*, 3rd ed. (Taipei: Lianjing, 2011), 41–65, 155–59; Nicolas Tackett, *The Origins of the Chinese Nation: Song China and the Forging of an East Asian World Order* (Cambridge: Cambridge University Press, 2017), 143–210.

16. Alexander Woodside, "Territorial Order and Collective-Identity Tensions in Confucian Asia: China, Vietnam, Korea," *Daedalus* 127, no. 3 (Summer 1998): 199; David C. Kang, *East Asia Before the West: Five Centuries of Trade and Tribute* (New York: Columbia University Press, 2010), 35.

17. 1488 HHJ, 356.

18. These texts are not accurate depictions of actual eleventh century BCE events; of relevance here is the received tradition of Kija, not northeast Asia's early history. Sima Qian, *Shiji (Xinjiaoben Shiji sanjiazhu bing fubian erzhong)* Scripta Sinica (Taipei: Dingwen shuju, 1981), 3, pp. 105–9; 4, p. 131; 38, pp. 1602–21, especially the Zheng Xuan 鄭玄 (127–200) commentary on page 1620. See also the commentaries on the *Zhoushu* 周書 in part 12 of the *Shangshu zhushu* 尚書註疏 in SSJZS 167a–b. See also Xu, *Reconstructing Ancient Korean History*, 29–36.

19. Chosŏn and Ming envoys had to grapple with these incoherencies in their numerous meditations. For a thorough discussion, see Pak Ch'unsŏp, *Chosŏn kwa Myŏng*, especially 61–79.

20. *Analects* 18.1.

21. Sima Qian, *Shiji*, 3, 108–9.

22. Michael Nylan, *The Five "Confucian" Classics* (New Haven, CT: Yale University Press, 2001), 139–40.

23. The 1450 envoy Sima Xun, for example, wrote "His loyalty and righteousness made him willing to depart with Weizi / his heart of benevolence was known only about Confucius" [忠義肯同微子去 仁心唯有仲尼知] and "for millennia, he has been venerated in an old temple in Chosŏn" [千載朝鮮享舊祠]. 1450 HHJ, 37. Nylan, *The Five "Confucian" Classics*, 132–36; 139–42.

24. Here, the Chinese reading of "Chaoxian" for 朝鮮 references Kija's state in the classics in order to distinguish it from Chosŏn Korea.

25. Chen Shou, *Sanguo zhi*, ed. Yang Jialuo, Scripta Sinica, Zhongguo xueshu leibian (Taipei: Dingwen shuju, 1980), 30, pp. 848–49.

26. 1476 HHJ, 234.

27. 1476 HHJ, 235. Other Chosŏn commentators were more direct in their criticism, calling Zhang Jin a "petty man" and "ignorant" for his interpretation of Kija. See Pak Ch'unsŏp, *Chosŏn kwa Myŏng*, 113–15.

28. 1450 HHJ, 37.

29. Hŏ Pong, "Hagok choch'ŏn'gi," in HMC 58:404c, 407a, 409a–b, 410a–b.

30. 1488 HHJ, 429–30.

31. Yi Manpu, *Siksan sŏnsaeng pyŏl chip*, 4 in HMC 179:93d.; *Yŏnsan'gun ilgi* 12:11a [1496/1/13, 6]. For travel inscription in Chosŏn, see Maya K. H. Stiller, *Carving Status at Kŭmgangsan: Elite Graffiti in Premodern Korea* (Seattle: University of Washington Press, 2021).

32. Hŏ Pong, "Hagok choch'ŏn'gi," in HMC 58:404c–d.

33. Yu Hong, *Songdang chip*, 2 in HMC part 2, 3:393a.

34. One rare early Chosŏn collection of epigraphic writing, the *Excellent Selection of Famous Epigraphs* (*Sŭngje yŏngsŏn* 勝題英選), featured Ming writing, all of which predates the 1560s and points to an aesthetic landscape untouched

by the devastation of the Imjin War. See *Sŭngje yŏngsŏn*, Kyujanggak Archives (Seoul National University) Ko (古) 3431–4, vol. 1, 3 (2 missing), 3 vols., 16th century.

35. 1537 HHJ, 582. For a discussion of this trope, see Sixiang Wang, "The Filial Daughter of Kwaksan: Finger Severing, Confucian Virtues, and Envoy Poetry in Early Chosŏn," *Seoul Journal of Korean Studies* 25, no. 2 (December 2012): 204–5.

36. Ŏ Sukkwŏn, *A Korean Storyteller's Miscellany: The Paegwan Chapki of O Sukkwon*, trans. Peter H. Lee (Princeton, NJ: Princeton University Press, 1989), 174; Ŏ Sukkwŏn, *P'aegwan chapki*, in TDYS 1:732, 1:759. A rubbing of the plaque with Gong Yongqing's calligraphy survives in the Kyujanggak archives in Korea. The original inscription, which reads "Fishing village" 漁村, is not mentioned in other textual records. See Gong Yongqing, *Ŏch'on kakcha*, Stone rubbing, 1537, Kyu 28156, Kyujanggak Archives (Seoul National University).

37. *Sejo sillok* 32:24a [1464/2/22, 4]. It is unclear whether the order from 1464 applied to other missions. Nevertheless, requests by Ming envoys to see Korean writing underwent court approval. The casual disclosure of Korean works was discouraged, if not altogether prohibited. See *Chungjong sillok* 84:20b [1537/3/14, 4]; Yu Hŭi-ch'un, *Miam sŏnsaeng chip*, 6 in HMC 34:250c.

38. Ŏ Sukkwŏn, *A Korean Storyteller's Miscellany*, 245–46; Ŏ Sukkwŏn, *P'aegwan chapki*, in TDYS 1:780–81.

39. Hŏ Kyun, *Sŏngsu sihwa*, in Hong Manjong and Chŏ Sŏngjik, *Shihua conglin*, 284. Anthologized in nearly all Korean *hansi* anthologies premodern and modern, it reads: "After a rain on the long dike, grasses are thick. / With a sad song I send you off to the South Bank. / When will the Taedong River cease to flow? / Year after year my tears will swell the waves" [雨歇長堤草色多 送君南浦動悲歌 大同江水何時盡 別淚年年添綠波], translation by Richard J. Lynn in Peter H. Lee, trans., *Anthology of Korean Literature: From Early Times to the Nineteenth Century* (Honolulu: University Press of Hawai'i, 1981), 58. See also Nam Yong'ik, *Jiya jiaozhu*, ed. Zhao Ji (Beijing: Zhonghua shuju, 2008, 74–77.

40. Yi Saek's poem managed to do just that when it received the acclaim of the 1567 envoy Xu Guo. See Hong Manjong and Chŏ Sŏngjik, *Shihua conglin*, 176, 153.

41. For the physical inscription of *ciyun*, see Judith Zeitlin, "Disappearing Verses: Writing on Walls and Anxieties of Loss in Late Imperial China," in *Writing and Materiality in China*, ed. Judith Zeitlin and Lydia H. Liu (Cambridge, MA: Harvard University Asia Center, 2003), 73–125.

42. It is difficult to confirm whether this or any other piece that was "left as an inscription" necessarily ended up adorning a Chosŏn edifice on a permanent basis, but Ming envoys did expect to see the writings of their predecessors.

Sejong sillok 127:31a [1450/1a/19, 3]; Ni Qian, *Chaoxian jishi*, Congshu jicheng chubian 3240 (Beijing: Zhonghua shuju, 1985), 17–18; Li Dongyang, *Huailu tang ji*, SKQS 1250 (Kanseki Repository, 1516), 29:16b. For Chen, see *Tanjong sillok* 2:27b [1452/8/24, 3]; for Zhang, 1460 HHJ, 115, 133. Zhang Ning, *Fengshi lu*, Congshu jicheng chubian 2142 (Shanghai: Shangwu yinshuguan, 1936), 12.

43. In 1522, the court ordered its printing agency 校書館 to enlist more scribes and good calligraphers to prepare the writings of two especially prolific envoys so that local officials could then have them carved in time for the envoy's departure. *Chungjong sillok* 45:30a [1522/7/3, 2].

44. *Sejo sillok* 33:24a [1464/6/2, 4].

45. 1488 HHJ, 382: "Over and over, the envoys have come to Pyŏkche Station; / On its walls are ink, thick with poems left in leisure. / Ascending the pavilion, in the snow and mist, he once composed; / The strength of Lord Ni's brush rivals that of Han Yu" [紛紛使節來碧蹄 壁間濃墨閒留題 登樓雪霽作長賦 倪公筆力凌昌黎].

46. Few, if any, of these pieces survived the Imjin War. Nonetheless, such plaques accorded a Ming envoy lasting visibility. Inscriptions by the 1606 envoy Zhu Zhifan remain to this day. Most notable is his plaque hanging in the Confucian temple at the National Academy, now on the grounds of Sungyungwan University. For Zhu's work in Korea, see Kim Hongdae, "Chu Chibŏn [Zhu Zhifan] ŭi pyŏngo sahaeng (1606) kwa kŭ ŭi sŏhwa yŏn'gu," *Onji nonch'ong* 11 (2004).

47. The sobriquet survives well into the colonial period.

48. The other was "Hwaryŏng" 和寧, which refers to Yi's hometown. *T'aejo sillok* 2:15a [1392/11/29, 1], 3:3b [1393/2/15, 1]. Han, "Kija Worship," 358–59.

49. By the mid-Koryŏ period, a transhistorical idea of Korea was already represented with names such as Haedong (East of the Sea 海東), Ch'ŏnggu (Verdant Hills 青邱), Samhan (Three Hans 三韓), and Tongguk (The Eastern Kingdom 東國). These names linked geographical space to cultural and political continuity. They also transcended dynastic time. Notably, Chosŏn was not one of them, being a distinct name of earlier states. It was associated specifically with Koryŏ's western capital, P'yŏngyang, and referenced the "Three Chosŏns" of Tan'gun, Kija, and Wiman. See Remco E. Breuker, *Establishing a Pluralist Society in Medieval Korea, 918–1170: History, Ideology and Identity in the Koryŏ Dynasty* (Leiden: Brill, 2010), 30–57. For Koryŏ use of titles, see Chŏng Inji, *Koryŏ sa*, 14:14a–15b (hereafter KS), 1:1b, 90:13a–b. For three Chosŏns, see Iryŏn and Yi Pyŏngdo, *Samguk yusa* (Seoul: Tugye haksul chaedan, 1999), 1:1a–b. For P'yŏngyang as a western capital, see KS 58:29a–30b.

50. Liu Ju, *Jiu Tangshu*, ed. Yang Jialuo, Scripta Sinica (Taipei: Dingwen shuju, 1981), 199, 5320.

51. Hyung-Wook Kim, "An Ancient and Glorious Past: Koguryŏ in the Collective Memories of the Korean People" (PhD diss., University of California, Los Angeles, 2012), 20–30; Breuker, *Establishing a Pluralist Society*, 98–102; Han, "Kija Worship," 352–3. See also KS 94:4b–5a, 7:33a–34b.

52. The Liao court chronicler Yelü Yan 耶律儼 (?–1113) referred to Koryŏ as "Silla," implying a refusal to recognize Korean claims to Koguryŏ. Jiang Weigong, "Liaoshi dilizhi Dongjing Liaoyangfu tiao jishi miuwu tanyuan," *Zhongguo bianjian shidi yanjiu*, no. 2 (2011): 123–127.

53. Shim, "A New Understanding of Kija Chosŏn," 299–305.

54. See the commentaries of Du Yu 杜預 (222–285) in Sima Qian, *Shiji*, 38, pp. 1609, 1621.

55. The envoy-author was Guo Yongxi 郭永錫. Why his poem was mentioned in the KS is puzzling, but most likely, the verse was intended to augur the Yuan's doom. KS 11:13a–13b [1366/12]

56. *Sŏnjo sillok* 165:18a [1603/8/13, 1].

57. This scholar, Shi Guifang 史桂芳 (fl. 1558), argued Kija's association with Chaoxian only emerged in later Warring States period texts, not authentic classics. Yi Kyŏngnyong, "Myŏngdae chisigin ŭi Chosŏn insik kwa yangguk ŭi pangbuk chŏngch'aek," *Myŏng-Chŏng sa yŏn'gu* 25 (April 2004): 88–89.

58. The Shandong tomb cast a long shadow over the issue. The late Chosŏn scholar Chŏng Yagyong 丁若鏞 (1762–1836) noted that "many are confused regarding [the location] of Kija's Chaoxian, [believing it to be] in Liaodong," but he was convinced from his research that it was in fact in Korea. He consulted the *Gazetteer of the Ming's Great Unification*; found no mention of other tombs; and was convinced the one in P'yŏngyang was genuine, arguing "there was no reason for Kija to be reburied in China" after having established a state in Korea, a position adopted by his contemporaries. Chŏng did not consult more local Chinese gazetteers, however. They continued to mention a Kija tomb through the late Qing. See Chŏng Yagyong, *Yŏyudang chŏnsŏ* 6, chirijip 1 in HMC 286:230a–231a. See also Hong Kyŏngmo, *Kwanam chŏnsŏ* 16 in HMC part 2, 113:45a–465d; Du Zhao and Yue Jun, *Shandong tongzhi*, Yongzheng, Zhongguo fangzhi ku (Beijing: Airusheng, 2009), 32:37a, 7506. The Guangxu period editors of one gazetteer harbored doubts about their local Kija tomb, stating they would "await those who love antiquity to investigate the evidence" before weighing in; see Meng Guanglai and Chen Siliang, *Caozhoufu Caoxian zhi*, Guangxu [1884] (Beijing: Airusheng, 2009), 1:14b, 155.

59. *Sejong sillok* 3:16b [1419/2/25, 6]; Pyŏn Kyeryang, *Ch'unjŏng sŏnsaeng munjip*, 12 in HMC 8:147a; Han, "Kija Worship," 361–62.

60. *Sejong sillok* 39:13b [1428/1/26, 5]; *Sejong sillok* 3:16b [1419/2/25, 6]. The relevant entries in the *Veritable Records* are split between 1419 and 1428.

61. *Sŏngjong sillok* 29:5b [1473/4/18, 3].

62. *Sŏnjo sujŏng sillok* 16:9a–b [1582/11, 1].

63. Yi I, *Yulgok sŏnsaeng chŏnsŏ*, 34 in HMC 45:321a–b. Han Young-woo argues Yulgok's text, along with Yun Tusu's stabilized the Chosŏn view of Kija; see Han, "Kija Worship," 368–69.

64. Yi I, *Yulgok chŏnsŏ*, 14 in HMC 44:292a–294a.

65. The "eight points" first appear in Fan Ye, *Hou Hanshu*, ed. Li Xian and Yang Jialuo, Scripta Sinica, Zhongguo xueshu leibian (Taipei: Dingwen shuju, 1981), 85, p. 2817.

66. For example, the P'yŏngan Sŏnu 平安 鮮于氏 descent group. Korean genealogies can be reliable, but claims of ancestry before the fourteenth century are often specious or undocumented. Claims of ancestry to the second millennium BCE, such as the Sŏnu did with Kija, were certainly invented traditions. See *Sŏnjo sillok* 165:18a [1603/8/13, 1]; Yun Tusu, *Kija chi*, Asami Collection (University of California, Berkeley), Asami 22.1, vol. 1–3, 1879, segye 世系 1a–4b; Eugene Y. Park, "Old Status Trappings in a New World The 'Middle People' (Chungin) and Genealogies in Modern Korea," *Journal of Family History* 38, no. 2 (April 2013): 166–87.

67. Besides well-known classical texts, Yun also drew on the authority of recent scholars, such as the Ming prince Zhu Quan 朱權 (1391–1448, better known as Hanxuzi 涵虛子). See Yun Tusu, *Oŭm sŏnsaeng yugo*, 3 in HMC 41:545b–d. See also Yun Tusu, *Kija chi*, where the assessments of past authorities worked as definitive textual evidence.

68. The shrine to Tan'gun also supported the idea that Chosŏn was continuous with Kija's Chaoxiao. As an autochthonic progenitor (*sijo* 始祖) of the first Korean kingdom who also lived during the time of the ancient Sage King Yao, Tan'gun asserted that Chosŏn existed before Kija's arrival. Ming envoys, however, were dubious of Tan'gun's historicity. Tang Gao, for example, wrote of Tan'gun's shrine, "[When he] established [his] kingdom, [it was a time] so faint / [It was then,] with this ancestor that Chosŏn first began" [開國何茫然 朝鮮此鼻祖]. 1521 HHJ, 522. See also 1537 HHJ, 597, 600; Pak Ch'unsŏp, *Chosŏn kwa Myŏng*, 42–45, 101–9.

69. 1457 HHJ, 55–56.

70. 1459 HHJ, 110; 1476 HHJ, 213. See similar statements in 1537 HHJ, 755.

71. 1539 HHJ, 935.

72. 1537 HHJ, 595; Eighteenth- and nineteenth-century publications that included maps of P'yŏngyang identify the locations of these fields. These also used Ming envoy writings. See Sŏ Myŏngŭng, *Kija oegi*, Harvard-Yenching Rare Books, TK 3483.4 2980 (P'yŏngyang, 1776), 3:24a–40b; Han Yŏngho and Yun Tusu, *Kija yuji*, Harvard-Yenching Rare Books Movable type, [1878] (Kisŏng [P'yŏngyang],

1922), 4:1a–13b. For well-field maps, see Sŏ Myŏng'ŭng, *Kija oegi*, prefatory pages; illustrations in Yun Tusu, *Kija chi*, 1–3: to 圖 5a–5b. See also *Jitian kao* 箕田考 in Han P'aekkyŏm, *Chosŏn chi*, Siku quanshu cunmu congshu, Shi bu (part 2) 255 (Tainan: Zhuangyan wenhua, 1996), 401–408; Nuri Kim, "Making Myth, History, and an Ancient Religion in Korea" (PhD diss., Harvard University, 2017), 49–53.

73. Anthony Grafton, *Worlds Made by Words: Scholarship and Community in the Modern West* (Cambridge, MA: Harvard University Press, 2009), 146–47; Prys Morgan, "From a Death to a View: The Hunt for the Welsh Past in the Romantic Period," in *The Invention of Tradition*, ed. E. J. Hobsbawm and T. O. Ranger (Cambridge: Cambridge University Press, 1983), 45–47.

74. For the connection between forgery, philology, and political claims, see Charles Garfield Nauert, *Humanism and the Culture of Renaissance Europe* (Cambridge: Cambridge University Press, 1995), 176–77, especially the case of Valla and the Donation of Constantine. See also Anthony Grafton, "Invention of Traditions and Traditions of Invention in Renaissance Europe: The Strange Case of Annius of Viterbo," in *The Transmission of Culture in Early Modern Europe*, ed. Anthony Grafton, Ann Blair, and Shelby Cullom Davis Center for Historical Studies (Philadelphia: University of Pennsylvania Press, 1990), 9–24. Forgeries were less to assert historical truths than to illustrate, through antiquarian examples, received narratives; see Alfred Hiatt and British Library, *The Making of Medieval Forgeries: False Documents in Fifteenth-Century England* (London: British Library and University of Toronto Press, 2004), 5–11, 136–55; Peter H. Wilson, *Heart of Europe: A History of the Holy Roman Empire* (Cambridge, MA: The Belknap Press, 2016), 429.

75. *Sejong sillok* 3:16b [1419/2/25, 6]

76. Sima Qian, *Shiji*, 38, 1620. The 1457 envoy Chen Jian tried to erase this ambiguity by including the direct object pronoun *zhi* 之 to the original phrasing of the *Shiji*: 周封箕子於朝鮮而不臣之; see 1457 HHJ, 55–56.

77. A sobriquet for virtuous officials.

78. 1488 HHJ, 356.

79. Fu Sheng, *Shangshu dazhuan*, SKQS (Kanseki Repository, 1778), 3:4a–4b: 箕子既受周之封 不得無臣禮 故於十三祀來朝.

80. Ouyang Xiu and Song Qi, *Xin Tangshu*, ed. Yang Jialuo (Taipei: Dingwen shuju), 100, pp. 3932–33.

81. Pyŏn Kyeryang, *Ch'unjŏng chip* 12 in HMC 8:147a.

82. Pyŏn's version phrase combines the phrasing of the *Mao Commentaries* with the *Shangshu jingyi* commentaries of the *Great Plan* to create an entirely new meaning. The former uses 不臣之志 in a negative sense, while the latter understands 遂其不臣 to be more of a gesture of magnanimity on the part of the

Zhou king. See Duan Changwu 段昌武, *Maoshi jijie* 毛詩集解, SKQS Zhong-guo jiben guji ku (Beijing: Airusheng, 2009), 20:1a–b, 289; Huang Lun 黃倫, *Shangshu jingyi* 尚書精義, SKQS (Kanseki Repository, 1180), 28:10b.

83. Pyŏn also ascribed Korea's cultural parity "entirely" to Kija's teachings, implicitly diminishing the civilizing influence of later imperial dynasties. Therefore, Kija allowed for Korean cultural difference, without conceding inferiority.

84. 1488 HHJ, 358, 356. This interpretation remained dominant through the end of the Chosŏn period. When Chosŏn intellectuals rejected Qing moral authority and saw themselves as the rightful heirs of the classical tradition, Hong Chikp'il 洪直弼 (1776–1852) took this logic one step further and rejected even the *Grand Historian* account. In the essay, "Disputing the tribute to Zhou" (*Choju pyŏn* 朝周辯), written in 1834, he asserted that King Wu and Kija were both "sages" and treated each other as equals, which implied that Wu would never have invested Kija in the first place. Therefore, the *Grand Historian* must have confused Kija with a different Shang prince due to an exegetical error. Hong also maintained that Kija never paid tribute to the Zhou and ruled his kingdom, Korea, as a sovereign. Hong Chikp'il, *Maesan sŏnsaeng munjip*, 27 in HMC 296:6a–7a; Han Yŏngho and Yun Tusu, *Kija yuji*, 7:4a–5a. For Kija and the rejection of Qing legitimacy, see Hyung Il Pai, *Constructing "Korean" Origins: A Critical Review of Archaeology, Historiography, and Racial Myth in Korean State-Formation Theories* (Cambridge, MA: Harvard University Asia Center, 2000), 113–14.

85. See 1460 HHJ, 136–37; Zhang Ning, *Fengshi lu*, 2, 20–21. Zhang Ning's essay was inscribed at Kija's shrine and quoted by later Chosŏn scholars; see Yu Hŭiyŏng, *Kyogam p'yoje ŭmju Tongguk saryak*, Kojŏn charyo ch'ongsŏ 85–2 (Kyŏnggi-do Sŏngnam-si: Han'guk chŏngsin munhwa yŏn'guwŏn, 1985), 1; Sŏ Myŏng'ŭng, *Kija oegi*, 3:8a–10a.

86. Dong Gao, QTW, 587, pp. 5927a–b.

87. 1521 HHJ, 515.

88. 1521 HHJ, 518.

89. 1521 HHJ, 518.

90. Yi wrote, "In the past when the Zhou did not make Kija a subject / his enfeoffed land was by the edge of the River P'ae" [昔周之不臣夫子兮 胙茅土於浿之澨]. 1521 HHJ, 515. For further discussion of the *buchen* and investiture issue, see Pak Ch'unsŏp, *Chosŏn kwa Myŏng*, 61–67, 95–100, 269–70.

91. Lefebvre, *The Production of Space*, 33.

92. Schmid, *Korea Between Empires*, 175–188; Henry Em, *The Great Enterprise: Sovereignty and Historiography in Modern Korea* (Durham, NC: Duke University Press, 2013). Kija's effacement was a process that was more gradual than usually appreciated, as Kojong's use of Kija demonstrates, see *Kojong sillok* 25:57a [1888/11/25, 1].

93. See Sun Weiguo, "Chuanshuo, lishi yu rentong: Tanjun Chaoxian yu Jizi Chaoxian zhi suzao yu yanbian," in *Cong zhoubian kan zhongguo*, ed. Ge Zhaoguang 葛兆光 et al. (Beijing: Zhonghua shuju, 2009), 313–15, for historicity of Kija, 320–23 for Tan'gun myth, 330–35 for both in colonial period. For Tan'gun's entry into mainstream history, see Pai, *Constructing "Korean" Origins*, 111–121. For a process intertwined with the emergence of the Taejonggyo, see Kim, "Making Myth," 27–44, 230–44. For Kija's relics in North Korea, see Sergei O. Kurbanov, "North Korea's Juche Ideology: Indigenous Communism or Traditional Thought?," *Critical Asian Studies* 51, no. 2 (April 2019): 299–301; Vladimír Glomb and Eun-Jeung Lee, "Between Ruins and Relics: North Korean Discourse on Confucian Academies," in *Confucian Academies in East Asia* (Leiden: Brill, 2020), 466.

94. Cho Uyŏn, "Chungguk hakkye ŭi 'Kija Chosŏn' yŏn'gu wa kŭ pip'an e taehan kŏmt'o," *Ko Chosŏn Tan'gun hak*, no. 26 (May 2012): 457–516; Yi Sŏnggyu, "Chungguk sahakkye esŏ pon Ko Chosŏn" 49 (August 2011): 25–28. For the connection between Kija and irredentism, see Cho Wŏnjin, "Kija Chosŏn yŏn'gu sŏnggwa wa kwaje," *Ko Chosŏn Tan'gun hak*, no. 20 (May 2009): 395–441.

95. A view linked to the status of Koguryŏ as ancestral to modern Korea. Kija has also become a battleground for the nature of early Chinese influence on Korea, but unlike Koguryŏ's "national" identity which once escalated to the level of diplomatic confrontation, Kija is for now largely relegated to the footnotes of scholars. See Donghun Jung, "Chinese Academic Research on the History of Sino-Korean Relations: The Work of Chen Shangsheng," *The Review of Korean Studies* 24, no. 1 (2021): 340–41. For Koguryŏ in modern Korea, see Kim, "An Ancient and Glorious Past," 123–63; Andre Schmid, "Rediscovering Manchuria: Sin Ch'aeho and the Politics of Territorial History in Korea," *The Journal of Asian Studies* 56, no. 1 (February 1997): 26–46. For the Koguryŏ debate and its relationship to modern Chinese and Korean nationalism, see Mark E. Byington, "A Matter of Territorial Security: China's Historiographical Treatment of Koguryŏ in the Twentieth Century," in *Nationalism and History Textbooks in Asia and Europe—Diverse Views on Conflicts Surrounding History* (Seoul: The Center for Information on Korean Culture, Academy of Korean Studies, 2005), 147–75.

CONCLUSION: THE MYTH OF MORAL EMPIRE

1. *Sŏnjo sujŏng sillok* 25:14a–b [1591/5, 3]. Perhaps evidence of Chosŏn loyalty to Ming, or simply not being oblivious to this textbook ruse of "borrowing a path to attack Guo" 假道伐虢.

2. David C. Kang, *East Asia Before the West: Five Centuries of Trade and Tribute* (New York: Columbia University Press, 2010), 93–98; Kenneth Swope, *A*

Dragon's Head and a Serpent's Tail: Ming China and the First Great East Asian War, 1592–1598 (Norman: University of Oklahoma Press, 2009), 50, 62–64; Nam-lin Hur, "The Celestial Warriors: Ming Military Aid and Abuse During the Korean War, 1592–8," in *The East Asian War, 1592–1598: International Relations, Violence and Memory*, ed. James B. Lewis (New York: Routledge, 2014), 243; James B. Lewis, ed., *The East Asian War, 1592–1598: International Relations, Violence and Memory* (New York: Routledge, 2014), 264–67.

3. Du Huiyue, *Mingdai wenchen chushi Chaoxian yu "Huanghuaji"* (Beijing: Renmin chubanshe, 2010), 256–260.

4. *Sŏnjo sillok* 27:6b–8a [1592/6/13, 7].

5. MSL *Shenzong* 250, 4648–49 [1592/7/3]

6. See *Sŏnjo sillok* 33:6b [1592/12/8, 2]; Sin Kyŏng, *Chaejo pŏnbang chi*, 2 in TDYS 36:36b–37a; Gari Ledyard, "Confucianism and War: The Korean Security Crisis of 1598," *Journal of Korean Studies* 6, no. 1 (1988): 82–85.

7. Some Ming officials continued to oppose Ming involvement, even after the emperor had committed his troops. One Jiang Yingke 江盈科 (1553–1605) treated the war as a pointless military venture, comparing it to the Yongle emperor's invasion of Vietnam; see Jiang Yingke, *Xuetaoge ji* (Beijing: Xichu Jiangshi, 1600), 6:24a–28a. See also Ledyard, "Confucianism and War," 86–88.

8. Pak Tongnyang, *Kijae sach'o* 2 in TDYS 10:47b.

9. Sin Kyŏng, *Chaejo* 2 in TDYS 7: 37a

10. Chŏng Konsu, *Paekkok sŏnsaeng chip* 3 in HMC 48:447b-449d.

11. The results would have been unclear if *naebu* had been enacted, but direct imperial administration under a *junxian* model is possible. See *Sŏnjo sillok* 27:8b [1592/6/14, 5], 27:10a [1592/6/16], 27:17b [1592/6/26], 28:15a [1592/7/11, 5].

12. *Sŏnjo sillok* 34:18b–19a [1593/1/12, 3].

13. As Nam-lin Hur argues, the "Ming-Chosŏn relationship had never been clearly defined in terms of reciprocal security arrangements." For Ming discussions of intervention, see Hur, "The Celestial Warriors," 238–45.

14. JaHyun Kim Haboush, *The Great East Asian War of 1592 and the Birth of the Korean Nation*, ed. William Joseph Haboush and Jisoo M. Kim, 93–105 (New York: Columbia University Press, 2016); Swope, *A Dragon's Head*, 187–95. *Sŏnjo sillok* 8 47:26b [1594/1/27, 5], 48:1b [1594/2/2, 3], 48:3a [1594/2/4, 2], 48:10b [1594/2/8, 3], 55:20b [1594/9/15, 4], 61:23a [1595/3/26, 2].

15. Masato Hasegawa, "Provisions and Profits in a Wartime Borderland: Supply Lines and Society in the Border Region Between China and Korea, 1592–1644" (PhD diss., Yale University, 2013), 107–131.

16. Sixiang Wang, "Loyalty, History, and Empire: Qian Qianyi and His Korean Biographies," in *Representing Lives in East Asia, China and Korea 1400–1900*,

ed. Ihor Pidhainy, Grace Fong, and Roger Des Forges, 321–29 (Ithaca, NY: Cornell University East Asia Program, 2018).

17. Seung B. Kye, "In the Shadow of the Father: Court Opposition and the Reign of King Kwanghae in Early Seventeenth-Century Choson Korea" (PhD diss., University of Washington, 2006), 42–55.

18. As proposed by Xu Guangqi 徐光啓 (1562–1633) and others. King Kwanghae and his envoys protested these proposals. See Xu Guangqi, *Xu Guangqi ji* (Shanghai: Zhonghua shuju, 1963), 3, 111; Kye, "In the Shadow of the Father," 198–218.

19. *Sŏnjo sillok* 44:6b [1593/11/9, 3], 109:27b [1599/2/19, 2]; Kye, "In the Shadow of the Father," 238–45; 261–65.

20. Adam Bohnet, *Turning Toward Edification: Foreigners in Chosŏn Korea* (Honolulu: University of Hawai'i Press, 2020), 135–51.

21. For an account, see Na Man-gap, *The Diary of 1636: The Second Manchu Invasion of Korea*, trans. George L Kallander (New York: Columbia University Press, 2020).

22. To be sure, direct administration was not a prerequisite for entering the imperial fold. For more about the Mongol nobles, see Nicola Di Cosmo, "Qing Colonial Administration in Inner Asia," *The International History Review* 20, no. 2 (1998): 287–309.

23. The Samjŏndo stele, also known as the "Accomplishments of the Great Qing Emperor" stele 大清皇帝功德碑. See "Tae Ch'ŏng hwangje kongdŏk pi" (stele rubbing, 1639), 20, Asami Collection (University of California, Berkeley).

24. To be sure, direct administration was not a prerequisite for entering the imperial fold. For more about the Mongol nobles, see Di Cosmo, "Qing Colonial Administration."

25. Yuanchong Wang, "Claiming Centrality in the Chinese World: Manchu-Chosŏn Relations and the Making of the Qing's Zhongguo Identity, 1616–1643," *Chinese Historical Review* 22, no. 2 (November 2015): 31–49.

26. A stele whose text and ritual use was a product of Qing and (reluctant) Korean coproduction, see Pae Usŏng, *Chosŏn kwa Chunghwa: Chosŏn i kkum kkugo sangsang han segye wa munmyŏng* (Kyŏnggi-do P'aju-si: Tolbegae, 2014), 33–55.

27. Peter Galison, "Trading Zone: Coordinating Action and Belief," in *The Science Studies Reader*, ed. Mario Biagioli (New York: Routledge, 1999), 138.

28. Joshua Van Lieu, "The Politics of Condolence: Contested Representations of Tribute in Late Nineteenth-Century Chosŏn-Qing Relations," *Journal of Korean Studies* 14, no. 1 (2009).

29. Takemichi Hara, "Korea, China, and Western Barbarians: Diplomacy in Early Nineteenth-Century Korea," *Modern Asian Studies* 32, no. 2 (May 1998):

389–430; Kirk W. Larsen, "Comforting Fictions: The Tribute System, the West-phalian Order, and Sino-Korean Relations," *Journal of East Asian Studies* 13, no. 2 (May–August 2013): 242–47; Jihoon Chun, "Late Nineteenth Century Ching-Chosŏn Union of Upper State and Subject State" (Choson History Society, Los Angeles; Bochum, October 26, 2021).

30. John King Fairbank, ed., *The Chinese World Order: Traditional China's Foreign Relations* (Cambridge, MA: Harvard University Press, 1968); Peter Weber-Schafer, *Oikumene und Imperium: Studien zur Ziviltheologie des chinesischen Kaiserreichs* (Bern: Peter Lang, 1968); Takeshi Hamashita, Linda Grove, and Mark Selden, *China, East Asia and the Global Economy: Regional and Historical Perspectives* (New York: Routledge, 2008); Fuma Susumu, *Chōsen enkōshi to Chōsen tsūshinshi* (Nagoya: Nagoya daigaku shuppankai, 2015); Huang Zhilian, *Dong Ya de liyi shijie: Zhongguo fengjian wangchao yu Chaoxian bandao guanxi xingtai lun* (Beijing: Zhongguo renmin daxue chubanshe, 1994); Yuanchong Wang, *Remaking the Chinese Empire: Manchu-Korean Relations, 1616–1911* (Ithaca, NY: Cornell University Press, 2018); Wang Hui, *Ya Zhou shi ye: Zhongguo lishi de xushu* (Hong Kong: Oxford University Press, 2010); Zhao Tingyang. "Rethinking Empire from the Chinese Concept 'All-Under-Heaven' (Tianxia)," in *China Orders the World: Normative Soft Power and Foreign Policy*, ed. William A. Callahan and Elena Barabantseva (Washington, DC: Woodrow Wilson Center Press, 2011); Zhao Tingyang, *Tianxia tixi: Shijie zhidu zhexue daolun* (Nanjing: Jiangsu jiaoyu chubanshe, 2005); Jiang Shigong, "Yiguo zhi mi: Zhongguo vs. Diguo," *Gongfa pinglun*, November 15, 2008; Jiang Shigong, "Chao daxing zhengzhi shiti de neizai luoji: 'diguo' yu shijie zhixu," Ai Sixiang, April 16, 2019; Jiang Shigong, "Jiang Shigong, 'Empire and World Order,'" trans. David Ownby, *Reading the China Dream*, accessed January 27, 2022; Timothy Brook, "Great States," *The Journal of Asian Studies* 75, no. 4 (November 2016).

31. Ludwig Wittgenstein, *Philosophical Investigations*, 4th ed., ed. P. M. S Hacker and Joachim Schulte (Oxford: Wiley-Blackwell, 2009), 65–66.

32. An observation made by Devin Fitzgerald upon reading an earlier version of this draft in December 2021. See also Devin Fitzgerald, "The Ming Open Archive and the Global Reading of Early Modern China" (PhD diss., Harvard University, 2020), 22–39.

33. That is, what "world empire" should look like, as described in Carl Schmitt, *The Nomos of the Earth in the International Law of the Jus Publicum Europaeum*, trans. G. L. Ulmen (Candor, NY: Telos, 2006).

34. The problem of empire making is one that transcends the issue of state making (even if an imperial order relies on powerful nation states to enforce its rules), as suggested in Michael Hardt and Antonio Negri, *Empire* (Cambridge, MA: Harvard University Press, 2000).

35. Pei Wang and Daniel A. Bell, *Just Hierarchy: Why Social Hierarchies Matter in China and the Rest of the World* (Princeton, NJ: Princeton University Press, 2020), 132–140.

36. Story by H. R. McMaster, "How China Sees the World," *The Atlantic*, May 2020; Howard W. French, *Everything Under the Heavens: How the Past Helps Shape China's Push for Global Power* (New York: Knopf Doubleday Publishing Group, 2017); Michael Schuman, "What Happens When China Leads the World," *The Atlantic*, October 5, 2020.

37. Vincent Garton, "Jiang Shigong's Chinese World Order," *Palladium* (blog), February 5, 2020.

38. Note the aspirational optimism in Paek Yŏngsŏ, "Zhonghua diguo zai dongya de yiyi: tansuo pipanxing de Zhongguo yanjiu," *Kaifang shidai*, 2014. To see Chosŏn Korea as imperial stakeholders also helps explain the seemingly contradictory diplomatic posture of the Chosŏn court and its elites in the face of Qing rule. They denied Manchu Qing legitimacy and asserted Ming loyalism, even as they sought to remain the Qing Empire's first and most loyal vassal. But if Chosŏn was deeply maintaining a normative notion of what a proper empire should be (not ruled by Manchus) and also seeking to preserve its preeminent place in the imperial order (as its first vassal), then these actions, however inconsistent they might first appear, in fact speak to the continuous sense of Korean investment in the imperial project in the longue durée.

Bibliography

DATABASES

Chosŏn Wangjo sillok 朝鮮王朝實錄, https://sillok.history.go.kr/.
Scripta Sinica, 漢籍全文資料庫計畫, http://hanchi.ihp.sinica.edu.tw/.
Han'guk kojŏn chonghap DB, 한국고전종합DB, https://db.itkc.or.kr/.
Zhongguo fangzhi ku, 中國方志庫, http://server.wenzibase.com/.

WORKS CITED

Agamben, Giorgio. *State of Exception*. Chicago: University of Chicago Press, 2005.
Ahn, Juhn Y. *Buddhas and Ancestors: Religion and Wealth in Fourteenth-Century Korea*. Seattle: University of Washington Press, 2018.
Akin, Alexander. "Printed Maps in Late Ming Publishing Culture: A Trans-Regional Perspective." PhD diss., Harvard University, 2009.
Allsen, Thomas T. *Culture and Conquest in Mongol Eurasia*. Cambridge: Cambridge University Press, 2001.
——. "The Rise of the Mongolian Empire and Mongolian Rule in North China." In *The Cambridge History of China Volume 6: Alien Regimes and Border States, 907–1368*, ed. Herbert Franke and Denis C. Twitchett, 321–413. Cambridge: Cambridge University Press, 1994.
Alston, Dane. "Emperor and Emissary: The Hongwu Emperor, Kwŏn Kŭn, and the Poetry of Late Fourteenth Century Diplomacy." *Korean Studies* 32 (2008): 101–47.
Alston, William P. *Illocutionary Acts and Sentence Meaning*. Ithaca, NY: Cornell University Press, 2000.

Ames, Roger T. *Confucian Role Ethics: A Vocabulary*. Beijing: Chinese University Press, 2011.

An Changni. "Chosŏn chŏn'gi 'Hwanghwajip' mit Myŏng sasin ŭi Chosŏn kwallyŏn sŏjok ch'ulp'an e taehan yŏn'gu" 朝鮮 前期『皇華集 』및 明使臣의 朝鮮關聯書籍 出版에 대한 연구. *Kugŏ kyoyuk* 107 (2002): 347–71.

Anderson, Benedict R. *Imagined Communities: Reflections on the Origin and Spread of Nationalism*. New York: Verso, 1991.

An Kihyŏk. "Yŏmal Sŏnch'o tae Chungguk kwan'gye wa Kugwang siho" 여말선초 대중국관계와 國王諡號. *Yŏksa wa hyŏnsil* 104 (June 2017): 229–62.

Ariffin, Yohan, Jean-Marc Coicaud, and Vesselin Popovski, eds. *Emotions in International Politics: Beyond Mainstream International Relations*. Cambridge: Cambridge University. Press, 2017.

Arkush, R. David, and Leo Ou-fan Lee. *Land Without Ghosts: Chinese Impressions of America from the Mid-Nineteenth Century to the Present*. Berkeley: University of California Press, 1989.

Atwood, Christopher P. "Legal Norms and Apocalyptic Dreams: Inter-Polity Relations in the Long Mongol Century." Unpublished manuscript, last modified September 6, 2019.

——. *The Rise of the Mongols: Five Chinese Sources*. Indianapolis, IN: Hackett, 2021.

Austin, John Langshaw. *How to Do Things with Words*. London: Oxford University Press, 1975.

Baldanza, Kathlene. "The Ambiguous Border: Early Modern Sino-Viet Relations." PhD diss., University of Pennsylvania, 2010.

——. "De-Civilizing Ming China's Southern Border: Vietnam as Lost Province or Barbarian Culture." In *Chinese History in Geographical Perspective*, ed. Jeff Kyong-McClain and Yongtao Du, 55–70. Lanham, MD: Lexington, 2013.

——. *Ming China and Vietnam: Negotiating Borders in Early Modern Asia*. Cambridge: Cambridge University Press, 2016.

Bang, Peter F., and C. A. Bayly, eds. *Tributary Empires in Global History*. New York: Palgrave Macmillan, 2011.

Bang, Peter F., and Dariusz Kołodziejczyk, eds. *Universal Empire: A Comparative Approach to Imperial Culture and Representation in Eurasian History*. Cambridge: Cambridge University Press, 2012.

Barber, Karin. *The Anthropology of Texts, Persons and Publics: Oral and Written Culture in Africa and Beyond*. Cambridge: Cambridge University Press, 2007.

Barkey, Karen. *Empire of Difference: The Ottomans in Comparative Perspective*. Cambridge: Cambridge University Press, 2008.

Bayly, C. A. *Imperial Meridian: The British Empire and the World, 1780–1830*. London: Longman, 1989.

Bell, Catherine. *Ritual: Perspectives and Dimensions*. Rev. ed. New York: Oxford University Press, 2009.

Benite, Zvi Ben-Dor, Stefanos Geroulanos, and Nicole Jerr, eds. *The Scaffolding of Sovereignty: Global and Aesthetic Perspectives on the History of a Concept*. New York: Columbia University Press, 2017.

Benton, Lauren A. *A Search for Sovereignty: Law and Geography in European Empires, 1400–1900*. Cambridge: Cambridge University Press, 2010.

Berger, Peter L., and Thomas Luckmann. *The Social Construction of Reality: A Treatise in the Sociology of Knowledge*. New York: Penguin, 1967.

Bohnet, Adam. "Ruling Ideology and Marginal Subjects: Ming Loyalism and Foreign Lineages in Late Choson Korea." *Journal of Early Modern History* 15, no. 6 (November 2011): 477–505.

——. *Turning Toward Edification: Foreigners in Chosŏn Korea*. Honolulu: University of Hawai'i Press, 2020.

Bol, Peter K. *Neo-Confucianism in History*. Cambridge, MA: Harvard Asia Center, 2008.

Bourdieu, Pierre. *Language and Symbolic Power*, ed. John Brookshire Thompson, trans. Matthew Adamson and Gino Raymond. Cambridge: Polity Press, 1991.

Breuker, Remco E. *Establishing a Pluralist Society in Medieval Korea, 918–1170: History, Ideology and Identity in the Koryŏ Dynasty*. Leiden: Brill, 2010.

——. "Koryŏ as an Independent Realm: The Emperor's Clothes." *Korean Studies* 27, no. 1 (January 2003): 48–84.

——. "The Three in One, the One in Three: The Koryŏ Three Han as a Pre-Modern Nation." *Journal of Inner and East Asian Studies* 2, no. 2 (December 2005): 144–67.

——. "Within or Without? Ambiguity of Borders and Koryŏ Koreans' Travels During the Liao, Jin, Song, and Yuan." *East Asian History*, no. 38 (2014): 47–62.

Brook, Timothy. *The Confusions of Pleasure: Commerce and Culture in Ming China*. Berkeley: University of California Press, 1998.

——. "Great States." *The Journal of Asian Studies* 75, no. 4 (November 2016): 957–72.

Brook, Timothy, M. C. van Walt van Praag, and Miek Boltjes, eds. *Sacred Mandates: Asian International Relations Since Chinggis Khan*. Chicago: University of Chicago Press, 2018.

Brose, Michael C. "Uyghur Technologists of Writing and Literacy in Mongol China." *T'oung Pao*, Second Series, 91, no. 4/5 (January 2005): 396–435.

Buc, Philippe. *The Dangers of Ritual Between Early Medieval Texts and Social Scientific Theory*. Princeton, NJ: Princeton University Press, 2009.

Burbank, Jane, and Frederick Cooper. *Empires in World History: Power and the Politics of Difference*. Princeton, NJ: Princeton University Press, 2010.

Byington, Mark E., ed. *The Han Commanderies in Early Korean History*. Illustrated ed. Cambridge, MA: Korea Institute, 2014.

——. "A Matter of Territorial Security: China's Historiographical Treatment of Koguryŏ in the Twentieth Century." In *Nationalism and History Textbooks in Asia and Europe—Diverse Views on Conflicts Surrounding History*, 147–75. Seoul: The Center for Information on Korean Culture, Academy of Korean Studies, 2005.

Cai Meihua, and Zhao Ji, eds. *Hanguo shihua quanbian jiaozhu* 韓國詩話全編校注. Beijing: Renmin wenxue chubanshe, 2012.

Callahan, William A. *Sensible Politics: Visualizing International Relations*. New York: Oxford University Press, 2020.

——. "Tianxia, Empire, and the World: Chinese Visions of World Order for the Twenty-First Century." In *China Orders the World: Normative Soft Power and Foreign Policy*, ed. William A. Callahan and Elena Barabantseva. Washington, DC: Woodrow Wilson Center Press, 2011.

Cha, Hyewon. "Was Joseon a Model or an Exception? Reconsidering the Tributary Relations During Ming China." *Korea Journal* 51, no. 4 (Winter 2011): 33–58.

Cha, Javier. "To Build a Centralizing Regime: Yangban Aristocracy and Medieval Patrimonialism." *Seoul Journal of Korean Studies* 32, no. 1 (2019): 35–80.

——. "The Civilizing Project in Medieval Korea: Neo-Classicism, Nativism, and Figurations of Power." PhD diss., Harvard University, 2014.

Ch'a Ch'ŏllo 車天輅. *Osan sŏllim ch'ogo* 五山說林草藁. Reprint [17th century]. TDYS. Kyŏngsŏng [Seoul]: Chosŏn kosŏ kanhaenghoe, 1909.

Chan, Hok-lam. *Legitimation in Imperial China: Discussions under the Jurchen-Chin Dynasty (1115–1234)*. Seattle: University of Washington Press, 1984.

——. "Wang O (1190–1273)." *Papers on Far Eastern History* 12 (September 1975): 43–70.

Chan, Hok-lam, and Laurie Dennis. "Frenzied Fictions: Popular Beliefs and Political Propaganda in the Written History of Ming Taizu." In *Long Live the Emperor!: Uses of the Ming Founder Across Six Centuries of East Asian History*, ed. Sarah Schneewind, 15–33. Minneapolis: Society for Ming Studies, 2008.

Chang, Howard. *After Eunuchs: Science, Medicine, and the Transformation of Sex in Modern China*. New York: Columbia University Press, 2018.

Chang Tongik. *Songdae Yŏsa charyo chimnok* 宋代麗史資料集錄. Seoul: Sŏul taehakkyo ch'ulp'anbu, 2000.

——. *Wŏndae Yŏsa charyo chimnok* 元代麗史資料集錄. Seoul: Sŏul taehakkyo ch'ulp'anbu, 1997.

Chen, Jack W., and David Schaberg, eds. *Idle Talk: Gossip and Anecdote in Traditional China*. Berkeley: University of California Press, 2014.

Chen, Li. *Chinese Law in Imperial Eyes: Sovereignty, Justice, and Transcultural Politics*. New York: Columbia University Press, 2016.

Chen Long and Shen Zaiquan. "Chaoxian yu Ming Qing biaojian waijiao wenti yanjiu" 朝鮮與明清表箋外交問題研究. *Zhongguo bianjiang shidi yanjiu* 20, no. 1 (2010): 61–68.

Chen Qiyou, ed. *Han Feizi* 韓非子. Beijing: Zhonghua shuju, 1958.

Chen Shou 陳壽. *Sanguo zhi* 三國志. Ed. Yang Jialuo. Taipei: Dingwen shuju, 1980.

Chen Xuelin [Chan Hok-lam]. *Mingdai renwu yu chuanshuo* 明代人物與傳說. Hong Kong: Zhongwen daxue chubanshe, 1997.

Chen Yiqiu. "Cong Chaoxian shichen de Zhongguo xingji kan Mingdai zhonghouqi de Yuhe guan: yi Huitong guan tiduguan wei zhongxin" 從朝鮮使臣的中國行紀看明代中後期的玉河館—以會同館提督官為中心. *Nanjing xiaozhuang xueyuan xuebao* 3 (2014): 57–76.

Cho Uyŏn. "Chungguk hakkye ŭi 'Kija Chosŏn' yŏn'gu wa kŭ pip'an e taehan kŏmt'o" 중국학계의 '箕子朝鮮' 연구와 그 비판에 대한 검토. *Ko Chosŏn Tan'gun hak* 26 (May 2012): 457–516.

Cho Wi 曺偉. *Maegye chip* 梅溪集. Reprint [1718]. HMC 16. Seoul: Minjok munhwa ch'ujinhoe, 1988.

Cho Wŏnjin. "Kija Chosŏn yŏn'gu sŏnggwa wa kwaje" 기자조선 연구의 성과와 과제. *Ko Chosŏn Tan'gun hak* 20 (May 2009): 395–441.

Cho Yongch'ŏl. "Chosŏn ch'ogi Yŏjin kwan'gye ŭi pyŏnhwa wa tongbungmyŏn chiyŏk chinch'ul kwajŏng: Sejong 14 nyŏn (1432) Yŏngbukchin sŏlchi ijŏn sigi rŭl chungsim ŭro" 조선 초기 여진 관계의 변화와 동북면 지역 진출 과정—世宗 14 년 (1432) 영북진 설치 이전 시기를 중심으로. *Yŏksa hakpo* 233 (2017): 39–73.

Cho Yŏngnok. "Sŏnch'o ŭi Chosŏn ch'ulsin Myŏngsa ko—Sŏngjong cho ŭi tae Myŏng kyosŏp kwa Myŏngsa Chŏng Tong–" 鮮初의 朝鮮出身 明使考—成宗朝의 對明交涉과 明使 鄭同–. *Kuksagwan nonch'ong* 14 (1990): 107–34.

Cho Yŏngsŏk 趙榮祏. *Kwanajae ko* 觀我齋稿. HMC (sok) (續) 67. Seoul: Minjok munhwa ch'ujinhoe, 2008.

Ch'oe Chongsŏk. "Chosŏn ch'ogi yŏngjorye unyŏng kwa Pŏn'guk ŭiju" 조선초기 迎詔禮 운영과 『蕃國儀注』. *Yŏksa wa tamnon* 86 (April 2018): 139–77.

——. "Chosŏn ch'ogi kukka wisang kwa 'Sŏnggyo chayu'" 조선초기 국가 위상과 '聲教自由.' *Han'guk sa yŏn'gu* 162 (September 2013): 3–44.

——. "Chosŏn ch'ogi 'siwang chi che' nonŭi kujo ŭi t'ŭkching kwa chunghwa pop'yŏn ŭi ch'ugu" 조선초기 "시왕지제(時王之制)" 논의 구조의 특징과 중화 보편의 추구. *Chosŏn sidae sahakpo*, no. 52 (2010): 5–59.

——. "Koryŏ malgi, Chosŏn ch'ogi yŏngjo ŭirye e kwanhan saeroun ihae mosaek 'Pŏn'guk ŭiju ŭi sogae wa pogwŏn'" 고려말기, 조선초기 迎詔儀禮에 관한 새로운 이해 모색-『蕃國儀注』의 소개와 복원-. *Minjok munhwa yŏn'gu* 69 (2015): 269–309.

Ch'oe Hang 崔恒, and Sŏ Kŏjŏng 徐居正, eds. *Kyŏngguk taejŏn* 經國大典. Asami Collection (University of California, Berkeley) 18.10, vol. 1-4. Seoul, 1603 [15th century].

Ch'oe Pu 崔溥. *Ch'oe Pu's Diary: A Record of Drifting Across the Sea*, trans. John Thomas Meskill. Tucson: University of Arizona Press, 1965.

——. *Kŭmnam chip* 錦南集. Reprint [1676]. HMC 16. Seoul: Minjok munhwa ch'ujinhoe, 1988.

——. "P'yohae rok" 漂海錄. In *Kŭmnam chip*. Reprint [1676]. HMC 16. Minjok munhwa ch'ujinhoe, 1988.

Chŏn Haejong 全海宗. "Han-Chung chogong kwan'gye kaeron—Han-Chung kwan'gyesa ŭi chogam ŭl wihayŏ—" 韓中朝貢關係概觀—韓中關係史의 鳥瞰을 위하여—. In *Kodae Han-Chung kwan'gyesa ŭi yŏn'gu* 古代漢中關係史의 研究. Seoul: Samjiwŏn, 1987.

——. *Han-Chung kwan'gyesa yŏn'gu* 韓中關係史研究. Seoul: Ilchogak, 1970.

Chŏng Hwan 丁煥. *Hoesan sŏnsaeng munjip* 檜山先生文集. Reprint [1765]. HMC (pt. 2) 2. Seoul: Minjok munhwa ch'ujinhoe, 2005.

Chŏng Inji 鄭麟趾. *Koryŏ sa* 高麗史. Ed. Hŏ Sŏngdo 허성도. Pukhan sahoe kwahak wŏn, 1998. http://www.krpia.co.kr/product/main?plctId=PLCT00004467.

Chŏng Konsu 鄭崐壽. *Paekkok sŏnsaeng chip* 栢谷先生集. Reprint [1710]. HMC 48. Seoul: Minjok munhwa ch'ujinhoe, 1989.

Chŏng T'aesang. "Myŏng ŭi Ch'ŏllyŏngwi wa Koryŏmal kukkyŏng ŭi chaegŏmt'o" 明의 철령위와 고려말 국경의 재검토. *Inmun kwahak yŏn'gu* 58 (September 2018): 189–216.

Chŏng Taham. "Chŏngpŏl iranŭn chŏnjaeng / Chŏngpŏl iranŭn chesa" 征伐이라는 戰爭/征伐이라는 祭祀. *Han'guksa hakpo* 52 (August 2013): 271–306.

——. "'Sadae' wa 'kyorin' kwa 'Sochunghwa' ranŭn t'ŭl ŭi ch'osiganjŏgin kŭrigo Ch'ogonggganjŏgin maengnak" '事大'와 '交隣'과 '小中華'라는 틀의 초시간적인 그리고 초공간적인 맥락. *Han'guksa hakpo* 42 (2011): 287–323.

——. "Yŏmal Sŏnch'o ŭi Tongasia chilsŏ wa Chosŏn esŏ ŭi Hanŏ, Hanimun, Hunmin Chŏngŭm" 麗末鮮初의 동아시아 질서와 朝鮮에서의 漢語, 漢吏文, 訓民正音. *Han'guksa hakpo* 36 (2009): 269–305.

Chŏng Tonghun. "Koryŏ-Myŏng oegyo munsŏ sŏsik ŭi sŏngnip kwa paegyŏng" 高麗-明 外交文書 書式의 성립과 배경. *Han'guk saron* 56 (2010): 139–207.

——. "Myŏngdae chŏn'gi oegyo sajŏl ŭi sinbun chŭngmyŏng pangsik kwa kukkagan ch'egye" 明代前期 外國使節의 身分證明 方式과 國家間 體系. *Myŏng-Ch'ŏng sa yŏn'gu* 10 (October 2013): 1–34.

——. "Myŏngdae ŭi yeje chilsŏ esŏ Chosŏn kugwang ŭi wisang" 명대의 예제 질서에서 조선국왕의 위상. *Yŏksa wa hyŏnsil* 84 (June 2012): 251–92.

Chŏng Ŭnju. *Chosŏn sidae sahaeng kirokhwa: yet kŭrim ŭro ingnŭn Han-Chung kwan'gye sa* 조선시대 사행기록화: 옛 그림으로 읽는 한중관계사. Seoul: Sahoe p'yŏngnon, 2012.

Chŏng Yagyong 丁若鏞. *Yŏyudang chŏnsŏ* 與猶堂全書. Reprint [1934-1938]. HMC 281–86. Seoul: Minjok munhwa ch'ujinhoe, 2002.

Ch'ŏnsang yŏlch'a punya chi to 天象列次分野之圖. 1395. Stele. Ch'angdŏk 12937. National Palace Museum of Korea, Kukbo 228.

Chu Changmin. *Kwanghae, Wang i toen namja* 광해: 왕이 된 남자. CJ Entertainment, 2012.

Chun, Hae-jong. "Sino-Korean Tributary Relations in the Ch'ing Period." In *The Chinese World Order; Traditional China's Foreign Relations*, ed. John King Fairbank and Ta-tuan Ch'en, 90–111. Cambridge, MA: Harvard University Press, 1968.

Chun, Jihoon. "Late Nineteenth Century Ching-Chosŏn Union of Upper State and Subject State." Presented for the Choson History Society, Los Angeles; Bochum, October 26, 2021. https://www.youtube.com/watch?v=qNM1uX-ehq4.

Clark, Donald N. "Sino-Korean Tributary Relations under the Ming." In *The Ming Dynasty, 1398–1644, Part 2*. The Cambridge History of China. Cambridge: Cambridge University Press, 1998.

Cover, Robert M. "The Supreme Court, 1982 Term—Foreword: Nomos and Narrative." *Harvard Law Review* 97 (1983): 4–63.

Da Yuan shengzheng guochao dianzhang 大元聖政國朝典章. Scripta Sinica. Taipei: Guoli gugong bowuyuan, 1976.

Dai, Yingcong. "A Disguised Defeat: The Myanmar Campaign of the Qing Dynasty." *Modern Asian Studies* 38, no. 1 (February 2004): 145–89.

Dardess, John W. *A Ming Society: T'ai-Ho County, Kiangsi, in the Fourteenth to Seventeenth Centuries*. Berkeley: University of California Press, 1996.

Deng Yunlong 鄧雲龍 and Li Yourong 李友榕. *Sanshui xianzhi* 三水縣志. Jiaqing 嘉慶本. [1819] Zhongguo fangzhi ku. Beijing: Airusheng, 2009.

Deuchler, Martina. *The Confucian Transformation of Korea: A Study of Society and Ideology*. Cambridge, MA: Council on East Asian Studies, 1992.

——. *Under the Ancestors' Eyes: Kinship, Status, and Locality in Premodern Korea*. Cambridge, MA: Harvard Asia Center, 2015.

D'Haeseleer, Tineke. "Tang Taizong in Korea: The Siege of Ansi." *East Asian History*, no. 40 (August 2016): 1–17.

Di Cosmo, Nicola. "Qing Colonial Administration in Inner Asia." *The International History Review* 20, no. 2 (1998): 287–309.

Diamond, Norma. "Defining the Miao: Ming, Qing, and Contemporary Views." In *Cultural Encounters on China's Ethnic Frontiers*, ed. Stevan Harrell, 92–116. Seattle: University of Washington Press, 1995.

Diao Shuren. "Jingtai, Tianshun nianjian Jianzhou sanwei Nüzhen yu Ming chao, Chaoxian guanxi" 景泰、天順年間建州三衛女真與明朝、朝鮮關係. *Shixue congkan* 1 (2010): 101–7.

Diao Shuren, and Bu Zhaojin. "Lun Yuanmo Mingchu Zhongguo yu Gaoli, Chaoxian de bianjie zhi zheng" 論元末明初中國與高麗、朝鮮的邊界之爭. *Beihua daxue xuebao (Shehui kexue ban)* 2, no. 1 (March 2001): 51–55.

Diao Shuren and Wang Jian. "Ming chu Maolian wei yu Chaoxian de guanxi" 明初毛憐衛與朝鮮的關係. *Dongbei shidi* 1 (2006): 252–68.

Dong Gao 董誥. *Quan Tang wen* 全唐文. Scripta Sinica. Beijing: Zhonghua shuju, 1987.

Dong Yue 董越. "Chaoxian zazhi" 朝鮮雜志. In *Shi Chaoxian lu*, ed. Yin Mengxia and Yu Hao. Beijing: Beijing tushuguan chubanshe, 2003.

——. *Chosŏn pu* 朝鮮賦. Trans. Yun Hojin. Sosu sŏwŏn pon 紹修書院本. Kkach'i, 1995.

Doyle, Michael W. *Empires*. Ithaca, NY: Cornell University Press, 1996.

Dreyer, Edward L. *Early Ming China: A Political History, 1355–1435*. Stanford, CA: Stanford University Press, 1982.

Du Huiyue. *Mingdai wenchen chushi Chaoxian yu "Huanghuaji"* 明代文臣出使朝鮮與「皇華集」. Beijing: Renmin chubanshe, 2010.

Du Zhao 杜詔 and Yue Jun 岳濬. *Shandong tongzhi* 山東通志. Yongzheng 雍正本. Zhongguo fangzhi ku. Beijing: Airusheng, 2009.

Duan Changwu 段昌武. *Maoshi jijie* 毛詩集解. SKQS. Zhongguo jiben guji ku. Beijing: Airusheng, 2009. http://server.wenzibase.com.

Dudden, Alexis. *Japan's Colonization of Korea: Discourse and Power*. Honolulu: University of Hawai'i Press, 2005.

Duncan, John B. *The Origins of the Chosŏn Dynasty*. Seattle: University of Washington Press, 2000.

——. "The Problematic Modernity of Confucianism: The Question of 'Civil Society' in Choson Dynasty Korea." In *Korean Society: Civil Society, Democracy and the State*, ed. Charles K. Armstrong. New York: Routledge, 2002.

——. "Proto-Nationalism in Premodern Korea." In *Perspectives on Korea*, ed. Duk-Soo Park and Sang-Oak Lee. Sydney: Wild Peony, 1998.

——. "The Social Background to the Founding of the Chosŏn Dynasty: Change or Continuity." *Journal of Korean Studies* 6 (1988): 39–79.

——. "Uses of Confucianism in Modern Korea." In *Rethinking Confucianism: Past and Present in China, Japan, Korea, and Vietnam*, ed. Benjamin A. Elman, John B. Duncan, and Herman Ooms, 431–62. Los Angeles: UCLA Asian Pacific Monograph Series, 2002.

Duthie, Torquil. *Man'yōshū and the Imperial Imagination in Early Japan*. Leiden: Brill, 2014.

Dyke, Jon M. Van. "Legal Issues Related to Sovereignty over Dokdo and Its Maritime Boundary." *Ocean Development & International Law* 38, no. 1–2 (July 2007): 157–224.

Egan, Ronald. *The Problem of Beauty: Aesthetic Thought and Pursuits in Northern Song Dynasty China*. Cambridge, MA: Harvard Asia Center, 2006.

Elman, Benjamin A. *A Cultural History of Civil Examinations in Late Imperial China*. Berkeley: University of California Press, 2000.

Em, Henry. *The Great Enterprise: Sovereignty and Historiography in Modern Korea*. Durham, NC: Duke University Press, 2013.

Fairbank, John King, ed. *The Chinese World Order; Traditional China's Foreign Relations*. Cambridge, MA: Harvard University Press, 1968.

Fan Ye 范曄. *Hou Hanshu* 後漢書. Ed. Li Xian and Yang Jialuo. Scripta Sinica. Taipei: Dingwen shuju, 1981.

Fan Yongcong. *Shida yu baoguo: Yuan Ming zhi ji de Zhong Han guanxi* 事大與保國: 元明之際的中韓關係. Hong Kong: Xianggang jiaoyu tushu, 2009.

Fang, Jun. *China's Second Capital: Nanjing Under the Ming, 1368–1644*. New York: Routledge, 2014.

Farmer, Edward L. *Zhu Yuanzhang and Early Ming Legislation: The Reordering of Chinese Society Following the Era of Mongol Rule*. New York: Brill, 1995.

Feng Keyong 馮可鏞 and Yang Taiheng 楊泰亨. *Cixi xianzhi* 慈谿縣志. Guangxu 光緒本 [1899], Zhongguo fangzhi ku. Beijing: Airusheng, 2009.

Fitzgerald, Devin. "The Ming Open Archive and the Global Reading of Early Modern China." PhD diss., Harvard University, 2020.

Franke, Herbert. *From Tribal Chieftain to Universal Emperor and God: The Legitimation of the Yüan Dynasty*. München: Verlag der Baerischen Akademie der Wissenschaften, 1978.

French, Howard W. *Everything Under the Heavens: How the Past Helps Shape China's Push for Global Power*. New York: Knopf Doubleday, 2017.

Friday, Karl F. *Samurai, Warfare and the State in Early Medieval Japan*. New York: Routledge, 2004.

Frigo, Daniela, ed. *Politics and Diplomacy in Early Modern Italy: The Structure of Diplomatic Practice, 1450–1800*. Trans. Adrian Belton. Reissue, Cambridge University Press, 2011.

Fu Sheng 伏勝. *Shangshu dazhuan* 尚書大傳. SKQS. Kanseki Repository, 1778. https://www.kanripo.org/edition/SBCK/KR1b0059.

Fubini, Ricardo. "Diplomacy and Government in the Italian City-States of the Fifteenth Century (Florence and Venice)." In *Politics and Diplomacy in Early Modern Italy: The Structure of Diplomatic Practice, 1450–1800*, ed. Daniela Frigo, trans. Adrian Belton, 25–48. Reissue, Cambridge University Press, 2011.

Fuma Susumu 夫馬進. *Chōsen enkōshi to Chōsen tsūshinshi* 朝鮮燕行使と朝鮮通信使. Nagoya: Nagoya daigaku shuppankai, 2015.

Galison, Peter. "Trading Zone: Coordinating Action and Belief." In *The Science Studies Reader*, ed. Mario Biagioli, 137–60. New York: Routledge, 1999.

Gao Dengxian 高登先 ed. *Shanyin xianzhi* 山陰縣志. Chinese Rare Book Collection (Library of Congress). 1662. https://lccn.loc.gov/2012402983.

Gao Yanlin. "Ming chao yu Chaoxian wangchao zhi jian de shichen wanglai" 明朝與朝鮮王朝之間的使臣往來. The final research results supported by the KFAS international scholar exchange fellowship program, 2003–2004, August 13, 2004.

Garton, Vincent. "Jiang Shigong's Chinese World Order." *Palladium* (blog), February 5, 2020. https://palladiummag.com/2020/02/05/jiang-shigongs-vision-of-a-new-chinese-world-order/.

Ge Zhaoguang. *Lishi Zhongguo de nei yu wai: youguan Zhongguo yu zhoubian gai nian de zai chengqing* 歷史中國的內與外: 有關「中國」與「周邊」概念的再澄清. Hong Kong: Xianggang zhongwen daxue chubanshe, 2017.

——. *Zhaizi Zhongguo: chongjian youguan Zhongguo de lishi lunshu* 宅茲中國: 重建有關中國的歷史論述. 3rd ed. Taipei: Lianjing, 2011.

Ge Zhenjia, ed. *Cui Pu "Piaohai lu" pingzhu* 崔溥《漂海錄》評註. Beijing: Xianzhuang shuju, 2002.

Geertz, Clifford. *Negara: The Theatre State in Nineteenth-Century Bali*. Princeton, NJ: Princeton University Press, 1981.

Glassman, Jim. *Drums of War, Drums of Development: The Formation of a Pacific Ruling Class and Industrial Transformation in East and Southeast Asia, 1945–1980*. Leiden: Brill, 2018.

Glomb, Vladimír, and Eun-Jeung Lee. "Between Ruins and Relics: North Korean Discourse on Confucian Academies." In *Confucian Academies in East Asia*, ed. Vladimír Glomb, Eun-Jeung Lee, and Martin Gehlmann, 456–492. Leiden: Brill, 2020.

Goertz, Gary, and Paul F. Diehl. "Toward a Theory of International Norms: Some Conceptual and Measurement Issues." *The Journal of Conflict Resolution* 36, no. 4 (1992): 634–64.

Gong Yongqing 龔用卿. *Ŏch'on kakcha* 漁村刻字. 1537. Stone rubbing. Kyu 28156. Kyujanggak Archives, Seoul National University.

——. *Shi Chaoxian lu* 使朝鮮錄. Nanjing: Taofeng lou, 1937.

Gordon, Stewart, ed. *Robes of Honour: Khilat in Pre-Colonial and Colonial India*. 3rd ed. New Delhi: Oxford University Press, 2003.

Graeber, David, and Marshall Sahlins. *On Kings*. Chicago: Hau Books, 2017.

Grafton, Anthony. "Invention of Traditions and Traditions of Invention in Renaissance Europe: The Strange Case of Annius of Viterbo." In *The Transmission of Culture in Early Modern Europe*, ed. Anthony Grafton, Ann Blair, and Shelby Cullom Davis Center for Historical Studies. Philadelphia: University of Pennsylvania Press, 1990.

——. *Worlds Made by Words: Scholarship and Community in the Modern West*. Cambridge, MA: Harvard University Press, 2009.

"Grand Secretariat Archives (Neige daku dang'an 內閣大庫檔案)." Taipei, Fusinian Library, 18th century. 106204; 287678; 117451; 056317. Academia Sinica. http://archive.ihp.sinica.edu.tw/mctkm2/index.html.

Guo Fei 郭棐. *Yue da ji* 粵大記. Wanli 萬曆本 [16th century]. Zhongguo fangzhi ku. Beijing: Airusheng, 2009.

Guo Jiahui. "Tianxia tongli: Mingdai binli de liuchuan yu yuwai shijian de fenzheng" 天下通禮: 明代賓禮的流傳與域外實踐的紛爭. *Taiwan shida lishi xuebao* 59 (June 2018): 1–40.

Ha, Yiming. "Public Discourse and Private Sentiment: Ritual Controversies, Ritual Authority, and Political Succession in Ming and Chosŏn." *Ming Studies* (May 2022): 1–26.

Haboush, JaHyun Kim. "Academies and Civil Society in Chosŏn Korea." In *La société civile face à l'État: dans les traditions chinoise, japonaise, coréenne et vietnamienne,* ed. Léon Vandermeersch, 383–92. Paris: École Française d'Extrême-Orient, 1994.

——. "Contesting Chinese Time, Nationalizing Temporal Space: Temporal Inscription in Late Chosŏn Korea." In *Time, Temporality and Imperial Transition: East Asia From Ming to Qing,* ed. Lynn A. Struve, 115–41. Asian Interactions and Comparisons. Honolulu: University of Hawai'i Press, 2005.

——. *The Great East Asian War of 1592 and the Birth of the Korean Nation.* Ed. William Joseph Haboush and Jisoo M. Kim. New York: Columbia University Press, 2016.

——. "Versions and Subversions: Patriarchy and Polygamy in Korean Narratives." In *Women and Confucian Cultures in Premodern China, Korea, and Japan,* ed. Dorothy Ko, JaHyun Kim Haboush, and Joan R. Piggott. Berkeley: University of California Press, 2003.

Halperin, Charles J. *Russia and the Mongols: Slavs and the Steppe in Medieval and Early Modern Russia.* Bucureşti: Ed. Academiae Romane, 2007.

Hamashita, Takeshi, Linda Grove, and Mark Selden. *China, East Asia and the Global Economy: Regional and Historical Perspectives.* New York: Routledge, 2008.

Han Chaeyŏn 韓在濂. *Koryŏ kodoching* 高麗古都徵. Reprint [1850]. Asea munhwasa, 1972.

Han Hyojung 韓孝仲, ed. *Chŏngju Han ssi chokp'o [sep'o]* 清州韓氏族譜[世譜]. Ko (古) 4650–74 Kyujanggak Archives, Seoul National University, 1617.

Han Hyŏngju. "Taemyŏng ŭirye rŭl t'onghae pon 15 segi Cho–Myŏng kwan'gye" 對明儀禮를 통해 본 15세기 朝–明관계. *Yŏsa minsok hak,* no. 28 (November 2008): 39–75.

Han Myŏnggi. *Imjin Waeran kwa Han-Chung kwan'gye* 임진왜란과 한중 관계. Seoul: Yŏksa pip'yŏngsa, 1999.

Han Sŏngju. *Chosŏn chŏn'gi sujik Yŏjinin yŏn'gu* 조선 전기 수직 여진인 연구. Seoul: Kyŏng'in munhwasa, 2011.

Han Yŏngho. "Chosŏn ŭi Hoehoeryŏkpŏp toip kwa 'Ch'ilchŏngsan oe p'yŏn'" 조선의 回回曆法 도입과『칠정산외편』. *Minjok munhwa* 45 (June 2015): 127–60.

Han Yŏngho, Yi Ŭnhŭi, and Kim Minjŏng. "Sejong ŭi yŏkpŏp chejŏng kwa 'Ch'ilchŏng san'" 세종의 역법 제정과『칠정산(七政算)』. *Tongpang hakji* 168 (2014): 99–121.

Han Yŏngho 韓榮浩 and Yun Tusu 尹斗壽. *Kija yuji* 箕子遺志. Harvard-Yenching Rare Books Movable type. [1878]. Kisŏng [P'yŏngyang], 1922.

Han, Young-woo. "Kija Worship in the Koryŏ and Early Yi Dynasties: A Cultural Symbol in the Relationship Between Korea and China." In *The Rise of Neo-Confucianism in Korea*, ed. William Theodore de Bary and JaHyun Kim Haboush, 349–71. New York: Columbia University Press, 1985.

Handel, Zev Joseph. *Sinography: The Borrowing and Adaptation of the Chinese Script*. Leiden: Brill, 2019.

Hara, Takemichi. "Korea, China, and Western Barbarians: Diplomacy in Early Nineteenth-Century Korea." *Modern Asian Studies* 32, no. 2 (May 1998): 389–430.

Hardt, Michael, and Antonio Negri. *Empire*. Cambridge, MA: Harvard University Press, 2000.

Hasegawa, Masato. "Provisions and Profits in a Wartime Borderland: Supply Lines and Society in the Border Region Between China and Korea, 1592–1644." PhD diss., Yale University, 2013.

Hawes, Colin S. C. *The Social Circulation of Poetry in the Mid-Northern Song: Emotional Energy and Literati Self-Cultivation*. Albany, NY: SUNY Press, 2005.

Heer, Philip de. *The Care-Taker Emperor: Aspects of the Imperial Institution in Fifteenth-Century China as Reflected in the Political History of the Reign of Chu Ch'i-Yü*. Leiden: Brill, 1986.

——. "Three Embassies to Seoul: Sino-Korean Relations in the 15th Century." In *Conflict and Accommodation in Early Modern East Asia: Essays in Honour of Erik Zurcher*, ed. Leonard Blusse and Harriet T. Zurndorfer. Leiden: Brill, 1993.

Hejtmanek, Milan. "The Familiar Dead: The Creation of an Intimate Afterlife in Early Chosŏn Korea." In *Death, Mourning, and the Afterlife in Korea: From Ancient to Contemporary Times*, ed. Charlotte Horlyck and Michael J. Pettid. Honolulu: University of Hawai'i Press, 2014.

Hennings, Jan. *Russia and Courtly Europe: Ritual and the Culture of Diplomacy, 1648–1725*. Cambridge: Cambridge University Press, 2016.

Henthorn, William E. *Korea: The Mongol Invasions*. Leiden: Brill, 1963.

Hevia, James Louis. *Cherishing Men from Afar: Qing Guest Ritual and the Macartney Embassy of 1793*. Durham, NC: Duke University Press, 1995.

——. "Sovereignty and Subject: Constituting Relationships of Power in Qing Guest Ritual." In *Body, Subject & Power in China*, ed. Angela Zito and Tani E. Barlow. Chicago: University of Chicago Press, 1994.

Hiatt, Alfred, and British Library. *The Making of Medieval Forgeries: False Documents in Fifteenth-Century England*. London: British Library and University of Toronto Press, 2004.

Ho, Ping-Ti. "In Defense of Sinicization: A Rebuttal of Evelyn Rawski's 'Reenvisioning the Qing.'" *The Journal of Asian Studies* 57, no. 1 (1998): 123–55.

Hŏ Pong 許篈. *Haedong yaŏn* 海東野言. Reprint [17th century]. TDYS. Kyŏngsŏng [Seoul]: Chosŏn kosŏ kanhaenghoe, 1909.

——. "Hagok sŏnsaeng Choch'ŏn'gi" 荷谷先生朝天記. In *Hagok chip*, Reprint [1707]. HMC 58. Seoul: Minjok munhwa ch'ujinhoe, 1990.

Hŏ T'aegu. *Pyŏngja Horan kwa ye, kŭrigo Chunghwa* 병자호란과 예, 그리고 중화. Seoul: Somyŏng ch'ul'pan, 2019.

Holcombe, Charles. *The Genesis of East Asia, 221 B.C.–A.D. 907*. Honolulu: University of Hawai'i Press, 2001.

Hong Chikp'il 洪直弼. *Maesan sŏnsaeng munjip* 梅山先生文集. Reprint [1866]. HMC 295–96. Seoul: Minjok munhwa ch'ujinhoe, 2002.

Hong Kyŏngmo 洪敬謨. *Kwanam chŏnsŏ* 冠巖全書. Reprint. HMC, Sok (續) 113–14. Seoul: Minjok munhwa ch'ujinhoe, 2011.

Hong Manjong 洪萬宗, and Cho Sŏngjik 趙成植. *Shihua conglin jianzhu* 詩話叢林箋注. Ed. Zhao Ji. Tianjin: Nankai daxue chubanshe, 2006.

Huang Lun 黃倫. *Shangshu jingyi* 尚書精義. SKQS Kanseki Repository, 1180. https://www.kanripo.org/text/KR1b0018/.

Huang Zhilian. *Dong Ya de liyi shijie: Zhongguo fengjian wangchao yu Chaoxian bandao guanxi xingtai lun* 東亞的禮義世界: 中國封建王朝與朝鮮半島關係形態論. Beijing: Zhongguo renmin daxue chubanshe, 1994.

Hucker, Charles O. *A Dictionary of Official Titles in Imperial China*. Stanford, CA: Stanford University Press, 1985.

Hunt, Lynn Avery, ed. *The Invention of Pornography: Obscenity and the Origins of Modernity, 1500–1800*. New York: Zone Books, 1993.

Hur, Joon. "The State and Identity Construction in Chosŏn Korea." PhD diss., University of California, Los Angeles, 2019.

Hur, Nam-lin. "The Celestial Warriors: Ming Military Aid and Abuse During the Korean War, 1592–8." In *The East Asian War, 1592–1598: International Relations, Violence and Memory*, ed. James B. Lewis, 236–55. New York: Routledge, 2014.

Idema, W. L. "Fighting in Korea: Two Early Narrative Treatments of the Story of Xue Rengui." In *Korea in the Middle: Korean Studies and Area Studies: Essays in Honour of Boudewjin Walraven*, ed. Remco E. Breuker, 341–58. Leiden: CNWS, 2007.

Im Hyŏnjin. "Yŏmal Sŏnch'o ŭi tae-Myŏng kwan'gye wa insin mu oegyo kwannyŏm" 여말선초의 對明 관계와 人臣無外交 관념. *Sahak yŏn'gu* 138 (2020): 213–54.

Iryŏn 一然 and Yi Pyŏngdo. *Samguk yusa* 三國遺事. Seoul: Tugye haksul chaedan, 1999. https://www.krpia.co.kr/.

Jeong Ho-hun. "Deconstructing the Official History of Koryŏ in Late Chosŏn." *Seoul Journal of Korean Studies* 26, no. 2 (December 2013): 335–60.

Jiang Shigong. "Jiang Shigong, 'Empire and World Order.'" Trans. David Ownby. *Reading the China Dream.* Accessed January 27, 2022. https://www.readingthe chinadream.com/jiang-shigong-empire-and-world-order.html.

——. "Yiguo zhi mi: Zhongguo vs. Diguo" 一國之謎: 中國 vs. 帝國. *Gongfa pinglun,* November 15, 2008. https://www.gongfa.com/html/gongfazhuanti/xiandaixing /20081115/41.html.

Jiang Weigong. "Liaoshi dilizhi Dongjing Liaoyangfu tiao jishi miuwu tanyuan" 《遼史·地理志》東京遼陽府條記事誤謬探源. *Zhongguo bianjiang shidi yanjiu,* no. 2 (2011): 119–29.

Jiang Yingke 江盈科. *Xuetaoge ji* 雪濤閣集. Beijing: Xichu Jiangshi 西楚江氏, 1600.

Jiang, Yonglin. *The Mandate of Heaven and the Great Ming Code.* Seattle: University of Washington Press, 2013.

Jiang Yueguang 姜曰廣. *Youxuan jishi* 輶軒紀事. Congshu jicheng chubian 3240. Beijing: Zhonghua shuju, 1985.

Jiao Hong 焦竑. *Guochao xianzheng lu* 國朝獻徵錄. Scripta Sinica. Mingdai zhuanji congkan 明代傳記叢刊 109–14. Taipei: Mingwen shuju, 1991.

Jin Yufu 金毓紱, ed. *Liaohai congshu* 遼海叢書. Shenyang: Liaoshen shushe, 1985.

Johnston, Alastair Ian. *Cultural Realism: Strategic Culture and Strategy in Chinese History.* Princeton, NJ: Princeton University Press, 1998.

Jorgensen, John. *The Foresight of Dark Knowing: Chŏng Kam Nok and Insurrectionary Prognostication in Pre-Modern Korea.* Korean Classics Library: Philosophy and Religion. Honolulu: University of Hawai'i Press, 2018.

Jung, Donghun [Chŏng Tonghun]. "Chinese Academic Research on the History of Sino-Korean Relations: The Work of Chen Shangsheng." *The Review of Korean Studies* 24, no. 1 (2021): 333–54.

——. "From a Lord to a Bureaucrat: The Change of Koryŏ King's Status in the Korea-China Relations." *The Review of Korean Studies* 19, no. 2 (December 2016): 115–36.

Kalmo, Hent, and Quentin Skinner. *Sovereignty in Fragments: The Past, Present and Future of a Contested Concept.* Cambridge: Cambridge University Press, 2010.

Kang Chaejŏl, and Yi Poggyu. "Orangk'ae (Oryanghap) ŏwŏn sŏlhwa yŏn'gu" 오랑캐 (兀良哈)語源說話 研究. *Pigyo minsokhak* 22 (February 2002): 181–218.

Kang Chehun. "Chosŏn ch'ogi hunch'ŏk Han Myŏnghoe ŭi kwanjik saenghwal kwa kŭ t'ŭkching" 조선 초기 勳戚 韓明澮의 관직 생활과 그 특징. *Yŏksa wa silhak* 43 (November 2010): 5–43.

Kang, David C. *East Asia Before the West: Five Centuries of Trade and Tribute.* New York: Columbia University Press, 2010.

——. "Getting Asia Wrong: The Need for New Analytical Frameworks." *International Security* 27, no. 4 (2003): 57–85.

Kang, David C., and Xinru Ma. "Power Transitions: Thucydides Didn't Live in East Asia." *The Washington Quarterly* 41, no. 1 (January 2018): 137–54.

Kang, Etsuko Hae-jin. *Diplomacy and Ideology in Japanese-Korean Relations: From the Fifteenth to the Eighteenth Century*. New York: Springer, 2016.

Kang Hŭimaeng 姜希孟. *Sasukchae chip* 私淑齋集. Reprint [1805]. HMC 12. Seoul: Minjok munhwa ch'ujinhoe, 1988.

Keliher, Macabe. *The Board of Rites and the Making of Qing China*. Oakland: University of California Press, 2019.

Kelley, Liam C. *Beyond the Bronze Pillars: Envoy Poetry and the Sino-Vietnamese Relationship*. Honolulu: University of Hawai'i Press, 2005.

——. "'Confucianism' in Vietnam: A State of the Field Essay." *Journal of Vietnamese Studies* 1, no. 1–2 (2006): 314–70.

Kim Allo 金安老. *Hŭiraktang ko* 希樂堂稿. Reprint. HMC 21. Seoul: Minjok munhwa ch'ujinhoe, 1988.

Kim An'guk 金安國. *Mojae chip* 慕齋集. Reprint [1687]. HMC 20. Seoul: Minjok munhwa ch'ujinhoe, 1988.

Kim Chinam 金指南. *T'ongmun'gwan chi* 通文館志. Ko. 古 5120-11, vol. 1–3. Kyujanggak Archives, Seoul National University, 1720.

——. *T'ongmun'gwan chi* 通文館志. Kyujanggak charyo ch'ongsŏ. Seoul: Sŏul taehakkyo Kyujanggak Han'gukhak yŏn'guwŏn, 2006.

Kim Chongsŏ 金宗瑞. *Koryŏsa chŏryo* 高麗史節要. Reprint [15th century]. Seoul: Minjok munhwa ch'ujinhoe, 1966.

Kim Chuwŏn. "Kugyŏk Chosŏn wangjo sillok e nat'anan pŏnyŏgŏ 'orangk'ae' e taehayŏ" 국역 조선왕조실록에 나타난 번역어 "오랑캐"에 대하여. *Han'guk ŏnŏ hakhoe haksul taehoeji* (December 2006): 54–62.

Kim Han'gyu. *Sa Chosŏn nok yŏn'gu: Song, Myŏng, Ch'ŏng sidae Chosŏn sahaengnok ŭi saryojŏk kach'i* 사조선록 연구: 송, 명, 청 시대 조선사행록의 사료적 가치. Seoul: Sŏgang taehakkyo ch'ulp'anbu, 2011.

Kim Hodong. *Monggol cheguk kwa Koryŏ: K'ubillai chŏngkwŏn ŭi t'ansaeng kwa Koryŏ ŭi chŏngch'ijŏk wisang* 몽골 제국 과 고려: 쿠빌라이 정권 의 탄생 과 고려 의 정치적 위상. Seoul: Sŏul taehakkyo ch'ulp'anbu, 2007.

Kim Hongdae. "Chu Chibŏn [Zhu Zhifan] ŭi pyŏngo sahaeng (1606) kwa kŭ ŭi sŏhwa yŏn'gu" 朱之蕃 의 丙午使行 (1606) 과 그의 서화 연구. *Onji nonch'ong* 11 (2004): 257–304.

Kim, Hyung-Wook. "An Ancient and Glorious Past: Koguryŏ in the Collective Memories of the Korean People." PhD diss., University of California, Los Angeles, 2012.

Kim, Jisoo M. *The Emotions of Justice: Gender, Status, and Legal Performance in Chosŏn Korea*. Seattle: University of Washington Press, 2015.

Kim Kihwa. "'Hwanghwajip' ŭi p'yŏnch'an kwa kanhaeng e kwanhan yŏn'gu" 「皇華集」의 編纂과 刊行에 관한 연구. *Sŏjihak yŏn'gu* 39 (June 2008): 201–53.

Kim Ku 金坵. *Chip'o chip* 止浦集. Reprint [1801]. HMC 2. Seoul: Minjok munhwa ch'ujinhoe, 1990.

Kim Kwiyŏng 金貴榮. *Tongwŏn chip* 東園集. Reprint [1935]. HMC 37. Seoul: Minjok munhwa ch'ujinhoe, 1988.

Kim Kyŏngnok. "Chosŏn ch'ogi t'ongsa ŭi hwaltong kwa wisang pyŏnhwa" 조선초기 통사의 활동과 위상 변화. *Han'guk hakpo* 26, no. 4 (December 2000): 53–91.

——. "Chosŏn sidae chogong ch'eje tae Chungguk sahaeng" 朝鮮時代 朝貢體制와 對中國 使行. *Myŏng Chŏng sa yŏn'gu* 30 (2008): 91–128.

Kim, Nuri. "Making Myth, History, and an Ancient Religion in Korea." PhD diss., Harvard University, 2017.

Kim Pusik 金富軾. *Samguk sagi* 三國史記. Han'guksa saryo yŏn'guso, 2004. http://www.krpia.co.kr.

Kim Pyŏngin. "Koryŏ Yejong ŭi t'ongch'i haengwi e nat'anan yuhyŏngjŏk t'ŭkching kwa kŭ chŏngch'ijŏk paegyŏng" 고려 예종의 통치행위에 나타난 유형적 특징과 그 정치적 배경. *Yŏksa wa kyŏnggye* 79 (June 2011): 35–74.

Kim, Seonmin. "Borders and Crossings: Trade, Diplomacy and Ginseng between Qing China and Chosŏn Korea." PhD diss., Duke University, 2006.

Kim, Sun Joo. "Culture of Remembrance in Late Chosŏn Korea: Bringing an Unknown War Hero Back into History." *Journal of Social History* 44, no. 2 (2010): 563–85.

——, ed. "Residence and Foreign Relations in the Peninsular Northeast During the Fifteenth and Sixteenth Centuries." In *The Northern Region of Korea: History, Identity & Culture*, 18–36. Seattle: University of Washington Press, 2010.

Kim Sunja. *Han'guk chungse Han-Chung kwan'gyesa* 韓國中世韓中關係史. Seoul: Hyean, 2007.

Kim Suon 金守溫. *Sigu chip* 拭疣集. Reprint. HMC 9. Seoul: Minjok munhwa ch'ujinhoe, 1998.

Kim T'aeyŏng. "Chosŏn ch'ogi Sejo wangkwŏn ŭi chŏnjesŏng e taehan ilgoch'al" 朝鮮초기 世祖王權의 專制性에 대한 一考察. *Han'guk sa yŏn'gu* 87 (December 1994): 117–46.

Kim Tangt'aek. *Wŏn kansŏp ha ŭi Koryŏ chŏngch'isa* 元干涉下의 高麗政治史. Seoul: Ilchogak, 1998.

Kim Tongch'ŏl. "Chosŏn hugi suugak muyŏk kwa kakkung kye kongin" 朝鮮後期 水牛角貿易과 弓角契貢人. *Han'guk munhwa yŏn'gu* 4 (December 1991): 55–110.

Kim Wihyŏn. *Koryŏ sidae taeoe kwan'gyesa yŏn'gu* 高麗時代對外關係史研究. Seoul: Kyŏng'in munhwasa, 2004.

Kim Wŏnjun. "Chosa wa ŭi ch'aunsi e nat'anan Chipong ŭi ŭisik: Chipong ŭi 'Hwang-hwajip ch'aun' ŭl t'onghae" 詔使와의 次韻詩에 나타난 芝峯의 意識-지봉의「皇華集次韻」을 통해-. *Hanminjok ŏmunhak* 44 (2004): 230–69.

Kim Yŏngdu. "Sillok p'yŏnch'an e nat'anan Sejo chŏngkwŏn ŭi chŏngdangsŏng ch'ugu" 실록 편찬에 나타난 세조 정권의 정당성 추구. *Han'guk sahak sahakpo* 27 (2013): 65–99.

Kim Yujin 김유진. *Sin'gijŏn* 신기전. CJ Entertainment, 2008.

Kim, Yung Sik. *The Natural Philosophy of Chu Hsi (1130–1200)*. Philadelphia: American Philosophical Society, 2000.

King, Ross. "Ditching "Diglossia": Describing Ecologies of the Spoken and Inscribed in Pre-Modern Korea." *Sungkyun Journal of East Asian Studies* 15, no. 1 (2015): 1–19.

——. "Nationalism and Language Reform in Korea." In *Nationalism and the Construction of Korean Identity*, ed. Hyung Il Pai and Timothy R. Tangherlini, 33–72. Berkeley: Institute of East Asian Studies, University of California, 1998.

——. "North and South Korea." In *Language and National Identity in Asia*, ed. Andrew Simpson, 200–34. Oxford: Oxford University Press, 2007.

Ko, Chong-sok, and Ross King. *Infected Korean Language, Purity Versus Hybridity: From the Sinographic Cosmopolis to Japanese Colonialism to Global English.* Amherst, NY: Cambria Press, 2014.

Ko Pyŏngik. *Tonga kyosŏpsa ŭi yŏn'gu* 東亞交涉史의硏究. Seoul: Sŏul taehakkyo ch'ulp'anbu, 1970.

Koo, Se-Woong. "Making Belief: Religion and the State in Korea, 1392–1960." PhD diss., Stanford University, 2011.

Kornicki, Peter. *Languages, Scripts, and Chinese Texts in East Asia*. Oxford: Oxford University Press, 2018.

Ku Manok. "Chosŏn wangjo ŭi chipkwŏn ch'eje wa kwahak kisul chŏngch'aek: Chosŏn chŏn'gi ch'ŏnmun yŏksanhak ŭi chŏngbi kwajŏng ŭl chungsim ŭro" 조선 왕조의 집권체제와 과학기술정책-조선전기 천문역산학의 정비 과정을 중심으로-. *Tongpang hakchi* 124 (2004): 219–72.

Ku Pŏmjin. "Tong Asia kukche chilsŏ ŭi pyŏndong kwa Chosŏn–Ch'ŏng kwan'gye" 동아시아 국제질서의 변동 과 조선-청 관계. In *Tong Asia kukche chilsŏ sok ŭi Han-Chung kwan'gyesa: cheŏn kwa mosaek* 동 아시아 국제 질서 속의 한중 관계사 : 제언과 모색, ed. Yi Ikchu, 293–380. Seoul: Tongbuga yŏksa chaedan, 2010.

Ku Toyŏng. "Chosŏn chŏn'gi oegyo kwan'gye ŭi hamsu, 'yeŭi chi kuk'" 조선 전기 朝明外交關係의 함수, '禮義之國'. *Taedong munhwa yŏn'gu*, no. 89 (2015): 159–204.

Kuhn, Felix. "Much More Than Tribute: The Foreign Policy Instruments of the Ming Empire." *Journal of Chinese History* 5, no. 1 (January 2021): 59–82.

Kurbanov, Sergei O. "North Korea's Juche Ideology: Indigenous Communism or Traditional Thought?" *Critical Asian Studies* 51, no. 2 (April 2019): 296–305.

Kuwano Eiji. "Chōsen Chūshūdai niokeru shūkei benfu mondai no sainen" 朝鮮中宗代における宗系弁誣問題の再燃. *Bulletin of Faculty of Literature, Kurume University. Intercultural Studies* 25 (2008): 51–78.

——. "Kōrai makki no girei to kokusai kankyō tai Min yōhai girei no sōshutsu" 高麗末期の儀礼と國際環境-对明遥拝儀礼の創出. *Bulletin of Faculty of Literature, Kurume University*. 21 (2004): 61–105.

Kwŏn Inyong. "Myŏng chunggi Chosŏn ŭi ip-Myŏng sahaeng—So Seyang ŭi 'Pu Kyŏng ilgi' rŭl t'onghayŏ" 明中期 朝鮮의 入明使行—蘇世讓 의 「赴京日記」를 통하여. *Myŏng- Ch'ŏng sa yŏn'gu* 19 (2003): 109–34.

——. "Myŏng chunggi Chosŏn ŭi Chonggye pyŏnmu wa tae Myŏng oegyo" 明中期 朝鮮의 宗系辨誣와 對明外交. *Myŏng-Ch'ŏngsa yŏn'gu* 24 (October 2005): 93–116.

Kwŏn Kŭn 權近 et. al., ed. *Koewŏn tŭngnok* 槐院謄錄. Jangseogak Archives (Changsŏgak 藏書閣) k2-3465., thirteenth to seventeenth centuries.

Kwŏn Kŭn 權近. *Tonggukki* 東國記. Kyujanggak Archives (Seoul National University) 가람古貴951-G995d., 1460.

——. *Yangch'on chip* 陽村集. Reprint [1674]. HMC 7. Seoul: Minjok munhwa ch'ujinhoe, 1990.

Kwŏn Pŏl 權橃. *Ch'ungjae sŏnsaeng munjip* 冲齋先生文集. Reprint [1752]. HMC 19. Seoul: Minjok munhwa ch'ujinhoe, 1988.

Kye, Seung B. [Kye Sŭngbŏm]. "Huddling Under the Imperial Umbrella: A Korean Approach to Ming China in the Early 1500s." *Journal of Korean Studies* 15, no. 1 (2010): 41–66.

——. "In the Shadow of the Father: Court Opposition and the Reign of King Kwanghae in Early Seventeenth-Century Choson Korea." PhD diss., University of Washington, 2006.

Kye Sŭngbŏm. *Chosŏn sidae haeoe p'abyŏng kwa Han-Chung kwan'gye: Chosŏn chibae ch'ŭng ŭi Chungguk insik* 조선시대 해외 파병과 한중 관계: 조선 지배층 의 중국 인식. Seoul: P'urŭn yŏksa, 2009.

Lam, Joseph S. C. "Huizong's Dashengyue, a Musical Performance of Emperorship and Officialdom." In *Emperor Huizong and Late Northern Song China: The Politics of Culture and the Culture of Politics*, ed. Patricia Buckley Ebrey and Maggie Bickford, 395–452. Cambridge, MA: Harvard Asia Center, 2006.

——. "The Presence and Absence of Female Musicians and Music in China." In *Women and Confucian Cultures in Premodern China, Korea, and Japan*, ed. Dorothy Ko, JaHyun Kim Haboush, and Joan R. Piggott, 97–120. Berkeley: University of California Press, 2003.

Lan Hongyue. "'Di guo' gainian zai Hanwenquan de fanyi yu liuchuan: Cong Mumo Riben dao Qingmo Zhongguo" 「帝國」概念在漢文圈的翻譯與流傳: 從幕末日本到清末中國. *Zhongyang yanjiuyuan lishi yuyan yanjiu jikan* 93, no. 1 (March 2022): 213–72.

Larsen, Kirk W. "Comforting Fictions: The Tribute System, the Westphalian Order, and Sino-Korean Relations." *Journal of East Asian Studies* 13, no. 2 (May–August 2013): 233–57.

——. *Tradition, Treaties, and Trade: Qing Imperialism and Chosŏn Korea, 1850–1910.* Cambridge, MA: Harvard Asia Center, 2008.

Ledyard, Gari. "Confucianism and War: The Korean Security Crisis of 1598." *Journal of Korean Studies* 6, no. 1 (1988): 81–119.

——. "The International Linguistic Background of the Correct Sounds for the Instruction of the People." In *The Korean Alphabet: Its History and Structure,* ed. Young-Key Kim-Renaud, 31–87. Honolulu: University of Hawai'i Press, 1997.

——. *The Korean Language Reform of 1446.* Seoul: Singu Munhwasa, 1998.

——. "The Korean Language Reform of 1446: The Origin, Background, and Early History of the Korean Alphabet." PhD diss., University of California, 1966.

——. "Korean Travelers in China over Four Hundred Years, 1488–1887." *Occasional Papers on Korea,* no. 2 (March 1974): 1–42.

——. "Two Mongol Documents from the Koryŏ Sa." *Journal of the American Oriental Society* 83, no. 2 (1963): 225–39.

Lee, Eun Hee. "Korean Astronomical Calendar, Chiljeongsan." In *Handbook of Archaeoastronomy and Ethnoastronomy,* ed. Clive L. N. Ruggles, 2157–62. New York: Springer, 2015.

Lee, Iksop, and S. Robert Ramsey. *The Korean Language.* Albany, NY: SUNY Press, 2000.

Lee, Jin-Han. "The Development of Diplomatic Relations and Trade with Ming in the Last Years of the Koryŏ Dynasty." *International Journal of Korean History* 10 (December 2006): 1–24.

Lee, Ji-Young. *China's Hegemony: Four Hundred Years of East Asian Domination.* New York: Columbia University Press, 2016.

——. "Diplomatic Ritual as a Power Resource: The Politics of Asymmetry in Early Modern Chinese-Korean Relations." *Journal of East Asian Studies* 13, no. 2 (May–August 2013): 309–36, 377.

Lee, Jongmook. "Establishing Friendships Between Competing Civilizations: Exchange of Chinese Poetry in East Asia in the Fifteenth and Sixteenth Centuries." In *Rethinking the Sinosphere Poetics, Aesthetics, and Identity Formation,* ed. Nanxiu Qian, Richard J. Smith, and Bowei Zhang. Amherst, NY: Cambria Press, 2020.

Lee, Kang Hahn. "Discussing David M. Robinson's *Empire's Twilight: Northeast Asia Under the Mongols.*" *International Journal of Korean History* 16, no. 1 (2011): 1–24.

——. "Shifting Political, Legal, and Institutional Borderlines Between Koryŏ and the Mongol Yuan Empire." *Seoul Journal of Korean Studies* 29, no. 2 (2016): 239–66.

Lee, Ki-baik. *A New History of Korea.* Seoul: Ilchogak, 1997.

Lee, Peter H. *A History of Korean Literature.* New York: Cambridge University Press, 2003.

——. *Songs of Flying Dragons: A Critical Reading*. Cambridge, MA: Harvard University Press, 1975.

Lefebvre, Henri. *The Production of Space*. Malden, MA: Wiley, 1992.

Lewis, James B., ed. *The East Asian War, 1592–1598: International Relations, Violence and Memory*. New York: Routledge, 2014.

Lewis, Mark E. "Warring States: A Political History." In *The Cambridge History of Ancient China*, ed. Michael Loewe and Edward L. Shaughnessy, 587–650. Cambridge: Cambridge University Press, 1999.

Li Bo. "Maolian wei yu Ming, Chaoxian de guanxi yanjiu" 毛憐衛與明、朝鮮的關係研究. Master's thesis, Dongbei shifan daxue, 2011.

Li, Chunyuan. "Transition Under Ambiguity: Koryŏ-Mongol Relations around 1260." *International Journal of Korean History* 25, no. 1 (February 2020): 123–56.

Li Dongyang 李東陽. *Huailu tang ji* 懷麓堂集. SKQS 1250. Kanseki Repository, 1516. http://kanripo.org/text/KR4e0120/.

——. *Li Dongyang ji* 李東陽集. Changsha: Yuelu shushe, 1984.

Li, Gertraude Roth. "State Building Before 1644." In *The Cambridge History of China*, ed. Willard J. Peterson, vol. 9, 9–72. Cambridge: Cambridge University Press, 2002.

Li Shanhong. "Mingdai Huitongguan dui Chaoxian shichen menjin wenti yanjiu" 明代會同館對朝鮮使臣門禁問題研究. *Lishixue yanjiu* 132, no. 3 (2012): 143–46.

Li Shenghua. *Chu Ming shige yanjiu* 初明詩歌研究. Beijing: Zhonghua shuju, 2012.

Li Tao 李燾. *Xu zizhi tongjian changbian* 續資治通鑑長編. Scripta Sinica. Beijing: Zhonghua shuju, 2004.

Liang, Li. "Tables of Sunrise and Sunset in Yuan and Ming China (1271–1644) and Their Adoption in Korea." In *Editing and Analysing Numerical Tables: Towards a Digital Information System for the History of Astral Sciences*, ed. Matthieu Husson, Clemency Montelle, and Benno van Dalen, 253–85. Turnhout, Belgium: Brepols, 2021.

Lin Yaoyu 林堯俞, ed. *Libu zhigao* 禮部志稿. SKQS 597–98. Taipei: Taiwan Shangwu yinshuguan, 1983.

Liu, Jing. "Beyond the Land: Maritime Interactions, Border Control, and Regional Powers Between China and Korea, 1500–1637." PhD diss., Syracuse University, 2019.

Liu, Jing, and Yan Piao. "Expansion, Contestation, and Boundary Making: Chosŏn Korea and Ming China's Border Relations over the Yalu River Region." *International Journal of Korean History* 25, no. 2 (August 2020): 105–42.

Liu Ju 劉昫. *Jiu Tangshu* 舊唐書. Ed. Yang Jialuo. Scripta Sinica. Taipei: Dingwen shuju, 1981.

Liu, Lydia H. *The Clash of Empires: The Invention of China in Modern World Making*. Cambridge, MA: Harvard University Press, 2004.

———. *Translingual Practice: Literature, National Culture, and Translated Modernity: China, 1900–1937*. Stanford, CA: Stanford University Press, 1995.

Logie, Andrew. "Diagnosing and Debunking Korean Pseudohistory." *European Journal of Korean Studies* 18, no. 2 (2019): 37–80.

Lu Qiguang 魯琪光 and Shao Ziyi 邵子彝, eds. *Jianchang fuzhi* 建昌府志. Tongzhi 同治本 [19th century]. Zhongguo fangzhi ku. Beijing: Airusheng, 2009.

Lü Weiqi 呂維祺. *Siyi guan zengding guanze* 四夷館增定館則. Beijing University Library: China-America Digital Academic Library (CADAL), 1675. https://archive.org/details/02087264.cn.

Ma Guangzu 馬光祖. "Jingding Jiankang zhi" 景定建康志. In *Song-Yuan fangzhi congkan* 宋元方志叢刊, ed. Zhou Yinghe 周應合. Shanghai: Zhonghua shuju, 1990.

Mair, Victor H. "Buddhism and the Rise of the Written Vernacular in East Asia: The Making of National Languages." *The Journal of Asian Studies* 53, no. 3 (1994): 707–51.

Mancall, Mark. "The Ch'ing Tribute System: An Interpretive Essay." In *The Chinese World Order: Traditional China's Foreign Relations*, ed. John King Fairbank, 63–90. Cambridge, MA: Harvard University Press, 1968.

McClymond, Kathryn. *Ritual Gone Wrong: What We Learn from Ritual Disruption*. New York: Oxford University Press, 2016.

McMaster, H. R. "How China Sees the World." *The Atlantic*, May 2020. https://www.theatlantic.com/magazine/archive/2020/05/mcmaster-china-strategy/609088/.

Meng Guanglai 孟廣来 and Chen Siliang 陳嗣良. *Caozhoufu Caoxian zhi* 曹州府曹縣志. Guangxu 光緒本 [1884]. Zhongguo fangzhi ku. Beijing: Airusheng, 2009.

Meskill, John Thomas. "A Record of Drifting Across the Sea: P'yohaerok." PhD diss., Columbia University, 1959.

Messick, Brinkley Morris. *The Calligraphic State: Textual Domination and History in a Muslim Society*. Berkeley: University of California Press, 1993.

Meyer, Christian. "Negotiating Rites in Imperial China: The Case of Northern Song Court Ritual Debates from 1034 to 1093." In *Negotiating Rites*, ed. Ute Hüsken and Frank Neubert, 99–115. London: Oxford University Press, 2012.

Miao Dong. "Yuandai shichen yanjiu" 元代使臣研究. PhD diss., Nankai University, 2010.

Milburn, Olivia. "Headhunting in Ancient China: The History of Violence and Denial of Knowledge." *Bulletin of the School of Oriental and African Studies* 81, no. 1 (February 2018): 103–20.

Millward, James. "How Mongolia Matters: War, Law, and Society." In *How Mongolia Matters: War, Law, and Society*, ed. Morris Rossabi, 19–34. Leiden: Brill, 2017.

Morgan, Prys. "From a Death to a View: The Hunt for the Welsh Past in the Romantic Period." In *The Invention of Tradition*, ed. E. J. Hobsbawm and T. O. Ranger, 43–100. Cambridge: Cambridge University Press, 1983.

Mosca, Matthew W. *From Frontier Policy to Foreign Policy: The Question of India and the Transformation of Geopolitics in Qing China*. Stanford, CA: Stanford University Press, 2013.

Muir, Edward. *Ritual in Early Modern Europe*. Cambridge: Cambridge University Press, 2005.

Mun Chungyang. "15 segi ŭi 'p'ungt'o pudongnon' kwa Chosŏn ŭi koyusŏng" 15세기의 '風土不同論'과 조선의 고유성. *Han'guk sa yŏn'gu* 162 (September 2013): 45–86.

——. "'Hyangnyŏk' esŏ 'Tongnyŏk' ŭro: Chosŏn hugi chagungnyŏk ŭl katkoja hanŭn yŏlmang" '鄉曆'에서 '東曆'으로 : 조선후기 自國曆을 갖고자 하는 열망. *Yŏksa hakpo* 218 (June 2013): 237–70.

Na, Man-gap. *The Diary of 1636: The Second Manchu Invasion of Korea*. Trans. George Kallander. New York: Columbia University Press, 2020.

Nam Yong'ik 南龍翼. *Jiya jiaozhu* 箕雅校注. 1688. Ed. Zhao Ji. Beijing: Zhonghua shuju, 2008.

Nappi, Carla. *Translating Early Modern China: Illegible Cities*. London: Oxford University Press, 2021.

Nauert, Charles Garfield. *Humanism and the Culture of Renaissance Europe*. Cambridge: Cambridge University Press, 1995.

Needham, Joseph. *The Hall of Heavenly Records: Korean Astronomical Instruments and Clocks, 1380–1780*. Cambridge: Cambridge University Press, 2004.

Ni Qian 倪謙. *Chaoxian jishi* 朝鮮紀事. Congshu jicheng chubian 3240. Beijing: Zhonghua shuju, 1985.

——. *Liaohai bian* 遼海編. Reprint [1469] In *Shi Chaoxian lu*, ed. Yin Mengxia and Yu Hao. Beijing: Beijing tushuguan chubanshe, 2003.

Nielsen, Niels Christian. *Fundamentalism, Mythos, and World Religions*. Albany, NY: SUNY Press, 1993.

Nishijima Sadao. *Chūgoku kodai kokka to Higashi Ajia sekai* 中国古代国家と東アジア世界. Tokyo: Tōkyō Daigaku Shuppankai, 1983.

Nylan, Michael. *The Five "Confucian" Classics*. New Haven, CT: Yale University Press, 2001.

Ŏ Sukkwŏn 魚叔權. *A Korean Storyteller's Miscellany: The Paegwan Chapki of O Sukkwon*. Trans. Peter H. Lee. Princeton, NJ: Princeton University Press, 1989.

——. *Kosa ch'waryo* 攷事撮要. [1554] Asami Collection (University of California, Berkeley) 35.7. Seoul, 17th century.

——. *P'aegwan chapki* 稗官雜記. Reprint [1472]. TDYS. Kyŏngsŏng [Seoul]: Chosŏn kosŏ kanhaenghoe.

Oakley, Francis. *Kingship*. Oxford: Blackwell, 2005.

Oh, Hang Nyeong. "The Meaning of Ritual Practices in the Compilation of the Chosŏn Sillok." In *The Institutional Basis of Civil Governance in the Chosŏn Dynasty*, ed. John Duncan, 161–79. Seoul: Seoul Selection, 2009.

Oh, Young Kyun. *Engraving Virtue: The Printing History of a Premodern Korean Moral Primer*. Leiden: Brill, 2013.

Olberding, Garret P. S., ed. *Facing the Monarch: Modes of Advice in the Early Chinese Court*. Cambridge, MA: Harvard Asia Center, 2013.

Ong, Alexander Eng Ann. "Contextualising the Book-Burning Episode During the Ming Invasion and Occupation of Vietnam." In *Southeast Asia in the Fifteenth Century: The China Factor*, ed. Geoff Wade and Laichen Sun, 154–65. Hong Kong: Hong Kong University Press, 2010.

Ouyang Xiu 歐陽修 and Song Qi 宋祁. *Xin Tangshu* 新唐書. Ed. Yang Jialuo. Taipei: Dingwen shuju, 1981.

Owen, Stephen. *Readings in Chinese Literary Thought*. Cambridge, MA: Harvard University Press, 1992.

——. *Traditional Chinese Poetry and Poetics: Omen of the World*. Madison: University of Wisconsin Press, 1985.

Pae Usŏng. *Chosŏn kwa Chunghwa: Chosŏn i kkum kkugo sangsanghan segye wa munmyŏng* 조선과 중화: 조선이 꿈 꾸고 상상한 세계와 문명. Kyŏnggi-do P'aju-si: Tolbegae, 2014.

Paek Yŏngsŏ [Bai Yongrui]. "Zhonghua diguo zai dongya de yiyi: tansuo pipanxing de Zhongguo yanjiu" 中華帝國在東亞的意義: 探索批判性的中國研究. *Kaifang shidai*, 2014. http://www.opentimes.cn/bencandy.php?fid=373&aid=1783.

Pagden, Anthony. *Lords of All Worlds: Ideologies of Empire in Spain, Britain and France c. 1500–c. 1800*. New Haven, CT: Yale University Press, 1995.

Pai, Hyung Il. *Constructing "Korean" Origins: A Critical Review of Archaeology, Historiography, and Racial Myth in Korean State-Formation Theories*. Cambridge, MA: Harvard Asia Center, 2000.

Pak Chŏngmin. "Yŏnsan'gun—Myŏngjongdae Yŏjinin naejo ŭi chaegŏmt'o" 연산군—명종대 여진인 來朝의 재검토. *Yŏksa hakpo* 222 (June 2014): 37–65.

Pak Ch'unsŏp. *Chosŏn kwa Myŏng nara munsadŭl ŭi Kija tamnon ŭi chŏn'gae: "Hwanghwajip" yŏn'gu* 조선과 명나라 문사들의 기자 담론의 전개: "황화집" 연구. Seoul: Pangmunsa, 2018.

Pak Hŭihyŏn. "Kakkung kwa hwasal ŭi chejak" 각궁과 화살의 제작. *Han'guk minsok hak* 10 (December 1977): 177–215.

Pak Sŭngim 朴承任. *Sogo sŏnsaeng munjip* 嘯皋先生文集. Reprint [1600]. HMC 36. Seoul: Minjok munhwa ch'ujinhoe, 1999.

Pak Tongnyang 朴東亮. *Kijae sach'o* 寄齋史草. Reprint [1472] TDYS 10. Kyŏngsŏng [Seoul]: Chosŏn kosŏ kanhaenghoe, 1909.

Pak Wŏnho[hyo]. *Ch'oe Pu P'yohaerok yŏn'gu* 崔溥《漂海錄》研究. Seoul: Koryŏ tae-hakkyo ch'ulp'anbu, 2006.

——. *Myŏngch'o Chosŏn kwan'gyesa yŏn'gu* 明初朝鮮關係史研究. Seoul: Ilchogak, 2002.

——. "Myŏngch'o Chosŏn ŭi Yodong kongpŏl kyehoek kwa Chosŏn p'yojŏn munche" 明初 朝鮮의 遼東攻伐計劃과 朝鮮表箋問題. *P'aeksan hakpo* 19 (1975).

——. "Myŏngch'o ŭi munchaok kwa Chosŏn p'yojŏn munje" 明初의 文字獄과 朝鮮 表箋問題. In *Myŏngch'o Chosŏn kwan'gyesa yŏn'gu*, Seoul: Ilchogak, 2002.

Pak Yunmi. "Koryŏ chŏn'gi oegyo ŭirye esŏ kugwang 'sŏmyŏn' ŭi ŭimi" 고려 전기 외교의례에서 국왕 '서면(西面)'의 의미. *Yŏksa wa hyŏnsil* 98 (December 2015): 69–102.

Park, Eugene Y. *A Family of No Prominence: The Descendants of Pak Tŏkhwa and the Birth of Modern Korea*. Stanford, CA: Stanford University Press, 2014.

——. *A Genealogy of Dissent: The Progeny of Fallen Royals in Chosŏn Korea*. Stanford, CA: Stanford University Press, 2018.

——. "Old Status Trappings in a New World: The 'Middle People' (Chungin) and Genealogies in Modern Korea." *Journal of Family History* 38, no. 2 (April 2013): 166–87.

Park, Hyun Suk. "The Government Courtesan: Status, Gender, and Performance in Late Chosŏn Korea." PhD diss., University of Chicago, 2015.

Park, Jae Woo. "Early Koryŏ Political Institutions and the International Expansion of Tang and Song Institutions." *Korean Studies* 41 (2017): 9–29.

Park Kwon Soo. "Calendar Publishing and Local Science in Chosŏn Korea." In *Science and Confucian Statecraft in East Asia*, ed. Francesca Bray and Jongtae Lim, 123–44. Leiden: Brill, 2019.

Park, Saeyoung. "Me, Myself, and My Hegemony: The Work of Making the Chinese World Order a Reality." *Harvard Journal of Asiatic Studies* 77, no. 1 (July 2017): 47–72.

Park, Seo-Hyun. "Dueling Nationalisms in North and South Korea." *Palgrave Communications* 5, no. 1 (April 2019): 1–8.

——. *Sovereignty and Status in East Asian International Relations*. Cambridge: Cambridge University Press, 2017.

Park, Si Nae. "The Sound of Learning the Confucian Classics in Chosŏn Korea." *Harvard Journal of Asiatic Studies* 79, no. 1 (2019): 131–87.

Peng Dingqiu 彭定求, ed. *Quan Tangshi* 全唐詩. Beijing: Zhonghua shuju, 1960.

Perdue, Peter C. *China Marches West: The Qing Conquest of Central Eurasia*. Cambridge, MA: Belknap Press, 2005.

——. "The Tenacious Tributary System." *Journal of Contemporary China* 24, no. 96 (November 2015): 1002–14.

Phan, John Duong. "Lacquered Words: The Evolution of Vietnamese Under Sinitic Influences from the 1st Century B.C.E. Through the 17th Century C.E." PhD diss., Cornell University, 2013.

Piao Zhongjin. *Zhongguo shifu waijiao de qiyuan yu fazhan* 中國詩賦外交的起源與發展. Beijing: Shizhi chanquan chubanshe, 2014.

Pines, Yuri. *Envisioning Eternal Empire: Chinese Political Thought of the Warring States Period*. Honolulu: University of Hawai'i Press, 2009.

Pines, Yuri, Michal Biran, and Jörg Rüpke, eds. *The Limits of Universal Rule: Eurasian Empires Compared*. Cambridge: Cambridge University Press, 2021.

Pollock, Sheldon. *The Language of the Gods in the World of Men: Sanskrit, Culture, and Power in Premodern India*. Berkeley: University of California Press, 2009.

Pomeranz, Kenneth. "Empire and 'Civilizing' Missions, Past and Present." *Daedalus* 134, no. 2 (Spring 2005): 34–45.

Pössel, Christina. "The Magic of Early Medieval Ritual." *Early Medieval Europe* 17, no. 2 (May 2009): 111–25.

Pratt, Mary Louise. *Imperial Eyes: Travel Writing and Transculturation*. London: Routledge, 1992.

Pyŏn Kyeryang 卞季良. *Ch'unjŏng sŏnsaeng munjip* 春亭先生文集. Reprint [1825]. HMC 8. Seoul: Minjok munhwa ch'ujinhoe, 1990.

Qian, Nanxiu, Richard J. Smith, and Bowei Zhang, eds. *Rethinking the Sinosphere: Poetics, Aesthetics, and Identity Formation*. Amherst, NY: Cambria Press, 2020.

Qing shilu 清實錄. Scripta Sinica. Beijing: Zhonghua shuju, 1936.

Qiu Jun 丘濬. *Daxue yanyi bu* 大學衍義補. SKQS 712–713. Taipei: Shangwu yinshu guan, 1986.

Ravina, Mark. *To Stand with the Nations of the World: Japan's Meiji Restoration in World History*. Oxford: Oxford University Press, 2017.

Rawski, Evelyn S. *Early Modern China and Northeast Asia: Cross-Border Perspectives*. Cambridge: Cambridge University Press, 2015.

——. "Reenvisioning the Qing: The Significance of the Qing Period in Chinese History." *The Journal of Asian Studies* 55, no. 4 (November 1996): 829–50.

Reynolds, Graeme R. "Culling Archival Collections in the Koryŏ-Chosŏn Transition." *Journal of Korean Studies* 24, no. 2 (October 2019): 225–53.

Roberts, Luke S. *Performing the Great Peace: Political Space and Open Secrets in Tokugawa Japan*. Honolulu: Hawai'i University Press, 2015.

Robinson, David M. *Empire's Twilight: Northeast Asia Under the Mongols*. Cambridge, MA: Harvard Asia Center, 2009.

——. *Korea and the Fall of the Mongol Empire: Alliance, Upheaval, and the Rise of a New East Asian Order*. Cambridge: Cambridge University Press, 2022.

——. "Korean Lobbying at the Ming Court: King Chungjong's Usurpation of 1506: A Research Note." *Ming Studies* 41, no. 1 (Spring 1999): 37–53.

——. *Martial Spectacles of the Ming Court*. Cambridge, MA: Harvard Asia Center, 2013.

——. "The Ming Court and the Legacy of the Yuan Mongols." In *Culture, Courtiers, and Competition: The Ming Court (1368–1644)*, ed. David M. Robinson, 365–422. Cambridge, MA: Harvard Asia Center, 2008.

——. "Politics, Force and Ethnicity in Ming China: Mongols and the Abortive Coup of 1461." *Harvard Journal of Asiatic Studies* 59, no. 1 (June 1999): 79–123.

——. "Rethinking the Late Koryŏ in an International Context." *Korean Studies* 41 (July 2017): 75–98.

Robinson, Kenneth R. "Centering the King of Chosŏn." *The Journal of Asian Studies* 59, no. 1 (2000): 33–54.

——. "Organizing Japanese and Jurchens in Tribute Systems in Early Chosŏn Korea." *Journal of East Asian Studies* 13, no. 2 (May 2013): 337–60.

——. "Policies of Practicality: The Choson Court's Regulation of Contact with Japanese and Jurchens, 1392–1580s." PhD diss., University of Hawai'i, 1997.

Robinson, Michael. "National Identity and the Thought of Sin Ch'aeho: Sadaejuŭi and Chuch'e in History and Politics." *The Journal of Korean Studies* 5 (January 1984): 121–42.

Rogers, Michael C. "National Consciousness in Medieval Korea: The Impact of Liao and Chin on Koryŏ." In *China Among Equals*, ed. Morris Rossabi, 151–72. Berkeley: University of California Press, 1983.

——. "Notes on Koryŏ's Relations with Sung and Liao." *Chindan hakpo* 12 (1991): 310–35.

Roosen, William. "Early Modern Diplomatic Ceremonial: A Systems Approach." *The Journal of Modern History* 52, no. 3 (1980): 452–76.

Rossabi, Morris, ed. *China Among Equals: The Middle Kingdom and Its Neighbors, 10th–14th Centuries*. Berkeley: University of California Press, 1983.

——. *The Jurchen in the Yuan and Ming*. Ithaca, NY: Cornell University, China-Japan Program, 1982.

——. *Khubilai Khan: His Life and Times*. Berkeley: University of California Press, 1988.

Rothman, E. Natalie. *Brokering Empire: Trans-Imperial Subjects Between Venice and Istanbul*. Ithaca, NY: Cornell University Press, 2012.

Ruan Yuan 阮元 and Lu Xuanxun 盧宣旬, eds. *Chongkan Songben Shisanjing zhushu fu jiaokan ji* 重刊宋本十三經注疏附校勘記. Scripta Sinica. Taipei: Yiwen yinshu guan, 1965.

Ryu Kisu. "Hwanghwajip ŭi kanhaeng kwa suroktoen Myŏngsa e kwanhan koch'al" 皇華集의 刊行과 收錄된 明詞에 관한 考察. *Chungguk hak yŏn'gu* 47 (2009): 91–125.

Sayŏkwŏn 司譯院. *Sangwŏn cheŏ* 象院題語. Asami Collection (University of California, Berkeley) 18.61. Korea, 16th Century.

Schmid, Andre. *Korea Between Empires, 1895–1919*. New York: Columbia University Press, 2002.

——. "Rediscovering Manchuria: Sin Ch'aeho and the Politics of Territorial History in Korea." *The Journal of Asian Studies* 56, no. 1 (February 1997): 26–46.

Schmitt, Carl. *The Nomos of the Earth in the International Law of the Jus Publicum Europaeum.* Trans. G. L. Ulmen. Candor, NY: Telos Press, 2006.

Schneewind, Sarah. "Beyond Flattery: Legitimating Political Participation in a Ming Living Shrine." *The Journal of Asian Studies* 72, no. 2 (May 2013): 345–66.

——. *Community Schools and the State in Ming China.* Stanford, CA: Stanford University Press, 2006.

——, ed. *Long Live the Emperor!: Uses of the Ming Founder Across Six Centuries of East Asian History.* Minneapolis, MN: Society for Ming Studies, 2008.

——. "Pavilions to Celebrate Honest Officials: An Authenticity Dilemma in Fifteenth-Century China." *Journal of the Economic and Social History of the Orient* 65, no. 1–2 (2022): 164–213.

Schuman, Michael. "What Happens When China Leads the World." *The Atlantic,* October 5, 2020. https://www.theatlantic.com/international/archive/2020/10/what-kind-superpower-will-china-be/616580/.

Scott, James C. *Domination and the Arts of Resistance: Hidden Transcripts.* New Haven, CT: Yale University Press, 2008.

Seeley, Joseph A. "Reeds, River Islands, and Inter-Imperial Conflict on the Early Twentieth-Century Sino-Korean Border." *Water History* 12, no. 3 (September 2020): 373–84.

Seligman, Adam B, Robert P. Weller, Michael J. Puett, and Bennett Simon. *Ritual and Its Consequences: An Essay on the Limits of Sincerity.* New York: Oxford University Press, 2008.

Shi, Yunli. "The Korean Adaptation of the Chinese-Islamic Astronomical Tables." *Archive for History of Exact Sciences* 57, no. 1 (2003): 25–60.

Shim, Jae-Hoon. "A New Understanding of Kija Chosŏn as a Historical Anachronism." *Harvard Journal of Asiatic Studies* 62, no. 2 (December 2002): 271–305.

Shultz, Edward J. *Generals and Scholars: Military Rule in Medieval Korea.* Honolulu: University of Hawai'i Press, 2000.

Silverstein, Michael, and Greg Urban. *Natural Histories of Discourse.* Chicago: University of Chicago Press, 1996.

Sima Guang 司馬光. *Zizhi tongjian* 資治通鑑. Ed. Hu Sansheng. Scripta Sinica. Beijing: Beijing guji chubanshe, 1956.

Sima Qian 司馬遷. *Shiji (Xinjiaoben Shiji sanjiazhu bing fubian erzhong)* 史記 (新校本史記三家注并附編二種). Scripta Sinica. Taipei: Dingwen shuju, 1981.

Sin Kyŏng 申炅. *Chaejo pŏnbang chi* 再造藩邦志. Reprint [1693]. TDYS 35–39. Kyŏngsŏng [Seoul]: Chosŏn kosŏ kanhaenghoe, 1909.

Sin Sukchu 申叔舟. *Pohanjae chip* 保閑齋集. Reprint [1645]. HMC 10. Seoul: Minjok munhwa ch'ujinhoe, 1988.

Sin T'aeyŏng. *Myŏng nara sasin ŭn Chosŏn ŭl ŏttŏk'e poannŭn'ga: "Hwanghwajip"*
yŏn'gu 명나라 사신은 조선을 어떻게 보았는가: "皇華集" 研究. Seoul: Taunsaem,
2005.

——. "'Hwanghwajip' ŭi p'yŏnch'an ŭisik yŏn'gu - sŏmun ŭl chungsim ŭro"『皇華集』
의 편찬의식 연구 - 序文을 중심으로 -. *Hanmun hakpo* 5 (2001): 115–44.

Sivin, Nathan, Kiyosi Yabuuti, and Shigeru Nakayama. *Granting the Seasons: The
Chinese Astronomical Reform of 1280, with a Study of Its Many Dimensions and
a Translation of Its Records.* New York: Springer, 2009.

Sloane, Jesse D. "Mapping a Stateless Nation: 'Bohai' Identity in the Twelfth to
Fourteenth Centuries." *Journal of Song-Yuan Studies* 44 (2014): 365–403.

Smith, Paul J. "Irredentism as Political Capital: The New Policies and the Annexation of Tibetan Domains in Hehuang (the Qinghai-Gansu Highlands) Under
Shenzong and His Sons, 1068–1126." In *Emperor Huizong and Late Northern
Song China: The Politics of Culture and the Culture of Politics,* ed. Patricia Buckley Ebrey and Maggie Bickford, 78–130. Cambridge, MA: Harvard Asia Center,
2006.

Smith, Richard J. *Mapping China and Managing the World: Culture, Cartography
and Cosmology in Late Imperial Times.* London: Routledge, 2013.

Smits, Gregory. *Maritime Ryukyu, 1050–1650.* Honolulu: University of Hawai'i Press,
2019.

Sneath, David. *The Headless State: Aristocratic Orders, Kinship Society, and Misrepresentations of Nomadic Inner Asia.* New York: Columbia University Press, 2007.

Sŏ Inwŏn. "Chosŏn ch'ogi yŏksa insik kwa yŏng'uk insik: 'Tongguk yŏji süngnam' ŭl
chungsim ŭro" 朝鮮初期 歷史認識과 領域認識-『東國輿地勝覽』을 중심으로.
Yŏksa wa sirhak 35 (June 2008): 89–116.

Sŏ Kŏjŏng 徐居正. *P'irwŏn chapki* 筆苑雜記. Reprint [1472]. TDYS 1. Kyŏngsŏng
[Seoul]: Chosŏn kosŏ kanhaenghoe, 1909.

——. *Saga chip* 四佳集. Reprint [1705]. HMC 10–11. Seoul: Minjok munhwa ch'ujinhoe, 1988.

——, ed. *Tongmunsŏn* 東文選. Seoul: Kyŏnghŭi ch'ulp'ansa, 1966.

Sŏ Myŏng'ŭng 徐命膺. *Kija oegi* 箕子外紀. Harvard-Yenching Rare Books, TK
3483.4 2980. P'yŏngyang, 1776.

So Seyang 蘇世讓. "Yanggok pugyŏng ilgi" 陽谷赴京日記. In *Yŏnhaengnok chŏnjip* 燕行錄全集, ed. Im Kijung 林基中, [1534], vol. 2. Seoul: Tongguk taehakkyo
ch'ulp'anbu, 2001.

Song Ho Jung. "Old Chosŏn—Its History and Archaeology." In *The Han Commanderies in Early Korean History,* ed. Mark E. Byington, 49–80. Early Korean Project
Occasional Series. Cambridge, MA: Korea Institute, Harvard University, 2013.

Song Huijuan. *Qingdai Zhong-Chao zongfan guanxi shanbian yanjiu* 清代中朝宗藩
關係嬗變研究. Changchun: Jilin daxue chubanshe, 2007.

Sŏng Hyŏn 成俔. *Yongjae ch'onghwa* 慵齋叢話. Reprint [15th century] TDYS 1. Kyŏngsŏng [Seoul]: Chosŏn kosŏ kanhaenghoe, 1909.

Song Lian 宋濂. *Wenxian ji* 文憲集. SKQS 1223–24. Taipei: Shangwu yinshu guan, 1983.

——. *Yuan shi* 元史. Ed. Yang Jialuo. Scripta Sinica. Taipei: Dingwen shuju, 1981.

Song, Nianshen. "A Buffer Against Whom? Rethinking the Qing-Chosŏn Border Region." *Geopolitics*, December 21, 2020, 1–17.

——. "Northeast Eurasia as Historical Center: Exploration of a Joint Frontier." *Asia-Pacific Journal: Japan Focus* 13, no. 44.2 (November 2015): 1–18.

Sorenson, Henrik H. "Lamaism in Korea During the Late Koryŏ Dynasty." *Korea Journal* 33, no. 3 (1993): 67–81.

Spruyt, Hendrik. "Collective Imaginations and International Order: The Contemporary Context of the Chinese Tributary System." *Harvard Journal of Asiatic Studies* 77, no. 1 (July 2017): 21–45.

——. *The World Imagined: Collective Beliefs and Political Order in the Sinocentric, Islamic and Southeast Asian International Societies*. Cambridge: Cambridge University Press, 2020.

Stary, Giovanni. *A Dictionary of Manchu Names: A Name-Index to the Manchu Version of the* "Complete Genealogies of the Manchu Clans and Families of the Eight Banners." Wiesbaden: Harrassowitz, 2000.

Steininger, Brian. *Chinese Literary Forms in Heian Japan: Poetics and Practice*. Cambridge, MA: Harvard Asia Center, 2017.

Stiller, Maya K. H. *Carving Status at Kŭmgangsan: Elite Graffiti in Premodern Korea*. Seattle: University of Washington Press, 2021.

Stoler, Ann Laura, Carole McGranahan, and Peter C. Perdue, eds. *Imperial Formations*. Santa Fe, NM: School for Advanced Research Press, 2007.

Stollberg-Rilinger, Barbara. *The Emperor's Old Clothes: Constitutional History and the Symbolic Language of the Holy Roman Empire*. Trans. Thomas Dunlap. New York: Berghahn, 2015.

Su Che 蘇轍. *Luancheng ji* 欒城集. SKQS 1112. Taipei: Shangwu yinshu guan, 1983.

Su Shi 蘇軾. *Dongpo quanji* 東坡全集. SKQS 1107–1108. Taipei: Shangwu yinshu guan, 1983.

Suh, Soyoung. "Herbs of Our Own Kingdom: Layers of the 'Local' in the Materia Medica of Early Choson Korea." *Asian Medicine* 4, no. 2 (December 2009): 395–422.

Sun Weiguo. "Chuanshuo, lishi yu rentong: Tanjun Chaoxian yu Jizi Chaoxian zhi suzao yu yanbian" 傳說, 歷史與認同: 檀君朝鮮與箕子朝鮮歷史之塑造與演變. In *Cong zhoubian kan Zhongguo*, ed. Ge Zhaoguang 葛兆光, Fudan daxue wenshi yanjiuyuan 復旦大學文史研究院, Elman Benjamin A., and Wenshi yanjiu yuan 文史研究院, 313–36. Beijing: Zhonghua shuju, 2009.

——. *Cong "zun Ming" dao "feng Qing": Chaoxian wangchao dui Qing yishi de shan-bian (1627–1910)* 從「尊明」到「奉清」: 朝鮮王朝對清意識的嬗變 (1627–1910). Taipei: Taiwan daxue chuban she, 2019.

——. "Lun Mingchu de huanguan waijiao" 論明初的宦官外交. *Nankai xuebao*, no. 2 (1994): 34–42.

——. *Ming Qing shiqi Zhongguo shixue dui Chaoxian de yingxiang: jian lun liangguo xueshu jiaoliu yu haiwai Hanxue* 明清時期中國史學對朝鮮的影響: 兼論兩國學術交流與海外漢學. Shanghai: Shanghai cishu chubanshe, 2009.

——. "'Ming shilu' yu 'Chaoxian wangchao shilu' zhi bijiao yanjiu" 《明實錄》與《朝鮮王朝實錄》之比較研究. In *Ming Qing shiqi Zhongguo shixue*.

——. "Shi shuo Ming dai Xingren" 試說明代行人. *Shixue jikan*, no. 1 (1994): 11–16.

Sun Weiran. "Qiantan Tang-Luo zhanzheng zhong de 'Maixiaocheng zhi zhan'" 淺談唐羅戰爭中的買肖城之戰. *Dongbei shidi* 2 (2010): 43–44.

Sŭngje yŏngsŏn 勝題英選. Kyujanggak Archives (Seoul National University) Ko (古) 3431–4. Vol. 1, 3 (2 missing)., 16th century.

Sŭngmunwŏn 承文院, ed. *Tongmun hwigo* 同文彙考. Han'guk saryo ch'ongsŏ 24. Seoul: Kuksa p'yŏnch'an wiwŏnhoe, 1978.

Swope, Kenneth. *A Dragon's Head and a Serpent's Tail: Ming China and the First Great East Asian War, 1592–1598*. Norman: University of Oklahoma Press, 2009.

Szonyi, Michael. *The Art of Being Governed: Everyday Politics in Late Imperial China*. Princeton, NJ: Princeton University Press, 2017.

Tackett, Nicolas. *The Origins of the Chinese Nation: Song China and the Forging of an East Asian World Order*. Cambridge: Cambridge University Press, 2017.

"Tae Ch'ŏng hwangje kongdŏk pi" 大清皇帝功德碑. Stele rubbing, 1639. Asami Collection (University of California, Berkeley) 20.

Tao, Jing-shen. *Two Sons of Heaven: Studies in Sung-Liao Relations*. Tucson: University of Arizona Press, 1988.

Teng, Emma. "Other as Self? The 'Civilized Barbarian' in Dong Yue's *Fu on Korea*." In *Travels in and out of Pre-Modern Korea*, ed. Marion Eggert, 63–84. Bochumer Jahrbuch zur Ostasienforschung. Bochum, Germany: Fakultät für Ostasienwissenschaften, Ruhr-Universität Bochum, 2012.

Throness, Aaron Wesley. "To Govern the State and Bring Peace to the Realm: Qiu Jun's (1421–1495) Geographic Statecraft Thought in 15th Century Ming China." Master's thesis, University of British Columbia, 2022.

Tianhua caizi 天花才子 and Siqiao jushi 四橋居士. *Kuaixian bian* 快心編. Taipei: Tianyi chubanshe, 1985.

Truschke, Audrey. *Culture of Encounters: Sanskrit at the Mughal Court*. New York: Columbia University Press, 2016.

Tsai, Shih-shan Henry. *The Eunuchs in the Ming Dynasty*. Albany: SUNY Press, 1996.

U Kyŏngsŏp. *Chosŏn Chunghwa chuŭi ŭi sŏngnip kwa Tong Asia* 조선 중화주의의 성립과 동아시아. Seoul: Yuni sŭt'ori, 2013.

Van Lieu, Joshua. "Chosŏn-Qing Tributary Discourse: Transgression, Restoration, and Textual Performativity." *Cross-Currents: East Asian History and Culture Review*, no. 27 (June 2018): 79–112.

——. "Divergent Visions of Serving the Great: The Emergence of Chosŏn-Qing Tributary Relations as a Politics of Representation." PhD diss., University of Washington, 2010.

——. "A Farce That Wounds Both High and Low: The Guan Yu Cult in Chosŏn-Ming Relations." *Journal of Korean Religions* 5, no. 2 (December 2014): 39–70.

——. "The Politics of Condolence: Contested Representations of Tribute in Late Nineteenth-Century Chosŏn-Qing Relations." *Journal of Korean Studies* 14, no. 1 (2009): 83–115.

——. "The Tributary System and the Persistence of Late Victorian Knowledge." *Harvard Journal of Asiatic Studies* 77, no. 1 (July 2017): 73–92

Wade, Geoff. "Civilizational Rhetoric and the Obfuscation of Power Politics." In *Sacred Mandates: Asian International Relations Since Chinggis Khan*, ed. Timonthy Brook, M. C. van Walt van Praag, and Mike Boltjes, 75–81. Chicago: University of Chicago Press, 2018.

——. "Engaging the South: Ming China and Southeast Asia in the Fifteenth Century." *Journal of the Economic and Social History of the Orient* 51, no. 4 (2008): 578–638.

Wagner, Edward W. "The Literati Purges: Case Studies in the Factionalism of the Early Yi Dynasty." PhD diss., Harvard University, 1959.

——. *The Literati Purges: Political Conflict in Early Yi Korea*. Cambridge, MA: Harvard University Press, 1974.

Wakeman, Frederic E. *The Great Enterprise: The Manchu Reconstruction of Imperial Order in Seventeenth-Century China*. Berkeley: University of California Press, 1985.

Walker, Hugh D. "The Yi-Ming Rapprochement: Sino-Korean Foreign Relations, 1392–1592." PhD diss., University of California, Los Angeles, 1971.

Walzer, Michael. *Just and Unjust Wars: A Moral Argument with Historical Illustrations*. New York: Basic Books, 2015.

Wang, Ban. *Chinese Visions of World Order: Tianxia, Culture, and World Politics*. Durham, NC: Duke University Press, 2017.

Wang Gungwu. "The Cambridge History of China." In *Ming Foreign Relations: Southeast Asia*, ed. Denis C. Twitchett and Frederick W. Mote, vol. 8. Cambridge: Cambridge University Press, 1998.

——. "The Rhetoric of a Lesser Empire: Early Sung Relations with Its Neighbors." In *China Among Equals: The Middle Kingdom and Its Neighbors, 10th–14th Centuries*, ed. Morris Rossabi, 47–63. Berkeley: University of California Press, 1983.

Wang Hui. *Ya Zhou shiye: Zhongguo lishi de xushu* 亞洲視野：中國歷史的敘述. Hong Kong: Oxford University Press, 2010.

Wang Jianfeng. "Mingchao tidu Huitongguan zhushi shezhi tanwei" 明朝提督會同館主事設置探微. *Liaoning daxue xuebao: zhexue shehui kexue ban* 34, no. 6 (November 2006): 79–82.

Wang Jianxin 王檢心, Liu Wenqi 劉文淇, and Zhang Anbao 張安保, eds. *Chongxiu Yizheng xianzhi* 重修儀徵縣志. Daoguang 道光本 [1890]. Zhongguo fangzhi ku. Beijing: Airusheng, 2009.

Wang Keping. "Shifu waijiao zai Ming chao yu Chaoxian guanxi shi shang de zuoyong" 詩賦外交在明朝與朝鮮關係史上的作用. *Yanbian daxue xuebao* 44, no. 1 (February 2011): 88–92.

Wang, Pei, and Daniel A. Bell. *Just Hierarchy: Why Social Hierarchies Matter in China and the Rest of the World*. Princeton, NJ: Princeton University Press, 2020.

Wang, Sixiang. "Chosŏn's Office of Interpreters: The Apt Response and the Knowledge Culture of Diplomacy." *Journal for the History of Knowledge* 1, no. 1 (December 2020): 1–15.

——. "Co-Constructing Empire in Early Chosŏn Korea: Knowledge Production and the Culture of Diplomacy, 1392–1592." PhD diss., Columbia University, 2015.

——. "Compiling Diplomacy: Record-Keeping and Archival Practices in Chosŏn Korea." *Journal of Korean Studies* 24, no. 2 (September 2019): 255–88.

——. "Emotions in Koryŏ-Mongol Diplomacy: From Covenants of Affect to the Paternal Simile." Unpublished manuscript, December 1, 2021, typescript.

——. "The Filial Daughter of Kwaksan: Finger Severing, Confucian Virtues, and Envoy Poetry in Early Chosŏn." *Seoul Journal of Korean Studies* 25, no. 2 (December 2012): 175–212.

——. "Korean Eunuchs as Imperial Envoys: Relations with Chosŏn Through the Zhengde Reign." In *The Ming World*, ed. Kenneth Swope, 460–80. New York: Routledge, 2020.

——. "Loyalty, History, and Empire: Qian Qianyi and His Korean Biographies." In *Representing Lives in East Asia, China and Korea 1400–1900*, ed. Ihor Pidhainy, Grace Fong, and Roger Des Forges. Ithaca, NY: Cornell University East Asia Program, 2018.

——. "The Sounds of Our Country: Interpreters, Linguistic Knowledge and the Politics of Language in Early Chosŏn Korea (1392–1592)." In *Rethinking East Asian Languages, Vernaculars, and Literacies, 1000–1919*, ed. Benjamin A. Elman, 58–95. Leiden: Brill, 2014.

——. "Story of the Eastern Chamber: Dilemmas of Vernacular Language and Political Authority in Eighteenth-Century Chosŏn." *Journal of Korean Studies* 24, no. 1 (March 2019): 29–62.

——. "What Tang Taizong Could Not Do: The Korean Surrender of 1259 and the Imperial Tradition." *T'oung Pao* 104, no. 3–4 (October 2018): 338–83.

Wang Yinglin 王應麟. *Yu Hai* 玉海. SKQS 943–48. Taipei: Shangwu yinshu guan, 1983.

Wang, Yuanchong. "Claiming Centrality in the Chinese World: Manchu-Chosŏn Relations and the Making of the Qing's Zhongguo Identity, 1616–1643." *Chinese Historical Review* 22, no. 2 (November 2015): 95–119.

——. *Remaking the Chinese Empire Manchu-Korean Relations, 1616–1911*. Ithaca, NY: Cornell University Press, 2018.

Wang, Zhenping. *Ambassadors from the Islands of Immortals: China-Japan Relations in the Han-Tang Period*. Honolulu: University of Hawai'i Press, 2005.

——. *Tang China in Multi-Polar Asia: A History of Diplomacy and War*. Honolulu: University of Hawai'i Press, 2017.

Weber-Schäfer, Peter. *Oikumene und Imperium: Studien zur Ziviltheologie des chinesischen Kaiserreichs*. Bern: Peter Lang International, 1968.

Wechsler, Howard J. *Offerings of Jade and Silk: Ritual and Symbol in the Legitimation of the T'ang Dynasty*. New Haven, CT: Yale University Press, 1985.

Wen, Xin. "The Road to Literary Culture: Revisiting the Jurchen Language Examination System." *T'oung Pao* 101, no. 1–3 (August 2015): 130–67.

Westad, Odd Arne. *Empire and Righteous Nation: 600 Years of China-Korea Relations*. Cambridge, MA: Harvard University Press, 2021.

Wheaton, Henry. *Elements of International Law*. Ed. Richard Henry Dana and Theodore Dwight Woolsey. Gale, *Making of Modern Law*, 1866.

Wilkinson, Endymion Porter. *Chinese History: A Manual*. Cambridge, MA: Harvard Asia Center, 2000.

Wills, John E., ed. *China and Maritime Europe, 1500–1800: Trade, Settlement, Diplomacy, and Missions*. Cambridge: Cambridge University Press, 2011.

Wilson, Peter H. *Heart of Europe: A History of the Holy Roman Empire*. Cambridge, MA: Belknap Press, 2016.

Wittgenstein, Ludwig. *Philosophical Investigations*. 4th ed. Ed. P. M. S. Hacker and Joachim Schulte. Oxford: Wiley-Blackwell, 2009.

Womack, Brantly. *China and Vietnam: The Politics of Asymmetry*. Cambridge: Cambridge University Press, 2006.

Wong, Bin. *China Transformed: Historical Change and the Limits of European Experience*. 1st ed.. Ithaca, NY: Cornell University Press, 2000.

Wong, King Kwong. "All Are the Ruler's Domain, but All Are Different: Mongol-Yuan Rule and Koryŏ Sovereignty in the Thirteenth and Fourteenth Centuries." *Seoul Journal of Korean Studies* 34, no. 1 (2021): 1–30.

Woodruff, Phillip H. "Foreign Policy and Frontier Affairs Along the Northeast Frontier of the Ming Dynasty, 1350–1618: Tripartite Relations of the Ming Chinese,

Korean Koryo, and Jurchen-Manchu Tribesmen." PhD diss., University of Chicago, 1995.

——. "Status and Lineage Among Jurchens of the Korean Northeast in the Mid-Fifteenth Century." *Central and Inner Asian Studies* 1, no. 1 (1987): 117–54.

Woodside, Alexander. "Territorial Order and Collective-Identity Tensions in Confucian Asia: China, Vietnam, Korea." *Daedalus* 127, no. 3 (Summer 1998): 191–220.

Wright, Eloise. "History and Autoethnography: Accounting for the Indigenous Population of Yunnan, 1550–1650." *Journal of Colonialism and Colonial History* 22, no. 1 (2021).

Wu Yue. "Waijiao de linian yu waijiao de xianshi: yi Zhu Yuanzhang dui 'buzhengguo' Chaoxian de zhengce wei zhongxin" 外交的理念與外交的現實—以朱元璋對 "不征國" 朝鮮的政策為中心. *Mingshi yanjiu* 11 (2010): 26–54.

Xia Yan 夏言. *Guizhou xiansheng zouyi* 桂洲先生奏議. Siku quanshu cunmu congshu, Shi bu (part 2) 史部 60. Tainan: Zhuangyan wenhua, 1996.

Xiao Qiqing. *Nei Beiguo er wai Zhongguo: Meng-Yuanshi yanjiu* 內北國而外中國: 蒙元史研究. Beijing: Zhonghua shuju, 2007.

Xiao Tong 蕭統 and Li Shan 李善, eds. *Wenxuan* 文選. Shanghai: Shanghai guji chubanshe, 2005.

Xu Dongri. *Chaoxian chao shichen yanzhong de Zhongguo xingxiang: yi "Yan xing lu" "Chao tian lu" wei zhongxin* 朝鮮朝使臣眼中的中國形象: 以《燕行錄》《朝天錄》為中心. Beijing: Zhonghua shuju, 2010.

Xu Guangqi 徐光啓. *Xu Guangqi ji* 徐光啓集. Shanghai: Zhonghua shuju, 1963.

Xu Jing. *A Chinese Traveler in Medieval Korea: Xu Jing's Illustrated Account of the Xuanhe Embassy to Koryo.* Trans. Sem Vermeersch. Honolulu: University of Hawai'i Press, 2016.

Xu Qixiong. "Shida zhicheng—Cong 16 shijimo 'Zhaoxue guoyi' he 'Renchen qingyuan' kan Chaoxian Li Chao zhengzhi hexin dui Zhongguo de xiangxiang he qixu" 事大至誠—從16世紀末 "昭雪國疑" 和 "壬辰請援" 看朝鮮李朝政治核心對中國的想象和期許. In *Cong zhoubian kan Zhongguo,* ed. Ge Zhaoguang 葛兆光 and Wenshi yanjiu yuan 文史研究院, 337–45. Beijing: Zhonghua shuju, 2009.

Xu Song 徐松, and Wang Deyi 王德毅, eds. *Song huiyao jigao* 宋會要輯稿. Scripta Sinica. Taipei: Zhongyang yanjiuyuan lishi yuyan yanjiusuo, 2008.

Xu, Stella. *Reconstructing Ancient Korean History: The Formation of Korean-Ness in the Shadow of History.* London: Lexington Books, 2016.

Xu Yikui 徐一夔. *Da Ming jili* 大明集禮. Jiajing 嘉靖本. Scripta Sinica, 1530.

——. *Ming jili* 明集禮. SKQS 649–50. Taipei: Shangwu yinshu guan, 1978.

Xu Yuanmei 徐元梅. *Shanyin xianzhi* 山陰縣志. Ed. Zhu Wenhan 朱文翰. Jiaqing 嘉慶本. Zhongguo fangzhi ku. Beijing: Airusheng, 2009.

Xue Yingqi 薛應旂. *Fangshan xiansheng wenlu* 方山先生文錄. Dongwu shulin jiaokan ben 東吳書林校刊本 [1544]. Siku quanshu cunmu congshu, jibu 集部 102. Jinan: Qilu shushe, 1997.

Xue Yingqi 薛應旂 and Hu Zongxian 胡宗憲, eds. *Zhejiang tongzhi* 浙江通志. Jiajing 嘉靖本 [16th century]. Zhongguo fangzhi ku. Beijing: Airusheng, 2009.

Yan Congjian 嚴從簡. *Shizhi wenxian tongbian* 使職文獻通編. National Central Library (Taiwan), 1565.

——. *Shuyu zhouzi lu* 殊域周咨錄. Reprint. Beijing: Gugong bowuyuan tushuguan, 1580. https://ctext.org/library.pl?if=en&res=2263.

——. *Shuyu zhouzi lu* 殊域周咨錄. Ed. Yu Sili. Beijing: Zhonghua shuju, 1993.

Yang Bojun 楊伯峻. *Chunqiu Zuozhuan zhu* 春秋左傳注. Beijing: Zhonghua shuju, 1981.

Yang Junqing 楊儁卿 and Cheng Kai 程楷. *Pinghu xianzhi* 平湖縣志. Tianqi 天啟 [17th century]. Zhongguo fangzhi ku. Beijing: Airusheng, 2009.

Yang, Shao-yun. *The Way of the Barbarians: Redrawing Ethnic Boundaries in Tang and Song China*. Seattle: University of Washington Press, 2019.

Yang Yulei. *Yanxing yu Zhong-Chao wenhua guanxi* 燕行與中朝文化關係. Shanghai: Shanghai cishu chubanshe, 2011.

Yao Cha 姚察, Xie Gui 謝炅, Wei Zheng 魏徵, and Yao Silian 姚思廉. *Liang shu* 梁書, ed. Yang Jialuo. Zhongguo xueshu leibian 中國學術類編. Taipei: Dingwen shuju, 1980.

Yao Sui 姚燧. *Muan ji* 牧庵集. SKQS 1201. Taipei: Shangwu yinshuguan, 1983.

Ye Quanhong 業泉宏. *Mingdai qianqi Zhong Han guojiao zhi yanjiu: 1368–1488* 明代前期中韓國交之研究. Taipei: Shangwu yinshuguan, 1991.

Yi Aedŭk. "Chosŏn sidae Yŏnsan'gun ŭi yŏak chedo e kwanhan koch'al" 조선시대 연산군의 여악제도에 관한 고찰. *Muyong hakhoe nonmun chip* 50 (2007): 159–77.

Yi Hwang 李滉. *T'oegye chip* 退溪集. Reprint [1843]. HMC 29–31. Minjok munhwa ch'ujinhoe, 1989.

Yi I 李珥. *Yulgok sŏnsaeng chŏnsŏ* 栗谷先生全書. Reprint [1814]. HMC 44–45. Minjok munhwa ch'ujinhoe, 1989.

Yi Ik 李瀷. *Sŏngho sŏnsaeng sasŏl* 星湖先生僿說, ed. Yi Tonhyŏng 李暾衡. Han'guk kojŏn chonghap DB. Seoul: Han'guk kojŏn pŏnyŏgwŏn, 1978. https://db.itkc .or.kr/.

Yi Ikchu. "Koryŏ Ch'ungnyŏl wangdae ŭi chŏngch'i sanghwang kwa chŏngch'i seryŏk ŭi sŏngkyŏk" 高麗 忠烈王代의 政治狀況과 政治勢力의 性格. *Han'guk saron* 18 (1988): 155–222.

——. "Koryŏ, Wŏn kwan'gye ŭi kujo e taehan yŏn'gu- sowi 'Sejo kuje' ŭi punsŏk ŭl chungsim ŭro" 고려, 원관계의 구조에 대한 연구 - 소위 "세조구제"의 분석을 중심으로-. *Han'guk saron* 36 (1996): 1–51.

———. "Koryŏ-Monggol chŏnjaeng ch'ogi (1231–1232) ŭi Kanghwa hyŏpsang yŏn'gu" 고려-몽골 전쟁 초기(1231~1232)의 강화 협상 연구. *Han'guk sa yŏn'gu* 180 (March 2018): 1–31.

Yi Kyŏngnyong. "Myŏngdae chisigin ŭi Chosŏn insik kwa yangguk ŭi pangbuk chŏngch'aek" 명대 지식인의 조선 인식과 양국의 防北정책. *Myŏng Ch'ŏng sa yŏn'gu* 25 (April 2004): 67–96.

Yi Kyubo 李奎報. *Tongguk Yi Sangguk chip* 東國李相國集. Reprint. HMC 1–2. Minjok munhwa ch'ujinhoe, 1990.

Yi Kyuch'ŏl. "Chosŏn Sŏngjŏngdae oegyo ŭirye pyŏn'gyŏng e taehan nonŭi wa tae Myŏng ŭisik" 조선 성종대 외교의례 변경에 대한 논의와 대명의식. *Yŏksa wa hyŏnsil*, no. 98 (December 2015): 169–97.

———. "Sejo tae Moryŏnwi chŏngpŏl ŭi ŭimi wa tae Myŏng insik" 세조대 모련위 정벌의 의미와 대명인식. *Han'guksa yŏn'gu* 158 (September 2012): 121–58.

Yi Manbu 李萬敷. *Siksan sŏnsaeng pyŏl chip* 息山先生別集. Reprint [1813]. HMC 178–179. Seoul: Minjok munhwa ch'ujinhoe, 1995.

Yi Myŏngmi. "Koryŏ-Mongol kwan'gye wa Koryŏ kugwang wisang ŭi pyŏnhwa" 고려-몽골 관계와 고려국왕 위상의 변화. PhD diss., Seoul National University, 2012.

Yi Saek 李穡. *Mogŭn'go* 牧隱藁. Reprint [1626]. HMC 3–5. Seoul: Minjok munhwa ch'ujinhoe, 1990.

Yi Sangjŏk 李尚迪. *Yŏnhaeng sarye* 燕行事例. Fonds Maurice Courant, Manuscrits coréens n5258 KS 42. Paris, 1857.

Yi Sŏkhyŏng 李石亨. *Chŏhŏn chip* 樗軒集. Reprint [1587]. HMC 9. Seoul: Minjok munhwa ch'ujinhoe, 1988.

Yi Sŏnggyu. "Chungguk sahakkye esŏ pon Ko Chosŏn" 중국사학계에서 본 고조선. *Han'guksa simin kangjwa* 49 (August 2011): 21–71.

Yi Sugwang 李睟光. *Chipong sŏnsaeng chip* 芝峯先生集. Reprint [1633]. HMC 66. Seoul: Minjok munhwa ch'ujinhoe, 1996.

Yi Sŭngso 李承召. *Samt'an sŏnsaeng chip* 三灘先生集. Reprint [1515]. HMC 11. Seoul: Minjok munhwa ch'ujinhoe, 1996.

Yi, T'ae-jin. *The Dynamics of Confucianism and Modernization in Korean History.* Ithaca, NY: East Asia Program, Cornell University, 2007.

Yi To 李祹. *Sejong ŏje Hunmin chŏngŭm ŏnhae* 世宗御製訓民正音諺解. Reprint. Kyujanggak Archives 가람 古 411.1-H899s. Seoul, 1568.

Yi Yŏnghun. *Sejong ŭn kwayŏn sŏnggun inga* 세종은 과연 성군인가. P'aju: Paengnyŏn tongan, 2018.

Yin Mengxia, and Yu Hao, eds. *Shi Chaoxian lu* 使朝鮮錄. Beijing: Beijing tushuguan chubanshe, 2003.

Yŏngjŏp togam 迎接都監. *Yŏngjŏp togam toch'ŏng ŭigwe* 迎接都監都廳儀軌. Kyujanggak Archives (Seoul National University) Kyu 14545, 14546. Seoul, 1608.

——. *Yŏngjŏp togam toch'ŏng ŭigwe* 迎接都監都廳儀軌. Kyujanggak Archives (Seoul National University) Kyu 14559. Seoul, 1634.

Yoo, Jamie Jungmin. "Networks of Disquiet: Censorship and the Production of Literature in Eighteenth-Century Korea." *Acta Koreana* 20, no. 1 (2017): 249–80.

Yoshikawa Kōjirō. *Five Hundred Years of Chinese Poetry, 1150–1650: The Chin, Yuan, and Ming Dynasties*. Princeton, NJ: Princeton University Press, 1989.

Yu Hong 俞泓. *Songdang chip* 松塘集. Reprint [1642]. HMC Sok (續) 3. Seoul: Minjok munhwa ch'ujinhoe, 2005.

Yu Hŭi-ch'un 柳希春. *Miam sŏnsaeng chip* 眉巖先生集. Reprint [1869]. HMC 34. Seoul: Minjok munhwa ch'ujinhoe, 1989.

Yu Hŭiyŏng 柳希齡. *Kyogam p'yoje ŭmju Tongguk saryak* 校勘標題音註東國史略. Kojŏn charyo ch'ongsŏ 85–2. Kyŏnggi-do Sŏngnam-si: Han'guk chŏngsin munhwa yŏn'guwŏn, 1985.

Yu Pada. "Chosŏn ch'ogi ŭngchoch'ik kwallyŏn ŭiju ŭi sŏngnip kwa Cho-Myŏng kwan'gye" 朝鮮 初期 迎詔勅 관련 儀註의 성립과 朝明關係. *Yŏksa minsok hak*, no. 40 (November 2012): 123–60.

Yu Sŭnghyu 李承休. "Chewang un'gi" 帝王韻記. In *Koryŏ myŏnghyŏnjip*, Reprint [1287] [1939]. Seoul: Sŏnggyun'gwan taehakkyo Taedong munhwa yŏn'guwŏn, 1973.

Yu Sŭngju. "Chosŏn chŏn'gi tae Myŏng muyŏk i kungnae sanŏp e mich'in yŏnghyang: 15 segi tae Myŏng kŭmŭn chogong kwa kungnae kŭmŭn kwangŏp ŭl chungsim ŭro" 조선전기 대명무역이 국내산업에 미친 영향 - 15세기 대명금은조공과 국내 금은광업을 중심으로 -. *Asea yŏn'gu* 32, no. 2 (July 1989): 29–66.

Yuan Gaoli jishi 元高麗紀事. Taipei: Guangwen shuju, 1972.

Yun Chŏng. "Sukchongdae Tanjong ch'upok ŭi chŏngch'isajŏk ŭimi" 숙종대 단종 추복의 정치사적 의미. *Han'guk sasang sahak* 22 (June 2004): 209–46.

Yun, Peter. "Confucian Ideology and the Tribute System in Chosŏn-Ming Relations." *Sach'ong* 55, no. 9 (2002): 67–88.

——. "Rethinking the Tribute System: Korean States and Northeast Asian Interstate Relations, 600–1600." PhD diss., University of California, Los Angeles, 1998.

Yun Tusu 尹斗壽. *Kija chi* 箕子志. Asami Collection (University of California, Berkeley), 22.1. Vol. 1–3., 1879.

——. *Oŭm sŏnsaeng yugo* 梧陰先生遺稿. Reprint [1635]. HMC 41. Seoul: Minjok munhwa ch'ujinhoe, 1989.

Yurdusev, A. Nuri. *Ottoman Diplomacy: Conventional or Unconventional?* New York: Palgrave Macmillan, 2004.

Zarakol, Ayşe. *Before the West: The Rise and Fall of Eastern World Orders*. Cambridge: Cambridge University Press, 2022.

Zeitlin, Judith. "Disappearing Verses: Writing on Walls and Anxieties of Loss in Late Imperial China." In *Writing and Materiality in China*, ed. Judith Zeitlin and Lydia H. Liu, 73–125. Cambridge, MA: Harvard Asia Center, 2003.

Zhang Fangping 張方平. *Lequan ji* 樂全集. SKQS 252–255. Taipei: Shangwu yinshuguan, 1970.

Zhang, Feng. *Chinese Hegemony: Grand Strategy and International Institutions in East Asian History*. Stanford, CA: Stanford University Press, 2015.

——. "Confucian Foreign Policy Traditions in Chinese History." *The Chinese Journal of International Politics* 8, no. 2 (June 2015): 197–218.

Zhang Ning 張寧. *Fengshi lu* 奉使錄. Congshu jicheng chubian 2142. Shanghai: Shangwu yinshuguan, 1936.

Zhang Shizun. "Ming Qing Chaoxian shituan 'xiamayan' he 'shangmayan' kaoshi" 明清朝鮮使團 "下馬宴" 和 "上馬宴" 考釋. *Anshan shifan xueyuan xuebao* 21, no. 5 (2019): 33–40.

Zhang Tingyu 張廷玉. *Ming shi* 明史. Beijing: Zhonghua shuju, 1974.

Zhang, Ying. *Confucian Image Politics: Masculine Morality in Seventeenth-Century China*. Seattle: University of Washington Press, 2017.

Zhao Ji. *Zuben Huanghua ji* 足本皇華集. Nanjing: Fenghuang chubanshe, 2013.

Zhao Tingyang. "Rethinking Empire from the Chinese Concept 'All-Under-Heaven' (Tianxia)." In *China Orders the World: Normative Soft Power and Foreign Policy*, ed. William A. Callahan and Elena Barabantseva. Washington, DC: Woodrow Wilson Center Press, 2011.

——. *Tianxia tixi: Shijie zhidu zhexue daolun* 天下體系: 世界制度哲學導論. Nanjing: Jiangsu jiaoyu chubanshe, 2005.

Zhao Zan 趙瓚. *Hongzhi Guizhou tujing xinzhi* 弘治貴州圖經新志. Hongzhi 弘治本 [15th century]. Zhongguo fangzhi ku. Beijing: Airusheng, 2009.

Zheng Wenbao 鄭文寶. "Nan Tang jinshi" 南唐近事. In *Wudai shishu huibian* 五代史書彙編, ed. Fu Xuancong 傅璇琮. Hangzhou: Hangzhou chubanshe, 2004.

Zhu Changtai 朱昌泰 and Li Ruizhong 李瑞鍾, eds. *Changshan xianzhi* 常山縣志. Guangxu 光緒本 [1908]. Zhongguo fangzhi ku. Beijing: Airusheng, 2009.

Zhu Xi 朱熹. *Dianjiao sishu zhangju ji zhu* 點校四書章句集注. Beijing: Zhonghua shuju, 1983.

Zhu Yuanzhang 朱元璋. *Huang Ming zuxun* 皇明祖訓. Siku quanshu cunmu congshu, shi bu (part 2) 264. Tainan: Zhuangyan wenhua, 1996.

Zhu Zhanji 朱瞻基. *Da Ming Xuanzong huangdi yuzhi ji* 大明宣宗皇帝御製集. Siku quanshu cunmu congshu, ji bu (part 4) 24. Tainan: Zhuangyan wenhua, 1997.

Zito, Angela. *Of Body and Brush: Grand Sacrifice as Text/Performance in Eighteenth-Century China*. Chicago: University of Chicago Press, 1998.

Zurndorfer, Harriet T. "Prostitutes and Courtesans in the Confucian Moral Universe of Late Ming China (1550–1644)." *International Review of Social History* 56, no. S19 (December 2011): 197–216.

Index

Abca, 113–14, 117

abdication:, 51, 100, 102–3, 108, 158–59, 161–62

academic poetry, 210–12, 346n36

accountability, 164–66, 168–69

administration, politics of, 10–11

aggressive diplomacy, 341n74

Ai Pu, 189

Ancestral Injunctions, 52, 160

ancestry, in Korea, 358n66

ancient history, 30–31, 63–64, 200, 211–13, 248–49, 252–54, 265–69

animals: as tribute, 99–100, 103

Anp'yŏng (prince), 89, 106

aristocracy, 18–19, 24–25, 102–3, 110, 125, 199, 296n7, 301n67

Asia: Central, 16, 70, 74, 143–44; culture of, 126–27; East Asian languages, 11; Europe and, 7, 83; feudalism in, 31; reunification in, 33–34; sovereignty in, 13–14; Western culture and,

11–12, 322n4. *See also* East Asia; *specific topics*

Assembled Rituals of the Great Ming (Da Ming jili), 188

asymmetrical politics, 57, 97, 109, 150–51, 174, 277

Austria, 265

authority: in China, 113; over Chosŏn Korea, 78–80, 152–54, 157–58, 172–74, 182–88; in civilization, 217; cosmic, 126; cultural, 222; in culture, 66; diplomacy and, 166–67, 172–73, 197–200; due process and, 168; in dynasties, 105–6; idioms of, 340n44; in imperialism, 115–16, 186, 269, 308n49; in imperial tradition, 21, 47, 62; over Korea, 154–57, 355n37; in Koryŏ territory, 178, 347n40; over memorials, 47–48; in Ming dynasty, 51–54, 71–78, 81–82, 97–98, 102, 120–21, 124–25; in monarchy, 17,

authority (*continued*)
125–26, 270, 339n39; in Nanzhao empire, 33; in political autonomy, 138; politics and, 27–28; power of, 18; propriety with, 185–86; rhetoric of, 177; ritual and, 58–62, 64, 185–86; of Sejo, 110–13, 119; of Sejong, 67–71, 85–88; sovereignty and, 63–67; in succession charts, *101, 104*; of T'aejong, 54–57, 183; *zhongtong*, 42

autoethnography, 18–19, 37–38, 128, 132, 151, 153–56, 198, 223–25, 249–51, 269–74

axioms, 131, 133–34

Bai Yong, 127–28
Ban Chao, 190
barbarians (*yi*): to Chosŏn Korea, 40–41; to civilization, 4–6, 124–25, 130, 214–15; foreignness of, 152–53; identity of, 38, 66, 138, 140, 151; to Korea, 166; in monarchy, 52; Mongols as, 213–14; reputation of, 141; sovereignty and, 131
Barber, Karin, 151
Barkey, Karen, 18
Beijing. *See* China; Ming dynasty
biao. See p'yo
Bigan, 252–53
bilateralism, 32, 57, 109
Book of Songs, 38, 203, 220–24, 308n49. See also *Brilliant Flowers Anthology*
Botasiri (princess), 27–28
bribery, 133, 140, 144–45, 236, 244; as "personal feeling," 92–93.
Brilliant Flowers Anthology (poetry): civilization in, 221–24; diplomacy in, 195, 199–200, 204, *205–6*, 207–9,

224–26; education from, 201–3, 214–22, *215, 218*; as encomium, 211–212; female music in, 231–32; history in, 209–14, 248, 251; landscapes in, 256–57; poetry in, 242–43; reception of, 241; reputation in, 229; relationship to Towers and Pavilions style, 209–11, versions of, 344n7, 344n18
Brook, Timothy, 282–83
buchen (rebellion), 266–68
Buddhism, 28, 75, 93
bureaucracy, 10, 31–32, 78, 102, 134, 139, 142–51, 169, 174–75
Byzantine empire, 5

Caesar, Julius, 265
calendars, 49–50, 59–60, 69–71, 141, 183, 279, 310n73,
calligraphy, 208, *218*, 244, *257–58, 257–59, 258–59*, 355n36, 356n43
Cao Jixiang, 96
censorship, 228, 317n16
Central Asia. *See* Asia
Ceremonial Protocols for Vassal States, 177, 184–85, 188
ceremony. *See* ritual
Champa kingdom, 317n11
Chan, Hok-lam, 47–48
Chaoxian. *See* Chosŏn Korea; Korea; Koryŏ territory
Chaoxian fu. See Description of Chosŏn
Ch'ang (prince), 161
ch'aun (rhyme-matched verses), 204
cheguk. See empire (concept).
Chen Bangcheng, 143–45, 148, 150
Chen Dun, 183–87, 194, 255–56, 340n56
Chen Jian, 202, 233–34, 351n53, 359n76
Chen Jiayou, 111–14, 264

and, 11–13; of Korea, 30–35, 152–54, 341n82; of Koryŏ territory, 67–68, 248–49; literary, 198–99, 240, 345n22; of Ming dynasty, 197–200, 224–26, 243–44, 309n54; reputation and, 241–45; ritual in, 339n33; in *Selections of the East*, 40–41; of Song dynasty, 34, 251; suburban, 177–81; of Tang dynasty, 61, 299n34; in *Veritable Records*, 170, 192–93; of Vietnam, 344n11; Western, 11–13, 322n4; women in, 219–20, 313n111. See also *specific topics*
Cungšan (chief), 111, 123–25, 128
curfews, 142–43

Daidu. *See* Beijing
Dali empire, 16
Da Ming jili. See Assembled Rituals of the Great Ming
Dashengyue, 37
Dayu Mo. See Counsels of Yu
daurgaci, 10, 41, 181
Daxue yanyi bu. *See Supplement to the Extended Meaning of the Greater Learning*
Description of Chosŏn (Dong Yue), 198–99
diguo. See empire (concept).
diplomacy: agency in, 148–49; aggressive, 341n74; authority and, 166–67, 172–73, 197–200; bribery in, 133, 140, 144–45, 244; in *Brilliant Flowers Anthology*, 195, 199–200, 204, *205–6*, 207–9, 224–26; Chen Jiayou in, 111–13; with China, 339n33; with Chosŏn Korea, 133–34, *139*, 241–45, 248–49, 280–84, 329n14; in Confucian culture, 30–31; culture

and, 188–94, 229–34; diplomatic memorials, 302n77; diplomatic policy, 140–41; double truths in, 95–100, *101*, 102; with dynasties, 85–87, *87*, 106–7; ecumenical language in, 151; façade truth in, 109, 117; in Han dynasty, 341n74; history of, 2–3, 352n3; honorifics in, 149–50; idioms in, 30; in imperial tradition, 89–93, 131; infringement in, 59–60; interpreters in, 129–30, 143–44, 321n73; investiture and, 102–6, *104*; isolation in, 28; Kija and, 254–59, *256–58*, 269–71, 360n84; kinship in, 141–42; with Korea, 35–40, 52, 166–71, 294n1; by Kwŏn Kŭn, 6–7, 18–19; language of, 282–83; literary, 199–200, 202–3; Ma Jian in, 117–24; in memorials, 42, 49–50, 302n77; with Ming dynasty, 29, 128, 157–66, 227–29, 245–47, 259–64, *261*, 273–80, 314n126, 315n7; monarchy and, 44–45, 93–95; with Mongolia, 179; notices in, 114; personal feelings in, 92–93; political reputation and, 234–41; politics of, 4; practice of, 81–84; protocol in, 332n56; with Qing dynasty, 13, 281–82, 302n77; after Qubilai, 45; rhetoric in, 66–67, 117–18, 134–37, 149–50; ritual in, 170–71, 174–77; scholarship on, 17–21; with suburban culture, 177–81; with Suyang, 87–89, 175–76; systems of, 315n10; titles in, 112–13; tributary systems and, 250, 288n20; in tributary systems paradigm, 8–9; with Yuan dynasty, 260–61; Zhang Ning in, 113–17; with Zhu Yuanzhang, 305n9

impeachment, 144–45, 148
imperialism: authority in, 115–16,
186, 269, 308n49; bureaucracy in,
142–51; to China, 271; dynasties
and, 310n71, 365n34; in East Asia,
177–78, 326n87; economics of,
137–38, *139*, 140–42; excess in,
300n45; expansion in, 292n50;
formality in, 290n34; hierarchies in,
181, 215; history of, 280–83; ideology
of, 273–74, 283–84, 365n33; after
Imjin War, 274–80; imperial envoys,
338n24; imperial institutions, *139*; to
Ming dynasty, 203; in Mongolia, 10,
14, 17, 25, 110; rhetoric of, 133–34,
151; ritual and, 128; stakeholders of,
365n38
imperializing mode: defined, 19, as
used in diplomacy, 42–44, 132–37,
141–42, 148–51, 154–57, 162–66, 194,
274–77
imperial tradition: authority in, 21,
47, 62; to China, 13–14, 18, 33; in
Chosŏn Korea, 31–32, 108–10,
113–17, 128, 273–74; civilization
in, 44–45; in Confucian culture,
9–16; diplomacy in, 89–93, 131;
emperor-states in, 63; history of,
19, 49–50; identity with, 53–54;
ideology of, 10–11, 15–16, 245–46;
imperial transmission, 40–45; kin in,
103–4; Korea and, 1–6, 25, 116–17;
memorials and, 39–40, 46–47;
military in, 23–24; in Ming dynasty,
10, 84, 117–24, 154–57, 280–84;
monarchy in, 14–15, 45–46, 111–13;
religion in, 13; rhetoric in, 19–20;
violence in, 124–28
information, in Chosŏn Korea, 86–87

Injo (king), 191–93, 278–79
injŏng (gifts), 90–93
interlocutors, 268–69
international law, 1–2, 13, 282
interpreters, 18, 83–86, 114–15, 129–30,
143–44, 294n69, 302n78, 321n73;
in Ming Translator's Institute, 46,
302n78
investiture, 3–4, 7, 28–29, 32–33, 37,
51–52, 64–66, 81–82, 85–88, 97,
102–6, *104*, 158, 165, 183–84, 223,
253, 266–69, 282, 334n18, 334n22
irredentism, 17–19, 32–35, 40–41,
54–57, 212–14, 266–69, 280
Islam, 175, 312n101

Japan: China and, 55; dynasties in, 108–
9; Korea and, 57, 274–78; monarchy
in, 290n36; Mongolia and, 131;
Vietnam and, 225
Jiajing (emperor), 46, 189
Jiang Shigong, 282
Jiang Yingke, 362n7
Jiang Yueguang, 191–94, 243–44,
341n82
Jianwen (emperor), 51–52
Jian Yi, 136
Jianzhou Guards, 109–10, 118–24; war
with, 124–128, 142
Jiaqing (emperor), 246
Jin empire, 109
Jingtai emperor, 85–87, *86*, 96–98
Jin Shi, 233–34, 240
Jurchen people, 40, 56, 76, 109–10, 127;
diplomatic interactions with 82,
90–91, 93, 99 111–14, 118–24, 191,
278; as ecumenical "others," 146,
167, 176. *See also* Jianzhou Guards,
Maolian Guard.

memorials of, 304n89; Ming dynasty and, 23–25, 175; monarchy in, 27–30, 32, 41–42, 178–79; to Mongolia, 42–44, 55, 180, 279–80, 310n73; political loyalty in, 180–81; Qubilai leadership in, 42–45; Six Obligations and, 41–42; to Song dynasty, 40; Yuan-Koryŏ imperial universalism, 6

küregen, 23, 180–181

Kwanghae (king), 277–78

Kwŏn Kŭn, 1–2, 5–7, 18–19, 25, 134–36, 204

Kwŏn Pŏl, 152–53

Kwŏn Ŭng'in, 255

Kwŏn Ye, 228

Kye, Seung B. (Kye Sŭngbŏm), 165

Kyrgyz people, 32–33

ladies-in-waiting, 321n88

landscapes, 209–14, 254–59, 256, 345n22, 355n34

Lang Borghan, 113–17, 121–22, 124

language: alphabets, 71–76; Chinese, 15; and correct phonology, 72–75; connotations of, 266–68; of diplomacy, 282–83; in East Asia, 11; ecumenical, 151; emotive, 238–39; etymology, 11–12, 14; history of, 11–12; idioms, 11–13, 30, 59, 81–82, 133–34, 291n39, 340n44; interlocutors, 268–69; interpreters, 83–86, 114–15, 129–30, 143–44, 294n69, 302n78, 321n73; in memorials, 45–46; politics of, 14, 148; romanization of, 323n14

Latin America, 19

Ledyard, Gari, 73

Lee, Ji-Young, 189–90

Lefebvre, Henri, 249, 353n8

Lê Quý Ly, 54–55

Liadong Regional Commission, 89–93

Liaodong military, 318n41

Liaoyang, 2

Li, Chen, 63

Li Dongyang, 244, 346n36

Li Duri, 122

Li Jing, 98

Li Manju, 113, 121–25, 128

Li Shangyin, 33

literary culture, 198–99, 240, 345n22

literary diplomacy, 199–200, 202–3

literary Sinitic. See Sinographic cosmopolis

Literary Selections, 35–36

Literary Selections of the East (Sŏ Kŏjŏng), 35–36, 45–46, 48–49

literati identity, 190–91, 235–36

Liu Yong, 236

Liu Zongyuan, 267–68

liyi zhi bang. See "country of propriety and righteousness"

loose rein, 111

Lu Yong, 230–31

Ma Jian, 117–24

Manchu Qing empire, 16, 109

Mao Cheng, 163

Maolian Guard, 109–11, 113–15, 117–25, 128

maps: Chosŏn Korea, xxiv; Koryŏ and Ming territory, xxv; overland envoy route, xxvi

marriage: and diplomacy, 9, 27–28, 97–98, 102–4, between Koryŏ and Mongols. See küregen

mediation, rhetoric of, 121

memorials: of aristocracy, 301n67; authority over, 47–48; diplomacy in, 42, 49–50, 302n77; history of, 329n12; imperial tradition and, 17, 39–40, 46–47; in Korea, 59; of Koryŏ territory, 304n89; language in, 45–46; monarchy and, 41; *p'yo*, 143, 151; in Song dynasty, 36–37; tributary systems and, 35–40, 300n44

Mencius (philosopher), 30–31

men of the wilds (*yain*), 93, 99, 112, 118, 120–22, 319n49

military: of China, 211–12; in imperial tradition, 23–24; intelligence, 122, 316n15; in Korea, 57; Liaodong, 318n41; of Ming dynasty, 110, 362n7; of Mongolia, 27; of Qing dynasty, 291n39; rivals, 32–33; of Tang dynasty, 212–13

Ming dynasty: authority in, 51–54, 71–78, 81–82, 97–98, 102, 120–21, 124–25; bureaucracy of, 174–75; calligraphy in, 257–59, *258–59*; Champa kingdom to, 317n11; China and, 261–62; civilization to, 254–59, *256–58*; commercialization in, 235–36; compliance with, 189–90, 194–95, 221–22; conspiracy to, 28, 158–59; culture of, 197–200, 224–26, 243–44, 309n54; deference to, 94; diplomacy with, 29, 128, 157–66, 227–29, 245–47, 259–64, *261*, 273–80, 314n126, 315n7; ecumenical boundaries for, 129–32; embassies of, *205–6*, 217; emperors in, 14–15; eunuchs in, 140, 199–200; frontier policies of, 135–36; Great Rites Controversy in, 144–45; Heavenly

Altar in, 67–68; history of, 130–31, 165; identity in, 135–36; ideology in, 24; imperial institutions of, *139*; imperialism to, 203; imperial tradition in, 10, 84, 117–24, 154–57, 280–84; interpreters for, 302n78; Korea and, 45–50, 56–57, 97, 134–35, 146–47, 172–74, 211–12; Koryŏ territory and, 23–25, 175; Kwŏn Kŭn's embassy to, 1–2, 6, 47–48; leadership in, 52–53; military of, 110, 362n7; Ming Messenger's Office, 82; Ming territory, *xxv*; monarchy to, 59, 184–85; peace to, 53–54; politics in, 65–66, 117, 248–49, 264–69; Qing dynasty and, 7–8, 165, 365n38; relations with, 2–5, 18–19, 82–83; rhetoric of, 152–54; righteousness in, 137–38; ritual authority in, 64; ritual to, 188–94; Sejo to, 102–7, *104*; trade with, 16; war in, 124–28; Yan Song for, 46; Zhu Yuanzhang for, 3. See also *specific topics*

Ming History, 130–31, 165

Miscellaneous Records of the Brush Garden, 240

mock memorials, 36–39. See also *p'yo*

modernity, 13, 20–21, 53–54

monarchy: abdication in, 51, 100, 102–3, 108, 158–59, 161–62; ambition in, 57; authority in, 17, 125–26, 270, 339n39; barbarians in, 52; in Chosŏn Korea, 12, 46, 53, 65–66, 81–82, 85–89, 94–95, 99–100, *101*, 143, 176, 234–41, 269–71; civilization in, 167–68; coup d'états in, 95–100, 102, 157–58; diplomacy and, 44–45, 93–95; feudalism in, 31–32; Five Dynasties

and Ten Kingdoms period, 33;
in Han dynasty, 50; in imperial
tradition, 14–15, 45–46, 111–13;
in Japan, 290n36; in Khitan Liao
empire, 40; in Koryŏ territory,
27–30, 32, 41–42, 178–79; loose
rein in, 111; marriage in, 181–82;
memorials and, 41; to Ming dynasty,
59, 184–85; to Mongolia, 60–62;
mourning rituals in, 183–86; nobility
in, 64; poetic sociability in, 20–21;
politics of, 11, 36, 115–16; reform in,
61–62; regicide, 106–7, 153–54, 160–
61; righteousness of, 127–28; ritual
in, 182–88; stakeholders in, 19–20;
in Tang dynasty, 59; in *Veritable
Records*, 88–89; women in, 103–5,
217; *yukpu* system in, 61
Mongolia: China and, 62, 296n7;
diplomacy with, 179; Great Wall
to, 306n19; history of, 23–24, 41;
imperialism in, 10, 14, 17, 25, 110;
Japan and, 131; Korea and, 8–9;
Koryŏ territory to, 42–44, 55, 180,
279–80, 310n73; military of, 27;
monarchy to, 60–62; Mongols,
213–14; Mongol-Yuan patronage,
6; Mongol Yuan empire, 16; Persia
and, 15; in Sino-Korean relations,
4–5, 23–25; sovereignty to, 182; Tang
dynasty and, 58
moral influence (*feng*), 308n49
moral transformation, 65
mourning rituals, 84–85, 94, 154,
156–57, 183–86, 191–93
muhua zhuyi. See Sinocentrism
Munjong (king), 88, 94, 183
music: in Chosŏn Korea, 47; female,
231–34; musicians, 76–78; songs,

37–39, 232–33. See also *Brilliant
Flowers Anthology*
Myŏngjong (king), 188

Nam Kon, 162–64, 238, 275
Nanzhao empire, 16, 33
National Academy (Korea), 120
nationalism: in historiography, 17–18,
53–54, 71–72, 78–79, 251, 269–71
neoclassicism, 296n13
Neo-Confucianism, 25, 79, 346n31
neologisms, 11–12
nianhao. See calendars
Ni Qian: legacy of, 201–2, 204,
211, 217–19, *218*; on poetry, 255;
reputation of, 87–88, 90, 105, 187,
338n23; Sima Xun and, 240; women
to, 231–32. See also *Brilliant Flowers
Anthology*
nobility. See *specific topics*
nomads, 155, 185–186,
norms in diplomacy, 9–10, 15, 19,
43–45, 109, 170–73, 194–95, 231–34,
235–39, 246
*Nosan'gun ilgi. See Chronicles of Prince
Nosan*
notices (*p'aemun*), 114
Nüzhen. See Jurchen people
Nurhaci, 191
Nylan, Michael, 252

outside relations, 81–82
overland envoy route, *xxvi*
Owen, Stephen, 210–11
Ŏ Segyŏm, 126, 326n85
Ŏ Sukkwŏn, 129, 238

p'aemun (notices), 114
Pae Usŏng, 5

Pagden, Anthony, 11
Pak Sŭngim, 153–54, 166–69, 172
Pak Wŏnho, 47–48
Pak Wŏnhyŏng, 112, 222–23, 234
Park, Seo-Hyun, 194
performativity, 302n70
Persia, 15–16
personal feelings, 92–93
philosophy, 65, 126–27, 155
poetic sociability, 20–21
poetry. See *Brilliant Flowers Anthology*
political autonomy, 66, 138, 180, 267–69
political ideology, 9, 20
political legitimacy, 83, 96–97, 165
politics: accountability in, 168–69; of administration, 10–11; asymmetrical, 150–51; authority and, 27–28; of bilateralism, 32; cabals in, 105–6; in Chosŏn Korea, 18, 28–29, 95–97, 124–25; in Confucian culture, 233; of conquest, 290n32; corruption in, 148; of coup d'états, 102–3; of diplomacy, 4; of dynasties, 11; of history, 264–65; image, 244; of Imjin War, 236–37; of impeachment, 144–45; in Korea, 114; of language, 14, 148; legitimacy in, 64–65; in Ming dynasty, 65–66, 117, 248–49, 264–69; of monarchy, 11, 36, 115–16; of reputation, 229, 234–41; rhetoric in, 169–70; of sovereignty, 326n85; of tributary systems, 8; of Yuan dynasty, 24
Pratt, Mary Louise, 18–19
private relations, 81–82
Privilegium Maius, 265
procedure, 77–78, 115–16, 145, 148, 152–53, 168
proclamation (*cho*), 187–88

public and private, 77, 81–82, 146, 191, 233
"public transcripts," 108–9, 159
Pyŏn Kyeryang, 68, 262, 265–69, 360nn82–83
pyŏnmu. See "disputing slander campaign"
p'yo: concepts in, 306n25; memorials, 143, 151; performativity in, 302n70; tradition of, 36, 40–41, 43–44, 47, 49–50, 58–60. *See also* diplomacy; memorials
P'yŏngyang, 89, 211–13, 216, 248–53, 256–59, 259–64, 269–71
P'yŏngyang Morandae, 256

Qian Hongchu, 33–34
Qing dynasty: China and, 270; Chosŏn Korea and, 342n4, 360n84; diplomacy with, 13, 281–82, 302n77; history of, 279–80; Manchu Qing empire, 16, 109; military of, 291n39; Ming dynasty and, 7–8, 165, 365n38; records of, 242; restrictions in, 331n50; Vietnam and, 245; *yi-ness* of, 286n10
Qing Taizong, 278–79
Qing Taizu, 191
Qin Shihuangdi, 55
Qi Shun, 207–9, 212–14, 216–17, 232–34, 239–40, 242, 350n46
Qiu Jun, 65
Qubilai Khan, 42–45, 64

Rawski, Evelyn, 16
rebellion (*buchen*), 266–68
reciprocity, 31–34, 44, 83, 153, 155–56, 168–71, 268
Record of an Embassy to Chosŏn, 189

Zhao Gong, 178
Zhao Samboo, 123
Zhang, Ying 235
zhengfa (retributive violence), 125–26
Zheng He, 175
Zheng Xuan, 304n87
zhongtong, 42
Zhòu (king), 48, 252
Zhou, Duke of, 162
Zhou dynasty, 48, 66, 210, 221–24,
    252–53, 262, 265–69
Zhu Di, 51–52
Zhuge Liang, 209
Zhu Mengxian, 230

Zhu Quan, 358n67
Zhu Xi, 66, 156, 295n10
Zhu Yuanzhang (emperor): Chosŏn
    Korea to, 64–65; diplomacy
    with, 305n9; Korea and, 3–4, 49;
    leadership of, 23–24, 52–53; for
    Ming dynasty, 3; reputation of,
    51–52; Yi Sŏnggye and, 28–29,
    67–68
Zhu Yunwen, 51. *See* Jianwen
    (emperor)
Zhu Zhanji, 104. *See* Xuande (emperor)
Zhu Zhifan, *257–58, 258,* 356n46
zongfan system, 282